Understanding ECONOMICS TODAY

Understanding ECONOMICS TODAY

SIXTH EDITION

GARY M. WALTON

President, Foundation for Teaching Economics
Professor of Management and Economics
University of California, Davis

FRANK C. WYKOFF

Elden Smith Professor of Economics
Pomona College and Claremont College Graduate School

Irwin
McGraw-Hill

Boston, Massachusetts   Burr Ridge, Illinois   Dubuque, Iowa
Madison, Wisconsin   New York, New York   San Francisco, California   St. Louis, Missouri

Irwin/McGraw-Hill

A Division of The **McGraw·Hill** Companies

Understanding Economics Today

Copyright © 1998 by The McGraw-Hill Companies, Inc. All rights reserved. Previous editions 1996, 1994, 1991, 1989, and 1986 by Richard D. Irwin, Inc. Printed in the United States of America. Except as permitted under the United States Copyright Act of 1976, no part of this publication may be reproduced or distributed in any form or by any means, or stored in a data base or retrieval system, without the prior written permission of the publisher.

This book is printed on acid-free paper.

2 3 4 5 6 7 8 9 0 DOC DOC 9 0 0 9 8

ISBN 0-256-24651-3

Publisher: Gary Burke
Development editor: Wendi Sweetland
Marketing manager: Nelson Black
Project manager: Terri Wicks
Production supervisor: Rich DeVitto
Text and cover designer: Lorna Lo
Compositor: GAC/Shepard Poorman
Typeface: Times Roman
Printer: R. R. Donnelley & Sons Company

Library of Congress Cataloging-in-Publication Data

Walton, Gary M.
    Understanding economics today / Gary M. Walton, Frank C. Wycoff.
    — 6th ed.
       p.   cm.
    Includes index.
    ISBN 0-256-24651-3
    1. Economics.   I. Wykoff, Frank C., 1942– . II. Title.
  HB171.5.W23   1997
  330—dc21   97-27679
                                         CIP

http://www.mhhe.com

To Linda and Jane

CONTENTS

𝒫 PART I
MACROECONOMICS   226

PREFACE

THE PURPOSE OF LEARNING ECONOMICS

Learning economics empowers us. It helps us make better and more reasoned decisions as private individuals and as participating citizens in a world of scarcity. It increases an appreciation of the importance of incentives in shaping people's decisions, and it develops an understanding of how complex economic systems work.

This empowerment of understanding is not easily accomplished. Many people have taken courses in economics and yet have no idea how to apply economics to the problems and issues facing them on a daily basis. Economics applies to business, government, medicine, science, the military, law, politics, sports, religion, and many other aspects of modern life. We are amazed and delighted at the ability of our profession to contribute to a better understanding in these diverse areas of study. Indeed, George Stigler, the 1982 Nobel laureate in economics, has called economics the "imperial science."

The purpose of this book is to help people learn economics. To meet this goal we attempt to show the usefulness of economic analysis and help develop the skills of economic reasoning.

Almost all texts in economics will tell you that economics is the study of how individuals and nations, through their governments, make choices about how to use their scarce resources to fulfill their wants. This definition focuses largely on economics as a problem of constrained maximization—getting the most out of limited resources. Another useful perspective is to view economics as a study of commercial societies engaged in producing and exchanging and of the outcomes of these activities, including the effects of laws, policies, institutions, and organizations on social interactions through markets.

The principal advantage of economics for most people is not the many complex models, concepts, terms, and institutions that professional economists use and study; rather, it is the improved decision making on personal matters and guidance to citizens on matters of policy that sound economic reasoning provides. To repeat, economic understanding empowers individuals with insight into how large social systems characterized by extensive division of labor are coordinated. This essential understanding is best achieved by nurturing and developing an economic way of thinking, a perspective stated early in this century by John Maynard Keynes:

> [E]conomics does not furnish a body of settled conclusions immediately applicable to policy. It is a method rather than a doctrine, an apparatus of the mind, a technique of thinking which helps its possessor to draw correct conclusions.

This "apparatus of the mind," or economic way of thinking, follows logically from *five basic propositions* of human nature and well-accepted truths.

FIVE PROPOSITIONS FOR ECONOMIC REASONING

1. *People choose, and individual choices are the source of social phenomena.* People make choices based upon their perceptions of the expected costs and benefits of alternatives. Choices involve risk; outcomes cannot be guaranteed because the consequences of choices lie in the future.

2. *Choices impose costs.* People incur costs when making decisions. Choices involve trade-offs among alternatives. People weigh marginal gains against marginal sacrifices. Ultimately, the cost of any decision is the next best alternative that must be forgone. Reasoned decision making leads to an increase in any activity in which expected benefits exceed expected costs, and a decrease in any activity in which expected costs exceed expected benefits.

3. *Incentives matter.* Incentives are rewards that encourage people to act. Disincentives discourage actions. People respond to incentives in predictable ways; when incentives change, behavior changes in predictable ways.

4. *The "rules of the game" impact people's choices.* Laws, customs, moral principles, and cultural and institutional characteristics impact individual choices and shape the economic system.

5. *Understanding based on knowledge and evidence imparts value to opinions.* The value of an opinion is determined by the knowledge and evidence upon which it is based. Statements of opinion should initiate the quest for economic understanding, not end it.

In *Understanding Economics Today*, we cover many topics that are vigorously debated, issues over which economists have divergent views and different approaches. We identify these diverse viewpoints and use basic models to show how these different approaches work.

We begin with the fundamental tools of choice—demand and supply—for individuals and for businesses and see how their choices affect actions in the marketplace. This is *microeconomics*. From decision making by individuals and businesses we proceed to choices that are national in scope—the issues of inflation, aggregate unemployment, and economic growth. This is *macroeconomics*. In *international economics* we examine how U.S. government policies can affect economic conditions worldwide as well as at home.

To repeat, our objective in this book is to bring some joy to the study of economics and to provide some basic tools of economic reasoning and analysis so that more effective economic choices and better insights into local, state, national, and international economic issues can be made.

It is important at the outset to realize that teaching objectively about social issues and at the same time presenting some fundamental tools of reasoning and analysis is a challenge in a one-semester course. It is impossible to cover all the topics of economics and include all the tools. Hard choices must be made; for every tool of analysis presented, an example must be sacrificed. Every practical example studied sacrifices time for tool building. A week devoted to the study of monopolies loses a week to discuss the deficit.

Since each professor's taste for various topics differs, we have built in flexibility to allow choice of emphasis among various topics. Still, we start from the premise that the objective of a one-semester economics course is to show how economists think about important issues. Our view is that students need a basic tool kit of reasoning for dealing with practical problems. We try to avoid a course filled with mathematical equations and daily doses of data, tables, and graph shifting. Geometry, algebra, statistics, and other tools of the trade are used sparingly and only to support analysis of problems. Thus, we develop only the tools needed to think clearly about the problems most likely studied. In this book we focus on the economic analysis of problems and issues that can be learned in one semester. To this end, we have picked problems, examples, and issues that we think capture immediate interest. Our view is that tools are learned most effectively when used to deal with an interesting or important problem.

Another primary aim of this text is to provide a balanced perspective. Basic fundamentals of economics are applied to many issues of current and historic interest and divided evenly among the micro and macro sections. Furthermore, there is a balanced perspective in the political rhetoric presented; every effort has been made to make this book politically neutral. To accomplish this, differences of opinion are noted, revealing where opinion and scientific findings diverge.

We begin with microeconomics to introduce the traditional tool of economics as applied to individual markets. We present a basic circular flow model to provide the basis for the analysis of product and resource markets. We emphasize markets as arrangements of social cooperation and describe their workings, limitations, and possibilities for failure. The role of government when markets fail is included along with some of the problems of government intervention. International trade issues and the tool of comparative advantage conclude Part I. In Part II, we move to macroeconomics and develop the circular flow model further to show the roles of money, taxes, banking, and government policy. We conclude the book with policy analyses of international trade and finance.

Despite the long development period for the body of knowledge, or tool kit, known as *microeconomics*, its development and range of applications continues apace. In recent years three fields in economics—*economic history, law and economics*, and *public choice*—have witnessed extraordinary extensions of scholarly work based primarily on microeconomic theory. Also recently, leaders in these fields have received Nobel prizes in economic science. The chapters on microeconomics are written in the spirit of these vibrant fields of applied microeconomics. Although sources of disagreement are noted, the consensus among economists on the theoretical foundations of microeconomics is comparatively strong.

It is widely recognized, however, that there is much less consensus among economists on macroeconomic models. Monetarists, Keynesians, new classical macroeconomists, rational expectations, and supply siders all get pretty excited when discussing each others' papers at conferences. The public dialogues between Feldstein, Friedman, Greenspan, Stein, Stiglitz, Laffer, Bosworth, Tyson, and others are shattering the view that we have a working macro model.

Despite professional differences about an effective macro model, we do have a body of knowledge that is vital to students. The basic idea that various markets interconnect in subtle ways is an essential ingredient to national economic policy analysis. Thus, our approach to macro is to first teach the body of information on which we do have consensus: the measures of macro performance, the importance of government budget policy, the role of money and banking in our economy, the consequences of inflation, the importance of unemployment, and the difficulties in designing policies to foster growth and stability.

We have striven to deal as fairly as possible with the different schools of thought about macroeconomic theory and policy. Rather than ignore the differing macro interpretations and perspectives, we use the circular flow model as a vehicle for presenting Keynesian, monetarist, new classical macro, and supply-side views. This approach minimizes the mathematics, geometry, and statistics needed, allowing choice on which view best captures the workings of the national economy and how each perspective contributes to our economic intuition.

Our approach to macro policy is to explain different views and identify their key differences. We avoid strong advocacy. This allows instructors to develop macro policy issues in a context in which students can read about the views and critiques of each. We welcome correspondence and advice from both teachers and students.

Understanding
ECONOMICS TODAY

PART I

MICRO-ECONOMICS

What are you going to do today? What are your plans for next year? Every day each of us makes choices on how to spend our time and our money. More wealth and time increase our options and range of choices, but no one has unlimited amounts of these things. Choices are forced upon us because scarcity is a fact of life for all of us. And scarcity imposes costs on us by requiring the sacrifice of one thing (money or time) to get another (a piece of apple pie or a suntan).

Nations face scarcity, too—a scarcity of resources that makes choices on national policy inevitable. Nations cannot produce everything for every citizen. Greater defense will require fewer other things, perhaps fewer automobiles, schools, hospitals, or less free time. Scarcity and choice are central to *economics, which is the study or science of human behavior in a world of scarcity.*

In economics we assume that people pursue what they feel is in their own self-interest. We all prefer more to less and usually make decisions that we hope will improve our well-being. We hasten to add that this assumption of self-interest does not imply greed or selfishness. These qualities may be involved, but when people make decisions to better their circumstances, their motives may be to help others as well as themselves. If you were offered $100 from the government or a generous stranger to use as you please, would you turn it down? Would anyone? How about if the amount were $1,000? Our self-interest would certainly urge us to take it, perhaps to help a friend, or to save it for a rainy day.

Most important, the self-interest assumption, used in economics to portray human behavior and to predict outcomes, greatly helps us understand the importance of incentives as they influence our choices. Adam Smith, the father of modern economics, recognized that the motivation of self-interest helps to explain and predict human behavior.

We are now embarking on microeconomics, which is the part of economics that deals with individual and collective choice and decision making in markets. It involves the study of quantities (and quality) of goods and services produced, sold, and bought, and the study of how prices are determined. We shall also see how government policies can affect prices and the quantities exchanged in the marketplace.

Simply stated, the distinction between microeconomics and macroeconomics (discussed in Part II) is that microeconomics studies the pieces while macroeconomics studies the whole. Microeconomics studies the trees; macroeconomics views the forest. So, in microeconomics we study individual market participants—individual consumers, individual businesses, and distinct markets—such as the markets for home computers or movies or bicycles. We focus on the parts of the economy rather than on the whole. A key feature of Part I (and indeed of the entire book) is the role that self-interest plays in determining economic outcomes: what is produced, how it is produced, and for whom it is produced.

Some of the material in this part of the book is controversial. Should government ban boxing? Should smoking be prohibited at outdoor sporting events? What would be the effects of such a policy on baseball ticket prices? Should bank interest rates be controlled, or should banks be allowed to set any rate they choose? What keeps local shoe stores from doubling the prices of shoes? Or from cutting prices in half?

These and many other issues and questions appear in the chapters ahead. There you will find some, but not all, of the answers; some answers cannot be based on analysis alone. The "right answer" often depends on our individual value judgments of right and wrong, or good and bad. Each of us, reasonable as we may be, can honestly disagree with others on issues involving values. We hope you will gain useful insights into how the economic forces in our world work.

CHAPTER 1

The Economics of Personal and Social Choice

꠱ CHAPTER PREVIEW

At the beginning of each school term, notices appear on campuses of sign-up and meeting times for sports and other extracurricular activities. Whether you choose cross-country running, football, student government, the debate team, or a job, you quickly recognize that your commitment is costly. The involvement costs time, energy, nervous tension, anxiety, and sometimes even pain. And yet the decision not to join a team or activity also has its costs: missing out on the fun, new friends, and the personal growth that come from making such commitments. Living is costly; so is just existing. Sound judgment and good choices can improve your well-being.

1. What are the costs to you to take this course in economics?
2. What benefits will you gain from this course?

NEW CONCEPTS

Choice
Opportunity Costs
Trade-off
Privatization
Property Rights
Productive Resources
Scarcity
Centralized Economic Systems
Decentralized Economic Systems
Positive Economics
Normative Economics

𝕴 CHAPTER OBJECTIVES

After studying this chapter, you should be able to:

1. Engage in economic reasoning.
2. Determine opportunity costs and compare them to benefits in order to make choices.
3. Recognize key differences between centralized and decentralized economic systems.
4. Recognize the role of the economic resources of land, labor, capital, and entrepreneurship.
5. Understand the difference between positive and normative economic assertions.

ECONOMICS AND YOU

No matter how we use it, our time has costs. Economics is the study of choice and decision making in a world with limits. Every **choice** we make costs us some forgone alternative. Every morning we all face the choice of when to get up. Some people are deliberate and conscious of this simple daily routine; they use an alarm clock or a clock radio and arise at a predetermined time. Others (like one of the authors) awake from natural forces, when the spirit moves them. But as soon as a semiconscious state is reached, the question of when to get out of bed must be faced. Often the decision is postponed—a wish for "just 10 minutes more." Sometimes the 10 minutes multiply. Whether the choice to "sleep in" is made consciously or habitually, the costs of the choice are unavoidable. The discipline of economics shows us that even this daily choice—when to get up—implies cost. The 10 minutes more in the morning leaves 10 fewer minutes for other things.

CHOICE is the act of selecting among alternatives.

An essential first step toward understanding economics is learning to engage in economic reasoning.

ECONOMIC REASONING PROPOSITION: *People choose, and individual choices are the source of social phenomena.* People make choices based on their perceptions of the expected costs and benefits of alternatives. Choices involve risk; outcomes cannot be guaranteed, because the consequences of choices lie in the future.

Economics formally recognizes the relationship between choice and costs in terms of **opportunity costs.** The opportunity cost of a bicycle is measured in terms of other goods and services that must be sacrificed (or forgone) in order to get the bicycle. The money you pay for the bicycle plus the value of your time spent shopping for it reflect the sacrifice (cost) of your choice.

𝍤 𝍤

OPPORTUNITY COST results from choice and is the highest-valued alternative forgone.

Consider the opportunity costs of taking a course in sociology. There are other courses to take and other subjects to study. By making the choice to take sociology, you give up some other course or activity. By reading a book, you are forgoing the opportunity to read and study other subjects, watch TV, or use your time in some other way. Every choice implies an opportunity cost, and choices are unavoidable because your time is limited.

Trade-offs and Weighing the Alternatives

Although you can never be absolutely certain, you have a pretty good idea of which college courses are hard and which ones are easy. Students, like other people, prefer the path of least resistance. They also prefer good grades.

For the sake of analysis, suppose you are taking economics, French, and three other courses. Further, assume that you are unable to devote more than *10 hours a week* of study to both economics and French. Assume also that your objective is to get the highest grade point average (GPA) possible. How can you *maximize your GPA* for these two subjects?

The numbers in Table 1–1 represent the time you will have to study in order to earn any given grade. An A in French and a C in economics is the best grade combination you can attain with 10 hours of study. You can raise your grade in economics from a C to a B by shifting 2 more hours of study time to economics, but this **trade-off** will cost you a drop from an A to a C in French. To get an A in economics instead of a B costs another 3 hours, leaving no time for French, and you get an F there. We do not rule out the possibility that such a trade-off may be preferred. Maximizing your GPA is not the only worthy objective. You may prize an education in economics, wish to major in it, or have a bet that you can do better than a C in the course. This example of trade-offs in grades illustrates the problem of choice and costs in terms of time and performance. Of course, a more complete analysis would consider a wider range of alternatives and trade-offs. The 10 hours of combined study in French *and* economics could be increased at the cost of study time in other subjects, and total study time could be increased at the expense of time spent jogging, playing cards, dancing, or working.

TABLE 1–1   The Trade-off in Grades for 10 Hours of Study

Hours per Week Studying French	Grade in French	Hours per Week Studying Economics	Grade in Economics
5	A	10	A
4	B	7	B
3	C	5	C
2	D	3	D
1	F	1	F

This example shows the hours of study needed to obtain various grades in economics and in French. If 10 hours is the total amount of study devoted to both, the best grades possible result in a B average (5 hours to each subject for an A in French and a C in economics). Any change in this allocation of time between the two subjects lowers the grade point average.

TRADE-OFFS reveal the exchange opportunities of selecting one thing rather than another.

Now let's add another economic reasoning proposition, one worthy of repeated review, perhaps even memorization and challenging contemplation.

ECONOMIC REASONING PROPOSITION: *Choices impose costs. People incur costs when making decisions.* Choices involve trade-offs among alternatives. People weigh marginal gains against marginal sacrifices. Ultimately, the cost of any decision is the next best alternative that must be forgone. Reasoned decision making leads to an increase in any activity in which expected benefits exceed expected costs, and a decrease in any activity in which expected costs exceed expected benefits.

Pondering the many choices you make each day and recognizing the trade-offs involved and the opportunities forgone (opportunity costs) are steps toward understanding the fundamental nature of costs and the role of choice in economics. But now let's turn from personal considerations to a global perspective on choice and trade-offs.

GLOBAL AND NATIONAL PROBLEMS TODAY

Boris Yeltsin, president of Russia, inherited a colossal problem from the former Soviet Union's previous leader. As Mikhail Gorbachev stated on January 27, 1987, in a speech to the Communist party's Central Committee: "At some point the country began to lose momentum, difficulties and unresolved problems started to rise up, and there appeared elements of stagnation and other phenomena alien to socialism."

Gorbachev saw the problem as one of reforming the system and making the Soviet economy more productive, without bearing unacceptable costs of change and without abandoning too many fundamental communist ideologies.

"Those who do not learn to change in life are left behind," Gorbachev told former East German leader Erich Honecker shortly before the Berlin wall began coming down in 1989. But by 1991, not long after a failed coup attempt against Gorbachev by old guard communists, the Soviet Union had splintered and Yeltsin was elected president of Russia by democratic means.

The loss of momentum and economic stagnation noted by Gorbachev manifested itself in many ways. For example, poor standards of public hygiene and sanitation, and extraordinary levels of alcoholism, especially among males, had led to a sharp reduction in Russian men's life expectancy. It fell by almost eight years, from the high point of the 1970s, to about 56 years today. In agriculture the huge collectives and centrally planned state farms had persistently produced below expectation. It bears remembering that a century ago, before the Russian Revolution of 1917, Russia was one of the two largest grain exporters in the world. In contrast, during the 1970s and 1980s the Soviets had to import tens of millions of tons of wheat and corn each year. To increase agricultural production, agricultural workers were allowed to farm on small (approximately one-acre) private plots. These plots occupied a mere 4 percent of the country's arable land but accounted for nearly 25 percent of Soviet agricultural output. The positive incentives for work gained from these steps away from collective ownership and to private holdings were apparent to Gorbachev and to other central planners. But private property as the "means of production" was in conflict with communist ideology.

Despite economic deterioration in many spheres of Russia in 1990, the country had a bumper crop in wheat that year. Yet the record output of wheat was accompanied by acute shortages of bread in the cities. Shelves were empty and long bread lines formed daily. How could that be? Can you imagine a bumper crop of wheat in the Midwest and bread shortages in Chicago? It's unthinkable. People with trucks would fetch the wheat, surely, and sell it to flour millers, who in turn would sell it to bakers. But in Russia the distribution system was breaking down, and this was not a reflection of road conditions. The rules of the game in Russia were not working effectively for the Russian people, and the incentives to work and exchange goods in a socially cooperative way were absent, or nearly so.

ECONOMIC REASONING PROPOSITION: *Incentives matter.* Incentives are rewards that encourage people to act. Disincentives discourage actions. People respond to incentives in predictable ways; when incentives change, behavior changes in predictable ways.

> ℐℐℐℐℐℐℐℐℐℐℐℐℐℐℐℐℐℐℐℐℐℐℐℐℐℐℐℐ
>
> ECONOMIC REASONING PROPOSITION: *The "rules of the game"*
> *affect people's choices.* Laws, customs, moral principles, and cultural and
> institutional characteristics impact individual choices and shape the
> economic system.

Individuals in the former Soviet Union did not have the same incentives to harvest, distribute, and process the wheat into bread as we do in the United States. This is because there were no private property rights to the wheat, trucks, gasoline, mills, flour containers, bakeries, and all of the other inputs that go into bread production. These were all owned collectively. Why should one person work hard when the return to effort was so widely shared? The self-interest of workers in the former Soviet Union encouraged shirking, and as the policing of work effort by authorities faltered, productive coordination and output declined. The absence of private property and very limited freedom to exchange discouraged the social cooperation generated through markets (the buying and selling) that we take for granted in the United States. Gorbachev, and more clearly Yeltsin, had come to realize this, but Gorbachev's choice for gradual change was fraught with political costs, as the coup attempt against Gorbachev in 1991 made clear.

For every problem there is an opportunity and, as Yeltsin knows, crises are the mothers of heroes. To heighten motivation and productivity and restructure the Russian Republic's failing command-and-control system, Yeltsin has attempted **privatization** reforms; these involve the selling of state-owned assets to private individuals or corporations. First popularized by Margaret Thatcher in Great Britian in the 1970s and adopted worldwide, privatization has been rapidly underway in Russia, the Czech Republic, Slovakia, Hungary, Poland, Bulgaria, and other countries behind the broken iron curtain. The process of privatizing is filled with political and economic hazards, however, as entrenched bureaucrats and managers of state enterprises resist change and as workers—fearing job losses—fight for the status quo. Although Yeltsin was reelected to office in October 1996, millions of workers in both state-owned and privatized forms were being paid in the goods they produced rather than with money. The government was behind in its payroll by several months, even to soldiers, who in November were being paid in heads of cabbage (which they could barter). Figure 1–1 graphically shows the growth of taxes unpaid and that a large portion of the tax collection problem was traceable to huge, state-owned firms who simply refused (or could not) pay. To close these firms down would impose great political risk. In addition, privatized enterprises, that often had the government as their main buyer, were not getting paid in cash either. Therefore, they couldn't pay taxes or the wages of their workers; note the vicious cycle here. Moreover, many private businesses were under threat from organized-crime elements demanding "protection money." Such developments clearly underscore the importance of establishing secure property rights and the need for enforcing legal contracts. Privatization is a necessary step toward building a market economy, but it

FIGURE 1–1   The Russian Tax Collector's Nightmare

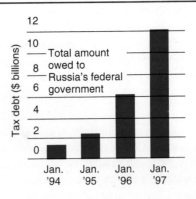

Company	Business	Tax Debt (in Millions)*
Avtovaz	Car maker	$504.1
Noyabrskneftegaz	Oil and gas producer	252.1
Nizhevartovskneftegaz	Oil producer	198.1
Uraltransgaz	Gas transporter in the Urals	180.0
Volgotransgaz	Gas transporter in the Volga	144.0
Norilskgazprom	Gas supplier	144.0
Orenburgneft	Oil and gas producer	126.0

*As of Jan. 1, 1997.

Avtovaz, Russia's largest car maker, may be a big tax debtor, but it is not alone. Many other companies have helped contribute to the sharp growth of Russia's federal tax debt.

Sources: Russian Ministry of Finance; Russian State Tax Service.

cannot assure success without the proper institutions to support it. This point merits elaboration.

In the United States and other advanced market economies, the legal system is often taken for granted. The economies of the former Soviet republics do have legal systems, primarily criminal codes on murder, theft, and so on. However, their legal systems are woefully weak on economic transactions and enforcement of contracts. Now that the new world of private property rights and free exchange has emerged, the legal systems are straining to cope. In the United States we have lawyers, courts, and judges who rely on our Uniform Commercial Code to resolve contractual economic and business disputes, as well as centuries of experience of rules of law.

PRIVATIZATION is the transfer of activities from the public sector to the
private sector. It entails a move from common or government ownership to
private ownership of property and a reduction of government regulations
that constrain individual rights to the use of resources. Privatization
changes the rules of the game.

Despite our relatively advanced market system, challenges remain for the United
States too. Consider Charles Gomez, a city manager in southern California, who is
facing a tough choice. He is taking a lot of criticism because the costs to local
residents for city garbage collection have been rising. A recent study makes it clear to
Gomez that privatizing garbage collection would save money for both the residents
and the city government. But he has to get the City Council's approval before he can
lay off the city garbage collectors and contract with private firms to pick up and haul
the trash. A couple of council members were supported in their election by unions
who oppose privatization schemes. Gomez figures the majority of the council, however, will support his plan because they want to use the money that will be saved to
remodel City Hall. The choice to privatize garbage collection is tough because it has
its costs (layoffs and lost political support), but the trade-off, a sharp-looking, remod-
eled City Hall, strengthens Gomez's case. City managers face choices and weigh
trade-offs like these daily.

ECONOMICS AND NATIONAL PROBLEMS YESTERDAY

Inflation and Price Controls

When confronted with escalating costs and prices, such as those we have experienced in the medical sector (e.g., hospital, physician, and pharmaceutical expenses)
in the United States in recent years, some policymakers recommend price freezes to
stop the price increases. Price controls to contain the costs of medical services were
proposed by the Clinton administration in 1994 as part of the president's proposal on
national health care. Such controls have been used sporadically for centuries (especially during wartime), usually having results surprising to the advocates of price
controls. A good case in point is President Nixon's recommendation in the early
1970s for mandatory wage and price controls as a means to combat rising prices.
Figure 1–2 traces a decade of inflation (the yearly percentage increase in prices
overall) and reveals the experience of wage and price controls during the Nixon
years. Nixon's opinion at the time was that the controls would benefit the economy
by stopping inflation. But opinions, even those of a president, should only be the
beginning of a discussion, a contention that brings us to another economic reasoning
proposition.

FIGURE 1–2 Inflation and Nixon's Price Controls

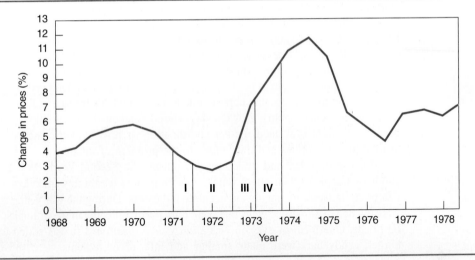

Source: U.S. Department of Commerce Statistical Abstract, 1978, p. 483.

> ECONOMIC REASONING PROPOSITION: *Understanding based on knowledge and evidence imparts value to opinions.* The value of an opinion is determined by the knowledge and evidence upon which it is based. Statements of opinion should initiate the quest for economic understanding, not end it.

What was the evidence and the effectiveness of price controls? As shown in Figure 1–2, Nixon's controls were imposed in August 1971, when the inflation rate was 4.5 percent. The peak precontrol rate of inflation had been 6 percent in early 1970, so the rate was actually falling at the time controls were imposed. The inflation rate then continued to decline and stabilized at around 3 percent throughout 1972, then as some sectors of the economy had their prices freed it started to rise more steeply in 1973. By the time controls were completely lifted in early 1974, the inflation rate was 10 percent and still rising.

On the surface, it appears that the controls did little to stop inflation. At most, the controls appear to have delayed the price explosion.[1] However, during the period of their effect, the price controls were both disruptive and inflationary. Price controls promoted waste by utilizing millions of government and industry labor hours to police and administrate the legal mandates. As market conditions changed, prices

---

[1]By contrast, a similar postcontrol price explosion did not occur during the Korean War. For more on this, see "Can Price Controls Work" by Hugh Rockoff in *Second Thoughts*, Donald N. McCloskey ed. New York: Oxford University Press, 1993, pp. 132–35.

remained the same, and so shortages, distortions, and other inefficiencies began to appear. For example, during the second and third periods of Nixon's controls, fertilizer and chemical firms sidestepped sales at artificially low prices in domestic markets by increasing exports. This hurt agricultural production at home, lowered food supplies, and caused food prices to increase. Since prices of imported goods were not regulated, many U.S. lumber firms first shipped wood products to Canada, and then reimported them for sale in the United States. Because poultry feed prices were not subject to controls, it became unprofitable to raise chickens for sale at fixed government prices; hence poultry growers slaughtered chickens by the millions. In short, because controls prevented market coordination of prices, inefficiencies lowered availability of supplies and thus added to the problem of inflation.

The use of wage and price controls during the Second World War provides another example of their effectiveness. One important lesson this episode teaches is that price statistics are not always accurate indicators. During the war years, controls were evaded in numerous ways that were only partly reflected in the official statistics on prices. One form of evasion was *quality deterioration*. Fat was added to hamburger, candy bars were made smaller and inferior ingredients were substituted, coarser fabrics were used in making clothes, maintenance on rental properties was reduced, and so on. Sometimes whole lines of low-markup, low-quality merchandise were eliminated from stores, forcing poor customers to purchase more costly high-markup, high-quality lines. And, of course, black markets developed, like the illegal markets for drugs today. Finally, when price controls were lifted in 1946, Americans experienced their highest spurt of inflation in the 20th century.

When wage and price controls are imposed, people face new and greater constraints on how they can use or exchange what they own. Private **property rights** are diminished when price or wage limits are imposed. It is another example of changing the rules of the game.

PROPERTY RIGHTS specify the conditions of ownership of an asset—the rights to own, use, and sell it.

Here again, economic analysis assists our understanding of the problem. Separating results (smaller, more costly supplies) from intentions (lower inflation) is extremely useful, and economics plays a powerful role in the assessment of the results of proposed policies.

SCARCITY AND CHOICE FOR EVERYONE

Whether the focus is on the present or the past, whether the problems considered are personal or those of nations, the necessity of choice is inevitable. No matter what the form of government or social organization, no matter what the amount of wealth or **productive resources,** each nation must address certain fundamental problems in providing goods and services. Economists usually talk about four major categories of productive resources:

1. Labor is the workers' time weighted to take account of their skills and knowledge. Increases in both the number and the skills of workers improve a nation's ability to produce.

2. Land and natural resources consist of the land for farming and forestry, bodies of water for fishing and transportation, and deposits of minerals such as iron or other ores.

3. Capital is the stock of machinery, equipment, and buildings. These allow labor, along with land and natural resources, to produce more goods and services than would otherwise be possible.

4. *Entrepreneurship* refers to the special human abilities needed to employ the other resources in order to produce goods and services. It involves finding the most economically efficient (profitable) use of the resources available within an economy. The entrepreneur risks suffering a loss in an attempt to make a profit from reorganizing market resources from lower-valued to higher-valued uses.

> **PRODUCTIVE RESOURCES** are the inputs of labor, land and natural resources, capital, and entrepreneurship used to generate new goods and services.

Because these resources, no matter how plentiful, are scarce relative to society's wants, finding the best uses for resources is a perplexing and difficult problem. The undeniable permanent fact of **scarcity** (the condition of being in limited supply) necessitates choice and creates costs. Scarcity always has and always will impose costs on all individuals, most commonly—though not solely—in terms of limits on time and money. Whether the social order is communistic, socialistic, or capitalistic, resources are never adequate to produce all the goods and services wanted by everyone.

> **SCARCITY** is the fact that human wants and needs are unlimited and the resources to satisfy those wants and needs are limited. Scarcity defines a relationship between the amount of something we want and the amount that is available. It is the condition of being in limited supply.

All nations must face the problem of how to allocate their limited resources. It is a matter of choices. Economics encompasses the study of this allocation of scarce resources.

There are numerous examples, contemporary and historical, of many different systems of allocating resources. Indeed, when comparing nations, there is a nearly continuous spectrum of resource allocations systems, but to simplify, for the present let's consider two polar extremes:

- **Centralized economic systems** with common property ownership and centralized direction and control of production and distribution.
- **Decentralized economic systems** emphasizing private property and the freedom to change through markets to supply and distribute goods and services.

Centralized economic systems emphasize central planning and government control of production and distribution, whereas decentralized economic systems rely mostly on markets and individual decision making within markets to produce and distribute goods. Also, decentralized systems are usually characterized by private ownership of capital and land, while centralized systems are characterized by public

---

TOOL KIT

DISTINGUISHING BETWEEN VALUE JUDGMENTS AND SCIENTIFIC STATEMENTS

It is important to realize that scientific analysis is not always free of value judgments. It is essential that value judgments be distinguished from economic propositions that are independent of personal beliefs or feelings. The instinct to question statements and propositions, to ask specifically if they are opinions, should be developed. Recognizing the difference between expressions of how things ought to be and statements of cause and effect is important.

Positive economics pertains to objective value-free inquiry. Positive economics is a statement of what is, not of your or my or anyone else's values or subjective feelings. An example of a positive economic proposition is "If the price of ice cream rises relative to the prices of other goods, people will buy less ice cream." It doesn't say that the outcome (less ice cream consumption) is good or bad; it just states the expected result. This can then be tested and verified (or disproved) by the facts. As a rule, however, it is often difficult to stick to value-free positive economics. Therefore, we must be wary of letting feelings guide analysis. We must recognize others' feelings and be accountable for our own as well.

When we allow values to enter the economic analysis, we leave the world of positive economics and enter that of **normative economics.**

ownership of these means of production. Neither system exists in a pure form. Each system reflects characteristics of both centralization and dispersion, and each involves tremendous social cooperation and coordination.

The People's Republic of China, although it is rapidly turning toward more market orientation, is still a good example of an economic system that emphasizes methods of central control. Government officials there decide what part of the productive mechanism is to be devoted to providing consumer goods and services; what part is to be used to make capital goods; and what part is to be allocated for research, for military use, and so on. Lesser officials in the hierarchy make the more detailed decisions on allocations. The results may or may not parallel or satisfy the wishes of consumers. Although prices are assigned to goods and services, they serve the main purpose of keeping accounts and informing and guiding planners. Nevertheless, consumers are free to choose among the goods produced. Since the late 1980s decentralized choice has been growing in this and other centrally planned economies.

In more decentralized enterprise economies, such as those of the United States, Canada, Germany, Japan, and Mexico, the allocation of resources occurs mainly through market forces and legal restraints. Individuals influence the marketplace

Normative economics is economic analysis that contains value judgments, either implicitly or explicitly. If we add to the positive economic statement about less ice cream consumption that "ice cream prices should not be allowed to rise," we have slipped into the realm of normative economics. This has added a value judgment that less ice cream consumption is bad. Keep on guard for the words *should* or *ought to.* They almost always signal that values have entered the analysis.

Both positive and normative economics are important. So is distinguishing one from the other. Positive economic statements are capable in principle of being refuted by empirical evidence, independently of opinion. Normative economic statements inherently cannot be confirmed or rejected; they are subject to agreement or disagreement of opinion, not to scientific testings. And yet the two kinds of statements often become mixed and are capable of reinforcing each other.

For instance, you may value most highly a goal of helping teenagers, perhaps with the specific remedy of raising the incomes of teenagers. Given your goal, consider asking Congress to raise the *minimum wage.* A minimum wage is set by law to establish the lowest hourly wage that can be paid. Will this policy remedy (a choice) serve your policy goal (another choice)? Studying the positive economics of the minimum-wage law reveals that higher minimum wages tend to reduce the employment of teenagers. The teenagers who work will earn more, but others will fail to get jobs. Therefore, raising the minimum wage may not be consistent with your goal, as established by your values. Positive economics can help you decide which remedies are helpful and which are harmful to realizing your objectives or the policy goals of the nation.

by their investments and consumer decisions. They also offer productive resources—their labor, capital, land, and entrepreneurship—for hire. All these individual and collective choices occur in a complex web of competitive and cooperative interaction.

Whatever the basic method or system of resource allocation, the fundamental problem of choice remains, for all people, in all places, for all times. This is true for individuals, families, groups of all kinds, towns, cities, states, and nations. Choosing, either individually or collectively, is the inevitable consequence of scarcity. Indeed, it is the only way to cope with it.

ECONOMIC ANALYSIS AND VALUE JUDGMENTS

How do we know if some choices are better than others? How do we select among the many choices possible? Here is where *economic theory* and economic tools become important. They assist in understanding the world around us. For example, the concept of opportunity costs is an extremely valuable tool. With economic analysis you can compare costs to benefits. There are many other economic tools that can be applied to policy issues and economic problems.

Economics is a social science that uses the same methods of analysis used in biology, physics, and chemistry. Like other sciences, economics relies on models and theories to give simplified representations of the real world. These models and theories clarify the issues to aid understanding. Indeed, they are essential to explain and predict economic phenomena in the real world. Economic models do not attempt to explain how people think, however. Instead, a model generalizes human behavior to predict how people will act—which may be far different from how they *say* they will act.

Economics uses a different emphasis from that used in the other social sciences. Political science concentrates on how power relationships within informal and formal political settings and institutions shape people's actions. Psychology takes special note of how personalities and motivations shape human behavior and interpersonal activity. In contrast, economics stresses how the facts of scarcity and necessity of choice influence people's actions. In developing economic models, you should be aware of this special emphasis.

USING THEORY IS YOUR ONLY CHOICE

When Columbus said he could reach the Orient by sailing west from Spain, he postulated that the world was round and that it was smaller than the sages of his day believed. Many others believed the world was flat. His model, or theory of the world, was testable. He said there were no edges for him to fall off. Columbus tested his theory with a long ocean journey.

The assumptions he used for his theory were simple representations of the real world. *Assumptions* are simplified abstractions from the real world used to state a theory. Think of all the detail Columbus left out—the winds, the currents, the color of the oceans, their depth, contents, and on and on. His abstractions or simplifications illustrate the two essential features of the development and use of theory.

First, no model or theory is ever complete; all the details and interrelationships that exist are never captured in full. Assumptions "simplify" reality to a manageable dimension. The key to scientific model building is to identify only the essential relationships needed to analyze the problem being addressed. What is essential is a matter of study and choice. Because theories ignore nonessential detail, they lack realism. Yet they are realistic if they clarify the central forces at work. We shall observe this clash of "reality and unreality" as economic theory is developed and used.

Second, theories must be useful. To be useful, they have to be testable. A theory must be observed in action in order to determine if it is consistent (i.e., proves to be correct) with what we are trying to understand and explain. In short, the theory is useful if it serves to predict results and to explain how the real world works. Can economic theories predict what will happen in the world around us? In the chapters to follow, we develop the answer: a qualified yes.

🎞 CHAPTER REVIEW

The concepts and economic reasoning propositions introduced in this chapter have been applied to several national, as well as personal, issues. However, the relevance of these concepts, terms, and propositions is far wider than the illustrations and applications given here. The specific examples of privatization and of price controls are less important than the concepts and propositions themselves. Indeed, these tools of understanding are applicable to all societies throughout the history of mankind. This alone emphasizes their importance.

The necessity of choice and the importance of clarifying trade-offs and opportunity costs of any action (or inaction) are undeniable. These truisms apply to governments that emphasize either centralized economic systems or decentralized systems. Scarcity of productive resources—the land, labor, capital, and entrepreneurship—makes choices unavoidable at the national level. Scarcity of time and income makes choices unavoidable at the personal level. Incentives impact personal decisions and social outcomes.

Explicit use of economic theory and simplifying assumptions are basic to sound economic analysis. It is important, however, to distinguish between positive and normative economic analysis. Positive economics is objective and is tested by the facts, while normative economics rests, at least in part, on subjective value judgments.

𝒿𝓇 MULTIPLE-CHOICE SELF-TEST 𝒿𝓇 𝒿𝓇 𝒿𝓇 𝒿𝓇 𝒿𝓇 𝒿𝓇 𝒿𝓇 𝒿𝓇 𝒿𝓇 𝒿𝓇 𝒿𝓇 𝒿𝓇 𝒿𝓇 𝒿𝓇 𝒿𝓇

1. Which of the following is a productive resource of an economy?

   a. A sewing machine.
   b. An unskilled 16-year-old.
   c. An acre of rocky land.
   d. All of the above; they are all productive resources.

2. If you can get a wage of $5 per hour for working some extra hours, then that must mean:

   a. You face a trade-off between earning money and having more leisure hours at a cost of $5 per hour.
   b. Leisure is worth more than $5 per hour to you.
   c. Leisure is worth less than $5 per hour to you.
   d. You can't afford any more leisure.

3. "Lowering corn prices in Mexico will lead poor people to buy more corn." This statement involves:

   a. Positive economics.
   b. Normative economics.
   c. A choice of policy goals.
   d. A value judgment.

4. Property rights are:

   a. Defined and enforced by individuals in a decentralized economy and by government in a centralized economy.
   b. The rules that determine who has the right to use and to exchange particular goods and services.
   c. All owned by government in a centralized economy.
   d. All the above are true.

5. An economic model is a good one if it:

   a. Predicts economic outcomes well.
   b. Includes all the forces influencing earning behavior.
   c. Is both positive and normative.
   d. Uses a set of simplified assumptions about how economic forces operate.

𝒿𝓇 STUDY QUESTIONS

1. Should you spend the same amount of study time on each course in order to maximize your GPA? Explain.

2. Before there were federally supported loans to students from the government, it was almost impossible for students to borrow money from banks on the

promise to pay out of future earnings. How does the concept of property rights help to explain this?

3. Are campsites scarce where you go camping? How are they allocated to users?

4. Is it cheaper to travel by train or by plane from New York City to San Francisco? What is critical to the answer?

5. What are some of the trade-offs you must consider when deciding how to spend Saturday evening?

6. Can economic theory be good in theory but not good in practice? Explain.

ﾟﾚ PROBLEM

Elena and Luis have invested their substantial savings in machinery for their small company, which builds wooden planter boxes. Business has been slack for some time. The company has been earning enough money to pay the wages of its employees, but it is paying nearly nothing back to Elena and Luis. They are trying to decide whether to stay in business or to give up and sell off their equipment. Their friend Jack tells them it would be silly to sell the equipment. "After all," he points out, "you own it, so it's not costing you anything. It would be different if you had borrowed money from the bank to buy it. Then it would cost you something to keep holding onto it." What is wrong with Jack's analysis? How would you counsel Elena and Luis.

CHAPTER 2

Scarcity and the Economic Problem

𝒥𝒞 CHAPTER PREVIEW

Imagine being so productive and earning so much per hour that you can't afford to go to lunch. Is that what people really mean when they say they're too busy to have lunch—that their opportunity costs are too high?

Everyone must face up to scarcity. (Even the wealthiest people have limited time.) Each choice we make imposes an opportunity cost in terms of time and money. And all nations are constrained by limited resources too. It is the finite amounts of land (and other natural resources), labor, capital, and entrepreneurship that limit productive capacity and cause the scarcity of goods and services. Even modern technologies cannot overcome the constraints of limited resources and economic scarcity.

If scarcity could be overcome, economic problems would disappear. But, of course, this is hardly conceivable. Overcoming the limits imposed by nature is only a part of the problem. Our wants, which continuously expand and grow, also contribute to the conditions of scarcity. If we were all content to consume like primitive peoples do but used the most advanced technologies to produce at the maximum, many of our economic problems would subside. What we observe, however, is that as our productive capacity grows so does the reach of human wants and expectations. Indeed, in societies such as ours, where social status is often linked with the possession of goods, scarcity has a strong psychological dimension. It is human nature to desire to possess more and more. No matter the make or reliability of the car we drive, it is normal behavior to want a newer or more expensive model. If our purchasing power permits, linoleum floors turn into tile or carpet; a small walk-up apartment is vacated for a six-room condo with a view; an open football stadium is replaced with a climate-controlled sports arena.

1. Despite the many, many timesaving appliances and devices available today, we seem busier than ever. Why is this?
2. Does competition in the marketplace make more products and services available, and does it mean lower prices to the consumers?
3. Does a decentralized market economy provide for a fair distribution of income?

𝒥𝓇 CONCEPTS REINTRODUCED

Centralized Economic Systems 16
Choice 6
Decentralized Economic Systems 16
Normative Economics 16
Opportunity Cost 6
Positive Economics 16
Property Rights 14
Scarcity 15
Trade-off 8

𝒥𝓇 NEW CONCEPTS

Economic Specialization
Division of Labor
Production Possibilities Curve
Rising Opportunity Costs
Unemployment
Economic Growth
Market Economy
Economic Problem
Input Markets
Output Markets
Circular Flow Model
Capital-Intensive Methods
Labor-Intensive Methods
Transaction Costs
Externalities
Public Goods
Income Distribution
Monopoly

📯 CHAPTER OBJECTIVES

After studying this chapter, you should be able to:

1. Use the production possibilities curve to illustrate economic growth, unemployment, efficient production, and opportunity costs.
2. Use the circular flow diagram to illustrate the market for goods and services and the related markets for productive resources.
3. Recognize externalities (positive and negative).
4. Recognize public goods. Realize the strengths and weaknesses of the market (price) system.

FACING UP TO SCARCITY

Scarcity is attributable both to nature and to human behavior. Economics is concerned both with the stinginess of nature that limits productive capacity and with the expansion of individual and social appetites.

Part of facing up to scarcity is recognizing that *scarcity necessitates rationing.* Suppose a kindly pizza maker who is also an invited speaker enters a college classroom at 11:30 AM with a small, piping hot pizza (no anchovies) to give to the 50 students there. The professor agrees to let the guest speaker distribute it, even though there's clearly not enough for more than one or two people. The problem is; How to ration the pizza? Some of the rationing alternatives might be:

1. Need
2. Merit
3. Lottery
4. Age
5. Looks
6. A contest
7. Teacher's choice
8. A committee's choice
9. Money price (auction)
10. First come, first served

Each method of rationing has its strengths and weaknesses. For example, need sounds like an excellent, fair, and kind method, but is need best determined by who is the poorest, hungriest, or has the best appetite and fondness for pizza? How could the guest speaker know or find out who this is? If merit is the criteria, how should we define merit? Best citizen? Smartest student? Teacher's pet? The lottery method is fair, but may put the pizza in the hands of someone who hates pizza. She or he could give it to a friend, or maybe sell it, thereby ultimately relying on money price as the way of rationing it. Using money price to ration the pizza also has disadvantages. People with little money are at a disadvantage. However, money price has one distinct advantage over all the other methods. It is the one method that financially rewards the supplier and encourages the pizza maker to provide more pizzas in the future. Other methods, like waiting in line (first come, first served) offer little advantage to suppliers, but money price does have its advantages. Money-price rationing, then, is the one method that offers incentives to providers to supply goods and services to satisfy buyers' wants. Incentives do matter —and in predictable ways. Money-price rationing also encourages specialization and division of labor, which lower the cost of goods and services, broaden the range of choices, and encourage economic and social cooperation.

Specialization and Economic Cooperation

Before examining the impact of scarcity and the economic problems it creates, it is important to note the productive strength that results from cooperative effort. The degree of our cooperation is often overlooked, especially in advanced economies. Only a few "hermits" adopt the individual approach to overcome scarcity; the rest of us join together, often unknowingly, in a common cause. The gains from these cooperative efforts to produce and exchange are tremendous. Cooperation allows the concentration of effort in a particular activity that we either enjoy or are best suited to perform. This focused effort is called **economic specialization.** As we specialize in activities in which we are individually proficient and productive, our collective output increases. Cooperation also allows the expansion of collective knowledge in science, the humanities, and the arts. It allows us to share and enjoy each other's abilities and special talents—such as those of Michael Jordan, Rush Limbaugh, Hillary Clinton, Luciano Pavarotti, Julia Child, Jackie Joyner, and you and me.

ECONOMIC SPECIALIZATION is the act of concentrating on a few particular tasks or producing only one or a few items.

The significant gains in production that result from these forms of cooperation have been recognized since the American Revolution. Adam Smith, a Scot, labored for 12 years to produce a timeless book, *The Wealth of Nations.* In this classic work (published in 1776), the great economist emphasized that when individuals pursue their own self-interest, the end result is an increase in the welfare of society.

In Smith's own words:

> [An individual] . . . neither intends to promote the public interest, nor knows how much he is promoting. . . . He intends only his own gain, and he is . . . led by an invisible hand to promote an end which was no part of his intention. . . . By pursuing his own interest he frequently promotes that of the society.

ECONOMIC REASONING PROPOSITION: *Social phenomena and outcomes emerge from choices people make in response to expected benefits and expected costs to themselves.*

Again, as noted in Chapter 1, in using the term *self-interest* we do not imply selfishness or greed as a motivation. Some people may base their decisions principally on such a motive, and perhaps all of us are a little selfish some of the time. But this is not implied. Other human motives that are consistent with self-interest are altruism; philanthropy; and caring for others, family, friends, the nation, and the environment.

The assumption that people follow their self-interest works less well in interactions among friends and family, but very well indeed when analyzing choices and human interactions among strangers. Market decisions are typically of this latter type. Economists have found that self-interest is a good predictor of individual behavior. Self-interest is a basis for human choices and strivings. To a worker, self-interest means preferring higher wages and better, safer working conditions; to a consumer, the most satisfaction for time and income spent; to a businessperson, maximum profits (revenues minus costs); to a landlord, renting for the highest amounts possible. Because of competition, however, we are not free to set just *any* price in order to sell what we own: our labor, our land, our capital, or our entrepreneurial capabilities. We are affected by others who are also pursuing their self-interests and competing with us. Their decisions influence the price we can charge.

INFLUENTIAL ECONOMIST

ADAM SMITH, 1723–1790

In 1776, when influential Americans signed the Declaration of Independence and were engaged in war against Great Britain, a revolutionary book entitled *The Wealth of Nations* was published in England. It has secured for its author, Adam Smith, as close to a state of immortality as can be obtained by any economic writer.

Adam was born in Kirkcaldy, Scotland, a few months after the death of his father. He entered the University of Glasgow at the tender age of 14. Three years later he went to Oxford University for six more years of study. He then returned to Scot-

land, first to the University of Edinburgh (teaching literature and economics) and then to the University of Glasgow (as a professor of logic and as holder of the chair of moral philosophy).

In 1763 he traveled through Europe as special tutor to the young Duke of Buccleuch. Residing mainly in Paris, Adam Smith had the opportunity to meet many of the leading intellectuals of the day. He had a close friendship with the great philosopher David Hume, also a Scot, who introduced him to illustrious men such as Voltaire, Turgot, and Quesnay. Smith had already earned a

Self-interest constrained by competition results in a greater voluntary supply of goods than would otherwise occur. Rather than abusing each other, we are guided by self-interest as if "by an invisible hand" to produce what others desire. Producers respond to people's purchases. Collectively, we offer and receive more resources, goods, and services. In the weeks before the 1984 Olympics, the news media reported anticipations of traffic jams and immense parking problems near the main Olympic site at the University of Southern California. On the opening day of the games, traffic moved smoothly, but the price to park all day in most nearby lots was $30 to $40. On the second day, many homeowners in the vicinity saw opportunities to make money and sold all-day parking places in their front and back yards for $10 each. By the third day, and throughout the remaining days of the games, traffic continued to move smoothly, and in the Olympic site area the typical all-day parking fee dropped to $5. Homeowners, following their own self-interest, added parking space for anxious automobile drivers attending the games. Society benefited. Self-interest also contributed to the smooth flow of traffic and lack of congestion on the freeways. Many people who otherwise would have vacationed or visited southern California at the time of the Olympic games went elsewhere or stayed home. Many Los Angeles residents left town in anticipation of problems, and a historical rarity occurred at Disneyland and at Magic Mountain; there were no waiting lines for their highly popular rides. The result of these people pursuing their own self-interest was greater space and less congestion for everyone.

Adam Smith presented a compelling argument that a society of individuals operating from self-interest maximizes the social well-being: When human and nonhuman resources are combined in a business, more effective **divisions of labor** become

reputation for excellence as a scholar by his first book *Moral Sentiments* (1759), but he wished to provide a more complete treatise on economics and political philosophy as well as on ethics and moral philosophy. He worked on *The Wealth of Nations* for 12 years.

In that book, Smith changed the face of economics. At that time, during the revolution in America when men were fighting for liberty and political independence, Smith's book also advocated freedom—the economic freedom to sell one's own labor and to enjoy the fruits thereof. Smith argued that this was enough to increase output for society and to guarantee prosperity. He said, "The natural effort of every individual to better his own condition, when suffered to exert itself with freedom and security, is so powerful a principle, that it is alone,

and without any assistance . . . capable of carrying on the society to wealth and prosperity." He revealed that a market system of competing individuals, free of government intervention, would be guided by an "invisible hand" to allocate productive resources to their most useful ends and distribute commodities efficiently for the best interests of society. His work showed how markets operate and how interference in these markets by government can sometimes have ill effects.

Five years after completing *The Wealth of Nations*, Smith became commissioner of customs for Edinburgh, like his father, who had been comptroller of the customs of Kirkcaldy just before Adam was born. Compared to the revolution in economic thinking that *The Wealth of Nations* created, Adam Smith's final years were quiet and uneventful.

possible. He first illustrated the gains from the division of labor with this classic illustration of an 18th-century pin factory:

> One man draws out the wire, another straightens it, a third cuts it, a fourth points, a fifth grinds it at the top for receiving the head; to make the head requires two or three distinct operations; to put it on is a peculiar business, to whiten the pins is another; it is even a trade by itself to put them into the paper. (*The Wealth of Nations,* 1776)

Whereas one worker at that time could produce no more than 20 pins a day toiling alone, 10 workers, each specializing in a single task, could produce up to 48,000 pins in one day. For 10 workers, the jump in output was from 200 pins to 48,000! No greater skills were required, just greater interdependence and productive cooperation.

TOOL KIT

THE PRODUCTION POSSIBILITIES CURVE

To visualize the choices involved in our individual and cooperative efforts in production, let's divide the total goods and services produced into two categories: (1) food and (2) shelter. Measured in physical units, the production possibilities for 1998 can be diagrammed as shown in Figure 2–A. Points *A, B, C,* and *D* represent different combinations of food and shelter that can be produced during the year. More precisely, these and other points on the production possibilities curve show the maximum amounts that can be produced during 1998, using the available resources of land, labor, capital, and technology. Point *E* conveys one extreme, in which all resources are committed to food production. Point *A* is the opposite extreme, with no resources used to produce food. Points *B, C,* and *D* represent more realistic combinations, in which both food and shelter are produced.

Figure 2–A shows that the basic economic problem stems from scarcity and illustrates once again the problem of choice. Should society locate at point *B,* at point *C,* or at some other point? *What*

bundle of goods should be produced? This is the first question of the basic economic problem that all societies face. Clearly, a choice must be made, and each choice implies a cost, an opportunity cost.

To show this cost, let's take a closer look at the production possibilities curve at points *B* and *C.* First, we see that a choice to produce more food implies that less shelter is produced. The opportunity cost of more food is the reduction of shelter. Alternatively, we can get more shelter only by shifting resources away from food production. An opportunity cost faces us at each point. At point *B,* if the production of shelter is reduced, food production is increased. A like change in production of shelter at point *C* results in an increase in food production. Both changes in food production show the opportunity costs of more shelter. The second thing to note is that the opportunity cost of more shelter is greater at point *B* than at point *C.* It takes a greater reduction in food production at point *B* to increase output of shelter to that point. At point *C* the sacrifice of food is less.

DIVISION OF LABOR is the assigning of specific tasks to workers and productive resources; it is a reflection of economic specialization.

The specialization of tasks and division of labor can also lead to the possibility for great economic mischief. Abundance is conditional; it depends upon the cooperation of great numbers of workers. Certain groups of workers and segments of the economy assume a special importance—their withdrawal from the productive effort affects the rest of us. The failure of some small groups to perform their economic function can cause disruptions to production and dislocations in distribution. It was this fact that motivated air traffic controllers to strike for higher wages and shorter hours in 1981.

FIGURE 2–A   The Production Possibilities Curve

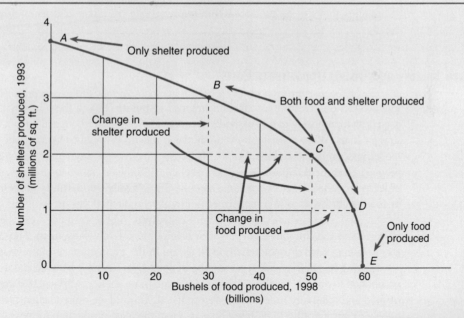

The production possibilities curve shows the different maximum amounts of shelter and food an economy can produce, using the available resources of land, labor, capital, and technology. It sets the boundaries of maximum production possibilities. At points *B, C,* and *D,* combinations of food and shelter are produced.

And it was the threat to the economy's performance that President Reagan used as the basis for firing the strikers and replacing them quickly. This example and many others, like the baseball strike in 1994, are reminders that individual and national riches are dependent on our personal accomplishments, talents, and efforts, and on the effective social cooperation we achieve through market forces and legal directives.

How we each pursue our individual self-interest and achieve productive cooperation is a recurring theme in this book. For the moment, however, we skip the process and the factors that guide these cooperative efforts. We leave the invisible hand as a teasing mystery, temporarily taking these efforts (and output) for granted.

OUR PRODUCTION POSSIBILITIES

Even with economic specialization and division of labor, choices must be made in a world of scarcity. How can we best combine our productive resources to achieve maximum output of goods and services? What are the economic trade-offs between, say, guns and butter? Economists use the **production possibilities curve** as a tool to analyze these and other questions.

> The PRODUCTION POSSIBILITIES CURVE shows the maximum amounts that can be produced with the available resources and technology.

Specialized Factors and Rising Opportunity Costs

The production possibilities curves developed in Figure 2–A in the "Tool Kit" have been drawn purposely to reflect modern reality. They are bowed out and are not simply straight lines. What does the bowed-out shape mean? Why is it characteristic of our modern economy? It reflects the fact that costs increase for anything when we try to produce more of it. Note that as more shelter is produced, more food is given up in order to increase shelter by the same amount. These **rising opportunity costs** in terms of food occur because in a modern economy the productive resources of labor, land, capital, and entrepreneurship are often specialized. These resources can be interchanged and substitutions made, but they cannot be perfectly substituted. Those in use for producing food are not equally well suited to the production of other goods.

Moving in small, equal steps, starting at point *D* in Figure 2–A, consider a shift in production to point *C* that results in less food and more shelter. At point *D*, a great deal of food and relatively little shelter are produced. To produce more shelter, factors are released from farming to building houses. First, the least productive farmers with the poorest soils and outmoded equipment are shifted to building houses. The increase in houses (1 million square feet more) leads to a loss of food (7 billion bushels). The next bundle of farm resources diverted—the farmers with better skills, better equipment, and more fertile soils—causes a larger drop in food production (20 billion bushels) for an equal gain in houses built (1 million square feet of shelter). The move from point *C* to point *B* imposes a greater sacrifice of food for shelter than from point *D* to *C*. Thus, further diversions of farm resources, those more specialized and more productive, cause even greater losses in food production. When extremely specialized farming resources are transferred to building houses, very large sacrifices in food production result. The more specialized the factors are to farming, the greater the loss in food output as the resources are shifted to other uses. In addition, the specialized farming factors are very likely to be less productive elsewhere. Some types of farm equipment and farming talents are helpful in building houses; others, such as knowledge of planting and the use of threshers, are almost worthless for building houses. Ultimately, at point *B* and beyond, the best farmers—those with the most knowledge, using specialized equipment, and working the most fertile soils—are shifted. The reduction in food production becomes very great indeed.

RISING OPPORTUNITY COSTS are the rise in per-unit costs as more is produced.

Consider another example of the same problem. Suppose there is a huge migration of young college-bound people into the country. To get more teachers, recently retired professors are rehired, and graduate students are reassigned to teaching more classes. Because few other goods and services are lost, the opportunity cost for these resources is low. Next, lawyers, accountants, and economists are called upon to teach classes; then engineers and scientists are called from industry. Although their teaching skills may be quite good, reallocation of these talents results in the loss of their efficiently produced goods and services. Here the opportunity costs begin to rise sharply; the production possibilities curve for education and other goods (and services) bends as we move along it. When individuals much less qualified to teach are called upon, little is gained in educational output, and loss of output elsewhere still results; graphically, the curve bends even more sharply. These differences in ability and specialization of talents and their imperfect substitutability ensure the curve's bowed-out shape.

Looking at the opportunity costs of shifting specialized productive factors to other areas shows us another part of the economic problem. In addition to determining *what* to produce, all societies must decide on *how* to produce their bundles of goods at the lowest cost possible.

Unemployment and Economic Growth

In the mid-1960s, the United States increased its military efforts in the Vietnam War. President Lyndon Baines Johnson, in a nationally televised speech, assured the American people that the United States could meet its military commitments abroad and wage a War on Poverty at home. He implied that we could provide the guns, planes, and ammunitions for war *and* could expand, even initiate, new social

FIGURE 2–1   Being Inside the Production Possibilities Curve

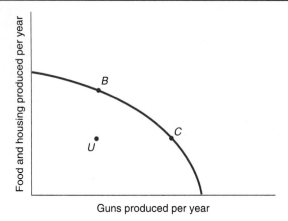

When unemployment or underutilization occurs, the economy is producing at less than the maximum production possibilities (perhaps at point *U*). This places the level of production, *U,* inside the production possibilities curve.

programs—all without sacrifice! By using a production possibilities curve, we can see that these assurances were ultimately misleading. Figure 2–1 shows that a move from *B* to *C* to get more guns leaves less food and housing for social programs. If the economy is producing at full capacity (implied in the production possibilities curve), more guns can only come from the sacrifice of food and housing. If, however, there is *unemployment,* the actual level of production is less than the maximum production possibilities; the actual production level would be located inside the production possibilities curve—perhaps at point *U.* **Unemployment** occurs when some workers who are willing and able to work and who are actively seeking work are not employed. Moving toward full employment can lead to a higher production level. Then it is possible to have more guns *and* more food and housing, simultaneously. At the time Johnson made his assurances, however, there was full employment. In outlining his program, Johnson did not contend that there was unemployment nor did he contend that there were other sources of inefficiency that could be wiped out to allow production increases for both types of goods.

A second possibility for increasing production of not only guns, but also food and housing, occurs when there is rapid growth in the economy. When a nation experiences **economic growth,** the boundaries of the maximum production possibilities curve shift out, as shown in Figure 2–2. In this case, more can be produced of guns and housing and food, simultaneously.

ECONOMIC GROWTH is a sustained increase in output or output per person.

FIGURE 2–2   Economic Growth and the Production Possibilities Curve

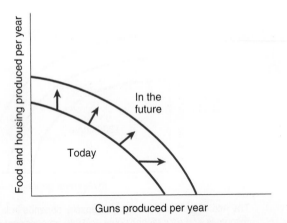

A shift of the production possibilities curve can result from economic growth. An increase in the factors of production—the amount of resources—or advances in productivity will boost the total amounts that can be produced and push out the boundaries of the production possibilities curve.

Economic growth occurs because of increases in productive resources or because of new technologies, more specialization, or other efficiency gains. But economic growth takes time. It does not occur automatically. Time- and resource-consuming investments are needed to develop the human skills to build new plants and equipment or to perform research leading to new technologies. If these investments are made, then the production possibilities curve will shift out. President Johnson, however, did not have growth in mind when he spoke. Rather, he emphasized the immediate ability to produce more of not only food and housing, but also guns. Rather than considering it a reflection of economic reality, we attribute President Johnson's remark largely to political rhetoric.

As we pass through the 1990s, the political rhetoric continues and so does the applicability of the production possibilities curve. This curve applies to the debate on the trade-offs between a government spending reduction and a tax increase by the federal government in its quest to reduce the federal budget deficit. It also applies to our future as a nation.

Current and past decisions do have long-run consequences. They bear on the future in an important way. A nation's future looks quite different when trade-offs between investment goods and consumer goods are considered. This is shown by yet another version of the production possibilities curve (Figure 2–3). We see that in 1980 an unavoidable choice was made between more consumer goods, point *X*, and more investment goods, point *Y*. At point *X*, more TVs, stereos, good food, wine, travel, and entertainment are produced and enjoyed. At point *Y*, there are fewer comforts from the consumer goods, but more resources are directed toward

FIGURE 2–3   Present Choices and Long-Run Growth

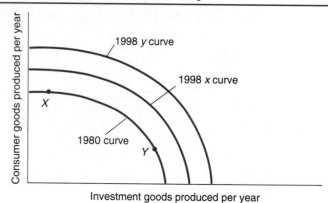

The rate of growth of productive capacity depends in large measure on developing productive resources and new technologies. In 1980 an economy at point *Y* was directed more toward research, study, and construction than the same economy at *X*. Choosing greater production of investment goods will increase the rate of economic growth in the future. The choice of *Y* will lead to future production possibilities that have more goods (1998 *y* curve instead of 1998 *x* curve) than the choice of point *X* will result in.

study, research, producing machines, and toward constructing roads, bridges, planes, and buildings. We see that if in 1980 the economic choice had been made for the investment goods, point *Y,* the production possibilities curve would have shifted further—to 1998 *y* rather than to 1998 *x*. So, present choices are important for future generations. The political debates of the 1992, 1994, and 1996 elections noted this repeatedly: the importance of rebuilding the nation's infrastructure, improving education, and the like. Whether the long-run or the short-run view is taken, at any point in time scarcity exists, no matter how much past growth has occurred. Which is preferable: a little more today or a lot more tomorrow? We always face trade-offs.

THE ECONOMIC PROBLEM AND THE MARKET ECONOMY

How does a **market economy** work to solve the **economic problem** all societies face? Prices send signals to producers (sellers) and buyers (both consumers and investors) about the values of goods, services, and resources. Another term for market economy is *price system.* Sometimes this term is used interchangeably with the terms *market economy* and *market system.*

A MARKET ECONOMY is an extremely decentralized system in which many buyers and sellers interact.

𝜋. 𝜋.

The ECONOMIC PROBLEM involves three basic questions: What goods and services will be produced? How? For whom?

Because there are billions of items and services that people desire, what factors determine which things get produced and which do not? Because there are also many different ways to produce desired goods or services, *how* will they be produced? By which particular methods? How shall the inputs be mixed and organized? Should a business that sells tree-trimming (and -removal) services (1) use several workers with a few ladders and handsaws, or should it (2) use only a few laborers, a truck with a movable platform (nest), and chainsaws?

Once the goods are produced, *who* gets them? What factors determine how the goods and services are distributed—and why some consumers get more than others?

A market economy is a decentralized system that relies on prices resulting from the interactions of millions of individuals. A model helps to simplify these interactions and allows us to assess the basic characteristics of market systems. (The model of markets we use here is simplified to exclude government exchanges, and yet it reveals the basic features of market exchange.)

People live in *households* and earn income in one of two ways: by selling their labor services or by selling use of their property (capital, land, or natural resources). They sell these in **input markets,** where the resources of production are exchanged. Money flows are generated by these exchanges as households receive income from the businesses that pay out money to obtain productive factors. This selling and buying involves quantities (hours worked, square footage of space rented or leased, machine-hours used) and prices (hourly wages, monthly rents, interest paid for capital, and profits).

Households, too, confront a variety of prices in the **output markets,** where goods and services are exchanged. The flow of goods and services from businesses to the output markets and on to households (consumers) is matched by a flow of money in return. Again, these exchanges are made in terms of quantities (autos, haircuts, tacos, or textbooks) and prices.

Both the input and output markets combine to form the **circular flow model** of market exchange (Figure 2–4). This model shows the money flows between households and businesses and the interdependent relationship between the input and output markets of a market economy. The relationship between incomes and prices determines the standards of living for individuals and for the society. As prices for goods and services fall relative to wages and other earnings, households become better off; if wages rise relative to prices for goods and services, households are also better off. They can buy more with their income from the input market. In any economy, choices are continually being registered in both input and output markets. As Figure 2–4 illustrates, these markets are interdependent.

The choices households make are telegraphed to businesses by price and quantity changes through sales or inventory fluctuations. Businesses respond to these shifting messages from households by changing their purchases or productive

𝕁ℛ FIGURE 2–4   The Circular Flow Model of Market Exchange

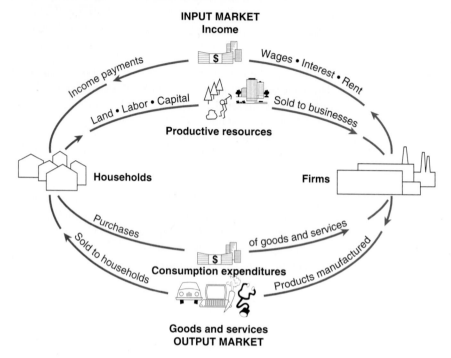

The input and output markets are connected and interdependent. The circular flow model diagrams the flow of money from businesses to households in exchange for the productive resources of land, natural resources, labor, and capital. The money flow in the opposite direction from households to businesses represents consumption expenditures made in exchange for goods and services.

resources in the input markets. These changes, in turn, influence households' incomes and expenditures.

𝕁ℛ 𝕁ℛ

THE CIRCULAR FLOW MODEL shows the money and real exchanges in both the input and output markets.

The market economy allocates the limited resources according to the choices registered by both the households and the businesses. Each group's decisions are both causes and effects. Business choices about what to produce are determined by what they perceive consumers will buy. Businesses hire the resources to produce those goods, which determines the income that different households have at their disposal to buy goods. Each decision maker in each of these groups acts according to self-interests on the basis of information sent through the markets. It is all high drama of social coordination and cooperation on the basis of clear private property rights and freedom to exchange.

What

The questions of *what* and *how much* are produced are answered by the results of millions of independent decisions by individuals in households and in businesses. If enough households buy an item at a price high enough to cover costs, businesses respond by producing more. When businesses learn or perceive that households will not pay enough to cover the costs of production for a product, they will produce something else. Businesses will stop offering products that have "no market." Such decentralized decisions are ultimately part of the success stories of digital watches, videocassettes, jogging shoes, and home computers, or of the product failure stories of the DeLorean auto, *Us* magazine, Kaypro computers, and the United States Football League.

How

Because it is in their own self-interest, businesses keep production costs at the lowest levels possible. They do this by combining, at the least cost, the resources they own with other inputs available for hire. Many different combinations of input mixtures are possible. In the United States we emphasize **capital-intensive methods.** We see many self-service machines—coin-operated laundries and vending machines for mass-transit tickets, cigarettes, food, drinks, and cash. In other countries, such as China, India, Vietnam, or Cambodia, we see far fewer self-service machines. Labor is relatively abundant in such countries, and numerous salespeople work in small shops or sell and process tickets. Similarly, in agriculture in the United States we see the extensive use of heavy machinery operated by few workers. The capital-labor ratio is typically high. This is in large measure because U.S. capital is cheap relative to labor. Not so in Asia and other populous countries, where more **labor-intensive methods** are commonly used and where the capital-labor ratio is usually low. Why? Again, it is a matter of markets and relative prices involving millions of decision makers. The question concerning *how* we produce, just as *what* we produce, is answered by the market economy.

CAPITAL-INTENSIVE production methods reveal a high quantity of capital per worker.

> ⌘⌘⌘⌘⌘⌘⌘⌘⌘⌘⌘⌘⌘⌘⌘⌘⌘⌘⌘⌘⌘⌘⌘⌘⌘⌘⌘⌘⌘
>
> LABOR-INTENSIVE production methods reveal a low quantity of capital per worker.

In an economy in which labor is expensive relative to capital, businesses economize on labor and combine inputs differently than in an economy where labor is cheap relative to capital. Advances of technology expand the range and opportunities for new and different combinations of the input mix. For instance, automatic drive-through car washes in the United States clearly illustrate the uses of new technology to replace the labor-intensive hand car wash. This change to the automatic car wash lowered overall costs. Car washing by hand is still the prevailing least-cost method in China and India, however.

To Whom

In a pure market economy, money price is the method used to ration scarce goods and services, and households receive goods and services only if they can pay for them. The amounts household members can afford depend on their income, which in turn depends on what inputs they own and the price at which they can sell those inputs. People in households holding few marketable skills and with no land or capital to sell will fare poorly. Alternatively, households owning valuable resources—fertile land, stands of timber, oil wells, or plants and equipment—and having special talents (like those of Michael Jordan or Madonna) will have high incomes. For them steak dinners will be routine; a Porsche, a Mercedes, and a beach home will be within their reach.

The question of income distribution always raises the issue of fairness, and with it, the issues of normative economics. You may or may not accept the distribution of income generated by market forces as equitable. Some see justice from the viewpoint that households receive what they earn from voluntarily selling their property and labor to others. Here the essential requirement for fairness (or market justice) is that the opportunity to exchange exists and that the exchanges and contracts are voluntary. Households then receive value for the items they provide to and exchange with others. Their incomes differ as a result of different natural talents, other inputs owned, and the different choices they make.

In contrast, if you emphasize *distributive justice*, you will view the distribution of income through markets as sometimes unfair. Talents, skills, ownership of resources, opportunities, and just plain luck vary among households in ways we may or may not be able to influence. The fact that our income depends on this is not necessarily fair, and the market does not systematically correct for this.

Much of the disagreement among economists—indeed, among all of us—stems from the different values and priorities given to the issues of income distribution, opportunity, and efficiency. Markets, though often viewed as unfair because outcomes are unequal for some, generally are efficient and get the most from productive

⚡ **TABLE 2–1**   Conceptualizing the Economic Problem

Source of the Problem	Imposes and Requires Basic Choices	Answered by Economic Systems Varying in Form between Two Extreme Types
Scarcity	What to produce	The centralized planned economy
	How to produce	The decentralized market economy
	Distribution of products (to whom)	

This illustrates the components of the economic problem that all societies face: Scarcity imposes basic choices of what to produce, how to produce, and to whom the goods and services are distributed. The two extreme alternatives, organizing the economy as a centrally planned system or as a decentralized market system, entail the same constraints of scarcity and result in our having the same basic choices to make. Of course, there are many variations of these polar extremes of organizing the resources.

resources. One role of government is to interfere when the market outcomes result in inherent and unacceptable inequality among population segments.

Table 2–1 diagrams the components of the basic economic problem faced by all societies. The two extreme forms of organizing resources for its solution are shown—the decentralized solution and the centralized one. Most economies lie somewhere in between these two extremes, but the U.S. case emphasizes the decentralized market solution.

Markets, Prices, and Information

In any economy, information is one of the most precious items to possess. Before the American Revolution, an English merchant trying to compete with Yankee traders in the West Indies lamented: "You time things there better than we, get there faster and with what is needed." How true that was, especially following hurricanes. By the time the news of such disasters reached England, Yankee traders from the North American colonies were already docked at the West Indies harbors with their ships full of lumber and other essentials for rebuilding.

The value of business and economic information is no less today. In modern economies like that of the United States, prices send signals and provide information to decision makers. Typically, prices are not determined through negotiations or by one-to-one bargaining; they are advertised or listed. Buyers simply shop for the lowest price on a particular item. This system of setting and responding to prices is efficient and keeps the costs of shopping time low.

Suppose that somewhere the demand for oil increases, or its supply diminishes. As users we do not know that there is a problem. We do not know where the most urgent demand is or where the fall in supply may have occurred. It matters not to you or me which has happened; we only observe that the price for oil is going up. Through the market's many intermediaries, this relevant and much-needed information of price change is communicated to each of us as consumers. We react to this signal of a price increase by buying less oil and by using substitutes. As producers or storers of oil, we will be encouraged to sell more oil. These varied individual reactions assist the market in alleviating the temporary oil shortage. The market acts as a whole, despite the fact that almost none of us know or have a broad perspective on the market and its sources of supply and demand. This illustration may cause us to recall the ordeals of the Organization of Petroleum Exporting Countries (OPEC) and the oil and gas shortages of the 1970s. However, it is paraphrased from another example stated nearly four decades ago by F. A. Hayek, distinguished economist and 1974 Nobel Prize winner in economics.[1]

MARKET DEFICIENCIES AND IMPERFECTIONS

Although in a market economy the cost of transmitting information is reduced, information is not free. Ignorance still abounds and mistakes are made. People who have the property rights of their own labor, capital, land, ideas, and other resources may err in how they use these productive factors. They may make unsound decisions on how they combine their resources with others or on how they allocate them to specific uses. After all, thousands of businesses fail each year. Markets do not operate perfectly or guarantee profits for everyone. There are costs, sometimes significant ones, in operating in markets in the real world. Let's consider some of the sources of market deficiencies and other economic problems that arise in markets.

Transaction Costs

First, there are costs of negotiating exchanges (**transaction costs**), and these make markets work imperfectly. For instance, in business dealings there are costs of making up contracts, gaining legal advice, keeping records to protect against defaults, and other, similar information-gathering activities. Many specialized entities (e.g., advertisers, newspaper want ads, government agencies) strive to lower the costs of information for buyers, sellers, and others, but it is seldom that information is generated without cost. Even finding out about the weather imposes time costs. Transaction costs exist for market economies and for command economies, too. In addition, households do not communicate their preferences perfectly or without cost. Have you ever gone to a movie, only to find that you cannot get in because all the tickets are sold? Or have you ever been unable to go to a movie, even where there are many empty seats, because the ticket price was too high? In these instances, the transaction costs prevented you and the theater owner (who has property rights on entrance and ticket sales) from making the mutually beneficial exchanges that might have led to

---

[1]F. A. Hayek, "The Use of Knowledge in Society," *American Economic Review* 35 (September 1945), pp. 519–20.

your seeing the movie for a price. The imperfections caused by transaction costs are characteristic of all types of economic systems, including the market economy.

For one additional example, consider the differences in the transaction costs of buying a new car versus a used one. A used car presents a lot more uncertainty (absence of information) for a buyer. How many owners have there been, has the car even been in an accident, how has it been maintained and serviced? Can you trust the owner to tell you truthfully all about these and other issues? There is not perfect availability and accuracy of information about a new car either, but consumer guides and warranties help buyers lower transaction costs on new cars relative to used cars.

TRANSACTION COSTS are the costs of making an exchange, including human time costs of shopping, exclusive of the price of the item exchanged.

Externalities

Second, markets are imperfect when some of the costs of consumption or production are imposed on others. Litter strewn on the countryside, smog from exhaust fumes, and polluted rivers and streams impose harm on all of us. The people who cause these damages hurt the rest of us. If most people receive innoculations against a communicable disease, the possibility of an epidemic is reduced. Even those who are not immunized benefit from this practice. These third-party effects are called **externalities.** When the externality is positive, the activity causing the benefits should be encouraged beyond the level resulting from people following their own self-interest. When the externality is negative, the activity should be discouraged.

These statements should be viewed as general guidelines, but caution is warranted. For example, if coal fuel used in steel production causes only slight air pollution and the costs of changing fuels are very high, it may be best for the community to live with the air pollution. This might be the best alternative, for instance, if the population density is low and the higher clean-fuel costs elminate many jobs. If the costs of reducing the pollution exceed the gain in benefits, society loses by insisting on eliminating the pollution. If the population density is very high, however, the costs of the pollution will be much higher, and the community might benefit greatly by switching fuels. A tax on coal will encourage such a switch. So will a subsidy on the next best alternative fuel. The key is to reduce the pollution when the benefits (better health, cleaner environment) from reducing it are greater than the costs (changing fuels) of reducing it. Each situation is unique, and judgments must be made.

The underlying problem here is the right to use the air, which we all own as common property. When everyone owns the rights to air—to breathe and fill with smog from autos and pollution from factories—the costs to society often exceed the costs to individuals who act in their own self-interest. Because ownership of common property (e.g., the air) gives incentives for people to overuse it, and because the costs of monitoring peoples' actions are high, we typicaly resort to government regulations as a means of reducing air pollution. As we shall see in Chapter 9, economics is useful for finding the least-cost method of reducing pollution.

For another example of the benefit-cost trade-off problem posed by externalities, consider the environmental impact of disposable diapers. Environmental groups point to them as a major culprit in the filling up of landfill space with nondegradable materials, and campaigns to ban them have been waged in various states and localities.

Environmentalists stress that the convenience that consumers purchase when they buy a box of disposable diapers comes at too high a price. That convenience costs not merely the $8 or $9 per package paid at the cashier's stand, but also includes the environmental destruction caused by the nearly 16 billion used disposable diapers added to landfills annually.

Although it sounds enormous, actually these 16 billion diapers represent merely 2 percent of all garbage produced by households each year. If wasteful habits are to be curbed, paper products (37 percent) and yard waste (20 percent) merit attention, too.

Furthermore, the use of cloth diapers has its environmental costs as well, and these are typically ignored in the discussion of cloth versus disposable. In particular, cloth diapers would be less appropriate in a community where water to wash them is in short supply, or which is lacking adequate sewage treatment facilities. And the air pollution generated by the vans and trucks used to pick up and deliver cloth diapers to each household must be considered as well.

If the abundance of disposable diapers, like other garbage, results in a shortage of landfill space, then the market value of land will increase and thereby increase the cost of using landfill space for all garbage. This will raise the cost to households of disposables relative to cloth, resulting in fewer disposable diapers used. Or will people selfishly use the roadside to dispose of paper diapers? The answer depends on social values and/or the enforcement strategies and capabilities available.

EXTERNALITIES are costs or benefits that affect third parties.

Public Goods

Third, some goods and services would almost never be produced without collective action by government. Choices expressed through a market economy do not generate armies, agencies of law and order, or flood-control programs. For these **public goods** and other valued public services, centrally planned collective action is needed to ensure their supply. Private suppliers will fail to produce these public goods, because there is little or no possibility for these suppliers to collect revenue for them from users.

PUBLIC GOODS are goods that cannot be withheld from people, even if individuals do not pay for them; therefore, they are normally provided by government.

Income Distribution

Fourth, when a market economy (or any other economic system) gives rise to extreme income inequality or lack of opportunity for personal economic advancement, such as is revealed by the number of the homeless or destitute poor, interference to correct for these inequities is justified. Even if the market economy provided high overall prosperity, correction to reduce extreme inequalities in **income distribution** would still be needed in order to enable all households to maintain the standards of living consistent with that society. *Income distribution* refers to the distribution of income among people for a given time period, such as one year.

Monopoly and Economic Concentration

Finally, if there is an absence of competition, unfair advantages will accrue to the lucky one or few who hold a **monopoly** on the production or sale of certain goods. Monopoly power and economic concentration are possible in a market economy, although historically, they have most often come from government decree.

A MONOPOLY is a market with only one supplier.

The Case for the Market Economy

One of the main arguments for using the decentralized market economy to overcome scarcity and to answer the three basic questions of *what, how,* and *to whom* is that the decentralized market economy emphasizes individual freedom. Each household or business aspires to sell its services or resources for as much as possible. The competition that we impose on each other constrains these possibilities. Sellers may conspire to raise prices. But, if some sellers wish to expand their sales or if new suppliers are encouraged to enter the business, the conspiracy to raise prices is unlikely to succeed. Some buyers may conspire to ruin a seller through a boycott. But those buyers who wish speedy service, who prefer an uncrowded shop, or who prefer lower prices are there to counter the conspiracy. The more employers there are, the greater the freedom that workers possess and the greater their choices. In this sense, effective and impersonal market competition serves to protect individual freedom. And this freedom of choice and enterprise (meaning freedom from directives from a central authority) generally leads to selection of the least-cost methods of production. Except for the imperfections noted, competition through markets is not only responsive to individual and collective wants, but also creates minimal waste. Prices provide the signals and the incentives to sell what is wanted at the lowest costs possible. Moreover, as our wants change, inputs are transferred from low-valued to higher-valued uses. This responsiveness and flexibility, based on individual incentives, was noticeably absent in the former Soviet Union and its satellite countries. The economic failings of those nations are now clearly understood. Although there are pros and cons to any economic system, including a market economy system, evaluation and perception of the efficacy and fairness of any economy depend on both positive and normative economic issues. We shall focus on these issues in the chapters to follow.

CHAPTER REVIEW

All individuals and societies face the basic economic problem caused by scarcity. These include three choices: What to produce? How? And, for whom?

The production possibilities curve (a "Tool Kit" item) shows the problem of choice and reveals the opportunity costs of choice. It also illustrates unemployment, economic growth, and the prevalence of increasing costs resulting from economic specialization in society. Such specialized uses of resources cause much interdependence and reflect substantial cooperation in production and exchange. Individuals following their own self-interests generate items and services the rest of us want. This benefits society.

The circular flow model shows the workings of a market economy system. It emphasizes the principal features of market exchange, in both input and output markets, and the determinants of income and our material standard of living.

The decentralized market economy approach to solving the economic problem has pros and cons. Transaction costs, externalities, monopoly, economic concentration, and the need for public goods are some of the market deficiencies that arise. Income distribution is a matter of normative economics that leads some to view market outcomes as unfair. All these factors address the issue of the role of government in society.

𝕵 MULTIPLE-CHOICE SELF-TEST 𝕵 𝕵 𝕵 𝕵 𝕵 𝕵 𝕵 𝕵 𝕵 𝕵 𝕵 𝕵 𝕵 𝕵 𝕵 𝕵

1. Which of the following is *not* true of competition?
   a. It keeps households and firms from charging prices higher than the level caused by scarcity.
   b. Its absence is a reason for government to intervene in a market.
   c. It means that there are many buyers and many sellers in a market.
   d. It guarantees the highest wages for workers and the highest prices for firms.

2. Production possibilities curves show economic growth:
   a. As resulting from high levels of consumption.
   b. As a shifting out of the curves.
   c. As a reduction in opportunity cost.
   d. As output choices outside the curve.

3. The circular flow model shows:
   a. The transactions of the economy as a flow of money in one direction and goods and services in the other.
   b. That households are buyers and businesses are sellers in both the output and input markets.
   c. That the final sales revenues received by businesses are greater than the incomes earned by households.
   d. That income levels, not prices, determine how much goods and services households will be able to buy.

4. Which of the following does *not* show prices serving as an accurate information signal of relative scarcity?
   a. Wages rise in the United States; many textile plants move their operations to poor nations.
   b. The cost of producing silver tableware rises; more new households buy stainless steel tableware, instead.
   c. Burning trash, which emits wastes into the air, is cheaper than garbage collection; most households burn their trash.
   d. The population of Phoenix, Arizona, rises; apartment rents rise; numerous people move out to smaller cities and towns.

5. Which of the following is *not* a market failure?
   a. Two firms that produce gymnasium seats agree to merge so that they can charge higher prices.
   b. Government provides funding for research into the nature of matter because little such research is done.
   c. Keith Johnson sleeps in a doorway in Chicago because his mental illness makes him an unsatisfactory job candidate.
   d. The price of beef in the United States rises dramatically; consequently, most Americans eat less beef.

☜ STUDY QUESTIONS

1. If the production possibilities curve were a straight line, would there be increasing, decreasing, or constant costs of society's outputs?

2. If tickets to the Super Bowl are being "scalped" for $1,000 and you are given one ticket free, what does it cost you to see the game in person rather than watch it on TV?

3. Are you willing to search longer and incur higher transaction costs to find and purchase an automobile rather than an ice cream cone? A refrigerator rather than a university education? Why?

4. Is the Statue of Liberty a private or a public good? Why?

5. What is the basic economic problem, and what causes it?

6. How do decentralized market economies and centralized economies differ in their approaches to the determination of what and how to produce?

〜 PROBLEMS

1. Draw and mark on your diagram a production combination that a nation might choose after a change in the production possibility curve. Draw the new curve so that the only change in productivity is in the availability to grow food; it still takes the same amount of resources to make only manufactured goods. Does this mean that the new choice can only involve more food, not more manufactured goods?

2. War has broken out in the Middle East, sharply reducing the supply of oil to the United States. The government has decided to order a 20 percent reduction in the production of gasoline for motor vehicle consumption in order to save petroleum. Before the outbreak of war, average annual consumption of gasoline for motor vehicles in the United States had been 120 billion gallons. It must now be reduced to 96 billion gallons. You are responsible for designing a system to allocate the reduced supply of gasoline. How will you do it?

CHAPTER 3

The First Law of Economics

𝔍𝔍 CHAPTER PREVIEW

Almost every Saturday night in Hollywood you will find hundreds of young people in souped-up cars, "dragging Main Street." Cruising Main Street on Saturday night is a favorite pastime in many U.S. towns. It's people-watching at its best, and everybody enjoys being where the action is. But "dragging the Main" really guzzles gas, and the amount of slow cruising in hot rods, pickups, and cherried rigs is strongly influenced by the price of gas. Because young people's allowances or incomes are limited, rising gas prices cut deeply into their pocketbooks. Cruising the Main, in the spirit of the great old movie *American Graffiti,* was tremendously popular in the 1950s and the 1960s, as it was in the 1980s and is in the 1990s. It was much less popular in the 1970s when gasoline prices were much higher and young people frequently sought other things (substitutes) to do with their time on weekend nights.

1. Are changes in the popularity of dragging the Main due only to fads and changing customs?
2. How is a movie a substitute for gasoline?

𝕵 NEW CONCEPTS

Law of Demand
Quantity Demanded
Demand Curve
Nonprice Determinants of Demand
Normal Goods
Inferior Goods
Substitutes
Complements
Change in Demand
Change in Quantity Demanded
Price Elasticity of Demand
Price Inelastic
Unitary Elastic
Price Elastic
Total Revenues

⚞⚟ CHAPTER OBJECTIVES

After studying this chapter, you should be able to:

1. Recognize the law of demand and the demand curve.
2. Understand the determinants (causes) of the demand curve that shift it right or left.
3. Understand the difference between a change in the quantity demanded and a change in demand.
4. Recognize the difference between "normal" and "inferior" goods.
5. Calculate price elasticity of demand.
6. Distinguish among elastic, unitary elastic, and inelastic demand situations.
7. Compute total revenue.
8. Recognize the relationship between price elasticity of demand and total revenue.

PRICES COUNT

It seems a matter of common sense that if the price of pizza falls, some people will buy more of it. The **price** of something is the amount of money (or other things) that you have to give up in order to get it. People buy more when price falls—not because of increased hunger, but because for the same sacrifice they now can obtain more pizza. People will surely take advantage of the improved option, perhaps buying fewer tacos, less fried chicken, or fewer hamburgers. We say the fall in price leads to substitution: more pizza, fewer other goods. Also, for pizza consumers, a fall in the price leaves them with more money for expenditures in general, including pizza.

Everyday expressions such as, "I need a Coke," or "The car needs a paint job," or "The city needs a new fire station," do not make sense if the word *need* is strictly interpreted. A cola drink, a paint job, and a fire station are goods, and all require sacrifices to get them. Are they really a matter of necessity, worthy of unlimited sacrifice either of money or other goods? Don't prices matter?

Parents with children pleading their "need" for a Coke might prudently respond, "Cokes are too expensive, but you can have some lemonade or a 7UP." Would the children still "need" the Coke? Or suppose the front porch or the living room "needs" painting much more than does the car, or that there is a strong argument for new draperies. These and many other possibilities are the sacrifices implicit in the "need" to paint the car. What if the costs of painting the car are extremely high? Should the car be painted if it means skipping meals or doing without heat in the winter? Similarly, is the city's best choice a new fire station? Or would a new park, increased crime prevention, or other services be a better use of the money in the city's budget? There is no escaping the fact that each so-called need incurs a sacrifice, and greater sacrifices raise the cost of the need.

The notion that people will buy more of something if less is sacrificed in order to obtain it is the basis of much of economic analysis. We know from human nature and observation that people prefer more to less; substitutes can be found for almost everything, and people are capable of making choices among and substitutions for the things they want. These traits of human nature provide us with one of the most useful analytical tools in economics, and perhaps in all of the social sciences. This empirically established analytical tool is so powerful that it is called the **law of demand.** This law is humanly made, but has never been legislated. However, great mischief occurs when government policy or business decisions ignore it.

The LAW OF DEMAND states that more of any particular good or service will be purchased as its price falls; less will be purchased as its price rises.

Many people believe that a business can raise its revenues merely by raising prices. But as the law of demand shows, higher prices discourage buying, and fewer sales lower revenues. Will the fall in quantities sold reduce revenues more than a price rise increases them? Clearly, business decision makers must carefully consider consumer responses to any price changes.

If a city government passes legislation restricting the number of taxis and sets a "fair" *maximum price* on taxi services, what happens if the city's population grows dramatically? Would the city law prevail? Or would other, more fundamental forces push the price above the "fair" set price? What happens if it becomes "politically impossible" to change the city law in order to expand the number of taxis or to legislate higher rates? In the former Soviet Union prices of consumer goods were set by government, and shortages were pervasive because official prices were set very low, allegedly to help the needy. But rationing cannot be avoided, and rationing by nonprice means caused trouble for Soviet planners and consumers. News of renewed supplies led to a stampede of consumers to stores, and long lines of people waiting were a normal sight in the cities. Bribes were also common, because official prices were rigid and could not rise to reduce the quantities demanded by anxious customers. When prices are set too low to properly ration available supplies among consumers, lines (first come, first served), bribes, or other rationing means develop. Moreover, as emphasized in Chapter 1, none of these nonprice means of rationing goods encourages suppliers to increase supply. Commands or force become necessary.

The law of demand not only aids our understanding of human behavior but it also often helps anticipate the problems that will occur if it is ignored, or if new conditions emerge.

The Law of Demand Restated

The law of demand deals with the relationship between the quantity demanded of a good (or service) and its price. The **quantity demanded** is the amount purchased at a particular price for a given time period, such as a month or a year. The law of demand asserts that there is an inverse relationship between the quantity of anything people will buy and the price (or sacrifice) they must pay to get it. An *inverse relationship* between two things means that they move in opposite directions. That is, as one goes up, the other goes down. At higher prices, lower quantities will be demanded; at lower prices, higher quantities will be purchased.

This inverse relationship between price and quantity is best understood when it is isolated from other factors that also affect the demand for a good or service. (The other factors affecting demand will be covered below in great detail.) First, keep in mind that the quantity demanded is a specific amount (e.g., 10,000 bicycles) demanded at a particular price (say, $125 per bicycle). Second, the quantity demanded always has a time dimension (e.g., 10,000 bicycles per month), and it is vital to keep the time periods consistent when making comparisons. Finally, the quality of the good is assumed to be unchanged during the time period analyzed.

The Demand Schedule and the Demand Curve

To illustrate the law of demand, Figure 3–1 shows a hypothetical demand schedule for cola drinks. This schedule shows the maximum amounts buyers will purchase per year at different prices. The schedule reveals that at $2 per 16-ounce cup consumers' yearly demand is less than half of what it would be at $1.50. Similarly, at $1 per 16-ounce cup, consumers will buy twice as much as they would at the $1.50 price.

The information of the demand schedule can be translated graphically into a **demand curve,** also shown in Figure 3–1. The demand curve here is downward-sloping from left to right. This negative, or downward, slope comes from the inverse relationship between price and quantity demanded. The graph is read by selecting various points (price-quantity combinations) on it: Point *A* shows that at the $2 price, the demand is 4 billion cola drinks per year; when the price drops to $1 (at point *C*), the demand increases to 20 billion cola drinks per year.

The DEMAND CURVE graphically shows the relationship between prices and the corresponding quantities demanded per time period.

The "Other Things" that Determine Demand

The law of demand relates the price and the quantity demanded of a good (or service). Price is not the only thing that determines the quantities purchased. What relevant other things have we held constant in listing the demand schedule and drawing the demand curve? What things besides the price of cola soft drinks determine the quantity demanded?

FIGURE 3–1 A Hypothetical Demand Schedule and Demand Curve for Cola Drinks

Price per 16-Ounce Cup of Cola	Demanded Quantity of 16-Ounce Cups Purchased per Year (billions)	Price/Quantity Combination Point
$2.00	4	A
1.50	10	B
1.00	20	C
0.50	35	D
0.25	45	E

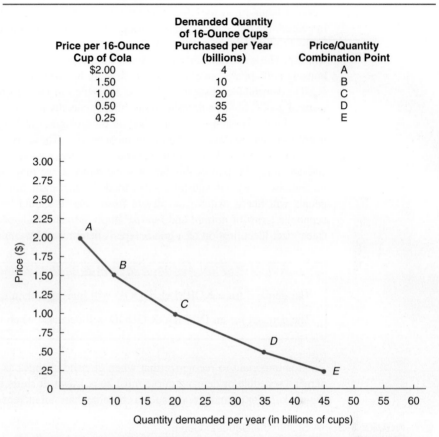

The schedule shows hypothetical amounts of cola drinks demanded annually at alternative prices. The inverse relationship between price and demanded quantity is graphed on the demand curve. It illustrates that, at higher prices, lower quantities are demanded; at lower prices, higher quantities are demanded. It is assumed that other things are held constant and that only prices change. Check the demand curve yourself to be sure that the combination points (*A–E*) are precisely where they ought to be on the demand curve.

The five key **nonprice determinants of demand** are:

1. Income.
2. Prices of related goods.
3. Expectations about future prices.
4. Population size.
5. Tastes and preferences.

Income

The relationship between income and demand was first tabulated by Ernst Engel, a German landlord in the 19th century who observed that as his tenants' incomes increased, the *percentage spent* on food fell; that spent on clothes and housing held fairly steady; and that spent on education, medicine and health care, and recreation went up. These relationships in percentage terms generally still hold true—except for housing and apparel, markets for which there has been considerable expansion.

The demand for most goods will rise as people's incomes increase. These are called **normal goods,** because the demand for them generally increases as income increases. A cola drink is certainly a normal good for most people, but there are some goods that people will choose less of when their incomes rise. These are called **inferior goods.** Macaroni and dry milk are possible examples of inferior goods. If macaroni is inexpensive and a regular part of the diet of some families, we may anticipate that, as their income rises, they will substitute other foods for macaroni. Similarly, as incomes rise, people will likely switch from dry to fresh milk. It should be emphasized that the economic terms of *normal* and *inferior* imply no value judgments on the items they categorize. Identification of a goods type is determined by empirical evidence.

The demand for a NORMAL GOOD will increase when incomes increase.

The demand for an INFERIOR GOOD will decrease when incomes increase.

It is important to recognize that when demand changes as income changes, the demand schedule or demand curve must be redrawn. It shifts position, as shown in Figure 3–2. For normal goods, such as baseball bats, an increase in income will shift

FIGURE 3–2   A Shift in the Demand Curve

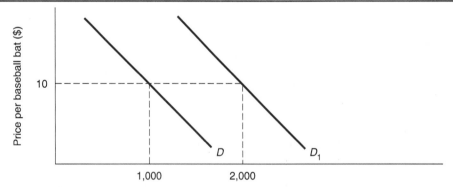

When one of the *other determinants of demand* (other than the price) changes, the demand curve shifts position. When income increases, demand increases for baseball bats, a *normal* good (*D* shifts to D_1). When income falls, demand for baseball bats decreases (D_1 to *D*).

the demand curve upward and to the right (from D to D_1); a fall in income will shift it downward and to the left. For an inferior good, an increase in income will shift the demand curve downward and to the left (from D_1 to D); a fall in income will shift it in the opposite direction.

Prices of Related Goods

When we draw a demand curve, we hold the prices of all other items constant. We then determine the effect of the price change relative to other prices. A demand curve for cola drinks is drawn assuming that the prices of noncola drinks and other items remain unchanged. These are obviously related goods; the demand for cola and the demand for noncola drinks are interdependent. When we apply the law of demand to popcorn, we hold the price of butter constant, because the demand curves for popcorn and for butter relate to each other.

These are examples of two general types of related goods: **substitutes** and **complements.** It is good practice to determine whether one good is a substitute or a complement to another, or whether it is simply unrelated. To be sure that one good is a substitute rather than a complement for another, we must consider how a change in price for one thing affects the demand for the other, as shown in Figure 3–3.

Consider cola and noncola drinks again. If each drink (16-ounce cup) costs $1 and the noncola drink falls in price to $0.75 per cup, people will undoubtedly buy fewer cola and more noncola drinks (other things remaining equal). Why? They are good *substitutes.* The lower cost of one leads to a substitution by the other—not totally, but at least partially. The fall in the price of noncola drinks shifts the demand curve for cola drinks inward, to the left (from D_1 to D in Figure 3–2). A jump in noncola prices has the opposite effect, shifting the demand curve for cola soft drinks outward, to the right (from D to D_1 in Figure 3–2).

FIGURE 3–3 Price Effects on Related Goods

A Substitutes			B Complements			C Unrelated		
Price of cola drinks	↑ ↑	Demand for noncola drinks	Price of movie tickets	↑ ↓	Demand for cola drinks	Price of pillows	↑	Demand for cola drinks unchanged
Price of noncola drinks	↓ ↓	Demand for cola drinks	Price of movie tickets	↓ ↑	Demand for cola drinks	Price of pillows	↓	Demand for cola drinks unchanged

Related goods are substitutes or complements. When two goods are substitutes, a price increase in one will cause the demand for the other to go up. When the price of one good goes up and the demand for the other falls, the two goods are complements. If a price change in one does not change the demand for another, they are neither substitutes nor complements; they are unrelated.

> 𝕵𝕵
>
> For SUBSTITUTES, a price change for one leads to a shift in the same direction in the *demand* for the other.

The reverse occurs with complementary goods—for example, tennis racquets and tennis balls, popcorn and butter, movie tickets and cola drinks. If the price of popcorn goes up sharply, the price of popcorn and butter in combination is higher. People will buy less of the combination, another way of applying the law of demand. Or think of it as a shift downward and to the left in the demand for butter. Less butter is demanded, because the price of popcorn has risen. These are *complements*. Higher-priced movie tickets shift the demand curve for cola drinks (as well as candy and popcorn) downward and to the left. Higher-priced tennis racquets discourage newcomers to the game and reduce the demand for tennis balls.

> 𝕵𝕵
>
> For COMPLEMENTS, in contrast to substitutes, a price change for one leads to a shift in the opposite direction in the *demand* for the other.

Expectations about Future Prices

It is sometimes argued, mistakenly, that the law of demand does not hold, because of speculative buying. This occurs when people buy something in the hopes that its price will rise and they can sell at a profit. Consider the situation when the price of orange juice rises and people buy more of it. Isn't that contrary to the law? Suppose that they buy because they anticipate further price increases in the future because a hard freeze has hit the Citrus Belt. Alternatively, if the price of portable radios falls today, people might buy fewer radios if they think the price will go still lower next week.

A closer inspection shows that, rather than being exceptions, these occurrences are consistent with the law of demand. If today we see a new, higher price on a good but speculate that the price will soon be even higher, we decide that the price now is low relative to the future. We buy more now. We buy at today's relatively lower price, and we will buy less in the future at the expected higher relative price. In general, if a rise in future prices is expected (other things remaining unchanged), we purchase more now—the amount demanded increases now. Alternatively, if we speculate that future prices will be lower, we may buy less today, even though the price may have fallen somewhat already. For the moment, demand has fallen; we defer our purchases.

Population Size

If average incomes remain unchanged, an increase in population usually shifts the demand curve upward and to the right (D to D_1 in Figure 3–2). The number of buyers and the total purchasing power increase, and hence the demand for most goods increases as well. Alternatively, if population declines, demand will decline. The example of the emergence of a frontier boomtown and its decline to a ghost town helps in visualizing these population effects. Alternatively, there are age-specific changes that alter demand conditions—a baby boom or an aging population. Baby booms obviously affect demand for certain types of goods: diapers, baby food, and child care facilities. An aging population brings greater demands for nursing homes, medical care, and "oldies-but-goodies" records.

Tastes and Preferences

This leads us to the issue of tastes. Just as spending patterns stem from demographic changes, consumers (at any age) change their tastes and preferences for goods and services for other reasons. When "Beatlemania" hit in the mid-1960s, long hair became the rage and the demand for haircuts dropped off considerably. An upswing of interest in soccer in the United States in the 1980s and 1990s brought greater demand for soccer balls and possibly a decline in the demand for baseballs. Economists generally have little to say about what causes tastes or preferences to change. They leave to marketers, psychologists, and others the determination of why people buy certain brands or styles of goods rather than other brands or styles. In any case, major changes in tastes, especially fads, can have big effects on demand in certain markets.

Change in Demand versus Change in Quantity Demanded

One of the most common sources of confusion in economic analysis stems from the failure to distinguish between a **change in demand** (when the entire demand curve shifts) and a **change in quantity demanded** (when the curve does not shift, but the price has changed). Consider the following contradictory but seemingly plausible statements:

- The price went up, so demand went down.
- Demand went up, so price went up.

The first statement errs, confusing a movement upward along the demand curve (a fall in the quantity demanded because of a price increase) with a downward shift in the curve (change in demand). Figure 3–4 illustrates this important distinction.

A CHANGE IN DEMAND results from a change in one of the nonprice determinants and causes a shift in the position of the demand curve.

A CHANGE IN QUANTITY DEMANDED comes from a price change and involves a movement along the curve.

FIGURE 3–4   Change in Quantity Demanded (Panel A) versus Change in Demand (Panel B)

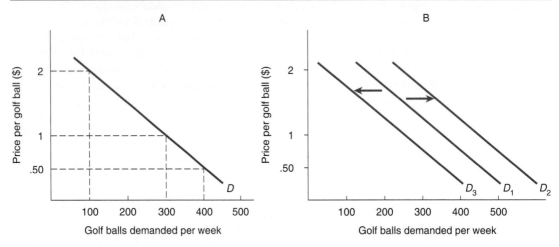

The distinction between a change in the quantity demanded and a change in demand is illustrated here. In Panel A the graph shows the alternative quantities of golf balls demanded as price changes. If the price rises from $1 to $2, other things remaining constant, a *change in quantity demanded* will occur, from 300 to 100. In B a change in demand is illustrated and the entire demand curve shifts, either an increase from D_1 to D_2 or a decrease from D_1 to D_3. Changes in other things—tastes, population, expectations of future prices, income, prices of substitutes and complements—cause a *change in demand* (Panel B).

In Panel A the demand curve shows changes in quantities demanded resulting from price changes (other things being constant). A rise in price from $1 to $2 will not change demand, but the quantity demanded will fall from 300 to 100; alternatively, a fall in price from $1 to $0.50 will increase the quantity demanded from 300 to 400. In both cases, however, no change in demand has occurred; that is, the curve has not shifted.

In contrast, Panel B shows changes in demand—actual shifts in the demand curve as one or more of things other than price change. An increase in demand and shift in the demand curve from D_1 to D_2 might be caused by any of several factors:

• Taste change (greater preference).
• Greater population.
• Expectation of a future price rise.
• Increase in income (if a normal good).
• Fall in income (if an inferior good).
• Price of a substitute rises.
• Price of a complement falls.

What factors would cause a decrease in demand, such as from D_1 to D_3?

The Demand for Cabs in New York City

There are not enough cabs in New York City, and catching a cab is difficult, especially on cold or rainy days. New York City limits the number of licensed cabs on the streets by requiring each one to have a medallion (certificate of operation). The number of medallions has been frozen for decades at 11,787, and this property right to own and operate a cab has become quite valuable. Partly, this is because in New York City private cars are an extreme luxury. In addition, the deterioration of the subways and the rise of New York's business population has increased the demand for cabs greatly. A medallion that once cost around $200 is worth over $100,000 today. Furthermore, as taxi fares (rates) are regulated and fixed by a commission to meet normal demand, temporary jumps in demand don't cause prices to rise. People wait longer for rides. During rainstorms or in freezing weather, people who otherwise would walk take cabs. This additional demand causes people to stand for long times waiting to find a vacant cab. Scuffling and angry words from wet or cold taxi demanders fighting to jump into cabs are commonplace in New York City. Rationing of the limited taxi services is accomplished by longer waiting periods instead of by higher prices.

Price Responsiveness and Price Elasticity

The law of demand tells us that the quantity demanded will increase as price falls. But how much will it increase? Will a fall in the price of bananas by 10 cents per pound lead to a large increase in the quantity demanded? Will the 10-cent-per-pound price decline lead to a greater increase of bananas bought than a fall in the price of gasoline by 10 cents a gallon will increase the consumption of gas? How can changes in the quantity demanded of bananas and of gasoline be compared when one is measured in pounds and the other in gallons?

The **price elasticity of demand** measures the buyers' response to a price change. It is a measure based on *percentage changes* and therefore allows comparisons for all items, despite vast differences in the units used to measure and sell them. The formula states

$$\frac{\text{Percent change in quantity}}{\text{Percent change in price}} = \text{price elasticity of demand} \qquad (3\text{--}1)$$

It measures in percentage terms the purchase responsiveness of buyers to price changes. The result is always expressed as a positive value, despite the inverse (negative) relationship and opposite change in the direction (or sign) of price and quantity. Consequently, a 10 percent fall in the price of gasoline, which leads to a 5 percent increase in gas purchased, reveals a price elasticity measure of 0.5:

$$\frac{\text{Percent change in } Q}{\text{Percent change in } P} = \frac{5}{10} = 0.5$$

Whenever the result is less than 1.0, as in this example, we say it is **price inelastic**, because the purchase responsiveness is low. The *price inelastic* case has an elasticity measure less than 1. Alternatively stated, the quantity response in percentage terms is less than the price change in percentage terms. All such cases are price inelastic. When the price elasticity measure is exactly 1.0, where the percent change in Q equals the percent change in P, it is **unitary elastic.** A unitary elastic case has an elasticity measure equal to 1. For cases where the responsiveness is greater and in which the percentage change in quantity exceeds the percentage change in price, the measure is said to be *price elastic*. Price-elastic cases have elasticity measurements greater than 1. For example, a price increase from $1 to $1.25 is a 25 percent increase [(1.25 − 1.00)/$1 = 25%]. If the quantity demanded falls from 1,000 to 700, a 30 percent decline [(1,000 − 700)/1,000 = 30%], the demand is price elastic (30%/25% = 1.2).[1] If the quantity decline is to 750 (a 25 percent decline), the demand is unitary elastic (1.0). A lesser quantity decline would reveal a price-inelastic section of the demand curve. The words *section of the demand curve* are emphasized because the price elasticity measure is not constant for the whole demand curve. In fact, the elasticity measure changes as you measure different points on the same demand curve. Time spent in measuring elasticities for the various price-quantity relationships in Figure 3–1 will reveal this characteristic.

PRICE ELASTICITY OF DEMAND is the percentage change in the quantity demanded divided by the percentage change in price.

Applications of the Price Elasticity Concept

The concept of price elasticity has many practical and analytical uses. For instance, it will answer the question: Will an increase in price raise revenues? Consider the problem of a university athletic director and head football coach who want to increase revenues for their home games. Costs to clean up and maintain the stadium and other incidental costs do not change significantly as the number of people in attendance changes, at least over a certain range. In this special case, increases in revenues directly and totally increase profits. If ticket prices to home games are increased from $5 to $6, a 20 percent jump, revenues will rise, stay the same, or fall, depending on the price elasticity of demand.

---

[1]We note one additional consideration for those seeking greater precision to the elasticity measure. Ideally, the measured computation should be the same up or down the demand curve between two points, but $1 to $1.25 is a 25 percent increase, whereas $1.25 to $1 is a 20 percent decrease. And 1,000 to 700 is a 30 percent decrease, whereas 700 to 1,000 is a 300/700, or 43 percent increase. One way to obtain greater precision is to use a *geometric mean* of the two prices (and quantities). Start with $0.25 (the price change) and divide it by [($1 + $1.25)/2] (the average of the two prices). This gives a percent change of 22 percent. Similarly, the percent quantity change can be calculated as 300 divided by 850 [(1,000 + 700)/2], or about 35 percent. This more precise measure gives an elasticity of 35/22.5, or about 1.5. For small price changes, the gain in precision from this method is slight, but the gain in precision grows with larger price and quantity changes. In the computations that follow, we stick with the simple, but less precise, measure of computation.

🏈 FIGURE 3–5 The Price-Elastic Case

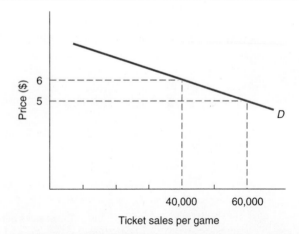

Ticket sales per game

A price hike on football tickets from $5 to $6 is a 20 percent jump and is less than the fall in ticket sales, which decline from 60,000 to 40,000, or 33 percent. The elasticity measure in this case is *price elastic,* and total revenues fall because of the price increase.

If there are many other things to do on Saturday afternoons besides watch football (lots of good substitutes), the price elasticity of demand for football may be quite high. Depending on where you live, you may be able to choose among ski trips, rock festivals, a beach party, a homecoming in a neighboring town, movies, and the football game. Figure 3–5 shows the price-elastic case for a football game, where there is a drop in attendance from 60,000 to 40,000. This attendance (quantity) decline, because of the 20 percent price increase, exceeds 20 percent. Therefore, **total revenues** per game fall. They fall from $300,000 to $240,000. Alternatively, if "it's the only game in town," in the sense that there isn't much else to do for entertainment on Saturday afternoons, then the price elasticity may be quite low.

🏈🏈🏈🏈🏈🏈🏈🏈🏈🏈🏈🏈🏈🏈🏈🏈🏈🏈🏈🏈🏈🏈🏈🏈🏈🏈🏈

TOTAL REVENUES are measured by price times quantity.

In Figure 3–6 the drop in quantity demanded from 60,000 to 55,000 (a drop of only 8 percent) is lower than the percentage increase in price (20 percent). In this case, total revenues rise because of the price hike, from $300,000 to $330,000.

The life of a head football coach can sometimes be hard. Suppose the university president and the board of trustees put pressure on the athletic director to bring in more money and the athletic director in turn tells the head coach he wants the stadium filled—completely—and that ticket prices are also going up to $7. Woe be it

FIGURE 3–6   The Price-Inelastic Case

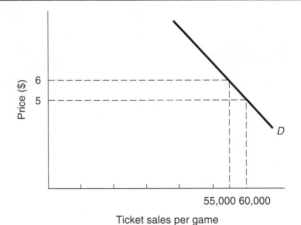

A price hike from $5 to $6 (20%) reduces football ticket sales from 60,000 to 55,000 (e.g., by 8%). In this case the elasticity measure is *price inelastic,* and total revenues rise because of the price increase.

for the coach if the price elasticity of demand is high. If the demand is *D,* as shown in Figure 3–7, the coach must somehow shift the demand curve out to the right (to D_1) or he won't fill the stadium (70,000 capacity). The coach might argue that the price should be $4 instead of $7. At the initial demand situation of *D,* the coach could fill the stadium at a price of $4. And $280,000 ($4 × 70,000) in revenues is better than $210,000 ($7 per ticket with only 30,000 attending). In addition, the alumni and students will be pleased by the low price and large crowd. But the athletic director may insist on more, such as a championship team, one good enough to shift the demand curve from *D* to D_1. Then a full stadium will be possible at $7 and total revenues will be $490,000.

Even with the higher demand of D_1, however, the question remains: Will revenues be maximized at the price of $7? Again, it depends on the price elasticity of D_1. If it is price inelastic, a full stadium will not maximize revenues. A higher price with some empty seats will raise revenues if the demand is price inelastic.

The ideal demand curve for the athletic director, and for every business decision maker, is mythical. It is vertical, like the one shown in Figure 3–8. This peculiar demand curve would allow higher and higher prices to be charged, with no reductions in quantity demanded. Indeed, it defies the law of demand. And yet, this mythical demand curve is repeatedly implied: "We need another fire station." "I need a Coke." "The car needs painting." But there really is no such thing as a perfectly inelastic demand curve, that is, one that is vertical. Some demanders will reduce their purchases as prices advance; everyone will cut spending at sufficiently large price changes (other things being equal). (In certain rare and special instances,

🏈 FIGURE 3–7   Shifting the Demand for Football Tickets

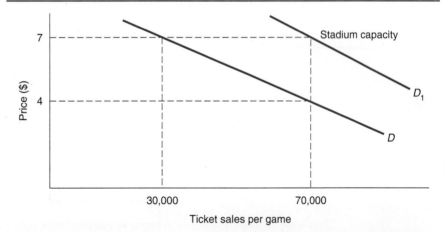

If the athletic director raises the price of football tickets from $4 to $7 and insists the stadium be filled at 70,000 capacity, the head football coach will not be able to meet this objective if the demand curve is *D*. However, if the team becomes a championship team or other factors increase demand to *D₁*, the stadium can be filled at $7 per seat.

such as a need for organ transplants, the demand curve may be vertical over a considerable but not unlimited range.) Despite this obvious point, the media are filled with statements implying complete inelasticity of demand. Daily we hear or read the terms *basic needs, absolute necessities,* and *essential requirements* applied to a whole array of proposals. Upon close inspection, these needs are seen to be not really so absolute and their demand curves not really so inelastic as the statement makers might insist. The use of these terms is transparent rhetoric. Be on guard for such terms when they are used in advocacy of things you oppose. And be prepared to defend your assertions if you are challenged for using such rhetoric yourself.

Factors Influencing Elasticity

As the examples imply, one of the most important factors affecting the price elasticity of demand is the availability and range of good substitutes. The greater the availability of good substitutes, the more elastic is the demand. Another factor is how important an item is in your budget. If expenditures on an item are large relative to your income, you will be much more sensitive to price changes than if the expenditure is an insignificant portion of your budget. If your family spends $200 a month on one thing and only $20 a month on something else, a 10 percent increase in price will be more acutely felt on the large-expenditure item. There will be strong incentives to reduce the quantity of the large-expenditure item. Finally, time is an important factor. In the short run, price changes do not bring about the quantity response that will occur in the long run. First responses to a price change may be very slight. Although

 **FIGURE 3–8**   The Perfectly Inelastic Case

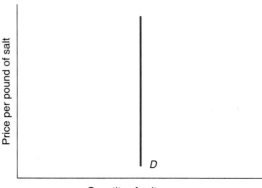

This is the demand curve implicit in frequently heard rhetorical statements about "absolute needs," "necessities," and "essential requirements." It is perfectly inelastic, with no change in quantity demanded, no matter the level of price.

we are creatures of habit, as consumers we eventually find substitutes for items that are rising in price. Or, producers will devise them for us. When OPEC curtailed oil sales in 1973 and raised gasoline prices dramatically worldwide, people in the United States initially reduced their use of gasoline only modestly. However, after more fuel-efficient cars were produced and people found other means to conserve on gasoline (and other fuels), the quantity reduction in demand because of the higher

INFLUENTIAL ECONOMIST

ALFRED MARSHALL, 1842–1924

Today the United States is the center of learning in economics; it is where most of the leading research and instruction is undertaken by the world's most influential economists. At the turn of the century, however, England was the center of learning in economics, and Alfred Marshall was the world's most influential living economist.

Alfred's father, a cashier at the Bank of London, wanted his son to enter the ministry. Alfred had other ideas, however, and turned down a scholar-

ship to study theology at Oxford. Instead he studied math at Cambridge, graduating with an MA in 1865. His interest in ethics and concern for improving people's lives led him to economics, and two years later he began his studies of economics.

By 1880 he was recognized as the key figure in the development and professionalization of economics. He employed his mathematical training to build on the works of earlier classical writers. Marshall added rigor to economics; the tools of analysis price was much larger. In the short run, the price elasticity was small; in the long run, it was considerably more. The need for gasoline was actually much less absolute in the long run than OPEC and many consumers and policymakers proclaimed. The truth is that there are substitutes for nearly everything, and time and imagination help us to find them. Even a movie can substitute for gasoline, as young people seek less expensive ways to entertain themselves than dragging the Main.

For the purpose of raising revenues, governments throughout history have sought to tax items that are highly price inelastic: alcohol, tobacco, or salt. For such items, when the tax is imposed and the price rises, the fall in the quantity demanded is slight. Tax revenues jump dramatically. In the case of salt, Adam Smith in *The Wealth of Nations* notes that "salt is a very ancient and very universal subject of taxation." Why? As he further notes: Salt is one of "the necessities of life"; and "the quantity annually consumed by any individual is so small; . . . that nobody . . . could feel very sensibly even a pretty heavy tax upon it." We translate Smith's observations to mean the following:

- There are few good substitutes for salt.
- Expenditures on salt are typically a small fraction of an individual's income.

Even salt, however, has some price elasticity, more so in the long run than in the short run. Consumers may buy more foods with high natural salt ingredients and fewer salt additives if salt rises significantly in price. In cold, icy regions where rock salt is used in winter to deice walkways and streets, sand and charcoal chips may be used instead if salt prices rise sharply.

It is comforting that the power to take advantage of the low price elasticity of demand for salt is limited because of competition among suppliers. No single producer has complete control over all the salt for sale. Therefore, if Safeway raises the price of

he developed broke new ground in bringing forth understanding and solution of many problems.

His most important work, the *Principles of Economics,* appeared in 1890 and, in his lifetime, reappeared through eight editions, the last in 1920. *Principles* became the standard text for English-speaking economists. It was both an original contribution to knowledge, suggesting areas for future research, and a broad exposition of the problems that interest economists. The modern student can still learn much from reading Marshall's *Principles.* Indeed, it provides the basis for most textbooks in economics.

In *Principles* Marshall developed the concept of elasticity of demand and the convergence of the law of demand and the law of supply (to be introduced in Chapter 4). Marshall initiated the systematic use of the principles of demand and supply as the central basis of economic science. He first stated this combination of demand and supply in the second edition of his *Principles:*

In spite of a great variety in detail, nearly all the chief problems of economics agree in that they have a kernel of the same kind. This kernel is an inquiry as to the balancing of two opposed classes of motives, the one consisting of desires to acquire certain new goods, and thus satisfy wants; while the other consists of desires to avoid certain efforts or retain certain immediate enjoyment. . . . In other words, it is an inquiry into the balancing of the forces of demand and supply.

its brand, people can turn to other brands, such as Lady Lee or Morton's. For *any brand,* price elasticity is extremely *high* because there are many excellent substitutes. Indeed, one brand is almost identical to another. Therefore, a tax would generate little revenue if it were placed on only one brand or at one sales outlet. For example, suppose all brands were taxed but at only one chain, say, Safeway. Following their own self-interest, people would buy salt at pretax prices at other outlets, such as 7-Eleven, White Owl, Lucky, and neighborhood stores. The problem for government and producers aspiring to extract money from people by raising prices on price-inelastic items is that, generally, substitutes are plentiful, even for necessities. Furthermore, multiple suppliers mean that control over price becomes difficult to initiate and impossible to sustain.

We conclude with one last example. Surely economists will agree that water is a necessity of life. Perhaps, but of the 350 gallons used daily by an average family of four in the United States today, how many are used for drinking? A few, possibly! But think of the uses of water for gardens, toilets, showers, washing clothes (and cars), sports, and frolicking entertainment. Is a baseball bat a substitute for water? Yes, asserts a parent whose house has just been metered for water use (a fee charged per gallon used) and tells the children to stop the garden-hose water fight. "Go play ball in the park," they are told. The truth is, there are substitutes for everything.

⅏ CHAPTER REVIEW

The main topic of this chapter is the law of demand, which states that at lower (higher) prices, larger (smaller) quantities will be demanded, other things being equal. Price and quantity demanded are therefore inversely related; if price goes up, quantity demanded goes down.

The demand curve is downward-sloping from left to right, and it shifts if any of the nonprice determinants of demand change. These nonprice determinants of demand are income, prices of related goods (substitutes or complements), expectations about future prices, population size, and tastes.

A change in demand is not the same thing as a change in quantity demanded, which can occur from a price change. A change in demand occurs only when the nonprice determinants change. An increase in demand (a shift to the right) may result from a taste change (increased preference), a larger population, expectations of a future price increase, an increase in income (for a normal good), a decrease in income (for an inferior good), a rise in the price of a substitute, or a fall in the price of a complement.

The degree or extent of the responsiveness of the quantity demanded to a price change is measured as follows: Price elasticity = (percent change in *Q*) ÷ (percent change of *P*). When this measure is more than 1, it is called *price elastic,* and a decline in price will lead to larger revenues (price times quantity). When the price elasticity measure is less than 1, it is called *price inelastic,* and a price increase will lead to larger revenues. When the measure is exactly 1, it is called *unitary elastic,* and total revenues thus remain unchanged with a price change.

🙐 MULTIPLE-CHOICE SELF-TEST 🙐🙐🙐🙐🙐🙐🙐🙐🙐🙐🙐🙐🙐🙐🙐

1. Medical care costs have risen tremendously and continue to rise.
   a. This has no effect on the calculation of the number of hospital beds an area needs.
   b. The high and rising prices cannot deter people from purchasing medical care, because this is not a voluntary choice.
   c. Because the use of medical care has not declined much despite large price increases, it is a good bet that the demand curve for medical care is inelastic.
   d. Purchases of medical care have risen over the decades, even though prices were rising. This situation is an exception to the law of demand.

2. The price of down rises, and consumers cut back on their purchases of down jackets. This is best explained as a:
   a. Downward shift in the demand curve for down jackets.
   b. Decrease in quantity demanded.
   c. Change in tastes.
   d. Decline in demand.

3. The price of lamb chops rises slightly, and the quantity of lamb chops purchased increases. Which of the following is the best explanation for this situation?
   a. The price of pork rose.
   b. People's incomes rose, and lamb chops are a normal good.
   c. American consumers seem to be seeking more variety in the meats they eat.
   d. All the above are reasonable explanations for why the whole demand schedule for lamb should shift up.

4. Which of the following could explain why the demand for tobacco is inelastic?
   a. Tobacco is a luxury.
   b. Tobacco purchases are a significant part of many people's incomes.
   c. There are not very close substitutes for tobacco.
   d. The demand is quite inelastic for a short period but becomes more elastic as buyers have time to make adjustments.

5. An increase in the demand for a good:
   a. Is shown by a movement along the demand curve.
   b. Can be the result of a decrease in price of a substitute good.
   c. Is basically caused by a decrease in price of the good.
   d. Means that people are willing to pay more than before for any given quantity of the good.

📖 STUDY QUESTIONS

1. What substitutes and complements influence your demand for ice cream? For orange juice? For camping trips?

2. If the price of gasoline doubles, what will happen to the demand for and value of automobiles in the United States? For bicycles?

3. If there is a large bumper crop of oranges and the price of orange juice falls, will the demand for orange juice necessarily change? Why or why not?

4. If the price of movie tickets jumps from $3 to $3.50 and attendance slips from 2,000 per week to 1,800, what happens to the theater owner's weekly revenues? Compute them.

5. Refer to Question 4. In this price range, what is the price elasticity of demand implied?

6. What substitutes or complements influence the price elasticity of demand for tickets to see movies?

⚖ PROBLEM

Here's a common situation in cities around the world: The public transit system is running significantly in the red. City government officials argue over whether to raise fares to combat the deficits. One usual argument against a fare increase is that it will create hardship for lower-income people who have no other means of transport. Another issue is often overlooked: How much of a fare increase will it take to resolve the problem? Suppose that the current bus fare is $0.75 and the government is considering raising it to $1. If this reduces the number of trips purchased from 10,000 to 8,000:

1. What is the elasticity of demand for bus trips?

2. What does this elasticity of demand suggest to you about what will happen to total revenue earned by the bus system?

3. Check your answer to Question 2 by calculating the total revenue earned when the fare is $0.75 cents and when it is $1. Does the fare increase resolve the deficit problem as well as you (or the city officials) might have thought? Why or why not?

CHAPTER 4

The Law of Supply and Market Price

𝕁𝕁 CHAPTER PREVIEW

Burt Hansen, a farmer in the Midwest, learned that several neighboring farms were switching from corn to soybeans. Not a daily price watcher, Burt simply kept his eye on some of the most successful farmers in his region. In checking around, Burt learned that soybean prices had moved up, thus providing strong encouragement for farmers to increase their soybean production. Burt's kids liked to play hide and seek among the cornstalks, but Burt rationalized that with the extra income from soybeans, he could buy them some new things—maybe some video games or a horse. He had made a similar production change a few years earlier when a prominent agricultural professor visiting a statewide 4-H Club rally told the 4-H members, among them Burt's oldest daughter, about a new pesticide spray that would also stop fungus. Burt's corn had been plagued with fungus for several years, so it was an especially important technological breakthrough for him to consider. He recalled that his average yields per acre had jumped nearly 15 percent that year, and the new spray had cost little more than the old one. Burt's income had jumped nicely too; maybe the switch to soybeans now would do the same thing. Soybeans could possibly raise his income well above what he could get from corn, and his land was well suited for either crop. Yes, he would definitely switch; Burt expected the soybean prices to stay high. Burt is increasing soybean production in response to price increases. The higher revenue will raise his own income, so he is acting in his own self-interest. In addition, by supplying more of the good whose market value has risen, Burt also helps society. This shows how markets are institutions of social cooperation and how responses by individuals to market signals are acts of social cooperation.

1. What role does self-interest play in supplying the goods that are demanded in the marketplace?

2. In a market economy does either demand alone or supply alone determine the market price of an item?

3. If market prices for corn and soybeans were set by law and not permitted to change, would Burt Hansen have any incentive to switch crops in the event of soybean shortages?

4. What is the best way to ration soybeans if a shortage develops?

CONCEPTS REINTRODUCED

NEW CONCEPTS

Law of Supply
Supply Curve
Cost Determinants of Supply
Technological Advances
Change in Supply
Change in Quantity Supplied
Elasticity of Supply
Markets
Surplus
Shortage
Equilibrium
Market Clearing Price
Equilibrium Price
Disequilibrium
Commodity Futures

🎓 CHAPTER OBJECTIVES

After studying this chapter, you should be able to:

1. Recognize the law of supply and the supply curve.
2. Distinguish between a change in supply and a change in the quantity supplied.
3. Recognize the determinants of supply that shift the supply curve to the right or left.
4. Understand how market price equilibrium is determined.
5. Measure shortages and surpluses and determine their causes.

INFORMATION AND SUPPLY

Businesses continually seek information. Sources of useful information seem unlimited. Television, radio, and newspapers; church socials; Rotary, Kiwanis, and 4-H Club meetings; tavern gossip; weekend drives; e-mail; and the U.S. Departments of Commerce and Agriculture all generate information useful to business decision makers.

Burt's story illustrates how producers (suppliers) acquire and use information on productive techniques, costs, and selling opportunities. However, such information usually boils down to an array of prices. So common and systematic are the reactions of suppliers to price changes that there is another economic law—the law of supply. It is combined with the law of demand to show how market price is determined.

THE LAW OF SUPPLY

Like the law of demand, the **law of supply** is not the result of legislation; it comes from observation and the study of human behavior. It states the relationship between price and quantity, or more specifically, the relationship between various prices and actual quantities that are offered for sale. It is based on the repeated observation that people usually act in their own interests. To improve their income and wealth, people take advantage of opportunities and they respond to incentives.

> The LAW OF SUPPLY states that at higher prices, the quantities supplied will increase, other things held constant. Alternatively, at lower prices, smaller quantities will be supplied, other things being equal.

As the law of supply states, there is a direct relationship between quantity and price. As the price goes up, the quantity supplied goes up, too. In contrast, the law of demand conveys there is an inverse, or negative, relationship between quantity and price.

The positive relationship between price and quantity supplied is due in part to substitution possibilities in production. Like Farmer Hansen, producers often can substitute among items they produce, even in the short run. When producers can change and switch among items to be produced, they will supply less of those things that fall in value (corn, perhaps) and more of those things that have increased in price (say, soybeans). Greater profits are thus gained, or losses reduced. Sellers want to cover costs and earn a profit, and like buyers, they take advantage of opportunities for gains. As the law of supply explicitly states, we are holding other things constant here—most importantly, technology, wages for labor, taxes or subsidies, and prices for other inputs such as capital and land.

There is another reason that quantities supplied are directly related to prices. From Chapter 2, recall the production possibilities curve and note that as more and more of a particular thing (e.g., houses) are produced, increasing costs are incurred. The sacrifices of one thing for another eventually become greater and greater because factors of production are typically specialized and cannot be perfectly substituted for each other. Moreover, some inputs are fixed and relatively unexpandable, especially over short periods. If costs per unit do rise as more units are produced, higher prices become necessary to allow producers to cover these rising costs. When conditions of increasing costs do prevail, producers are unwilling to produce more and incur additional costs unless higher market prices encourage them. It should be clear also that the law of supply is consistent with cost increases as production rates are speeded up. Chapter 6 presents a more thorough discussion of costs and production.

It is especially important to recognize that supplies are limited by costs. If buyers wish to obtain more of a particular item, suppliers must be encouraged to supply more of it. Higher prices provide this encouragement for suppliers to move resources from an existing use into the production of items more urgently wanted. Moving resources from one use to another reminds us that costs are opportunity costs, that is, real forgone alternatives.

The Supply Schedule and the Supply Curve

Similar to the law of demand, the law of supply can be illustrated as a schedule relating prices to quantities supplied. In Figure 4–1 several price and quantity combinations for cupcakes highlight the direct relationship between quantities supplied and price. As the price of cupcakes increases, bakeries respond by producing more cupcakes (and perhaps fewer doughnuts or other items). At a price of 5 cents per cupcake, no one produces cupcakes for sale, but at 10 cents, 500 cupcakes per week are produced and offered for sale. Higher prices elicit even more production and possibly even the start-up of new bakeries.

In summary, at very low prices the bakeries produce little, because of the problem of covering costs. At higher prices, costs are more completely covered, and at sufficiently high prices profits will be earned. As resources are attracted by these price rises, the supply expands.

FIGURE 4–1   A Supply Schedule and Supply Curve for Cupcakes

Price per Cupcake	Quantities Supplied per Week
$.05	0
.10	500
.15	1,500
.20	2,500
.25	4,000
.30	6,000

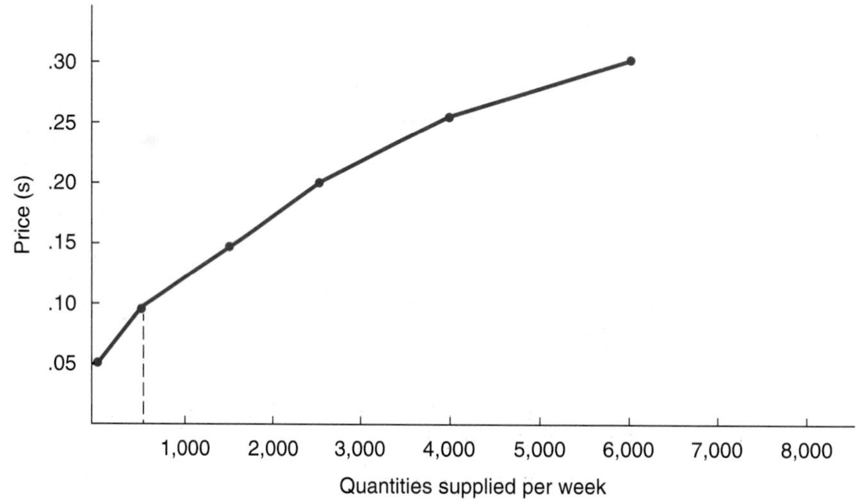

This supply schedule illustrates the law of supply: There is a direct, positive relationship between price and quantity supplied. In graphing the figures from the supply schedule into a supply curve, the law of supply is again apparent; more is supplied as the price goes up, and less is supplied as prices decrease.

These positive supply responses to higher prices are graphed in Figure 4–1 as a **supply curve.** As in the graph for demand, price is shown on the vertical axis. Each of the combinations of price and quantity traces out the supply curve, which has a special slope. The supply curve slopes upward and to the right, which is another way of saying that at higher prices larger quantities are supplied.

> The SUPPLY CURVE graphically shows the quantities supplied at each price for a given time period.

Cost Determinants of Supply

Price, of course, is only one of the main determinants of the quantity supplied. What other factors influence the amounts supplied? What are the **cost determinants of**

supply that we have assumed to be constant in stating the law of supply and in graphing the supply curve? The major cost determinants of supply are:

- Technology.
- Wages and other input prices for productive resources, such as capital, land, and raw materials.
- Taxes or subsidies.
- Prices of certain other goods produced and offered for sale.
- Expected future prices.

First, new discoveries and **technological advances** can cause significant changes in the costs of production. A technological advance results in more output produced with a given quantity of the inputs; or fewer inputs are needed to produce a given level of output. In the early 1800s, steam power was introduced in inland water carriers in the United States. Other improvements to steamboats quickly followed. The supply of water transportation expanded dramatically (especially upstream). Life on the Mississippi and other waterways was permanently altered by the fall in costs from these production improvements. Farms and plantations spread west, and New Orleans and St. Louis became major cities. Smaller towns also sprang up along the rivers where people settled and steamboats traveled.

Today there are many similar examples of cost reductions and far-reaching supply changes resulting from advances in technology. The cost of computers has fallen enormously, in large measure because of technological advances. Improved production techniques have greatly increased agricultural crop yields per acre. An average farmer in the United States can feed over 60 people today, compared to only 15 in 1950.

Second, if producers have to pay higher wages to workers, or higher prices for capital, land, or raw materials, these cost increases will cause producers to reduce supply. They supply less each time the price goes lower. Alternatively stated, suppliers require higher prices to supply the same quantity; if input costs fall, then supply will increase for a given price.

Third, if a product is taxed, the unit costs of production rise from the perspective of the supplier; this lowers the profits, and therefore fewer units are supplied. In contrast, if government offers a subsidy, production costs fall from the viewpoint of the supplier, and more units are supplied.

Fourth, if the price of doughnuts increases while the price of cupcakes remains unchanged, the opportunity costs of supplying cupcakes increase. The supply of cupcakes will fall as bakeries strive to take advantage of the new, improved opportunities for gain in supplying doughnuts. Alterations in the production mix, from fewer cupcakes to more doughnuts, are generated by the relative fall in the price of cupcakes.

Finally, if the item produced can be easily stored, a change in the expected future price will change today's supply. If the expected future price increases, fewer items will be supplied today in order to sell more later at the higher expected prices. Future prices are relevant opportunity costs to sellers selling today.

If any of these cost determinants changes to lower the cost of supply, the number of suppliers will increase and the quantities supplied by established suppliers will increase also (to a point to be explained later in the chapter). The fall in costs, relative to price, increases the profitability of production and encourages the increase in supply. An increase in costs lowers the profitability of operations and encourages a reduction in supply.

Change in Supply versus Change in Quantity Supplied

As in the case of demand analysis, confusion may develop if the distinction between a **change in supply** and a **change in quantity supplied** is not clearly maintained. In the change of quantity supplied there is simply a movement along the supply curve, with a price advance causing a movement up a given supply curve. No change in supply has occurred, and yet the quantity supplied has increased, just as the law of supply assures. No change in supply will occur unless there is a change in one of the cost determinants: technology, input costs, taxes or subsidies, prices of certain other goods, or prices expected in the future. If these remain unchanged, the supply curve will not shift.

A CHANGE IN SUPPLY results from a change in one of the cost determinants of supply and causes a shift in the position of the supply curve.

A CHANGE IN QUANTITY SUPPLIED may result from a change in supply or in price involving only movement along the curve.

Figure 4–2 shows in Panel A the change in quantity supplied as a result of a change in price and in Panel B a change in supply, or an actual shift of the supply curve. In A, the price rise generates greater quantities supplied, other things being equal. In B, one of the other things, that is, one of the cost determinants, has changed. A shift of the supply curve outward to the right, denoting an increase in supply, may come from changes in one or several of the cost determinants of supply:

- A technological advance requiring fewer inputs to produce the same output.
- A fall in wages or other input costs.
- A fall in a tax (or a rise in a subsidy) on the item produced.
- A fall in the price of a related item that affects the opportunity cost of the good (e.g., doughnuts versus cupcakes).
- A fall in the expected future price.

Changes in any of these cost determinants in the opposite direction will cause costs to rise and shift the supply curve upward and to the left. When this occurs, supply has changed or, more specifically, has fallen.

FIGURE 4–2   Change in Quantity Supplied (Panel A), Change in Supply (Panel B)

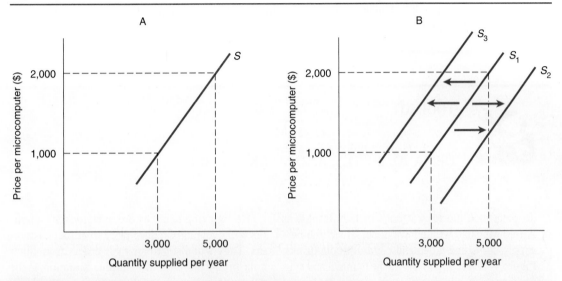

Panel A. This graph illustrates the law of supply, the direct relationship between price and quantity supplied. As price increases from $1,000 to $2,000 (other things unchanged), quantity supplied increases from 3,000 to 5,000 per year. No change in supply has occurred, but a change in quantity supplied has resulted.

Panel B. This graph shows changes in supply. The shift outward and to the right, from S_1 to S_2, reveals an increase in supply. The shift upward and to the left from S_1 to S_3 (or S_2 to S_1, or to S_3) denotes a fall in supply. A technological advance that lowers production costs will cause supply to advance, shifting S_1 to S_2. A rise in wages will cause supply to fall; S_1 shifts to S_3.

Elasticity of Supply

Just as with demand, the question arises regarding how significant the supply responses will be to price changes. Again, the concept of elasticity determines this. The **elasticity of supply** measure is identical conceptually to the price elasticity of demand. It is a measure of quantity responsiveness to a price change, and is defined:

$$\frac{\text{Percent change in quantity}}{\text{Percent change in price}} = \text{price elasticity of supply} \qquad (4\text{–}1)$$

The ELASTICITY OF SUPPLY is the percentage change in the quantity supplied divided by the percentage change in price.

Applying this to the supply information for cupcakes in Figure 4–1, we find that as price changes from 15 cents to 20 cents per cupcake, the elasticity of supply is calculated as follows:

TOOL KIT

DEMAND, SUPPLY, AND MARKET PRICE

To determine the market price of cola drinks, as Alfred Marshall would have done, let's combine a supply curve and a demand curve for cola drinks. Figure 4–A (see p. 79) shows the demand and supply curves of cola drinks. Both curves are derived from the schedules of quantities supplied and demanded. Recall that the curves and the schedules both convey the same information; only the forms of the price and quantity information are different.

The demand curve and the supply curve can be graphed together because their variables are the same. The vertical axis shows the prices per 16-ounce cola drink, and the horizontal axis shows the quantities per month, either demanded or supplied. The demand curve tells us the quantities that buyers will purchase at varying prices, and the supply curve shows the amount supplied at each price.

To see how market price is determined, let's consider the situation at a price of $1.25. Moving along this price line horizontally to the right, we see that the quantity demanded (at *A*) is less than the quantity supplied (at *B*). At this price, $1.25, a *surplus* develops as buyers fail to buy all that is produced. This surplus, which is the difference between the quantity supplied and the quantity demanded at $1.25 per drink, is calculated in the schedule as 25,000 per month. It is the quantity difference between points *A* and *B*. Suppliers will find their inventories growing, as their store shelves and stockrooms bulge with unsold cola.

Recognizing that they are overstocked, suppliers will eventually reduce price to attract customers. They will also reduce their orders from other cola producers. For this surplus situation to be corrected, prices must fall, perhaps first with so-called sales but ultimately with more permanent price reductions. When price does decline, say, to $1, larger quantities will be demanded and fewer supplies will be produced. A surplus situation continues, but at a smaller level. Downward pressures on price continue as long as the surplus situation persists.

Consider now a price of 25 cents, resulting in 45,000 units (at *X*) being demanded per month and 5,000 units (at *Y*) being supplied. Thirsty customers will find store shelves frequently empty and vendors will say, "Sorry, we are all out of cola." Eventually the word will get out that there is a shortage of cola. The shortage is measured horizontally in Figure 4–A as the quantity difference between points *X* and *Y* and is calculated as the amount 40,000. When shortages occur, there is little likelihood of suppliers offering "sales." Instead, suppliers will be inclined to raise the price, figuring there will still be enough customers to buy the cola. But as prices rise, say, to 50 cents, the quantity demanded will fall and the quantity supplied will rise. The shortage is reduced by the price rise, but at 50 cents per cola a shortage continues, albeit at a lower level. Here

$$\frac{\text{Percent change in } Q = \dfrac{2,500 - 1,500}{1,500} = \dfrac{2}{3}}{\text{Percent change in } P = \dfrac{.20 - .15}{.15} = \dfrac{1}{3}} = 2$$

again, upward pressures on price continue until the shortage situation no longer exists.

In this market example for cola soft drinks, 75 cents is the *equilibrium* or *market clearing price*. We see that 75 cents is the unique price that "clears the market" and equates the quantity demanded to the quantity supplied. Graphically, it is where the supply and demand curves cross (at *E*) in Figure 4–A.

📊 **FIGURE 4–A**   Supply and Demand Schedule and Curves for Cola Drinks

Price per 16-Ounce Cola	Quantity Demanded per Month	Quantity Supplied per Month	Quantity Supplied minus Quantity Demanded	Market Condition
$0.25	45,000	5,000	−40,000	Shortage
0.50	37,000	22,000	−15,000	Shortage
0.75	30,000	30,000	—	Equilibrium
1.00	22,000	36,000	14,000	Surplus
1.25	15,000	40,000	25,000	Surplus

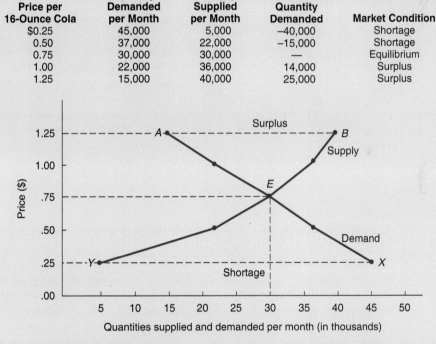

The schedule shows the quantities supplied and demanded at each price and the subsequent shortages or surpluses. It is also clear that 75 cents is the unique price that results in equilibrium, the market clearing price where the quantity supplied and the quantity demanded are equal. In the graph, the supply and demand curves intersect at *E*, at the price of 75 cents. At prices higher than 75 cents, surpluses occur; at prices lower than 75 cents, shortages occur.

This specific elasticity measure is *only* for this price-change segment of the supply curve. Over different price-quantity ranges, the elasticity measure typically changes. For example, the elasticity of supply as price changes from 20 cents to 25 cents per cupcake is

$$\frac{\dfrac{4,000 - 2,500}{2,500} = \dfrac{3}{5}}{\dfrac{.25 - .20}{.20} = \dfrac{1}{4}} = 2.4$$

Further checking will show that there are other elasticity calculations at other prices.[1]

The suppliers' responsiveness to price changes is influenced greatly by time. The longer producers have to make production adjustments, the greater the supply response as price changes. In the short run, possible changes are limited. If the price of soccer balls rises, inventories can be reduced, and some changes in the production mix (fewer volley balls, more soccer balls) or a speedup of production rates can occur. But in the short run, per-unit production costs rise more sharply than in the long run (analyzed in detail in Chapter 6). To speed up production in the short run, overtime pay may be required, or additional, hard-to-locate raw materials may be needed, or outmoded machinery may not be immediately replaceable.

In due time, however, more workers can be hired at regular pay, new sources of raw materials found, and better machinery introduced. Indeed, new suppliers may enter the business and supply additional quantities, if high profits in producing soccer balls encourage them. Consequently, for any price change, when a longer time is allowed for production adjustments, the quantity change from suppliers is more extensive. In short, the longer the timeframe considered, the larger the elasticity of supply.

Markets

Markets are often thought of as particular places or networks in which buyers and sellers interact to exchange goods and services for money. Neighborhood stores, the New York Stock Exchange, the docks or fields where labor services are bought and sold, catalogs, and vending machines illustrate the tremendous range in the forms that markets take. Rather than emphasize space or location, however, economists view markets as a network of transactions and a process of competitive bids and offers.

Our interest here, consequently, is not in the many different physical forms of markets and their locations but rather in how market prices are determined. We have analyzed the laws of demand and of supply; now we want to merge the two. By combining the demand and supply curves, we dramatically advance our powers and

---

[1]As a reminder, a gain in the measured computation of elasticity can be obtained by using the geometric mean of the prices and quantities. See Chapter 3, footnote 1, page 60.

range of economic analysis. In this way we can see how **surpluses** and **shortages** arise and how they are eliminated by price changes.

A SURPLUS occurs when the quantity supplied exceeds the quantity demanded at a given price.

A SHORTAGE occurs when the quantity demanded exceeds the quantity supplied at a given price.

CHANGES IN DEMAND AND SUPPLY AND MARKET PRICE

The market is said to be in **equilibrium** at the **market clearing price** when neither buyers nor sellers are inclined to change their price offers or purchases. It is not necessarily a condition of happiness or contentment. Buyers would prefer lower prices if they could still get the amount they want. Sellers would prefer higher prices if only the customers would buy no less. But the **equilibrium price** is the lowest price possible without buyers having to face shortages and the highest price possible without suppliers having to endure surpluses. At the equilibrium price there are no compelling market forces pressuring suppliers to raise or lower the price. Production flows match purchases, and the market continues to clear—unless demand or supply changes.

EQUILIBRIUM is a condition of the quantity supplied equaling the quantity demanded so that the market clears at the existing price.

The Effect on Price of a Change in Demand

We return to our cola example. If income or population increases or the price of root beer or other substitutes rises or if tastes change or the price of a complement to cola falls, then demand increases. The demand curve for cola will shift outward and to the right, and more will be demanded at each price, as shown in Figure 4–3 by the relocation of D to D_1. The market is now initially in **disequilibrium.** The increase in demand causes a shortage to develop initially, which in this instance is the quantity demanded of 47,000 minus that supplied of 30,000. The shortage encourages suppliers to raise price and expand supplies. This upward pressure on price and quantity, spurred by the demand increase, continues until the equilibrium price of $1 is reached. The market clears, with production just matching purchases at higher levels, and there is no incentive urging suppliers to change production rates further or to alter price.

There are now more resources committed to the production of cola. These added resources were pulled from competing uses. The higher cola price ($1) covered their opportunity costs, something the $0.75 price did not do. In this example, suppliers have responded to buyers' personal desires for more cola. By raising price and

---

DISEQUILIBRIUM occurs when either a surplus or a shortage develops; the quantity demanded does not equal the quantity supplied at the going price.

FIGURE 4–3   The Effect on the Price of Cola from Changes in Demand

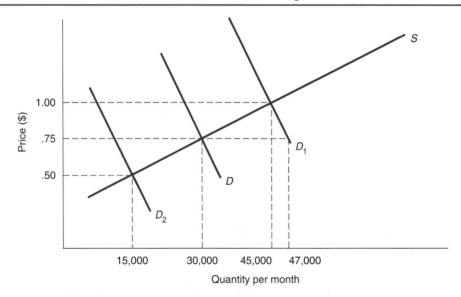

An increase in demand from *D* to *D*₁ (as one of the nonprice determinants of demand—such as income—for cola changes) will cause the equilibrium market clearing price to rise from 75 cents to $1 per cola. Larger quantities will be demanded and supplied, but there has been no change in supply. In contrast, a reduction in demand from *D* to *D*₂, perhaps because of a change in tastes, will reduce the equilibrium price from 75 cents to 50 cents. There has been no change in supply, but the quantity supplied is reduced in response to the price fall, and the quantity demanded now is less, too. It should be noted that supply has not changed, because none of the cost determinants of supply have changed.

producing more, suppliers were doing what was in their own self-interest. No government mandates, town meetings, or business conferences were required. The emerging market shortage and upward price changes provided the signals to suppliers for more cola, and they responded by supplying larger quantities to demanding customers. How often we fail to see these responses as acts of social cooperation!

Now suppose that because of a change in tastes, from soft drinks to natural juices, there is a fall in the demand for cola from D to D_2 (see Figure 4–3). This will lead to a set of market adjustments in the opposite direction. From the initial equilibrium price of 75 cents, a surplus market situation soon develops. Prices slip downward as suppliers strive to attract customers and sell their supplies of soft drinks. As prices decline, less is produced and supplied, and resources are diverted to other uses or simply idled. This process of price decline and resource shift ends when a new equilibrium price is reached. At 50 cents per cola the quantity demanded equals the quantity supplied once again, but at a lower level. No further pressures for price or quantity change are evident. Again, the changed personal preferences of individuals as buyers have precipitated the surplus and ultimately the price change. Suppliers observing these price changes and market activity act in their own self-interest and respond by providing less cola. Society's desire for cola fell, and the price change signaled suppliers to produce less.

It is important to emphasize that in these two examples of demand change, no change in supply occurred. Price changes led to changes in quantities supplied, but none of the cost determinants of supply changed. Consequently, the supply curve did not shift even though resources did. Furthermore, an increase in demand raised price and quantity supplied; a decrease in demand lowered both.

The Effect on Price of a Change in Supply

If technological advances or a fall in wages or other input costs occurs, then supply will increase. An increase in supply can also occur if a tax on cola is lifted or if the prices of other soft drinks decline. Figure 4–4 shows that if one of these things happens, the supply curve for cola will shift downward and to the right, from S to S_2, resulting in more being supplied at each price. The initial equilibrium price of 75 cents, where S and D intersect, is no longer a market clearing price, and the added supplies generate surpluses. However, when the price falls, the surplus is reduced, and when the price of 60 cents is reached, production equals purchases once again. In this example, more cola production resulted from a change in costs of supply, not from a change in demand. An advance in technology or other sources of cost reductions changed supply. Suppliers did not necessarily cause these changes, but by acting in their own self-interest, they provided happy results for cola lovers. Buyers drank more cola at lower prices.

FIGURE 4–4   The Effect on the Price of Cola from Changes in Supply

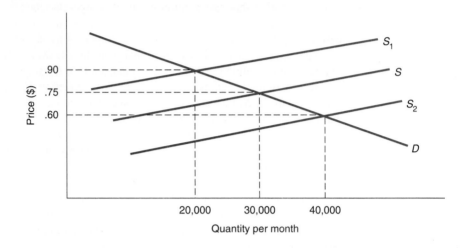

An increase in supply from S to S_2, as one of the cost determinants of supply for cola changes (e.g., the new, improved technology), will cause the equilibrium market clearing price to fall from 75 cents to 60 cents. Larger quantities will be demanded and supplied, but there has been no change in demand. Alternatively, a reduction in supply from S to S_1 (perhaps because of higher wages or more costly raw materials) will raise the equilibrium price from 75 cents to 90 cents per cola. There has been no change in demand, but the quantity demanded is less because of the higher price. The quantity supplied is also less now, but demand has not changed. That is because none of the nonprice determinants of demand have changed.

In contrast, suppose that labor costs rise because of higher wages. This change in labor's opportunity costs will reduce supply, and S shifts to S_1. At the initial equilibrium price of 75 cents a shortage emerges. At 75 cents the quantity demanded remains unchanged, but now less is supplied. This shortage situation puts upward pressures on price, and as prices inch upward, smaller quantities will be demanded (i.e., there is a movement along D), and more will be supplied (i.e., there is a movement along S_1). Upward pressure on price is sustained until the new equilibrium price of 90 cents is reached. This is where S_1 and D intersect, and the market clears. With the quantity demanded equal to the quantity supplied, there are no further pressures for price adjustments.

Although the fall in supply was not "ordered" or induced by cola drinkers, their willingness to endure the price increase to 90 cents led to larger quantities supplied than if the price had remained at 75 cents. In a sense, cola drinkers assisted the suppliers in overcoming the increase in labor costs caused by higher wages. The higher costs of cola production also encouraged a shifting of resources away from cola and into other, competing uses. This further illustrates the social cooperation generated by markets.

In summary, when demand does not change but supply does, two variations can occur. If supply increases, price falls and quantities demanded increase. If supply falls, price increases and quantities demanded decrease.

The Functions of Prices

Prices assist our social cooperation in three ways. First, prices provide information about values. We consider the price of an item when contemplating a purchase. Is the item worth more to us than the money price? To sellers, the question is price versus costs (per unit). Is the price enough to cover costs? Second, price changes are signals of values changing, and these signals provide incentives for us to change—and these changes are predictable! Higher prices encourage some (or all) buyers to be more judicious and buy less, and urge some (or all) producers to make and sell more. Finally, prices ration goods. Prices ration a good among people, giving it to those who are able and willing to pay for it, rather than to others who value it less than the price charged. Through these three functions of prices, goods and resources are channeled to their highest-valued uses.

Speculation and Prices

Because the future is always uncertain, people speculate, deliberately or not, about the prices of **commodity futures.** Such speculations impact current prices. Recall from Chapter 3 that if demanders expect future prices to rise, they demand more today. Suppliers will supply less if they expect future prices to rise. Both the demand and supply curves change, raising prices today. For example, consider this question: Should corn chip makers (e.g., Fritos) increase or reduce their inventories of raw corn needed for production? Specialists who buy and sell corn futures help them make the correct decision. Buyers and sellers of corn futures are specialists who study weather patterns, and planting and harvesting information worldwide in order to predict corn prices in the future. If they predict a lower than expected harvest, perhaps as a result of growing expectations of a below-normal rainfall in the Midwest, they buy futures because they expect a poor harvest will raise corn prices. Their purchases today of corn futures push up corn futures prices today. The corn chip makers can read these price changes for corn futures daily in the newspaper and act accordingly. If prices of corn futures rise, they know the "experts" on corn are predicting price increases and will conclude that their corn inventories will rise in value. This encourages them to slow production today and hold off selling on the market somewhat until prices rise in the future. They also will hasten to add to their inventories today by buying now rather than in the future. These decisions reduce supplies for use today and drive up corn chip prices.

> COMMODITY FUTURES are contracts to buy or sell a specified amount of a particular commodity at a specified future date at a price agreed upon now.

Of course, not all speculators predict the future correctly. Consistently wrong speculators usually become ex-speculators, and they do not serve society positively. Speculators who do predict the future correctly, however, help society as does a ship captain at sea who puts his crew on rations immediately upon finding spoiled food and inadequate amounts to sustain present daily rations. Changing prices of futures—in grains, oil, metals, foreign currencies, and many other items—guide our decisions today. For example, if oil futures rise rapidly today because of a threat of war in the Middle East or Persian Gulf, prices of oil and gas at the pump move up as well, almost instantly. Inventory holders of oil hold onto their oil and lower their sales today—they do so on the basis of the information supplied by rising prices of oil futures. And this changes prices at the pump quickly and encourages consumers to use less gas—long before the oil ships arrive back in port with less oil for gas refining than was expected when they first left.

Markets, Price Flexibility, and Social Cooperation

In each of the above examples of changes in demand and changes in supply, resources are shifted among competing alternatives. Recall that Adam Smith described this process as an "invisible hand" guiding the resources to their most valued uses. Price changes provide signals to suppliers to produce more when buyers demand more and to produce less when buyers demand less. Moreover, if supply falls (costs rise), then buyers assist the market by buying less as prices rise. Or if supply increases (costs fall), buyers respond to price reductions by buying more.

These adjustments to market forces by demanders and suppliers generate social cooperation and systematic coordination. But the decisions are made individually, and people are not actually conscious of cooperating to find a new market equilibrium or market clearing price. Indeed, economists disagree on the effectiveness of markets to use resources fully and effectively. Some, like Adam Smith, view markets as basically efficient vehicles for properly channeling scarce resources among competing alternative uses. They see markets as effective and responsive to changing conditions. Others point to the problems of lengthy periods of resource idleness and unemployment when some markets shrink. Clearly, there are cases in which prices are slow to adjust and the time period of moving from one equilibrium to another may be quite long. Some theorists, such as Karl Marx, argue that most markets are chaotic and that socioeconomic advances that are fair to all can be obtained only by planning and government controls. Still others, such

FIGURE 4–5   Price Changes as a Demand Increase Is Followed by a Supply Decrease

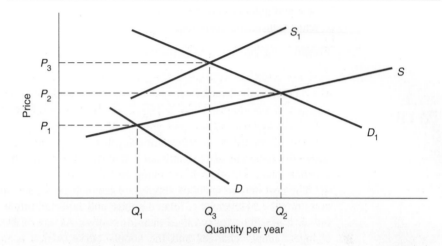

A sequence of demand and of supply changes, from *D* to *D₁* and from *S* to *S₁*, respectively, may cause the period of disequilibrium to be an extended one, as price first moves up from P_1 to P_2 and then upward still to P_3.

as Friedrich von Hayek, argue that most market failings are caused by too much government interference. In fact, markets are seldom entirely free of some type of government controls or regulations.

Reasonable people disagree on the role of markets in a society and how reliant we should be on them. Changing conditions, which cause disequilibriums, are frequent real-world occurrences. Oftentimes the conditions of disequilibrium are merely transitory, as market adjustments continue and price movements sluggishly shift from one equilibrium to another. As illustrated in Figure 4–5, a sequence of demand and supply changes, from D to D_1 and then from S to S_1 (and there are many other possible variations), respectively, can send prices upward from P_1 to P_2 and then upward further to P_3.

In very active markets, such as the stock market, equilibrium adjustments are speedy and prices can change swiftly. Whether the markets and market prices are promptly responsive or sluggish, the concept of equilibrium is neither trivial nor useless; it is extremely useful for analytical purposes. Certainly, the laws of supply and demand are beyond dispute. The concept of equilibrium helps to anticipate and predict the direction of price and quantity changes as markets are disturbed. It also helps to better understand markets when special complicating conditions emerge:

- When market clearing prices are disallowed by legal restraints.
- When government policies purposely change the allocation of resources away from free-market outcomes.
- When transaction costs rise.

Conditions of shortages and surpluses are indeed prevalent, as we shall see in Chapter 5.

𝒯𝓇 CHAPTER REVIEW

The law of supply states the relationship between price and quantity supplied and shows this to be a positive relationship; that is, more of something will be supplied as its price increases, other things being equal.

The cost determinants of supply are technology, wages and other input costs, taxes or subsidies, prices of related goods, and expected future prices (the opportunity cost of selling today rather than tomorrow). As any of these cost determinants changes, supply changes and the supply curve, which is upward-sloping, also changes position.

The supply response to a price change is measured by the elasticity of supply. Supply is more elastic in the long run than in the short run. Supply and demand together determine market price.

Market equilibrium exists where the quantity demanded and the quantity supplied are equal at a particular price. This is the market clearing price, and it occurs where the demand and supply curves intersect. At all other prices, either a shortage or a surplus will occur. These disequilibrium conditions lead to price adjustments and resource shifts.

If demand increases (i.e., the demand curve shifts to the right), price will rise and the quantity supplied will increase. If demand falls, price will decline and the quantity supplied will fall.

If supply increases (i.e., the supply curve shifts to the right), price will fall and quantity demanded will increase. If supply falls, price will rise and quantity demanded will fall.

Economists disagree on the benefits and effective responsiveness of markets. But the influence of market forces and the importance of the laws of supply and demand are beyond dispute. Moreover, markets generate acts of social cooperation among buyers and sellers and are vehicles for progress and change.

𝕴 MULTIPLE-CHOICE SELF-TEST 𝕴 𝕴 𝕴 𝕴 𝕴 𝕴 𝕴 𝕴 𝕴 𝕴 𝕴 𝕴 𝕴 𝕴 𝕴

1. Which of the following kinds of information *could not* be signaled to tire producers by either input or output prices?

    a. Oil, used to make synthetic rubber, is becoming scarcer.

    b. Demand for cars, and therefore tires, has fallen.

    c. A new technique for tire making with robotic equipment is available, but it costs more than current methods.

    d. All the above information can be signaled by prices.

2. Which of the following is *not* a reason that supply curves slope upward?

    a. As the price of the good falls, some producers may switch to the production of other goods.

    b. As the price of the good rises, the elasticity of supply increases.

    c. As producers all expand their production, the cost of producing the good rises.

    d. As the price of the good rises, some new producers will start producing it.

3. Fewer VCRs will be produced at every price:

    a. If a new and more expensive technology is introduced.

    b. Is a way of saying that supply has decreased.

    c. If the price of similar goods also produced by VCR firms falls.

    d. If demand for VCRs declines.

4. Disequilibrium in a market:

    a. Is an unusual state.

    b. Shows that a market is not functioning efficiently.

    c. Occurs for a while every time supply or demand conditions change.

    d. Shows that the concept of equilibrium is not useful.

5. When a market is in equilibrium:

    a. Quantity supplied equals quantity demanded at the current price.

    b. Market price may be pushed up, but it won't decline.

    c. Market price may tend to decline, but it won't rise.

    d. The supply and demand curves are identical.

𝒲𝒫 STUDY QUESTIONS

1. How would an increase in theft from your neighborhood stores affect the prices of the items they sell? Explain your answer.

2. Is supply for cotton shirts or blouses more elastic in the long run than in the short run? Why?

3. What are the conditions for equilibrium in a market for potato chips? Graph it.

4. When a shortage of peanut butter prevails, what forces are at work to bring about equilibrium?

5. How does self-interest lead from disequilibrium to equilibrium in a market where there are shortages (or surpluses) of bicycles? Peanut butter?

6. If a demand increase for movie tickets does not raise price, what does the supply curve look like? Graph it.

🎜 PROBLEM

Housing construction firms can produce new housing over a year's time at the prices indicated, as shown by QS in the following supply schedule. Beneath the QS row is the demand data for housing a few years ago, with the quantities shown as QD_1. Then a recession occurred. As household income fell a little and more people were unemployed, the demand for new housing declined so that only the amounts shown as QD_2 were demanded at each possible price. (The number of houses is measured in thousands.)

Price	$40,000	$45,000	$50,000	$55,000	$60,000
QS	300	400	500	600	700
QD_1	750	700	650	600	550
QD_2	600	550	500	450	400

1. On an accurately drawn graph, mark the price-quantity combinations shown for the supply of new houses, and draw a supply curve to connect them.

2. Draw in the initial demand curve, D_1. What was the equilibrium price of new houses, and how many would have been built that year?

3. Draw in the recession demand curve, D_2. What happened to the equilibrium price and quantity of new houses?

CHAPTER 5

Shortages, Surpluses, and Prices

᛭ CHAPTER PREVIEW

Throughout the history of the United States the federal government has often intervened in markets, sometimes to control prices and sometimes to help businesses. In the 19th century the government gave large public land grants to companies to build privately held railroads. In the late 1970s the federal government came to the aid of the Chrysler Corporation, the Boeing Aircraft Corporation, and the Continental Illinois Bank. With government financial aid the companies were able to maintain their financial solvency through difficult times. Since World War II, government intervention in housing, energy, and agriculture has been extensive. Yet the problems, particularly in agriculture, have hardly lessened.

Today, special interest groups routinely approach government for assistance. American businesses want a level playing field to compete with Japanese and European producers as well as with each other. Farmers in Illinois and Iowa want protection from the vagaries of weather and other uncertainties. Bankers in New York want the freedom to compete, but they also want federal insurance and assistance in case savers should start a run on banks. Renters in New York want low rents and cry out for continued rent controls. In these, and many other cases, politicians react to pressures—sometimes with new legislation.

1. Why don't butter, milk, and cheese prices fall when vast quantities of these products are spoiling in government warehouses?

2. Controls are imposed on rents in New York City and Berkeley, California, and on farm production in Iowa. How do these controls impact prices and production, and how do they affect buyers and sellers?

CONCEPTS REINTRODUCED

Change in Quantity Demanded 57
Change in Quantity Supplied 76
Choice 6
Demand Curve 52
Disequilibrium 82
Equilibrium 81
Markets 80
Normative Economics 16–17
Opportunity Cost 7
Positive Economics 16–17
Price 50
Property Rights 14
Shortage 81
Supply Curve 74
Surplus 81

NEW CONCEPTS

Price Controls
Price Ceiling
Price Floor
Rent Controls
Tie-in Sales
Price Supports
Acreage Controls
Target Prices

🖋 CHAPTER OBJECTIVES

After studying this chapter, you should be able to:

1. Recognize the production and income effects of price controls.
2. Distinguish between price ceilings and price floors.
3. Use the demand and supply diagrams to analyze price floors (e.g., agricultural price supports) and price ceilings (e.g., rent controls).

PRICE MOVEMENTS

For most products, prices are left free to move and to adjust in response to changes in market forces. If the demand for orange juice increases because people become more health-conscious, an increase in the price of orange juice will choke off excess quantities demanded and stimulate supply in order to alleviate the emerging shortage. If new oil fields are discovered, oil supplies will increase. Suppliers will be forced to lower oil prices in order to sell more oil. The lower prices will dampen the quantity supplied and stimulate the quantity demanded. This will reduce the glut of oil. Prices are like a communications network. Flexible prices responding to market changes send signals to us all.

Shortage and *surplus* are familiar terms. We would have to deal with the situations they describe much more frequently if prices were not free to move up and down. Nevertheless, price, as a means of solving the problem, is commonly ignored. The news media frequently report problems of shortages and surpluses, but they rarely address the cause or consider the role of price in the solution. This is not surprising in television coverage. Visual aids in today's TV news coverage are paramount, and few viewers have the patience to listen to lengthy analyses. Camera crews bring us pictures of oil tankers anchored offshore, unable to unload their cargo at capacity-filled storage yards and refineries. Or they show us near-empty water reservoirs in areas of drought. Quite naturally, this type of coverage leads us to believe that shortages or surpluses are caused by the physical absence or physical abundance of things. But an oil surplus or a water shortage is as much a pricing problem as a physical problem. Similarly, news photos and TV clips of empty shelves in grocery stores announce a shortage of, say, peanut butter. A box-office cashier closing the window to long lines of customers for a Bruce Springsteen concert reveals a high demand for tickets. These visuals record the physical consequences of shortages or surpluses, but they rarely depict the solution. A price adjustment sufficient to clear the market and equate the quantities supplied to quantities demanded is a rapid and efficient solution—but alas, reporting this would be less interesting visual material for news cameras.

Market Disorder

Two aspects of shortages and surpluses are the (1) time and (2) the size of the price adjustment needed to clear markets. And there are winners and losers to consider. With shortages, buyers lose, and those holding inventories win; with surpluses, the reverse holds. Economists, like other people, make different normative judgments on whether the government should assist those who might be seriously hurt financially by price changes. They also disagree on the method of help. For example, if a very rapid and steep price rise is needed to alleviate a shortage, the financial distress may be extreme for those who are highly dependent on the good. When gas prices rise, what about the effect this has on the schoolteacher who has a long commute? Or the college student who needs a car to get from school to a part-time job? Should government help them?

Should government help distressed firms that face bankruptcy when their product prices fall? In 1979, when the Carter administration came to the rescue of the Chrysler Corporation with a huge low-cost loan on favorable terms, this action was defended on the grounds that it saved jobs. The bailout overcame the personal costs and anxieties of workers who would have been forced into unemployment. It helped the stockholders, too. Was the Chrysler experience sufficiently unique to warrant such unusual financial interference by the government in a private market? Another favored entity in the late 1970s was the New York City government; the federal government helped bail out the financially distressed city government when it was on the verge of bankruptcy. Similarly, in 1995 it did the same for Washington, D.C. Should the government have done this in 1995 for bankrupt Orange County, California? Where was government in the time of need for the great number of small businesses that failed that year, and indeed fail every year? How does government decide whom to rescue and whom to let fail?

Government occasionally steps into various markets to interfere with prices: rent on apartments, interest on loans, prices of gasoline, and prices on farm goods. The use of supply and demand analysis helps us to understand the economic consequences of government intervention and limitation on price movements. We can see how government controls affect market conditions. Political, social, and other relevant issues also play a role in these types of government activities.

PRICE CEILINGS AND PRICE FLOORS

Selective **price controls** have been enacted by government to address specific problems and help certain groups of people.[1] When government imposes an upper limit on prices, there is a **price ceiling** that prevents prices from rising above the legally

---

[1]There also have been times when the government has interfered with market prices generally and unselectively. In World War II, the government enforced a policy of comprehensive wage and price

selected limit. In contrast, when government imposes a lower price limit, or **price floor,** prices are prevented from going below the legally specified level.

A PRICE CONTROL sets an upper or a lower legal limit on a price.

A PRICE CEILING sets an upper legal limit on price.

A PRICE FLOOR sets a lower legal limit on price.

When price ceilings are applied, the government is generally trying to help buyers (consumers) by restraining the producer or seller from charging "too much" for goods or services. Alternatively, when government imposes a price floor, it is usually trying to help suppliers by not letting the price get "too low." One familiar example of a price ceiling is rent control—legalized in New York City, Washington, D.C., and in Berkeley and Santa Monica, California. Another example is the upper limits that are set on consumer loan interest rates in most states. Ceilings on petroleum prices in the 1970s are another practical example.

Examples of price floors are the price supports on many agricultural products—corn, cotton, milk, butter, cheese, peanuts, and other items. The minimum wage for labor is another example of a price floor.

The effects of selective price controls do not always correspond to the intentions of government policymakers. Sometimes there are undesired side effects. Rent controls may help some families but hurt others. Price supports on dairy items help some farmers, but at the same time they hurt consumers of milk, ice cream, and cheese.

Rent Controls and Housing Shortages

In 1979, after more than a decade of general price advances (inflation) and rising rents in particular, residents of Santa Monica, California, voted in favor of **rent controls.** In Washington, D.C., controls have been around since the 1960s. In New York City, rent controls have been in effect ever since 1942. The legal aspects of rent controls vary among these cities, but the general effects are the same. Landlords are constrained from raising rents, and those occupying the rental units pay lower rents. Although alleged "rent gouging" is supposedly eliminated by the law, other difficulties arise. The use of supply and demand analysis, as given in Figure 5–1, aids in understanding the causes and sources of these difficulties.

---

controls; in 1971, the Nixon administration imposed wage and price controls throughout the economy. These broad-based policies are discussed in Chapters 1, 14, and 19.

📖 FIGURE 5–1   A Price Ceiling Case: Rent Controls and Housing Shortages Resulting from Demand Increases

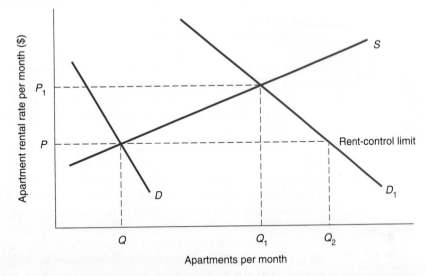

When demand increases and *D* shifts to D_1 the rent-control limit (*P*) will create a shortage equal to ($Q_2 - Q$) in apartments. The market clearing price, P_1, is above *P* but is disallowed by the law—hence, the shortage. Price does not ration the housing space; other means of rationing develop, including "key" fees, "side" payments, and personal preferences.

RENT CONTROLS set upper limits on rents charged to tenants by owners,

Assume that an increase in population, such as has occurred in New York City since the 1940s, has caused an increase in demand for rental housing. Figure 5–1 illustrates this shift in the demand curve for rental housing as *D* to D_1. Assume further that rent controls have been set and that they impose an upper limit on the rental rates that landlords can charge.[2] Let this ceiling be *P*. The shift in the demand curve causes a shortage of rental units, but no increase in rental rates above *P* can occur to ration the limited number of apartments among the many people wanting them. But given scarcity, some form of rationing must occur. If price could rise to P_1, no shortage would be sustained, and the quantity supplied would increase from *Q* to

---

[2]Although rents for apartments obviously vary by location, size, and quality, when rent-control laws are imposed, they generally freeze the prevailing rental rates. Consequently, the simplification here of an average rate and standard rental unit is appropriate for any particular apartment or set of apartments.

Q_1. However, because the maximum rental rate is P, the shortage of rental housing becomes the difference between Q_2 and Q.

Those renters who already have apartments benefit from the government-placed lid on rents (P rather than P_1). In contrast, landlords are hurt because the rental returns on their property are less at P than they would be at P_1, and potential renters, who want space but cannot obtain it, are frustrated in their search. Future renters will find the shortage uncorrected. In the fall of 1987, several thousand (mostly new, entering) University of California students could not find housing in rent-controlled Berkeley. There simply wasn't any housing available at the legal rental rates, and new supplies did not develop. Many students temporarily slept in the Harmon Gymnasium on cots for $10 per night.

Because price fails to ration the housing space available, other means evolve. When vacancies develop, landlords are in a position to select their tenants from among the many renters seeking housing because of the shortage of units. Landlords might discriminate on the basis of religion, race, sex, or age. Or they might select or reject tenants by other criteria—whether they are college students, whether they have children or pets, or whether they are willing to pay "under-the-table" (key) money just to get a key to the apartment. The greater the shortage created by rent ceilings, the greater the ability of landlords to discriminate by whatever means they may choose. Thus, the greater are the incidences and kinds of discrimination that arise. Other laws against such discrimination may discourage the use or effects of such personal preferences in selecting new tenants, but personal choices undoubtedly increase in importance when price is lost as a rationing device.

In reality, rent control creates a political property right in occupancy of a rent-controlled apartment. But to enjoy the property right you have to occupy the apartment. Even wealthy celebrities, such as actress Mia Farrow, singer Carly Simon, and TV commentator Alistair Cooke, are among rent-regulated tenants in New York City. In the mid-1980s average midtown Manhattan controlled rents were under $500 per month, but small studio apartments with uncontrolled rents went for nearly $1,000 a month. People frequently hang onto their Manhattan apartments even while buying large houses in Connecticut. The artificially low price provides incentives to do this, and, often, tenants who have to move attempt to sublet their units for special key money or other payments.

Owners also try to improve their circumstances. If the costs of maintenance rise when rents are legally fixed, landlords may neglect maintenance on apartments. As they attempt to lower the real costs of upkeep, the quality of rental units declines. Present and future renters lose in the process. Sometimes owners convert their apartments into condominium units to avoid the law. This reduces the quantity of rental units available. After controls were imposed in Washington, D.C., the conversion of apartments to condominiums increased nearly tenfold between 1970 and 1979. Incentives do matter.

All these experiences have been common in New York City, in Washington, D.C., and wherever rent-control laws exist. The problems develop as buyers and sellers, acting in their own self-interest, try to find ways to improve their own circumstances in the face of the law. When increases in demand, requiring new, higher equilibrium prices, are not allowed, changes toward equilibrium occur anyway—by a fall in the value (quality) of housing at the legal price.

Sometimes additional laws are passed to correct these circumstances and problems. Subletting and charging key money have long been prohibited in New York, and laws have been passed to require proper maintenance of buildings. Yet a 1960 survey in New York City showed that nearly a fourth of the renters in rent-controlled apartments were routinely paying more than was legally allowed. (This was exclusive of bribes and also did not account for reductions in maintenance and housing quality.) Moreover, the building of new apartments cannot be legislated. Since 1945 there has been almost no construction of apartments subject to rent control in New York City.

Further, as a result of advancing deterioration because of lack of maintenance and because of rising property taxes, many landlords have simply abandoned their apartments altogether. Tens of thousands of apartment units were abandoned in the 1960s and 1970s in the Bronx and in the Lower East Side of Manhattan. Large numbers of apartments were also abandoned in neighborhoods not far from the White House in the nation's capital. Consequently, like the effect of landlords converting their apartments into condominiums, abandonment of tens of thousands of buildings reduced the availability of rental units, worsened the rental shortage, and reduced the tax base. With a smaller tax base, either tax rates have to be raised or government services lessened.

All these effects are the results of market forces at work when price is constrained from reaching equilibrium. But some type of equilibrium is approached in any case, and the creative forms these spontaneous adjustments take are both surprising and discouraging.

The negative experiences of rent controls do not always discourage their popularity, however, as is shown by their adoption in Santa Monica in 1979. Because current renters benefit from rent controls, and because landlords and future renters suffer, the political lines on rent control are clearly drawn. However, future renters are often too young or too distant to have a voice in the matter and are unaware that they will be adversely affected by rent controls. Because current tenants significantly outnumber landlords, defeat of rent-control measures usually depends on the effectiveness of landlords in convincing nonrenters to vote in their favor. Because landlords individually have more at stake and have more wealth than tenants do, landlords are usually willing to invest more dollars to convince others of the ill effects of rent controls. In 1983 a Los Angeles County rent-control initiative was defeated by a 60/40 vote. The "war chest" of the advocates, who called themselves the Coalition for Economic Survival, totaled a meager $60,000. The landlord groups, though fewer in number, spent $1.6 million to oppose the measure. Historically, landlords have defeated a high percentage of proposed rent-control referenda. Nevertheless, when rents increase rapidly, new proposals for rent controls invariably arise.

FIGURE 5–2   Interest Rates and Price Ceilings: Two Cases

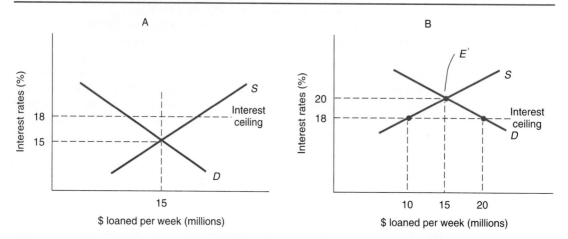

In Panel A, all of the demand for loans can be satisfied at market clearing interest rates below the interest rate ceiling of 18 percent. Here the legal interest ceiling is only a potential constraint. In Panel B, when market forces push the market clearing price on interest rates to 20 percent, all of the demand for loans cannot be met at the legal constraint rate. Only $10 million per week in loans are supplied, leaving another $10 million unsupplied. Thus a ceiling constraint on price fails to ration the quantity of loans supplied.

Usury Laws and Getting a Loan

Since earliest times money lending has been the subject of special attention. Interest on loans was labeled unjust by religious leaders in the Middle Ages, and many state laws limit the interest rates that can be charged for consumer loans and home mortgages. These legal upper limits on interest charges are generally referred to as usury laws.[3] *Usury* is an excessive or exorbitant interest charge, and the law sets the upper limits on interest rates.

Politicians find it popular to pass usury laws that "assist" small borrowers and protect them from "usurist" lenders. The laws supposedly prevent borrowers from being victimized into accepting loans and falling into debt at very high rates of interest. But do these laws help borrowers? Who gains because of usury laws?

In Figure 5–2, two alternative supply and demand situations are shown, along with a legally imposed interest rate ceiling of 18 percent. In Panel A the equilibrium rate of interest of 15 percent is below the 18 percent legal ceiling. The quantity of loans ($15 million) supplied equals the quantity of loans demanded, and no shortages or surpluses of funds prevail. Whenever a legal upper limit exceeds the market clearing price, the ceiling is only a potential, not an actual binding constraint.

---

[3]There are biblical admonitions against usury, and in the Middle Ages the Catholic Church viewed *any* interest charge at all as usury. Philosophers and theologians argued over matters such as the "just price" of things.

However, as shown in Panel B, when the market forces of supply and demand increase the equilibrium price above the legal ceiling, perhaps to 20 percent (E'), a shortage is caused by the interest rate ceiling. At the ceiling rate of 18 percent, loans of $20 million per week are demanded. However, the supply of loanable funds is only $10 million at an interest charge of 18 percent. A shortage of $10 million per week is evident.

Institutions supplying loanable funds are inclined to introduce new, special "handling costs," which previously were covered by the interest charges. For instance, a mortgage loan may be quoted as 17 percent, plus a one-time charge of 3 "points" for getting the loan. (A *point* is 1 percent of the amount loaned.) Legal restrictions may prevent this means of rationing the limited supply. If price (the interest rate plus possible other charges) is prevented from rationing the available supply, banks will then sharply discriminate among customers. The most common form of this selectivity is to eliminate "risky loans." Because the risk of an individual's not paying back the loan depends significantly on the person's wealth or income, refusals of loans to low-income people will increase. High-income people will get loans at 18 percent instead of at higher rates, and low-income people will get a "thank you for applying, but we are sorry to inform you" letter of refusal. Again, some form of rationing is unavoidable.

No Consensus on Usury Laws

What outcomes do politicians expect when passing usury laws? The laws do keep some poor people from getting loans at interest rates that some politicians judge to be too high. However, some poor people evidently prefer to borrow at those rates, even though they are high, rather than be refused a loan altogether. And some may turn to underground loan sharks and face danger and very high interest rates to get needed loans. Evaluating the outcomes is obviously a normative issue, but the positive economic analysis enables us to understand the effects of usury laws. Economists (and others) disagree on these normative matters. Should people be left free to judge what is in their own best interests? Or should government intervene to protect certain people from possible mistakes and errors of judgment? And, if government does intervene, who should be protected?

Gasoline Shortages in the 1970s

In 1973 the Organization of Petroleum Exporting Countries (OPEC), which controlled most of the world supply of oil, was led by its Arab members to reduce the supply of crude oil to most Western countries. OPEC's reduced supply of crude oil resulted in sharply higher prices and profits on petroleum products.[4] The Arab-led slowdown in production and control of shipments was mounted to protest the West-

---

[4]Total revenues from oil increased because demand was price inelastic in the short run.

FIGURE 5–3   Price Ceiling and a Fall in the Supply of Gasoline

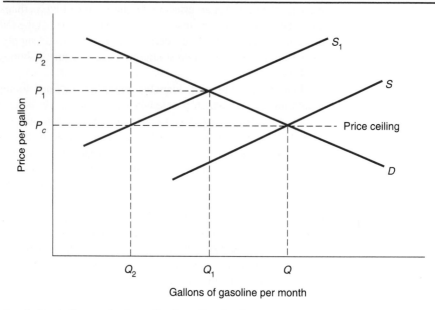

A reduction in the supply of gasoline from S to S_1 when a price ceiling of P_C is in effect will create a shortage equal to $Q - Q_2$. People would be willing to pay P_2 per gallon for the quantity supplied of Q_2. Because price does not ration the gasoline, other means develop. In the 1970s these other means included gas lines, tie-in sales, and other rationing methods.

ern nations' favorable policies toward Israel. The results were viewed as high drama by the media, and many feared that the oil-dependent industrial nations were going to be pretty much at OPEC's mercy.

There were economic dislocations in many countries as the price of crude oil rose and, with it, the prices of oil derivatives such as gasoline and home heating oil. In Europe, however, the economic repercussions were less apparent and more easily adjusted to than in the United States. Gasoline prices increased, and European motorists faced higher costs of filling up the tank. Those drivers were concerned and, quite expectedly, complained. Nonetheless, those who paid received gasoline, and price effectively served its role to ration the available supplies of gasoline among the many users. In Europe motorists were a little poorer, but they pretty much conducted business as usual, as did gasoline station owners and attendants there.

U.S. Price Controls and Gasoline Lines

U.S. legal mandates prevented gasoline (and heating oil) prices from rising to new market clearing heights. In 1971, President Richard M. Nixon tried to fight inflation by imposing price and wage controls on almost all industries. This policy was phased out by 1974, but controls on gasoline and heating oil prices were maintained.

As OPEC reduced the supply of crude oil to refiners, this automatically led to a decrease in the supply of gasoline. Figure 5–3 shows this reduction in the shift of *S* to S_1. Prices could not legally rise above the price-controlled ceiling, P_c. Consequently, the quantity supplied fell, not just from Q to Q_1 but all the way to Q_2. Because the quantity purchased cannot exceed the quantity supplied for sale, the price people were willing to pay for Q_2 greatly exceeded P_c. This price is shown as P_2 in Figure 5–3. Various measures to get around the law sometimes made the effective cost to buyers of gasoline actually approach P_2.

American drivers of the 1970s experienced a number of changes and ordeals.[5] Services that had previously been given free—pumping gas, oil checks, and windshield cleaning—were withdrawn or priced separately. First-come–first-served policies replaced price rationing and the gas line became a way of life for American motorists waiting to fill up. People shopped around for shorter lines and waiting periods, but in many cases lines were already formed when gas stations opened for business. Fights sometimes broke out if someone tried to drive to the front of the line or get around others who were having difficulty starting their cars after waiting with their engines turned off. On several occasions shootings and killings resulted from these disputes. Busy husbands and wives argued about who should "waste their time" waiting in the gas line. Physicians in some areas were given special exemption from waiting because of "patient needs." In short, the time costs of "fill-ups" rose dramatically. Unlike price increases, however, these costs on consumers were generally not benefits to suppliers (e.g., oil producers).

Some gas stations, however, did attempt to get some of the additional money people were willing to pay to get speedy fill-ups. Sometimes they used **tie-in sales** to ration the gasoline and increase the effective price of gas. Tie-in sales require that two (or more) things be purchased simultaneously. Customers who parked their cars at the station (for a healthy fee) were given full-tank fill-up privileges without the wait. Before the law cracked down, one station in Chicago was selling rabbit-foot charms for $10 each for the right to fill up the tank at price-ceiling prices. Because gas was in such short supply, stations sharply reduced their pumping times, and "no gas" signs were seen everywhere. Tips and favors to station owners and attendants became common, especially for fill-ups after closing times.

These and other forms of rationing raised the true effective price of gasoline. Although the monetary price ceilings were set with the intent of helping those who "needed" gas, the results were widely seen as ineffective. Those with lower-than-average personal time values were hurt less relative to those with highly valued time. Figure 5–3 shows that the effective price (P_2) actually exceeded the equilibrium monetary price (P_1) that would have prevailed in the absence of a price ceiling. The chaos that came when prices were not allowed to signal the appropriate scarcity of gasoline was extensive indeed.

---

[5]There were actually two quite severe shortage periods, in 1974 and again in 1979, shortly following OPEC's major price advances.

Price Ceilings and Food Shortages

Sometimes government controls do more than create chaos—they can cause death. Government policies in Ethiopia in the 1980s are a good example. The government there set price controls on agricultural crops, undoubtedly to keep the cost of food low. Such controls, coupled with periods of drought, however, resulted in shortages of food and widespread starvation. The drought created food shortages, but government price controls did not give incentives to farmers to provide more food. Indeed, it encouraged hoarding there. Government interference in distributing food gifts to the starving further hurt those in distress. Generous people from all over the world attempted to supply food and aid to starving Ethiopians, often in the face of government resistance and intervention. The shortages of available food resulted in millions of people starving.

A similar occurrence faced General George Washington at Valley Forge during the winter of 1777. With his army in great need of food and provisions, he was unable to purchase them because of government policy. The legislature of Pennsylvania, in an attempt to lighten the burden (taxes) of war on the population, imposed price ceilings on foods and commodities needed by the army. The prices of these goods, when sold illegally, were many times higher than the legally mandated prices. Most farmers refused to sell at the artificially low legal prices. Instead they preferred to hoard their highly valued foodstuffs and provisions until they could sell them at real market values. Washington tried in vain to secure food and provisions in 1777, and he and his men suffered through a torturous winter. Only afterward did the Pennsylvania legislature see the error it had made, and the next year it abandoned price controls altogether.

Price Supports and Surpluses in Agriculture

In 1933, when farmers and others were suffering the economic distresses of the Great Depression, the Agricultural Adjustment Act was passed. The act set price floors on many agricultural items, including wheat, cotton, and feed grains. Later adjustments to the 1933 act and other legislative actions increased the range of agricultural products given price floors. Other changes were made in order to deal with problems of surpluses. Agricultural **price supports** are applied in increasingly complicated ways, but whatever the legislative formula, the effects are fundamentally the same. In 1996, major agricultural items like wheat, cotton, rice, corn, barley, sorgum, peanuts, and feed grains enjoyed some form of government price support. From the time of the Great Depression, the main features of U.S. farm policy have been price supports and acreage controls, and, since 1973, target prices.

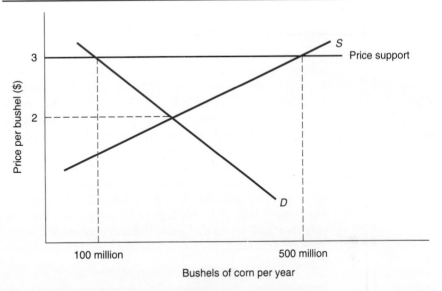

FIGURE 5–4   A Price Floor Case: A Guaranteed Price Support in Agriculture

If the government sets a price support (legal price minimum) of $3, the quantity supplied (500 million bushels) will exceed the quantity demanded (100 million), and a surplus of 400 million will result. The government then purchases and stores the surplus corn.

PRICE SUPPORTS are simply price floors on certain crops.

Figure 5–4 illustrates the effects of price supports in the corn market. If the market equilibrium price is $2 per bushel and a government price support of $3 sets a price floor of $3, farmers have an incentive to supply more corn (500 million bushels) than demanders will buy (100 million). The surplus (400 million) is purchased by the government and then stored. In actual practice, today farmers store the corn temporarily themselves. A farmer with 10,000 bushels stores it and applies for a loan from the Commodity Credit Corporation equal to the price support ($3) times the number of bushels, or $30,000. If the market price rises above the price-support level, the farmer can sell at the higher price and repay the loan. If not, the farmer can simply let the government take the corn. The effect is that government guarantees the farmer that the price will be no less than the price-support level. In this example, the taxpayers' total cost is $3 × 400 million bushels (transfer to the farmers) plus the storage costs. It should be noted that the greater the price inelasticities of demand and supply, the smaller will be the surplus and quantities purchased by government.

Because surpluses are typically added to surpluses year after year, government policy soon began to impose **acreage controls.** Today these are called *acreage limitation* programs or *reduced acreage* programs, and, of course, they are used to reduce supply and to shift the supply curve to the left.[6] Because of the price inelasticity of demand for farm products, lower supplies will raise prices sharply and increase total revenues to farmers as a whole. Farmers today are required to reduce their planted acreages by a certain percentage (of a base-year acreage amount) in order to be eligible for the government price supports. In the early 1980s President Reagan boosted this effect with the Payments in Kind (PIK) program. This program gives government-stored crops back to farmers who keep their fields fallow. These farmers then sell the surplus commodities in the marketplace. This program reduces output produced and the costs of storage, and, given the inelasticity of demand, raises income for farmers. It was implemented in part because acreage controls have generally been ineffective in reducing supply, and surpluses have been the rule rather than the exception. Productivity advances in agriculture have more than offset the output reductions from holding some lands fallow, and it has been in the farmers' self-interests to voluntarily remove only their least productive acres. Because only the best soils are planted and more intensely cultivated, the output reductions of acreage controls have typically been negligible.

ACREAGE CONTROLS set limits on acres in production.

Another outcome of agricultural policy has been higher prices of foodstuffs (and fiber) to consumers. Since 1973, **target prices** have been applied on some items to try to help farmers without raising prices to consumers. Figure 5–5 illustrates that at a target price of $3, farmers will supply 500 million bushels. Under this system the government lets the farmers sell their corn on the market at a price sufficient to sell all of it. The price that consumers are willing to pay for all of it is $1. The government then pays the farmer the difference between the market price ($1) and the target price ($3). This difference of $2 times 500 million is the total subsidy. Again note that, in this case, the higher the price inelasticity of demand, the greater is the price decline to the consumer and the greater the burden on the taxpayers.

TARGET PRICES are a special type of price support for agriculture.

With target prices, the surplus problem is eliminated, and consumers are better off than with price supports, and they also recive lower prices than would prevail in a

---

[6]In our example in Figure 5–4, a supply shift to the left by enough to cross the demand curve at the $3 price would be viewed as ideal by policymakers.

FIGURE 5–5 A Guaranteed Target Price in Agriculture

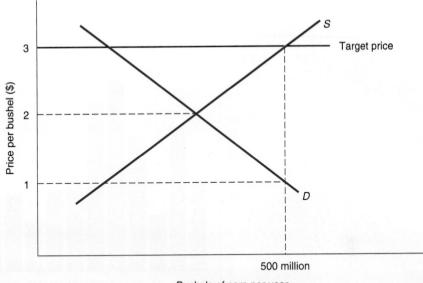

If a target price for corn is set at $3 and farmers produce and sell 500 million bushels at the price demanders will pay for all of it, the market price will be $1 per bushel. There is no surplus, but the government will pay farmers the difference between the guaranteed target price of $3 and the market price of $1 times 500 million bushels. The corn subsidy is thus $2 per bushel, or $1 billion in total.

market without government interference. The farmer is just as well off as with price supports.[7] Who pays the subsidy? A third party does—the taxpayer.

Politics and Payments to Farmers

Figure 5–6 shows the recent history of government price support payments to U.S. farmers. The year of greatest payments was 1986, about $26 billion. In 1994 the government gave farmers $10 billion in subsidies at a cost of $90 per taxpayer. These benefits to farmers were not distributed equally among the states. Table 5–1 lists the payments in 1993 to the five highest and five lowest benefiting states.

---

[7]Alternatively, the effect of the PIK program was very negative on many agricultural businesses, such as seed suppliers and other input and processing businesses. These businesses felt the drop in demand for their services as farmers cut back production to qualify for surplus crop benefits from government. Although, this government policy was helping some farmers, it was hurting other, related businesses, especially sellers of fertilizers and other agricultural inputs.

FIGURE 5–6   Total Farm Price Supports Paid by Government

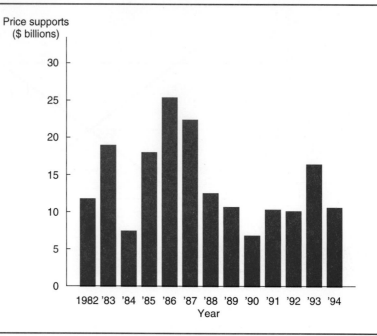

Source: *The Economist,* February 11, 1995.

TABLE 5–1   Farm Subsidies, in 1993, by State
(in thousands of dollars)

States that received the most in government payments:	
Texas	1,420,830
Iowa	1,229,544
Illinois	851,190
Minnesota	823,250
Nebraska	806,273
States that received the least:	
Rhode Island	140
Alaska	1,789
New Hampshire	1,942
Connecticut	2,892
Hawaii	3,131

Source: U.S. Department of Agriculture.

FIGURE 5–7   Kansas Farms, Size and Number, 1951–93

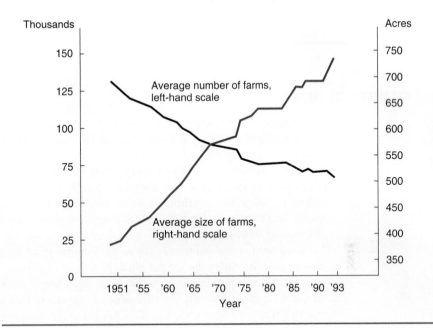

Source: *The Economist,* February 11, 1995.

It is important to emphasize that not all farmers receive subsidies. Indeed, only 30 percent of the 1.9 million U.S. farmers in 1995 received subsidies. The payments are based on selected crops (e.g., corn and rice) and are not based on need, income, or wealth. The larger the output though, the greater the payments received. This, along with other forces, has helped increase the size of farms and reduce their number from 5.9 million in 1945 to 1.9 million in 1995. Figure 5–7 traces these contrasting trends for a typical farm state, Kansas. There and throughout the nation small, family farms have become more and more rare. Most that remain are part-time enterprises, often worked by people whose main line of work is elsewhere. Big corporate farms produce the bulk of our food and fiber today. In 1940 the largest 2 percent of farms accounted for 50 percent of total U.S. farm production. In 1992, 3 percent produced half of total farm output.

Why should a small portion of farmers, most of whom are rich, receive subsidies when small businesses do not? That is one of 53 questions Senator Richard Lugar of Indiana asked in early 1995 as he chaired hearings of the Senate Agriculture Committee.

Despite historical opposition by agricultural interests—who have been long accustomed to public assistance—price support, target prices, and acreage restrictions were eliminated by Congress in a bill signed into law by President Clinton shortly before the 1996 presidential election. The law, however, guarantees farmers who have received subsidies in the past a continuance of federal payments through 2002 in excess of what they would have received under the previous program. Exceptions were granted for sugar and peanut subsidies, which continued under the old programs. The political question hanging is this: Will the old program be reinstated in 2002 once the guaranteed payments run out?

🏦 CHAPTER REVIEW

When changes in demand or supply occur, prices normally adjust to ration the item and to establish a new equilibrium to clear the market. In some markets, government price controls prevent the equilibrium price from being reached. Some controls, such as rent controls and usury laws, set price ceilings that do not allow prices (rent or interest) to rise above the legally imposed level. When the price ceiling is below the equilibrium price needed to clear the market, a shortage results, and forms of rationing other than price evolve. Scarcity makes some form of rationing unavoidable.

In contrast, some controls, such as agricultural price supports (and minimum wages), set price floors that do not allow prices (or wages) to fall below the legally set level. When the price floor is above the equilibrium price needed to clear the market, a surplus will result. Because of price supports in U.S. agriculture, surpluses in agriculture have been common. This has led to other controls (including acreage controls), to higher prices for food and fiber to consumers, and to higher taxes for taxpayers.

𝕵𝕽 MULTIPLE-CHOICE SELF-TEST 𝕵𝕽 𝕵𝕽 𝕵𝕽 𝕵𝕽 𝕵𝕽 𝕵𝕽 𝕵𝕽 𝕵𝕽 𝕵𝕽 𝕵𝕽 𝕵𝕽 𝕵𝕽 𝕵𝕽 𝕵𝕽 𝕵𝕽

1. Which of the following effects *should not* be expected from rent controls?
   a. Some landlords will be unable to afford repairs on their buildings.
   b. People will search less for apartments to rent, because they will more quickly find apartments they can afford.
   c. "Less desirable" tenants will find it harder to find apartments.
   d. The quantity of rental housing supplied will not grow as rapidly as it would without controls.

2. The government of Burma had a price ceiling on rice. Which of the following should you have been surprised to see going on?
   a. People waited in long lines to buy rice.
   b. To overcome the effects of low price, Burmese farmers rapidly expanded their rice output per acre.
   c. Shopkeepers sometimes sold rice only to customers who also bought canned goods at a high price.
   d. None of the above is a surprising outcome.

3. When the federal government puts price floors on agricultural products, which of the following is *not* used to deal with some of the problems created?
   a. Government pays farmers to leave some land unplanted.
   b. Government lets farmers borrow money against unsold crops, then takes the crops in payment for the loan.
   c. Government buys up the unsold amounts and stores them to be used in case of famine or international shortfalls.
   d. Government uses all the above methods to prevent farmers from being left with crops they can't sell.

4. Which of the following gainers or losers from U.S. oil price controls are *not* correctly identified?
   a. Most people who heated their homes with oil gained.
   b. Some drivers lost more from waiting times and difficulty getting gas than they gained from low prices.
   c. Oil companies gained large profits from controls.
   d. Owners of large-engine vehicles gained more than owners of small-engine vehicles.

5. If a shortage of paper exists:
   a. The current market price for paper must be too high.
   b. Consumers will have to cut back on their purchases of paper in order to solve the problem.
   c. An increase in price will end the shortage.
   d. A government price floor is probably the cause.

⚅ STUDY QUESTIONS

1. If a law were passed requiring that milk be given away free, how much milk would be available in the long run?

2. What would the law freezing milk prices do to the supplies of butter, cheese, and other milk-processed foods? How would this affect the market for milk substitutes?

3. Will the quantities supplied and demanded be changed if a legal price floor is set below the equilibrium price? Explain.

4. If a price ceiling is set on gasoline that is below the market clearing equilibrium price, what other means of rationing gas will likely occur? How will this affect the gasoline market? Use the supply and demand curves to illustrate your answer.

5. From Question 4, who gains and who loses from price controls?

6. What happened to the demand for health care services when the Medicare and Medicaid health care programs (nearly free health services) were legislated? What happened to the quantity demanded? What happened to health care costs? Use supply-demand curves to illustrate your answer.

7. What is the key characteristic of the demand for wheat that causes acreage limits to raise wheat farm incomes? Explain.

𝒯𝒫 PROBLEMS

1. Since the surgeon general and others have been urging Americans to stop smoking, demand for tobacco products has decreased. At the same time, the Department of Agriculture has been providing price supports to farmers who grow tobacco. The following table shows some of the results of these price supports.

    a. Draw a demand curve and a supply curve from the following demand and supply schedule. Quantities are in tons.

Price	$6,000	$8,000	$10,000	$12,000
Quantity demanded	10	9	8	7
Quantity supplied	4	6	8	10

    b. What is the equilibrium price? The quantity sold?
    c. Draw in a price floor of $12,000 per ton. How much tobacco now will be demanded? How much will be produced? What is the size of the surplus?
    d. If the government handles the surplus problem by buying up all the unsold tobacco at the support price and burning it, how much will the government have to buy? How much will it pay?
    e. Suppose, instead, the government decided to solve its problem by offering to buy all the farmers' tobacco at $12,000 per ton and then selling it to consumers for whatever price it could get. What amount would it then end up paying out?
    f. Options *d* and *e* have different groups paying more of the cost of the price-support program. Which one is preferable from the point of view of all taxpayers? Which is preferable from the point of view of tobacco consumers?

2. From Figure 5–1, p. 97, can you find the maximum price renters would be willing to pay for *Q*, given D_1? Hint: It is not on the graph (Figure 5–1), but the answer is logically the same as P_2 in Figure 5–3, p. 102.

CHAPTER 6

Production, Profits, and Marginal Analysis

🎵 CHAPTER PREVIEW

The driving force behind the billions of business decisions made each year in market economies is the profit motive. Business firms must make at least enough money to cover costs. Plus they would like to make a bit more—profit. They do not always succeed, but profit seeking is as American as apple pie.

Business decision makers in the pursuit of profits keep a keen eye on sales and the costs of production. Firms increase production if demand increases and sales advance. Firms change production methods if the relative costs of inputs change. Managers and business owners constantly seek the most profitable level (or rate) of production for their firm and the least costly input combinations. This may mean producing more or less, or possibly just holding production at an existing level.

If costs of certain inputs change, then businesses are compelled to change production methods. They can do this because inputs can generally be combined in various ways. A baseball field can be mowed in a day by (*a*) 10 people pushing hand mowers, (*b*) 5 people pushing power mowers, (c) 2 people riding power mowers, or (d) 1 person driving a tractor rig pulling a rack of mower blades. If the costs of capital equipment decline relative to wages (labor costs) then methods c and d become more common and methods a and b less so.

The Wall Street Journal, Business Week, and other media usually report only those business activities that are big, newsworthy events: a new plant, sensational profits, a bankruptcy, or big layoffs. However, important day-to-day business operations usually involve rather modest adjustments—decisions made at the margin, such as hiring another worker and increasing production.

1. What incentives would encourage you to start a business?
2. If you decided to open a small restaurant, what costs would you incur to start and run the business?
3. What conditions would encourage you to expand the business? To close down?

𝒥𝓇 CONCEPTS REINTRODUCED

Elasticity of Supply 77
Opportunity Cost 7
Capital-Intensive Methods 37
Labor-Intensive Methods 38
Law of Supply 72
Price 50
Productive Resources 15
Quantity Demanded 51
Total Revenues 61
Substitutes 56
Supply Curve 74

𝒥𝓇 NEW CONCEPTS

Production Costs
Fixed Inputs
Fixed Costs
Variable Costs
Profits
Short Run
Long Run
Marginal Analysis
Law of Diminishing Marginal Productivity
Marginal Physical Product of Labor
Marginal Cost

🎗 CHAPTER OBJECTIVES

After studying this chapter, you should be able to:

1. Distinguish between fixed and variable costs.
2. Distinguish between short-run and long-run costs.
3. Define and compute marginal cost.
4. Define the marginal physical product of labor.
5. Understand the law of diminishing marginal productivity.

PRODUCERS KEEP AN EYE ON THE MARKET

Shopping can be fun, hectic, or disappointing. Nevertheless, the buying decisions we make as customers send important signals to producers on what goods to produce and what services to provide. When we go shopping, we buy from *retailers* who sell items and services in relatively small quantities to consumers. These retailers in turn must restock their store shelves, so they order goods in volume from *wholesalers* who specialize in selling to retailers. Some retailers may also buy in bulk directly from primary producers that make the items we buy.

Although the process is indirect, if we buy more, the retailers and wholesalers then order more from manufacturers. Consequently, decisions on what and how much to produce are based ultimately on customer orders and on forecasts of customer buying. Businesses also watch closely what it costs to produce the goods we buy, for most businesses operate to make a profit. To do this, their revenues from sales must exceed the costs of production.

If orders pick up, businesses are encouraged to produce more, but they must consider the effect of costs on these production increases. Will the additional revenues from sales be more or less than the additional costs of production? This is the key question: Only if added revenues exceed added costs will profit rise with expansion. Will the business be able to fill the orders and sell the goods at the same established price, or will rising costs cause a fall in profit if price is not also rising?

As emphasized in Chapter 4 in the discussion of the law of supply, suppliers are limited by costs. To induce present and potential suppliers to produce more of the things we want, we must pay them enough to cover all their **production costs.** Only then will they shift resources from other uses to production of the things we want. Unless they can cover the opportunity costs of the additional resources, producers will be neither willing nor able to reallocate resources to supply the items we want to buy.

As implied by the law of supply, increasing costs of production are the general rule—at least in the short run. But why do costs rise in the short run? Why do supply curves rise more steeply in the short run than for long-run periods? These issues were introduced in Chapter 4 in the discussions of the elasticity of supply and increasing costs. Now the analysis of rising costs will be extended.

Combining Inputs

Production transforms raw materials and semiproduced goods into final products, or labor and other inputs into services. Efficient production is achieved by systematically combining land, labor, and capital in ways that minimize the total costs of the inputs for any given output.

For example, baking an apple pie is an act of production, and Table 6–1 gives a favorite recipe and production guide of Linda Walton's that gives exceptionally favorable results. This particular combination of inputs—raw materials, labor, and capital—constitutes the minimum inputs needed to prepare and bake the pie. Increasing the inputs produces more pies. Changing and substituting the inputs (buying and then baking a frozen pie in order to save on labor) or the ingredients (cherries for apples, margarine for butter) alter the quality, form, and quantity of the outputs. Even pie production allows alternative combinations of inputs.

Usually there are specific instructions (or a single recipe) on how to combine inputs, but there are alternative processes or input combinations for most of the things produced. A magazine article or a legal brief can be typed slowly using a typewriter or entered quickly on a word processor. The first method is relatively labor intensive compared to the second. If labor is cheap and capital expensive, as in China, manual typing may be the least-cost method. However, if labor costs are high relative to capital, then a more capital-intensive word processor method may be more cost-effective.

Brush painting a house is more time-consuming than is spray painting it with a few brush touch-ups. Whether it is best to use labor-intensive brushes or capital-intensive spray compressors depends on the prices of the various inputs. The least-cost method depends on the relative costs of labor and capital. Even baseball teams combine talents in different proportions. Some emphasize pitching, while others emphasize strong hitting. And all professional teams use pitching machines rather than "honest labor" for batting practice.

TABLE 6–1   Linda Walton's Recommended Input Requirements for a Class A Apple Pie

Raw Materials	Other Capital	Labor
2 cups flour	1 large pie pan	1 hour 20 minutes labor:
1 cup shortening	Rolling pin	20 minutes to shop for ingredients
1 teaspoon salt	Measuring cup and spoons	½ hour to peel, core, slice apples
¼ cup water	Oven	15 minutes to mix and roll dough
6 large apples	(Energy) 1 hour 5 minutes at 350°	15 minutes to assemble
1 cup sugar	Sharp knife	
4 tablespoons flour	Table	
2 teaspoons cinnamon		
¼ cup butter		

Added to this recipe for a Class A apple pie are other ingredients, additional minimum capital, and creative labor skills needed to make and bake it. Of great value in its own right, the recipe also illustrates the process of combining inputs for a particular method of production.

Variations in the way inputs are combined extend beyond production for sale. During the Vietnam War, the Vietcong and North Vietnam forces relied on labor-intensive fighting methods. They used manual labor and hand shovels to dig tunnels for penetrating enemy lines and for protection. For them, labor was relatively plentiful, whereas capital was comparatively scarce. Alternatively, the U.S. forces utilized much more capital-intensive fighting units. They used tractors and bulldozers to clear protection zones. In the United States, labor is costly relative to capital. These relative costs of inputs were reflected in the news media reports of battle losses. U.S. newspapers (and official U.S. casualty reportings) emphasized labor losses—the dead and wounded. The enemy's loss of men sounded enormous compared to U.S. losses. Vietnam news media, on the other hand, gave greater emphasis to capital losses, planes shot down, bridges destroyed, roads and villages taken, and the like. To a considerable extent, the emphasis of wartime news mirrored the relative input scarcities of the two societies.

Businesses and Productive Resources

Although production is often done privately (e.g., home cooking) or by government (e.g., first-class delivery of mail), production for sale in markets is most often done by businesses. Businesses are organized by *entrepreneurs* (a word of French origin meaning "undertaker") to bring together the other different productive resources—land, labor, and capital—to produce and sell for a profit. They vary in size and form—from small individually owned firms to large corporations.

When an entrepreneur organizes a firm to produce something or provide a service, he or she must provide credible guarantees to pay workers, to pay rent, to deliver goods, and to make good on other promises and contracts. In this way the productive resources are combined. These promises and contracts vary in length of time from long periods (e.g., for hiring workers, buying raw materials, leasing or buying buildings) to as short as a day or less (e.g., for hiring a repair technician).

Consequently, the firm views some inputs as fixed and others as variable. Suppose a firm sells typing services for term papers, legal documents, and other professional reports. Assume the firm, No-Ink, Inc., leases for one year a 500-square-foot office equipped with desks and word processing equipment. No-Ink signs a one-year contract for these leased inputs, regardless of the level of production. These are **fixed inputs,** which impose **fixed costs** on the firm. These costs do not vary whether 1 or 100,000 documents are produced. However, No-Ink also purchases paper, carbon ribbons, and other supplies; hires word processor operators; and pays for mailing, marketing, telephone, and other expenses that vary with the level of production. Costs associated with inputs that vary with the rate of production are called **variable costs.**

FIXED INPUTS cannot be changed for a given time period.

𝕁𝕁 𝕁𝕁

FIXED COSTS for that time period are unavoidable and do not vary with output.

VARIABLE COSTS increase or decrease directly with the level of production.

The cost to the entrepreneur must also be considered. When providing funding for the new business enterprise, the entrepreneur loses the opportunity to use those funds in other ways. In particular, interest could have been earned by purchasing bonds or by providing the funds for another business enterprise. The cost to the entrepreneur is the income that could have been earned with those funds in their next-best use. Those forgone earnings are the opportunity costs of that capital.

The owner-manager's time is also a cost. If the owner spends 50 hours a week managing the business, other alternatives are forgone. The opportunity cost of being the owner-manager is the forgone income of this person's next most productive use. It is just as much a real cost to No-Ink's owner as if someone else had been hired to manage the office,

Consequently, profit is more than the mere difference between the actual cash the firm takes in and the actual cash it pays for its inputs. Although an accountant would define *profits* as the difference in cash flow between cash revenues and expenses, to economists **profits** are the difference between all revenues and all explicit and implicit costs—the full opportunity costs of all inputs. The small mom-and-pop business may appear to earn a significant profit from the accountant's perspective and yet earn little or no profit from the economist's perspective. To an economist, the opportunity cost of the time spent by the family in the business is a real cost, even though no explicit money payments change hands within the family unit.

To illustrate the computation of profits from an economist's perspective (according to the definition here), we will consider the following circumstances: Julie White, a recent college graduate, turns down a $30,000 dollar-a-year job in order to open her own business. She borrows $150,000 to buy a small shop (sales outlet) and equipment. Total salaries (plus benefits) paid to other workers are $140,000 for the year, and raw materials totaled $50,000. Annual interest on the loan is $15,000 (10%), and insurance costs are $10,000. Total revenues from sales for the year are $250,000.

Profits equal revenues minus all costs—namely, total revenues of $250,000 minus the following:

$140,000	labor
40,000	materials
15,000	interest
10,000	insurance
30,000	Julie's opportunity cost
$235,000	total costs

Thus, Julie's firm makes $15,000 in profits. Clearly, Julie's firm has a positive value, at least temporarily. And, upon seeing Julie's example, another college grad with similar opportunity costs and skills may be inclined to open a similar business.

PROFITS for a given period of time equal total revenues minus total costs (including all implicit opportunity costs).

Short Run versus Long Run

Every firm like Julie White's that has some fixed costs or is under contract for inputs for a specified period is operating in the **short run.** Let's suppose that instead of borrowing $150,000, Julie rented the building and equipment for a minimum of two years at $1,250 per month and bought insurance at six-month intervals paying $5,000 each six months. Julie's short run of operations was at least two years when she signed the lease for the shop and equipment, because she contracted to pay $1,250 each month regardless of success (profits) or failure (losses).

After that contract period ends, Julie must decide among several choices:

1. Stay in or quit the business.
2. Buy or sell fixed inputs.
3. Sign new contracts or leases.

The time period up until everything can be recontracted is the short run.

The SHORT RUN is the period during which some inputs are fixed.

The LONG RUN is the period during which all inputs are variable.

The length of the short-run time period varies greatly from industry to industry and firm to firm—even over the life of a single firm. Although the terms *short run* and *long run* are imprecise in a calendar sense, they are quite necessary to a discussion of sound business decisions. It is important to understand the factors in each category. The reason for this is that, in the short run, existing inputs (costs) and past commitments constrain firms more than they do in the **long run.** Production costs behave differently in the short run than in the long run because there is less flexibility in the short run in the way a firm can combine inputs. In addition, in the short run some costs (the fixed costs) have no bearing on current business decisions! For these reasons some scholars like to emphasize that firms tend to *operate* in the short run and *plan* in the long run. To see why, we turn to the use of **marginal analysis.**

ANOTHER LAW: THE LAW OF DIMINISHING MARGINAL PRODUCTIVITY

Another maxim of economics is the **law of diminishing marginal productivity.** This law addresses the empirical relationship between variable inputs and outputs in the short run. This is a recognized law in economics because of the consistent results that develop when variable inputs are increased relative to fixed inputs—noting a distinct relationship between additions (marginal) of an input and the additions (marginal) to output. This law is also known as the *law of diminishing marginal returns.* It was first empirically verified in England over a century ago, after repetitive observations revealed diminishing marginal returns in agricultural production when increasing inputs of labor were applied in relation to fixed amounts of land and capital.

The LAW OF DIMINISHING MARGINAL PRODUCTIVITY states that if all factors of production are held constant except one, equal additions of that one variable factor will eventually increase output in decreasing increments.

The recognition of diminishing marginal productivity extends beyond the realm of economics and business. In World War II, British Prime Minister Winston Churchill argued that there were diminishing marginal returns to dropping bombs on German factories and transportation and communication facilities. He was confident that third and fourth raids rendered comparatively little additional damage; they merely rearranged the wreckage caused by earlier, more effective attacks. For him, diminishing marginal returns meant that the increase in damage to enemy industry diminished with each bombing.

Consider a very different example: insulating the attic of a house. To maintain a desired temperature, the first six-inch layer of insulation will reduce energy use (for heat in winter and cool air in summer). Adding another six-inch layer will further reduce energy use, but not by as much as did the previous layer. In fact, the fourth or fifth layers may reduce energy use only slightly, if at all.

The law of diminishing marginal productivity is illustrated in Figure 6–1, using a classical example from agriculture. In the agriculture example, land and a given amount of capital—seed, machinery, and fertilizer—are held constant, but additional inputs of labor increase the total output. These additions to output are the **marginal physical product of labor.**

The MARGINAL PHYSICAL PRODUCT OF LABOR is the added output that occurs when one new worker is added to the production process while all other inputs are held fixed.

FIGURE 6–1   Illustrating Diminishing Marginal Productivity of Labor in Onion Production

(1) Capital Investment	(2) Land (acres)	(3) Labor Input (number of workers for one month)	(4) Total Output per Season (bushels of onions)	(5) Marginal Physical Product of Labor per Season (bushels of onions)
$1,000	10	1	100	100
1,000	10	2	260	160
1,000	10	3	360	100
1,000	10	4	440	80
1,000	10	5	500	60
1,000	10	6	540	40
1,000	10	7	560	20
1,000	10	8	550	—10

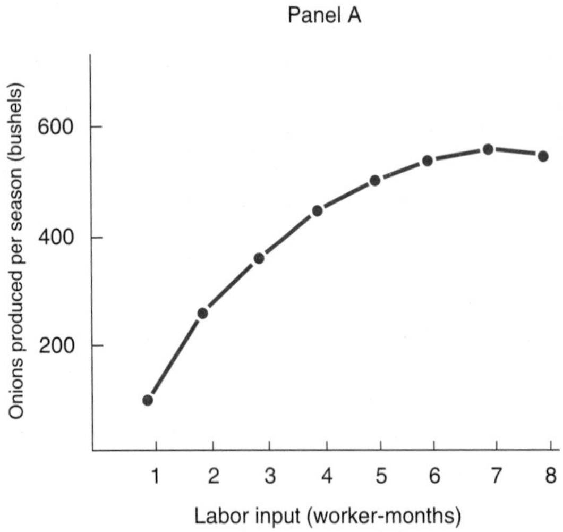

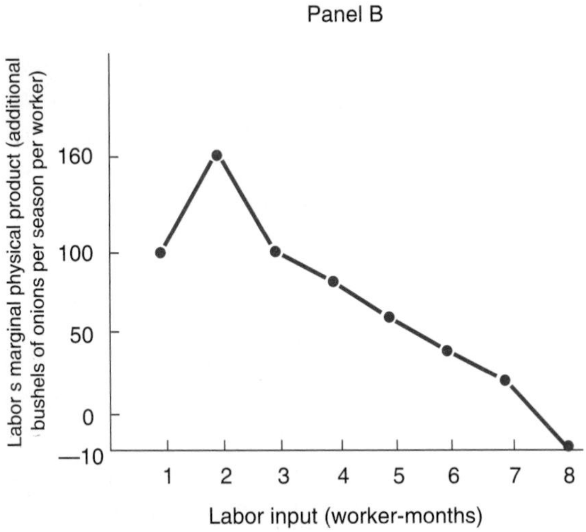

Panel A   Panel B

The law of diminishing marginal productivity is illustrated here, using a classical case from agriculture. In this hypothetical case for onion production, the amount of land (column 2) and the amount of equipment, fertilizer, and seed (column 1) remain constant, while additions of labor (column 3) are made. Total output at harvest time is given in column 4. In column 5 the change in output per additional worker, that is, the marginal physical product of labor, is shown. It diminishes after the second worker, showing the law of diminishing marginal productivity in effect.

Panels A and B illustrate the production function when relating output to input. The horizontal axes measure the number of workers, and the vertical axes measure output. Panel A shows total output, while Panel B shows the additional output from adding more workers, one at a time.

As this example of onion production shows, at the beginning the marginal productivity of labor (the variable factor) may increase. Realistically, one worker may not have high output results if there are too many machines to run and too much land to cultivate all alone. In this case, two workers may produce more than double the output of one. With two workers, each one may be able to specialize in certain tasks, leading to higher marginal product results—at least, up to a point. However, when workers are increased to the point at which each worker on average has fewer and fewer machines (and smaller amounts of land) to work with, labor productivity will fall.

As shown in Figure 6–1, one unit of labor (one worker for one month) realizes a total product of 100 bushels of onions. A second worker raises the total product to 260. As labor is increased from zero to one, the marginal product of labor is 100; an increase of labor from one unit to two generates a marginal product of 160 (260 – 100). The marginal product of adding a third worker is 100; a fourth, 80. Total product increases at a diminishing rate until the marginal product of labor becomes zero or turns negative. In the example, the marginal product of adding an eighth worker is negative.

Marginal Costs in the Short Run

Firms bound by fixed-cost, contractual arrangements (a short-run situation) face the problem of adjusting their production rate with variable inputs only. Generally, the fixed costs arise from a plant of fixed capacity, and a set number of acres of land or of machines and equipment. The key question then is this: Will the increase in revenues from more sales exceed, equal, or be less than the increase in variable costs? To return to our example: When onion production rises from 360 to 440 bushels after labor input is increased from three to four workers, how does the cost for added labor compare with the value of extra onions produced? Suppose workers are paid $400 per month and onions sell for $10 per bushel. The added cost of hiring a fourth worker is $400, but the added revenue is $10 times the 80 bushels of onions produced by the fourth worker—$800.[1] Clearly, the added revenue exceeds the added cost, so that profits increase. A fifth worker adds another $400 to costs, and the added revenue is $600 ($10 × 60 bushels). The marginal product of labor when a sixth worker is hired is 40 bushels, and the added value to output is $400 ($10 × 40), an amount just equal to the wages paid for the extra labor. Profits remain unchanged by the addition of a sixth worker; further additions of labor actually lower profits, because the marginal product of labor is below 40 bushels and below $400 in value. The most profitable output when onions sell for $10 per bushel is 540 bushels, the level at which six workers are hired at $400 each per month.

There is another way of comparing changes in costs to changes in revenues in order to make decisions about profitable production levels. This alternative solution focuses on the added cost to produce one more bushel (unit of output). This added cost per bushel is compared to the revenue received, which is equal to the price per bushel ($10). If the added costs are less than the revenues added, it is profitable to produce more; however, if the added costs to produce one more unit are more than the revenue received for it, then it is more profitable not to produce the extra unit.

---

[1]The multiplication of the output price by the marginal physical product of labor is called the *value of the marginal product of labor* (discussed more thoroughly in Chapter 8).

Economists call these changes in costs, as output is increased one unit, **marginal cost.** Using this important term, a competitive firm's managers can apply the following rules of thumb to raise profits:[2]

- If price exceeds marginal cost, produce more. Each addition to output adds more to revenues than to costs.
- If price is less than marginal cost, produce less. Each reduction in output lowers costs more than it lowers revenues.
- The most profitable level of production for competitive firms that do not control market price is the level at which price equals marginal cost.

JL JL JL JL JL JL JL JL JL JL JL JL JL JL JL JL JL JL JL JL JL JL JL JL JL JL

MARGINAL COST is the increase in total costs as one more unit is produced.

Marginal Physical Product and Its Mirror Image—Marginal Cost

When the marginal physical product of the variable input declines, as the law of diminishing marginal productivity ultimately assures, the marginal cost of output increases. In the strictest sense, marginal cost and marginal physical product are inversely related, the "mirror image" of each other.

For example, from the illustration of onion production, at $400 per month per worker, when workers are increased from three to four, the marginal cost per bushel of onions is $5. This is calculated by dividing the added output of 80 bushels into the added costs of labor ($400 ÷ 80 = $5). Alternatively stated, the change in cost from adding one more worker ($400) divided by the change in output from adding one worker (80 bushels) equals marginal cost ($5). The extra cost of increasing output from 360 to 440 (80 bushels) is one month's wages. The added wage cost ($400) divided by the marginal physical product of labor (80 bushels) equals the marginal cost ($5). Therefore, if the wage stays the same (at $400) and the marginal product of labor falls with added workers, the marginal cost must rise. For instance, a fifth worker adds $400 to costs, and the marginal product is 60 bushels. Therefore, the marginal cost per bushel is $6.67 ($400 ÷ 60). A sixth worker adds 40 bushels, for a marginal cost of $10 ($400 ÷ 40).

Now let's consider another type of firm and how marginal product and marginal costs are related. If a firm leases a pizza shop with two ovens for a year, hires workers, and each week buys pizza ingredients, the marginal physical product of labor and materials combined, when added to the fixed capital of two ovens, eventually declines.

---

[2]These general rules hold *only* for firms that sell in competitive markets where prices are taken as given by the market forces of supply and demand. Modifications of these rules, for firms with degrees of monopoly and price-setting power, are given in Chapter 7.

Even if the prices paid per ingredient and the wages paid per worker do not change, the marginal cost per pizza will rise as additional workers cause crowding and the production of fewer and fewer pizzas per worker. At the extreme, it is possible for too many workers to be hired and for the operation to become too large for the pizza shop. The marginal costs may become very high indeed when the workers crowd each other, possibly burning themselves or each other. Pizzas cannot be baked, tempers flare, and pizzas are wasted. In this extreme situation, the marginal physical product of the variable inputs may become zero or possibly negative. At this point the marginal cost of a pizza becomes astronomical. There are no advantages to the shop owner or to consumers from pushing production that far. Pizza parlor owners, as well as the owners of all firms, ignore the law of diminishing marginal productivity (or its counterpart, the law of rising marginal cost in the short run) at their own financial peril.

Comparing Marginal Cost to Price

As just noted and as shown in Figure 6–2, when marginal costs are less than price, revenues go up more than costs do as production increases. In this onion-production example, we see that the marginal cost of onions is $5 when a fourth worker is added. When the fifth worker is added, the marginal cost of onions rises to $6.67; for a sixth, to $10. If the price per bushel is $10, the extra revenue exceeds the added costs up to the point where the sixth worker is hired. Therefore, given the fixed costs, which must be paid no matter what the level of production, we see that 540 bushels is the most profitable output level in the short run.[3] This method of equating marginal cost to price gives exactly the same profit-maximizing results that we found by comparing added costs to added revenues. As we observed in that example, it didn't pay to hire a seventh worker, because the marginal product was too low. Figure 6–2 shows this too. A seventh worker brings a marginal product of only 20 bushels valued at $200 (20 × $10) but costs $400 to hire. We also see that the fall in the marginal product to 20 raises the marginal cost to $20 per bushel ($400 ÷ 20 = $20), twice the price received. Adding the seventh worker certainly lowers the profitability of the firm. However, if the price of onions suddenly jumped to $20 per bushel, then a marginal product as low as 20 would be justified. This would equate marginal cost to price. Alternatively, if wages fell from $400 to $200, a seventh worker would add as much to revenues (20 × $10) as to costs ($200).

Fixed Costs in the Short Run

Because fixed costs must be paid regardless of the level of production, fixed costs do not reflect any forgone opportunities. In the short run, the decision maker views fixed costs (whether owned or under contract) as *sunk.* For example, the case where Julie

---

[3]Depending on the fixed costs, the firm is making either profits or losses; therefore, the most profitable output here means either the greatest profits or the least losses.

FIGURE 6–2   Hiring the Profit-Maximizing Number of Workers

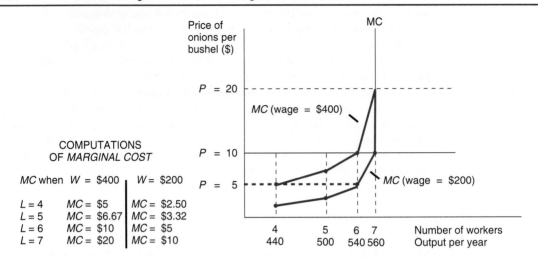

COMPUTATIONS
OF *MARGINAL COST*

MC when *W* = $400	*W* = $200
L = 4 *MC* = $5	*MC* = $2.50
L = 5 *MC* = $6.67	*MC* = $3.32
L = 6 *MC* = $10	*MC* = $5
L = 7 *MC* = $20	*MC* = $10

Given price (*P*) equal to $10 and the wage (*W*) equal to $400, the firm maximizes profit by hiring workers up to and including the sixth, because each of these workers adds more to total revenue than to total cost; thus, each causes profits to increase (or losses to decrease). The sixth worker, in fact, adds just as much to revenue as to cost, resulting in no change in profits. However, hiring any additional workers would result in a decrease in profits. The seventh worker, for example, adds $400 ($20 per bushel) to costs and only $10 per bushel to revenues. This would be a $10 decrease in profits for each bushel added from hiring the seventh worker. However, if the price of onions increased to $20 per bushel, or if the wage rate fell to $200, then the firm would gain by hiring the seventh worker as well.

TOOL KIT

USING MARGINAL ANALYSIS TO SET PRODUCTION LEVELS
THAT MAXIMIZE PROFITS IN THE SHORT RUN

If a business decision raises revenues more than it raises cost, profits rise and management is pleased. Similarly, if a decision leads to cost reductions relative to revenues, profits increase. Although managers often do not explicitly recognize that they use marginal analysis to set profit-maximizing levels of production, they do use rules of thumb that are dis- guised applications of marginal analysis. In economics we generalize these rules of thumb to arrive at explicit operational propositions on profit-maximizing production levels.

When some inputs and costs are fixed—in the short run—the law of diminishing marginal productivity tells us that as variable inputs are added,

White leased a shop and equipment for two years and bought insurance each six months had sunk costs in insurance of up to six months. After six months, Julie could reconsider whether or not to buy coverage and stay in business another six months. She had sunk costs of $1,250 per month in the lease for two years; after two years, she could sustain or quit that contractual obligation. These are not marginal costs except at the time of renewal, then they are sunk again.

Fixed costs have no bearing on decisions to produce a little more or a little less, and revenues may or may not be sufficient to cover them in the short run. Once the decision is made to buy or contract for a fixed input, the only production options open are to introduce changes in the variable inputs or to shut down or sell out. Revenues in the short run must be sufficient to pay for the variable costs—the out-of-pocket expenses—or it is preferable to quit the business. For example, if revenues from Julie's business cover the labor, materials, insurance, and her opportunity cost *plus some, but not all,* of the monthly fixed costs for the lease, she will prudently stay in business and then exit when the lease expires. Of course, if she does that, she is assuming and counting on the fact that the past will repeat itself. If she anticipates a rise in revenues, she may gamble optimistically and resign the lease (and perhaps she can negotiate a lower rental rate).

In our example of onion production, the landowner could eventually sell or lease the land. However, until that happens, the landowner has no alternatives to its use. Until the land is sold or leased out, the costs of the land are fixed. The fixed land costs do not influence the landowner's production decisions, because in the short run there are no alternative uses of the land.

total output will rise at a decreasing rate. To determine the profit-maximizing level of production, the added revenues from selling more must be compared to the variable costs from producing more.

The law of diminishing marginal productivity means that the value of the additional output (revenues) decreases for any given addition to costs (addition of variable inputs). Alternatively put, it states that the addition to costs will rise at an increasing rate for any given increase in output (revenues).

We should expand production when the revenues from the added output exceed the addition to costs. We should reduce production when the decline in revenues (from the fall in output) is less than the decline in costs. The profit-maximizing level of production occurs at the point at which the addition to revenues from adding one more variable input equals the addition to costs.

Expressing this marginal analysis in an alternative way, we should expand production when price exceeds marginal cost. We should reduce production if price is less than marginal cost. The production level to maximize profits is where price equals marginal costs. At that point, a change in production up or down will lower profits (with conditions explained in footnote 2).

Similarly, the pizza shop owner who buys a new cash register adds to the other fixed costs of the firm. A cash register may improve the accounting process, and the purchase may be a good business decision. However, once it is bought (or leased), the cash register has no immediate alternative uses for the pizza shop owner. Even using it does not significantly affect its value for resale, as a gift, or as a decoration. For all practical purposes, the purchase of the cash register is irrelevant in determining how many pizzas to bake. The cash register costs the pizza shop owner the same for 1,000 pizzas sold as for 100 sold.

To give one final example, any business that buys liability insurance adds to its sunk costs, once the insurance contract is signed, until the period of coverage is over. During this interval, these and other sunk costs are irrelevant to business decision makers in determining levels of production. Only the costs that can be added or subtracted bear on production-level decisions. In the short run, these are limited to variable costs, costs that are future oriented. Past decisions will have determined sunk costs; present choices have consequences and costs that lie in the future. The burden of the entrepreneur is to compare expected revenues to expected costs in an uncertain world.

All Costs Vary in the Long Run

Businesses are constantly renewing contracts (as contract periods end) and making new commitments on fixed inputs. These long-run considerations are critical in determining whether to stay in business. They are related to, yet different from, decisions on production levels for a short period of time. If the revenues from sales do not cover *all costs* in the long run, the firm will alter its operations or quit the business. In the long run all costs must be covered, or decision makers will not sign contracts, buy fixed inputs, and plan to hire and purchase variable inputs.

To return to our example of onion production, if rent paid for the land is $1,000 a year, and if seed, fertilizer, and machinery costs are $1,000, total fixed costs equal $2,000. We observed that, in order to maximize profits, six workers should be hired for one month at $400 each ($2,400). Let's treat the farm manager as one of the hired workers in this example, with an opportunity cost for her labor equal to $400, the wages paid to other labor. Total costs therefore equal $2,000 plus $2,400, or $4,400. The value of sales at $10 per bushel equals $5,400 ($10 × 540 bushels). The farm operator receives $1,000 as profits plus his opportunity cost of $400.[4] Given no foreseeable changes in these conditions, it would be profitable to recontract and stay in business for another year.

---

[4]If the opportunity cost of the farm manager were $500 rather than the $400 we calculated, then the profit would be $900 rather than $1,000. Profit is the difference between revenues and all costs, including full opportunity costs.

However, if total rental costs increased by more than an additional $1,000 or if prices fell or wages increased enough to erase the profits, it would not be profitable to recontract at the existing terms. If profit expectations are negative, decision makers in the long run can choose to avoid any losses by leaving the business. *And all opportunity costs must be covered in the long run.* If not, a business can reallocate the resources under its control to other uses in order to receive higher monetary rewards.

Supplier Responses in the Short Run and in the Long Run

As emphasized in Chapter 4, the elasticity of supply is greater in the long run than in the short run. The supply curve rises more steeply in the short run than in the long run because of fixed input constraints in the short run. The fixed inputs cause the law of diminishing returns to be in effect. Figure 6–3 uses the example of cassette production to illustrate the difference with a long-run supply curve, S_{LR}, that is less steeply sloped than its short-run counterpart, S_{SR}.

In the onion-production example, for instance, the fixed and limited amount of land and machines (plus seed and fertilizer) imposes limits on the productivity of labor. The land limitation causes (*a*) the marginal product of labor to decline after a second worker is added and (*b*) the marginal product of labor to fall to zero (and less) when an eighth worker is added. Therefore, the marginal cost of production rises as a third worker is added and continues to rise more steeply with the addition of each worker. With the fixed input constraints, less land and fewer machines are available to each worker for use in producing onions. This causes the diminishing marginal productivity and the rising marginal costs in the short run.

Marginal costs can also rise in the long run, but because inputs are generally variable in the long run, no fixed inputs constrain productivity through the law of diminishing returns in the long run.[5] However, inputs do vary in quality, and the best quality of land for onions may not be in unlimited supply, even in the long run.

For example, in the pizza case, if the shop can be enlarged, especially its preparation area, and if more ovens can be installed in proportion to the number of workers added, production may possibly be increased without diminishing marginal productivity of labor. In this situation, increases in the demand for pizza will lead to a supply response that is very elastic.

Using a cassette-production example, in Figure 6–3, S_{LR} illustrates an elastic long-run supply case. In the long run, with little if any capacity constraint, demand can increase without sharp price increases. However, in the short run, if fixed inputs constrain production severely and diminishing marginal productivity leads to sharply falling marginal products of the variable inputs, then the supply

---

[5]If there is only one manager, or if a single public service, such as a road, exists to constrain production, then this type of fixed factor can still lead to diminishing marginal returns, even for very long periods.

FIGURE 6–3   Supply in the Long Run and in the Short Run

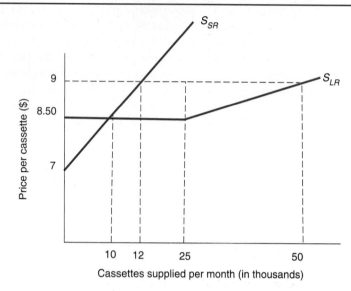

Fixed inputs in the short run constrain the supply response and make the supply curve in the short run (S_{SR}) more inelastic than in the long run (S_{LR}) when all inputs are variable. For any given price increase, then, more will be supplied per month in the long run than in the short run.

response will be quite inelastic. The supply curve will resemble S_{SR}, and price will rise sharply with a demand increase. The supply response will be more limited in the short run than in the long run. In the long run all inputs are variable, and production is not constrained by fixed inputs causing limited short-run capacities. For that reason, as emphasized in this chapter, the elasticity of supply depends greatly on time.

CHAPTER REVIEW

Fixed inputs cause supply conditions to differ between the short run and the long run, because fixed inputs set practical limits on how much firms can produce. In the short run, producers alter production levels by changing only the variable inputs. Therefore, costs per unit rise more steeply in the short run than in the long run. Competitive firms that cannot set price independent of the market-determined price find their most profitable production levels where marginal cost equals price.

Marginal cost is defined as the change in costs that results from a change in one unit of output. Marginal cost is calculated by dividing the price of a variable input into the marginal product of the variable input.

As stated by the law of diminishing marginal productivity, the marginal product of variable inputs eventually declines in the short run, because as each variable input is added there are fewer fixed inputs to work with. It is this decline in the marginal product of the variable input that causes a rise in the marginal cost of production. Although fixed costs are relevant to the long-run decision to recontract, sign leases, and continue in business, the sunk costs have no bearing on the decision of how much to produce in the short run.

In the short run, revenues must cover variable costs. In the long run, however, revenues must exceed or at least equal all costs, including full opportunity costs, or the business will be unprofitable and will ultimately fail.

🎵 MULTIPLE-CHOICE SELF-TEST 🎵 🎵 🎵 🎵 🎵 🎵 🎵 🎵 🎵 🎵 🎵 🎵 🎵 🎵 🎵

1. The short run is the time period:
   a. That lasts one year or less.
   b. In which firms must ignore variable costs and make production choices based on whether or not they can cover fixed costs.
   c. In which firms must make production decisions without being able to change the levels of some of their inputs and costs.
   d. In which firms have lower costs of production.

2. Which of the following costs should cause a firm to change its level of production over the next six months?
   a. The property tax on the buildings the firm owns has just doubled.
   b. An office buys an expensive computer and then discovers that none of the staff can or will use it.
   c. The repair costs on the firm's conveyor belt system ended up being far less than the firm had expected when it undertook the repair job.
   d. None of these costs should cause the firm to change the level of production it had chosen before these changes occurred.

3. If a firm's marginal cost of producing a good is increasing:
   a. The firm should cut back its production until marginal cost levels off.
   b. That is a sign the marginal physical product of some inputs is decreasing.
   c. The firm should increase its production.
   d. The firm must be operating at a loss.

4. In the short run, but not in the long run:
   a. A firm may do better by producing at a loss rather than by shutting down.
   b. Firms face rising marginal costs.
   c. Firms' supply curves are more elastic.
   d. Firms can vary all their inputs.

🎵 STUDY QUESTIONS

1. You own a McDonald's fast-food restaurant franchise. What are the fixed costs and what are the variable costs?

2. What do economists mean by the *short run*? Why do production costs rise more steeply in the short run than in the long run?

3. If inputs are fixed, then is supply likely to be more or less elastic?

4. Why do marginal costs rise in the short run? Give two real-world examples of increasing short-run marginal costs.

5. Give one example of the law of diminishing marginal productivity. Explain in detail.

6. You own a yogurt shop with three yogurt machines. How would marginal analysis help you determine the level of yogurt production for maximum profits?

✒ PROBLEM

Classy Closets is a new firm just started up by a friend of yours. It makes closet-organizing units. Your friend is seeking your advice about the best level of production to plan on, given some changing market conditions. Some starting information on the firm's costs that your friend can give you is in the table below:

Number of units	1	2	3	4	5	6
Fixed cost	$500	—	—	—	—	—
Variable cost	$300	$500	$700	$1,000	$1,400	$1,900
Total cost	—	—	—	—	—	—
Marginal cost	—	—	—	—	—	—

1. Fill in the blanks in the table.

2. Draw a graph of marginal cost. (Put marginal cost on the vertical axis, quantity on the horizontal axis.)

3. Suppose the going price for closet units is $300. How many closet units per week should your friend's firm make? What if the price rises to $350? To $400?

4. Draw lines on your marginal cost graph at each of the three prices named in 3. Label the points of intersection of the price lines and the marginal cost line *A, B,* and *C* for the $300, $350, and $400 prices, respectively. Check that the production level at each of these points is the same as your answers to the questions in 3.

CHAPTER 7

Competition and Monopoly

Over 16 million U.S. businesses currently compete for consumer dollars. Each of us is among the millions of consumers who interact with these businesses to make transactions and purchase goods and services. It appears to us as customers that prices are "set" by businesses, and in some instances, we are correct. In general, though, the actual degree of control over price varies greatly among industries. Some businesses enjoy considerable price-setting capability, whereas others have no power to set the prices they would like.

1. Can a monopolist raise profits by producing less and selling at a higher price?
2. For society, why are competitive businesses generally preferable to monopolies?
3. Where do you get better service: McDonald's, your local supermarket, or the Department of Motor Vehicles?

𝕁𝓇 CONCEPTS REINTRODUCED

Elasticity of Supply 77
Marginal Analysis 120
Marginal Cost 124
Price 50
Price Elasticity of Demand 60
Profits 120
Substitutes 56
Total Revenues 61

𝕁𝓇 NEW CONCEPTS

Market Structure
Pure Competition
Pure Monopoly
Price Taker
Price Searcher
Marginal Revenue
Monopolistic Competition
Oligopoly
Rule of Rational Choice

𝕁𝕃 CHAPTER OBJECTIVES

After studying this chapter, you should be able to:

1. Distinguish among four basic market structures: pure competition, monopolistic competition, oligopoly, and monopoly.
2. Distinguish between price takers and price searchers and their decision criteria for maximizing profit; describe how firms determine the quantity to produce that has maximum profit; and describe how price searchers find the price that maximizes profit.
3. Recognize the relationship between total revenue and marginal revenue.

MARKET STRUCTURE AND SETTING PRICES

The amount of competition that prevails among sellers largely determines how much control each business has over its price. Competition regulates markets by making sellers responsive to buyers' wishes, by rewarding the most cost-efficient producers and sellers with revenues equal to or in excess of costs, and by encouraging entrepreneurs to allocate resources to their most highly valued uses. Although some firms operate in extremely competitive markets, others may have all the market to themselves. Between these extremes are many variations of competitiveness and price-setting power. Economists study markets to see how they work and to determine their **market structure.**

> **MARKET STRUCTURE** is a classification system for grouping firms according to the degree of competition they face in the marketplace.

In practical application the distinctions among different market structures is often hazy. The geographical boundary of a market, that is, the size of the area where buyers and sellers interact, is often fuzzy. The boundaries may be local, regional, national, or global. Restaurant markets are local, banking is regional, the stock market is national and international. Some markets are truly global: oil, computers, and wine, for example. Such differences are important, but the fuzziness of market structure remains.

If you own and operate the only restaurant in a town, you will have more control over price than if there are other restaurants competing with you for customers. Even if you have the only restaurant in town, there may be restaurants in nearby towns to give you regional competition. A second market-structure classification problem arises when you try to determine which substitute items (or services) compete with each other in a specific market. Do grocery stores and home cooking compete with restaurants? Do Kentucky Fried Chicken restaurants and other fast-food places compete with a gourmet Chinese restaurant? Do radio, television, stereo records, tape recorders, or video and computer games have overlapping services and qualities that place them in competition with each other? Does Joe's Used Cars compete with a General Motors (GM) new car dealer?

Economists, lawyers, and others disagree on how to characterize real-world markets. Nevertheless, the concept of market structure is frequently used in arguments in our courts, especially in antitrust cases. Economists regularly use market-structure specifications to analyze problems and draw conclusions on how effectively suppliers respond to consumers or how efficiently they allocate and combine resources. Two opposite extremes of market structure that are frequently used for analysis are **pure competition** and **pure monopoly.** These very different alternatives represent the cases of (1) many sellers of identical goods and (2) one seller. We will analyze these two extreme market structures and then consider intermediate forms.

In PURE COMPETITION there are many sellers selling the same product, and no seller can set the price.

In PURE MONOPOLY one seller controls the entire market.

Pure Competition: The World of Price Takers

When the number of buyers and the number of sellers of an item (or service) are large enough, the price of that item (or service) is taken for granted. Each of the market participants is a **price taker,** because no single individual or combination of sellers (or buyers) is able to set price or to change it. The price depends entirely on the forces of supply and demand and emerges from the market as a given. These price takers (suppliers and demanders) simply view the price as something beyond their control. A buyer may attempt to buy at prices below the market price, but sellers would not gain from accepting such offers. If some buyers refuse to pay the market price, they most likely will end up empty-handed. Likewise, a seller may set a price above the market price, but buyers can conveniently buy from others selling at the lower market price. Such a seller will find no customers.

A PRICE TAKER is a seller (or buyer) that takes the market price as a given.

Pure competition, where everyone is a price taker, exists when no single supplier (or buyer) has sufficient influence on the total supply (demand) to significantly change the conditions of supply (demand). If a firm quits the business or withholds all its supplies or if a new firm enters the market, the impact on market price is negligible. The action will not affect the market clearing price.

Besides being price takers, purely competitive businesses are free to enter or leave the market. Existing firms cannot block entry of potential firms, and there are no legal restrictions that limit or block exit from the market.

Examples of purely competitive markets include the various financial markets: stock, bond, and futures. Many agricultural markets also have characteristics of pure competition. This does not negate the fact that government policy greatly alters the conditions of supply and prices in agricultural markets. Typically, farmers are price takers and have no sense of rivalry with their competitors. They even call them neighbors. Taxicab services, haircuts, video rentals, cleaners, grocery stores, and many, many other groups of competing firms also fit the pure competitive model, except in isolated areas.

Because each business firm is a price taker in purely competitive markets, the firm's main decision is how to adjust output. It can produce more or less or nothing at all. One important implication of purely competitive market structures is that very high (above-normal) profits or losses are only temporary, because market forces constantly adjust price and minimize the difference between revenues and costs. If demand increases and price advances, unusual profits may occur in the short run. However, freedom of entry means that the long-run elasticity of supply is very high—much higher than in the short run.[1] New entrants will appear to compete for customers and earn some of the above-normal profits. These additions to supply will tend to reduce market price and drop profits back to minimal levels. New entrants will continue to appear until price has fallen sufficiently to erase all above-normal profits. Although high profits can occur in the short run, free entry assures their eventual disappearance.

Alternatively, losses won't prevail very long, either. If a fall in demand leads to a fall in price and costs exceed revenues, some firms will eventually quit or go into another type of business. As emphasized in Chapter 6, in the long run all resources must be paid their full opportunity costs. Business decision makers will not endure losses indefinitely. As firms leave the business, the reduction in supply tends to raise price and eliminate the losses. Exit will continue until eventually losses are entirely eliminated. One consequence of pure competition, then, is supply flexibility, as guided by profit opportunities and losses. Changes in consumer desires, which pre-cipitate changes in both demand and price, are met by supply responses.

Another important result of pure competition is that, in the long run, price will be as low as possible, given costs. Price will be no higher than is needed to cover the costs of production and distribution. Any price higher than this encourages entry, increases quantities supplied, and lowers price; any price lower than this causes losses, spurs exit, reduces quantities supplied, and raises price. In short, competitive

---

[1]Freedom of entry or exit does not mean this movement is accomplished without cost. Resources must be compensated for in order to enter a business, and inputs may be idled when the business exits. If these costs are met, the firm may enter or exit the business.

markets expand when demand increases and contract when demand declines. Price in the long run is as low as possible, but is sufficient to cover all the costs of the good (or service). Very high profits (or losses) may occur temporarily from time to time. Entry and exit will erode them and bring about normal payments to all resources in the long run—payments that just cover their opportunity costs.

Pure Monopoly: The World of Price Searchers

Pure monopoly is the opposite extreme of pure competition. A combination of two Greek words, *mon* and *polein*, monopoly ("sole seller") refers to a market structure totally lacking competition. There is only one seller, and entry into the market is restricted, legally or otherwise.

Although a monopoly may have all the market to itself and thus can set the price, the market demand curve limits the opportunities on sales and revenues. If a monopolist raises price too high, sales may disappear. If a monopolist expands production to sell more, the price must be lowered. Figure 7–1 shows that the basic options of a monopolist selling bottles of a secret health serum are to sell less at a higher price (500 bottles at $6 each) or to sell more at a lower price (600 bottles at $5 each).

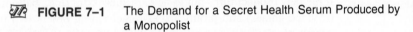 **FIGURE 7–1**   The Demand for a Secret Health Serum Produced by a Monopolist

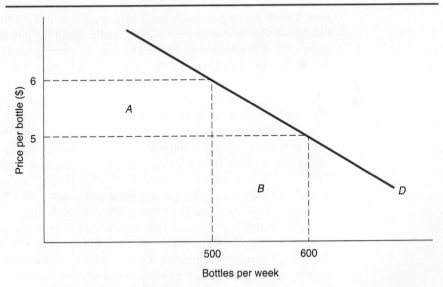

A monopolist can raise price, but the quantities for sale must be lowered in order to sell at the higher price. Areas *A* and *B* represent the impact on total revenues from a change in price and quantity. Raising the price from $5 to $6 gains some revenues (*A*) from buyers now paying more per bottle but loses some revenues (*B*) by the reduction in sales.

Raising the price from $5 to $6 loses area *B* in revenues (100 units sold at $5 each) but gains area *A* ($1 on each of the 500 bottles sold).

The demand curve shows the maximum prices the monopolist can charge for various quantities. The monopolist's control over price and revenue depends on the elasticity of the demand curve. Remember that the elasticity of demand depends primarily on the number and availability of close substitutes. That is why blocking entry of others into the market is of vital importance to a monopolist. Preventing competition and the emergence of substitute goods (or services) assures that the monopolist gets all the market's demand. Blocking entry and preventing the appearance of substitute items make the monopolist's demand curve less elastic.

Several key barriers to market entry permit monopolies to persist. Privileged information, such as a secret formula or a special technology or process, is one such barrier. Another is the control of an essential raw material required in a production process. For example, bauxite mines were once closely held by the Aluminum Corporation of America (Alcoa), which thus controlled one of the essentials for entry into aluminum manufacture, but it is difficult to find similar cases today.[2] Another, more common entry barrier is patent protection. Patent holders retain 17 years of exclusive rights to the production of a patented item. Such exclusive rights are granted to encourage invention and to spur economic progress. Patents help to assure property rights in ideas and to spur creativity, but if the new product turns out to be very successful (e.g., ballpoint pens, computers, or video games) and profits are extremely high, others will try to develop close substitutes not covered by the patent. This often limits monopoly power and sometimes causes patent holders to incur large legal fees to fight for their patent rights. Finally, another barrier to market entry occurs when the government grants exclusive rights of production to a particular firm for other reasons. One such case was that of American Telephone & Telegraph (AT&T), which had a monopoly on the sale of phone services for many years, until legal actions in the 1970s broke up the company into competing units. Sometimes the government maintains the monopoly rights for itself, as in first-class mail services.

City governments often grant monopoly rights to such businesses as garbage collection firms or utility companies. These monopolies are tolerated when resource savings are apparent from allowing one firm to supply all a market's demand, that is, when one large company can meet the market demand at lower total costs than several small firms can. One garbage collection center with a fleet of trucks following a well-designed schedule of routes and collection times often is more efficient (lower in cost) than many separately owned trucks competing as do taxicabs. Securing such monopolies usually does not carry with it the right to set monopoly prices. Typically, a regulatory commission must approve "appropriate rates" to be charged to customers. What rates are appropriate and whether monopolies try to keep costs as low as possible are topics of considerable disagreement among consumers, regulators, managers, and others.

---

[2]This was one of the reasons a 1937 complaint was filed against Alcoa for monopoly practice. A decade later the case was still unresolved, although eventually Alcoa lost.

Although monopoly power clearly has revenue-enhancing advantages, it should be emphasized that, even with a monopoly, profits are not automatically assured. The demand for a monopolized item may be so low that costs are not covered at any price. Millions of items have been patented for which no market has developed. The inventor who develops and patents a new gadget that no one wants has a monopoly but no market. Production of such unwanted gadgets will be economically futile—it will only render losses.

The monopolist is constrained by demand conditions in the market and must live with the law of demand. Given the inverse relationship between the quantity demanded and price, the higher the monopolist sets price, the lower will be the quantities sold. For this reason, we call a monopolist and others with varying degrees of control over price **price searchers.** The problem for the monopolist is to find the particular price-quantity combination that is most profitable—-the one that results in the greatest difference between total revenues and total costs. This maximizes profits.

𝜋 𝜋

PRICE SEARCHERS are sellers that have some degree of monopoly power and can set price.

The Profit-Maximizing Monopolist

Profit maximizing is the art of finding a price-quantity combination to maximize the difference between total revenues and total costs. The key rule to maximizing profits or minimizing losses is to expand production when *the addition to revenues exceeds the addition to costs.* Alternatively, a firm wishing to minimize losses or maximize profits should cut back on production when the decrease in costs exceeds the fall in revenues.

A change in total costs as output changes by one unit is marginal cost. We now add the idea of **marginal revenue.**

𝜋 𝜋

MARGINAL REVENUE is the addition to total revenue as one additional unit is produced and sold.

Table 7–1 illustrates the profit-maximizing effects of equating marginal revenue to marginal cost and shows the process of measuring marginal revenue for a monopolist selling bottles of a health serum (e.g., liquid DHEA). The demand schedule is given in columns 1 and 2. When price and quantity are multiplied, we obtain total revenues, column 3. As the quantities of the health serum sold increase from 100 to 200 bottles per week, total revenues increase from $1,000 to $1,800. The price has fallen somewhat, but the quantity sold has doubled, and the change in total revenues is $800 for the additional 100 units sold. Therefore, marginal revenue per bottle for

TABLE 7–1   Determining the Profit-Maximizing Price-Quantity Combination for a Price Searcher

(1) Price per 8-Ounce Bottle	(2) Quantity of Bottles Demanded per Week	(3) Total Revenues	(4) Marginal Revenues per 8-Ounce Bottle	(5) Marginal Cost per 8-Ounce Bottle	(6) Increase or Reduction in Profits per 100 Bottles
$10	100	$1,000		$2	$ 800
9	200	1,800	$ 8	2	600
8	300	2,400	6	2	400
7	400	2,800	4	2	200
6	500	3,000	2	2	0
5	600	3,000	0	2	−200
4	700	2,800	−2	2	−400
3	800	2,400	−4	2	−600
2	900	1,800	−6	2	

This example illustrates the effects on profits of selecting various price-quantity combinations. Profits are maximized at the point at which marginal revenue equals marginal cost. Columns 1 and 2 show the demand schedule, the quantities of bottles purchased at each respective price. Column 3 gives total revenues (price times quantity). To calculate the increase or reduction in net revenues (column 6), we first calculate marginal revenues (column 4). Marginal revenue is the change in total revenue divided by the change in output. Marginal cost (column 5), which is the change in cost from changing output, is constant in this example, at $2. When marginal revenue exceeds marginal cost, an expansion of production (and sales) adds more to revenues than to costs. Therefore profits increase. Alternatively, when marginal costs exceed marginal revenues, a reduction in output (and sales) reduces costs by more than it reduces revenues. Therefore profits are again increased. They are maximized in this example at the point at which marginal cost and marginal revenue are equal (at $2). Selling 500 bottles at $6 is the profit-maximizing combination for this monopolist.

the second 100 bottles produced per week is $8 ($800 ÷ 100). When price is lowered from $9 to $8, sales increase to 300 bottles, and total revenues rise from $1,800 to $2,400. The change in total revenues is $600. The marginal revenue per bottle over this range of bottles produced (201 to 300) is $6 ($600 ÷ 100).

For the purpose of analysis, assume that the marginal cost of the health serum is $2 per bottle, whether 100 bottles or 900 bottles are produced per week. What price and quantity maximize profits?

If the price searcher drops price from $8 to $7, total revenues increase by $400, bringing $4 per bottle in marginal revenue for every bottle produced and sold between 301 and 400. As we increase production, $2 per bottle is added to costs. The consequence of expanding production (and sales) by 100 bottles while marginal revenue is $4 and marginal cost is $2 is to increase profits by $200 (column 6). Expansion of production and sales from 400 to 500 bottles, however, adds no more to total revenues than it does to total costs. At 500 bottles per week, marginal revenue and marginal cost are the same, $2. Therefore, profits are maximized. Expansion beyond 500 units reduces profits. At 600 bottles marginal revenue is zero while marginal cost is still $2. Marginal revenue is zero because there is no change in total revenues as output and sales increase from 500 to 600 bottles.[3] The price reduction effect is exactly offset by the quantity expansion effect, as can be calculated from the price-quantity information in Table 7–1. The revenue lost from reducing price from $6 to $5 on all bottles sold ($1 × 500) can be compared to the revenue gained by selling more bottles (600 rather than 500) at the lower price ($5 × 100). These effects exactly offset each other over this range, so that total revenues do not change. Marginal revenue is zero. Further expansions of production and sales would require additional price reductions and would reduce total revenues, making marginal revenues negative.

The profit-maximizing monopolist will neither produce in the range where the addition to revenues is negative nor produce bottles for sale where the addition to costs exceeds the addition to revenues. The profit-maximizing price-quantity combination exists where marginal cost equals marginal revenue. In our example, marginal cost equals marginal revenue at the production rate of 500 that can be sold at $6.

Marginal Revenue for Price Searchers and Price Takers

For firms operating in purely competitive markets, the addition to total revenue from selling one more unit is the price prevailing in the market. These price takers, as dictated by market circumstances, have no control over price. An addition to revenues from an additional sale equals the market price. Market price and marginal revenue are identical for firms in purely competitive markets. That is why, as was shown in in Chapter 6, profits were maximized for the competitive onion producer when price equaled marginal cost. For competitive sellers (price takers) price is the marginal revenue, so that equating price (marginal revenue) to marginal cost maximizes profits.

For a price searcher in a monopolized market, however, price and marginal revenue are not the same. Price exceeds marginal revenue. As detailed in Figure 7–2, a reduction in price by a monopolist has two offsetting effects on revenues. As price is lowered from $9 to $8, sales advance from 200 to 300 bottles. The lowering of the price gains some revenues (area *B*) for the monopolist because of the additional sales, but some revenues are lost (area *A*) because all buyers now pay $8 instead of $9. As a result of this price reduction and addition to sales, marginal revenue is positive because area *B* exceeds area *A*. Alternatively, a price reduction from $3 to $2 adds 100 bottles to total sales. But the gain in revenues (area *Y*) from more sales is less than the revenue lost (area *X*) as a result of all buyers paying the lower price.[4]

In Figure 7–3 the marginal revenue is graphed along with the monopolist's demand curve. As price is lowered, offsetting revenue effects occur similar to those

---

[3]A discerning eye will detect that profits in our example are the same at a 400-per-week rate of production as at a 500-per-week rate. However, this is because of the discrete breaks and jumps in quantities by 100 units (and in prices by $1 amounts). A smooth, continuous demand curve with price changes by 1 cent and by 2 units per 1-cent change would lead to the 500-per-week profit optimum.

[4]These offsetting areas are equal over the range where marginal revenue is zero; in this case, it is where production and sales advance from 500 to 600.

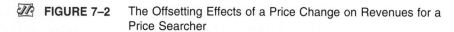

FIGURE 7–2   The Offsetting Effects of a Price Change on Revenues for a Price Searcher

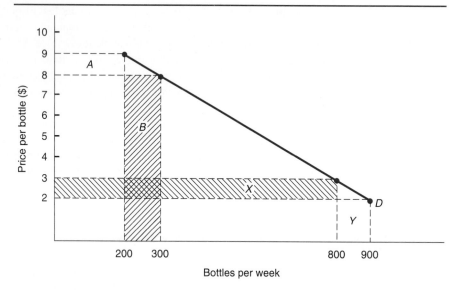

Areas *A* and *B* show the offsetting revenue effects of lowering price from $9 to $8. Area *A* reveals revenues lost from charging all buyers the lower price, whereas area *B* shows the gain in revenues from the additional sales. Because area *B* exceeds area *A,* marginal revenue is positive. Alternatively, these offsetting effects generate a negative marginal revenue for a reduction in price from $3 to $2. This is because area *X* is greater than area *Y.*

in Figure 7–2, making marginal revenue less than price per bottle sold. At a price of $8, the marginal revenue of an additional bottle sold is $6 (also see Table 7–1), $2 below the selling price. A drop in price to $7 generates an addition to sales (400 instead of 300) and marginal revenue of $4, again less than the price of $7.

As guided by the rule on how to maximize profits, the monopolist will seek the price-quantity combination that equates marginal revenue to marginal cost. As shown in Figure 7–3, this is at the price of $6 and sales of 500 bottles. At this production (and sales) rate, marginal cost and marginal revenue are equal at $2.

After a monopolist equates marginal revenue to marginal cost in order to maximize profits, the decision maker then sells the quantity produced at the highest price the market will allow—in our example, $6 at point *B* (Figure 7–3). Consequently, *for a price searcher, price is greater than marginal revenue* and also greater than marginal cost. In competitive situations, however, profits are maximized when price and marginal cost are equal. *For the price taker, marginal revenue is price.*

If production costs are the same for both the monopolist and the competitive firm, the price will be higher under conditions of monopoly. In addition, given the inverse (negative) relationship between quantity demanded and price, the higher price of the

FIGURE 7-3   Price, Marginal Revenue, and Marginal Cost Together for
the Monopolist

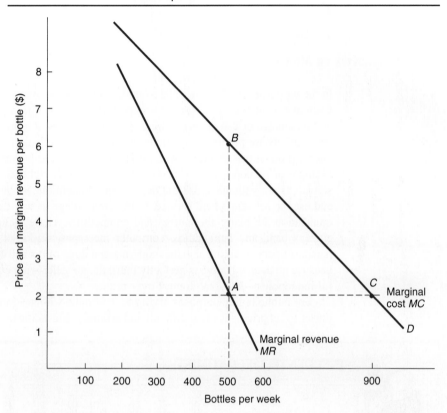

On the basis of the information given in Table 7–1 the marginal revenue (*MR*) curve is drawn,
along with the demand curve. Also shown is the marginal cost curve. For the monopolist,
marginal revenue is less than the price charged. Because marginal revenue exceeds
marginal cost over the range of sales up to 400 bottles per week, additions to net revenues
occur by expanding production over this range. Profits are maximized where the marginal
revenue curve intersects the marginal cost curve at point *A*. This is where marginal revenue
equals marginal cost at $2, a price of $6 is charged, and 500 bottles are sold.

monopolist means lower output and lower sales than under the competitive system.
In competition, the price would be $2 and quantity would be 900 (point *C* in
Figure 7–3).

In short, a monopolized market results in a more limited output and higher prices
than is true for competitive markets. Competitive markets generally result in maximized output and the lowest prices possible. Therefore, consumers are generally
worse off under monopoly than under competition. This is a major reason that

consumer groups usually oppose increases in monopoly power and that it is considered necessary for government to regulate the power of monopolies and to enforce the provisions of the antitrust laws, to be discussed in Chapter 9.

Some Perspectives on Monopoly Power

In the world of business, most firms have some control over the prices they charge. Even in reasonably competitive markets, firms can sometimes enjoy a special location advantage or can enter new or expanding markets at a profitable time. In fact, few markets are purely competitive or purely monopolistic. Few monopolists produce a product or service for which there are no close substitutes. Even the classic example of monopoly, the U.S. Postal Service's sole rights to sell first-class mail service, is not without significant degrees of competition. No buyer is forced to buy and use the first-class mail service. In the broad range of services constituting communication are many alternatives and competitors. These include Western Union, citizens band and ham radios, computer messages, walkie-talkies, old-fashioned person-to-person talking, and the modern technology of fax and e-mail. Furthermore, because no demand curve is perfectly inelastic, no seller—not even the most powerful monopolist—has total control over price.

For public policy purposes, trying to determine who has monopoly power—the power to set price—is often difficult and arbitrary. Elasticities of demand depend on

INFLUENTIAL ECONOMISTS

JOAN ROBINSON, 1903–1983; GEORGE STIGLER, 1911–1992

At the time of her death in 1983, Joan Robinson was one of the world's leading contemporary economists. Like Alfred Marshall, her academic home was Cambridge University, where she taught for more than 40 years.

Robinson's best-known book, *The Economics of Imperfect Competition,* was published in 1937. In it she developed theories of "imperfect competition"—explaining markets dominated by a relatively few large corporations. At the same time, an American economist, Edward Chamberlin, working independently, came out with a similar study. Central to their findings was that in markets where only a limited number of producers oper-

ate, competition is only partial. Firms can differentiate their products from others competing in the same market through brand names and other distinguishing product attributes.

In later studies, Robinson argued that, although the growth of monopolies has tended to reduce competition within countries, competition among industries and corporations from different nations has increased. She asserted that "modern industry is a system not so much of monopolistic competition as of competitive monopolies."

Robinson was sharply critical of modern capitalism and orthodox economists. She argued that most economists "are impeded by a theoretical the range and number of substitutes, so that the more good substitutes there are, the more elastic is the demand. Monopoly power is inversely related to the elasticity of demand; the broader the range and category of goods (or services) considered, the less powerful the monopoly. The more narrowly specific markets are defined, the greater is the perception of monopoly. Does Joe's Used Cars compete with a General Motors dealer? Perhaps yes in some cities and regions. Perhaps no in others. Good arguments are possible on both sides. Economists generally agree that artificial barriers to market entry reduce output, raise prices, and reduce market responsiveness to changes in buyers' preferences.

Price Searchers and Price Discrimination

The fact that the market demand curve slopes downward suggests that people differ in their ability and willingness to pay. Some people are willing and able to pay high prices, whereas others won't buy unless the price is low. If a price searcher can separate demanders for their good or service into distinct groups, they can sometimes charge different prices to different groups of people. Laws generally prevent discrimination by race or sex, but allow different treatment of people in many market exchanges.

Consider movie theaters and student price discounts, child and adult prices, and senior citizen discount prices. Owners lower the prices for those groups that they can identify as having a high price elasticity of demand. These are highly price-sensitive

---

scheme which (with whatever reservations and exceptions) represents the capitalist world as a kibbutz operated in a perfectly enlightened manner to maximize the welfare of all its members."

The policy implications of government intervention and regulation inherent in Robinson's work stand in sharp contrast to those rendered by the work of George Stigler. In a pathbreaking study in 1963, Stigler offered evidence contrary to the then-accepted economic thought. For more than a century economists agreed that government regulation of public utilities served the general good by keeping prices low and fair. Stigler's findings showed, however, that rates controlled by state regulatory commissions were neither lower nor more equitable than free-market rates. The solid empirical basis to Stigler's work strongly challenged the prevailing view about the benefits of government intervention in the private sector of the economy.

Following his example, many other scholars have subjected government regulation to close scrutiny. Most of these studies confirm Stigler's findings that the costs of regulation exceed the benefits. The Reagan administration endorsed Stigler's view that open and competitive markets establish broadly beneficial price structures, a significant departure from the public policies of earlier administrations. The trend, as initiated by the Carter administration and continued by the Reagan administration, has been toward deregulation of industries, most notably in transportation (airlines and trucking), energy, banking, and communications.

In 1981 Stigler was awarded the Nobel Prize in economics. His research and teaching at the University of Chicago School of Business were legendary and remain so. He died in 1992.

people. A small price reduction will significantly increase the quantity demanded by them (e.g., students, senior citizens, and children), thereby raising revenues. A majority of other adults with higher-than-average opportunity costs of their time typically have a much more inelastic demand for movies, and prices can be increased (within limits) without significant reductions in ticket sales to them. This will increase revenues, too. The problem for the movie theater owners is to identify the groups and find the right prices to maximize revenues. Student IDs and age identifications help the theater owners separate the groups and prevent low-price purchasers from buying in place of high-price ticket purchasers. Selling tickets to each individual, who must show an ID in order to get a discount price, is how movie theater owners prevent resale. Note, however, that price discrimination doesn't work for the candy, popcorn, and drinks sales inside the theater. Prices for these things are high inside compared to prices for these items in stores because the owner has a temporary local monopoly, but the high prices charged are the same for everyone, old and young alike. Price discrimination here fails, because it is much harder to prevent resale. If adults were charged more for candy and popcorn than were children or students, adults would let the children and students buy their candy and popcorn for them while they waited in their seats.

Airlines typically practice price discrimination, too, separating more price-inelastic demanders (e.g., business travelers with very high opportunity costs of their time) from more price-elastic travelers (e.g., vacationers, and nonurgent travelers). They separate the groups by lead time and dates of travel. Prices for midweek travelers (those who leave on Monday, return on Thursday) or who buy shortly before they travel, pay much more for the same flight than those who buy three weeks in advance and who are willing to take a Saturday night stayover. Here again, raising prices for inelastic travelers raises total revenues, and lowering prices for elastic travelers raises total revenues.

Colleges and universities that offer full and partial scholarships for some students while charging full tuition and fees for others are also engaging in price discrimination tactics. Examples of price discrimination abound but, in order to succeed with price discriminations, the seller must meet three criteria:

1. Be a price searcher.
2. Identify and separate demanders into at least two categories, with different price elasticities of demand.
3. Prevent resale.

Market Structures between Pure Monopoly and Pure Competition

The pure monopoly model and the pure competitive model are adequate for analyzing many market structures, even though the actual market conditions may be slightly different. Many firms that sell different goods (or services) but that are approximately alike can have some control over price. These are price searchers in a market structure called **monopolistic competition.** Colgate, for example, can charge more for its toothpaste than Kmart can for its brand, because they are not operating in a perfectly competitive market. As long as Colgate is able to convince toothpaste buyers that its brand is superior to Kmart's, buyers will be willing to pay a premium for Colgate. Candy bars, toothpastes, soaps, breakfast cereals, hamburgers, and shoes are a few examples of monopolistically competitive markets. However, if there is freedom of entry and exit, these firms, each producing items that have unique attributes, will not earn above-normal profits in the long run. Freedom of entry will assure supply adjustments that ultimately equate revenues to costs. Consequently, the competitive model tells us much about these markets, even though the firms may advertise and act in a limited way as price searchers.

In MONOPOLISTIC COMPETITION there are a large number of firms selling similar but differentiated products, with no significant barriers to entry.

Alternatively, the monopoly model may work well in certain cases where there is more than one firm. For example, in the 1970s the obstructive collusion and other actions of OPEC led to output reductions and price increases of oil and other forms of energy. (See pages 101–103 in Chapter 5 for review.) The monopoly model can explain the results of such collusion.

Oligopolies—The Near Monopolies

There are market structures, however, in which the models of monopoly and competition do not serve well. Some markets are dominated by just a few firms, such as the market in new automobiles. To be sure, GM, Ford, Chrysler, and the foreign automakers do compete, but they appear to be extremely interdependent. Their sense of rivalry is keen, and a price change by one typically results in quick, sometimes unpredictable, reactions by the other firms. Entry is difficult. These types of market conditions, with high degrees of market concentration and firm interdependence, are referred to as **oligopoly** markets. Because price adjustments in these markets often precipitate unpredictable results and are highly risky, the companies often prefer to compete with each other by using quality variations or advertising campaigns. Consequently, prices tend to be less flexible or variable in oligopolistic markets.

In an OLIGOPOLY market structure just a few firms normally control a high percentage of total sales.

Marginal Analysis—The Decision Maker's Tool

Decision makers in market structures of all varieties routinely search for ways to realize gains for the firm: The rule of thumb in order to maximize profits in the long run for almost all business decision makers, no matter the market structure, is to apply marginal analysis. Recall that marginal analysis compares the results of small, incremental changes: quality variations, advertising campaigns, or quantity and price adjustments. When the addition to revenues is expected to exceed the addition to costs, expand. When the reduction in costs is expected to exceed the reduction in revenues, contract. Even more generally, if the expected benefits exceed the expected costs of a choice, proceed; if the expected costs exceed the expected benefits, contract. Let's call this the **rule of rational choice**.

THE RULE OF RATIONAL CHOICE
For any decision, when the additional benefits exceed the additional costs, proceed. When the additional costs exceed the additional benefits, contract.

Ironically, this widespread practice and use of marginal analysis is not always done consciously, at least in the form of equating marginal cost to marginal revenue. The question raised by businesses considering a change is this: Will it add more to revenues than to costs? Whether or not this is consciously realized by the decision maker, it still represents marginal analysis at work.

CHAPTER REVIEW

This chapter has analyzed the problems of maximizing profits of firms that operate in different market structures, but with emphasis on the cases of pure competition and pure monopoly. In markets that are purely competitive there are many sellers of identical goods (or services), and no one seller can influence price. All competitors are price takers, and the market forces of supply and demand determine price.

In contrast, in a pure monopoly there is only one seller. Monopolists can set price according to the demand for the good. The monopolist is a price searcher who maximizes profits by producing the quantity at which marginal revenue and marginal cost are equal. Price is then set as high as possible (on the demand curve) but just low enough to sell all that is produced.

The competitive firm also maximizes profits by producing the amount at which marginal cost and marginal revenue are equal; however, for competitive price-taking firms, price and marginal revenue are identical.

Compared to the results in a competitive market, a monopoly firm produces a smaller quantity and charges a higher price.

Most market structures lie between the two extremes of pure competition and pure monopoly. Monopolistic competition is a market structure with no barriers to entry, but the firms produce items with similar, but not identical, attributes (e.g., toothpaste, hamburgers). Oligopoly is another special structure in which a few firms, each producing a similar product (e.g., automobiles, computers), control most of the supply.

Whatever the market structure, marginal analysis helps decision makers determine profit-maximizing solutions. The rule of thumb to maximize profits or reduce losses is this: When the addition to revenues (marginal revenues) exceeds addition to costs (marginal costs), increase production (expand); when the reduction in costs exceeds the reduction in revenues, reduce production (contract).

𝒥𝓏 MULTIPLE-CHOICE SELF-TEST 𝒥𝓏 𝒥𝓏 𝒥𝓏 𝒥𝓏 𝒥𝓏 𝒥𝓏 𝒥𝓏 𝒥𝓏 𝒥𝓏 𝒥𝓏 𝒥𝓏 𝒥𝓏 𝒥𝓏 𝒥𝓏 𝒥𝓏 𝒥𝓏

1. In a competitive market in the short run:
   a. Firms may earn high profits.
   b. Firms must be free to enter and exit.
   c. The firms will have neither losses nor large profits.
   d. Individual firms have some influence on market price.

2. High profits:
   a. Can't pull new firms into a monopolistically competitive market.
   b. Are guaranteed in monopoly markets because of the lack of competition.
   c. Are a signal for other firms to enter into a competitive market, expanding output in the long run.
   d. Can exist in monopolistically competitive markets in the long run.

3. A monopoly market exists in *all but* which of the following cases?
   a. Reductions in demand have driven all but one firm out of the market for canned lemon slices.
   b. The government grants a firm a patent on a formula for a powerful new glue.
   c. A county government has designated one firm to be the water provider for the rural part of the county.
   d. One firm owns all five known deposits of a rare mineral.

4. Find the *false* statement about the rules for maximum profits.
   a. The rule in all kinds of markets is to produce until marginal revenue equals marginal cost.
   b. The rule in competitive markets is to produce until marginal cost equals price.
   c. The rule in monopolistically competitive markets is to produce until price equals marginal cost.
   d. The rule in oligopoly markets is to produce until marginal cost equals marginal revenue.

5. Find the *false* statement about a monopolistically competitive market.
   a. One of its most important features is that the good is produced in many varieties.
   b. Each firm faces a downward-sloping demand curve.
   c. There are more than two or three firms in the market.
   d. The number of firms in the market is fixed.

𝒥𝓏 STUDY QUESTIONS

1. In what type of market structure does McDonald's operate? GM? Merrill Lynch? The New York Yankees? AT&T? American River Community College? Joe's Bar and Grill?

2. Using marginal analysis, how does a price taker determine the level of production that maximizes profits?

3. Using marginal analysis, how does a price searcher determine the level of production that maximizes profits?

4. If International Business Machines (IBM) bought up all its competitors in order to form a monopoly, what would happen to the quantity supplied, the quantity demanded, the price, and the profits in the industry?

5. From Question 4, who gains and who loses?

6. You sell computer diskettes. Using marginal analysis, what general rule should you follow to determine whether to expand or reduce your business advertising programs?

𝕁𝔯 PROBLEM

Riverbottom Cement Company has a local monopoly on cement production. Its marginal cost for producing additional cement is currently $50 per hundred tons, and the demand schedule it faces is given in the following table. (Quantities are in hundreds of tons, and prices are per hundred tons.)

Price	Quantity	Total Revenue	Marginal Revenue	Marginal Cost	Change in Profits (*MR* – *MC*)
$90,000	1	$	$		
$80,000	2	$	$	$40,000	$
$70,000	3	$	$	$50,000	$
$60,000	4	$	$	$50,000	$
$50,000	5	$	$	$50,000	$
$40,000	6	$	$	$55,000	$
$30,000	7	$	$	$60,000	$

1. Calculate the total revenue, marginal revenue, and change in profits for each level of production.

2. What is the best cement-output level for Riverbottom?

3. Draw a graph of marginal revenue, marginal cost, and price. Check to see that your graph indicates the same best level of production that you determined in 2, above.

CHAPTER 8

Jobs and Wages

𝒥𝒥 CHAPTER PREVIEW

Firms express their demands for workers in many ways, ranging from placing "help-wanted" ads in shop windows to hiring specialized "head-hunting" firms that seek out top executives. Job vacancies with specified qualifications for the jobs are routinely listed in the help-wanted sections of newspapers, in government bulletins, and in trade magazines.

How we land a job varies greatly. It may be just a matter of being there first. Often it helps to know someone who has a connection; a friend or relative who can put in a good word for you. Many jobs require interviews with personnel officers who check on your qualifications, probe for your shortcomings, and try to determine your worth to the company. Many college seniors undergo intensive job interviews by business recruiters who visit campuses in search of prospective employees. The business recruiter's responsibility and basic objective is to hire people who will contribute services and output worth more to the business than is the salary paid. It's their application of the rule of rational choice—hire more workers when the expected added revenues exceed the expected added costs.

The employer's objective is to realize a familiar economic principle—the maximization of profits for the firm. If a particular job pays $2,000 per month, the recruiter wants to make sure the person hired can contribute no less than $2,000 in services to the business and, it is hoped, much more than that. Essentially, job seekers should be able to persuade the interviewer that their employment will bring in more revenues to the business than the salary offered for the job.

The help-wanted sections of newspapers in San Diego, Houston, Chicago, Memphis, Detroit, Tampa, and Syracuse all list job openings for computer operators. Although the requirements and job descriptions are similar, the starting salaries range from $24,000 to over $30,000 per year.

The number of jobs available in particular lines of work and the wages paid for these jobs are the result of supply and demand forces interacting in labor markets.

1. Why do starting salaries vary so much?
2. What effects do minimum-wage laws have on the availability of part-time jobs?

𝄞 CONCEPTS REINTRODUCED

Demand Curve 52
Law of Diminishing Marginal Productivity 121
Marginal Analysis 120
Marginal Cost 124
Marginal Physical Product of Labor 121
Market Structure 136
Opportunity Cost 7
Profits 120
Pure Competition 137
Pure Monopoly 137
Rule of Rational Choice 150
Short Run 120
Shortage 81
Supply Curve 74
Surplus 81

𝄞 NEW CONCEPTS

Labor Markets
Derived Demand
Marginal Revenue Product of Labor
Craft Unions
Industrial Unions
Right-to-Work Laws

𝒥𝒦 CHAPTER OBJECTIVES

After studying this chapter, you should be able to:

1. Explain how a firm decides whether or not it is profitable to hire more workers.
2. Understand the difference between marginal physical product of labor and marginal revenue product of labor.
3. Understand the relationship between product demand and labor demand.
4. Understand how wages are determined by market forces.
5. Recognize the effects of wage controls on earnings and employment.
6. Recognize the role and effects of unions in labor markets.

LABOR MARKETS: BUYERS, SELLERS, AND WAGES

Business decision makers try to assess the value of a worker's contribution to the firm. They want to make the right hiring choice for the firm because the choice—selecting Elizabeth Wykoff, perhaps, instead of Ashley Walton for the job—is an opportunity cost. Workers make career choices and decide whom to work for; their choice also imposes an opportunity cost.

Although some argue that it is dehumanizing, labor time is bought and sold in markets in much the same way that goods and services are exchanged. The wage plus fringe benefits is the price paid for labor and is determined through the interaction of demand and supply. In **labor markets** businesses and governments are the primary buyers of labor, and individuals in households are the main sellers. In goods and services markets, the reverse is true.

𝒥𝒦 𝒥𝒦

A LABOR MARKET is the exchange of human skills and time for wages and benefits.

The law of demand prevails in labor markets, and the demand curve for labor is downward-sloping. Businesses are willing to hire more workers at lower wages; they tend to reduce the number of workers hired if wages increase. The law of supply also is in effect, and the supply curves for particular types of labor services and skills are upward-sloping. For example, higher salaries for professors encourage more people to pursue academic careers and attempt to qualify as professors. Higher wages for carpenters raise the quantity of carpentry services supplied. In short, higher wages for any career (or job) attract people because the opportunity costs of other jobs and activities have risen.

Figure 8–1 illustrates the determination of the market clearing wage for word processors. As in previous graphs of supply-demand curves, the number of word processors per time period is shown on the horizontal axis, and the wage paid is shown on the vertical axis. The market clearing wage of $1,800 per month is

FIGURE 8-1   The Market for Word Processors in the Miami, Florida, Area

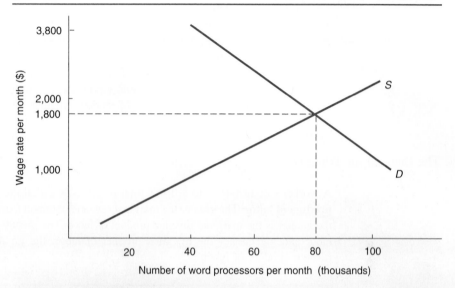

The market clearing monthly wage for word processors is determined by the intersection of the demand and supply curves for word processors. Any "going wage" above $1,800 per month would cause a surplus of word processors and ultimately reduce the wage downward to $1,800. Any wage below $1,800 would cause a shortage and put upward pressure on the wage.

determined where the quantity of word processors demanded equals the quantity supplied. Any other "going wage" would cause either a temporary shortage or a surplus and would eventually lead to a wage and employment adjustment.

The Derived Demand for Inputs

The demand for any productive resource, including labor, derives from the demand for the good or service that the input is capable of producing. Word processors have jobs because there is a demand for letters, documents, manuscripts, and other forms of written communications. Construction workers have jobs because of the demand for new homes and other buildings. Professors teach only if students are enrolled in their courses. In short, the demand for labor is not an end in itself; it is valued as a means to produce goods and services that are valued in the marketplace. For that reason we say that the demand for labor is a **derived demand.**

DERIVED DEMAND is a reflection of the demand for the product or service the resource produces.

Consequently, the wages that firms are willing to pay for labor depend on the dollar value of what labor produces. The value of labor's contribution depends on the market's value of the output (both price and quantity). The greater the price paid for the item produced, the higher will be the workers' pay; or the greater the physical product per worker, the higher will be the wage. Both price and the productivity of workers influence the wage that a firm offers. This is true whether the market structure is competitive or degrees of monopoly power exist, but the demand curve for labor is downward-sloping, regardless of market structure.

The Demand for Workers

A worker's contribution to a firm's total revenues is called the **marginal revenue product of labor.** The greater the marginal revenue obtained from selling the output, the greater is the marginal revenue product of labor. The greater the productivity of labor and the greater the marginal product of labor, the greater is the marginal revenue product of labor.

> The MARGINAL REVENUE PRODUCT OF LABOR is the multiple of two variables: (1) the marginal physical product of labor and (2) the marginal revenue received from selling another unit of output.

In the short run, the marginal revenue product of labor declines because of the law of diminishing returns. As more and more workers are added to a set of fixed factors, at some point the extra, or marginal, physical product of labor declines. Even if the price of the output remains unchanged,[1] this fall in the marginal physical product of labor assures that the marginal revenue product of labor will also decline as output increases.

Furthermore, in monopolized markets (and other price-seeking market situations, such as oligopoly) firms face downward-sloping demand curves for their products, and additional supplies can be sold only if the price is reduced. The price decline that occurs when more is supplied and sold reduces the revenue returns to labor's added production. More can be sold only at lower prices, and because the goods that the added labor produces must be sold for less, additional workers are worth less to the firm.

These sources of decline in the marginal revenue product of labor as more workers are added are illustrated graphically in Figure 8–2. Here we see another version of the rule of rational choice and the principle of maximizing profits. This rule encourages firms to hire workers as long as they contribute more to the revenue

---

[1]This would occur for a competitive price-taking firm that produces a little more. In this case price and marginal revenue are the same.

📊 FIGURE 8–2　　The Marginal Revenue Product of Labor

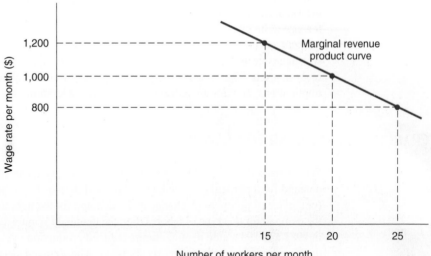

The marginal revenue product of labor is the marginal physical product of labor times the marginal revenue received from selling another unit of output. The marginal revenue product curve slopes downward because of the law of diminishing returns and the decline of the marginal physical product of labor that occurs when more and more workers are added to fixed factors of production. Given a market wage of $1,000, the hiring of 20 workers maximizes profits for the firm. If the marginal revenue product exceeds the wage, the addition to revenues exceeds the addition to costs. Then it pays to hire more workers. If it is below the wage, the addition to revenues is less than the addition to costs, and profits are increased by hiring fewer workers. A fall in the wage (to $800) will lead to more workers hired (25). An increase in the wage (to $1,200) will cause fewer workers to be hired (15). Hence, the quantity of workers hired varies inversely with the wage. Note also, this is another application of the rule of rational choice.

of the firm than the wages they are paid. A firm will hire workers up to the point at which the marginal revenue product of labor equals the wage. As Figure 8–2 shows, if the going wage is $1,000 per month, the firm will maximize profits by hiring 20 workers. Twenty workers is the level that equates the marginal revenue product of labor to the wage. At the margin, the revenues from labor's contribution just equal what the firm pays for labor. If a larger labor crew is in place, the firm can increase total profits by cutting back to 20 workers. If only 15 workers are hired, an additional worker will contribute more to total revenues than to costs, and profits will expand. Hiring more than 20 workers will cause profits to be less than maximum, because each worker added contributes less to total revenues than to costs. If the wage falls to $800, this increases the number of workers that can be profitably hired. At $800 the new maximizing level is 25. Alternatively, a wage of $1,200 will decrease the maximizing level to 15.

In conclusion, whether the market structure is competitive or not, all firms have demand curves for labor that are negatively sloped. Wages are prices; they provide information and impact incentives. More workers will be hired if the wage falls; fewer will be hired if the wage rises. This general conclusion of a downward-sloping demand curve for labor is important. As a tool of positive economic analysis, it advances our understanding of wage determination and the effect of interference in labor markets. The downward-sloping demand curve for labor has important policy implications, as well as important welfare considerations for workers.

CHANGING THE DEMAND FOR LABOR

What causes the demand for labor to increase, and what can cause it to decline? The demand for a particular specialized labor skill derives from the demand for the item (or service) it produces. A change in the demand for the item (or service) will change the demand for that type of labor. When the demand for autos fell in the United States in 1981 and 1982, auto manufacturers reduced production rates. As auto workers saw it, the demand for their services dropped. The demand curve shifted to the left. Automobile prices fell relatively and so did the value of auto workers. When auto sales advanced sharply in 1983, however, the demand curve for auto workers shifted to the right. Similarly, as the demand to watch football increased, especially in the 1960s and in the early 1980s, the demand for football players increased. New leagues were formed, such as the American Football League (AFL), the Canadian Football League, and the United States Football League (USFL), and players' salaries grew. In effect, the demand curve for football players shifted to the right as their output rose in value. Alternatively, as the primary school-aged population dropped in the 1970s, the demand for elementary and high school teachers also declined. In short, a change in the demand for a good or service produced by special types of labor will change the demand for those particular labor skills.

Figure 8–3 shows that a change in demand for labor means a shift in the demand curve for labor. When the price of an item increases, the demand for the labor skills that produce it shifts upward, from *A* to *B*. A fall in the price of the item will lead to an opposite shift, from *B* to *A*. (Recall that a *change in demand* is different from a *change in the quantity demanded*.)

Several other factors can cause the demand curve for labor to shift. One is the price of other inputs that can be substituted for labor. Because businesses seek least-cost methods of production, they continually assess their costs of production. If machines (or other capital) can be substituted for labor, a fall in the price of machines will reduce the demand for labor (*B* to *A*). If the capital costs of automated car washes decline, the demand for labor to wash cars will decline, as occurred in the 1950s. Less expensive automated toll booths on highways or at bridge crossings will reduce the demand for people who collect tolls by hand. However, when capital-for-labor substitution occurs and fewer workers are hired, those remaining employed usually receive higher wages. This is because each worker has more capital to work with, which makes the workers more productive.

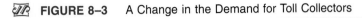

FIGURE 8–3 A Change in the Demand for Toll Collectors

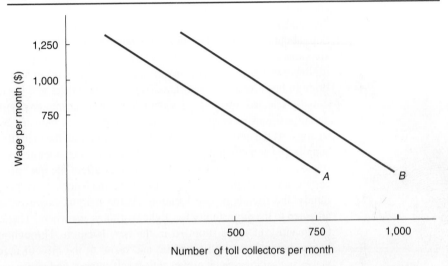

An increase in the demand for a particular labor skill means a shift to the right (and upward) of the demand curve for this type of labor. This shift, from *A* to *B*, occurs when the value of labor's contribution increases. This can result from an increase in the price of the output produced by this labor skill, by an increase in the productivity (marginal physical product) of this type of labor, or by an increase in the cost of using other inputs as substitutes for labor. Alternatively, a fall in the price of the output, a decline in labor productivity, or a fall in the cost of using other inputs (e.g., machines in place of workers) will shift the demand curve for labor downward and to the left.

Technological advances also usually have a mixture of effects. Advances in computer technology have increased the demand for programmers, information systems experts, and other related kinds of skilled labor. The marginal physical product of these workers has been increased by advances in computer technology. Alternatively, other workers, such as people who count inventories by hand and keep records manually, have seen reduced demand for their services. Advances in technology increase the demand for some workers and reduce it for others.

SUPPLIES OF LABOR SKILLS

The law of supply, as applied to labor markets, says that more people are willing to work at higher wages. There is a direct relationship between the wage rate for particular, specialized skills and the number of workers supplying those skills. Higher wages for car mechanics raises the opportunity cost of potential car mechanics doing other jobs.

The wage, however, is not the only consideration in selecting a career or in choosing a job. Nor is it the only determinant of the supply of specific labor skills. Personal preferences, psychological rewards, locational preferences, and expectations about the future all influence the quantity of various labor skills supplied. These are valued subjectively and differently by people. Some people are willing to work for lower wages in one type of work because of prestige or a sense of self-fulfillment. Pride in one's work is important. Yet many scientists and business professors who initially selected lower salaries in universities over higher-paying research or managerial positions in corporations are being drawn to industry by advancing relative salaries. At the margin, changes in wages will affect the quantity of specialized skills supplied by some people, even though personal considerations may predominate for others. For example, locational preferences affect the quantity of labor supplied to certain areas. Higher earnings elsewhere may not attract people who are tied to family and friends in one location. At the margin, however, some people will be attracted to the opportunity for higher earnings elsewhere. Those who move increase the quantity of labor supplied in the new location. Throughout American history people have abandoned farm life and taken to the city, in part, because of higher wages in the cities. Such moves reflect self-interest and new, changing opportunities.

In summary, although many nonwage factors influence conditions of supply, the law of supply holds for specialized labor skills. Higher wages bring forth greater supplies of labor; therefore, the supply curves for specific labor skills are upward-sloping. Moreover, the demand curves for specific labor skills are of the usual form; they are downward-sloping. The importance of these conclusions becomes increasingly evident as we use supply and demand analysis to assess policies affecting labor markets.

The Shortage of Accounting Professors

In Chapter 5 the conditions and sources of market shortages were analyzed for several commodities. The analysis revealed that prolonged periods of shortages are caused when prices are prevented from rising to market clearing levels. The price adjustment needed to clear a market is sometimes prevented by a government-imposed price restraint. However, institutional price inflexibility may also cause shortage conditions to continue. A good example of this is the past and present market shortage of accounting PhDs in the United States.

With the continuing growth of regulations and the greater complexity of the tax laws and other financial matters, the demand for accountants and financial analysts has advanced sharply. This reveals again the concept of derived demand. Salaries for accountants have increased, and partners in some accounting firms currently command annual salaries of several hundred thousand dollars. The rising salaries for CPAs (certified public accountants) have increased the number of students enrolling in business schools and accounting programs. In the 1980s and early 1990s, for example, the number of graduates majoring in accounting increased nearly tenfold.

This supply response, precipitated by higher relative salaries for accountants, reveals the pursuit of self-interest. Because of the sharp increase in this demand for accounting courses, there was an increase in the demand by business and management schools for accounting professors, especially for those with PhDs in accounting (again illustrating derived demand). The PhD requirement has been maintained because a high proportion of PhDs on the faculty is required for accreditation by the American Assembly of Collegiate Schools of Business (AACSB). These PhD requirements are part of the standards set by the AACSB.

Although the demand has advanced greatly, the supply of PhDs in accounting has increased only modestly. This shortage continues to be a primary headache and concern of deans of business schools, and despite higher salaries for accounting professors, the PhD shortage persists. This is largely the result of infrequent and modest wage adjustments in this segment of the academic market. Because of the abundance of PhDs in many areas—in history, English, and sociology, for example—university administrators have been slow to realize the extent of the shortage of accounting professors. Furthermore, although the shortage was eventually recognized, preferentially high salaries for accounting PhDs have been difficult for many administrators to approve. That is because university administrators must consider the issues of pay equity among academic disciplines, and their decisions on salaries are often constrained by faculty reviewing committees and faculty collective bargaining agreements. Salaries for accounting professors have risen higher and faster than salaries for professors in many other academic disciplines. Today, assistant professors in accounting frequently receive higher salaries than experienced full professors in the humanities. Nevertheless, salaries for accountants in business have risen even faster than salaries for accounting PhDs in academics. Therefore, most students in accounting are content to acquire bachelor's or master's degrees and to take promising high-paying jobs in business. Why pursue a PhD and an academic career? The salary restraints imposed by institutional factors and university administrators have sustained an accounting PhD shortage for more than a decade. Nationwide the number of open faculty positions in accounting continues to exceed the number of applicants.

Minimum-Wage Laws and Labor Surpluses

In Chapter 5 we found that prolonged surpluses occur when prices fail to fall to market clearing levels. When legal limits maintain prices above market equilibrium levels, surpluses can be sustained indefinitely in commodity markets and in labor markets, too.

In 1996, the Republican Congress, upon the recommendation of President Clinton, passed legislation raising the hourly minimum wage nationally from $4.25 to $5.15, with the total increase of $0.90 per hour to occur in two increases in increments of $0.45 per hour each year over two years. State laws sometimes set even higher legal wage minimums (e.g., California, Massachusetts) and whichever is higher, state or federal, sets the lower limit that can be paid.

FIGURE 8–4   The Prospective Surplus-Causing Effects of the New Minimum-Wage Law

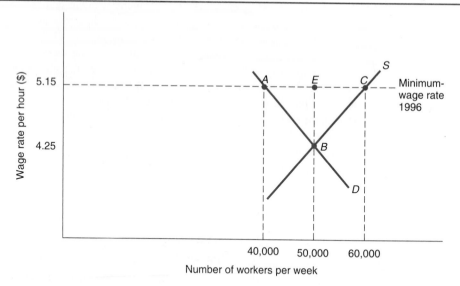

Let's assume the market clearing wage is $4.25 for unskilled workers, which is determined by the intersection of the demand and supply of these workers at point *B* (50,000 workers). When a minimum wage of $5.15 is imposed, the quantity demanded is reduced to 40,000 workers (point *A*). The distance *A–E* measures the reduction in employment, which is smaller than the total surplus (excess supply) of workers (the distance *A–C*). The distance *E–C* is the increase in the quantity of labor supplied as more workers enter the market because of the higher wage.

Figure 8–4 illustrates the surplus-causing effects of raising the minimum wage above market clearing wage rates. It also reveals that some workers benefit while others do not. In Figure 8–4, the higher minimum wage reduces the quantity demanded to 40,000 workers and increases the quantity supplied to 60,000. The surplus of 20,000 workers is greater than the number of workers who are displaced or who lose their jobs.[2] That is because additional workers enter the market and prefer to work more hours when the new, higher minimum wage is imposed. This surplus is measured as distance *A–C* in Figure 8–4, and these "surplus workers" add to the total number of people who are classified as unemployed. In passing the $5.15 minimum wage, Congress and President Clinton argued that higher minimum wages will help workers. But not everyone agreed.

Economists widely agree on the consequences of minimum wages. Who gets the higher wages and benefits and who becomes unemployed and loses out depend on actual market conditions. It is very important to distinguish between the long-run and the short-run effects of a minimum-wage policy. Short-run supply and demand curves are less elastic than long-run curves. Therefore, the displacement effects and

---

[2]The reduction in the quantity of labor demanded will result from a reduction in the number of firms using low-wage labor and in the number of workers employed by each firm.

𝒥ℛ **FIGURE 8–5**   Teenage Unemployment and the Real Minimum Wage

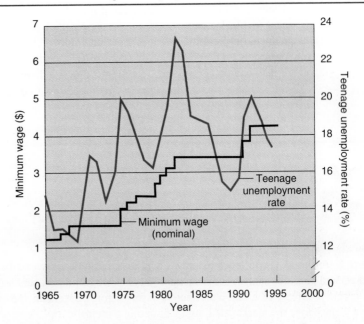

Jumps in teenage unemployment closely correlate with hikes in the minimum wage.

Source: Bureau of Labor Statistics.

the surplus-labor results of minimum wages are greater in the long run than short-run observations suggest.

Numerous studies have demonstrated the unemployment and distribution effects of minimum wages. These studies show that higher minimum wages reduce the teenage share of employment in the low-wage categories. Higher minimum wages reduce the quantity demanded for full-time teenage workers, thus forcing many such workers into part-time employment or into unemployment. This is illustrated in Figure 8–5, which shows the changes in teenage unemployment rates associated with past hikes in the minimum wage. Among adult males the picture is mixed, with some gaining, and others losing. Because the gainers approximately match the losers among adult males in the low-wage category, there is no net gain among them from a higher minimum wage. According to the studies, adult women in the low-wage group tend to gain; those making more money because of the higher minimum wage have outnumbered those who are displaced or lose work because of the law.[3]

Overall, it is clear that higher minimum wages largely redistribute income from some "have-nots" to other have-nots. The major losers are young, unskilled workers

---

[3]For reference see Donald Deere, Kevin Murphy, and Finis Welch, "Employment and the 1990–91 Minimum Wage Hike," *American Economic Review,* vol. L5, no. 2, May 1995, pp. 232–37.

with little, if any, job experience. The high levels of teenage unemployment in the 1980s and 1990s, nearly 20 percent for white teenagers and approximately 40 percent for black teenagers, are in part the result of the minimum wage. Because the law reduces on-the-job training of these unemployed young workers, it also reduces their prospects for higher lifelong earnings. Another disadvantage for young people is that if they have no prior work record or if they are displaced after a very short period on the job, they are not covered by unemployment compensation.

TOOL KIT

THE INTERDEPENDENCE OF MARKETS AND THE IMPACT OF UNIONS ON WAGES AND EMPLOYMENT

Figure 8–A shows the interdependence of labor markets and provides analyses of the employment and earnings effects of a union's effectively setting a wage above the market clearing level in the hotel industry. For the sake of analysis, this example is limited to workers who clean and prepare rooms for occupancy. The hotel workers are unionized; the motel workers are not. If the union succeeds in setting a wage at $6.50 per hour for hotel workers (diagram A), the supply of workers must be restricted by limiting entry to the union by increasing apprenticeship periods, by imposing high union dues, by using a seniority system, or by other means. The effect is to raise the earnings of those union members who retain employment in hotel work and who receive $6.50 per hour. However, those displaced (diagram B) increase the supply of workers with similar skills in the open labor markets. There is an increase of supply in the labor market for workers who clean and prepare motel rooms. The outcome is a fall in the wage rate for motel workers from $5 to $4.50 per hour.

The actual extent of the fall in wages in the nonunionized sector, of course, depends on the elasticity of demand for labor there and on the increase in the supply of workers. The actual number of workers displaced because of the wage hike depends on the elasticity of demand for workers in the unionized sector. The more inelastic the demand for workers forming the union, the less severe the problem of rationing jobs and the fewer the number of workers displaced when the wage increases. Consequently, unions have historically been successful in labor markets in which select labor skills face few substitutes and in which the demand for labor skills is relatively inelastic.

It should be emphasized that the formation of unions and their successes in setting wages above market clearing levels do not always result in existing workers being displaced. Does this refute the existence of a downward-sloping demand curve for labor? Not at all! We live in a dynamic world, and the demand curves for labor skills periodically shift to the right at the same time that unions win higher wage settlements because of buoyant commodity markets, for instance. If this occurs, the problem of rationing jobs is lessened, and possibly no union workers are displaced. Nevertheless, others who would prefer to work in the unionized area at the lower market clearing wage rather than to work elsewhere at even lower wages are prevented from doing so.

Unions and Workers

The history of unions is a fascinating subject dating back to the guilds of the Middle Ages. Originally these early guilds had mainly religious and social goals. However, in time, the merchant and craft guilds adopted economic goals, and the labor movement began. The American labor movement, in particular, started with local **craft unions.** These are exclusive combinations of workers in individual trades such as

---

Some people argue that unions set precedents for higher wages that help all workers, union and nonunion. There is no basis of economy theory for this, however, and the negative slope of the demand curve generally shows the redistributive outcome of union wage setting described here.

Although unions have clearly improved work conditions and earnings for union members, other workers with similar skills who are either displaced or forced into competing areas of work with enlarged supplies of labor can be made worse off.

FIGURE 8–A   Wages and Employment in Two Labor Markets

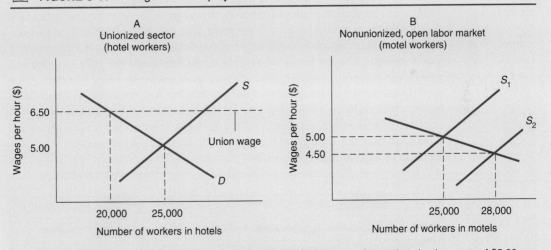

Diagram A illustrates the union's success in raising wages by $1.50 above the market clearing wage of $5.00 per hour for hotel workers. This reduces the quantity of labor demanded for hotel work (cleaning and preparing rooms for occupancy), however, by 5,000 workers. These displaced workers lose, but those retaining work gain higher earnings. In addition, however, others in competing, open labor markets also lose. As the displaced hotel workers from the union sector add to the supply of labor services in open markets (nonunionized motel workers), wages soften and decline there. This is shown in diagram B as a shift (increase) in the supply of motel workers—from S_1 to S_2—and a fall in the wage there to $4.50.

printers, shoemakers, and bakers. Like the early craft guilds, most modern craft unions require new entrants to complete apprenticeship programs and meet other requirements to gain membership and work. In this and other ways, craft unions are able to influence and control, at least partially, the total supply of workers with competing skills. Their ability to influence and reduce the supply of workers in various trades improves earnings and raises wages and fringe benefits above levels that would prevail if there were open competition for jobs.

Industrial unions emerged later than craft unions but are a major source of union strength today. Industrial unions are inclusive combinations of workers in an entire industry, regardless of the type of job performed. They include the powerful Teamsters Union and the United Auto Workers (UAW). Industrial unions are the principal components of the American Federation of Labor–Congress of Industrial Organizations (AFL-CIO). The AFL-CIO, as its name suggests, is an umbrella type of organization comprising both craft and industrial unions.[4] Its aim is to further the common interests and increase the economic status of all union members.

Early court judgments involving unions frequently were unfavorable to unions. Before 1830, judges viewed unions as conspiracies to prevent or restrain trade. Without the legal right to strike and bargain collectively, unions had little power. Because of this, union membership remained limited. At the turn of the century, fewer than 1 worker in 20 was in a union. As Table 8–1 shows, throughout the first third of the 20th century, only 1 in 18 workers (about 6 percent) was a union member. With the coming of the Wagner Act (also called the *National Labor Relations Act*) in 1935, union membership jumped to nearly 16 percent of the labor force. Since 1945, union workers typically have made up more than one-fifth of the total workforce. The Wagner Act, popularly called *labor's Magna Carta,* was vital to the upsurge of union strength. The act legalized collective bargaining and the right to strike and provided a peaceful means of gaining union recognition. In 1947, however, union growth was slowed by the passage of the Taft-Hartley Act, which allowed individual states to pass **right-to-work laws.** This act was passed because of the unusually high number of work stoppages that occurred in 1946. It was vigorously opposed by unions. The act also disallowed the closed shop, which required workers to join the union in order to obtain employment.

RIGHT-TO-WORK LAWS make it illegal for union membership to be a requirement for continued employment.

The right to strike and the threat of strike provide unions with a powerful bargaining tool with which to negotiate wage settlements with employers and to change

---

[4]In 1978 there were 174 unions in operation, with 108 of these affiliated with the AFL-CIO. The AFL-CIO was formed in 1955 when the American Federation of Labor, comprising craft unions, merged with the Congress of Industrial Organizations.

TABLE 8–1   Union Membership, 1900–1990

Year	Union Membership (millions)	Civilian Workers in Unions (%)
1900	0.8	2.7
1910	2.1	5.6
1920	5.0	12.1
1930	3.6	7.4
1940	8.9	15.9
1950	15.0	22.9
1960	18.1	24.5
1970	20.6	24.1
1980	22.8	21.8
1990	16.7	15.0

The growth of union membership in the United States in the 20th century reached a peak during the late 1960s, when nearly 25 percent of all civilian workers belonged to unions. By the 1990s, only about one in seven workers was unionized.

Source: L. Davis et al., *American Economic Growth* (New York: Harper & Row, 1972), p. 220; and U.S. Department of Labor, Bureau of Labor Statistics.

employees' working conditions. To win and maintain a wage and fringe benefits settlement above market clearing levels means, however, that the available number of jobs must be rationed among the larger number of workers wishing to work in unionized jobs. In recent decades union members have received wages and fringe benefits that are typically about 20 percent above those of nonunion workers in comparable jobs.

Nevertheless, union membership has been falling since 1980, and as Table 8–1 shows, the decline was dramatic throughout the 1980s. By 1997 only about one in seven workers was a union member. Growing international competition, with lower labor costs (e.g., in automobile and steel), and factory relocations from the northeastern and north central states (strong union areas) to the South and the Southwest (weak union areas) have contributed to these declines in union strength. Increased new foreign-owned factories in weak union areas in the United States has also added to this decline. The low proportion of workers in unions in the United States stands in contrast to higher membership proportions in other advanced economies: 24 percent in Japan, 29 percent in Canada, 35 percent in England, and 82 percent in Sweden.

PATCO's Gamble

One of the most dramatic moments in union wage negotiations in modern times occurred on August 3, 1981, when the Professional Air Tower Control Organization (PATCO) struck for higher wages, shorter hours, and a better retirement package. Because of the special public-sector status of air traffic control, the strike was illegal. However, the 15,000 air controllers knew how vital their services were to the nation, and risking their jobs with average yearly pay of $35,000 (about $48,000 today) appeared worth it. PATCO made three demands: a $10,000 pay hike for all controllers, a 32-hour work week, and retirement after 20 years of service at 75 percent of the highest year's salary. President Ronald Reagan promptly warned that any striker not back to work by August 5 would be fired; 11,345 defied his ultimatum and were fired.

The PATCO gamble was extremely costly to those fired. Surveys of former controllers found most of them earning less than $25,000 per year several years after the strike. Estimates of the difference between what they had earned as controllers and their new earnings totaled nearly $170 million per year in the mid-1980s. Better working conditions and less stress in the new jobs apparently did not compensate for the pay loss. As one former controller stated, "It's hard to get it out of your blood. It's the most exciting thing that most of us will ever do."[5]

PATCO's gamble failed, mostly because the union confused the lack of substitutability of air traffic control services with the easy substitutability of air traffic controllers. Of course, the airports would close down without air control services. But the job requires no college degree, and the workers' $35,000 average yearly earnings in 1981 exceeded the average yearly earnings of full professors in universities and colleges nationwide. When the openings for 11,345 jobs were announced, 200,000 people applied.

Jobs Forecast

Ever since the Industrial Revolution began in England in the late 18th century, people have been predicting that machines would destroy jobs. In the late 1940s, Norbert Weiner, a pioneer in computing, forecast that the new technology of computers would destroy enough jobs to make the Great Depression of the 1930s look like a picnic. Today, the revolution in information technology is redefining the workplace at a rapid pace, destroying jobs, changing the location of work from office to home, but also creating new kinds of jobs.

The pace of technological change has surely varied over the decades, and it has almost certainly increased since the Industrial Revolution. The historical record is reassuring, however, because the evidence is clear that general unemployment has not risen over time. Individuals do get displaced and sometimes suffer severe hardships if their alternatives for work are few. But new technologies create work and opportunities, reminding us again that with change there are winners and losers.

Forces that dramatically affect supply and demand in markets—for example, technological and demographic changes—alter the prospects for work. When thinking about a career and reviewing the prospects for employment, it is prudent to anticipate changes in labor market opportunities. Figure 8–6 provides a forecast of market changes by the year 2005 and suggests where jobs are being created and

---

[5]Roger Lowenstein, "For Fired Air-Traffic Controllers, Life's OK But Not Like Old Times," *The Wall Street Journal* (August 1986), p. 1.

FIGURE 8–6   Winners and Losers, Job Changes by 2005

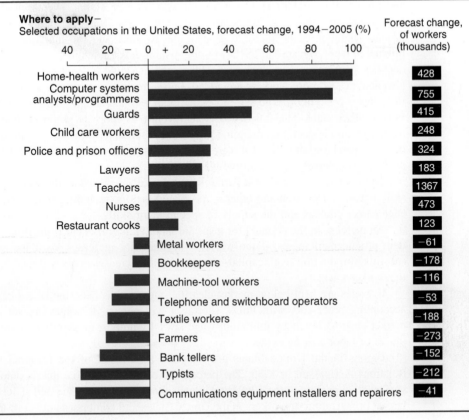

Where to apply—
Selected occupations in the United States, forecast change, 1994–2005 (%)

Forecast change,
of workers
(thousands)

Occupation		(thousands)
Home-health workers		428
Computer systems analysts/programmers		755
Guards		415
Child care workers		248
Police and prison officers		324
Lawyers		183
Teachers		1367
Nurses		473
Restaurant cooks		123
Metal workers		−61
Bookkeepers		−178
Machine-tool workers		−116
Telephone and switchboard operators		−53
Textile workers		−188
Farmers		−273
Bank tellers		−152
Typists		−212
Communications equipment installers and repairers		−41

Source: Bureau of Labor Statistics.

where they are being lost. These forecasts reflect the impact of technological change, the aging of the American population, changing preferences and income, and other forces, global and domestic. Consistent with long-run trends of the past, it suggests that in the years ahead there will be a net gain in the number of jobs.

CHAPTER REVIEW

This chapter shows the workings of demand and supply forces in labor markets. Private-sector employers hire workers for profit-maximizing purposes because it is in their self-interest to do so. They attempt to hire workers who contribute more to the firm (in revenues) than the wages paid. The demand for a worker's labor services is not an end in itself, but is derived from the demand for the items (and services) that the worker produces.

The wage is determined by the intersection of the supply and demand for labor, and firms will hire labor up to the point at which the marginal revenue product of labor equals the wage. This maximizes the profits of the firm. The marginal revenue product of labor is the multiple of marginal revenue and the marginal physical product of labor. Because of the law of diminishing returns, labor's marginal product declines as more workers are added. Hence, the marginal revenue product of labor also declines as more workers are added. Furthermore, for the price searcher, who must lower price in order to sell more, marginal revenue is less than price and also falls as price falls. The fall in marginal revenue as more is produced and sold, together with the declining marginal product of labor, determines the negative slope of the demand for labor by price searchers. For these reasons the demand for labor by all firms is inversely related to the wage.

The quantity supplied of a particular labor skill increases as the wage for that skill increases. Location and other work-related factors, including education, influence career choices and the supply of special labor skills.

An increase in the demand for a special labor skill will occur if the price of the item produced increases, if the worker's productivity increases, or if the cost of substitute production (e.g., capital-using) methods increases. This will tend to raise the worker's wages.

If wages are kept below market clearing rates, as has been the recent case for accounting professors with PhDs, shortages will persist. If wages are set above market clearing levels by minimum-wage laws, by unions, or by other means, surpluses of labor will be evident.

Unions in the United States grew rapidly as a result of the National Labor Relations Act passed in 1935. The percentage of the labor force that is unionized peaked at 25 percent in the 1960s and is now about 14 percent. The AFL-CIO is the largest organization of workers in the United States and comprises both craft unions (specific trades) and industrial unions (all trades in an industry).

✍ MULTIPLE-CHOICE SELF-TEST ✍ ✍ ✍ ✍ ✍ ✍ ✍ ✍ ✍ ✍ ✍ ✍ ✍ ✍ ✍ ✍

1. For price-searching firms, the marginal revenue product of labor:
   a. Declines as more workers are hired, because the marginal revenue earned from additional output declines.
   b. Equals the price of the product multiplied by the marginal physical product of labor.
   c. Is reduced by an increase in demand for the firms' product.
   d. Is greater than the wage they pay their workers.

2. The general rule for the number of workers to hire in order to maximize profits is:
   a. Hire workers as long as their marginal revenue product is positive.
   b. Continue to hire more workers until an additional worker would no longer add to total revenue.
   c. Hire additional workers until the marginal revenue product the last one adds is equal to the wage.
   d. Hire the number of workers that maximizes the marginal revenue product of labor.

3. Which of the following *would not* decrease the demand for horticultural (flower-growing) farmworkers?
   a. The demand for fresh flowers decreases.
   b. Automated flower-picking machines are found to cut flowers rapidly and with little damage.
   c. New, higher-wage job opportunities open up for unskilled laborers.
   d. The price of weed control chemicals falls.

4. Those who lose by the imposition of a higher minimum wage include:
   a. Employers only.
   b. All workers.
   c. No workers.
   d. Teenage workers.

5. A higher wage set by a union (above the market clearing wage):
   a. Is somewhat like a wage floor.
   b. Is intended to combat racial discrimination.
   c. Will tend to increase employment in the occupations it affects.
   d. Requires equal wages for jobs requiring equivalent levels of skill and responsibility.

✍ STUDY QUESTIONS

1. Can an exemption from the minimum-wage law for teenagers help teenagers as a group? How?

2. If firefighters make $2,500 per month and clerks make $1,500 per month, what will a new government-enforced pay scale that equates these salaries at $2,000 do to the quantity of clerks demanded? The quantity of clerks supplied? The quantity of firefighters demanded? The quantity of firefighters supplied?

3. Given the information in Question 2, how will the jobs for clerks be rationed if the wage is $2,000? Who will pay for it?

4. If 10 baseball bat–producing firms that are competitive are made into one large monopoly, what will happen to the demand for labor to produce baseball bats?

5. What happens to total wages paid to labor in the automobile industry if the demand for labor there is inelastic and a union bargains and receives a wage hike? What if the demand is elastic?

6. What determines the elasticity of demand for labor in an industry?

𝒯ℛ PROBLEM

For each of the following situations, draw a demand-supply graph of the labor market to show what is happening and its effects on wages and quantity of labor employed in:

1. The market for lumberers: A housing boom increases the demand for lumber for construction.

2. The market for secretaries, traditionally dominated by women: Many other new job fields become more open to women.

3. The market for stenographers (typists able to take shorthand dictation): Dictating equipment improves in quality and convenience and falls in price.

4. The market for lawyers: There is a 50 percent increase in the annual number of law school graduates.

CHAPTER 9

Market Failure and Government Failure

𝕵 CHAPTER PREVIEW

The first automobile show was held in the old Madison Square Garden in New York in 1900. The American Automobile Club was formed two years later. By 1920 Henry Ford's Model T had dramatically lowered the cost of auto use. But the roads of the times were inadequate for automobile travel. Farmers especially pressed for a system of roadways that would give them relief from the muddy, impassable conditions they faced most of the year. The Federal Highway Act of 1921 was enacted in response to this demand for paved roads. Later outlays for a highway system reflected this growth in demand for government services—a demand that is typical of modern times. Since the 1920s, federal government expenditures have grown from nearly 4 percent to almost 25 percent of total expenditures in the economy.

1. Why does the government, rather than some large corporation, pay to build our highways and roads?
2. What are the proper economic roles and activities of government in our society?
3. In what circumstances does government allocate resources more efficiently than do free markets?

𝓙𝓛 CONCEPTS REINTRODUCED

Economic Problem 35
Externalities 42
Income Distribution 43
Market Economy 34
Monopoly 43
Normative Economics 16–17
Positive Economics 16–17
Price 50
Property Rights 14
Public Goods 42

𝓙𝓛 NEW CONCEPTS

Private Costs
Social Costs
Social Optimum
Common Property
Antitrust Laws
Economic Regulations
Natural Monopoly
Private Goods
Exclusion Principle
Free Rider
Transfer Program
Cash Benefits
In-Kind Benefits
Social Insurance Programs
Public Assistance Programs

◨ CHAPTER OBJECTIVES

After studying this chapter, you should be able to:

1. Distinguish between a public good and a private good.
2. Distinguish between private cost and social cost.
3. Recognize the conditions for social optimum.
4. Recognize the types of market failure.
5. Understand the intent and rationale for antitrust laws.
6. Understand how free-rider problems occur, and how other sources of government failure occur.

THE ROLE OF GOVERNMENT

In the mid-19th century, the great French social critic Alexis de Tocqueville toured the United States and wrote a two-volume book titled *Democracy in America*. One of his observations, still true today, was that "there is no country in which everything can be provided for by the laws, or in which political institutions can prove a substitute for common sense and public morality" (Volume I, Chapter VIII). Scarcity is as much a reality in the public sector as it is in private life. It is equally true, however, that there is no country in which everything can be provided by markets. It is evident that private interests sometimes conflict with the common good and public morality. Similarly, the self-interests of elected officials and government employees also sometimes conflict with the common good and national interests. Social harmony and law and order require government intervention and activities in many forms, but the power of special interests in government decision making sometimes leads to interventions and market corrections that many (even majorities) would view as harmful. In short, there are both market and government failures. Economic reasoning helps us understand why.

The role and limits of government activity in society are matters of perennial debate involving many dimensions: philosophical, social, political, moral, and economic. The economic role of government in a market economy is perhaps the most controversial aspect and source of disagreement among economists and the rest of us. In large measure, our differences of opinion ultimately stem from differing values about what ought to be. These include issues of fairness and equity and personal views on individual versus social responsibility. This is the realm of normative economics. Disagreement also results, however, from differences in interpretation of evidence, differences in judgment on market efficiency, differences in views on income distribution, and even differences on the best means to achieve agreed-upon ends.

It is important to keep in mind that the definition of the *proper* role of government is highly subjective. Indeed, Charles Wilson's quip, "What is good for General Motors is good for the country," reminds us that even the familiar term *public interest* means different things to different people. Nevertheless, there is probably more agreement about certain responsibilities of government—enforcing contracts, maintaining law and order, keeping the peace, helping the disadvantaged, and the like—than there is about the best ways to meet these responsibilities.

THE MARKET SYSTEM RECONSIDERED

In Chapter 2, we defined the basic economic problem in terms of the fundamental questions of (1) what to produce, (2) how to produce, and (3) to whom the goods are distributed. In a market economy, social cooperation is obtained by having clear property rights (rules of the game) and freedom to produce and exchange. The pursuit of profits is a primary determinant of what and how much is produced. Business decision makers strive to combine land, labor, and capital to produce and sell at costs that are below market prices. The distribution of goods depends on our choices, which depend on and are constrained by our awareness, preferences, and ability to pay for the things produced. The price system rations goods and services to those of us who are willing and able to pay. Ability to pay, of course, depends largely on income, which is based on payments we receive for the land, labor, or capital that we own and sell (or on borrowings or transfer payments from government).

The market system (price system) generally allocates resources efficiently and responsively to changing cost constraints and personal preferences. But markets sometimes fail. Moreover, the market system does not distribute income and opportunities equally. We strive in our society to achieve equality for all before the law, but people are not born with equal abilities, talents, opportunities, or prospects.

It is also important to realize that individuals do not always do what is in their own best interests. Furthermore, society does not allow people the freedom to consume or do everything they want. Illegal drugs, tobacco, alcohol, gambling, and prostitution are goods and activities that societies often try to reduce or eliminate by government action. Alternatively, governments also try to stimulate and promote certain types of "socially redeeming" activities. In the United States, religion, education, amateur athletics, and farming are among the activities that are tax-exempt or that regularly receive subsidies or special government assistance.

POLLUTION AS AN EXAMPLE OF MARKET FAILURE

Sometimes business decision makers fail to put resources to their most highly valued uses because the market sends the wrong signals. This can occur when certain costs can be shifted onto others. For example, both the business firm that dumps its waste products into a nearby stream and the careless consumer who tosses litter on a public beach impose costs on society. When polluters do not bear the full costs of their actions, some resources will be misused and wasted. This is most likely to occur when the market sends an erroneous signal that dumping is free. It is not. This erroneous pricing signal leads to pollution and environmental damage.

An analytically useful way to view pollution—smoggy air or dirty water—is as a negative externality. When a business produces paint and in the process pays wages to workers, buys materials, and pays for rent and waste removal, the costs of these activities are **private costs.** In this case, the private costs and the costs to society for the paint are the same, and there are no externalities imposed on third parties. However, if this business begins to dump waste into a stream, fouling the quality of the water, the private costs of producing the paint are less than the **social costs.** People other than the producers and consumers of paint bear some of the costs of paint production. These external costs are not charged to the business, and consumers do not pay for them either. Instead, third parties (people who value the unpolluted stream) bear the burden of the costs, the negative externalities.

PRIVATE COSTS are the internal costs that are explicitly borne by the firm.

SOCIAL COSTS include the private (internal) costs plus the external costs.

External costs exist whenever private costs are less than social costs (total costs). Any product or service that generates external costs is actually being subsidized, because part of the costs of production is borne by others. This condition encourages excess production because the social costs exceed the price of what is produced. Resources are thus misused and wasted; the price people pay for the good is less than the cost to society to produce it. Alternatively stated, when negative externalities are present, the price of the good is less than the true marginal cost of production. Therefore, output will exceed the level that is a **social optimum.**

A SOCIAL OPTIMUM exists when all long-run costs are covered and price equals marginal cost.

Figure 9–1 illustrates the excessive production and resource misallocation that results when negative externalities are present. Shown are a demand curve and two supply curves for paint. The lower supply curve (S_1) includes only the private costs of production. The higher supply curve (S_2) is determined by adding the external costs of pollution to the private costs of production. If paint manufacturers are polluting and are permitted to ignore these external costs, the supply curve is S_1, giving an equilibrium price of $12.50 per gallon and a quantity supplied (and demanded) of 15 million gallons. The market is cleared, and the firms are profit-maximizing, but production is not at the social optimum. The social costs of producing another gallon at the level of 15 million gallons of paint are $16 per gallon, and yet people only value a marginal gallon at $12.50 (the price per gallon). However, if the external costs imposed on others are included in the producers' cost calculations,

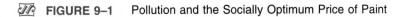

FIGURE 9–1   Pollution and the Socially Optimum Price of Paint

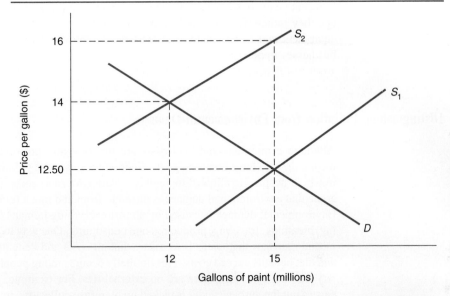

When external costs (e.g., pollution) occur, social costs are greater than private costs; the result is a level of production in excess of the social optimum amount. If the paint manufacturers ignore pollution costs that are imposed on others, their supply curve is S_1, resulting in an equilibrium price of $12.50 per gallon of paint and a production of 15 million gallons. However, the social costs per additional gallon are $16 for 15 million gallons. When all production costs are borne by producers, including the costs of pollution, the supply curve is higher (S_2). If consumers had to pay a price that covered all costs, the equilibrium price of paint would be $14 per gallon for 12 million gallons. This is the social optimum price and level of production.

or if the firms are required to pay for all their pollution costs, the supply curve including all costs is S_2. Accordingly, the price will rise to $14 per gallon, and the amount produced will drop to 12 million gallons. Consumers, then, rather than third parties, will pay the full cost of the paint.

We should also note that there are positive externalities as well as negative externalities. If a person buys and fixes up a run-down house, there may be benefits to the neighborhood as well as to the new owners. The social benefits exceed the private benefits, and unless the person is compensated, the supply of benefits resulting from the private-maximizing behavior of the person who repairs and improves the house will be less than the social optimum level.

When the market fails to send the proper cost signals, government may be compelled to "correct" the market signals. Otherwise, producers may find it in their self-interest to pollute and cause environmental damage. The problem is to change the signals so that the decision makers take into account all the costs of their actions. For this reason, some states compel motorists to have smog-control devices on their automobiles. This shifts more of the full cost of automobile use to the user. Similarly, in recent years, businesses have been taxed, at least partially, for the pollution damage they inflict. These taxes help provide incentives to install pollution-abatement equipment and to eliminate or at least reduce the negative externalities that these businesses impose.

Distinguishing Pollution from Environmental Damage

Although economists and ecologists are not typically portrayed as allies by the media, they do have common goals. Economics poses the pollution problem as one in which people are allowed to neglect certain (external) costs. Further, economists argue that environmental damage is different from and much broader than pollution. Environmental damage is caused by almost everything humans do, including walking, breathing, traveling, producing, and consuming. One way to justify the environmental damages that occur is to assure that all costs and benefits are accounted for and that benefits exceed costs. This normally occurs among people who make voluntary transactions when there are no externalities. For example, when my neighbor carries out the garbage and it is picked up by refuse collectors, my neighbor benefits, and the costs of the labor and added environmental damage to the dump site are paid (by taxes or fees). Thus, there is no pollution. However, if a dog tips over the garbage cans before they are emptied and the trash is spread around the neighborhood by a high wind, externalities have occurred. In short, *pollution* refers to costs imposed on others (third parties) without their consent.

Consider another example to distinguish between pollution and environmental damage. Suppose an airport like Dulles Airport (30 miles from Washington, D.C.) is built. It's noisy nearby, but no residential areas are close enough to be disturbed by the noise. Further suppose that a developer buys land near the airport, builds 10 houses, and sells them to new owners. Has the noise now become pollution? The economist argues no, that the house buyers purchase the houses knowing the negative amenities of the noise and pay less for the houses as a consequence. Both the developer and the buyers, we assume, are fully aware of the presence of the airport and the noise, and houses are priced accordingly. Another rhetorical question helps us to find the correct answer. Should we move Dulles Airport once the 10 houses are built? Would the costs of the airport relocation exceed the benefits to the 10 homeowners? Yes, no doubt.

Alternatively, the economist would argue that if the airport were built next to established neighborhoods, causing unwanted externalities, the homeowners should be compensated for the damage (property value losses). If these external costs plus the costs of constructing and operating the airport were less than the benefits provided by the airport, then the airport should not be built.

The core of the problem consists of the negative externalities, the costs imposed on others. Clearly the more "others" there are, the greater the external costs from any pollution activity. A smoke-belching plant built in a densely populated area imposes far greater external costs than the same plant (and smoke levels) built in a lightly populated area.

Ecologists and economists usually argue that efforts to reduce environmental damage should be focused on and aimed at targets of pollution where the benefits of pollution reduction exceed the cost of reducing it. Measuring benefits and costs, however, is a perennial source of disagreement.

Disagreements and Property Rights

It is important to emphasize the role of property rights in the pollution problem. Many would argue that the root of the pollution problem is property rights specifications. Who owns the air, lakes, rivers, streams, oceans, and open spaces? When waste is discharged into streams or lakes (because no one owns them exclusively), the polluter is treating these bodies of water as dump sites. This dumping is done on **common property.** Air is perhaps the best example of common property, because there are no individual ownership rights to it. The ocean is another good example of common property. When ownership (property) rights are unclear or indefinite, people have little or no economic incentive to consider the effects of their own actions on such common property. Conscience may encourage some people to refrain from polluting, but if only a few more people decide not to pollute the air, the total level of pollution is not significantly changed. Similarly, the quality of the oceans remains about the same even if one more ship cleans its oil containers at sea. However, the cumulative results can be dramatically damaging to the air and oceans—and to people. According to investigative reports, in developing countries, between 1.5 and 2 million people are poisoned every year from exposure to pesticides. The United Nations estimates that there are 10,000 pesticide-related deaths annually.

COMMON PROPERTY is collectively owned by all of us.

Most pollution occurs when people or businesses take advantage of common-property situations or when no well-defined property rights exist. When ownership rights to property do exist, owners can sue the polluter for damages to their property. Or rights to pollute can be sold between the parties affected. For example, a person who owns a lake can sell dumping rights to nearby homeowners who discharge effluents in the lake. This will internalize the external costs. These contracts are not made or enforced easily, however. That is why people who rent cars often do not drive them with the same care they would use in driving cars they own. That is also why people who conserve energy at home may leave lights on in the hotel rooms they occupy. Although everyone's costs are raised by such excesses, the full impact of these costs does not hit the pocketbooks of the wasteful individuals. In short, whenever private costs and social costs diverge, resources are misused, because decision

TABLE 9–1   Sulfur Dioxide Pollution: The Cost Alternatives of Reducing SO_2 by 30%.

(1)	(2)	(3)	(4)	(5)	(6)
Factory Type	Yearly SO_2 Emitted (tons)	Yearly Cleanup Cost/Ton (millions)	Resource Cost, Policy 1 (millions)	Resource Cost, Policy 2 (millions)	Resource Cost, Policy 3 (millions)
A	30	$5	$5 × 15 = $75	$5 × 9 = $45	$0
B	20	$4	$4 × 5 = $20	$4 × 6 = $24	$0
C	20	$3	$3 × 5 = $15	$3 × 6 = $18	$0
D	20	$2	$2 × 5 = $10	$2 × 6 = $12	$2 × 20 = $40
E	10	$1	$0	$1 × 3 = $3	$1 × 10 = $10
Totals	100		$120	$102	$50

Policy 1 limits pollution to 15 tons per firm; in policy 2 each firm cuts back 30 percent on SO_2 emitted (21 from A; 14 from B, C, and D; 7 from E); in policy 3 salable emissions rights equal 70 percent of the prior year's pollution, where tickets are distributed to the firms in proportion to the prior year's emissions (factory type A gets 21; B, C, and D get 14 each; and E gets 7). The least-cost method of reducing pollution by 30 percent is policy 3.

makers do not fully account for their actions. When externalities arise, cooperation through markets becomes more difficult, and resources may be misallocated.

Trading Pollution Rights

To reduce air pollution the federal government has frequently regulated the emissions of polluting firms. Sometimes the regulators set maximum emission limits and require use of abatement equipment to lower the emissions. Sometimes levels have been lowered by a certain percentage (i.e., 30 percent reduction). In the 1990s a new method was tried—set a target, a total acceptable emission level, and let the polluters trade pollution rights to find the least-cost way of meeting the target.

Table 9–1 compares these three approaches for five factory types emitting a total of 100 tons of SO_2 per year (column 2). Column 3 shows, in millions, that each factory type has different costs per ton to stop its pollution. First, let's consider the costs of reducing pollution 30 percent, to 70 tons, by policy 1, a regulation that sets a maximum pollution limit per factory at 15 tons. Column 4 shows the cost to each factory of cutting back to the 15-ton maximum. "Clean factory" type E bears no costs. "Dirty factory" type A bears the most ($5 × 15 tons). The total cost of policy 1 is $120 million, the sum of the costs to A, B, C, and D.

Policy 2 sets no pollution cap but requires a 30 percent reduction from each factory, or 3 tons less for every 10 tons initially emitted. Column 5 shows these costs. Factory A's costs are $45 million ($5 × 9 tons); B, C, and D bear less costs, because their cleanup costs per ton are less and the reduction required (6 tons each) is less. "Clean factory" E again bears the least cost, and the cost to the firms altogether is $102 million.

Now consider policy 3, where the right to emit one or more tons of SO_2. can be bought and sold, but 70 tons is the maximum amount of pollution the factories together can emit. Further suppose government gives tickets to the factories, whereby each ticket permits the polluter the right to emit 1 ton of SO_2. In order to limit total emissions to 70 tons, only 70 tickets are given. Let's assume the government distributes these in proportion to the pollution levels (7 tickets per 10 tons). Factory type A gets 21; B, C, and D get 14 each; and E gets 7. Now government says, trade if you wish, but if you emit more than the total tickets you hold, you'll be severely fined. "Dirty factory" type A needs 9 tickets, or it must pay $5 million per ton times 9 tons to clean up and comply. Factory type E can sell its 7 tickets to A and reduce all 10 tons of its emissions for $10 million. Factory type D can sell its 14 tickets and reduce all of its pollution (20 tons) at a resource cost of $40 million. In this case the total resource costs to clean up is $50 million (see column 6).

Why should factory D and factory E sell their tickets, and who will buy? They'll sell if the price is high enough, which for E is any price above $1 million per ticket—the opportunity cost of cleaning up. For D, the price must be above $2 million per ticket—it's the opportunity cost of cleaning up. To avoid cleanup costs on themselves, factory A needs 9 tickets, B needs 6, and C needs 6, too. Any ticket price above $2 million, but below $3 million, will provide the right incentives for D and E to sell (and clean up their pollution) and for A, B, and C to buy pollution rights rather than incur the higher cost of cleanup. The market exchanges transfer revenues among the firms, but all the firms gain from the exchange. Each firm is better off with policy 3 than with policy 1 or 2.

To see this, let's set the ticket price at $2.5 million, high enough to get D and E to sell and low enough to get C to buy. Factory type A buys 9 tickets for $2.5 million each for a total transfer to D and E of $22.5 million, half of the cost to A of cleaning up on its own ($5 × 9 tons = $45 million). B pays $2.5 million each for 6 tickets transferring $15 million to D and E. Again, the $15-million payment by B is less than its cost to clean up 6 tons ($24 million, see column 5). And C also gains, transferring $15 million to D and E. The total transfers, $52.5 million, exceed the $50 million costs to D and E to reduce their emissions by the 30-ton target. Everyone wins, and the target of a 30 percent reduction is met.[1]

Some could rightfully argue that 70 tons is too much. Changing the level, however, does not change the fact that policy 3 is the least-cost approach of meeting the target. It's the least-cost approach whatever level is set. And it may be more democratic, too. Suppose an environmental group wants to reduce the level to 65 tons. That group could buy 5 tickets and tear them up. This would raise the price of the tickets to at least $3 million, or enough to get factory C to clean up 5 tons in addition to D and E's 30 tons. Factory A and B would pay more for tickets, D and E would get more money, and C would win or lose depending on whether the ticket price was $3 million or more. And the air would be cleaner!

---

[1]If factories A, B, and C are adept bargainers they may get the price down close to $2 million, or if D and E are more clever, the price could move up near $3 million. Relative bargaining strength leaves this range of price uncertain.

Monopoly as a Market Failure

Market economies such as the U.S. economy are built on the philosophical understanding that competition and free markets are generally in the public interest. Two characteristics of monopolistic markets are (1) barriers to entry for potential competitors and (2) restriction of output to levels below the levels that would occur in competitive, open markets. Barriers to entry prevent some resources from being allocated to their highest valued uses; thus, entry barriers contribute to waste. The output restriction permits monopolists to charge higher prices than would prevail if they faced competition, and this situation is generally viewed as inherently unfair.

Because monopolies generally cause economic dislocations and prevent resources from flowing to their highest valued uses, government attempts to correct for these market failures. Basically, government uses two forms of intervention to address problems of monopoly: antitrust policy and economic regulation.

Antitrust Policy

Antitrust laws have existed since 1890. They were first enacted during an era when President Teddy Roosevelt took up "trust busting" against J. P. Morgan and others. They make illegal the practice of monopolization and the attempt to monopolize, such as when a firm attempts to acquire a large enough share of the market to control it. Antitrust laws also are designed to prevent the practice of forming combinations and conspiracies to restrain trade, such as when two or more firms conspire to fix price or establish exclusive sales territories that they individually monopolize. Antitrust laws make illegal the practice of monopolization, or attempts to monopolize a market.

Although antitrust enforcement is sometimes carried out by state governments, the primary responsibility for enforcement lies largely with the federal government through the Department of Justice and the Federal Trade Commission. Their authorities have been developed through five main legislative acts:

- The Sherman Antitrust Act (1890)
- The Federal Trade Commission Act (1914)
- The Clayton Act (1914)
- The Robinson-Patman Act (1936)
- The Celler-Kefauver Act (1950)

The administration and enforcement of these laws concentrate largely on the activities of rival firms, either on proposed mergers or buyouts or on allegations of price-fixing, price discrimination,[2] and other illegal acts. Antitrust actions are carried out on a case-by-case basis and are resolved either by a pretrial agreement (and discontinuance of an illegal practice) or by the courts. Consequently, the enforcement of the antitrust laws varies from administration to administration, depending in part on the interests and concerns of the president in office.

---

[2]Price discrimination occurs when two buyers are charged different prices for the same product. This is not always illegal, but it is held to be illegal if it weakens competition.

It is noteworthy that in the 1980s, despite some spectacular court decisions such as the breakup of AT&T, a significant decline in antitrust cases and enforcement occurred. This was a deliberate policy change ushered in by the Reagan administration and based on new legal and economic perspectives. The new thinking came from members of the so-called Chicago school of economists and legal scholars including Robert Bork, George Stigler, and Richard Posner. They contend that our antitrust laws often hurt consumers and actually inhibit U.S. companies' abilities to succeed in international competition. To illustrate their argument, suppose American steel producers, beset by low-price German, Japanese, and South Korean steel imports, persuaded Congress to raise trade barriers for one year. Then they met to decide on various plant closings and mergers, all of which would lower costs and make the U.S. firms more competitive when the trade barriers were lifted. Clearly, if such a reorganization lowered costs and enough competition remained after the barriers were lifted on foreign producers to bring prices down, consumers would be better off.

But, given the law now, some excluded small U.S. steel mills, and major buyers of steel, like the auto industry, could sue. The antitrust laws would be the basis for the suit and could prevent the cost-saving reorganization. In such cases, antitrust enforcement works detrimentally.

In 1995 the federal government and Microsoft, which produces the disk operating system (MS-DOS) and Windows software used in 80 percent of the personal computers in the United States, agreed on a settlement to reconcile antitrust charges against Microsoft. In rare legal action, federal judge Stanley Sporkin threw out the settlement, calling Microsoft a monopoly in a field "central to this country's well-being, not only for the balance of this century, but also for the 21st century." Others said Bill Gates, then age 39 and holder of $9.8 billion in Microsoft stock, should be praised not criticized. One of the ironies is that great creative success leads to growth, market dominance, wealth, and sometimes close legal scrutiny.

As discussed in Chapter 7, a major problem in analyzing monopolization and the application of antitrust laws in cases like Microsoft is the problem of market definition. This is a matter of great importance to the courts, for the broader a market's geographic boundaries and the greater the number of substitute items considered, the smaller the appearance of monopoly power. Because of these difficulties, the courts historically have been inconsistent in their interpretations and judgments.

In 1990, the nation celebrated the centennial anniversary of the Sherman Antitrust Act. The American Bar Association, the Western Economic Association, and other scholarly organizations held conferences to discuss the long-term effects of the act on the American economy. It is safe to conclude that no consensus has emerged from the continuing debate over the pros and cons of antitrust laws and their consequences.

Industry Regulation

Industries such as electric power, communications, gas pipelines, and others of special importance to the public interest are subject to government **economic regulations.** Firms in these highly regulated industries must seek approval from their regulatory commissions to change the rates they charge customers or to significantly alter the level or quality of services. New firms cannot begin operation, nor can old firms abandon service, without approval from the regulatory authorities. Examples of regulated industries and their governing commissions are given in Table 9–2.

ECONOMIC REGULATIONS are concerned with pricing, the control of entry into the market, the extension of service by established firms, and issues of quality control.

These transport and utility industries are clearly of special importance to the public interest. In addition, however, there is some economic justification for regulation when it is less costly to have the market's entire output produced by one large organization rather than by several small, competing firms. This special circumstance is referred to as a **natural monopoly.** A good example of a natural monopoly is a utility company. It is common for a utility company to incur very high start-up costs because of the vast amount of plant and equipment needed to apply advanced modern technologies. A modern electric power company must acquire land, install generators and other equipment, and erect and maintain power lines, as well as incur other operational costs. Because the fixed costs are large, the costs per kilowatt-hour drop sharply for large volumes of output. When the high fixed charges are spread (averaged) over many units, the average costs per unit decline. Therefore, one large company with sizable fixed costs may be able to produce in large volume for costs per unit that are far below those of several small, competing companies, each producing small volumes.

TABLE 9–2   Select Industries Subject to Regulation

Industry	Regulatory Commission and Activities
Electricity generation	Federal Energy Regulatory Commission (FERC) and agencies in 49 states control prices; agencies in 35 states certify service.
Natural gas transmission and retail distribution	FERC controls interstate transportation, and agencies in 49 states set rates for distribution.
Highway freight services	Interstate Commerce Commission (ICC) and agencies in 47 states regulate rates; ICC and agencies in 45 states control entry into common-carrier services.
Railroad services	ICC and agencies in 44 states set freight rates; ICC and agencies in 26 states certify entry into the provision of rail services.

Several major industries are closely regulated by state and federal regulatory commissions.

> A NATURAL MONOPOLY occurs when one producer can supply all of the market at lower costs than two or more producers can.

These conditions for a natural monopoly create a dilemma for society. Although lower per-unit costs are possible when one large producer exists, this natural monopoly situation obviously can work against the public interest if, for a monopolist, the power to price is allowed. To realize the resource savings of large-scale production and still ensure that "reasonable prices" prevail free of monopoly control, government has typically tried to regulate the market. It allows only one firm in the market and places that legal monopoly's operations under the scrutiny of a regulatory (public service) commission to ensure against the exploitation of monopoly power and to assure "reasonable profits." Alternatively, instead of regulation, government could set prices and invite competitive bids from firms for the exclusive rights to produce the output in that market. This method is used for the rights to sell food and lodging in Yosemite Park, California. The competitive bids help to minimize production costs and realize competitive prices without the need for a regulatory agency.

A critical aspect of all cases of industry regulation is the problem of setting rates (prices) to be charged. When regulated firms request a rate change from their regulatory commissions, the prices are usually determined and set on a cost-plus basis. Each commission's objective is to set price as low as possible and yet to allow the regulated firm to generate revenues sufficient to cover costs, including an adequate return to investors in the firm.

One major shortcoming of cost-plus pricing is the failure to promote sustained economic efficiency. There is little incentive for the regulated firm to cut costs in this situation, because prices ultimately would only be adjusted downward. An unregulated firm, however, has an incentive to cut costs, because it gains the full cost reductions as additions to profits.

Some businesses are also regulated, not because they are natural monopolies but simply because they are thought to be uniquely in the public interest. Radio and television (which can influence public opinion), railroads, motor and water carriers, and airlines (which provide vital linkages to the economy) are examples of the types of businesses that have been regulated in the name of serving the public interest. Other types of regulation are undertaken in the public interest but not on an industry-by-industry basis. These address special problems such as pollution, protection of consumers from faulty or unsafe products, provision of safe conditions for workers in the workplace, and issues of discrimination or affirmative action.

Critics of deregulation point to cases of poorer service and growing concentration in our national markets. In 1990, the eight largest airlines accounted for over 90 percent of the market—up from 80 percent in 1978. On a route-by-route basis, however, competition had increased from an average of 1.5 airlines per route in 1978 to 1.9 in 1988. In their book, *The Economic Effects of Airline Deregulation,* Clifford Winston and Steven Morrison of the Brookings Institute conclude that in the decade of the 1980s, average fares were 18 percent below typical prederegulation fares. This decline in rates saved passengers $6 billion (in 1988 dollars) for the decade—savings resulting from more competition and less government regulation.

Health, Safety, and Consumer Protection Regulation

The biggest explosion in regulation in recent decades has come in the health and safety of consumers and workers. The Environmental Protection Agency (EPA), the Consumer Product Safety Commission (CPSC), the Occupational Safety and Health Administration (OSHA), and the National Highway Traffic Safety Commission (NHTSC) are examples of some of the regulatory agencies that the U.S. government has created since 1960. These agencies are allowed to specify rules and regulations and to issue rulings and set fines and penalties for violations of their regulations.

To judge the effects of such regulations, the benefits and costs must be compared. Society benefits from the improved quality and safety of the workplace and its products, but placing an economic value on these benefits is often difficult. Consider the trade-offs people weigh. Some are willing to risk health in exchange for the pleasure of smoking cigarettes. Others determine that the pleasure of eating a double cheeseburger with mayonnaise outweighs the harm that cholesterol will do to their arteries. Some will live in a polluted city for a higher-paying job instead of moving to a healthier rural area. Many commute to and from work by driving on crowded, dangerous highways instead of facing the inconvenience of a safer bus trip.

The Deregulation Movement

In the late 1970s, a strong movement to deregulate business in the United States began. One of the reasons for deregulation was the failure of the regulatory agencies to keep up with changing market conditions. Oftentimes regulation suffers from a "regulatory lag"; in conducting investigations, holding hearings, filing lawsuits, and dealing with appeals, the regulatory process becomes inflexible. Some of the costs to society occur when newer technologies make regulations obsolete, such as when building codes and pollution scrubbers are required by law despite the development of new materials and devices. Again we see that *the inflexibility of regulation in dealing with change can impose costs on society.*

Another reason that regulation ultimately came under fire was the recognition that regulatory authorities can be manipulated by firms to effectively create a cartel. For example, regulation sometimes has been used to prevent entry of potential competitors. This occurred frequently in the airline and trucking industries. Before deregulation, the regulatory agencies [the Civil Aeronautics Board (CAB) and the Interstate Commerce Commission (ICC)] had to approve new routes and entrants. The regulatory mechanism often protected old established firms from new competition. Old firms worked regularly with the agencies, knew their personnel, and often hired away the regulators or supplied expertise to the commissions. Some critics would argue that the regulatory commissions often got "captured" by the industry. Indeed, who are the regulators? Often they are experts, previously employed by the industries they regulate.

Public Goods and "Total" Market Failure

Most goods are purchased and consumed by individuals for private use. When someone buys a new coat, other people are excluded from using it. Similarly, the owner of a new car has exclusive property rights to the car. Someone else wanting to use it must pay for it, by either renting it or buying it (or by making other arrangements with the owner to use it). Hamburgers, pizzas, clothes, houses, stoves, automobiles, and most of what is produced are called **private goods,** because the **exclusion principle** applies. The market system is capable of producing all kinds of private goods that can be bought and sold with exclusive rights to ownership and use.

A PRIVATE GOOD is owned exclusively, and it cannot be simultaneously used by others.

The EXCLUSION PRINCIPLE applies to goods that the owner can prevent others from using unless they pay.

A PUBLIC GOOD is one for which the exclusion of others is undesirable and unnecessary, impractical and difficult, or impossible.

There is another class of goods, however, for which the exclusion principle does not hold. These are goods for which the exclusion of others is undesirable and unnecessary, impractical and difficult, or impossible. These are called **public goods.** National defense is a clear example of a public good. Together, we are all consumers of national defense. One person's consumption of national defense does not reduce another's share of this public good. Each person's consumption of defense is the same as that of everyone else, although each of us may value it differently. Law and order, as provided by police protection and the legal system, is another public good available to everyone for collective consumption.

Public goods have special characteristics. Greater collective use does not increase the costs of providing the good. The marginal cost of greater use is zero; an increasing number of people can consume a public good without there being less available for others. Immigrants may enter the United States and share the benefits of national defense at no extra cost, but they do not reduce the amount of national defense available for the rest of us. "Pure" public goods are indivisible. (For example, you can't buy or sell $100 worth of national defense to each citizen.)

Television broadcasting signals are also a public good. Signals can be "scrambled" technologically to preclude viewing, but this is generally considered impractical or undesirable.[3] This is because the marginal cost of adding another viewer, once the signal is sent, is virtually zero. Furthermore, turning on an additional television set does not reduce the quality (or quantity) of reception by others.

As a practical matter some people may actually consume public goods in modestly greater (or lesser) amounts than others, but it is generally very difficult to charge people for a public good on the basis of how much they use. It is nearly impossible to determine how much anyone personally gains from or values police protection, fire protection, the rights to use the courts and the legal system, national defense, and the like. For these reasons, public goods cannot be or are not bought and sold in the marketplace. They are provided by the government.

The necessity of government's provision of public goods and the nature of the total market failure is illustrated by the example of national defense. A private company that wished to produce and sell national defense services would incur great costs. The company would face the high fixed costs of planes, tanks, training and maintaining soldiers, and all the other costs of military might. But how would it collect revenues? Who would buy the services? Most citizens realize that the amount of national defense supplied and the benefits received are independent of what they pay for it. The exclusion principle does not work, and people realize that they can consume about the same amount of national defense, regardless of whether they pay for it. Because public goods are consumed collectively, independently of individual payment, everyone has an incentive and opportunity to be a **free rider.**[4] Essentially, in many types of collective consumption in which free riding is possible because the exclusion principle does not apply, government itself must supply the good. The market fails completely in cases of "pure" public goods such as national defense.[5]

A FREE RIDER is one who receives something without paying.

PEOPLE IN POVERTY

When President Lyndon Johnson announced his War on Poverty in 1964, the Social Security Administration worked to provide a definition of *poverty*. Families were classified as poor if they had incomes smaller than three times the cost of providing a low-cost, nutritionally adequate diet. This poverty line was based on survey data indicating that low- and middle-income families spent about one-third of their incomes on food. By that definition, 20 percent of the population was poor in 1964, compared to almost 14 percent in 1996. A family of four in 1995 was classified as

---

[3]Cable TV uses special hook-ups to prohibit reception by those who do not pay.

[4]This term is not meant to include someone who receives a gift from someone else.

[5]Of course, if the national defense firm could forcibly collect tax revenues because of its military monopoly, it would become the government.

poor if its total income was less than $15,600; in that same year median income per household was nearly $34,000 in the United States.

Government and the Poor

Before providing a more detailed demographic profile on poverty, it is important to reveal how the government provides direct assistance to people classified as poor. This is done largely through **transfer programs.**

A TRANSFER PROGRAM is a program in which the government gives economic support to people without requiring that recipients supply any current goods or services in return.

The support provided by transfer programs is paid in one of two forms: (1) **cash benefits** or (2) **in-kind benefits.**

CASH BENEFITS are given as money, with no restrictions on how this money is to be spent.

IN-KIND BENEFITS are specific goods and services (e.g., food or medical care) given either free or at a reduced rate.

Profile on Poverty

With these means of assistance in mind, we now turn to the data on poverty. Figures 9–2, 9–3, and 9–4 provide an overview of poverty in the United States since World War II. Figure 9–2 gives the absolute number of individuals officially classified as poor. The number of people who were poor fell during 1959–69, held fairly steady 1970–81, then increased sharply during the 1981–82 recession, before sliding back until 1990, when the number rose once again. Figure 9–3 gives the proportion of people officially classified as poor. This percentage steadily declined until the mid-1970s, held steady until 1981, and since then has varied slightly at around 14 percent of the population. Figure 9–3 also shows total state and federal welfare spending in 1996 dollars. The sixfold increase in real expenditures for welfare recipients since 1964 stands in sharp contrast to the comparatively persistent poverty rate of about 13 or 14 percent.

Figure 9–4 disaggregates the data, first by race, showing in panel A, for 1990, that most poor Americans were white. Panel B gives the poverty rate (percent)

FIGURE 9–2   Official Number of Poor in the United States

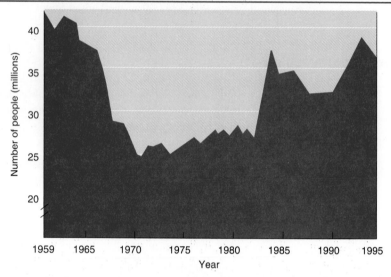

The number of individuals classified as poor fell steadily from 1959 through 1969. From 1970 to 1981, the number stayed about the same. It then increased during the 1981–82 recession, dropped off for a while, and has since risen in the 1990s.

Source: U.S. Department of Labor.

FIGURE 9–3   Welfare Spending and the Poverty Rate

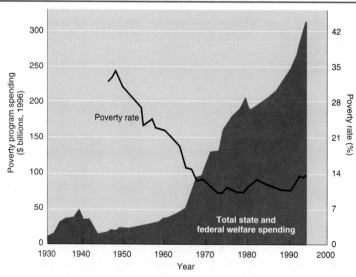

Welfare spending has increased dramatically since the late 1960s, whereas the measured poverty rate has remained relatively stable.

Sources: U.S. Departments of Commerce and Health and Human Services.

FIGURE 9–4   Profiles of Poverty

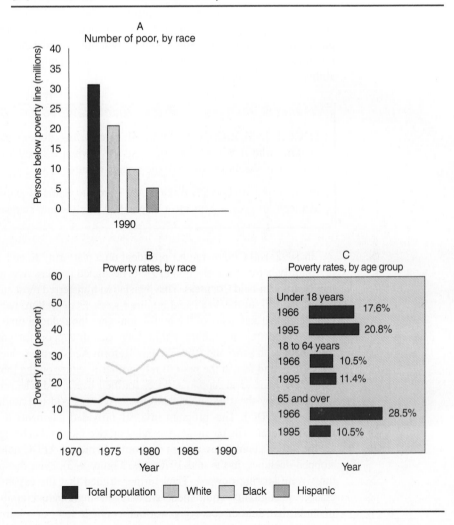

A
Number of poor, by race

B
Poverty rates, by race

C
Poverty rates, by age group

Under 18 years
1966   17.6%
1995   20.8%
18 to 64 years
1966   10.5%
1995   11.4%
65 and over
1966   28.5%
1995   10.5%

■ Total population   ▨ White   ▢ Black   ▨ Hispanic

showing the rate for blacks to be more than double the rate for whites. Panel C compares poverty rate changes between 1966 and 1995 by age group. A major change in the profile in poverty has been the marked reduction in the poverty rate for senior citizens. The main area of concern in the 1990s is the large fraction of children who are poor. Many of these poor children are raised in households headed by single women. The poverty rate for single women–led households has ranged between 55 and 45 percent (1970–90) for blacks and has held at close to 25 percent for whites. Meanwhile, from 1970 to 1991 the percentage of illegitimate births (defined as children born without fathers present at home) rose from 5.7 percent to 21.8 percent for whites and from 37.6 percent to 67.9 percent for blacks.

To help those in poverty the government uses transfer programs that fall into two categories: **social insurance** and **public assistance.** Social insurance comprises nearly four-fifths of government transfers (Social Security, Medicare, and Unemployment Compensation). Some well-known public assistance programs are Aid to Families with Dependent Children (AFDC), food stamps, housing assistance, disability payments, and Medicaid.

SOCIAL INSURANCE PROGRAMS are for everyone, regardless of income, who receives economic assistance when a specific event (e.g., retirement, disability, or unemployment) occurs.

PUBLIC ASSISTANCE PROGRAMS are programs of economic assistance available to people who meet a specified low-income standard.

In 1992, Bill Clinton ran for president on a platform "to end welfare as we know it." Shortly before his reelection in 1996, he signed into law new legislation passed by the Republican-held Congress. That legislation transferred most authority over welfare payments back to the states and required work from welfare recipients in return for benefits. Other key parts of the legislation were the reduced time limits on how long people could stay on welfare and no increases in support for young women having more babies. In short, the 1996 Welfare Reform Act sharply reduced federal authority for welfare and forced the poor to rely primarily either on the job market, their families, or state and local support services for their livelihood. The principal program that was altered by the 1996 Welfare Reform Act was Aid to Families with Dependent Children (AFDC). This program in 1991 provided payments to mothers of over 8 million children. The payments depended on two factors: (1) being classified poor and (2) the father's being absent from the house. Critics of AFDC noted that poverty rates stopped declining in the mid-1970s (see Figure 9–3), even though welfare expenditures were soaring upward. They further argued that the expansion of benefits and changes in eligibility requirements encouraged single-parent families and rising illegitimate births while discouraging work at available low- or minimum-wage jobs.

Critics of the new law fear especially the short-run consequences of such a policy shift and object to proposals for abolishing welfare. They claim that unemployment and stagnant wages during the 1970s were the principal causes of the lack of improvement in the poverty rate. Only the income-maintenance programs, they claim, prevented poverty from increasing further. In his weekly radio address in early July 1997, however, President Clinton said "welfare caseloads fell by 3.1 million between January 1993 and April of this year . . . this is the largest decrease in the welfare rolls in history giving us the lowest percentage of our population on welfare since 1970."[6]

---

[6]For a critique of the argument for abolition of the welfare state, see Robert Greenstein, "Losing Faith in 'Losing Ground,' " *The New Republic,* March 25, 1985, pp. 12–17.

GOVERNMENT FAILURES, TOO

The primary sources of market failure, in which voluntary exchanges through markets realize inefficient outcomes, occur when externalities are significant, when monopoly prevails, or when public goods are desired. To correct for these market failures, we often turn to government.[7]

However, the coercive actions we take through government to correct for market failures are subject to shortcomings and failures too. To see this, let's begin by assessing citizens as voters and our government representatives as guardians of the public interest. At the core of the problem in the public sector are the costs of obtaining and acting on information—by politicians, bureaucracies, vested interest groups, and voting citizens. The analysis to follow is based on elements of a core of theory recently developed called *public choice theory.*[8]

Politicians, Bureaucracies, and Vested Interests

Do elected officials act impartially in the public interest, or do they act in their own interest, as economic theory indicates for people making choices in markets? Do people's instincts and motives fundamentally change when they move from academia, business, or the professions into public service? Let's leave these questions begging, but recognize that elected officials clearly act as if a primary objective is to get reelected. To do this requires money, favorable media visibility, party support, and at least 50 percent plus one of the votes on election day.

We first note that planning horizons for public policy (and to get reelected) are limited by election intervals, which are no more than two years for congressional representatives. Representatives and their staff must show results before the next election; thus, actions with long-term results, no matter how promising, will be avoided in favor of policies with quick results. Second, politicians act on information, and the supply of information stems principally from two sources. Let's use agriculture as an example. For established programs, agricultural bureaucracies within and outside the Department of Agriculture supply representatives with information about price support programs, subsidies, food stamp issues, trade restrictions, and many others. In addition, farm groups form special interest groups (e.g., the Grange) to lobby for and provide information on their "needs." Typically, bureaucratic heads are paid more if their staffs are larger. Will they find it in their interests to enlarge their programs and provide information to support a larger range of government activity? Yes, quite likely; expanded programs would certainly be in the bureaucracies' private best interests. The same is true, of course, of the vested interest group lobbying to redistribute income in its own favor. In contrast, although the

---

[7]Poverty, economic stabilization (and other macroeconomic issues), and other reasons also justify government intervention in economic life.

[8]James Buchanan of George Mason University received the Nobel Prize in economic science in 1989 for his pioneering work in this field.

gains to bureaucracies and vested special-interest groups are substantial and clear to them, the average taxpayer bears only a small fraction of the increase in the costs of the enlarged and expanded program.

It is hardly in the best interests of the average citizen to spend time and money to add information and counterarguments to those given by the bureaucracies and vested interests. The dichotomy of incentives among bureaucracies, vested interests, and taxpayers prejudices the information received by our representatives. The persistent prejudice is to vote in favor of the proposals of bureaucracies and vested special-interest groups. In addition, the prospects for redistributing income and benefits in their favor encourage the prejudice of the information they supply. None of this implies that farmers or administrators are dishonest or have no regard for the public interest. It only implies that they have a strong sense of self-interest.

The conflict between private and public interest can also be seen in another example. Suppose you are a member of the Food and Drug Administration (FDA), responsible for the introduction of new drugs adequately tested for safety and side effects. You must thoroughly test the drug before it is allowed on the market. You seek additional information to reduce the risk that someone will be killed or seriously harmed by an unanticipated side effect. How much testing should you require to reduce the risk? Clearly, there are costs as well as benefits attached to additional testing. The costs are the lives lost and the suffering not relieved because the drug is held off the market while it's being tested.

How will a typical FDA commissioner evaluate these two costs: the lives lost through premature introduction and the lives lost through excessive delay in introduction of new drugs? If an approved drug turns out to have harmful side effects, the commissioners will be blamed. If the FDA refuses to approve a drug that reveals disastrous side effects in other countries where it is used, the media will applaud the FDA members. However, few condemn the FDA for lives lost while a drug is being tested during an excessively lengthy period, or applaud (AIDS activists are a recent exception) the FDA for shortening the testing period to hasten a new drug to the market. How would you act on the commission? You would typically find it in your interest as an administrator to test drugs beyond the point at which the marginal benefit equals the marginal cost to patients or society. You would err on the side of slow market entry, and you would say you were requiring extra testing in the public interest.

Information and Democracy

The pull and tug of private interests in conflict with the public interest can potentially be corrected by citizens who have the power "to vote the rascals out." The free-rider problem, however, prevails in the election process just as it does in the case of public goods. The important responsibility of voting and being informed on election day is communicated and stressed greatly in democratic societies, especially in the United States, and yet in elections a majority of eligible voters often do not vote. Many voters are only partially informed on the many ballot issues and on the positions of politicians running for office. Economists and political scientists note that there is a rationality to voter ignorance. Most citizens, including well-read, public-spirited, dedicated citizens, step into the polling booth on election day equipped with only partial information on the host of decisions they face.

Our ignorance is rational, it is argued, because our impact on the outcome is so minimal. It doesn't pay for us to spend great amounts of time to inform ourselves so that we become experts on each issue, because our individual votes count for little among 200,000 or 100 million votes. It's not selfishness or lack of commitment that causes our rational ignorance. Failures of information occur even for the most committed, and the opportunity to free ride on election results discourages our participation in elections and our dedication to becoming better informed. Like markets, democracy works, but not perfectly. The perennial debate before us is to judge when social cooperation through markets works best and when government interference leads to better outcomes.

CHAPTER REVIEW

The proper role of government in the economy is a matter of perennial debate. Government's mandate to provide law and order and to control the use of large-scale force (the armed forces) is generally well recognized. These are public goods that would not be supplied by the marketplace through private initiative.

The exclusion principle does not hold for public goods. We receive them whether we pay for them or not. No private corporations could supply such goods, because they cannot be sold. Free riders would know that they could still get the public goods without paying for them. These public-good cases reflect extreme forms of market failure.

Another type of market failure takes place when social costs are greater than private costs, as in cases of pollution. In these instances, a negative externality exists. For example, when people discharge pollutants into a common-property source, such as the air or the sea, negative externalities occur, and the private costs of production are less than the social costs. The proper role of government is to attempt to equate the private and social costs and to minimize the environmental damages that result when pollution occurs. This is done either through regulation, by taxing the activity that causes the damage, or by subsidizing cleanup methods.

Monopolies are another form of market failure. Monopolies prevent resources from moving to their highest-valued uses for society. The antitrust laws and government economic regulations have been the two primary means of minimizing monopoly power in cases in which it has arisen. If one firm can produce at lower costs than several smaller, competing firms, a natural monopoly exists. This presents society with a dilemma. For a natural monopoly, such as a utility, the lowest-cost form of production is one large firm (rather than several small ones), but the utility must be regulated to avoid monopolistic practices. Regulatory commissions are often established for this purpose. Finally, government has developed a safety net for those who are significantly disadvantaged or caught in poverty.

A larger dilemma for a society that wishes to correct market failures through government intervention is the occurrence of government failures. Government failures arise because of the high costs of obtaining and acting on information and because of the potential conflict between private interests of politicians, bureaucrats, and vested interests and the public interest. Further, the free-rider problem encourages rational ignorance by voters and discourages them from seeking information and participating in elections.

𝒥𝒦 MULTIPLE-CHOICE SELF-TEST 𝒥𝒦 𝒥𝒦 𝒥𝒦 𝒥𝒦 𝒥𝒦 𝒥𝒦 𝒥𝒦 𝒥𝒦 𝒥𝒦 𝒥𝒦 𝒥𝒦 𝒥𝒦 𝒥𝒦 𝒥𝒦 𝒥𝒦 𝒥𝒦

1. If the government taxes electric utilities for the amount of sulfur they emit when burning oil to produce electricity, which of the following *would not* be expected?
   a. The amount of electricity produced declines.
   b. The price of electricity falls.
   c. Firms switch to using higher-priced, low-sulfur oil.
   d. Consumers pay more for their electricity.

2. Natural monopolies are:
   a. Prevented from emerging by antitrust laws.
   b. Cases in which one firm can produce all the output for a market at lower cost than competing firms could.
   c. Found in industries with low fixed costs.
   d. All the above are true.

3. When households and firms freely dispose of their liquid wastes in a river, making the water unusable for drinking, swimming, or fishing:
   a. This is a positive externality.
   b. The social and private costs of liquid waste disposal are equal.
   c. More liquid waste disposal is occurring than would occur if full social costs were charged.
   d. This is a positive externality to the households and firms and a negative one to swimmers, fishers, and so on.

4. Basic scientific research is a public good because:
   a. Each new finding can be used by many people simultaneously.
   b. It is of no economic benefit to private individuals.
   c. Government and nonprofit institutions pay for most of it.
   d. It is desirable for society to increase scientific knowledge.

5. A firm selling a public good might have difficulty getting paid enough to cover its costs because:
   a. Each person who uses it would prefer to be a free rider.
   b. The exclusion principle prevents people from paying for the good.
   c. Public goods are too expensive for private-sector purchases.
   d. All the above are true.

☜ STUDY QUESTIONS

1. Analyze the following statement: "People follow their self-interests in the private sector but work for the public interest in the public sector."

2. What is the economic distinction between a private good such as a bicycle and a public good such as the Statue of Liberty?

3. Could the Statue of Liberty be made into a private good if it were relocated from New York Harbor to another place on land? How?

4. Why is water pollution likely to result when a lake is common property, that is, available to be used by all? Could the lake be privatized? Explain.

5. Give an example of a natural monopoly. How would it function if unregulated? How do you recommend regulating it?

☜ PROBLEMS

1. Farmers make up only 3 percent of the American population. Use public choice theory to explain why Congress consistently votes to continue farm price supports and subsidy programs that provide benefits to relatively few Americans and impose costs on many. Are members of the House of Representatives or the Senate most susceptible to pressure from agricultural lobby groups? Why? Why might a legislator support aid to agriculture even if there are no farmers among his or her constituents?

2. The stainless steel products industry in an area emits mercury-bearing chemicals into the bay waters. These are gradually killing a valuable fish population. The government estimates that each pound of mercury emitted is causing $1,000 worth of damage. With current production techniques, each ton of stainless steel products produced is accompanied by the emission of 10 pounds of mercury. The area industry's supply schedule, based on its internal costs, and its demand schedule follows:

Price	$50,000	$50,000	$55,000	$60,000	$65,000
Quantity supplied (tons)	5	6	7	8	9
Quantity demanded (tons)	10	10	9	8	7

   a. Draw the current supply and demand curves. How many tons will the area's industry be producing?

b. Draw a social cost curve on the diagram that shows how much the price per ton should be if the external cost of mercury pollution were also included. How many tons would the industry produce if it had to take all costs into consideration? If the government were able to charge the firms a $1,000 tax for every pound of mercury they emitted, how much would the industry produce?

c. After the tax is imposed, the firms develop a new way to process their stainless steel. It cuts their mercury emissions in half, at a cost of $2,500 extra per ton of steel produced. If they use this new process, how much is the additional cost per ton compared to the cost before the tax was imposed?

d. Sketch in this new supply curve on the graph. About how much will the firms now produce, and what will be the price?

CHAPTER 10

Trade among Nations

𝕵 CHAPTER PREVIEW

Many of us awake each morning to the sound of clock radios made in Singapore. We don clothes made from cotton grown in India and assembled in Hong Kong. Our shoes are imported from Italy; our coffee was grown in Brazil. Our newspaper is composed of pulp from trees grown in Canada. Our car may have been manufactured in Japan, Germany, or Sweden and probably uses gasoline made from Saudi Arabian crude oil. The American way of life depends very much on international trade.

The total volume of international trade is enormous. Today countries around the world exchange more than $2 trillion worth of goods and services, and the volume is growing. The reason there is so much international trade is that it provides mutual benefits. It raises the standards of living of people in all parts of the world. Despite the apparent benefits of international trade, however, governments historically have erected a variety of barriers to free trade. New trade agreements in the 1990s, such as NAFTA and the General Agreement on Tariffs and Trade (GATT), are moving us closer to a world of free trade, albeit imperfectly.

1. Why do national governments often interfere with international trade?
2. What are the economic effects of the policies that governments use to restrict trade?

𝕁𝕃 CONCEPTS REINTRODUCED

Demand Curve 52
Free Rider 192
Opportunity Cost 7
Production Possibilities Curve 28–31
Public Goods 42–43
Supply Curve 74

𝕁𝕃 NEW CONCEPTS

Comparative Advantage
Terms of Trade
Tariff
Quota
Voluntary Export Restraint
Embargo

🎶 CHAPTER OBJECTIVES

After studying this chapter, you should be able to:

1. Determine comparative advantages in production between two trading nations.
2. Define *terms of trade.*
3. List instruments of protectionist policy and give examples of each.
4. Distinguish among the winners and losers of protectionist policies.

THE GAINS FROM TRADE

Although the transactions are more complex, the essential characteristics of international trade are identical to those of domestic exchange. As a rule, nations don't trade—individuals do—and when trade is voluntary, it will not occur unless both parties benefit. International trade provides mutual benefits because economies have differences that generate gains from trade:

- **Economies have different relative quantities and qualities of various productive resources.**

  The numbers of skilled and unskilled workers, the types of machinery, the amount of fertile land, and the availability of raw materials and energy sources are unique to each country. These differences can have implications for the production techniques that are used. In the United States, labor is relatively scarce and expensive, but arable land and productive capital are relatively abundant. Consequently, in the United States, rice producers use machinery and land intensively but economize on the use of labor. In Japan, arable land is very scarce, but labor is relatively abundant. Thus, rice growers in Japan use labor-intensive techniques that economize on the use of land. Each rice seedling may be transplanted by hand several times.

- **Economies differ in available production techniques because of patent protection or other barriers to the spread of technologies.**

  Pharmaceutical companies, for example, obtain patents that give them monopolies in the production of new drugs for many years. Producers in other countries cannot legally manufacture drugs that are protected by patents. Similarly, the Coca-Cola corporation closely guards the secret formulas for its world-famous soft drinks.

- **Economies differ in climatic conditions.**

  This is important for tourism and for agricultural production. It is hard to get a suntan in Iceland! Grains such as wheat are not well suited to rainy, tropical areas; bananas and cocoa beans cannot be grown commercially in arid, temperate climates.

- **The people of different countries have different tastes.**

This can result from differences in values, in income levels, or in cultural traditions. Tastes influence the kinds of goods people want and the production activities their countries engage in.

The Ricardian Approach

The gains from trade between nations were first demonstrated in a persuasive and complete way in 1817 by the English economist David Ricardo. To see how countries gain from trade, we use a very simple example, similar to the one presented by Ricardo. The example involves two countries, England and Portugal. Each country produces two goods, cloth and wine. For simplicity, labor is treated as the only productive resource used to make the two goods, and all workers within the same country have identical abilities. The number of hours of work required to produce one bottle of wine or one yard of cloth remains constant in each country, no matter how much of each good is produced. Finally, all workers are fully employed; therefore, each country is on its production possibilities curve.

The climate and available technologies in each country determine the productivity of workers in the two industries. To be specific, suppose that in Portugal it takes 8 hours of work to weave a yard of cloth but only 4 hours to produce a bottle of wine. In England, 2 hours of work yield either a bottle of wine or a yard of cloth. These conditions are also reported in Table 10–1.

Comparative Advantage and Opportunity Cost

English workers can produce one unit of wine or cloth in less time than their Portuguese counterparts can. The English thus have a lower *resource cost* (measured as hours of labor per unit of output) than do the Portuguese, in both industries. However, this is not the key determinant of the gains from trade or of the pattern of exports and imports. The key principle is one that is at the heart of all theories of international trade, the notion of **comparative advantage.**

Let us apply this idea to our example. Table 10–1 shows the amounts of labor needed to produce one unit of each good in England and Portugal. We can use this

TABLE 10–1 Hours of Labor Required to Produce One Unit

	Wine	Cloth
In England	2	2
In Portugal	4	8

The opportunity cost in hours to produce one more yard of cloth or one more bottle of wine is lower in England than in Portugal, but the opportunity cost of more cloth is relatively lower in England. In England the trade-off in production is one for one, in Portugal, it is two wine for one cloth.

𝕿 𝕿

> A COMPARATIVE ADVANTAGE for a country occurs if the country has lower opportunity costs in producing that good than other countries have.

information to find the opportunity cost in terms of cloth or wine in each country. If Portugal produces an additional yard of cloth, there are 8 fewer hours of labor available to make wine. The opportunity cost of a yard of cloth in Portugal is thus the two bottles of wine that could have been produced in the 8 hours. If England produces an additional yard of cloth, there are 2 fewer hours of labor available to make wine. The opportunity cost of a yard of cloth in England is thus one bottle of wine.

The English are more productive than the Portuguese in both industries. This seems to suggest that if the two countries start to trade, England should produce both goods, and Portugal should produce neither. However, this would waste the entire labor force available in Portugal. For any combination of wine and cloth that England could produce, the two countries could enjoy more of both goods if the Portuguese also engaged in production. If world output is to be maximized, the labor forces of both countries must be fully employed.[1]

But which country should produce which good? Suppose first that England and Portugal both produce wine and cloth, and there is no trade between the two countries. Each country produces as much cloth and wine as its production possibilities curve permits. Let's see if trade can make a more efficient pattern of production than can no trade. Suppose England increases its cloth production by three yards, and Portugal cuts its cloth production by two yards. This requires 6 hours of labor in England but makes available 16 hours of labor in Portugal. Portugal can now produce four extra bottles of wine, but only three bottles of wine are lost in England. Thus, the net gain in world output is one yard of cloth *and* one bottle of wine. This shifting of production could continue, with England producing more and more cloth, and Portugal producing more and more wine. The output of both goods increases each step of the way.

Will the process result in England's producing only cloth, and Portugal's producing only wine? It can, but not necessarily. If each country specializes in production of the good in which it has a comparative advantage, there may be excess supply of one of the goods and excess demand for the other. In that case, one of the countries will have to produce *both* goods, though each will continue to produce and export the good in which it has a comparative advantage. If there is relatively high demand for wine in the two countries, England may have to produce both wine and cloth. It will export cloth to Portugal in exchange for imports of wine to supplement its own production.

Let us summarize the link between opportunity costs and the gains from trade in a different way. Recall that England has a lower opportunity cost of producing cloth than Portugal's opportunity cost: The opportunity cost of cloth is one unit of wine in

---

[1]Moving the Portuguese labor force to England is assumed unfeasible.

England but two units of wine in Portugal. However, this implies that Portugal must have a lower opportunity cost of producing wine than does England: Wine costs one unit of cloth in England, but only one-half unit of cloth in Portugal. The key point is that England can get wine more cheaply by producing excess cloth (and trading it to Portugal for wine) than by producing the wine itself. Similarly, Portugal can get cloth more cheaply by producing excess wine (and trading it to England for cloth) than by producing the cloth itself. Hence, the two countries gain from trade.

The TERMS OF TRADE are the relative prices of goods and services traded in international markets.

How are the gains from trade divided between the two countries? This is determined by the **terms of trade.** If the prices of the imports of a country go up relative to the prices of its exports, its real income is lowered: It can no longer afford the level of imports that it could in the past. In our Ricardian example, if wine becomes less popular and its relative price drops, the Portuguese become worse off. For any amount of wine they export, they now get less cloth in return.

An excellent example of the importance of the terms of trade was provided by the world petroleum market in the 1970s. OPEC raised the price of crude oil dramatically at several points during that decade. In 1970 crude oil cost about $3 a barrel, but by 1980 it cost more than $30 a barrel.[1] This seriously hurt countries that imported petroleum products, including the United States. To lessen the immediate effects on their standards of living, countries such as Brazil borrowed abroad to pay for their imported oil and incurred enormous foreign debts in the process. In contrast, countries such as Saudi Arabia and Kuwait amassed huge fortunes.

Some Complications

The Ricardian model, like all models, is a simplification of reality. There are more than two goods in two countries in the world. And although labor averages between 60 and 80 percent of all costs, other inputs also contribute to costs.

Despite the model's simplifications, these key points remain valid:

- Comparative advantage depends on the relative opportunity costs of production in different countries.
- Comparative advantage determines which countries export which goods.
- The exploitation of comparative advantage through specialization and trade is the basis for worldwide gains from trade.
- Greater international trade combats and reduces domestic monopoly power.

---

[1] See Chapter 5 for discussion of other aspects of this problem.

We also note that if costs per unit decline as levels of production increase (rather than stay constant, as was assumed), greater specialization and trade lower costs further.

PROTECTIONISM VERSUS FREE TRADE: THE ISSUES

Although economic theory shows that free international trade is an ideal objective, much of the trade among nations is managed and constrained by government policies. Some of these protectionist policies are aimed directly at restricting foreign trade. **Tariffs** make imports more expensive and reduce the quantity of imports brought into a country. **Quotas** overtly limit the quantities of imports that can be brought into a country and thus drive up their prices. These barriers to foreign imports provide protection to domestic industries that compete with those imports.

INFLUENTIAL ECONOMIST

DAVID RICARDO, 1772–1823

David Ricardo crafted a most persuasive case for free international trade. This was one of many important contributions he made to economics in his masterpiece, *Principles of Political Economy and Taxation,* first published in 1817.

Along with Adam Smith (1723–1790) and John Stuart Mill (1806–1873), Ricardo is considered one of the great classical economists. A Dutch immigrant to Great Britain, Ricardo by age 26 became an incredibly successful financier and a millionaire. He retired in 1814 to devote his energies to economic analysis and to political service as a member of Parliament. Like Adam Smith, Ricardo was a strong advocate of the efficiencies of the free market. He had a vision of vast expansion of the British economy through industrialization and the accumulation of productive capital.

Ricardo aligned himself politically with the emerging industrial sector of the British economy. However, this placed him in opposition to the landowners who controlled British agriculture. This landed aristocracy had traditionally controlled Parliament and sought to preserve its own economic dominance by keeping the prices of grain and other agricultural products high. One way that agricultural prices were kept high was through the British Corn Laws, a set of barriers to the importation of foreign grains. The laws were intended to stabilize and to elevate the prices of grains by keeping out inexpensive foreign imports, just as some farm support programs do nowadays.

Ricardo was opposed to the Corn Laws on political and economic grounds, and he supported his position with rigorous economic analysis. He

They drive up not only the prices of the imports but also the prices of the domestically produced goods that are substitutes for the imports.

A TARIFF is a tax on imports.

A QUOTA is a quantitative restriction on imports.

Other trade policies include export subsidies, government procurement policies (e.g., "Buy American" campaigns), and product safety regulations that discriminate against foreign imports. Some government policies are basically aimed at the domestic economy, but they have powerful effects on foreign trade anyway. These include government tax breaks, subsidies, and other forms of assistance to certain industries. All these policies have been used extensively in the United States and Canada, in Europe, and elsewhere.

---

argued that higher grain prices would inhibit industrialization in Britain. British landowners would benefit, but at the expense of British workers and industrial entrepreneurs. Because accumulation of capital would be inhibited, Britain would not achieve the economic growth of which it was capable.

Ricardo based his attack on the Corn Laws on several specific theories. His analysis of *economic rent,* considered valid to this day, showed that higher grain prices would benefit landowners, but not the farmers who actually worked the land. As the price of grain increased, poorer quality land was put into cultivation in order to supply additional quantities of grain. The cost of a unit of grain on this poorer land was higher than the cost on more fertile land. Because all grain sold for the same price, however, owners of high-quality land earned a surplus, the economic rent on their land. Rural workers did not enjoy any of the benefits, because competition among them for work kept their wages uniformly low.

The high grain prices did not just affect agriculture. British workers in both agriculture and industry had to earn higher wages to be able to

afford enough grain to survive. However, higher wages put a squeeze on the profits of British industries. These industries could not compete with foreign producers who were not burdened with such high costs. The Corn Laws thus inhibited industrialization in England by preventing the importation of inexpensive grain, primarily from Prussia (eastern Germany).

Ricardo also used his arguments for free trade to counter the popular economic philosophy of *mercantilism.* For centuries mercantilists had argued that it was virtuous for a country to run a large surplus of exports over imports in order to accumulate gold and other precious metals. They felt that one country could gain from trade only at the expense of others. Mercantilists also argued for direct government intervention to restrict imports and to promote exports.

Ideas popular for centuries are hard to refute. Indeed, mercantilist sentiments linger to this day. Nevertheless, by showing that there are mutual gains from trade, Ricardo made a strong intellectual case for free international trade. We are indebted to him for this contribution.

GATT, EU, AND NAFTA

Over one hundred countries have been involved in talks concerning GATT in the "Uruguay Round" that began in 1986. The Uruguay Round of GATT, completed in 1993, reduced tariff barriers among members by 40 percent. This remarkable and complex agreement relies heavily on the notion of comparative advantage that tells us everyone involved will be better off in the long run if trade is relatively free from quotas and tariffs. It also formed a mechanism for continued negotiations, the World Trade Organization, and a mechanism for resolving disputes among member countries. GATT followed on the heels of several important regional agreements.

By 1993 most of the trade barriers between 12 nations of Europe, called the European Union (EU)—including Germany, France, England, and Italy—had been removed. Although each country maintains its culture, language, and national identity, members of the EU agree to prohibit tariffs among themselves. They also agree to common tariffs with the rest of the world. The Scandinavian nations, Austria, and Greece are also members, and in a few years, Poland, Hungary, and the Czech Republic may be included as well.

Meanwhile, in 1994 the United States, Canada, and Mexico signed NAFTA, which set the stage for "ratcheting down" trade barriers in North America. Ultimately, a massive new **free-trade** zone running from the Yucatan to the Klondike would serve the people of these nations. President Clinton and Republicans generally supported this trade agreement, but Ross Perot argued vigorously against it, fearing U.S. job losses to low-wage Mexican workers.

The trade agreements of the 1990s are far more complex and subtle than similar agreements in the 1950s. Trade is far more extensive now and involves very different types of countries in terms of economic development, traditions, and culture. NAFTA, for example, is an agreement including a relatively poor country, Mexico, and very advanced industrial powers, the United States and Canada. U.S. agreements with Asian trading partners involve complex issues such as protecting intellectual property rights, establishing environmental rules, and outlawing slave and child labor.

Until recently, Chinese and South Korean firms, with the evident acquiescence of their governments, were pirating U.S. compact-disk recordings of music and video performers for sale in their countries and even export to the United States. This pirating is disallowed under U.S. patent laws, so that comparable new legal arrangements have been repeatedly under negotiation between the United States and China and South Korea.

All these free-trade agreements will reduce barriers to the movement of inputs (labor and capital), technologies, and goods and services. However, these agreements are not as free as their titles imply, for they are really *managed trade agreements,* albeit less restrictive than prior arrangements. The management of trade continues, because in the process of opening borders to greater freedom to trade, there are losers as well as winners. And politicians, as we learned in Chapter 9, listen to vested interests in forming national policies.

The Political Economy of Protection

To put it more generally, economists agree that the worldwide benefits from free trade would exceed the worldwide benefits from restricted trade. However, different individuals and industries in a country can be affected by international trade in different ways: In the United States, most farmers would be winners with free trade; they would enjoy better access to foreign export markets. On the other hand, steelworkers would be losers if protection for them fell. They would face lower wages or fewer jobs because of greater competition from foreign imports. Because the worldwide gains from freer trade exceed the worldwide losses, there *ought* to be a way to redistribute the gains so that *everyone* would be made better off. To do this, the winners would have to compensate the losers enough to offset their losses. In reality, however, our political processes are not well suited to provide this kind of compensation. Thus, those who are hurt by free trade have a vested interest in getting the government to impose barriers to trade that work to their advantage. And yet, rarely, if ever, do trade barriers serve the general national interest. Consequently, our trade agreements stress managed trade, establishing rules that partially compensate losers, such as wage guarantees on retraining for displaced workers.

A Historical Case Study: The Faltering U.S. Steel Industry, 1960–1982

A striking example of these problems is provided by the contemporary history of the basic carbon steel industry in the United States. There were sharp declines in both output and employment in that industry from 1960 through the mid-1980s, as shown in Table 10–2. Of course, much of the downturn in employment from 1980 to 1982 was caused by the deep recession in the United States and the rest of the world. In addition, total world demand for steel grew very slowly over the previous decades, and there was rapid growth in competition from Europe, Brazil, and Japan and other East Asian nations. After the recovery from World War II, steel producers in these countries invested in more modern techniques and equipment than were used in most

TABLE 10–2 Workers in the United States Steel Industry, Selected Years (in thousands of workers)

1960	1970	1980	1982
571.6	531.2	398.8	239.4

Total employment in the U.S. steel industry declined gradually in the 1960s and 1970s, but nose-dived around 1980. Recession and increased import competition were the major causes.

Source: American Iron and Steel Institute.

TABLE 10–3   Average Hourly Compensation Costs for Iron and
Steel Workers

	Costs in U.S. Dollars		
	In 1978	**In 1982**	**Percentage Increase from 1978 to 1982**
United States	$13.56	$22.74	68
Canada	9.99	14.58	46
West Germany	10.74	11.57	8
Japan	9.38	9.90	6
South Korea	1.35	1.73	28

Not only did U.S. steelworkers earn much higher incomes in 1978 than did their foreign
competitors, but their compensation actually grew faster from 1978 to 1982 than did
compensation in any other country.

Source: U.S. Department of Labor, Bureau of Labor Statistics.

of the older U.S. steel mills. They also enjoyed lower costs for iron ore and coal
relative to American steelmakers.

Perhaps the most important reason for the difficulties of the post–World War II
U.S. steel industry was its high labor costs relative to foreign producers. Even though
foreign steelworkers became increasingly productive, their wages did not increase as
much as American steel wages. Table 10–3 shows the changes in average hourly
compensation—wages plus fringe benefits—to workers in the iron and steel industries of several countries between 1978 and 1982.

Although many factors contributed to the differences between U.S. labor costs
and the cost of labor in other countries in 1982, two factors should be emphasized:

1.   The U.S. steel industry traditionally had higher wages than other U.S. manufacturing industries, and this differential grew in the late 1970s.

In 1978 the average hourly compensation of workers in all U.S. manufacturing
industries was $8.30; in 1982 it was $11.68. These hourly costs were well below the
U.S. iron and steel industry labor costs shown in Table 10–3. Alternatively, as wages
in all U.S. manufacturing grew by 41 percent from 1978 to 1982, they grew 68
percent in the steel industry.

2.   The dollar rose in value against most foreign currencies from 1978 to 1982.

As we shall see in Chapter 20, this rise in the value of the dollar meant that if
wages in these countries had remained constant in their own currencies during this
period, they actually would have fallen in dollar terms.

To summarize, wages in the U.S. steel industry grew relative to the average U.S.
wage, but the average U.S. wage grew even faster relative to foreign wages because of
the higher value of the dollar. This would not have been a problem if U.S. steelworkers
had become more productive relative to workers in other U.S. industries and abroad.

However, productivity in the U.S. steel industry actually grew more slowly than in U.S. manufacturing overall and lagged even further behind some of the foreign steel producers. Steelworkers alone were not responsible for this sluggish productivity growth. Failures by management to invest in more efficient technologies and to organize production more efficiently had a lot to do with the problem. In any case, steelworkers who lost their jobs paid for these failures. Stockholders in U.S. steel corporations lost, too.

As a result of the growth of foreign competition after 1960, the steel industry and the United Steelworkers Union repeatedly asked the U.S. government for protection from foreign imports. They argued that workers in countries like Korea were paid unfairly low wages—wages they couldn't compete with. They also claimed that foreign governments gave subsidies and other unfair advantages to their own steel firms. Several of these requests for protection were granted. In 1982 the U.S. government imposed quotas on imports of steel from Western Europe. This action was intended to counteract subsidies given by European governments to their steel producers. In 1984 the U.S. government negotiated a **voluntary export restraint** agreement for steel with a number of countries. To justify the restraints, the U.S. government claimed that foreign countries had used "unfair trade practices" to promote their steel exports to the United States. By the 1990s, however, as noted above, the United States was moving toward freer trade policies.

A VOLUNTARY EXPORT RESTRAINT is identical to an import quota, except that the foreign government agrees *voluntarily* to limit exports from its country to our market.

Economic Costs of Protection

Despite its political appeal, protection can entail enormous economic costs, especially on consumers and exporters. The basic problem is that import barriers prevent a country from enjoying the full benefits of comparative advantage. Countries import goods because it is more costly to produce these goods at home than to produce other goods for export, sell them abroad, and use the revenues to purchase imports from foreigners. Thus, if a country imposes import barriers, its cost of acquiring these goods is higher.

A demand-supply diagram shows these effects. Suppose initially there is free trade in automobiles, as shown in Figure 10–1. The curve D shows domestic demand for autos. The curve S_1S_1 shows the domestic supply of autos, and S_1S_0 shows the total supply (domestic and foreign) to the market. (The S_0 segment of S_1S_0 indicates an extremely elastic supply of foreign autos at an $8,000 price.) At the equilibrium price of $8,000, consumers purchase 700,000 autos each year. Of that total, 400,000 cars are supplied by domestic producers, and the rest (300,000) are foreign imports.

FIGURE 10–1   Free Trade in Autos

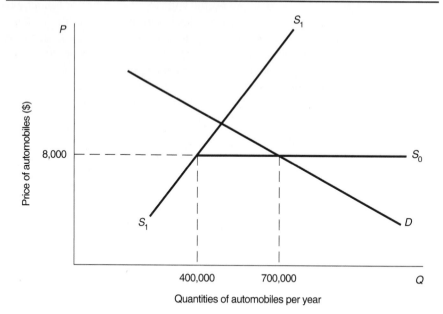

Domestic demand for autos is shown by *D*. Supply from domestic producers is S_1. With foreign imports added in, total supply to the market is S_0. At the equilibrium price of $8,000, domestic producers supply 400,000 autos, and consumers purchase 700,000 autos. The quantity of auto imports is 300,000.

Now, suppose that the government imposes a quota that limits all auto imports to 100,000. Figure 10–2 (see p. 217) shows its effects on price and the quantities of autos traded. Total supply is now determined by the domestic supply schedule S_1 plus 100,000. The quantity demanded equals the quantity supplied at point *A*; therefore, because of the quota, the price rises from $8,000 to $10,000, and the total quantity purchased by consumers falls to 580,000 autos. However, the quantity of autos supplied by domestic firms increases to 480,000.

Because of the higher price, domestic firms produce more autos, but consumers purchase fewer. Because the opportunity cost of importing the autos is less than the opportunity cost of producing them domestically, we can conclude that the quota creates economic inefficiencies. It causes domestic firms to produce too many autos, and domestic consumers to purchase too few. The new effect is a welfare loss, because the consumers, at the margin, value an auto at $10,000 whereas the cost of producing it in Japan is much less.

As noted earlier, in addition to quotas, tariffs are another form of protection to import competing firms. To compare the two alternatives, reconsider Figure 10–2, starting again from the equilibrium price of $8,000, and 700,000 autos bought and sold. A tariff of $4,000 on imports would drive a wedge between the buyer's price

▓ FIGURE 10–2 A Quota on Auto Imports

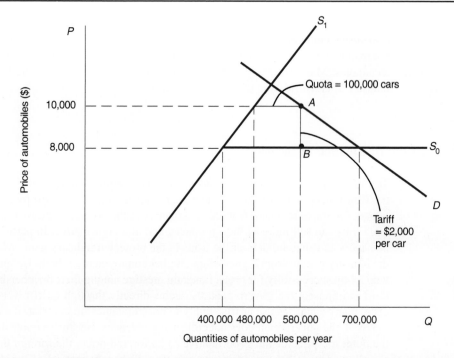

With a quota that limits imports to 100,000, total supply is limited to schedule S_1 plus 100,000. Price rises from $8,000 to $10,000, and the quantity of autos purchased falls from 700,000 to 580,000. The quantity supplied by domestic firms rises by 80,000. Notice that a quota on imported autos will result in consumers' paying more, and both domestic and foreign producers' earning more per automobile. If a tariff had been placed on imported autos rather than a quota, consumers would still pay more per auto purchased and domestic producers would earn more per auto, but foreign producers would earn less and the government would earn additional revenue. A tariff can have similar price and quantity effect. For example, a tariff of $2,000 would generate the same quantity supplied as the 100,000 quota. Price would rise to $10,000, U.S. auto suppliers would supply 480,000, and government would collect a tariff of $2,000 times 100,000 auto imports ($200 million).

of $10,000 and the foreign seller's price of $8,000. The $2,000 tariff is measured by the distance *A–B* ($10,000 to $8,000). This has the same effect on price and quantities as the 100,000 quota. Foreign suppliers supply 100,000 autos, and domestic suppliers supply 480,000. Consumers are just as poorly off with the tariff as with the quota; but the government, which now receives revenues or $2,000 times 100,000 autos or $200 million, is now better off. Clearly, foreign auto suppliers prefer quotas rather than tariffs, which is why we often see voluntary quotas being negotiated among rival trading partners. This has occurred frequently between the United States and Japan.

It is important to emphasize that higher trade barriers often generate unexpected consequences. Suppose we place a tariff on steel. If steel is used by other U.S.

industries, then these industries will incur higher costs. Protection of the steel industry hurts manufacturers of automobiles, machine tools, and farm equipment. Ironically, these industries are also threatened by foreign competition. Trade barriers also foster cumulative inefficiencies over time. If an industry is protected from international competition, it may not feel strong pressure to modernize its production techniques. Many have argued that this was a major problem with the U.S. steel industry after World War II.

Protection and the Distribution of Income

Tariffs and quotas have implications for the distribution of income within a country. Consumers of a protected product are obviously made worse off by tariffs and quotas. On the other hand, workers and owners of the protected industry are better off. Firms can sell more of their products, and at a higher price. In particular, the managers and shareholders of the firms in the protected industry gain. Workers in the industry benefit from higher wages, higher employment, or both. Union leaders who lobby successfully for protection gain prestige among their memberships. If a tariff is imposed, the government also gains directly through tariff revenues. Indeed, many countries use tariffs simply to raise revenues. In contrast, if a quota is imposed, the government does not collect any revenues. Because a quota drives up the domestic price of the good relative to its foreign price, the foreign firms that are allowed to sell the good in our country will benefit instead of the domestic government.

The voluntary export restraint agreement that the U.S. government reached with Japanese automobile producers in 1981 provides a nice illustration of all these effects. The agreement initially limited Japanese automobile sales in the United States to 1.68 million cars per year, down from the record 1.9 million units sold in 1980. With the quota on Japanese imports and recovery from the 1980–81 recession, profits of U.S. auto companies rose dramatically in 1983 and 1984. Their boards of directors awarded corporate managers huge bonuses early in 1984. In contract talks with GM later that year, the UAW negotiated only moderate wage increases but did get comprehensive job security guarantees.

There is also evidence that the quotas benefited the Japanese automobile companies. In Japan, intense competition among these companies keeps their profits low. However, under the export restraint agreement, they could each sell only a fixed number of cars to the U.S. market. This eliminated their incentives to cut prices so as to increase their market shares. Their profit margins were enhanced as a result. Japanese automobile producers also used the quotas as an opportunity to sell more expensive models in the United States—cars loaded with larger engines, air conditioners, power windows, cruise controls, and other expensive features. Everybody seemed to gain—except U.S. consumers, who wanted cheap transportation! In early 1985, President Ronald Reagan decided that the auto industry no longer required protection and suspended the restraints.

Popular Rationales for Protection

Despite the high economic costs of protection, many arguments have been made in favor of it. Although these arguments do address very real economic problems, we will see that protection is not the best policy in any of these cases.

One rationale is the *national security* argument: Protection can be used to maintain a minimum productive capacity in key industries. This makes us less vulnerable to import cutoffs in case of war, foreign export **embargoes** against us, or international price fluctuations. Protection is viewed as a sort of national insurance policy against import cutoffs. It turns out to be a very expensive policy. Although supply disruptions do occur from time to time, effective international embargoes are very rare. Even the United States has trouble making embargoes stick. In 1980 the United States suspended grain shipments to the then Soviet Union in retaliation for its invasion of Afghanistan, but the Soviets made up for their grain shortage by getting more grain from other countries.

An EMBARGO is a deliberate cutoff of supply, and is typically intended as a political statement.

The *infant-industry* argument is a second popular rationale for protection. The idea is that the government should allow emerging industries to grow in a market protected from harsh international competition. Over time, the industries can become more efficient. Their workers and managers can acquire valuable skills and experience. Their higher profits can be used to finance additional capital investments so that the industry enjoys the cost advantages of large-scale production. Interestingly, Japan has provided this sort of protection for many of its industries—such as telecommunications, computers, machine tools, and electronics—and several have become great success stories. Nevertheless, infant-industry protection can be justified on economic grounds only if there is some sort of market failure in the industry. For example, if entrepreneurs cannot convince lenders to provide funds for investments, even if there is long-run profit potential in the industry, there may be a basis for government assistance. Even so, protection is not the best policy.

Both the national security and infant-industry problems can be addressed more efficiently by providing direct subsidies to industries than by imposing trade barriers. These two problems require only that domestic production of a good be increased. Protection stimulates domestic production but lowers domestic consumption. Consumers are needlessly penalized. In contrast, a subsidy boosts production in the industry but does not lower consumption at all. Even with the budgetary costs added in, a subsidy is much less expensive to the economy overall. However, subsidies are not necessarily efficient remedies either and often are awarded for political rather than economic reasons. European governments provide massive subsidies to many of their basic industries at a far higher economic cost than can be justified by the economic benefits.

A third rationale for protection is the *employment* argument. Protection maintains employment levels in industries threatened by foreign imports, or at least allows workers in those industries to adjust more gradually to foreign competition. Even in this case, protection is an inefficient way to provide assistance. First, it probably costs more jobs in the long run in potential export industries than it saves in import-competing industries. In the long run, foreigners can afford to buy from us only an amount of goods and services that is equal in value to the goods and services they sell to us. If we cut back on our imports, then output and employment in our export industries will eventually have to fall, as well. Second, protection does not encourage workers and firms to adjust to the new realities of foreign competition. Clearly, such adjustment entails very real social and economic costs. Many workers who lose their jobs because of foreign imports are out of work a long time. Some must move their families to new parts of the country or get new job training. Nevertheless, protection inhibits this necessary adjustment—at a very high cost to the rest of us. It would actually be less costly to give the workers direct subsidies for moving and retraining. Trade adjustment assistance policies have been tried for this purpose in the United States, but have had many practical problems of their own.

Lastly, there is a fourth argument for protection (ambiguous, but based on cultural reasoning of recent vintage). The French and some other European commissioners of televised entertainment were insisting in 1995 that at least half of television entertainment in EU countries should be made in Europe. Cultural deprivation is the argument, and Hollywood (they say) is the source of the cultural decline. By this argument, freedom to choose has a damaging effect, and in fact, in 1994, 18 million viewers in Britain, France, Germany, Spain, and Italy watched *Baywatch* each week. Soaps one, Bach one-half.

Political Advantages of Protection

Why are trade barriers used so much more than other policies? Most of the answers are related to our political processes:

- **Direct subsidies require government expenditures, which readily attract the attention of critics.**

It is appropriate for these expenditures to be scrutinized by an informed public. However, the costs of trade barriers are not as obvious to the public as are the budgetary costs and fairness problems of subsidies. Trade barriers with effects more disguised to the general public, thus have a much better chance for enactment.

- **Trade barriers can be presented with an "us against the world" flavor in order to gain public support.**

In the U.S. Congress, one advocate of trade barriers has compared the flood of Japanese exports in the 1980s to the Japanese attack on Pearl Harbor in 1941.[2]

- **Trade policies seem more consistent with free-market attitudes held strongly in the United States.**

Direct forms of assistance, such as subsidies, appear to intrude much more deeply into the workings of our markets, even though they do not hurt consumers the way trade barriers do.

For rather different reasons, industries seeking protection generally prefer quotas (or voluntary export restraints) to tariffs: The price and sales effects are more disguised.

- **Tariffs are taxes on foreign importers; quotas generate extra profits for foreign importers.**

Tariffs are much more likely to trigger foreign retaliation. Voluntary export restraints are viewed as best of all, because they are imposed with the consent of the foreign government.

- **The effects of tariffs on prices are easily calculated (quotas affect prices indirectly).**

Quotas drive up prices just as tariffs do, but the price increases do not have to be officially announced. Quotas would thus be better for public relations.

- **If the world price of a commodity is highly volatile, a quota provides more reliable protection.**

If the world price of a good drops, a quota will limit the amount of foreign imports allowed in the country, thus holding the domestic price stable. On the other hand, even though a tariff keeps the domestic price of a good higher than the world price, if the world price falls sharply, the domestic price will drop too. The sugar market provides a nice example of this problem. U.S. quotas on sugar imports expired in 1974, though tariffs on sugar were retained. Shortly afterward, sugar prices plummeted around the world. So did U.S. sugar prices, even with the tariffs in effect. Within two years Congress installed a new set of trade barriers to protect sugar growers.

Lobbying for Protection

There is a final way to explain the prevalence of protectionist policies that are harmful to our national economic welfare. The explanation is ingeniously simple. It applies the economic analysis of public goods to our political process.

Think of the typical fight over protection of an industry as being waged by two opposing interest groups. The firms and unions of the industry make up a special

---

[2]Tom Redburn, "Trade Bomb Ticking for U.S., Japan," *Los Angeles Times,* January 16, 1983.

interest group that seeks protection; consumer groups and others represent the national interest. Which of these groups is best able to organize itself to lobby Congress?

The analysis in Chapter 9 of the free-rider problem suggests that the special interests will win most of the time. The basic idea is that all members of an interest group stand to benefit from a successful lobbying effort made on behalf of the group. Specifically, getting favorable treatment from Congress is a public good for the group. Anyone lobbying for protection will bear the full costs in time and money of that effort but cannot exclude others from enjoying the benefits. Therefore, nobody will be willing to lobby for legislation. Everyone wants to enjoy the benefits as a free rider—and to let someone else bear the costs of the effort.

To overcome this problem, a group must find a way to coerce each of its members to contribute to the lobbying effort. It is easiest to organize interest groups with few members, such as the firms and labor unions in a highly concentrated industry. Each member has a major stake in the success of the group as a whole. The temptation to be a free rider exists, but it is minimized. Of course, many of the industries that have sought protection have simply been around a long time and are thus more influential in Congress than are newer industries. Some are also concentrated geographically, which allows them to put strong pressure on a few key legislators from their areas. On the other hand, consumer groups usually consist of lots of members who each have very small stakes in the outcome. It is much harder to organize these diffuse groups in order to overcome the free-rider problem. In the battle for government action, the special interest group has the edge.

CHAPTER REVIEW

Countries gain from international trade because it allows them to produce on the basis of comparative advantage. This means that they should export the products for which they have a relatively low opportunity cost in comparison with other countries. The amount of benefits that any country gets from international trade depends on the prices of its exports relative to its imports. These terms of trade are determined by demand and supply conditions in world markets.

Despite the advantages of free trade, a vast number of restrictions have been imposed on international trade around the world. Tariffs, quotas, and other direct and indirect barriers to trade are used to protect industries from foreign competition. There are several economic rationales for such protection—the national security, infant-industry, and employment arguments—but from an economic standpoint there are better policies in each case.

Trade barriers have political advantages, however, over these superior policies. Moreover, pressures for protection and other benefits for special interest groups are very strong in political democracies because of the free-rider problem. Special interest groups with small numbers of members tend to be very successful lobbyists, to the detriment of the overall national interest.

✒ MULTIPLE-CHOICE SELF-TEST ✒ ✒ ✒ ✒ ✒ ✒ ✒ ✒ ✒ ✒ ✒ ✒ ✒ ✒ ✒ ✒

1. Suppose that California and Wisconsin each produce wine and cheese. Making a bottle of wine costs $3 in California but $12 in Wisconsin. On the other hand, making a pound of cheese costs $4 in California and $8 in Wisconsin. Under these conditions:

   a. California has a comparative advantage in production of both wine and cheese.

   b. California has a comparative advantage in production of wine, but Wisconsin has a comparative advantage in production of cheese.

   c. California has a comparative advantage in production of cheese, but Wisconsin has a comparative advantage in production of wine.

   d. Neither state has a comparative advantage in either industry.

2. If Japan has a comparative advantage in steel relative to the United States, then we should expect that:

   a. Japan will export steel to the United States *and* the United States will export steel to Japan.

   b. The United States will export steel to Japan.

   c. Japan will export steel to the United States.

   d. The given information is insufficient to determine the pattern of trade.

3. Which one of the following is *not* a form of protection, either obvious or disguised?

   a. Imposition of a tariff on foreign motorcycle imports.

   b. A large subsidy to domestic automobile producers.

   c. The easing of pollution standards for the domestic steel industry.

   d. Reducing corporate income taxes.

4. The idea that import protection can lessen a country's vulnerability to foreign export embargoes is known as:

   a. The *infant-industry argument.*

   b. The *national security argument.*

   c. The *employment argument.*

   d. The *unfair trade practice argument.*

5. Suppose that Japan could produce all goods more efficiently than the United States could. Then trade between Japan and the United States:

   a. Would benefit Japan but not the United States.

   b. Would result in the United States' buying many things from Japan but Japan's buying nothing from the United States.

   c. Both of the above are true.

   d. None of the above are true.

𝒥ℛ STUDY QUESTIONS

1. Suppose that England and Portugal satisfy the assumptions of the Ricardian model of international trade and that the hours of labor required to produce one unit of wine or cloth in the two countries are as follows:

	Wine	Cloth
In England	4	2
In Portugal	2	8

 a. Which country has a comparative advantage in cloth production? In wine production? Explain.
 b. If trade begins between the two countries, which would export cloth? Which would export wine?
 c. Suppose that there would be excess demand for wine and excess supply of cloth if each country specialized exclusively in production of the good in which it had a comparative advantage. Which country will have to produce both goods? Explain.

2. Table 10–1 shows that English workers can produce both wine and cloth in less time than can Portuguese workers. Could England ever have a comparative advantage in *both* goods? Explain.

3. Describe the "infant-industry" argument for protection. Why is a trade barrier not the best policy in this case? What is the best policy?

4. Industries that seek protection from foreign imports often seem to favor quotas over tariffs. Why?

𝒥ℛ PROBLEMS

1. Suppose that India and China both produce corn and rice, with the opportunity cost of 1 ton of rice being 2 tons of corn in India and 5 tons of corn in China. Before the opening of trade, the two countries produced the following amounts:

	India	China	Total
Corn	20 tons	50 tons	70 tons
Rice	100 tons	200 tons	300 tons

 a. If India gave up producing corn and switched all its resources to producing rice, how much rice could it produce? If China produced 25 tons more corn, how much rice would it have to give up? Draw up a new production table. What would happen to the total output produced by the two countries together?

b. Having specialized their production in order to trade, the two countries begin to trade. The terms of trade between rice and corn must lie somewhere between the ratios at which each country is able to produce the two—that is, 1 ton of rice for 2 tons of corn and 1 ton of rice for 5 tons of corn. Suppose that the trading rate settles at 1 ton of rice for 4 tons of corn, and India wants to buy exactly the same amount of corn that it used to produce, that is, 20 tons. Draw up a new table showing what each country will be able to consume because of specialization and trade. What do you notice about each country's total consumption *with* trade, as opposed to what each was able to produce and consume *without* trade?

2. Evaluate the following argument: "When the United States has international political disagreements with nations like South Africa, North Korea, or China, it is counterproductive to impose sanctions and cut off trading relations with the offending nation. Our interest, and indeed our long-term goals of fostering peace, democracy, and human rights, would be much better served if, instead, we did everything in our power to increase trade."

3. Suppose that, in exasperation over never-ending trade negotiations, the United States unilaterally removes *all* barriers to trade with Japan—all tariffs, all duties, all quotas, all reciprocal agreements—and declares all our markets open to Japanese products, regardless of whether or not the Japanese follow suit. Analyze the market for a specific product—Toyotas, for example—and predict the impact of such a unilateral declaration. Consider both short- and long-term effects and consequences for both the individual businessperson and the economy as a whole. Follow the chain of cause and effect as far as you can.

What's the stock market going to do? This question frequently confronts economists. They are also asked to forecast economic trends. But, in fact, most economists actually devote little time to forecasting. Nevertheless, they do enjoy trying to spot a trend or predict a turning point. Some put a few dollars into the stock market to test their savvy as forecasters. A few are even successful—John Maynard Keynes, an influential British economist, turned the modest endowment of Queens College Cambridge into a fortune by playing the stock market.

Answering the question, What's the stock market going to do? is complex because it requires knowledge of economics and of other disciplines—statistics, political science, sociology, meteorology, and psychology, to name a few. However, economists do deal with the heart of the question: What are the important national trends in the economy? Economists are concerned with understanding trends in output growth, unemployment, inflation, federal government budget policies, interest rates, taxes, industrial production, trade flows, and the like.

You are now embarking on a study of the part of economics that deals with the issues of output growth, unemployment, inflation, recession, and the trade balance. We shall describe and analyze federal government budget policies—spending, taxing, and deficits—and policies of the U.S. Federal Reserve System (the Fed), which is America's central bank. We will also discuss nonbudget government policies that influence the economy—industrial policy, technology policy, and managed trade policy. This part of the text will explore the study of economics in the large—macroeconomics.

Some of the material is quite controversial and generates heated political and theoretical debates—the appropriate level of defense spending, the impact of federal tax decisions, the influence of the Federal Reserve on interest rates, and the consequences of managed trade. When we come to such topics, we will explain the principal alternative views and analyze each. This approach will best equip you to critically evaluate from your own personal perspective national policy actions, economic trends, and the ideas of economists who hold different points of view—Keynesians, monetarists, neoclassicists, and supply siders.

A major theme in our discussion of microeconomics dealt with the role of relative prices in competitive markets. Prices in competitive markets lead private individuals and firms, operating in their own self-interest, to choose personally and socially constructive alternatives. We emphasized the ability, but not necessarily the will, of our political system to foster competitive behavior. Here, in macroeconomics, we see the government in a somewhat different light. Again a major theme is the ability of government, whether through its budget and nonbudget policies or through central bank policy, to constructively set a stable environment in which competitive markets can function efficiently to advance both private and social well-being.

As in Part I, we're not going to burden you with number crunching and technique grinding, though some is unavoidable. If you decide to really get down and grapple with economic model building and technique, you'll want to go on to a more advanced course later. Still, some ideas that you will study here are subtle and difficult. We hope that we have made them palatable for you.

CHAPTER 11

National Economic Problems

Stagnation, Inflation, Unemployment, and Competitiveness

🎵 CHAPTER PREVIEW

Two weeks into the semester, Antonio Buscaglia received an urgent message from his mother. She said that the General Dynamics missile design company back home had laid off 250 men and women and that Tony's father was among them. As a result, his family could no longer afford Tony's schooling. He would have to find a full-time job until his father was rehired. Although Tony had not especially liked classes, he knew that college held the key to a brighter future—perhaps even a future without layoffs.

Robin Westerfield had studied at City Junior College for two years and earned her degree in business economics. She had planned to open her own video games emporium ever since learning to model such games in her college computer class. Robin had earned an A– average, majoring in accounting and financial management. With the help of a $6,000 annual loan package from Imperial Valley Bank, she was able to open her store on Myrtle Street in Eugene, Oregon. Two years after opening, Robin's "Video Selections" company fell on hard times. Her new business was one of many companies staggering from the pressure of low-cost, high-tech games pouring out of Nintendo and offered at prices below Robin's costs. She struggled to bring in enough revenue to pay off her bank loan.

The Beaumont family dream had always been to send son Stanley to Duke University to study and play basketball for the Blue Devils. In 1996 Stanley was a B+ student and a 6-foot, 3-inch power forward with all-city honors from Damien

High School. Although Stanley was good enough to be eligible for a partial scholarship, his parents had known for some time that they would have to pay at least half his tuition and living expenses. Stanley's father and mother both worked, she as a grade school teacher and he as manager of the local Kmart in South Central Los Angeles. As early as 1985, they agreed to set aside Mrs. Beaumont's earnings to pay for college; her paychecks were deposited directly into a stock market fund. By 1996 the Beaumonts had accumulated enough resources to allow Stanley to afford Duke.

Economic growth during the late 1980s and middle 1990s, during which the stock market Dow Jones average increased from less than 3,000 to well over 7,000, generated growth in the family stock portfolio. Their savings plus earnings constituted the needed nest egg. Had a serious economic slowdown occurred or had the stock market collapsed before they withdrew the funds, the story might not have ended so happily.

Tony, Robin, Stanley, and their families share a common fate. Their economic situations partly reflect the results of national and international economic forces largely beyond their control. Though you may be bright, hardworking, and thrifty, outside economic forces may disrupt your life, causing unemployment, lost opportunities, and business failure. Conversely, seemingly unexpected windfalls can come your way. The bet-

ter you understand national trends, the better you can accommodate them in your plans.

1. Why is inflation a problem?
2. Can the government guarantee full employment?
3. What happened to productivity growth after the early 1970s?

𝒥𝒽 CONCEPTS REINTRODUCED

Law of Demand 51
Production Possibilities Curve (PPC) 29

𝒥𝒽 NEW CONCEPTS

Macroeconomics
Stagflation
Gross Domestic Product (GDP)
Real GDP
GDP Deflator
Nominal GDP
Inflation
Consumer Price Index (CPI)
Unemployment
Unemployment Compensation
Exports
Imports
Trade Balance
Labor Productivity

𝕵 CHAPTER OBJECTIVES

After studying this chapter, you should be able to:

1. Understand and define gross domestic product (GDP).
2. List some of the consequences of inflation.
3. Find the *real* dollar value of GDP and your personal earnings by using either the consumer price index (CPI) or the GDP deflator.
4. List some of the social problems caused by unemployment.
5. Use productivity figures to compare competitiveness between two countries.
6. Link growth in productivity to increases in living standards.

THE NATURE OF MACROECONOMICS

Macroeconomics studies broad trends in the economy, trends that are so widespread and general that their influence cuts across the various markets, regions, and sectors of our country. Because trends in growth, inflation, productivity, and unemployment affect so many parts of the economy, they are difficult to study in the same way that one individual market is studied.

A great many forces that influence our personal economic well-being originate at the national and even international levels. The large-scale economic forces—inflation, shifts in market pressures across international boundaries, changes in stock market valuations of industries, and advances in technology—are always felt locally and personally, but are most often caused at a macroeconomic level. In order to prepare yourself to deal effectively with these forces, you will want to have a broad understanding of how these macroeconomic systems work. For this reason, we are now turning to the study of the economic system from a distance rather than focus in on individual economic units, such as individuals, households, and firms. A better understanding of macroeconomic forces, fluctuations, cycles, and trends will empower you to become a proactive player in the marketplace rather than a helpless victim being driven by the winds of economic change.

Therefore, our perspective will now shift from emphasis on individual markets to the performance of the total national economy. Our focus moves from the family unit or the typical firm to all consumers as a group and to the entire business sector. In considering taxes, for example, attention is not directed toward specific taxes, such as a sales tax, but toward total taxes imposed on consumers and businesses. As another example, instead of studying supply and demand for one good, we will think about supply and demand for all goods combined into one total.

𝕵 𝕵

MACROECONOMICS focuses on the sum total of economic activity,
dealing with the issues of growth, inflation, unemployment, and productivity
and with national and international economic policies relating to these issues.

If you think of microeconomics as looking closely at each individual tree in the forest, then you can think of macroeconomics (or "macro," for short) as standing back and looking at the entire forest itself. Macro examines four big problem areas:

1. Stagnation—slow output growth or no output growth.
2. Inflation—widespread rising prices.
3. Unemployment—workers unable to find jobs and more generally idle resources.
4. Competitiveness—productive efficiency across countries.

Sometimes the economy suffers from all of these problems at once. This state of affairs is called **stagflation.**

In the next 10 chapters you will learn about these four big problem areas. We shall begin in this first macroeconomics chapter by identifying and evaluating several key economic indicators that are designed to inform us about some aspect of these dimensions of the economy. We shall look at an important measure of national production as an indicator of the level of living standards for the nation as a whole. We shall see how this measure has evolved over time.

We will also study measures of the cost of living, as indicted by inflation. In later chapters we shall study the forces that pressure the economy and make it more susceptible to inflation. These include pressures in product markets across the economy to demand more than can be produced and pressures in labor markets to push up input costs beyond their current productive efficiency.

We shall assess various magnitudes that indicate how well the labor market is working and, finally, in this chapter we shall look at indicators of relative economic efficiency among nations and over time. We will then link efficiency to incomes and wages in order to look at the implications for improvements in U.S. living standards.

FOUR BIG QUESTIONS OF MACROECONOMICS

As we noted above, the four basic questions to be considered each relate to one of the problem areas of macroeconomics:

1. What determines the output growth rate of an economy?
2. What happens when more is demanded from the economy than it is capable of producing?
3. Why are resources sometimes idle?
4. How can U.S. workers and firms compete in international markets?

The production possibilities curve (PPC) in Chapter 2 is helpful in illustrating these four basic questions. This will take up the rest of this section. Recall that the PPC encompasses all possible combinations of goods and services that the economy is capable of producing. When on its PPC, the economy is assumed to employ all of its resources efficiently and to incorporate the most appropriate technology.

The PPC discussion was developed in Chapter 2 to illustrate the concept of scarcity. The curve depicts various alternative combinations of the thousands of goods and services—stealth bombers, tennis shoes, strawberries, Chevrolets, or chicken soup—that the economy is capable of producing. Graphically, these thousands of products are represented by all combinations of two goods: food and shelter. (It may be helpful to return to Chapter 2 and review development of the production possibilities curve, because we now plan to use this tool of analysis to study the macroeconomic system.)

Figure 11–1 shows that the PPC for 1997 is a bowed curve that connects the axes for food and shelter. Each point on the PPC, such as point *A,* represents a pairing of food and shelter that the economy is capable of producing. If the economy were actually producing at point *A,* then it would be producing 500 billion bushels (F_a) of food and 150 million houses (G_a).

Figure 11–1 illustrates the first macro question: What determines the rate of growth of the economy? This question actually has two parts. In Figure 11–1, the 2000 PPC is above and beyond that for 1997. This indicates that the *potential* for production increases over the years. Such an increase in capacity is expected to occur over time, because the number of workers increases with population growth, because new machines and factories are added over the course of a few years, and because new technology and business methods develop. For growth to be *realized,* however, the economy must actually produce more, not just have the potential to produce more. Thus, as the PPC moves outward from 1997 to 2000, the economy must move out from point *A* to some point on the new PPC for 2000, such as point *B* in our illustration.

But what determines the level of economic production? What affects the extent to which the 2000 PPC will be beyond the 1997 curve? Could the PPC actually move inward instead of outward? Can policy measures be used to alter how fast the PPC expands? These questions are all related to the fundamental question: What determines the growth rate of output?

Figure 11–2 illustrates the second question: What happens when more is demanded from the economy than it is capable of producing? The country, in this example, is pressing to buy more food and more shelter simultaneously. We are trying to push beyond our capacity, which is represented by the production possibilities curve. In the aggregate, demand is pushing beyond the capacity of the economy. Thus, the macro question illustrated by Figure 11–2 is this: What happens if we demand too much?

Chapter 2 mentioned an important historical example of too much demand pressure in the aggregate economy. In 1965 President Lyndon Baines Johnson advocated increased Vietnam War spending, along with many new costly social programs, while the economy was already on the PPC surface. By definition, the PPC cannot bulge out, as it seems to do in Figure 11–2. The economy, therefore, will face too much demand in many markets and insufficient capacity to meet that demand. When demand rises and production cannot expand, then prices and costs must rise. Too many dollars chase too few goods, and when this situation prevails throughout the entire economy, prices increase. This is called *inflation.* Some countries have had particularly severe episodes of too many dollars chasing too few goods. In 1996 and 1997, for instance, the Bulgarian economy was driven into collapse and political chaos by inflation in excess of 100 percent per month. Inflation, when occurring at such extreme rates, is called

FIGURE 11–1   How Much Growth?

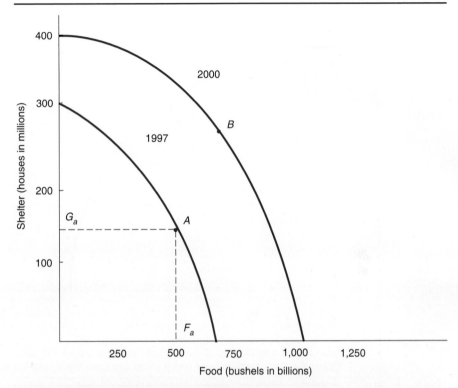

The 2000 production possibilities curve (PPC), representing the productive potential of the economy in 2000, lies beyond the 1997 PPC at point *A*. Potential output increases because of increases in manpower, capital, and improved technology. The economy must actually move out to the new PPC, for example, to point *B*, to realize growth. Thus, growth requires both the potential for improvement and its realization.

hyperinflation, and it often results in the collapse of the economic order, the destruction of people's savings, and often the collapse of the government. What are the consequences of various levels of inflation? Can we avoid it?

Figure 11–3 illustrates the third question of macro: Why are resources sometimes idle? The country in this example is producing at point *A*, inside its PPC. Because the economy has the capacity to produce along the frontier at points like *B*, *C*, or *D*, where it could be producing both more food and more shelter, production at point *A* is inefficient and wasteful. Why would any society allow itself to produce at an inefficient point?

An unpleasant fact of life is frequent nationwide and even worldwide slowdowns in production in which workers, machines, factories, and farms are idle. Why can't such slowdowns in the pace of economic activity be avoided? What are the costs of producing at points like *A*? These questions are related to the issue of idle resources.

FIGURE 11–2   What If Demand Exceeds Capacity?

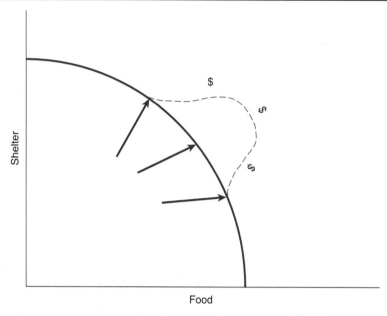

Here, the society is trying to expand beyond its PPC by demanding more food and more shelter than the economy can produce. Because the PPC cannot bulge out, the economy lacks the capacity to produce more of both food and shelter. Pressure from too much demand in many markets will drive up prices and costs throughout the economy.

U.S. competitiveness—say, vis-à-vis Japan and Germany—is important, but it is trickier to illustrate with the PPC diagram. First, in order to compare two countries, we need two PPC figures, one for each country. Second, the total potential of each country is not really relevant because one economy could be bigger but less efficient and less competitive than another. Russia, for example, is larger than Taiwan, but workers in Taiwan are more productive and thus enjoy a much higher living standard. We can correct for size by comparing the output level *per worker.* This is called *labor productivity.* Third, in comparing the competitiveness of two economies, we can consider both the levels of productivity (i.e., Which country produces more output per worker?) and the growth rate of productivity (i.e., Is one's growth rate outpacing the other?).

FOUR INDICATORS OF ECONOMIC HEALTH

A doctor who wants to evaluate your health measures several key indicators of your body's performance. The doctor may take your temperature, your pulse rate, and your blood pressure. When business executives, government officials, and other

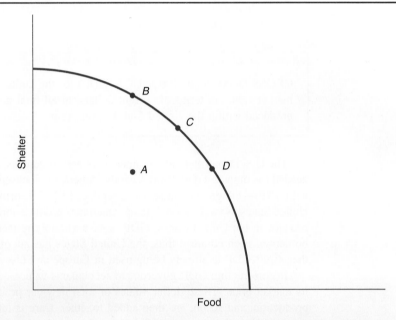

FIGURE 11–3   Why Are Resources Idle?

Here, the society is producing inside its PPC at *A*, thus wasting productive resources. It has capacity to operate along points *B, C,* and *D.* The result is idle capital and unemployment.

analysts wish to evaluate the economy's overall performance, they start with these four indicators:

1. Gross domestic product (GDP)
2. Consumer price index (CPI)
3. The unemployment rate
4. Labor productivity

These measures are the most frequently used indicators of economic performance. Each one is an important signal of some aspect of our economic well-being.

Growth and GDP

An economy's growth rate is an important gauge of its health. When an economy fails to grow, it is said to be *stagnant.* Stagnation can be a serious problem, because standards of living are not rising, and this can create significant social and political stresses. The basic measure of the economy's provision of new goods and services is **gross domestic product (GDP).** All final goods and services produced are included in GDP, ranging from new cars, blast furnaces, and oranges to college educations, restaurant meals, and attendance at professional sports events. If economists were forced to choose only one measure to indicate economic performance, they probably would choose GDP.

GROSS DOMESTIC PRODUCT (GDP) for the United States is the total market value, in terms of current dollars, of all final goods and services produced within the United States in one year.

The U.S. Department of Commerce collects, organizes, and analyzes all the data needed to compute GDP. Until recently, Americans focused on gross national product (GNP)—the goods and services produced by U.S. firms inside and outside the United States. Now, however, many Americans produce abroad and many foreigners produce in the United States. GDP more accurately reflects production within the borders of each country; thus, the United States has adopted the term *GDP* rather than *GNP*. GDP is already being used in Europe and elsewhere.

In constructing GDP, government accountants value one unit of each product by its market price. These dollar values of total new-car production, total hamburger production, and so on, are then added together. Care is taken not to count certain goods, such as the cotton used in current shirt production, because such products are *intermediate* to the production of final goods, and their worth will be included in the value of the shirt. Thus, the accountants avoid *double-counting* products. The final sum is total GDP measured in current dollars for the year in question.

Valuing different goods by their market prices enables measurement of all goods and services in the same units: current dollars. These dollar units are not chosen arbitrarily. In fact, in a market economy, the dollar price of one product relative to another reflects the relative cost of producing and buying that product. For example, if a new car sells for $12,000 and a new video recorder sells for $1,000, then the cost of a car is 12 times the cost of a video recorder. In its contribution to total GDP, then, 1 car is worth 12 video recorders, and the ratio 12 to 1 reflects the relative costs of the two products.

In a competitive market economy, these relative prices also reflect the values to consumers, who have expressed their preferences with their dollar "votes." Therefore, the different prices assigned to various products in constructing GDP reflect the relative importance assigned to these products by that society's dollar voters. As we shall see, this measure is flawed when we leave out important social costs such as environmental degradation and when certain social goods, such as clean, potable water, are ignored.

U.S. GDP in 1996 was $7,576,800,000,000.00, or roughly $7.58 trillion. After-tax personal income had reached an average of $21,040 per person.

Real GDP

GDP can be used to compare the performance of the U.S. economy over time. Consider, for example, the two years 1990 and 1991. GDP was $5,743.8 billion in 1990 and $5,916.7 billion in 1991, for a net increase of $172.9 billion. However, a

TABLE 11–1 GDP Measured in Current Dollars and Corrected for Inflation

Year	(1) Nominal GDP (current $ in billions)	(2) GDP Deflator (1992 = 100)	(3) Real GDP (1992 $ in billions)
1987	$4,692.3	83.1	$5,648.4
1990	5,743.8	93.6	6,138.7
1991	5,916.7	97.3	6,079.0
1992	6,244.4	100.0	6,244.4
1996	7,576.0	109.7	6,906.8

It is important to correct GDP figures for inflation before making comparisons among years. Column 1 is GDP measured in each year's current prices. Column 2 is the GDP deflator for each year relative to the base year 1992, which is set equal to 100. The 109.7 deflator for 1995 indicates that prices rose between 1992 and 1996 by 9.7 percent. The smaller deflator for 1987 indicates that prices were lower in 1987 than in 1992. Correcting for this difference in units, column 3 gives real GDP, which is measured in constant 1992 prices. Notice that *real* GDP fell by $59.7 billion from 1990 to 1991.

Real GDP is calculated as follows:

$$\text{Real GDP} = 100 \times \text{nominal GDP} \div \text{GDP deflator}$$

Source: Joint Economic Committee, *Economic Indicators* (Washington, D.C.: U.S. Government Printing Office, May 1997).

conclusion that the real domestic product increased by $172.9 billion would be a grave error. The error would be in ignoring the fact that the measurement units of GDP changed from 1990 to 1991. How can this be? Is GDP not measured in dollars each year? Yes, but 1991 U.S. dollars differ in value from 1990 U.S. dollars.

After a year of inflation, a 1991 dollar could buy fewer goods than could a 1990 dollar. In order to compare GDP figures over time, we must correct for inflation so that the GDP figures are all measured in the same units: constant dollars. The result is called **real GDP.** To measure real GDP, the Commerce Department publishes estimates of the percentage increase in the average price of products in GDP over a certain base year. The department now uses 1992 as the base year. This measure is called the **GDP deflator.** GDP measured in current prices is called **nominal GDP.** Nominal GDP figures for 1990 and 1991, along with the GDP deflators and real GDP, are presented in Table 11–1.

To deflate the nominal GDP figures, we merely divide GDP by each year's deflator and multiply by 100. The result is GDP measured in constant 1992 dollars. These real GDP figures appear in column 3 of Table 11–1.

Using the constant-dollar GDP figures in column 3, the performance of the U.S. economy from 1990 to 1991 can be sensibly compared. GDP fell from 1990 to 1991 by $59.7 billion in 1992 dollars. This indicates that rather than an average yearly gain of 3.0 percent, the economy from 1990 to 1991 actually declined by 0.97 percent. This conclusion contrasts sharply with the faulty conclusion drawn from uncorrected nominal GDP figures.

Although GDP is an invaluable indicator of economic activity, it can be overemphasized. GDP does not measure our total well-being. A country's well-being also depends on intangibles such as serenity and happiness, not counted in GDP. GDP also does not include a value for unpaid labor such as housework; nor does it include goods produced and marketed illegally, such as illicit drugs. Further, GDP does not measure the value of leisure time, safety in the workplace, or the polluting side effects of industrial production. GDP includes some products, such as nuclear bombs and hand guns, which many people think are "bad."

Inflation and the Consumer Price Index

High rates of **inflation** are rapid increases in the general level of prices, and they usually indicate that an economy is in trouble. Inflation was a stubborn problem for many countries in the 1970s, and the United States was no exception. While the U.S. inflation rates were modest by world standards, they were high by our own historical standards. In the 1950s and early 1960s prices rose at rates of 1 to 3 percent a year. In the late 1970s prices were rising at annual rates of 7 to 13 percent a year.

INFLATION is an increase in the overall level of prices over an extended period of time.

Historically, as noted earlier, rapid, out-of-control inflations, or hyperinflations, take place during wars and periods of severe political instability. The collapse of the Confederacy at the end of the Civil War was accompanied by hyperinflation, with rates running up to 250 percent per month. Political unrest in Germany after World War I brought with it a hyperinflation. Poland suffered severe inflation in the late 1980s, at 50 percent rates on a monthly basis, before the Solidarity government that replaced the communist regime was able to reform national economic policies. Much of Latin America in 1989 was in dire straits. The annual inflation rate in Peru reached 30,000 percent as radical terrorism shook urban centers. Argentina faced widespread rioting and death as inflation hit 200 percent in one month. Venezuela and Brazil also suffered severe instability because of hyperinflations.

Inflation Disrupts Economic Behavior

Inflation is a key indicator of economic performance. When an economy is incurring inflation, this indicates trouble in the underlying economic and political systems. Inflation, by itself, can do damage to the performance of the aspects of the economy. This damage reflects the fact that inflation usually obscures the underlying system of relative prices on which microeconomic decisions, as analyzed in Chapters 1 through 10, are based.

First, inflation erodes the value of currency: When the prices of goods and services that everybody buys are all going up, the purchasing power of the currency is declining. In other words, inflation is, by definition, depreciation of money. When inflation increases *unexpectedly,* then savings held in banks and savings institutions decline in *real* value. Unexpected inflation can destroy the buying power of savings, discouraging thrift. This problem is much less severe when inflation is *expected.*

Second, inflation tends to obscure the relative costs of different goods and services. Remember that relative prices of different goods are the signals from the marketplace telling buyers and sellers the relative costs of goods. If the price of apples rises relative to the price of oranges, then some consumers substitute oranges for apples. However, if the price of apples rises 20 percent, does this reflect inflation, or does it reflect an increase in the relative costs of apples to oranges? Confusion about price signals makes informed decisions difficult.

Third, inflation raises the effective burden of taxes on personal incomes and on business incomes. Effective tax burdens on families rise because inflation places families in tax brackets with higher tax rates. This tendency, called bracket creep, results from the progressive nature of our income tax system. In 1986 the personal income tax system started to be *indexed* so that the real tax burden would remain the same after inflation. In 1986 Congress replaced the system of 15 tax brackets with a system having only 3 tax brackets, then President Clinton in the early 1990s added 2 more brackets at the top end.

The most frequently cited indicator of inflation is the **consumer price index (CPI).** Thus, the CPI indicates the effect of inflation on consumer budgets. Detailed CPIs are also published for certain categories of goods, such as food, housing, and energy, as well as for different regions of the country and even for several major cities, such as Los Angeles, Chicago, and New York.

The CONSUMER PRICE INDEX (CPI) measures the average price paid for a market basket of goods and services for a typical U.S. consumer in comparison to the average price paid for the same basket in an earlier base period.

In constructing the CPI, the Bureau of Labor Statistics (BLS) selects a bundle of goods that are assumed to be in the shopping basket, so to speak, of the typical American consumer. The basket may contain a dozen eggs, one pair of tennis shoes, five loads of laundry, two movie tickets, 15 gallons of gasoline, and so forth. BLS arbitrarily sets the average value of the products in the basket for some base period, currently 1982–1984, equal to 100. In 1985–1989 the prices of the items in the basket had risen by 24 percent. Thus, BLS computed the 1985 CPI value to be 124.0.

By 1995 the average price of the goods in the market basket had increased over the early 1980s level by 50 percent, so that the 1996 CPI had reached 156.9.

TABLE 11–2   Inflation: Percentage Increases in the CPI, 1960–1995

Years	(1) Average Annual Inflation Rate (percent)	Year	(2) Average Annual Inflation Rate (percent)
1960–1964	1.3	1980	13.5
1965–1969	3.5	1982	6.2
1970–1974	6.1	1984	4.3
1975–1979	8.1	1987	3.6
1980–1984	7.5	1990	5.4
1985–1989	3.6	1993	3.0
1990–1994	3.5	1996	3.3

Column 1 illustrates the accelerating nature of U.S. inflation from 1960 to 1979 and the deceleration that began in 1980. Column 2 shows that inflation has declined after 1980 except in 1990.

Sources: *The Economic Report of the President* (Washington, D.C.: U.S. Government Printing Office, February 1995); and Joint Economic Committee, *Economic Indicators* (Washington, D.C.: U.S. Government Printing Office, May 1997).

Had your after-tax income in the early eighties, been $10,000, then your after-tax income by 1996 would have to have risen to $15,690 for you to have had the same purchasing power as before.

Some Inflation Experience

Table 11–2 presents the average yearly inflation rate figures, using the CPI, over five-year intervals for 1960 to 1994 and selected yearly rates from 1980 to 1996. The figures in column 1 show that inflation was accelerating from the early 1960s to the late 1970s. In the first five-year interval, 1960–1964, prices rose at 1.3 percent a year. Then prices started to rise at 3.5 percent a year, and by 1980 prices were rising at over 10 percent a year.

The consequences of inflation, such as reducing the purchasing power of incomes, discouraging thrift, distorting price signals, and raising effective tax burdens, created political pressures in the 1970s to slow inflation. We can see in column 2 that the rate of inflation fell from 13.5 percent in 1980 to 3.6 percent in 1987. Thus, although prices were still rising in 1987, they were doing so at a much slower pace.

A Warning about the CPI

Don't take CPI figures as indisputable, because the CPI tends to overstate inflation. It prices a fixed bundle of goods and thus ignores consumer substitution toward cheaper goods as prices rise unevenly. Many experts think the CPI is at least a 1% overstatement of the true cost of living increase. Some economists prefer the GDP deflator to the CPI, because the GDP deflator prices all products produced, not just consumer goods, and the deflator does not use a fixed market basket approach.

Idle Resources and the Unemployment Rate

Few problems plague modern economies more than that of underutilized and idle resources. The U.S. economy has enormous productive potential. This capacity to produce is reflected in a skilled and educated labor force; a large stock of factories, machines, and farm equipment; and an abundance of rich farmland, timber, and minerals. By the standards of history, these human and nonhuman resources can generate enormous quantities of goods and services. Yet, a portion of our productive resources—people, machines, and materials—frequently lies underused or idle. Businesses default, farms are foreclosed, and workers are unemployed.

The infamous case history of large-scale resource waste in America was ushered in by the great stock market crash of 1929. During the 1930s, the U.S. economy suffered from the deepest economic contraction of modern times. Unemployment increased from 3 percent in 1929 to 25 percent in 1933, and the real GDP fell by one-third. Net farm income declined 45 percent, and industrial production declined 37 percent. The Great Depression was a general, pervasive catastrophe. Yet, that catastrophe is only the most dramatic case of our country's frequent failure to use all its productive capabilities.

More than 50 years later, the United States still fails to utilize its potential fully. In 1982, for example, **unemployment** peaked at 11 percent. Nearly 12 million Americans were out of work. The utilization of factory capacity fell to 69 percent. This meant that nearly one-third of our factories and machines were idle. Net farm income fell by half, and corporate profits fell 30 percent. In the early 1990s, as a result of the abrupt end of the Cold War, many economies from Japan to Germany slumped. Unemployment throughout Europe was over 10 percent. How costly is this idleness, and how can it be avoided?

Idle resources, including idle labor, are a serious social problem:

1.   Failure to exploit potential production lowers living standards for everyone. If idle resources were put to work, they could generate more capital for future growth, they could produce additional services to improve the quality of leisure time, they could contribute to cleaning up the environment, they could enhance our military security, and they could contribute to paying the welfare bill.

2.   The persons who are actually unemployed—whether men, women, teenagers, or minorities—suffer disproportionately in an economic contraction. Loss of a job can mean a dramatic cut in income. Furthermore, being without work is depressing, infuriating, and frightening, and loss of a job can precipitate a myriad of family and personal troubles.

U.S. Unemployment Record

Table 11–3 contains U.S. unemployment rates and labor force statistics for select years from 1929 to 1996. The dramatic increase in unemployment in the early 1930s has already been discussed. In contrast, the lowest rate of unemployment for the United States was about 1 percent in 1944 when the economy was geared up for war. Perhaps 1955 and 1965, when unemployment was around 4.5 percent, were more typical years.

TABLE 11–3   Select Unemployment Figures, 1929–1995

Year	Unemployment Rate (%)	Year	Unemployment Rate (%)
1929	3.2	1979	5.8
1933	24.9	1982	9.7
1944	1.2	1985	7.2
1955	4.4	1990	5.6
1965	4.5	1995	5.6
1975	8.5	1996	5.4

Selected years of unemployment illustrate the performance of the U.S. economy in terms of this measure. The Depression stands out, with an unemployment rate of about 25 percent. During World War II, unemployment fell to about 1 percent.

Sources: *The Economic Report of the President* (Washington, D.C.: U.S. Government Printing Office, February 1995); and Joint Economic Committee, *Economic Indicators* (Washington, D.C.: U.S. Government Printing Office, May 1997).

TOOL KIT

DEFLATING PRICES WITH THE CPI

The CPI is a useful tool for comparing market prices of commodities over time. For example, gasoline prices from 1960 to 1985 increased considerably. Although it varied across the land, gasoline was roughly priced at about $0.38 a gallon in 1960 and at about $1.50 a gallon in 1985. It would appear as if gas prices had nearly quadrupled over 25 years. The law of demand suggests that gasoline demand would be severely dampened.

However, the law of demand compares quantity demanded to the price of a good relative to that of other goods in the market basket. Thus, in order to determine the true effect of more costly gasoline, we must correct the $0.38 and the $1.50 figures for differences in the costs of other items in the market basket itself.

The correct question for demand analysis is this: How much did gas prices change *relative* to the costs of other items in the market basket? To answer this question, we modify gas prices, using the CPI. We divide gas prices in each year by the CPI value and multiply the result by 100. The result, the cost of gas in each year relative to the cost of typical items in the consumer budget in that year, is presented in Table 11–A.

The uncorrected prices, which implied a quadrupling of costs, are divided by the respective CPI figures, to obtain corrected "relative" prices, or

$$\text{(Uncorrected price} \div \text{CPI)} \times 100$$
$$= \text{corrected relative price}$$

Based on the relative costs of gasoline, we conclude that the cost to a consumer of a gallon of

Relatively robust economic growth characterized the year 1979. However, by the standards of 1955 and 1965, the unemployment rate in 1979 was high—5.8 percent compared to the 4.5 percent of the earlier normal years. Relatively high unemployment during years of economic expansion became typical in the 1970s and the 1980s and was of great concern to policymakers.

Government undertakes numerous actions to reduce unemployment and ease the burden on those without jobs. After World War II the United States passed the Employment Act of 1946, which set full employment as a national policy goal. In 1974 Congress passed the Humphrey-Hawkins Act to reaffirm the federal commitment to full employment. Despite these official statements of intent and despite numerous programs and policies, the full-employment goal has been elusive.

A system of **unemployment compensation** eases the hardship from unemployment for those who are covered by it. Both firms and workers pay into the system. Then, when workers are laid off during slowdowns, they receive some payments in the form of unemployment compensation for up to 36 weeks.

Many economists agree that the unemployment rate is not a good measure of economic hardship. In 1982 a presidential commission chaired by Juanita Kreps pointed out that many workers earn inadequate income, as judged by government

gas increased by less than 50 percent from 1960 to 1980. Note also from the figures for 1970 that relative gas prices were actually lower in the 1960s. This helps explain the prevalence of so-called gas guzzlers among U.S. cars in the 1960s. By 1995, gas prices, corrected for inflation, were even lower than the 1960 levels. Gas-guzzling vans and campers were again popular.

Any time you want to compare consumer prices over time, you can apply this same method of correcting prices for inflation by dividing by the CPI.

TABLE 11–A   Correcting Consumer Prices with the CPI

Year	Uncorrected Gas Price	CPI (1962 = 100)	Corrected Relative Price
1960	$0.38	89	$0.43
1970	0.43	116	0.37
1980	1.50	247	0.61
1985	1.52	322	0.47
1995	1.22	450*	0.27

*CPI for 1995 was converted by the authors from the 1995 index (1982 – 1984 = 100) to the same base as previous years (1962 = 100).

Source: The gas prices are based on the fuel cost index taken from *The Economic Report of the President* (Washington, D.C.: U.S. Government Printing Office, 1986, 1996).

standards of poverty. These are called the *working poor.* Conversely, some unemployed workers are between jobs and not actually poor. *Hardship* denotes poverty whether one works or not.

U.S. Competitiveness and Productivity Growth

During the post–World War II era, from 1947 to the late 1970s, U.S. firms and workers produced more goods and services that were sold to foreigners than American consumers and firms bought from the rest of the world. When Americans sell goods abroad these are called U.S. **exports.** When Americans buy goods produced elsewhere, these are called U.S. **imports.** The difference is the trade balance. If U.S. exports exceed U.S. imports, then foreigners are buying more U.S. goods. We call that difference a *trade surplus.* If the United States imports more goods from the rest of the world than it exports to other nations, the United States runs a *trade deficit.*

U.S. Trade Deficits

Table 11–4 illustrates the U.S. **trade balance** from 1965 to 1996. The trade balance was in surplus from the end of World War II until the middle of the 1970s, when deficits began to occur. During the 1980s the U.S. trade deficits became much larger. The yearly trade deficits from 1985 to 1989 averaged –$122 billion, –$145 billion, –$160 billion, –$127 billion, and –$115 billion. The severe 1991 recession reduced imports so that the trade deficit fell to –$73 billion, but by 1993 it blew back up to the $100 billion range. In 1995 the trade deficit was –$187.7 billion.

Persistent trade deficits caused many analysts to fear that U.S. firms and workers had lost their ability to compete effectively in international markets. Trade imbalance between the United States and Japan drew particular attention because of the

TABLE 11–4   Average U.S. Trade Balance, Five-Year Intervals, 1950–1994, and 1996 (billions of $)

Years	Exports	Imports	Trade Balance
1965–1969	$ 31	$ 29	$ +3
1970–1974	61	63	–2
1975–1979	134	152	–18
1980–1984	219	273	–54
1985–1989	274	408	–134
1990–1994	441	562	–121
1996	612	799	–188

The U.S. trade balance has shifted dramatically from surplus to deficit since the early 1960s. The level of trade has grown rapidly as well.

Sources: *The Economic Report of the President* (Washington, D.C.: U.S. Government Printing Office, February 1995); and Joint Economic Committee, *Economic Indicators* (Washington, D.C.: U.S. Government Printing Office, December 1996).

noticeable successes of Japanese automobiles and consumer electronic products—for example, videocassette recorders (VCRs), compact disks (CDs), and advanced computer technologies. Were the United States' ability to create advanced technology and the country's competitive edge disappearing? Would Americans soon be poorer than the Japanese and perhaps the Germans? The top-of-the-line cars were the Japanese Lexus by Toyota and Germany's Mercedes-Benz. Nintendo dominated video toys, while the market values of top American firms like GM and IBM were in decline.

Labor Productivity Evidence

As indicated earlier, an important indicator of competitiveness is the productivity of workers in different countries. **Labor productivity** measures the ratio of output to the amount of labor input.

> LABOR PRODUCTIVITY measures the quantity of total output of goods and service produced on average by one hour of work.

According to one analyst, Angus Maddison, the real U.S. GDP was 37 times larger in 1986 than it was in 1874, 7 times larger than in 1919, and 3 times larger than in 1950. Labor productivity growth has been 2.1 percent since 1919, so that output per worker-hour is now nine times higher than it was in 1874 and double its 1950 level.

Although the concept of labor productivity is simple enough, actual measures are complex, because many very different types of outputs are produced in all countries and different types of labor inputs are used. Thus, in practice, productivity measures are the result of many practical decisions and conceptual problems in construction. Further, productivity varies over time quite considerably for any economy, as people are hired and fired and as output fluctuates.

Despite these difficulties, economists try to compare improvements in productivity among countries. Table 11–5 indicates some general trends in growth rates of productivity for five industrialized economies during this century. Each number in the table represents the average annual improvement, in percentage growth rate terms, in productivity for a country over an interval of several years.

Several pertinent facts are revealed by the table. First, productivity growth was positive for all these countries for over 100 years. This means that output growth was faster than labor input growth; as a result, living standards rose in all of these countries.

The United States enjoyed the fastest growth in productivity from 1870 until almost midcentury. However, the Great Depression of the 1930s and the disastrous war in the 1940s caused a severe collapse in living standards in the industrialized countries shown in Table 11–5. The capital stock of the United States fell, and the capital stocks, machines, factories, plants, and infrastructures of Europe and Japan were completely devastated. By 1950 the *levels* of productivity per worker in the

TABLE 11–5   Labor Productivity Growth Comparisons (average annual percentage growth rates)

	(1) 1870–1913	(2) 1913–1950	(3) 1950–1973	(4) 1973–1984	(4) – (3)* Slowdown
United States	2.0	2.4	2.5	1.0	−1.5
Japan	1.8	1.7	7.7	3.2	−4.5
Germany	1.9	1.0	6.0	3.0	−3.0
United Kingdom	1.2	1.6	3.2	2.4	−0.8
France	1.7	2.0	5.1	3.4	−1.7

*The difference between column 4 and column 3.

Source: Maddison, Angus, "Growth and Slowdown in Advanced Capitalist Economies," *Journal of Economic Literature,* June 1987, Vol. XXV, No. 2, p. 650, Table 2.

European countries were less than half that of American workers. Japan's output per worker was less than 15 percent that of the American worker.

From 1950 to 1973, labor productivity growth exploded in Japan and in Germany and was quite rapid elsewhere in Europe. By 1973 labor productivity in Europe had reached 75 percent of the American level, and in Japan had reached 45 percent.

After 1973 a disturbing trend developed: Labor productivity growth rates slowed down in all industrialized countries. The growth rate of worker productivity in the United States collapsed to 1 percent from 2.5 percent per year. Germany's and Japan's productivity fell to half of their previous levels. The U.S. growth rate, at one time the highest, was now the lowest.

The decline in productivity growth from 1973 on, which we have just seen in the data of Table 11–5, had major consequences for wage and income growth as well. Living standards cannot grow for the population as a whole if output per hour of work is rising. Just as the American worker's productivity stopped improving, the number of older Americans—potentially eligible for Social Security retirement benefits, other federal income support programs, and health care entitlements—began to grow. This increase in the aged dependent population reflected, in part, the longer life spans that were, in turn, a consequence of better living conditions.

The slower output per worker-hour growth rates, combined with increased pressures for Social Security, income, and health entitlements served to crunch the take-home pay of the working man and woman and led to a stagnation in the growth of family incomes. Table 11–6 shows the median family income (i.e., income of the family in the very middle of the income scale), corrected for inflation, for selected years from 1949 to 1996. It is evident from the table that incomes, measured in constant 1996 dollars, rose substantially for middle Americans from 1949 to 1973. After 1973, at the same time that the productivity growth slowdown was occurring, family income leveled off. Rather than continuing to grow rapidly, as it had from the end of World War II until the early seventies, income growth stalled. Inflation-corrected median family income in 1984 was only a little higher than it had been in 1973.

JR **TABLE 11–6**   Median Family Income (constant 1996 $)

Year	Income	Year	Income
1949	$18,283	1984	$38,772
1959	26,127	1988	41,470
1969	36,489	1990	41,223
1973	38,126	1993	38,980
1980	38,930	1996	41,239

Poverty level $15,950 (13.8% population) in 1996

Source: U.S. Commerce Department, Current Population Reports, 1950–1996.

Figure 11–4 illustrates the effects of slower productivity growth and more social dependents per worker on inflation-corrected average hourly and weekly earnings. In both panels A and B the slowdown of the early seventies is evident in the wage data. Panel B of Figure 11–4 shows that nonwage benefits, when added to the wage compensation of panel A continued to grow after 1973, but at a very much slower rate than before. As productivity declined, the proportion of nonwage benefits to wages continued to grow.

Though not shown in Table 11–6, the decline in wages for physical labor has been a major cause in the shifting of concentration of income distribution away from physical (blue-collar) workers toward analytical (white-collar) workers. Together, the slower growth of overall output per worker and the redistribution of income away from physical labor have been major contributing factors to increased levels of poverty, income disparity, and perhaps even homelessness.

Has the United States lost its competitive edge? Has America lost its ability to generate meaningful high-wage jobs for its low-skilled workers as manufacturing supremacy in autos, steel, and elsewhere has evidently shifted out of the United States to countries like Japan and Germany, and even to Korea, Taiwan, Mexico, and other nations?

JR CHAPTER REVIEW

Macroeconomics, which deals with national economic issues, focuses on four main problems: stagnation, inflation, idle resources, and noncompetitiveness. Four indicators of economic performance are:

1. GDP
2. CPI
3. The unemployment rate
4. Labor productivity

 **FIGURE 11–4**   Effects of Slower Productivity Growth

A. Average money earnings have declined since 1973.

Index of Average Hourly and Weekly Earnings Using 1973 as Base Year, 1947–1994

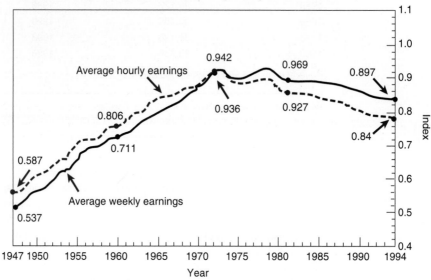

Note: Data for 1994 are from third quarter. All measures are adjusted for inflation using consumer price index—UX1.

Source: Bureau of Labor Statistics.

B. Though monetary pay has declined since 1973, compensation, including benefits, has grown.

Index of Hourly Compensation Using 1973 as Base Year, 1947–1994

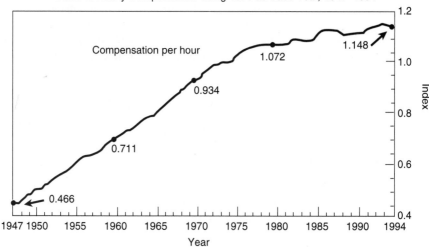

Note: Data for 1994 are from third quarter. Measures are adjusted for inflation using consumer price index—UX1.

Sources: Bureau of Labor Statistics. Panels A and B are from *Dollars and Cents* by Wallenberg, American Enterprise Institute.

We briefly reviewed some historical evidence about the U.S. economy, including data on these four indicators.

First, we reviewed the macroeconomic problems with a PPC. Growth means the curve is shifting outward; inflation occurs when we try to push the economy beyond the boundary too quickly. Unemployment and idle resources occur when we produce inside the boundary. Labor productivity divides output by the number of hours worked to obtain a gauge of worker efficiency.

GDP, when corrected for inflation, may be used to measure overall economic well-being. The most popular measure of inflation is the CPI, which measures the price of the average good in a consumer's market basket. The unemployment rate, although somewhat imprecise, is a politically sensitive indicator of idle resources. Labor productivity growth measures the growth of output relative to growth of labor, and this indicates the improved efficiency of an economy over time.

🎵 MULTIPLE-CHOICE SELF-TEST 🎵🎵🎵🎵🎵🎵🎵🎵🎵🎵🎵🎵🎵🎵🎵

1. GDP is measured:
   a. As the basis for estimating an economy's total output and the rate of growth of its output.
   b. As the dollar-valued aggregation of all goods and productive resources used in the economy.
   c. As the sum of the price of each kind of final good and output in the economy.
   d. As the final dollar value to consumers of all intermediate goods and services produced in the economy in a year.

2. The signaling function of prices:
   a. Is a microeconomic issue, not a macroeconomic issue.
   b. Is exaggerated by inflation, which makes all the price changes look bigger.
   c. Is unaffected by inflation, because inflation does not affect relative prices, but only the overall price level.
   d. Is hampered by inflation, because the meaning of a price increase becomes unclear.

3. A $600 weekly salary in a year when the CPI was 300 would be the same as what salary in the CPI base year?
   a. $900.
   b. $300.
   c. $200.
   d. None of the above.

4. A particularly unfortunate characteristic of unemployment as a macroeconomic problem is that:
   a. It is always a big problem, because it has never declined to zero.
   b. Much of the large burden of the problem is borne by the minority who become unemployed.
   c. It has little relationship to economic hardship.
   d. It is a problem for the economy as a whole, but it is not much of a problem for most of the unemployed.

5. The capacity utilization rate:
   a. Should nearly always rise and fall with the unemployment rate.
   b. Is less heard about because, unlike unemployment, it does not cause economic hardship for households.
   c. Measures a different kind of basic macroeconomic problem than does the unemployment rate.
   d. Is easier to measure than the unemployment rate, which must count people rather than machines.

6. When total output per hour of work rises in Germany faster than in the United States, this means:
   a. Germans produce more than Americans on average per hour.

    b. German worker efficiency is getting better faster than American worker efficiency.

    c. Americans are becoming poorer while Germans get richer.

    d. Productivity is higher in Germany than in the United States.

7. Income of the median family (the family in the middle of the income scale):

    a. Fell after 1973.

    b. Was highest in the "golden" sixties.

    c. Stagnated after 1973.

    d. Rose faster in the eighties and early nineties than in the fifties.

8. When Americans buy more goods and services from abroad than the rest of the world buys from the United States, we can say that:

    a. U.S. exports exceed U.S. imports.

    b. Japanese buy more goods from the rest of the world than from the United States.

    c. The United States runs a trade surplus.

    d. The United States runs a trade deficit.

STUDY QUESTIONS

1. Critically analyze GDP, the CPI, the unemployment rate, and U.S. productivity growth as indicators of economic performance.

2. What are the social costs of inflation?

3. Define *GDP*. What does it purport to measure? Is it a sound measure of human well-being?

4. In 1976 a tractor cost a farmer $9,100. In 1983 that same tractor cost $17,400. The CPI in 1976 was 170.5; in 1983 it was 298.4. How much did tractor prices rise from 1977 to 1983 when measured in constant prices?

5. How do rates of unemployment differ from hardship?

6. Why do you think that Japanese productivity growth was so much higher than that of the United States after World War II?

7. Do you see any connection between U.S. wage stagnation after the early seventies and slower U.S. labor productivity growth? Explain.

PROBLEM

Suppose your wage contract is indexed to the CPI. That is, your wage will automatically increase by whatever percentage the CPI increases. (Such an arrangement is now usually called a *COLA,* or *cost-of-living adjustment.*) Considering how the CPI measures true inflation, are you a little better off, a little worse off, or in just the same position in terms of purchasing power if the CPI and your wages go up by 10 percent? Might your answer depend on the particular bundle of goods that you buy, if they are rather different from the average bundle that the CPI is based on? Now consider bracket creep. Suppose the increase in your nominal income pushes you well into the next-higher tax bracket. Would your answer change? How?

CHAPTER 12

Overview of the National Economy

Cycles and the Circular Flow Model

𝒥𝒥 CHAPTER PREVIEW

A beggar came upon a fisherman and said, "Please give me a fish; I am hungry."

The fisherman, seeing that the beggar was weak from hunger, said, "Cut a willow branch and attach this line to it."

The beggar did so and said, "But I am still hungry."

"I know," replied the fisherman. "Here, attach this hook to your line."

The beggar did so and said, "But I am still hungry."

"I know," replied the fisherman. "Grab a grasshopper and attach him to your hook."

The beggar did so and said, "But I am still hungry."

"I know," replied the fisherman, patiently.

"Now toss your grasshopper into the stream."

The beggar did so, and soon he caught a fish.

The beggar was no longer hungry, and shortly thereafter, he became president of Allied Fish Company. He moved to Nob Hill, San Francisco, where he was elected president of the Rotary Club and was appointed chairman of the Symphony Orchestra Board. He married socialite Constance. . . .

Just as the beggar learned to feed himself, you can learn to evaluate the economy. But, just as being fed would have satisfied the beggar quicker, for us to tell you how the economy works might seem more satisfying to you than undertaking the effort to learn how to evaluate the economy yourself. But the skill of learning how economists think about the economy will be far more valuable and longer-lasting than simply knowing a few facts about today's economy.

1. Are business cycles a necessary reality? Can government prevent them altogether?
2. Does business investment spending depend on the pace of the economy, or does the pace of the economy depend on business investment spending?
3. Do exports expand the circular flow or contract it?

𝒥𝒮 CONCEPTS REINTRODUCED

𝒥𝒮 NEW CONCEPTS

Business Cycles
Expansion and Contraction Phases
Cycle Peaks and Troughs
Involuntary Unemployment
National Income
Dividends
Consumption Expenditures
Personal Savings
Retained Earnings
Investment Expenditures

📖 CHAPTER OBJECTIVES

After studying this chapter, you should be able to:

1. Describe the business cycle by listing and defining the phases of that cycle.
2. List some of the flows in the circular flow model and state the direction of these flows.
3. Understand some key forces that expand and contract the cycle.

THE NATIONAL BUREAU OF ECONOMIC RESEARCH (NBER) AND THE BUSINESS CYCLE

One of the most difficult and important questions in macroeconomics is this: Why do economies fluctuate over time? Why are there years when the economy performs sluggishly and other years when it performs quite well? Why does an economy suffer through years of inflation and then enjoy years of stability?

Chapter 11 presented four well-known indicators of the performance of different aspects of the national economy. They are (1) GDP, an indicator of growth; (2) CPI, an indicator of the rate of inflation or its absence; (3) the unemployment rate, an indicator of idle resources; and (4) productivity, an indicator of economic efficiency. A review of the statistics on these indicators shows that U.S. economic performance, although quite successful as a rule, is uneven. A severe depression lasted from 1929 to 1933. Inflation accelerated from 1965 to 1979. High unemployment and deep contractions marked the period of 1980 through early 1983. A rapid expansion started in 1983 and became the longest peacetime expansion in U.S. history, ending in the short recession of 1991. The 1990s saw another long expansion, beginning in 1992. Do slumps, such as those in 1929–1933, 1937–1938, 1973–1975, 1979–1983, and 1990–1991 have common features? Are the robust expansions, such as the ones in 1923–1929, 1960–1969, 1976–1979, and 1983–1989, 1992–? similar in some respects? Could the slumps, expansions, and differences between the two imply some overall coherence in national economic activity?

NBER Business Cycles

Our search for an explanation of these economic fluctuations begins with evidence provided by the National Bureau of Economic Research (NBER). A private research institute, NBER has collected, synthesized, and analyzed thousands of series of historical data on the U.S. economy.

Figure 12–1 illustrates the record of U.S. real GDP for 1900 to 1996. Two striking features derived from the graph are immediately apparent. The long-term trend in real GDP has been unmistakably upward, averaging over 3 percent a year, yet the actual path of GDP has been marked by short-term instability.

The long-run expansion of U.S. GDP should not come as a surprise. It reflects the fact that over time the number of workers and machines has increased, as has the use of materials, resources, and energy. In addition, the U.S. growth performance reflects advances in technology, innovation, education, skill development, and new managerial techniques. The economy has become increasingly sophisticated and advanced, both in the private and public sectors.

The instability and unevenness of the GDP growth path is also important. Figure 12–2 illustrates the fluctuations about the average 3.5 percent annual growth rate in GDP. The figure highlights the cyclical nature of economic performance. The long

FIGURE 12–1   U.S. Real GDP, 1900–1996

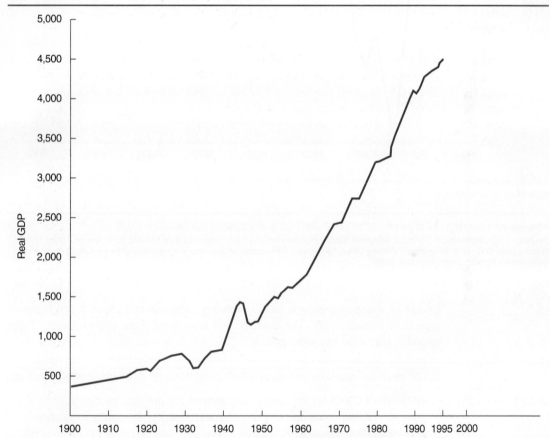

The growth path of U.S. real GDP in this century illustrates two important features of the economy: Growth has been upward with few major interruptions, and the path is jagged and uneven. Note that growth averaged over 3.5 percent per year from 1950 to 1970, as compared with a rate of 1.5 percent from 1929 to 1950, and to about 2 percent since 1975.

Sources: U.S. Commerce Department, *Historical Statistics of the United States, Colonial Times to 1970*, Bicentennial Edition, part I (Washington, D.C.: U.S. Government Printing Office, 1975); *The Economic Report of the President* (Washington, D.C.: U.S. Government Printing Office, February 1996); and Joint Economic Committee, *Economic Indicators* (Washington, D.C.: U.S. Government Printing Office, February 1997).

FIGURE 12–2 GDP Deviations about the Long-Run Trend, 1920–1996*

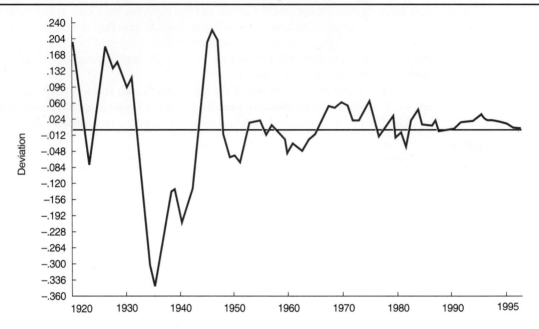

This figure focuses only on the fluctuating nature of the national economy. Market economies usually display this type of cyclical pattern.

---

*The average percentage rate of growth over the entire period has been subtracted from the data in Figure 12–1.

Source: U.S. Commerce Department, *Historical Statistics of the United States, Colonial Times to 1970.* Bicentennial Edition, part I (Washington, D.C.: U.S. Government Printing Office, 1975); and *The Economic Report of the President* (Washington, D.C.: U.S. Government Printing Office, February 1996).

swings of slump and growth as the economy contracts and expands are common aspects of economic life. The duration and severity of these episodes vary. These episodes are called **business cycles.**

> BUSINESS CYCLES are erratic and uneven but periodic swings in the pace of national economic activity, characterized by alternating expansion and contraction phases.

A business cycle is in an **expansion phase** when the economy is growing rapidly. Output is increasing, employment is rising, industrial production is increasing, and prices are tending to rise. Eventually, the pace of the expansion slows down until the economy levels off and ceases to expand. The cycle has now reached its **peak.**

FIGURE 12–3   Stylized Business Cycle

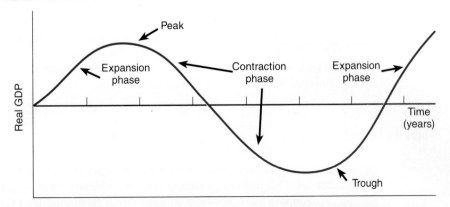

This hypothetical business cycle shows first the *expansion phase* of the cycle then, after the *peak,* the *contraction phase* leading to the *trough.* Actual cycles are never this smooth and easy to spot, nor do the cycles last a determined length of time. Economists argue, even today, about the causes of cycles.

The economy then begins to enter the **contraction phase.** GDP, employment, production, and prices are on the decline. The economic slowdown eventually comes to an end at the **trough** of the cycle. Then a new cycle can begin. A principal objective of macroeconomics is to understand what causes business cycles. In Figure 12–3, we illustrate the nature of cycles by drawing one complete hypothetical cycle, represented by the movement of real GDP over several years. Cycles are never this smooth and symmetrical, but are quite random and rough.

Difficulty in Predicting Turning Points in Cycles

As we have noted, actual economic behavior never mirrors the smooth cycle in Figure 12–3. The typical cycling process of an economy is uneven. In fact, the actual path is so erratic that the peak and the trough, the two key turning points of the cycle, can be identified and labeled only several months after they have occurred. Evidently, only luck allows some forecasters to predict these turning points with any degree of accuracy. Economists from the NBER study the past performance of the economy and decide, after the fact, that a *turning point* has taken place.

Economists would like to know why the economy cycles in an erratic and jagged pattern in its upward trend rather than moving up a smooth path. If turning points in the cycle could be anticipated, then perhaps policies could be recommended for smoothing out the pattern. Contractions in the cycle bring hard times. Unemployment increases, earnings fall, wages decline, profits are off, and farm incomes are lower. Furthermore, when the economy is erratic, life seems less secure and comfortable.

FROM MICRO MODELS TO MACRO BEHAVIOR

How can volatile economic activity be explained? If the slumps and booms of these sporadic fluctuations are studied with care, it may be possible to anticipate them, to devise protection from their ravages, or to modify their intensity. A scientific approach to understanding economic fluctuations requires trying to develop causal linkages between various economic activities.

Where to Begin?

In studying microeconomics we used the supply-and-demand model of an individual market. This model is a natural point of departure for building a macro model.

Suppose the supply-and-demand model were used for every good and service produced in the entire economy, from apples and shoes to medical degrees, computer chips, and blast furnaces. From these results, a comprehensive list could be prepared showing the quantities and prices of all goods and services produced. The value of yearly output in each market would be the market price per good multiplied by the equilibrium quantity of that good produced during the year. This would determine total output. If the final goods and services were selected and their values added together, the result would be total GDP measured at current market prices.

We now consider the markets for various types of workers. To know the number of carpenters employed and the wage rate for an hour of carpentry work, we would have to devise the demand and supply curves for carpenters. Equilibrium in the market for carpenters would be, of course, where the demand and supply curves intersected. This would yield the number of carpenters employed at the equilibrium market price for carpentry. If this process were repeated for every possible type of labor, then the total numbers of all types of workers employed, from carpenters to chiropractors, could be added together. This total would be the aggregate level of employment in the national economy.

INFLUENTIAL ECONOMIST

JOHN MAYNARD KEYNES, 1883–1946

The 20th century has been referred to as the "Age of Keynes." Indeed, few people have been more influential than this English economist. Lord Keynes was Chancellor of the Exchequer and represented Britain at Versailles following World War II. He married a famous actress for whom he established a theater and traveled among the lite-

rati of England (which included Virginia Woolf). He made fortunes both for himself and for Kings College by speculating in international currencies and commodities.

In 1935, Keynes published *The General Theory of Employment, Interest, and Money.* In this classic work Keynes set out to explain the cause

Unfortunately, simple, direct addition of all these equilibrium quantities is inadequate, because the total of all these additions does not square with what is happening in the national economy. The failure of adding up micro results to obtain the correct macro result illustrates the **fallacy of composition.** The most important inaccuracy of the summing up of micro supply-and-demand equilibrium results is the outcome that the national level of employment is in equilibrium. Yet national statistics on unemployment, studied in Chapter 11, clearly show numerous sustained fluctuations over time. The data, as well as surveys, also show that, during slumps in the business cycle, many workers suffer from unwanted periods of unemployment. John Maynard Keynes, one of the most influential economists of this century, called this outcome **involuntary unemployment.**

INVOLUNTARY UNEMPLOYMENT exists when potential workers who are able and willing to work at the existing market wage rate are unable to find jobs.

A second defect of the direct addition of micro results is that such simple summing up fails to capture the observed fluctuations in output and production from year to year. Something beyond market-clearing supply-and-demand analysis must be invoked to capture the essence of the fluctuating economy.

The objective now is to develop a new model for understanding why the national economy behaves in a more volatile way than implied by supply-and-demand equilibrium analysis. We will try to understand why GDP, unemployment, and inflation fluctuate in sporadic cycles rather than moving along smooth and steady paths. The model for use in this effort is the circular flow model introduced in Chapter 2.

---

of the Great Depression, which seemingly could not have happened according to pre-Keynesian classical economic doctrines.

This masterpiece became the fountainhead of modern macroeconomics. In it Keynes threw down the gauntlet, challenging conventional wisdom with a new view of the economic world. In so doing, he incurred the ire of the governing classes of the day. Both free marketers and socialists disagreed with Keynes's new teachings. Free marketers disliked the teaching because Keynes

argued that the private economy could not correct itself in depression. Radicals fought it because Keynes suggested that minimal government intervention could keep the capitalist system afloat.

Today many of Keynes's ideas are conventional wisdom, although some of his major proposals are rejected. Nevertheless, he has clearly altered the intellectual landscape of economics, as well as changing our perception of the appropriate role and responsibility of government in economic activity.

CIRCULAR FLOW MODELS AND CYCLES

Circular flow models will provide insight into the nature of economic fluctuations. These models are used to study the reaction of the national economy to outside shocks, such as a foreign war, a winter cold snap, a burst of government spending, or a contraction in the nation's money supply. Such shocks are seen to generate expansions and contractions in the pace of economic activity.

Version One

Circular flow model version one (shown in Figure 12–4) illustrates dollars flowing through the economy as transactions take place between households and firms. In particular, the model incorporates two important types of transactions: Households buy finished products (outputs) from businesses, and businesses buy input services from households. These input services include services of labor, management, land, loans, and capital. People in households own the inputs used by firms to produce the goods sold to the households. These inputs are called the *productive resources.*

As households buy economic goods and services (products), dollars flow from households to firms; as firms buy inputs, dollars flow from households to firms, back to households, and then around again, as shown in Figure 12–4.

The circular flow model actually contains two distinct flows: (1) the flow of dollars that runs counterclockwise from households to firms and back and (2) the flow of physical goods and services from firms to households and of physical input services from households to firms, which runs clockwise. The dollars are payments for the physical goods and services. The same dollars can flow through the circle several times while generating new household expenditures on goods and services and new income payments to households for inputs provided to firms.

To enrich understanding of the circular flow model, consider a typical family in the economy. When you go to the grocery store to buy food, you are passing dollars through the lower loop of the money flow from households to firms. Thus, dollars are seen to flow in a circle from your household to the grocery store. If a family member earns a wage or salary as a shoe store salesclerk, then the shoe store is passing dollars through the upper loop of the money flow from the firm to your household.

In the circular flow model, all payments made by firms to cover the costs of business and their profits are considered as payments made to households, because it is recognized that all these inputs are ultimately owned by households. The total dollar flow through the upper loop over a year is called annual **national income.**

NATIONAL INCOME is the total value of all earnings of the inputs (productive resources) that produce GDP. This includes wages, salaries, and fringe benefits of labor; rental income on all property; interest payments on loans; income of small individual proprietorships; and profit.

FIGURE 12–4   Circular Flow Model Version One: Households Transact with Firms

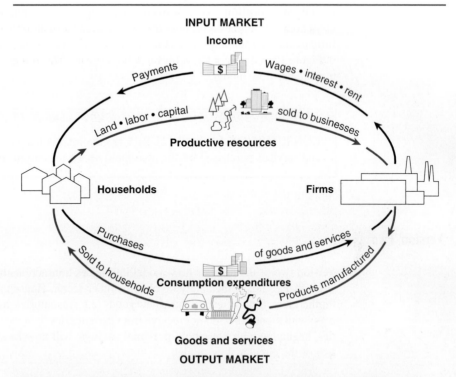

INPUT MARKET

Income

Payments

Wages • interest • rent

Land • labor • capital

sold to businesses

Productive resources

Households

Firms

Purchases

of goods and services

Sold to households

Products manufactured

Consumption expenditures

Goods and services

OUTPUT MARKET

We recall the circular flow model which illustrates the most rudimentary ingredients of an economy: Households buy goods and services from businesses in the output market; businesses buy productive resources from the households in the input market. The result is two flows: (1) a clockwise flow of physical goods and services and (2) a counterclockwise flow of dollars, which are the payments for the physical goods and services. In this simple case, the economy neither expands nor contracts—goods and services are simply exchanged for money.

If a family owns rental property, then it receives rent as payment for an input service—property. If a family earns dividends on stocks, then it receives a portion of the firm's profits (which is a return on capital). Virtually all input service payments disbursed by firms eventually end up in the hands of some household and are included in the upper loop of the money flow.

It is tempting to doubt this conclusion. After all, don't firms keep some of the money in profits? Yes, they certainly do. Some profits are retained by the firm and not passed on in the flow. Profits that are distributed, called **dividends,** do go to some households and thus do flow through the upper loop. Shortly, we will enhance our model in order to deal with the profits that are retained as a form of savings by the firm.

Every time a household buys a product, this purchase is included in the lower loop of the money flow. The total value of these purchases over a year is called annual **consumption expenditures.** Again, however, it might be asked: Don't households sometimes hold onto their income, rather than pass it on to firms in the form of current spending? Yes. Households save, and the simple circular flow model of Figure 12–4 does not allow for household saving. This brings us to version two of the circular flow model.

CONSUMPTION EXPENDITURES are the total dollar value of all goods and services purchased by the household sector for current use.

Version Two

Version two of the circular flow model introduces transactions by firms and households that do not immediately involve the other sector. Households and firms save. Furthermore, firms often purchase new goods (e.g., inventories, machines, and buildings) with money they do not receive from current sales to households. These activities, beginning with household **personal savings,** will now be shown with version two of the circular flow model.

PERSONAL SAVINGS are the difference between household income (after taxes) and consumption expenditures.

When households save some of their income, these dollars are withdrawn from the flow. Graphically, dollars withdrawn from the flow are represented, as in Figure 12–5, by an arrow pulling dollars out of the flow. Household saving is money that is not allowed to continue on in the flow of dollars to firms. Similarly, firms save in the form of **retained earnings.** Thus, another withdrawal arrow is seen in Figure 12–5 pulling dollars from the firm side of the flow. This arrow represents business saving.

Whereas households and firms withdraw revenues from the flow in the form of savings, firms periodically undertake new expenditures with money that is not usually received in the current period from households. These expenditures are accounted for as new injections into the flow. These expenditures by firms pay for the purchase of goods that are not for current sale. Such goods are called *capital goods,* and payments on them are called **investment expenditures.**

𝒥𝓇 FIGURE 12–5   Circular Flow Model Version Two: Savings and Investment

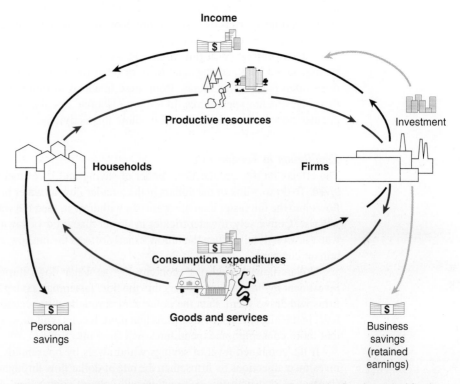

Some income that households receive is not passed on in the circular flow but saved for the future. Similarly, firms save some of their earnings. These financial activities are represented by arrows withdrawing expenditures from the circular flow. On the other hand, firms make investments that are not usually financed from currently earned business income. These investments are represented by an injection arrow.

INVESTMENT EXPENDITURES are dollars paid by firms on capital goods, which consist of factories, office buildings and other structures, machinery and equipment, inventories, and new residential housing construction. In general, investment spending is for goods and services used to produce other new goods or services.

In Figure 12–5, investment is depicted by an arrow injecting new dollars into the circular flow. As firms increase their investment spending, they pump new dollars into the circular flow. Thus, over time, dollars flow between households and firms through the upper and lower loops of the money flow. Some money is *withdrawn* in the forms of personal and business saving, and some is *injected* in the form of investment expenditures by firms. (*Technical note:* If investment is financed from current earnings, this is treated as a simultaneous withdrawal of business savings and injection of investment spending.)

It should be noted at this point that when people save, they usually put their savings into a bank, savings and loan, or other thrift institution. At the same time, firms often borrow this money from these financial institutions in order to finance their investment expenditures. In a more elaborate circular flow model, a financial circular flow loop could be added to show this activity.

Equilibrium in Version Two

The effects on the circular flow model of saving and investment can now be analyzed. To do so, think of the dollars in the circular flow as water in a bathtub. If water flows into the tub faster than the drain can withdraw it, then the water level in the tub will rise. Conversely, if water trickles in slower than it flows down the drain, then the water level will fall. When the inflow exactly offsets the outflow, the water level will remain constant.

Dollars flow through the economy just as water flows through the bathtub. If investment by firms injects dollars into the flow faster than saving by households and firms withdraws them, then the dollar flow throughout the economy, like the water level in the tub, will rise. This means that more income will flow into households and that more consumption expenditures will flow into firms.

If the combined level of savings withdrawals by households and firms exceeds investment injections by firms, then the rate of dollar flow throughout the system will contract. Along with this contraction will come a contraction in income and consumption expenditures. Only when investment injections and savings withdrawals are exactly offset will the dollar flow through the economy be constant, that is, without a tendency to either rise of fall. Only then will income and consumption expenditures be at a constant level. When the amount of injections of dollars into the circular flow exactly offsets the amount of dollar withdrawals for the system, and the overall level of spending is constant, then it is said that the system is in *equilibrium.*

In the special case of circular flow version two, equilibrium means that the level of injections from investment equals the level of withdrawals caused by the combined sum of personal savings and business savings. Put another way, in this model, the condition necessary for equilibrium is that total savings equal investment.

Shocks to Investment

Circular flow model version two is used to understand the fluctuating nature of the national economy. We will consider a shock to investment injections and see how the system responds. This provides some insight into how responses by firms and households to outside shocks will produce multiple reactions throughout the economy. The economy tends to move from one level of economic activity (equilibrium) to a different one. This aids our understanding of why the national economy is volatile.

Consider a shock that causes businesses to increase their expenditures on investment. This might be a burst of optimism, brought on by a favorable political climate in the Middle East, which leads the U.S. business community to expect an expansion of sales activity. As a result, firms decide to build up their inventories. They increase orders and add new goods to their shelves in preparation for the expected boom in sales. How will this affect the equilibrium of the circular flow?

Clearly, a new burst of investment causes an increase in the amount of dollar injections into the flow. The flow begins to expand. Because the firms are hiring new workers and using new tools and other productive inputs in order to produce the new capital goods, they are generating a new level of national income. This increased national income flows into the household sector. Households, in turn, use this higher level of national income in part to buy new goods and services in the form of increased consumption expenditures. Thus, consumption starts to increase, and this, in turn, means that new expenditures are flowing into firms—the flow is swelling up. The firms take the new dollars from the rising sales level of consumption goods and increase income payments to the inputs producing the new goods. The level of national income is rising.

When will the flow stop swelling? The answer has to do with the concept of equilibrium in the circular flow. The original outside shock that increased expenditures for investment started a rising tide of spending. If investment expenditures continue at the new, higher level, then national income will continue to swell as long as investment injections exceed saving withdrawals. However, the economy will naturally level off at a new equilibrium. As the level of national income flowing into households rises, the level of savings withdrawn will also rise. Similarly, as consumption expenditures flowing into firms rise, so do business savings. As savings levels rise with the tide, total savings withdrawals begin to reach the new, higher level of investment injections. Once this happens a *new equilibrium* level is reached: Total savings equal total investment.

Note that the new equilibrium is different from the old one. In particular, national income is greater, consumption expenditures are larger, personal and business savings have increased, and investment expenditures are higher. All boats have risen with the tide. This shows how investment expenditures can spur an economy into expansion.

Of course, just the opposite can happen, too. A shock from outside the model, such as fear of perverse world events, that drives down investment expenditures will generate a decline in the level of national income, consumption expenditures, and savings. Thus, as investment rises and falls, it produces multiplied expansions and contractions in national economic activity. This explains why a private market economy can be volatile over time.

How much will national income rise in response to some outside shock? If households pass on most of their income, then the flow will tend to rise more than it would if they immediately increased their savings levels. Similarly, firms can dampen the expansion by retaining most of their earnings.

To summarize, version two of the circular flow model explains how the economy can go through sustained periods of boom and bust when investment booms and busts. It also explains how the income level can sporadically jump about when shocks cause injections to jump about. This is not easily or clearly revealed by a purely micro-based supply-and-demand model. This circular flow model, however, can show how we attain different equilibriums at different levels of national income. This suggests that standards of living, employment, and consumption can be sustained at a variety of levels. There is no unique level of equilibrium income.

Finally, note that new investment expenditures generate periods of expansion that exceed the level of the new investment spending itself. The reason for this multiple expansion is that new injections generate subsequent increases in consumption expenditures, which compound as the flow swells. Thus, outside shocks can produce multiplied increases or decreases in the level of national income.

Version Three

Version three of the circular flow model introduces economic transactions between the United States and the rest of the world. Americans buy products from Japanese, German, Canadian, and Mexican producers, among others. These purchases of foreign-produced goods we call *imports*. We saw in Chapter 10 that countries, like people, trade voluntarily with one another in order to exploit each one's comparative advantage through specialization. This process enhances world living standards. Nonetheless, these flows of transactions influence the pace of economic activity over the course of the business cycle in each country.

When American consumers buy foreign-produced goods, they exchange their dollars for foreign currency that is used to pay for the foreign good. The actual real-world mechanism involves currency exchange by financial institutions, but from the point of view of the flow, imports of goods are a withdrawal from the circular flow. Imports result in expenditures' not being passed along by households in the domestic circular flow. Thus, imports are like savings in that dollar expenditures flow out of the economy. This may be represented by another arrow from the household sector leading away from the flow.

Some of what American workers and firms produce is exported to people in other countries. These exports are purchased by foreigners who, in effect, purchase American dollars with their own currencies. The American dollars then flow into the U.S. domestic circular flow. Thus, exports of goods and services, like investment expenditures by firms, are injections into the circular flow. When exports rise, they tend to expand the circular flow; dollars are pouring into the domestic economy through the business sector, causing increases in domestic income. Figure 12–6 illustrates imports as a withdrawal from and exports as an injection into the circular flow.

Note, at this point the exports involve the purchase of U.S. dollars by foreigners who use foreign currency on an exchange, whereas imports involve the selling of U.S. dollars by Americans, who buy foreign currency on an exchange. A question for your further consideration is this: What will be the net currency flow when exports and imports are equal?

FIGURE 12–6   Circular Flow Model Version Three: Imports and Exports

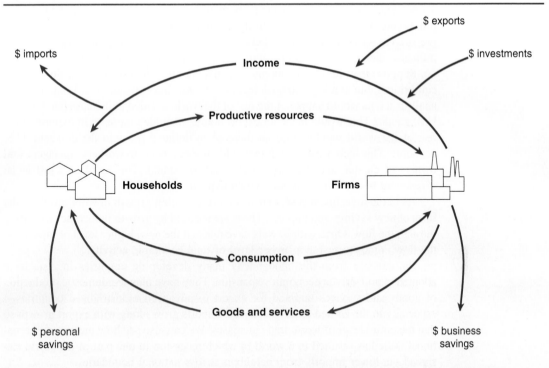

Some income recovered by households is used to import goods or services from the rest of the world. Imports act as a withdrawal of dollar expenditures from the flow because when households save the expenditures are not passed on in the flow. Exports, goods, and services produced in the United States and sold abroad inject new expenditures into the flow.

Equilibrium in Version Three

Recall from version two that when total injections equal total withdrawals the flow of money through the domestic economy is in equilibrium. This means, in this new version of the model, that the sum of all injections into the flow is exactly offset by the sum total of all withdrawals. Thus, investment expenditures plus exports equal the sum of imports and savings. We have the following equilibrium condition:

Total injections = total withdrawals
Investment + exports = imports and savings

It is important to realize that the circular flow can attain equilibrium without exports equaling imports, that is, without balance in foreign trade flows. However, total injections must equal total withdrawals. Suppose, then, that U.S. imports of foreign goods exceed U.S. exports. What does the equilibrium condition imply for domestic savings and investment? Because total injections equal total withdrawals, imports can exceed exports only if investment spending exceeds domestic savings. Thus, when a country is importing more than it exports, it is also investing more than it is saving, because only then will the circular flow be in equilibrium. We are now prepared to see how transactions between the U.S. economy and the rest of the world influence the pace of economic activity known as the *business cycle*.

Suppose that the U.S. economy was in a slump so that the circular flow was in equilibrium, but at a low, sluggish level of income and expenditures. What does our analysis tell us would happen if the rest of the world decided to increase purchases of U.S. goods? This would mean an export boom. A sudden increase in exports to the rest of the world would cause an increase in dollar flows into the domestic U.S. economy. This increase in spending would raise payments to workers, managers, and owners of capital, and the flow would start to expand. This would act just as an investment boom. The economy would expand.

As in the investment case, expansion brings with it growth in withdrawals in the form of new savings and imports. These are induced by growth in income circulating through the flow. Once withdrawals have reached the new, higher level of injections, the flow comes to rest at a higher level of total economic activity.

We can see from this model why many developing countries in Asia have adopted export-driven economic expansion. They have planned domestic production of goods and services targeted for export to advanced industrialized countries—especially to the United States. As a rule, imports grow along with export growth so that the entire level of world trade increases. We can also see how increased international trade has resulted in a world in which recession in one part of the world can spread via lower imports from neighbors across national boundaries.

🎢 CHAPTER REVIEW

Two important features of the national economy stand out when one inspects the performance of U.S. GDP over time: (1) GDP increases over the long term as the economy grows, and (2) the GDP growth path is sporadic, not smooth.

The NBER describes the paths of national economies as series of erratic cycles about the trend rate of growth. A major goal of macro is to explain these erratic cycles in the long-run growth trend.

The adding up of supply and demand from individual markets is not an adequate model of national economic activity. The sporadic nature of the national economy is simply not captured by adding supply-and-demand models together. The failure of adding up micro results to obtain the correct macro result illustrates the *fallacy of composition:* What may work for one market may not hold for all markets taken together. A noneconomic example is when one person stands up to see better at a football game, he can; but when all spectators stand up at once during an exciting play, no one can really see any better.

The circular flow model shows that firms buy inputs from households and households buy goods from firms. Investment by firms injects new spending into the flow, and saving withdraws spending from the flow. The flow is in equilibrium, with a constant level of national income, when injections equal withdrawals.

Increases in investment, in response to outside shocks, stimulate spending and cause increases in consumption and saving, and multiple increases in national income. Decreases in investment, conversely, dampen spending and cause multiple decreases in national income.

Exports to the rest of the world act as investment in that they stimulate the economy. Imports from abroad act as savings: They are withdrawals. These flows are part of how international trade influences domestic economies.

🎝 MULTIPLE-CHOICE SELF-TEST 🎝🎝🎝🎝🎝🎝🎝🎝🎝🎝🎝🎝🎝🎝🎝

1. Find the true statement about the nature of business cycles.
    a. The economy's growth during expansion phases has exceeded the declines in GDP that have occurred during contraction phases.
    b. Expansion phases end in a trough.
    c. The fact that the cycle has hit a peak or trough is easily recognized at the time that it happens.
    d. Little is known about what goes on during the course of a business cycle.

2. In the circular flow model, firms:
    a. And households form the two sides of the two types of markets, but firms are both suppliers and partial demanders in output markets.
    b. Are buyers in output markets and sellers in input markets.
    c. Make withdrawals from the circular flow, whereas households make injections into it.
    d. And households both invest and save.

3. The payments in the national income flow:
    a. Are only about half what firms receive in revenues.
    b. Will tend to be less, the higher profits are.
    c. Will tend to be higher, the higher the revenues are that firms receive.
    d. Have all the above characteristics.

4. In a simple model of the circular flow that includes just households and firms, equilibrium exists when:
    a. Injections equal withdrawals.
    b. The level of national income stops growing or shrinking.
    c. Investment spending equals the amount of savings.
    d. Any of the above is true.

5. According to the circular flow model, if firms decide to increase their investment expenditures, then:
    a. Income payments to households will decrease.
    b. Income will rise and households will end up saving more at a new equilibrium.
    c. This creates disequilibrium in the circular flow, and savings must decrease in order to create a new equilibrium.
    d. Consumption must decrease in order to balance the flow.

6. When a country exports more than it imports, then:
    a. Other countries must also export more.
    b. The rest of the world will slump.
    c. Domestic savings must exceed domestic investments in equilibrium.
    d. Domestic investment must exceed domestic savings in equilibrium.

𝒥𝓁 STUDY QUESTIONS

1. Use the circular flow model to analyze the effect on national income of a burst of new investment spending.

2. What is the relationship between micro models and business cycles?

3. Discuss the performance of employment and unemployment during the phases of a business cycle.

4. Why do you think the U.S. economy has followed a jagged path upward?

5. How do national income and GDP differ? How do they perform through the various phases of business cycles?

6. Can the circular flow model be in equilibrium when exports are not equal to imports?

𝒥𝓁 PROBLEM

Some economists are already predicting that, in the years following 2020, the savings rate of households will drop unusually low. Why? Because a rising fraction of the population will be of retirement age, a time when people do not save at all but rather consume more than their income by drawing upon past savings. Younger households will, of course, still be saving, but the overall amount saved out of everyone's income will decline. Illustrate this situation with a circular flow diagram in which you number the flows in the order in which they are affected. Write a description to explain your diagram.

CHAPTER 13

Government Fiscal Actions and the Pace of the Economy

𝕵 CHAPTER PREVIEW

"Ask 10 economists their opinions, and you'll get 12 different points of view." "Line all economists in the world up end-to-end, and they'll never reach a conclusion."

Indeed, to humorists it seems that no two economists agree. Vigorous debate marks discussion of industrial policy, tax reform, defense spending, merit pay for teachers, International Monetary Fund (IMF) bailouts, and Social Security benefits. The readers of *Time, Newsweek, Barron's,* and *The Village Voice* find a wide range of differing opinions.

No area reflects disagreement more than the *role of the federal government.* Consider, for example, the divergent views of two distinguished economists, John Kenneth Galbraith and Milton Friedman. Galbraith, Harvard professor emeritus, former U.S. ambassador to India, adviser to Democrats, and author of numerous books and articles, claims that the public sector is starved. In his most famous book, *The Affluent Society* (1958), Galbraith eloquently argued for increased social spending in a society characterized by uneven income distribution, bloated private wealth, and a starved public sector.

Nobel laureate, Milton Friedman, professor emeritus from the University of Chicago, fellow of the Hoover Institute, and an adviser to former President Ronald Reagan and former Prime Minister Margaret Thatcher, forcefully points to the U.S. government as an overblown octopus strangling the private market system. In *Capitalism and Freedom* (1962), he argued that less government results in improved productivity, greater economic well-being, and more human freedom.

The views of these two eloquent writers reflect two different political positions in the ongoing American debate over the appropriate role of government in our lives. House Speaker Newt Gingrich, and the 1994–1996 Republican Congress argue that the government interferes too much in the private lives of citizens and should be scaled back. They want less government assistance, fewer government programs, and less government spending. President Bill Clinton argues that a more activist government is needed and wants to spend more on welfare, highways, dams, and so forth, as well as guarantee universal coverage for medical care. Clinton and his advisers Laura D'Andrea Tyson and Vice president Al Gore prefer a more activist industrial policy favoring certain promising high-tech industries. Like President George Bush before him, however, President Clinton feels constrained by large budget deficits and has thus called for substantial tax increases. His Republican opponents favor tax decreases, arguing that higher tax revenues facilitate the political decisions to spend more.

The vast amounts of money involved in government spending and taxation raise numerous questions about how federal fiscal actions affect the pace of economic activity. What are the implications of government borrowing as an alternative to taxation in order to finance increased spending? Are federal deficits inflationary? Does government investment in infrastructure have consequences similar to those of government consumption expenditures? Our analysis here is not intended to promote a point of view that "government is good" or "government is bad"; our intention is to evaluate the economic effects of government fiscal actions.

1. Do increased taxes slow the economy?
2. Are federal deficits inflationary? Recessionary?
3. Is the trade deficit related to the budget deficit?

CONCEPTS REINTRODUCED

Bracket Creep 239
Business Cycles 254–256
Circular Flow Model 36
Equilibrium 81
Marginal Costs 124

NEW CONCEPTS

Government Expenditures
Transfer Payments
Government Budget Rule
Federal Debt
Entitlements
Marginal Tax Rate
Effective Tax Rate
Flat Tax
Payroll Taxes
Investment Tax Credit
Capital Gains
Excise and Sales Taxes
Structural Deficits
Cyclical Deficits
Gramm-Rudman-Hollings Law
Crowding Out
Twin Deficits

▨ CHAPTER OBJECTIVES

After studying this chapter, you should be able to:

1. Define *government expenditures, transfer payments,* and *entitlements* by giving examples of each.

2. Define the government *budget rule,* showing how the result can be a budget surplus, a balanced budget, or a budget deficit.

3. Define the federal debt.

4. List the four major revenue sources of the federal government.

5. Use a tax table to find the *marginal* tax rate and the *effective* tax rate for a given taxable income.

6. Use a tax table to list the various tax brackets and tell whether the tax rate is progressive, regressive, or proportional.

7. Define *fiscal policy.*

8. Use the formula for equilibrium in the circular flow model to show how an increase in government expenditures and/or transfer payments can crowd out private investment or can lead to an increase in the trade deficit.

GOVERNMENT ECONOMIC INTERVENTION

The argument over the appropriate role of the federal government extends well beyond U.S. borders. The great debates and upheavals in China, the Commonwealth of Independent States (the CIS), and Eastern Europe revolve around an intense dispute over central government ownership and control of the means of production: land, factories, machinery, and all resources. In Eastern Europe and the former Soviet Union, reformers such as Lech Walesa of the Solidarity Labor Union in Poland; Vaclav Klaus, Czech Republic leader; and Russia's Boris Yeltsin seek to disengage government monopoly of businesses by promoting private ownership and decentralized control of firms, farms, and property. The splitting of Czechoslovakia into the Czech and Slovak republics and the disintegration of the old Soviet Union into many independent states suggest that the transition to private markets may be difficult, uneven, and politically painful.

Western Europe is also going through a serious, complex debate over the role of government in the European Union (EU). How much authority should the independent nations—Germany, France, the United Kingdom, Denmark, Austria, Italy, and so on—have relative to the central economic authority in Geneva? Some see the European Common Market run by the European Union as an effective device for reducing tariffs and other trade barriers, but some see it as a nearly central government on the model of the United States with a single currency and uniform fiscal and monetary policies.

On the American political scene, libertarians stand on the right, holding the view that government's role should be minimal, rarely interfering in the personal lives of private citizens. To the left, socialists believe the government should own, control, or regulate major industries, using the dollars earned to provide benefits to citizens from birth to burial.

Most Americans, being pragmatic, don't hold doctrinaire political positions on the role of government. Although heated arguments continue, such as those over the level of strategic defense spending, the role of work in welfare programs, the breadth of medical coverage, the effectiveness in stabilizing the economy, and the viability of industrial policy, we have a rough social consensus that government should finance only the social programs that are not adequately provided by private markets. Most Americans agree:

- That the government should maintain an adequate defense system to protect our vital interests.
- That we need public support for Social Security, aid to education, environmental protection, unemployment insurance, and a poverty safety net.
- That there is a need for government to oversee the "rules of the game" for private enterprise through regulatory commissions (such as the Securities and Exchange Commission), the antitrust laws, and the courts.
- That government should build and maintain the infrastructure of public goods, such as highways, bridges, and dams.
- That government should help contribute to a stable economic environment.

In summary, most Americans, and most economists, agree that private enterprise efficiently satisfies many of our material needs and wants. Yet the need for some government economic intervention is widely recognized.

THE U.S. GOVERNMENT BUDGET IN PERSPECTIVE

Virtually every family, firm, and institution has a budget, and this includes the federal government. The federal budget is similar to your own budget in that two of its major features are expenditures or outlays and income or revenue. The outlay side of the budget has three parts: (1) government expenditures on goods and services, (2) transfer payments, and (3) **interest payments on federal debt. Government expenditures on goods and services** range from new missile systems, desks and typewriters, and the services of soldiers, technicians, and engineers to maintenance of the White House. In addition, government undertakes many payments that are not in exchange for goods and services; these payments are called **transfer payments.** Social Security payments are an example of transfer payments. Social Security accounts for about 75 percent of total transfer payments. Other transfer payments are unemployment compensation, Aid to Families with Dependent Children (AFDC), and agricultural subsidies. Finally, the federal government usually spends more money each year than it collects in tax revenues. The government borrows money and then pays interest on the loans.

GOVERNMENT EXPENDITURES ON GOODS AND SERVICES are dollar payments, made by the government, in exchange for currently produced products or work received.

TRANSFER PAYMENTS are outlays by the government for which no good or service is received in the current period. Thus, payments are received by private individuals, but government does not receive any good or service in exchange.

INTEREST PAYMENTS ON FEDERAL DEBT are dollar payments to those who hold government debt instruments called *securities.* These securities are held by banks, individuals, businesses, foreigners, and the Federal Reserve Bank.

The revenue side of the government budget comes from two alternative sources. The government can finance its expenditures either by collecting taxes or by borrowing money. When the government borrows, it issues a promise-to-pay note called a **U.S. government security.** Anyone holding such a security is, in effect, lending money to the federal government. These securities are financial assets and are held by financial institutions, corporations, private citizens, foreign governments, companies, and individuals.

A U.S. GOVERNMENT SECURITY is a loan instrument issued by the government, which promises to pay the lender a fixed rate of interest per year and repay the original loan at a fixed future date. (Variable-rate loans may be introduced in the future.)

Government fiscal activity must always satisfy the following condition: *Total outlays,* which are the sum of expenditures on goods and services (expenditures, for short), transfer payments (transfers, for short), and interest on the debt must equal *total revenue,* which is the sum of taxes and loans. This condition is called the **government budget rule.**

$$\text{Expenditures} + \text{transfers} + \text{interest} = \text{tax revenue} + \text{borrowing} \qquad (13\text{--}1)$$

Logically, the budget rule must always hold. When outlays exceed tax revenues, then

$$(\text{Expenditures} + \text{transfers} + \text{interest}) - \text{tax revenue} > \text{zero} \qquad (13\text{--}2)$$

The government must therefore borrow. This is called *deficit* spending. The deficit equals the difference between current outlays and tax revenues. Conversely, when the government spends and transfers less than it collects in taxes, it runs a *surplus.* When outlays equal tax revenues, the federal government has a **balanced budget.** If the flow of government fiscal activity over the course of a year results in a deficit, then the government adds to its stock of **federal debt.**

The FEDERAL DEBT is the current dollar sum of financial obligations, equal to all accumulated past deficits minus surpluses of the U.S. government.

People often try to draw analogies between their personal finances and the federal budget. Such analogies often lead to false conclusions. Some people think that because individuals either pay off their debts or face bankruptcy, the government must also someday have to pay off its debt or go bankrupt. This inference is false. People have relatively limited life spans; government does not. A more apt comparison is between the government and a corporation, because neither governments nor corporations are limited by human life spans. Large corporations finance much of their activity by borrowing. Because they do not have limited life spans, they need never retire all their debt. The same is true of the federal government. It need never retire its debt, because it does not have a finite life span. (The federal government is *not strictly* analogous to a firm, because unlike a firm, the government can print money. This will be studied in Chapters 14 and 15.) This does not mean a government can run deficits without consequences.

Deficit spending increases the debt, and interest payments on the debt grow each year that the government runs a new deficit. Therefore, the spending side of the ledger is rising. If the deficits are large enough, it is possible that interest payments will grow faster than the economy itself. Such a situation cannot be sustained. If interest costs rise faster than the ability to raise taxes, then the budget is unstable in the long run. Such a situation would require either a change in policy, such as less spending, or an economic crisis, such as inflation or flight from the currency in the form of a refusal to accept the currency in exchange for goods and services. Such events have occurred in many poorly run countries, and no country is immune to the realities of the budget constraint.

Historical Perspective on Federal Spending

Before the 1930s, federal fiscal activity was only a small part of the national economy. Except in wartime, federal expenditures were usually between 1 percent and 3 percent of GDP. The federal budget now hovers at about 25 percent of GDP. How did this growth come about?

The Depression and World War II

The most momentous change in the role of the federal government transpired during the tenure of President Franklin Delano Roosevelt (FDR) in response to the Great Depression. FDR dramatically increased and altered the role of the U.S. federal government (his program was called the *New Deal*). Until the 1930s, state and local governments financed projects in education, roads, dams, bridges, some medical and welfare assistance, police and fire protection, and sanitation. Their combined budgets vastly exceeded that of the federal government. The federal government managed the judicial system, administered interstate commerce, funded a relatively small peacetime army, and ran the national park system—and that was about it.

Under FDR, the federal government took a much more active role in supporting the unemployed, the retired, the poor, and others in need. His administration created major jobs programs, such as the Civilian Conservation Corps (CCC) and the Works Progress Administration (WPA). The government hired unemployed adults to undertake meaningful work. "New Dealers" established the Social Security system to offer retirement and disability benefits to workers and their families. The government became more actively involved in regulating financial institutions, insuring banks, and inspecting industrial firms. FDR created new federal agencies such as the National Recovery Agency (NRA) and the Federal Deposit Insurance Corporation (FDIC). Ten years after the 1929 crash, federal expenditures had increased by 225 percent in real terms. By the end of the 1930s, 7 percent of GDP went to federal government expenditures, compared to 2 percent in 1929, and three-quarters of this much larger federal budget was spent on nondefense programs.

World War II had a major impact on the federal budget, with observable effects on the U.S. economy. The growth of federal debt was enormous. To finance World War II, the government borrowed hundreds of billions of dollars by issuing U.S. government securities. By 1947, the federal debt held by the public was $225 billion, *nearly equal* to total GDP in that year. Because economic growth was so robust during the next 33 years, the ratio of federal debt outstanding to GDP declined.

The Early Postwar Period

At the end of World War II, the Cold War arms race and the explosion in the cost of modern weapons radically increased the overall level of federal spending and the proportion of the budget allocated to defense. Federal expenditures consumed, on average during the 1950s, 19 percent of GDP. About 85 percent of the growth in federal spending was on defense-related activity.

Lyndon Baines Johnson (LBJ), president from 1963 to 1968, presided over another major expansion in domestic federal spending. LBJ, believing that all Americans had a right to be free of poverty, launched the Great Society plan, with new and expanded social programs called **entitlements.** By far the largest and most expensive of these entitlement programs is Social Security. By 1997 Social Security alone would cost over $370 billion per year. Other important entitlement programs are Medicare for the aged, Medicaid for the poor, food stamps, and AFDC. AFDC is the principal welfare program in America. It is jointly funded by state and federal governments.

> ENTITLEMENTS are government transfer payments made to individuals having certain designated characteristics and circumstances, such as age, health, or need.

A major shift in the composition of the federal budget took place between 1960 and 1980. Defense fell from half of the federal budget to one-third. Transfer payments for social programs increased in share from one-quarter to one-half of the budget. The largest growth area of government spending was in Social Security.

Throughout the 1960s and 1970s, spending on entitlement programs continued to expand. These programs covered more people and provided more benefits to recipients. By the mid-1970s, these various cash income payments—Social Security, AFDC, medical care, education grants, and worker training—accounted for 40 percent of the federal budget, or $170 billion. The budget itself consumed some 20 percent of total GDP.

The Reagan-Bush-Clinton Years

The decades of the 1980s and the 1990s saw two major shifts in the pattern of federal spending. The first shift occurred when Ronald Reagan, elected president in 1980, reordered priorities away from social programs and toward defense spending. He reversed the decline in the Defense Department budget, slowed growth in entitlement programs, and cut nonretirement transfer payments. The second shift, which took place in the 1990s, during the administrations of George Bush and Bill Clinton, involved a reaction to the Reagan social cuts as well as a response to the evident disintegration of the Soviet empire.

The four pie charts in Figure 13–1 illustrate the changing composition of the budget from 1960 to 1980, the reversal of these trends through the second Reagan administration in 1988, and finally 1996.

From 1980 to 1984, President Reagan and the Republican Senate majority doubled defense spending. Despite legislated cutbacks in social programs, the recession of 1980–1982 forced social spending up via entitlements. By 1988 total government outlays for defense had grown from 21.6 percent of total outlays to 27 percent.

Shortly after George Bush took office, the Berlin Wall fell, under the pressure of a tide of East German immigrants flooding to the West. In short order, communist regimes in Poland, East Germany, Hungary, Czechoslovakia, and Romania collapsed, and reformers began to grope toward market economies. Soon the Soviet state itself collapsed and the former empire disintegrated into several independent republics. Russia has tried to turn toward democratic capitalism under Boris Yeltsin. The resulting collapse of the Warsaw Pact as a military threat to NATO forced downward pressure on U.S. defense spending, and soon cries for a "peace dividend" were heard in Congress.

FIGURE 13–1   Federal Expenditure Mix, for 1960, 1980, 1988, and 1996

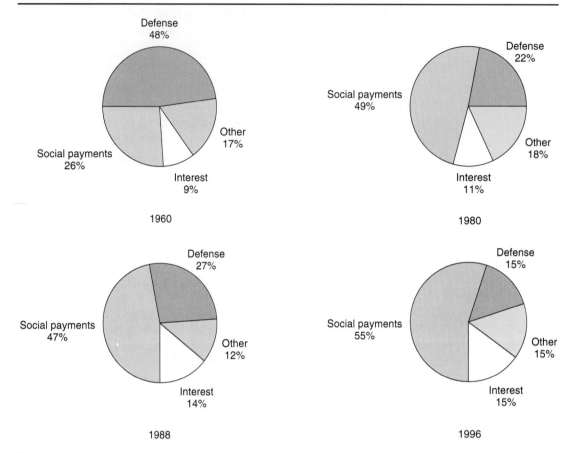

These pie charts indicate the allocation of the budget among several spending categories. From 1960 to 1980 defense spending fell from approximately 50 percent to 20 percent of the budget, whereas social payments increased from approximately 25 percent to 50 percent. The pie chart for 1988 indicates the Republican administrations' priorities: an increase in defense from some 22 percent to 27 percent while holding Social Security constant and reducing all other categories, except for interest payments on the national debt. The 1996 budget in turn reflects a return toward domestic social payments and a decline in defense—Democratic priorities.

Sources: Congressional Budget Office, *The Economic and Budget Outlook: Fiscal Years 1991–1995* (Washington, D.C.: U.S. Government Printing Office, January 1990); and *The Economic Report of the President* (Washington, D.C.: U.S. Government Printing Office, February 1995).

Divided Government

The collapse of the Soviet empire turned attention away from defense and foreign issues and toward domestic concerns. However, despite interest in domestic social problems—such as health care, crime, and poverty—persistent and large budget deficits spawned deep divisions in federal budget policy. Swinging from a Republican presidency and Democratic Congress, Americans elected Democrat Bill Clinton president, and in the 1994 midterm elections they sent a Republican majority to the House and Senate. Republicans controlled both houses of Congress for the first time in 40 years, but with slim margins.

Both sides tried to reduce the deficit by cutting programs, but fought over which ones to cut. The preeminent position of defense ended, with defense expenditures falling from 27 percent of the budget in 1988 to about 16 percent in 1996. As an oblique attack on social spending, Newt Gingrich and his fiscally conservative Republican colleagues sought a balanced budget amendment to the Constitution (an amendment that would require Congress to pass a balanced budget and would constrain its ability to raise taxes). Neither side seemed to have sufficient political power to resolve the persistent budget deficits. A slow but sustained growth did reduce the yearly deficit flow of red ink, but Congress still debated a Constitutional amendment to balance the budget.

Federal Budget Revenues

The explosion in federal expenditures from less than $3 billion in 1929 to a projected $1,630 trillion in 1997 required not only increased revenues from existing taxes but new tax sources altogether. In 1929, taxes on payroll (wages) did not exist, with two-thirds of federal revenues coming from taxes on personal income and corporate income (the latter being the larger of the two). The rest came from customs duties, excise taxes, and land sales. Historically, peacetime income-tax rates have been low. After every major war, military spending has fallen and Congress has reduced tax rates. Typically, however, Congress lowered tax rates less than the postwar decline in defense costs, and postwar budgets invariably registered surpluses. The period immediately after World War II proved no exception.

By 1950 the federal tax system relied on four major revenue sources:

1. Personal income taxes.
2. Corporate income taxes.
3. Payroll taxes.
4. Excise and other taxes.

Thirty years of congressional tax tinkering had, by 1985, produced an unintelligible and complex system of deductions, exclusions, and loopholes that greatly reduced the personal and corporate income-tax bases. In order to generate adequate revenue from the reduced base, Congress had either raised tax rates or allowed them to drift up via bracket creep. By 1980 the top rate was 70 percent, and many middle-class Americans paid tax rates ranging from 30 percent to 50 percent. The federal tax system had become an unintelligible and inefficient morass.

By 1985 Congress realized that the tax code had become too complex, inefficient, and unfair. Pervasive dissatisfaction with the system had led to criticism, tax avoidance, and political corruption. Congress finally felt compelled to overhaul the system. Following a remarkable 1984 Treasury report, *A Tax Proposal for Fairness, Equity and Efficiency,* Congress passed the **Tax Reform Act of 1986.** This act, the most revolutionary piece of tax legislation in 50 years, completely restructured the tax system, trading personal tax cuts for corporate tax increases so that net revenues were roughly unchanged.

The Personal Income Tax System

To illustrate some of the main structural changes in the 1986 Tax Reform Act, consider the personal income tax. By law the personal income tax system before 1986 was quite *progressive*—the more income a person earned, the higher the percentage of income that was paid in taxes.

To some people a progressive tax is seen as fair, because richer people can afford to pay a higher percentage of their incomes in taxes than can the poor. This equity benefit of a tax has to be weighed against its efficiency effects. *Efficiency* refers to the ability of the tax rule to collect revenues without unintentionally distorting private decision making. When a tax system is progressive, the tax rate charged on additional dollars earned is higher than the average tax rate up to that point. This is the concept of the **marginal tax rate.** The lowest marginal tax rate is zero, because at low income levels Uncle Sam collects no income tax. After that, tax rates gradually rise. The top marginal rate in 1979 stood at 70 percent for income over $85,000.

This means that were your income to reach $85,000, then every additional dollar you earned would be taxed at a rate of 70 percent. You would only get to keep 30 percent. In 1981 Congress adopted the Reagan plan to reduce the top marginal rate to 50 percent.

Reagan, when in his most successful years as an actor, found himself in the 90 percent tax bracket. If he got a new "gig" then of each new dollar he earned, he got to keep only 10 cents—the rest, 90 cents, going to Uncle Sam! When he became president, Reagan was determined to lower the top marginal tax rate, believing that high marginal rates were inefficient in that they discouraged work effort. In 1986 the top marginal rate was cut to 32 percent, thereby cutting the top rate by more than half in seven years.

The MARGINAL TAX RATE is the tax rate charged on the taxpayer's last additional dollar earned. If the tax system is progressive, then one's marginal tax rate is always greater than one's average tax rate.

Few taxpayers actually paid high-percentage marginal tax rates, however, because they were able to exploit various tax breaks. In practice, therefore, the personal income tax was only mildly progressive. After taking into account various tax breaks, the top **effective tax rate** was only about 33.5 percent, even for income over a million dollars a year. Horror stories about wealthy Americans paying no tax helped spawn the tax reform movement.

The key idea of the 1986 Tax Reform Act was the **flat tax**—a system in which one tax rate applies to all income. The Treasury plan called for a modified flat tax, with three brackets, ranging from 15 percent to 32 percent. Congress passed a three-rate system, but added a wrinkle—once the new law was phased into place in 1988, the bottom rate would be zero and most taxpayers would be in the 15 percent marginal tax bracket. Top income earners were to pay the top rate of 28 percent; however this rate would not just be their marginal rate but also their average rate. To get to this point with a top average and marginal rate the same, Congress had to force marginal rates to rise to a peak of 32 percent, then fall back down to 28 percent until all income of the very rich is taxed at the average rate of 28 percent. The new system also did away with many complex deductions and exclusions, so that almost all personal income is now taxed. The net effect, however, was a reduction in revenue from the personal income tax of about $200 billion per year.

In 1993 President Clinton and the Democratic Congress raised the top marginal tax rates to 42 percent, arguing that redistribution throughout the 1980s favored the top 5 percent of Americans at the expense of the poor. Clinton had originally favored a middle-class tax cut, but budget deficit realities made such a proposal impossible. The mid-1990s saw yet another attempt at lowering tax burdens, despite persistent budget deficits. The main platform plank of presidential candidate Senator Robert Dole (Republican–Kansas) was to reduce top marginal tax rates by 15 percent and move toward an even flatter tax.

Other Taxes

Before 1986 the **corporate income tax** rate was 46 percent for all income above very low levels. However, this statutory rate greatly exaggerated the tax burden on firms. Substantial tax breaks designed to encourage capital formation and risk taking dropped the effective tax rates well below 46 percent for most corporations. For banks and oil companies the effective rate was closer to 1 percent. For retail firms, it was anywhere from about 25 percent to about 40 percent. The actual rate depended on complexities such as the composition of capital, financial structure, and the nature of output. Some corporate giants actually paid no tax at all.

The Tax Reform Act of 1986 eliminated many corporate tax breaks in order to compensate for lost revenue from the personal income tax. The most important of these was the *investment tax credit,* which had allowed firms to reduce their tax payments to average rates well below those of persons. By eliminating these breaks, Congress could lower statutory rates to 33 percent and still raise corporate tax revenues to "pay for" the lower revenue from the personal income tax reform. Although many breaks were retained, Congress instituted a stiff minimum tax law that would ensure that big corporations paid a significant tax.

Social insurance taxes, which include the **payroll tax** and taxes for unemployment and medical insurance, take a flat percentage out of all earned income up to some maximum level. This type of tax is *regressive,* because it takes a higher percentage of income from low-wage earners than from those earning high wages. Furthermore, the government does not levy this tax on nonwage income. For these reasons, some analysts think the payroll tax is inequitable. They prefer a tax that is progressive or at least one that does not take less from the rich than from the poor.

Pressure to revert to a multirate income tax system began almost immediately after the passage of the 1986 flat-tax reform. One pledge of the Bush campaign had been to lower the tax rate applied to income from growth in the value of capital assets, such as stocks. The tax rate on these **capital gains** would be 15 percent, or about half of the top marginal tax rate. Advocates of this rate cut argued that a lower rate on capital gains would foster growth and encourage risky capital ventures. A capital gains tax rate cut came up again as part of the Republican Contract with America again in the 1996 presidential campaign and again in 1997. Opponents argued that the tax rate cut would be unfair in that immediate benefits would accrue to the rich. The implications for revenue of a cut in the capital gains rate have been debated vigorously; supporters argued that the cut would raise revenues by as much as $4 billion, and opponents argued that the same cut would reduce revenues by $4 billion. Statistical research has been unable to provide an unambiguous revenue prediction.

Some federal taxes come from a variety of sources, including **excise taxes** (taxes on specific products such as cigarettes and alcohol), license fees, import duties, and special charges for services rendered. The **sales tax,** levied on a wide variety of products, is restricted to the states.

The first pie chart in Figure 13–2 shows the relative importance in 1950 of these four tax categories. The largest source of federal taxes was the personal income tax—43 percent. The corporate income taxes contributed 27 percent, and social insurance taxes accounted for only 10 percent. The pie charts indicate two striking trends in the composition of federal taxes:

1. The corporate income tax fell as a source of federal revenues from 27 percent in 1950 to 8 percent by 1985. This reflects the growing importance of tax incentives for investment spending.
2. Social insurance taxes jumped in importance from about 10 percent to 36 percent of federal tax revenues. At first, the main tax in this category, the payroll tax, was used to support Social Security, but in the Johnson administration these taxes were placed into the general fund.

In 1986 these trends began to reverse somewhat. Corporate taxes now contributed more and personal income taxes less than before. Social insurance taxes continued to contribute about 36 percent of total federal tax revenue. Top tax rates were increased back above 32 percent, to 42 percent by President Clinton. Tax policy continues to be a contentious political issue.

Federal Deficit Spending

During the 32 years from 1958 to 1990, the federal government ran budget deficits in all but two years: 1960 and 1969. In absolute dollar terms, the size of federal deficits increased throughout the period. The largest deficit, in the early 1960s, was $7 bil-

FIGURE 13–2   Tax Revenues by Source, for 1950, 1980, 1985, and 1996

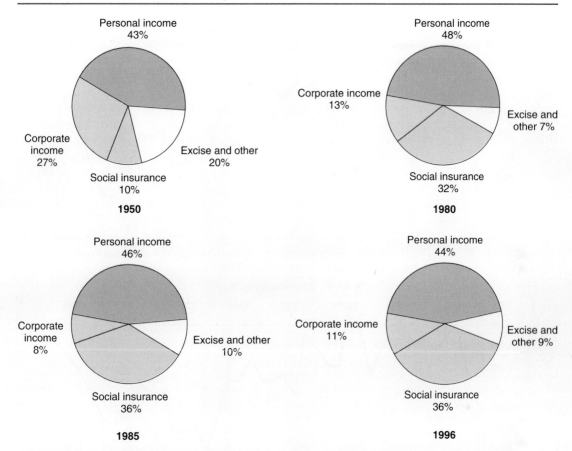

These pie charts illustrate changes in tax sources during the 40 years from 1950 to 1996. The most important changes are the decline in corporate income taxes and the increase in social insurance taxes.

Sources: Congressional Budget Office, *The Economic and Budget Outlook: Fiscal Years 1991–1995* (Washington, D.C.: U.S. Government Printing Office, January 1990); and *The Economic Report of the President* (Washington, D.C.: U.S. Government Printing Office, February 1995).

lion, and the peak of the Vietnam War brought a deficit of $25 billion. Deficits in the late 1970s ranged from $40 to $74 billion. In contrast, very large deficits of more than $200 billion a year occurred from 1982 through 1986, fell to the $150-billion range for a few years, then rose again to over $200 billion in the early 1990s. What do huge federal deficits imply for the government and the economy?

Figure 13–3 traces a picture of the deficit record from 1959 to 1996. The first diagram depicts the absolute dollar amounts of the deficits. The second diagram is really more revealing, because it deflates, or corrects, the deficit figures for the size of the economy by depicting the deficits as a percentage of GDP. Deficits and surpluses

FIGURE 13-3   Federal Deficits and GDP, 1959–1996

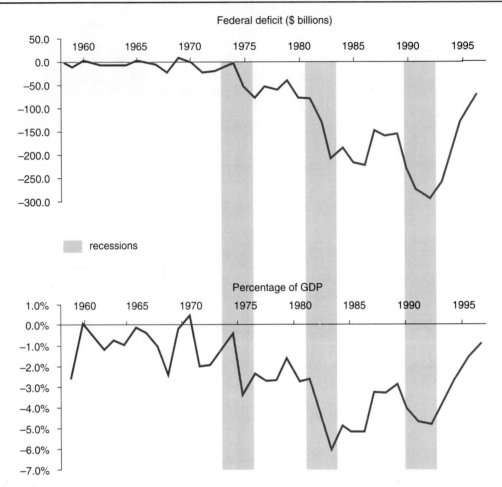

The first diagram illustrates that the absolute dollar size of federal government deficit spending increased over the 25-year period from 1959 to 1994. Forecasts indicate growing deficits unless major expenditure costs or tax increases are instituted. The second diagram puts these deficits into perspective, by showing them as a percentage of GDP.

Source: *The Economic Report of the President* (Washington, D.C.: U.S. Government Printing Office, February 1996).

fell within a range of 1.0 to −4.0 percent of GDP over the 25 years up to 1981. Surpluses and small deficits tended to characterize the years of strong overall economic performance: 1960–1961, 1965–1966, and 1969–1970. Large deficits tended to follow periods of economic slack, such as 1957–1958, 1974–1975, and 1981–1982. Each of these periods witnessed a major slump in the economy.

This pattern—larger deficits occurring during periods of economic slack—reflects the fact that government budgets suffer slumps just as personal budgets do.

Tax revenues decline, because the private sector generates less taxable income, and expenditures for social programs rise, because in slumps more people fall into need. Thus, federal budget deficits grow with slumps and decline with expansions. Another major cause of budget deficits is war. Governments invariably collect less in taxes than they spend to finance war efforts. The result is large deficits. In 1968, with heavy Vietnam War spending, the deficit was $25 billion.

However, the deficits for the 1980s and early 1990s have been very large by historical standards, despite strong economic performance. Furthermore, under current law entitlement spending will grow so fast in the early 2000s that within 20 years deficits will be over $400 billion per year. These facts pose another major policy issue: Are persistent, large federal deficits bad for the economy? If so, how can they be reduced? Persistent deficit finance implies a growing federal debt, and this includes increasing amounts owed to foreigners. Surprisingly, despite 22 years of deficit finance over a quarter century, the federal debt declined steadily as a proportion of GDP up to 1980. Figure 13–4 shows the time trend in the ratio of the federal debt to GDP from 1962 to 1995.

Since 1980 the trend of growth of the debt often has exceeded that of GDP. Economists call these new chronic deficits **structural deficits** because, unlike **cyclical deficits,** they persist regardless of economic performance. These structural deficits reflect the increase in defense spending without large corresponding reductions in domestic budget items and reflect continued cuts in corporate tax revenues. Personal tax rates were cut in 1981, 1982, and 1983, slowing the increase in personal tax revenues. The increase in interest on the debt is about $20 billion a year, enough to swamp modest budget cutting. The 1986 Tax Reform Act did not help to resolve the budget deficit, because President Reagan insisted that the act neither raise nor lower revenues.

To deal with the structural deficits, Congress passed the **Gramm-Rudman-Hollings law** in 1985, which mandated across-the-board cuts in spending in each year from 1986 through 1991 until the budget was balanced. The law allowed Congress and the president to agree on spending cuts in each fiscal year. If they failed to do so, then the law mandated general spending cuts.

The Gramm-Rudman-Hollings legislation was rather effective; it helped those in Congress, and the administration, who favored restraint to resist political pressure for new programs. Deficits as a percentage of GDP fell from 5 percent to 3 percent. President Bush, however, accepted a tax increase in 1990 in exchange for promises from Congress of future caps on spending increases through 1995. Gramm-Rudman-Hollings was rescinded.

Unfortunately, the economy fell into recession in 1991–1992, and deficits once again moved toward the 5 percent range. Bill Clinton defeated George Bush for the presidency in an election in which the federal deficit was a major issue. (Independent Ross Perot campaigned on a hard platform of balancing the budget.) Once in office, President Clinton reduced the deficit with a combination of tax increases and budget cuts so that by 1996 the deficit was less than 3 percent of a growing economy. Nonetheless, $200 billion deficits will persist. Republicans in Congress tried in 1996 but failed to drive spending down and cut the deficit without tax increases.

FIGURE 13–4   U.S. Federal Government Debt as a Percent of GDP, 1962–1996*

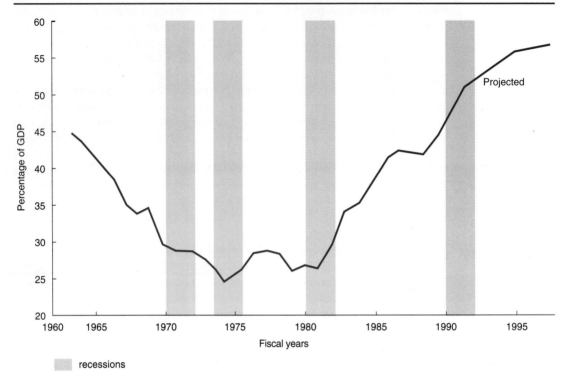

recessions

The ratio of federal debt to GDP indicates that the relative magnitude of the debt fell steadily until the mid-1970s. After 1980, the trend reversed, and debt relative to GDP started to climb. By the late 1980s, the trend leveled off— then started to rise in the 1990s.

*Figures for 1993 and later are projections.

Sources: Congressional Budget Office, *The Economic and Budget Outlook: Fiscal Years 1994–1998* (Washington, D.C.: U.S. Government Printing Office, January 1990); Joint Economic Committee, *Economic Indicators* (Washington, D.C.: U.S. Government Printing Office, March 1993); *The Economic Report of the President* (Washington, D.C.: U.S. Government Printing Office, February 1995); and *Economic Indicators,* June 1995.

TOOL KIT

KEY DATA SOURCES

The Economic Report of the President, issued each February, contains historical data on national economic activity. It may be obtained from the U.S. Government Printing Office, Washington, D.C., at a cost of about $15, or free from your legislator.

Three major policy issues concerning spending, taxes, and deficits arise from a historical survey of the federal budget:

1. What proportions of the GDP should go to defense, social spending, and the private sector?
2. What effect does our tax system have on the economy?
3. What effect does deficit spending have on the economy?

These questions are related to **fiscal policy.**

FISCAL POLICY refers to the federal government expenditure, tax, and borrowing decisions that affect the level of national economic activity and the mix of GDP.

Now that recent history on federal budgeting has been studied and some key fiscal policy issues have been identified, it is possible to analyze the relationship between fiscal policy and the level of economic activity and, finally, to analyze fiscal policy itself.

FISCAL POLICY AND THE CIRCULAR FLOW OF INCOME

The addition of fiscal policy to the circular flow model developed in Chapter 12 shows how that policy affects GDP. Remember that the budget rule dictates that any fiscal policy involves two actions. If government expenditures increase, they must be financed by either new taxes or new borrowing. Similarly, if taxes are cut, then something else in the budget rule must change—a rise in another tax, a cut in spending, or an increase in borrowing. The guiding rule of the budget rule, then, is that two simultaneous changes must always be accounted for in analyzing fiscal policy. As the historical record shows, tax collections rarely correlate with government spending levels.

Economic Indicators contains recent statistics on major macroeconomic indicators. It is published monthly by the Joint Economic Committee of Congress.

The Federal Reserve Bulletin, published monthly, contains historical financial data for the United States and some international statistics as well.

The Monthly Labor Review contains detailed data on the labor market and is available from the U.S. Labor Department, Washington, D.C.

The Survey of Current Business, a monthly printout by the Commerce Department, contains detailed data by industry. The July issue updates national income and production data.

Government may increase spending without levying new taxes. Congress may reduce taxes while maintaining old spending patterns. Consequently, deficits rise and fall often.

Spending and tax decisions are analyzed separately. Analysis of a change in government spending or taxing assumes a change in *deficit spending*. Thus, the two changes to be considered are first a direct spending or tax change and then the corresponding change in deficit spending.

The Impact of Government Taxation

We can analyze the direct effects of taxes by introducing taxes into the circular flow model. Figure 13–5, circular flow model version four, shows governments that tax the peasants, as did that of the Sheriff of Nottingham in the Robin Hood tales, put the revenue into coffers, and spend nothing. The taxes withdraw income from households and leave the people with less to spend. Consequently, taxes are a withdrawal of funds from the circular flow. Of course, businesses also pay taxes, so we show two tax withdrawals in the model: personal taxes and business taxes.

The first step in analyzing the effect of a change in taxes on the circular flow is to recall our Chapter 12 definition of *equilibrium:* the amount of income flowing through the system over time is constant. This condition occurs when total injections into the flow are exactly offset by total withdrawals. In this model, withdrawals equal injections whereas the sum of savings, imports, and taxes equals exports plus investment. We have the following equilibrium condition:

$$\text{Total withdrawals} = \text{total injections} \qquad (13\text{--}3)$$
$$\text{or}$$
$$\text{Imports} + \text{savings} + \text{taxes} = \text{investment} + \text{exports}$$

To understand how this works, consider the following example. If the government increases personal taxes, then people have less income with which to buy goods from firms, both foreign and domestic. Because fewer goods are purchased, firms are left with less income to pass on to households. Figuratively, because more income is drained from the flow, the pressure in the system falls, and the level of income flowing throughout the system declines. The income flow will also fall if business taxes are raised. Firms will then have to reduce payments to inputs, and the households will receive less income. The level of income passing through the flow will decline. As incomes and expenditures fall, "peasants" and firms have less to save. Thus savings will contract as well. Because imports depend on household income, imports will also fall.

How far will income fall, and how much will savings and imports decline? The answer depends on how firms react to the contraction. Firms may respond in one of two ways. They may think the contraction is short term and continue with existing investment plans. In this case, the decline in income will be just enough to pull savings and imports down to offset the higher taxes. At the new equilibrium, savings

FIGURE 13–5 Circular Flow Model Version Four: The Sheriff of Nottingham's Taxes

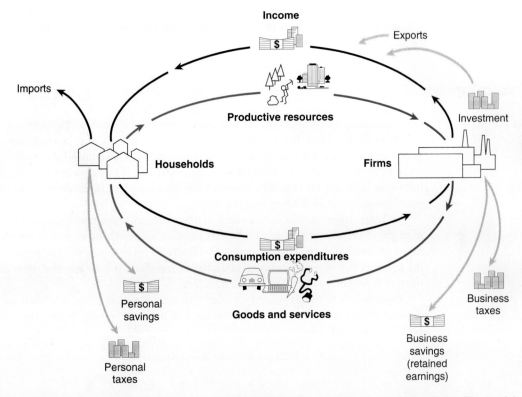

In this "Sheriff of Nottingham" model, the government taxes the private economy but spends nothing. The result is a drain on the circular flow of personal and business taxes. Personal and business savings and imports from the rest of the world also withdraw income from the flow. All taxes, imports, and savings are withdrawals. Investment pours income into the flow, and we call this an *injection*. Similarly, exports of goods and services are an injection. Equilibrium in this model occurs when total withdrawals equal total injections. Thus, the sum of taxes, imports, and savings equals investment expenditures plus exports at equilibrium.

plus imports plus taxes must equal the original level of investment plus exports. Alternatively, firms may respond to the contraction by reducing their own investment spending; fewer sales may induce fewer orders for new inventories. With lower investment injections and higher tax withdrawals, equilibrium income will fall even more. This is because savings and imports must contract until the new sum of lower savings and imports plus higher taxes combines to equal the new lower investment and export level. The new equilibrium is thus characterized by lower income, less in savings, fewer imports, higher taxes, and lower investment.

Regardless of how firms react, planned tax increases are *contractionary*: An increase in taxes implies a decline in national income. This process also works in reverse. A reduction in taxes increases national income. If investment rises and falls with the level of income in the flow, then income will fluctuate even more in response to planned tax changes. But the direction of the effect on income of a tax change remains the same. Increases in taxes slow the economy down, and decreases in taxes speed the economy up.

Transfer Payments

Government spending can now be introduced for circular flow model version five, shown in Figure 13–6. Recall the difference between government expenditures on goods and services and transfer payments. Government expenditures on goods and services result in increases in production and therefore act as investment expenditures—an injection into the flow. Figure 13–6 illustrates this injection by a government-spending arrow leading into the flow.

Transfer payments that do not result in new production are not injections but act as negative taxes. Just as a new tax lowers personal income, a new transfer payment raises personal income. Thus, transfers are illustrated by changing the designation of the personal tax arrow to personal taxes minus transfers. If transfers rise, then less income is withdrawn in taxes minus transfers.

Equilibrium in the expanded circular flow model still requires that total withdrawals equal total injections so that the level of income flowing through the economy is a constant.

$$\text{Total net withdrawals} = \text{total injections} \qquad (13\text{–}4)$$

or

$$\text{Imports} + \text{savings} + \text{taxes} - \text{transfers}$$
$$= \text{investment} + \text{government expenditures} + \text{exports}$$

It is important to realize that this equilibrium condition can occur at many different levels of income. Furthermore, it is important to realize that equilibrium does not require that the government balance its budget. Nor do private savings have to equal investment. The only condition necessary for equilibrium in this model is that the sum of all withdrawals equal the sum of all injections.

If for simplicity we momentarily leave out the rest of the world, an interesting implication of the model is illustrated by rearranging the elements of the equilibrium condition as follows:

$$\text{Savings} = \text{investment} + \left(\begin{array}{c} \text{government} \\ \text{expenditures} \end{array} + \text{transfers} - \begin{array}{c} \text{all} \\ \text{taxes} \end{array} \right) \qquad (13\text{–}5)$$

The expression in parentheses on the right-hand side of Equation (13–5) represents the government budget surplus or deficit. The equation says that, at equilibrium, private savings equal the sum of private investments and the surplus or deficit. Thus, for a closed economy with no foreign sector at any given equilibrium level, when the government raises the deficit, this leaves less investment per dollar of private

FIGURE 13–6   Circular Flow Model Version Five: Government Expenditures, Transfers, and Taxes

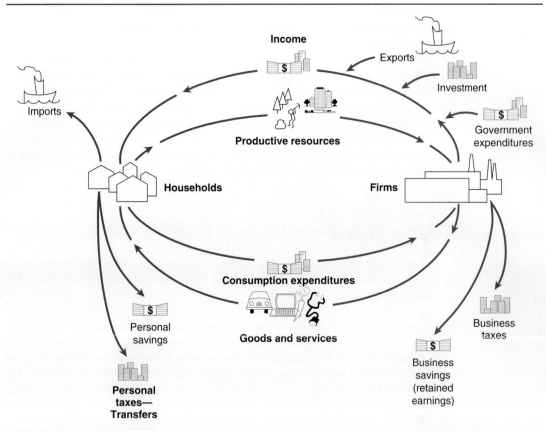

Government spending on new goods and services, which causes new production, is shown as an injection arrow labeled "Government expenditures." Transfers act as a negative tax and are shown as a withdrawal arrow. Equilibrium requires that total withdrawals equal total injections; thus

$$\text{Imports} + \frac{\text{personal}}{\text{savings}} + \frac{\text{business}}{\text{savings}} + (\text{personal taxes} - \text{transfers}) + \frac{\text{business}}{\text{taxes}} = \text{investment} + \frac{\text{government}}{\text{expenditures}} + \text{exports}$$

savings. This is why deficit spending can curtail investment spending. It competes for private savings with firms that want to invest. Deficits may compete with private investment spending under some circumstances.

Government Expenditures

What is the direct effect on equilibrium income of an increase in government expenditures? This depends in part on the initial condition of the economy. If government expenditures rise during a recession, then new production can occur, and the aggregate level of spending in the flow will rise. Firms that sell the new products will increase payments to inputs, which will cause new income to flow into households. The flow will continue to accelerate until it pulls savings and imports up enough to meet the new, higher level of total injections. If the economy is already in an expansion phase, at or near full employment, then the increased government expenditures cannot result in increased aggregate production. Thus, the increased demand is likely to create bottlenecks and put upward pressure on prices. Still, the government spending is expansionary in both cases. Increased government spending raises national income, whereas lowered government spending lowers national income.

Business executives may react to the increased pace of economic activity by increasing investment spending. When the economy expands, so do sales, profits, and prospects. This may induce investment spending. An increase in investment in response to an expansion may be called pulling in.

Deficit Finance and Crowding Out

Government expenditure and tax changes have indirect effects on changes in borrowing. These changes are mandated by the budget rule. If government increases spending and does not compensate for it either by reducing spending elsewhere or by increasing taxes, then borrowing must rise. How does the circular flow respond to increased government borrowing?

Supply-and-demand reasoning says that if government borrowing rises, this increased demand for loans will raise their price. The price of loans is the *interest rate.* Higher interest rates mean higher borrowing costs. Because firms often have to borrow in order to invest, some investment projects now may be unprofitable, and total investment may decline. Deficit finance may curtail private investment. The tendency for deficit finance to raise interest rates and curtail investment is called **crowding out.**

CROWDING OUT is the tendency for federal government, by deficit financing, to compete with firms for borrowed funds. Firms, unable or unwilling to borrow at higher rates of interest, then curtail their investment spending.

The effect of deficit-financed government spending increases is to raise income and *pull in* private investment. At the same time, however, the dollars borrowed to finance government expenditures will *crowd out* private investment. The net effect on equilibrium income will depend upon the relative strength of government spending and pulling in compared to the strength of the crowding-out effect of borrowing.

The relative strengths of pulling in and crowding out depend in part on the economic circumstances prevailing when the deficit occurs. In a deep recession, investment spending is usually low. When the economy is slack, pulling in is likely to dominate crowding out, because idle inputs can be put to work. In a rapidly growing economy, however, deficits are likely to crowd out private investment spending.

Generally, the crowding-out effect is unlikely to be powerful enough to offset both the increased government spending itself and the pulling-in effect. Each $1 of government expenditure that is financed by borrowing will crowd out, at most, $1 of investment. This will leave the total injections constant, and national income will not change. The level of income will not fall with an increase in government spending and may well increase. At the same time, crowding out of investment spending is a concern, because it means that fewer capital goods will be available in the future. Fewer capital goods, in turn, imply lower potential growth and lower realized growth.

Economics has not reached a consensus on the size of the crowding-out effect, but it is believed that $1 of government expenditure will crowd out less than $1 of investment, so that some net expansion in private expenditures occurs. Therefore, the overall effect of a deficit-financed increase in government spending is to stimulate the pace of current economic activity. How strong a stimulus this is continues to be a matter of debate.

The Budget Deficit and the Trade Deficit

If we reintroduce the rest of the world into the model, we see that the effects of budget deficits on the economy are more complex. First, we reintroduce exports as an additional injection and imports as an additional withdrawal, as in Equation (13–4). Just as we collected the government budget items on the right-hand side in Equation (13–5) so that savings equaled the sum of private investment plus the government budget deficit, we collect the trade terms on the left-hand side so that we have

$$\text{Savings} + (\text{imports} - \text{exports})$$
$$= \text{investment} + (\text{government expenditures} + \text{transfers} - \text{taxes}) \qquad (13\text{–}6)$$

Notice that the right-hand side term in parentheses is the budget deficit. The terms in parentheses on the left-hand side constitute the trade deficit so that

$$\text{Savings} + \text{trade deficit} = \text{investment} + \text{budget deficit} \qquad (13\text{–}7)$$

Recall that one concern about federal budget deficits was that they would drain private savings away from private domestic investment through crowding out. Now we see that the budget deficit could instead be offset by a trade deficit, leaving savings and domestic investment intact.

How can a trade deficit offset a budget deficit? Remember that a budget deficit means the government is borrowing to finance the excess of its expenditures over its revenues. The trade deficit is created by the United States' buying more goods from nations of the rest of the world than they buy from the United States. How are those excess goods from the rest of the world paid for? Basically, by American buyers giving foreigners net financial claims on future U.S. goods. These financial claims represent the fact that, to buy the excess goods, foreigners are offered more U.S. dollars than they need to purchase the American goods they want. What do foreigners do with these extra dollars? They do not have a use for them in their own countries, so foreigners use these dollars to make loans and financial investments in the United States. All that the economy requires is that the sum of injections equals the sum of withdrawals. With very high budget deficits, the government creates demand pressure for financial claims. Foreigners meet this demand by net saving—selling the United States more goods than we sell them and salting away the difference for the future. For this reason, many economists refer to the large budget and trade deficits as the **twin deficits.**

The term TWIN DEFICITS represents the belief that large budget deficits can in effect be financed by borrowing from the rest of the world. This takes the form of a trade deficit: We buy more foreign goods, and other countries accept claims on future U.S. goods in return.

CHAPTER REVIEW

Fiscal policy consists of federal government expenditure, transfer, and tax decisions that can influence the pace of economic activity. The history of fiscal policy indicates that the federal government frequently finances spending by borrowing. This is called *deficit spending,* and it contributes to a growing federal debt.

The ratio of federal debt to GDP fell from the end of World War II until 1980. In the 1980s, however, the planned growth of entitlement programs and defense spending, along with reductions in tax rates and business tax burdens, implied future growth of federal deficits, regardless of economic growth. This problem was not resolved by the mid-1990s.

Four major fiscal policy issues are highlighted in this chapter: (1) the proportion of GDP appropriated to defense versus federal social programs, (2) the consequences of the level and nature of taxation, (3) the effect on national income of deficit spending, and (4) the twin-deficits relationship between budget and trade deficits.

To aid in understanding fiscal policy, the circular flow model was used to show that government spending directly increases national income and that taxes directly contract national income.

However, complete analysis of fiscal policy requires paying heed to the budget rule, as well as consideration of the indirect effects of deficit finance implied by changes in government expenditures or taxes. Increases in government expenditures raise national income and crowd in investment spending, but the increased borrowing to finance new government expenditures can crowd out investment spending. The net effect depends on the relative strengths of crowding in and crowding out. Another important consequence of budget deficits is to attract foreign savings. When this happens, Americans import more goods than they export, resulting in a trade deficit.

MULTIPLE-CHOICE SELF-TEST

1. Government transfer payments:
   a. Are transferred to firms or individuals in exchange for services they provide.
   b. Are like gifts rather than purchases.
   c. Are payments for goods or services purchased by the government from another sector of government.
   d. Are a form of taxes.

2. The government budget rule can be expressed as:
   a. Expenditures plus transfers minus taxes equals borrowing.
   b. Taxes plus expenditures equals transfers plus borrowing.
   c. Expenditures equals taxes plus transfers plus borrowing.
   d. None of the above.

3. The U.S. government debt:
   a. Is equal to government spending plus transfers minus taxes.
   b. Is equal to one-tenth of GDP.
   c. Is the total of all the unpaid borrowing of the federal government.
   d. Is all the above.

4. The federal government's largest single source of revenue has long been:
   a. The payroll tax.
   b. The corporate income tax.
   c. The personal income tax.
   d. Borrowing.

5. A flat tax that charges the same marginal tax rate on all included income:
   a. Is by definition a proportional tax.
   b. Would reduce government revenues from the current system, which has higher marginal tax rates.
   c. Is a progressive tax if some initial amounts of income are excluded from taxation.
   d. Taxes all income with no deductions.

6. If domestic savings do not change, a larger government budget deficit will crowd out domestic investment, but this can be prevented if:
   a. Imports exceed exports, resulting in a trade deficit.
   b. Firms build up their inventories faster than the rate of fixed capital formation.
   c. The trade surplus increases because of more imports.
   d. People shift money into individual retirement accounts (IRAs).

7. An amendment to the Constitution to balance the budget would:
   a. Be opposed only by those who are fiscally irresponsible.
   b. Be supported by bond traders, who make their money trading U.S. government securities.

    c. Cost the taxpayers a lot more money.

    d. Shift some fiscal decision authority to the judicial branch of government.

🎓 STUDY QUESTIONS

1. Describe the major trends in tax policy from 1950 to 1986. Assess these trends, considering equity, efficiency, and deficit finance.

2. Assess the Republican position, endorsed by Alan Greenspan, that capital gains not be taxed.

3. Is government defense spending expansionary or contractionary, according to the circular flow?

4. Explain how *crowding out* works. Does any force offset this? Explain.

5. How has the role of government changed from the 1930s to the 1990s? What do these changes imply for the private economy?

6. What caused the change in the deficit-GDP ratio after the early 1980s?

7. How has Congress tried to deal with structural deficits in the budget?

8. What are the *twin deficits*?

𝕀𝕣 PROBLEM

The schedule of individual income tax rates for a married couple filing jointly in 1989 was as follows:

Taxable Income	Tax Rate on that Portion of Income (%)
$0–18,550	15
$18,550–44,900	28
$44,900–93,130	33
$93,130 and up	28

1. What marginal tax rate did a couple face if they earned the following amounts in taxable income? (I.e., income after deductions and exemptions of all allowable types were subtracted.)

   $2,000 per year

   $20,000 per year

   $50,000 per year

   $100,000 per year

2. What amount would a couple earning $20,000 per year in taxable income pay in income tax? What average income tax rate are they paying? What are the tax and the average tax rate for a couple with income of $50,000 per year? With income of $100,000 per year?

CHAPTER 14

Money, Money, Money

𝓙𝓁 CHAPTER PREVIEW

Money makes the world go 'round
It makes the world go 'round
The clinking, clanking sound of:
Money, money, money, money, money, money
Geta little, geta little
Money, money, money, money
A mark, a yen, a buck or pound,
That clinking, clanking, clunking sound
Is all it takes to make the world go 'round
It makes the world go 'round.

Cabaret
(Lyrics and music by Frank Ebb and John Kander.)

This chapter is about money, and making money is a favorite American pastime. Money is made in many, often extraordinary, ways. For example, superstar Michael Jordan earns about $45 million a year from product endorsements and personal appearances. Why? Because he is endowed with a unique skill. He can play basketball as no one else ever has. Fast, agile, graceful, and deadly accurate with a basketball, he can jump so high that he literally seems to float through the air above the heads of the other great players in the National Basketball Association. In addition, Michael Jordan is a generous and charming fellow, so that he is well liked by millions. Naturally sponsors want to associate their products with his grace, skill, and charm. Perhaps his unique talent justifies an annual income far in excess of the total cash awards given to all the Nobel Prize winners in any given year; perhaps not.

In contrast, the highest-paid federal officials, such as top State Department personnel, earn about $120,000 a year. Schoolteachers are lucky to earn half that amount. Chief executive officers (CEOs) of large U.S. corporations frequently earn annual incomes in the high triple digits—$750,000.

Ben Franklin is famous for his advice on handling money: "A penny saved is a penny earned." But from an economist's viewpoint, a penny saved and not invested is a penny losing earnings. Today's investor knows that money must earn a return.

You have learned to use supply-and-demand analysis to determine the relative prices of different goods: Schoolteachers are more plentiful than CEOs and have greater job security; thus, CEOs earn higher salaries. Even more rare are the greatly appreciated skills of the Michael Jordans. Each of these returns is expressed in a common unit, money, and all economic transactions occur in monetary units.

Society has strong ethical views on money. In the Bible, Jesus admonished the money changers to leave the temple. Today, we indict congresspeople and shun TV evangelists if their devotion to money is excessive. Money permeates politics, sports, business, and religion. People work for money, save it, borrow it, lend it, and steal it. Virtually every transaction, legal or illegal, involves money. Value is expressed in terms of "the coin of the realm," money.

1. Is money relevant to decision making in a rationally run economy?
2. Keynes once said that interest rates "rule the roost," meaning that they are the dominant influence on economic activity. Are they indeed the dominant influence?

CONCEPTS REINTRODUCED

Consumer Price Index (CPI) 239
Deficit Spending 284
Demand Curve 52
Equilibrium Price 81
GDP Deflator 237
Inflation 238
Opportunity Cost 7
Supply Curve 74

NEW CONCEPTS

Money
Transaction Accounts
M1
Savings Accounts
Time Deposits
M2
Exchange Value
Nominal Rate of Interest
Loanable Funds
Expected Real Interest Rate
Realized Real Interest Rate
Fisher Effect
Exchange Rates
Nonconvertible Currency
Reserve Currency

✐ CHAPTER OBJECTIVES

After studying this chapter, you should be able to:

1. Define *money* by listing the functions it serves.
2. Tell whether various items that serve a money function (e.g., currency, checking accounts, traveler's checks, and savings accounts) are part of M1; of M2, but not of M1; or of neither.
3. Define the price of money by its *intrinsic value, exchange value,* and *holding cost.*
4. Distinguish between real and nominal yields and interest rates.
5. List some of the factors that can shift demand for money.

WHAT IS MONEY?

To the layman the question, What is money? has a simple answer. Money is paper and coins. To economists, however, underlying this question are complex and subtle ideas. Money is not always paper and coins. For example, in the late 1980s the legal paper currency of Poland was the *zloty.* As the government printed more zlotys, a glut arose, and the purchasing power of the zloty declined rapidly. The people who held the zloty currency found their wealth eroding. Eventually the zloty was no longer accepted, so that it ceased to serve as the medium of exchange for goods and services. Instead, cigarettes and vodka were used, and items were quoted in cigarette or vodka units.

One pack of cigarettes acted as a dollar. The pack was the **unit of account** in transactions. If, for example, a pint of vodka were exchanged for five packs of cigarettes, then the pint of vodka was like a $5 bill. A carton of 10 packs of cigarettes was like a $10 bill. With 20 cigarettes to a pack, each cigarette acted as a nickel. Both vodka and cigarettes were actually exchanged in the marketplace for other goods. Agreements for future delivery were based on payments of cigarettes—that is, they were the **means of deferred payment.** Poles had to know the "price" of products in cigarette currency, not the zloty price. This example illustrates that **money** is whatever society uses to make transactions in the marketplace. This is not always the legal currency issued by the government.

> MONEY is the accepted common medium of exchange for goods and services in the marketplace. It also functions as the unit of account, a means of deferred payment, and a store of value.

Because they had no access to money, prisoners in World War II prisoner-of-war camps invented a system of currency based on items from CARE (Cooperative for

American Relief to Everywhere) packages sent by relief agencies. Again, packages of cigarettes proved useful as money; they were compact and divisible into smaller units, providing denominations for small transactions. Also, cigarettes did not deteriorate, so that given supply, they maintained their value and permitted **a store of value.** The purchasing power of a cigarette was low right after the Red Cross had made new deliveries; the number of cigarettes needed to buy an item was high. In the intervals between deliveries, the purchasing power of a cigarette rose. This occurred because cigarettes were smoked, which reduced the supply of the "money" and raised its purchasing power. The forces of supply and demand are clearly as applicable to the market for money as to other markets.

The Monetary Aggregates

In the United States today, purchases of goods and services are financed by paper dollars and coins (the **legal tender** mandated by the government) and by checks written on accounts in financial institutions. **Transaction accounts** consist of the total funds we may withdraw on demand from financial institutions such as banks, savings and loans, and credit unions. Money is important to the performance of a nation's economy. For that reason, it is important for us to be able to identify exactly what money is and to measure how much of it is in the economy. In subsequent chapters, this information will be shown to fit into our analysis of how macroeconomies work. Economists consider the U.S. money supply to consist of currency plus checking accounts. This is the narrowly defined money supply called **M1.** M1 includes several transaction accounts, including **NOW accounts** (for negotiable order of withdrawal), because these are used like checking accounts.

M1 consists of the total quantity of coins and paper currency classified as legal tender by government mandate that circulates in the hands of the public, plus traveler's checks and all checking account balances the public maintains in financial institutions.

Other financial accounts, similar to checking accounts, can be used to support purchases and these act very much like money. These include savings accounts and time deposits held in commercial banks, thrift institutions, savings and loans, credit unions, and other financial institutions. **Savings accounts** differ from checking accounts, because funds in savings accounts pay higher interest rates and cannot be withdrawn on demand by writing a check. **Time deposits** are held in a financial institution for a fixed time period (such as six months or a year). Early withdrawal from a time deposit account usually results in payment of a penalty fee.

Even in the United States the items that act like money (a medium of exchange, a store of value, a unit of account, and a measure of deferred payment) are evolving, along with innovations in other technologies such as telecommunications. New financial accounts similar to bank accounts sprang up in the late 1970s. **Money market mutual funds** are shares in institutional funds that invest in financial instruments such as U.S. Treasury securities, certificates of deposit (called *CDs*) in financial institutions, and commercial paper (IOUs of big corporations). Checks may be drawn on these share accounts, so in some respects they act like checking accounts. Economists include savings accounts, time deposits of less than $100,000, individually owned money market mutual funds, and similar *liquid assets* in their broadly defined money supply measure, called **M2.**

M2 includes all of M1 plus savings, small (less than $100,000) time-deposit account balances in financial institutions, and small money market mutual funds owned by individuals.

Other financial instruments are *near-monies.* These are less easy to convert into a medium of exchange and include large deposit accounts (of over $100,000) held by businesses, financial instruments created in the banking process (e.g., commercial paper), and financial instruments issued by government (e.g., U.S. savings bonds) and other institutions. These near-monies are sometimes included when economists refer to the monetary aggregates, but M1 and M2 are the two most frequently cited *monetary aggregates.*

These monetary aggregates are thought by most economists to be important indicators of economic policy, which we will be addressing soon. Thus, economists measure the growth rates of M1 and M2 in order to study how they influence macroeconomic activity. Table 14–1 shows the totals of M1 and M2, along with their annual growth rates for selected years from 1970 to 1996. Note that M2 had grown at a faster rate than M1 before 1985. In 1970, a third of M2 was the highly spendable M1-type accounts, but by 1985, M1 was less than a quarter of the total. Note also that M1 fell by 4.3 percent per year in 1996, whereas M2 grew at 4.9 percent. These figures show that M1 and M2 grow at different rates, implying that the composition of the financial instruments that act as money is constantly changing. This is natural, because the economic transactions system is always evolving. This means that the two different measures of the money supply behave differently over time. This difference, in turn, has some important implications in the evaluation of money and the economy. As will be seen to be important later, in August 1993, Alan Greenspan dropped these measures as specific policy targets for the central bank and began to focus more on an interest rate target. Many observers still use M1 and M2 as indicators of policy, so these numbers are studied carefully by lots of businesses and investors.

TABLE 14–1 U.S. Money Supply, M1 and M2

	Totals (in billions)		Annual Rates of Growth (%)	
Year	M1	M2	M1	M2
1970	$ 214.5	$ 628.1	5.1	6.5
1975	287.6	1,023.2	4.8	12.6
1980	412.2	1,633.3	6.8	8.9
1985	620.5	2,567.4	12.4	8.5
1990	827.2	3,355.9	4.0	3.5
1994	1,148.7	3,509.4	1.8	0.4
1995	1,124.9	3,662.3	-2.1	4.4
1996	1,081.0	3,833.1	-4.3	4.9

These totals are for the two most important monetary aggregates, M1 and M2. Note that their annual growth rates differ and, until recently, M2 usually grew faster than M1.

Sources: Joint Economic Committee, *Economic Indicators* (Washington, D.C.: U.S. Government Printing Office, August 1996), and *The Economic Report of the President* (Washington D.C.: U.S. Government Printing Office, May 1997).

Credit

How do the many transactions made with credit cards fit into the definition of money as the medium of exchange? At the time of purchase, neither cash nor check is used. To buy gasoline with your gasoline credit card you simply show your card to the attendant or computer, who records the purchase. Later the oil company bills you for the amount. You may hold other types of credit cards as well—American Express, Visa, Diners Club, MasterCard.

First, it is important to understand that money and credit are different concepts. Money is a specific, measurable magnitude; **credit** is the capacity to borrow money up to a specified limit under specified conditions. Thus, you may have a credit limit, say, of $1,500, on any particular credit card, or you may have a credit card from a specific company. The conditions for use of these credit cards are usually quite precise. You may have to pay an annual fee, be required to pay interest on outstanding balances, not purchase over a maximum limit, and so forth. In short, credit comes in many shapes and sizes.

Second, although some economists prefer to deal with the concept of total credit rather than with money supply, credit is more difficult to pin down and measure. Credit and money, however, are related. The amount of money circulating in the economy limits the availability and terms of credit extended by financial institutions and private corporations.

Third, when you make a credit purchase, the actual transfer of funds from your account is postponed until you, the buyer, pay off your account. This payoff eventually involves withdrawing funds from your bank balance. Thus, economists distinguish between the quantity of money as measured by M1 or M2 and the volume of credit, a capacity to borrow.

Some people think that someday money may cease to exist in a physical sense. In fact, banks maintain very little hard currency in their vaults now. The bank makes an electronic record on its computer of the money in your account. When you write a check, the bank reduces your balance electronically by the amount of the check. The recipient of your check (the issuer of the credit card) finds its bank account increased by the amount of your check. No pieces of paper changed hands in recording the transaction. Today, money used in many transactions exists in an accounting and electronic sense only, not in a physical sense. At the same time, the proportion of hard currency to M1 is rising. This may reflect an increase in tax avoidance schemes or in illegal transactions undertaken in cash form only.

WHAT PRICE MONEY?

Suppose you were transported to another planet where no one had heard of the dollar. In this locale, your dollars would be useless. Any money saved would be lost. Had you taken gold, cigarettes, or vodka, rather than paper dollars, your money, though unacceptable as a medium of exchange, would still have intrinsic value. Gold is ornamental, fills teeth, and is usable in industry; cigarettes may be smoked; vodka may be drunk. But paper money has zero intrinsic value. This is a unique and peculiar characteristic of paper money: It is intrinsically useless, yet people steal, lie, cheat, and work very hard to get it.

Money's Intrinsic Value

What is the price of this intrinsically useless item, money? The answer depends on what is meant by *price*. In one sense, the price of a dollar is always $1. In other words, when you ask the price of any good, you mean, How many dollars do I have to give up to get it? What is the price of a ticket to a Michael Jackson concert? Answer: $35. What is the price of a candy bar? Answer: 55 cents. But then, what is the price of a dollar? Answer: $1. Many times you hear that a dollar is not worth what it used to be. Ask the speaker what the dollar is worth now. If the answer is 25 cents, immediately pull out a quarter and exchange it for a dollar. Continue until you have all the speaker's dollars!

Money's Exchange Value

Money has another price, one that can change over time. Suppose we ask how many candy bars a dollar bought in 1960? The answer is about 10. In 1997, a dollar would buy fewer than two candy bars. In general, the dollar cost of any good in 1960 when compared to its dollar cost in 1997 was lower. The dollar now buys fewer goods and services than it did in 1960. The dollar buys less, because inflation between 1960 and 1997 lowered the **exchange value** of the dollar. The price of the dollar, in terms of its exchange value, is its purchasing power over goods and services in the marketplace. As a measure of this price, we use an index such as the CPI or the GDP deflator. Recall from Chapter 11 that the CPI measures the dollar price of the typical good in the market basket relative to its dollar price in some base year. If the CPI registers higher in 1997 than it did in 1960, then the dollar is cheaper and its exchange price is lower.

Money's Holding Cost

There is yet a third price of money: the cost of holding it. Now, you might think that holding money costs nothing. After all, if you stored $100 under your mattress, wouldn't you still have $100 when you got it out a year later? It would cost nothing to hold it right? Wrong! Inflation erodes the exchange price of money. If prices increased by 25 percent during the year, then your stored money would drop to 75 percent of its original value. Thus, one cost of holding money is the rate of inflation during the time the money was held.

Holding money has an additional cost, because even in the absence of inflation, you incur a cost by holding money. This cost is the forgone revenue that you could have earned had you put the money into productive use. When you do put your money to productive use, economists call the return you earn the **real rate of interest.** If you lend money to a business to finance a project, then the firm will be able to use your money to earn enough to pay back your money plus some interest and still keep some profit for itself.

Thus, when inflation is occurring, you bear two distinct types of costs by holding money. One is the cost because of inflation, which is eroding the purchasing power of your stored dollars, and one is the real rate of interest that you could have earned by putting your money to productive use. Thus, the total opportunity cost of holding money is the sum of these two costs.

The marketplace puts a value on this total opportunity cost—it is the *market rate of interest.* To distinguish this rate from the real rate of interest, economists call it the **nominal rate of interest.** The nominal rate of interest is the rate that you read about in the newspaper. The real rate of interest must be calculated by deducting from the nominal interest rate the loss of purchasing power of the dollar as a result of inflation.

How can you determine the opportunity cost of holding money? The answer lies in determining what you could have earned had you converted the money into an alternative asset. There are a great many available assets; a long-term CD, a U.S. government security, and a corporate bond are some of the possibilities. These alternative financial assets all yield interest income to the holders. Thus, you forfeit interest income by holding money. People and firms are constantly lending and borrowing money in the market that economists call the **market for loanable funds.** The market for loanable funds sets interest rates according to the supply and demand for loans. It works as does any other market. As Figure 14–1 illustrates, *D* is the demand for loanable funds by potential borrowers, and *S* is the supply of loanable funds by potential lenders. The price of the loan is the interest rate: the return to the supplier and the cost to the demander.

As shown in Figure 14–1, the quantity demanded and quantity supplied of loanable funds are at equilibrium at the interest rate of 6 percent. This implies that, at the margin, borrowers and lenders are satisfied with the interest rate. Borrowers are willing to pay 6 percent, because they expect to earn enough profit to pay off the loans, including interest costs. Lenders are also satisfied, because they expect a 6 percent interest rate will provide them a sufficient amount of interest to pay for their waiting as well as compensate them for expected inflation.

Interest Rates and Inflation

There is one important hitch in this market for loanable funds. When loans are made, no one knows for certain what inflation and profits will turn out to be. Thus, market interest rates reflect "expectations" of future real profits and inflation. The nominal interest rate, the rate that prevails in the marketplace, equals the sum of two distinct terms: the **expected real interest rate** and the *expected inflation rate*. In equation form

$$\begin{array}{ccc} \text{Nominal} \\ \text{interest rate} \end{array} = \begin{array}{ccc} \text{expected real} \\ \text{interest rate} \end{array} + \begin{array}{ccc} \text{expected} \\ \text{inflation rate} \end{array} \qquad (14\text{--}1)$$

If the nominal interest rate is 8 percent and if you expect inflation to be 5 percent per year, then you expect a real interest rate of 3 percent. Based on Equation (14–1)

$$8\% - 5\% = 3\%$$

Economists are very concerned about how inflation affects the expected real rate of interest. The expected real interest rate is the rate that firms must plan to cover with their profits. It is also the expected real cost of household credit. Thus, the expected real rate of interest is a central determinant in the decision making of the private sector.

Unfortunately, we cannot observe expected inflation and expected real rates. We can observe realized inflation only after the fact. Then, after the fact, we can subtract realized inflation from nominal interest rates to compute the **realized real interest rate:**[1]

---

[1]In general, all dollar values need to be corrected for inflation when one wants to make comparisons over time. To illustrate, suppose you live in a country in which inflation is usually fairly high, say 15 percent per year. Then, if you are a worker whose wages rise by 15 percent from one year to the next, the real increase in your income is actually zero. You are just keeping up with the cost of living, or inflation.

The following formula is used to determine the real increase in your living standards when inflation is occuring. This real increase is often called the *increase in income's purchasing power.*

% increase in purchasing power = % nominal increase − % change in price level

For instance, if your wages increased by 25 percent for one year, and the inflation rate had been 15 percent, then your wages increased in real purchasing power by 25 percent minus 15 percent, or by 10 percent. Similar corrections are needed in Social Security returns, dividend earnings, and, in fact, all dollar measures.

FIGURE 14–1   The Market for Loanable Funds

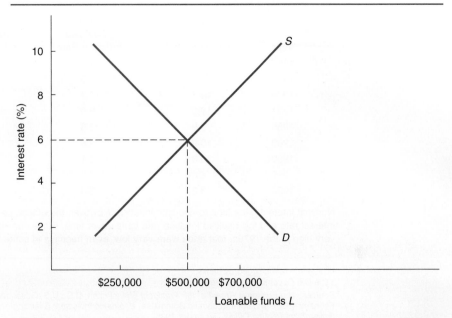

The market for loanable funds *L* sets the interest rate and the volume of loans at equilibrium. The interest rate at, say, 6 percent reflects the market assessment of expected inflation conditions and profit prospects.

$$\begin{array}{ccc} \text{Realized real} \\ \text{interest rate} \end{array} = \begin{array}{c} \text{nominal} \\ \text{interest rates} \end{array} - \begin{array}{c} \text{realized} \\ \text{inflation} \end{array} \qquad (14\text{–}2)$$

We illustrate the relation between realized inflation and nominal interest rates in Table 14–2. As the data indicate, when inflation rates are low—for example, 1.9 percent in 1965—market interest rates are also low: 4.5 percent. When inflation is higher, as in the 1970s, then interest rates are also higher: 7.9 percent in 1975 and 12.7 percent in 1979. When we subtract the inflation rates in column 2 from the nominal interest rates in column 1, we obtain the real rate of interest in column 3. These realized real rates of interest fluctuate just as do the nominal interest rates themselves. Real rates moved from 3.9 percent to 6.3 percent during the period from 1990 to 1995.

The Fisher Effect

Irving Fisher, professor of economics at Yale in the late 1920s, developed the idea that nominal interest rates accommodate expected inflation. He thought that when inflation was expected to increase, nominal interest rates would rise proportionately, leaving the expected real rate of interest unchanged. This effect of expected inflation

TABLE 14–2   Interest Rates and Inflation

Year	(1) Nominal Interest Rate*	(2) Realized Inflation Rate†	(3) Realized Real Interest Rate
1965	4.5%	1.9%	2.6%
1975	7.9	7.0	0.9
1979	12.7	13.3	−0.6
1981	18.9	8.9	10.0
1985	9.9	3.8	6.1
1989	10.9	4.6	6.3
1990	10.0	6.1	3.9
1995	8.8	2.5	6.3
1996	8.3	3.3	5.0

Nominal interest rates tend to rise with inflation. However, the difference between the nominal interest rate and the realized inflation rate varies over time. While nominal interest rates were very high in the 1970s, real rates were very low, even negative in some years, as in 1979.

---

*The prime rate charged by banks.
†The CPI December-to-December rate.

Sources: *The Economic Report of the President* (Washington, D.C.: U.S. Government Printing Office, February 1996): and Joint Economic Committee, *Economic Indicators* (Washington, D.C.: U.S. Government Printing Office, December 1996).

on nominal interest rates is called the **Fisher Effect,** and it implies that the expected real rate of interest, the important variable in private decision making, is a constant.

The evidence in Table 14–2 lends partial support to the Fisher Effect. Nominal interest rates rise with inflation. The market seems to partially compensate lenders for inflation. However, realized real rates of interest are by no means constant.

In the 1970s, inflation apparently outstripped nominal interest rates, resulting in very low real interest rates that actually became negative in 1979. In 1981, real interest rates suddenly jumped to 10 percent. A major economic slump marked the early 1980s, and many economists attributed this to the abnormally high expected real interest rates. Judging from the last column of Table 14–2, real interest rates remained relatively high throughout the 1980s. This may have contributed to the large foreign financial investments in the United States during this period and to the trade deficits.

WHY WE USE MONEY

Now that we have identified the price and cost of money, we are going to begin to develop a demand-and-supply model of the market for money. We begin here with the demand for money. We first discuss the demand for money in one economy, say, the United States. We then turn to the role of money in international transactions. In the next chapter we take up the supply side of the money market. The supply of money depends on specific institutional arrangements in various countries, and these institutions are sufficiently important that we need a chapter to carefully discuss them.

We have seen that money, even with zero intrinsic value, has an exchange price and a holding price. Why would people incur this holding cost when money has zero intrinsic value? Well, the virtue of money is that it buys things: It has purchasing power. As long as money has purchasing power, people will use it to buy goods and services.

Money can also be a temporary abode for savings; it is a store of value. The bottom line, then, is that money is a medium of exchange and a temporary store of value because its value is accepted by others in the marketplace. People demand money either to spend in the marketplace or to hold as a temporary *store of value*. The more people spend, the greater their demand for money. On the other hand, the higher the interest rate, the greater is the cost of holding money compared to making financial investments, and the less money people demand.

The Demand-for-Money Schedule

The quantity of money that people demand will be inversely related to the nominal interest rate, because this rate is the opportunity cost of holding money. The *demand-for-money schedule* is shown in Figure 14–2. If nominal interest rates rise, then the quantity of money demanded will decline, causing a movement along the demand schedule to the left.[2] This is shown in Figure 14–2 as the movement from *A* to *B* along the demand curve *D*.

As with any demand schedule, changes in factors (other than the interest rate) that affect the demand for money will shift the entire demand schedule. For example, if GDP rises, then the demand for money will increase, because people will need more money to support increased spending. This results in a rightward shift in the

---

[2]Keynes, when he analyzed money in his famous 1935 book, *The General Theory of Employment, Interest, and Money,* attacked the idea that the demand for money could be represented by a stable and predictable schedule. He did this by arguing that analysis such as ours, above, refers primarily to the *transactions demand for money.* People demand money in order to carry on transactions, so that if more transactions are needed more money is demanded. Keynes noted that people also hold money in the event they may need it for an unexpected event. He called this the *precautionary demand for money,* and he argued that this motive explained why people held more money than they actually used in transactions.

Keynes's truly innovative notion regarding money demand, though, was his idea of an unpredictable motive for holding money, which he called the *speculative demand for money.* This source of money demand was tied to interest rates, but in a complex and subtle way related to expectations and the desire to earn yields on financial assets. Keynes believed that speculators in bond and stock markets rapidly and unpredictably increased and decreased their holdings of money as they withdrew from or entered into risky financial investments. He felt this made the demand for money volatile and unpredictable.

In research papers written in the late 1950s and early 1960s, Milton Friedman argued that Keynes's partitioning of demand into three motives—transactional, precautionary, and speculative—was not helpful, and that one should simply view demand for money as a whole rather than as the sum of three motives.

money demand schedule. More money will be demanded at every interest rate. Figure 14–3 illustrates a rightward shift in the demand for money schedule, which could be caused by an increase in GDP.

Shifts in the Money Demand Curve

Some examples illustrate how changes in the behavior of firms, households, or government can lead to shifts in the money demand schedule. These examples will be expanded and further illuminated in Chapter 15 where the money market will be integrated into the circular flow model.

Suppose a boom in computer sales occurs. Full computer systems cost thousands of dollars, and buyers probably borrow money to finance their new purchases. This causes a rightward shift in the money demand curve.

Suppose the federal government increases spending or cuts taxes. Either of these actions will cause deficit spending and the government will borrow more money. Just as in the example in which the private sector increased its borrowing, the increase in federal deficit spending increases money demand. Again the result is a shift to the right in the money demand schedule.

Suppose firms become pessimistic and expect a decline in sales. Firms usually react to sales-decline projections by cutting new orders and selling off existing inventories (the stocks of goods on the shelves). When retail stores, such as department stores and auto dealers, cut inventories, their demand for borrowed money falls. Thus, declining inventory holdings cause a decline in money demand. This would be shown as a leftward shift in the money demand schedule.

TOOL KIT

PERSONAL INVESTMENT TIPS

The market for loanable funds offers many different ways to earn interest on your savings, from super NOW accounts to corporate stocks. These tips may help you choose.

1. *Balance risk against yield.* Insured accounts and small CDs in banks are secure, being insured by the Federal Deposit Insurance Corporation (FDIC), but yields are comparatively low. Higher-yielding alternatives, such as corporate bonds, are riskier. Your own attitude toward risk must guide you in trading off risk against potential yield. Some like to gamble; others do not.

2. *Diversify.* You can lose money even in a "safe" investment. In 1983 some retired couples lost most of their nest eggs when a Pacific Northwest public utility, nicknamed WHOOPS, filed for bankruptcy. The lesson is, spread your wealth around. For example, place some in a bank, some in a money market fund, and some in stocks.

3. *Be a skeptic.* You should view skeptically any adviser who assures you of an abnormally

Money in International Transactions

Transactions between citizens of different countries are complicated by the fact that the buyer and seller use different currencies. This means that in order to purchase or sell goods, they must exchange currencies. Thus, international demand for money is more complicated than domestic demand. Let us start thinking about the international money market here. A U.S. exporter who sells U.S. chemical products in Mexico will be paid in pesos, which must then be changed to dollars at a financial institution. The amount of dollars received per peso is called the **exchange rate** for pesos. On Monday, October 14, 1996, the exporter would have received about 13 cents, for each peso earned. If on that same day an American had purchased a Toyota Celica from an importer, the importer would have had to pay the Japanese producer in yen, even though the American purchased the car with dollars. Each $1 would have purchased 112 yen, and thus a $21,500 Toyota would have earned the producers in Japan 2,408,000 yen.

The EXCHANGE RATE is the price of one currency in terms of another. For example, one deutsche mark (DM) may equal $0.65, or $1 equals 1.5 DM.

---

high yield on any type of investment. Promises of extravagant yields should raise a flag of caution. Many local government entities lost a good deal of money in 1994 when Orange County, California, had to declare bankruptcy as a result of very risky investment strategies. Other municipalities had pooled their money with Orange County in order to earn extra-high rates.

4. *Be an incrementalist.* When you deal in stocks, it is safer to do so in small steps over time. Such a gradualist, or *incrementalist*, approach will protect you against big mistakes. On hearing of the October 1987 stock market crash just three days after she had put all her wealth into stocks, a friend panicked and withdrew all her funds the next day. She had bought at a market peak and,

compounding the error, then sold in a trough. She lost a lot of her wealth. A cautious incrementalist would move more slowly. Eventually, the market recovered and my friend's wealth would have been protected.

5. *Individual considerations.* Expected inflation, tax laws, and your personal goals of saving can influence your investment strategy. For example, under 1996 tax law, families with incomes under $25,000 could deduct a $2,000 IRA (individual retirement account) in determining taxable income. At a 15 percent marginal tax rate, they would gain an immediate tax saving of $300. The $2,000 and interest it earned would go untaxed until retirement.

FIGURE 14–2   The Demand-for-Money Schedule

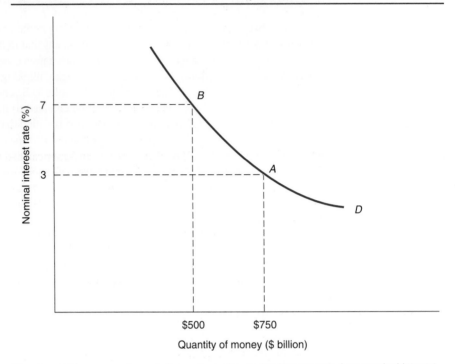

Quantity of money ($ billion)

The demand for money depends inversely on the market interest rate. Low nominal interest rates (at 3 percent) mean money is inexpensive to hold and that quantity demanded will be high ($750 billion). High interest rates (at 7 percent) mean that the cost of holding money is high and the quantity demanded will be low ($500 billion). This curve is sometimes called the *liquidity preference schedule.*

Sometimes countries agree to fix their exchange rates. Other times they let these rates fluctuate according to market forces. If one country has a lot of inflation, then its exchange value in terms of other currencies that are stable will go down. If the exchange rate has not been fixed by agreement, it will fall as the inflation reduces the exchange value of the currency. Sometimes governments try to fix their exchange rates even as their currencies are falling in value through inflation. Either such an attempt fails or the government ends up with a **nonconvertible currency**—a currency people will not buy at the official, government-controlled rate of exchange. Nonconvertible currencies are a serious impediment to foreign trade because they make exchange with foreigners awkward and expensive. The Hungarian forint, for instance, can be exchanged only at an artificially costly level imposed by regulation of the government.

In addition to importers and exporters of goods and services, investors also buy and sell currencies. A Brazilian who wishes to invest in Canada must exchange

FIGURE 14–3   An Increase in Money Demand

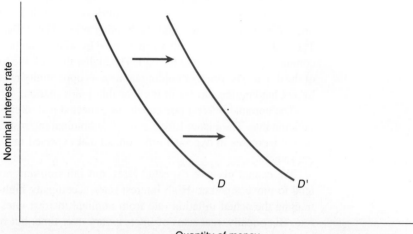

An increase in money demand causes a rightward shift in the money demand schedule. Money demand will increase if expenditures rise. This is illustrated by the shift from demand curve *D* to demand curve *D'*.

Brazilian cruzeiros for Canadian dollars at the going rate of exchange. When the Brazilian later cashes in the Canadian investment, or wants a return on it, the payment will be in Canadian dollars. If the investor wants to spend the earnings in Brazil, the Canadian dollars will have to be converted back into cruzeiros, at the rate of exchange that prevails in the new time period.

Many financial institutions hold foreign currencies and trade in them. Huge financial capitals of the world in New York, Tokyo, London, and elsewhere have vigorous markets in foreign exchange. Just as some people speculate in stock markets, others speculate on currencies.

The U.S. dollar, the DM, and the yen play special roles in the market for currencies. They are **reserve currencies,** which means that U.S. dollars, the DM, or the yen denominate many international transactions among other countries.

CHAPTER REVIEW

Money functions as the medium of exchange, the unit of account, a standard of deferred payment, and a temporary store of value. Any legal currency, such as the dollar, loses effectiveness if its purchasing power becomes unstable. Money can take the form of currency, transaction accounts in financial institutions, or such commodities as gold and cigarettes. In the United States today, money is M1—legal currency and spendable accounts at financial institutions. M2 comprises small, individually held savings and time deposit accounts added to M1.

Although paper money has zero intrinsic value, it has three prices: the dollar price, the exchange price, and the holding price. The dollar price of a dollar is $1. The exchange price of a dollar is measured by what it can buy in terms of an index of commodity prices, such as the CPI. The higher the CPI, the lower the exchange price of the dollar. The price of holding money, its opportunity cost, is the interest forgone by not lending the money in the loanable-funds market.

The nominal interest rate equals the expected real interest rate plus the expected inflation rate. The Fisher Effect states that nominal interest rates increase in proportion to increases in expected inflation, so that expected real rates of interest remain the same.

We cannot observe expected rates, but inflation and nominal interest rates do tend to move together. High interest rates accompany high-inflation periods. Subtracting the actual inflation rate from nominal interest rates gives the realized real rate. Historically, real rates of interest vary over time, but fluctuate much less than nominal rates.

People demand money to make transactions in the marketplace and as a temporary store of value. Thus, money demand depends on the pace of economic activity. It also depends inversely on market interest rates. Trade between people in different nations requires currency exchange. The U.S. dollar is traded for the Japanese yen, the DM for the British pound sterling, and so on. The units of account on most international transactions are either the U.S. dollar, the DM, or the yen.

ЛЛ MULTIPLE-CHOICE SELF-TEST ЛЛ ЛЛ ЛЛ ЛЛ ЛЛ ЛЛ ЛЛ ЛЛ ЛЛ ЛЛ ЛЛ ЛЛ ЛЛ ЛЛ ЛЛ ЛЛ

1. The key function that defines money is that:
   a. It is the legally recognized currency created by the government.
   b. It is a store of value.
   c. It serves as an economy's medium of exchange.
   d. It can be either currency, coins, or bank accounts.

2. The function(s) of money is (are) as:
   a. A store of value.
   b. A unit of account.
   c. A medium of exchange.
   d. A means of deferred payment.
   e. All of the above.

3. If an economy had no money, which of the following would occur?
   a. Greed would evaporate and people would behave better toward one another.
   b. Humankind would be freer from big businesses and rip-off artists.
   c. Transactions would be hampered, because there would be no accepted medium of exchange.
   d. Drug cartels would be unable to do business.

4. Checking account balances:
   a. Are a form of money and are included in both M1 and M2.
   b. Are a form of credit and are not included in money definitions.
   c. Are a form of credit and are included in M2 but not M1.
   d. Are a form of money and are included in M2 but not M1.

5. The value of money:
   a. Just for itself, is close to zero if the money is paper money.
   b. Will rise in purchasing power terms when there is deflation.
   c. Is less when there is unexpected inflation, both because of an increase in the opportunity cost of holding it and because of the change in purchasing power.
   d. Has all the above characteristics.

6. If the expected rate of inflation is 6 percent and the nominal interest rate is 10 percent:
   a. Then the expected real interest rate is 16 percent.
   b. Then the expected real interest rate is 4 percent.
   c. Then the realized rate of inflation must be below 6 percent.
   d. Then the realized rate of inflation must be 10 percent.

7. As people's incomes increase, they will demand:
   a. Less money, because they can do more of their buying on credit.
   b. More money, because they want to spend more to buy goods.

  c. Less money, because they can afford to invest their savings at higher interest rates.

  d. The same amount of money—it is changes in the interest rate that cause changes in the quantity of money demanded.

STUDY QUESTIONS

1. What are the functions of money?

2. Why do people have bank accounts that yield very low interest when they could earn much more interest by holding bonds or securities?

3. How does inflation affect interest rates when inflation is expected? When it is unexpected?

4. Why do economists talk about money rather than credit when they analyze the national economy?

5. When the economy starts out of a recession, demand for money starts to rise. How does this affect interest rates?

6. What is the Fisher Effect? How does Fisher explain the influence of expected inflation on investment decisions?

7. What would we expect to happen to the DM value of the Italian lira if Italy had a rapid inflation?

𝕿𝕽 PROBLEMS

1. In early 1990, the prime rate was 10 percent and the projected rate of inflation was 4.1 percent (according to the Council of Economic Advisers to the President). Can you tell what the expected real rate of interest was? The realized real rate of interest?

2. In 1996, the prime rate was 5.4 percent and inflation was expected to be about 3.3 percent. What was the expected real rate of interest? Comparing the expected real rate of interest in 1996 to that in 1990, how would you expect the rate of investment to differ between 1990 and 1996?

CHAPTER 15

The Fed and the Money Supply

𝕵𝕵 CHAPTER PREVIEW

We now turn to analysis of the supply side of the money market. We will focus on the banking system and the most important quasi-public agency in the sphere of regulating, supervising, and managing the banks, the U.S. Federal Reserve System—or *the Fed*, as it is called. As we shall see, the Fed has the power to determine and change the quantity of money in the economy, and the consequences of this power have resulted in criticism and praise of the Fed. Critics blamed the Fed for the persistent inflation of the 1970s and for the contractions of 1974–1975, 1980–1982, and 1990–1991. The accusation was that the Fed, rather than acting as a driver steering the economic car down the road, was a passenger in the back seat who reached forward on occasion and jerked the wheel, forcing the car to take a jagged path.

Defenders of Fed policies claim that the Fed has done its best to keep the economy on an even keel. They argue that it has been severe external shocks—oil embargoes, political crises, foreign competition, and financial disruptions—that have hammered and whipsawed the American economy. Political pressures have forced the Fed to respond with monetary expansion to offset slumps and with occasional contractions to fight inflation. To many economists, controlling inflation is (and should be) the number one priority of the Fed. Certainly, control of inflation is always on the minds of Fed policymakers.

In Chapter 13 we discussed what constitutes money in the United States, and we studied its unique feature as the *unit of account*. We then introduced the demand for money schedule. In this chapter we develop the supply side of the money market and then utilize supply-and-demand analysis, one of our most useful analytical tools, to learn how important money is to the pace of economic activity. You shall see that the quantity (supply) of money in the economy is determined largely by the Fed through a mechanism that, in turn, determines the ability of banks to make loans and to create bank deposits.

You will recall from Chapter 13 that the U.S. money supply, according to the narrowest definition, is M1, which consists of legal currency plus various transaction account balances at financial institutions. The broader definition, M2, also includes relatively small savings and time deposit accounts of individuals. The Fed controls these monetary aggregates M1 and M2, although inexactly and imperfectly. The Fed more directly controls the *monetary base,* which is the total quantity of dollars available in the form of bank reserves and currency outstanding. M1 and M2 are multiples of the monetary base, as is, in a broader sense, the total amount of credit available in the economy. Through control of the monetary base, the Fed influences M1, M2, and total available credit. These magnitudes, in turn, influence interest rates people pay for loans. This gives the Fed powerful influence over the pace of national economic activity.

1. Why do economists regard the Fed as important?
2. How does the Fed conduct monetary policy?

CONCEPTS REINTRODUCED

Circular Flow Model 289
Demand Curve 52
Interest Rates 307
M1 303
M2 304
Monetary Aggregates 303
Money 302
Savings 262
Supply Curve 74
U.S. Government Securities 276

NEW CONCEPTS

Federal Reserve (Fed)
Rolling Over the Debt
Federal Reserve Note (FRN)
Open-Market Operations
Bank Reserves
Fractional Reserve Banking
Money Multiplier
Currency Sterilization
Discount Rate
Federal Funds Rate

⚖ CHAPTER OBJECTIVES

After studying this chapter, you should be able to:

1. List the policy tools the Fed uses to control the money supply.
2. Tell how each of the policy tools could be used to change money-supply growth.
3. Find the money multiplier and the total quantity of money created from a given reserve requirement for bank deposits and an initial level of deposits.
4. See the connection between Fed policies and interest rates.

THE MONEY SUPPLY AND THE FED

In modern societies, governments issue legal currency in the form of paper money and coins. In the United States these are ten-dollar bills, one-dollar bills, Susan B. Anthony dollars, quarters, dimes, and so forth. Many transactions are paid with cash, but most expensive transactions are paid for with checks drawn on bank accounts. Thus, the total quantity of money in the economy is the sum of currency plus the amounts held in checking accounts in financial institutions, which include banks, savings institutions, credit unions, savings and loans, and other thrifts. For some purposes, economists also count the amounts held in savings accounts as part of the total supply of money. Constitutionally, in the United States the right and power to issue money and to control its quantity belong to the Congress. Congress in turn has delegated this responsibility to the **Federal Reserve System (the Fed),** the American equivalent of a central bank. The Fed issues currency and regulates the private banking system. The Fed's ability to issue currency and regulate banks makes it the key player in determining the supply of money in the economy. Thus, it is crucial for you to understand the nature of this institution.

The central bank has other obligations besides issuing currency. It regulates, inspects, and supervises commercial banks that are members of the Federal Reserve System. It also manages the payments system between banks. The Fed sets rules and restrictions on the types and composition of assets that banks can issue. It enforces limitations, which it also sets, on private banks' deposit accounts and on the relationship between these accounts and the structure of bank assets. The bank supervises and directly inspects the balance sheets of commercial banks that are Fed members. Thus, the banking industry, albeit private, is highly regulated and tightly controlled.

A thread of tension between populists and financiers weaves throughout American history. In colonial America, disputes arose between followers of Thomas Jefferson, who were mostly small farmers in the rural South, and followers of Alexander Hamilton, who were often bankers from the industrial North. In 1832 Andrew Jackson vetoed a bill to extend the charter of the second U.S. Bank. This veto of a *central* bank won him reelection. At the turn of the century, William Jennings Bryan, the great orator, was nearly elected president, because he stirred up populist sentiment against the gold standard. Nearly a century later, demonstrators marched on major

American banks to protest the Vietnam War. Even today, banks symbolize the American power structure. The historic undercurrent of distrust of banking and financial interests delayed the development of central banking in the United States and shaped today's system.

The Fed and Open-Market Operations

Although England established a central bank as early as the 17th century and stuck with it, early Americans tried to form central banks twice but abolished them both times. The second bank of the United States closed its doors in 1836. Our current central bank was formed by an act of Congress in 1913. The central bank is called the **Federal Reserve System**—not the Bank of the United States. This name itself indicates the structure of the Fed and the limitation of its power.

The Fed is not a single entity. The Fed is administered by the seven-member Board of Governors, each of whom is appointed by the president and approved by the Senate. One member is appointed every two years to serve a 14-year term. In addition, the country is divided into 12 Federal Reserve districts, with a regional Federal Reserve Bank located in each district (see Figure 15–1). Each of the 12 district banks has a nine-member board of directors, only a third of whom can come from the banking community. The most important policy-making group in the system is the **Federal Open Market Committee (FOMC).** This committee consists of the Board of Governors, the president of the Federal Reserve Bank of New York, plus presidents from four other district banks. These four district seats rotate annually. The FOMC calls the shots on monetary policy, including the amounts and timing of the buying and selling of securities necessary to carry out that policy.

> The FEDERAL RESERVE SYSTEM (the Fed) is the U.S. central bank. It is run by a Board of Governors, which is appointed by the president for overlapping 14-year terms and is technically independent of the executive and congressional branches of government. It is owned privately by its member banks. Thus it is a quasi-public agency. However, as a creation of Congress, the Fed can also be abolished by a stroke of the congressional pen.

Congress founded the Fed in such a way as to be relatively free of political influence, and legally independent of the executive, congressional, and judicial branches of government. Thus, the Fed is a quasi-public agency. Today, though, that independence is somewhat symbolic. The Fed owes its primary allegiance to Congress but rarely pursues policies at variance with the wishes of the president. In some democracies, the elected executive exerts direct control over central banking. However, in establishing the system, Congress felt the Fed could better pursue necessary,

FIGURE 15–1   Federal Reserve Districts and Branch Banks

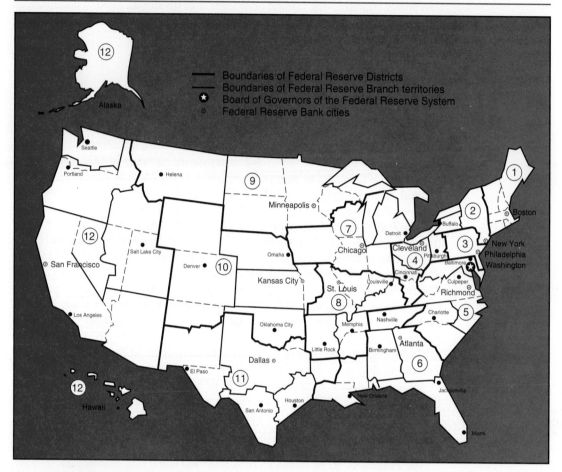

The Federal Reserve System is divided into 12 district banks across the country, ranging from Boston to San Francisco. However, power rests in the hands of the Board of Governors in Washington, D.C.

Source: Federal Reserve System.

and at times unpopular, policies only if isolated from day-to-day political pressures. Congress often expresses ambivalence about the Fed's independence and authority. Bills to force more Fed accountability, less Fed discretion, and more precise Fed reporting have frequently been introduced on the floors of Congress. For example, the Childs Bill, proposed in 1989, called on the Fed to set zero inflation as its only policy goal.

In addition to its congressional mandate to regulate the banking system and control the money supply, the Fed supervises and inspects banks. It also acts as the bankers' bank. Just as you keep deposit accounts in your bank, commercial banks keep deposit accounts with the Federal Reserve. Just as you may borrow from your bank, your bank may borrow from the Fed. The Fed also provides foreign exchange or dollars to the banking system as needed in day-to-day currency exchanges.

Essentially, the Fed controls the money supply (M1 and M2) through its power to manage the **monetary base.** The principal mechanism the Fed uses to change the monetary base is *open-market operations.* Following is an explanation of how this tool of the Fed works. Over the years, the Fed has become a large holder of U.S. government securities. Recall that these securities are IOUs sold by the U.S. Treasury to finance federal deficits. Individuals, firms, and banks buy U.S. securities to earn interest. In practice, interest and the original investment (principal) are paid back fairly quickly, in most cases within 60 to 90 days. (This reflects the fact that the primary security sold, the *Treasury bill,* has a maximum maturity of less than one year.) Consequently, each week the Treasury repays billions of dollars of securities. Typically, the Treasury does not retire billions of dollars of debt weekly; rather, it issues new debt to pay off the old. Wall Street calls this practice **rolling over the debt.**

The MONETARY BASE consists of the total quantity of currency in circulation outside of banks plus the currency held by banks or deposited by banks with the Fed.

Thus, the active market for federal securities involves many trading agents, including private companies, banks, individuals (both foreign and domestic), brokers, trust funds, other financial institutions, and the U.S. Treasury. This is the open market. When the Fed buys securities on the open market, it buys them by crediting the seller's bank with deposits at the Fed. Based on these deposit accounts at the Fed, the banks can draw claims on the Fed. These claims are non-interest-earning paper notes, which the Fed has the authority to print, called **Federal Reserve Notes (FRNs).** Just reach into your wallet and read the words across the top of a dollar bill: "Federal Reserve Note." The Federal Reserve Note is our paper money. Read further on the bill: "This note is legal tender for all debts, public and private."

The Fed injects currency or checkbook money into the economy when it buys U.S. government securities on the open market. Conversely, when the Fed sells securities, it reduces deposits of the buyers' bank at the Fed, and thus currency or checkbook money is taken out of the banking system. This security sale by the Fed contracts the monetary base. In short, the most important agency affecting the supply of money available to the economic system is the Fed. Its most important action is buying and selling U.S. securities on the open market—in transactions called **open-market operations.**

> OPEN-MARKET OPERATIONS are Fed purchases and sales of U.S. government securities. The Fed buys securities by crediting the seller's bank with deposits at the Fed. The banks may then draw on claims at the Fed, which include Federal Reserve Notes, the U.S. legal dollars. When the Fed sells securities, in effect, it withdraws dollars from the economy.

Some Federal Reserve Notes are held by the public, and these constitute the quantity of circulating legal paper currency. Some are held by foreign central banks, which assist their financial institutions in foreign exchanges. But great amounts are deposited in banks. Through its open-market operations the Fed can control the *monetary base,* which is the sum of bank deposits at the Fed, vault cash, and circulating currency.

Fractional Reserve Banking

We have now seen how the Fed issues and withdraws paper money from circulation through open-market operations. In Chapter 14, we saw that bank money—checking accounts and other transaction accounts—is much more important overall than paper money in the transactions process. The Fed also influences the *total amount of bank money* through its open-market operations. To understand how the Fed affects the amount of bank money, think of the Fed as the bankers' bank. When you wish to keep some money available, you deposit it at your bank. When your banker wishes to keep money on deposit, the money is either held in the bank vault or deposited at the Federal Reserve. These quantities are called **bank reserves.** You probably realize that when you deposit money in your account, your bank doesn't actually hold all that cash in the vault. Like most countries, the United States allows **fractional reserve banking.** This means that your bank holds only a fraction of your deposits on reserve, lending most of it to someone else who is willing to borrow and pay interest.

> BANK RESERVES are the total quantity of Federal Reserve Notes held in bank vaults or checkable deposits held by the banks at the Fed district banks.

Banks, like all businesses, try to maximize profits. Thus, the banks pay you a market interest rate for your deposits. Then, after setting aside some of your cash on reserve, as the Fed requires, they lend the rest to borrowers at a higher interest rate. The difference, or margin, provides the bank profits. Most of the money held on reserve is actually kept at the Fed. A small part is kept in the bank's vault, because banks need to have some working capital.

Imagine consolidating the accounts of all 15,000 U.S. commercial banks as if all deposit money were in one bank account. Obviously only a small portion of these deposits is held on reserve. Most of the money is loaned out to big corporations, small businesses, farmers, and private individuals. Thus, the entire banking system holds only a fraction of total deposits in reserves.

To be certain that the member banks maintain adequate reserves, the Fed sets a *legal minimum reserve requirement.* Banks must keep a certain fraction of deposits on reserve. This fraction is between 3 percent and 14 percent, averages 8 percent, and varies with the size of the bank. Originally, the Fed set minimum reserves to ensure adequate cash to meet possible withdrawals. If all depositors tried to withdraw deposits at once, the banks, lacking sufficient cash, would run dry. Usually, not all depositors withdraw cash at once, and bankers can estimate very closely the rates of deposit and withdrawal. When they do get surprise withdrawals, banks can borrow additional reserves from the Fed. Today the legal minimum reserve requirement primarily serves as a mechanism for control of the money supply.

Because so much of our cash is deposited in bank accounts, Fed open-market operations affect the total quantity of deposits and reserves as well as the quantity of cash in circulation. A simple example will illustrate the effect of open-market operations on bank reserves and deposits. This example will show that a small Fed purchase of U.S. government securities has a *multiple expansion* effect on the total supply of bank deposits.

Multiple Expansion of the Money Supply

Suppose the Fed buys a $1,000 U.S. government security on the open market. Figuratively, 1,000 new $1 bills are printed and used to buy the security from someone in the public. The Fed, in fact, creates the money electronically. It credits the bank of the security seller with $1,000 in deposit reserves at the Fed, and the bank credits the checking account of the seller with the $1,000. The Fed can buy the security from a private firm, a bank, or an individual, but regardless of who the seller is, that seller has $1,000 of new deposit money. (Note: The word *bank* is used in the generic sense for financial institution and the terms *bank money* and *deposits* are used in the generic sense for spendable checking-type accounts.)

In this example the Fed has increased both bank reserves and bank deposits by $1,000. Assume that this $1,000 is kept at First Bank of Detroit. Because of fractional reserve banking, the ultimate quantity of new bank money created will be much larger than $1,000. The First Bank of Detroit needs to keep only a fraction of the $1,000 on reserve. To maximize interest returns on loans, First Bank will lend as much of the $1,000 as possible. If the current reserve required is 10 percent of deposits, then First Bank need legally retain only $100 on reserve and can lend out $900. Assume First Bank lends $900 to Detroit Auto Mechanic, Inc., which orders tools. First Bank increases the checking account of Detroit Auto Mechanic by $900. The original Fed injection of $1,000 has increased the money supply by $1,900—$1,000 in the account of the security seller and $900 in the account of the auto shop.

Suppose the Detroit auto mechanic spends the $900 to buy tools from Great Lakes Hardware, a distributor. The hardware distributor places the $900 in its bank, Bank Two of Toledo. Bank Two, which must also obey the current legal reserve requirement of 10 percent, holds $90 in reserve and lends $810 to Dart Drugstore. The pharmacist's account is credited with $810. The total money supply has now increased to $2,710—$1,000 in the First Bank account of the security seller, $900 in the hardware distributor's account, and $810 in the pharmacist's account.

The original injection of $1,000 FRN is growing: $1,000, $1,900, $2,710. This multiplier process will continue, because the pharmacist will order stock, and Bank Three of Albany will receive new deposits of $810, keep $81 (10 percent of deposits) on reserve, lend $729, and so on. Notice that each additional round of loans is for a *smaller* amount of money: $1,000, $900, $810, $729. The total can actually be computed because it is known that each time the bank retains the current required reserve (in our example 10 percent) and lends the balance. The final quantity of money that can be created by the initial purchase of a $1,000 security is $10,000.

This $10,000 is the original $1,000 multiplied by the reciprocal of the 10 percent reserve requirement. This reciprocal is called the **money multiplier:**

$$\text{Money multiplier} = (1 \div \text{percent reserve requirement}) \qquad (15\text{--}1)$$

In our example, $1 \div 0.10 = 10$, so that the original $1,000 is multiplied by 10 to obtain the quantity of money created:

$$\$1,000 \times 10 = \$10,000$$

This equation illustrates the money multiplier. When reserve requirements are 10 percent, each $1 in new reserves may support $10 in bank deposits. If the reserve requirement were 15 percent, then each $1 in reserves would support $6.67 in bank deposits.

Put another way, once banks lend out all they legally can (90 percent) at each stage, each set of banks must retain 10 percent in required reserves. The entire original $1,000 pumped into the system by the Fed becomes required reserves. At 10 percent, total deposits grow to $10,000. In this way the Fed controls bank reserves through its open-market operations in our fractional reserve banking system.

Several questions arise about this process. First, what if the security seller had withdrawn this $1,000 from the First Bank, and spent it? We don't really have to worry about this, because had the seller spent the $1,000, the recipients would have put it in their banks and the process would have begun with those banks instead of First Bank of Detroit. If at any stage of the process someone withdraws money from the bank, this curtails the expansion process only if the cash does not work its way back into a bank. A withdrawal of cash that stays out of the banking system is a leakage from this process and reduces the money multiplier.

A second question arises: What role do reserve requirements play in the process? The 10 percent reserve requirement produced a tenfold multiple expansion of the initial $1,000. If the reserve requirement were 20 percent, then banks at each stage could lend only 80 percent, not 90 percent, and the quantity of money could rise to only $5,000. Instead of the sequence $1,000, $900, $810, $729 . . . , the sequence would be $1,000, $800, $640, $512. . . . An increase in the reserve requirement results in a *reduction* in the amount of bank money capable of being created by a given Fed security purchase. Working out some other numerical examples of your own based on different reserve requirements will show you how changes in the reserve requirement affect the total amount of money expansion.

The Fed sets the legal reserve requirement, and thus it possesses an additional tool to control the total money supply. It can increase the money supply by lowering the legal reserve requirement. What, for example, would happen to the $1,000 if the Fed reduced the reserve requirement to 5 percent of deposits? The answer is that a new multiple expansion of $950, $902.50, $857.38 . . . would occur, and the money supply would increase.

Foreign individuals, firms, financial institutions, and governments that hold dollars as reserves or for speculation may increase or decrease their demand for dollars. Consequently, dollars may unexpectedly flow into or out of the United States. When this happens, the Federal Reserve Bank will see an influx, for example, of dollars. The Fed can insulate the domestic money supply against undesired foreign flows by counteractive open-market operations. For example, to offset an inflow of dollars, the Fed could sell U.S. government securities, absorbing the foreign-supplied dollars. This type of Federal Reserve action is called **currency sterilization.**

The Safety of Our Banking System

A serious question arises under fractional reserve banking. Is it reliable? Because banks don't keep all deposited money on reserve, wouldn't they run out of money if depositors tried to withdraw all their funds? Wouldn't banks then have to declare bankruptcy? The blunt answer is Yes! If bank depositors all tried to withdraw funds at the same time, the banks would surely fail, because they don't have that much money on reserve.

Furthermore, if the public believes that a bank might fail, then depositors may run to their banks, pushing to the front of the line to withdraw their money. Because only a small fraction of money is kept on reserve, the bank will quickly run out of money. Such a panic produces a self-fulfilling prophecy: We expect our bank to fail, and our actions make it happen.

Bank failures became more frequent in the late 1980s. In part, this reflected increasing competition that was encouraged by the gradual adoption of new measures of the 1981 deregulation of the banking industry. But it also reflected financial instability—volatility in inflation, interest rates, and foreign currency-to-dollar exchange rates—and to some extent injudicious, illegal, and unprofessional banking practices under apparently inadequate supervision.

It became evident in the late 1970s that the entire U.S. savings and loan industry was buckling under great stress. Inflationary pressures in the 1970s had forced removal of protective regulations. Suddenly, the savings and loan associations (S&Ls) had to compete for deposits directly with banks. To boost revenues, S&Ls tried to diversify their portfolios away from traditional home loans. Partly as a result of offering high interest rates to attract new deposits, while holding low-earning mortgages from old housing loans, and partly as a result of investing in new, riskier types of assets, many S&Ls began to lose money. Some started to adopt riskier and riskier policies in order to remain solvent. Some turned to illegal practices, such as deceptive advertising, illegal investments in risky ventures, and outright fraud.

When various regions of the country slumped, weaker S&Ls collapsed altogether. In Texas, for example, where the oil exploration and real estate industries slowed simultaneously in the 1980s, numerous financial institutions collapsed, many under the cloud of corruption. S&L failures rose from 52 in 1980 to 551 in 1986.

Federal investigators discovered that both Congress and the S&L regulatory agency, the *Federal Savings and Loan Insurance Corporation (FSLIC),* had neglected warnings of dangerous financial arrangements and even corrupt investment practices. Some U.S. senators came under close scrutiny for serving on the Congressional Oversight Committee while receiving contributions from an indicted and convicted S&L executive, Charles Keating. The difficulties of the five senators illustrated the moral hazard problem of regulating financial institutions that are under extreme financial stress. The pressures to vitiate financial integrity can be enormous when financial disaster looms. The FSLIC is now defunct. S&Ls are now insured by the FDIC and are regulated by the Office of Thrift Supervision.

The S&L crisis raises the issue of how to regulate financial institutions so as to protect depositors and investors without placing the public budget at excessive risk. One lesson is that regulators must be able to fund large failures and to react quickly to avoid panics. Another is that public awareness of the conduct of regulators is essential to protecting public finances. A third is that although tough constraints on fiscal conduct of financial institutions may be necessary, they are difficult to enforce, especially if we fail to stay alert when watching the watchdogs.

INFLUENTIAL INSTITUTION

THE FEDERAL RESERVE SYSTEM, 1913–

Under the leadership of Paul Volcker, chairman of the Federal Reserve Board from 1979 to 1987, inflation from 1980 to 1986 fell from 13.5 percent to 1.1 percent per year. The Fed's tight money policy, combined with a high unemployment rate and high interest rates in 1981 and 1982, fueled the continuing debate over its independence. Here are some of the arguments:

Pro: The Fed must be independent of daily political pressures so that it can pursue unpopular but responsible policies. Professionals, not politicians, should determine the level of money and credit. If the Fed remains independent, two distinct policy agencies (the Fed and the executive branch) oversee the economic system. This prevents a monopoly of authority and minimizes

The Bush administration and Congress devised a bailout plan that would salvage the liquidity of depositors in failed S&Ls so as to assure confidence in the financial system. Estimates of the cost to taxpayers of the bailout plan ran into the hundreds of billions of dollars. Despite S&L difficulties, and some bank failures, public confidence in the banking system itself remains strong.

People now have confidence in the security of the U.S. banking system and the regulatory powers of the Fed. The Fed supervises and inspects banks to ensure safe banking practices. If individual banks become insolvent, the Fed arranges *takeovers* by healthy banks and protects the depositors in a sort of shotgun marriage. Even if a general panic unfolds, causing runs on many banks, the Fed (in principle) can combat this disaster by pumping new reserves into banks to cover withdrawals of deposits.

To prevent bank panics from becoming commonplace, Congress established the **Federal Deposit Insurance Corporation (FDIC)** in 1933. The FDIC insures all deposit accounts in member banks for up to $100,000 each. All Fed banks are also required to join the FDIC. Thus, even if a bank fails, depositors get their money back through FDIC insurance. Hypothetically, some utter disaster could produce a national panic, threatening many banks. The FDIC itself could become bankrupt. But even in such a case the Fed could pump new reserves into banks to shore up the system, or the Treasury could rescue the FDIC.

In summary, the Fed controls the money supply, measured as M1 or M2, through control of the monetary base, the total of outstanding cash and bank reserves. Two of the ways the Fed exercises control over these **monetary aggregates** are through the fractional reserve banking system and through the multiple-expansion process. The mechanisms the Fed uses are open-market operations and the reserve requirement.

The Fed has a third tool, which, though relatively unimportant, receives considerable attention in the press. A bank may borrow reserves from the Fed just as you can borrow funds from your bank. The interest the bank pays for a loan from the Fed

---

potential damage from errors of policy. Furthermore, an independent Fed allows pursuit of tight money policies without the president's taking the heat.

Con: The Fed should be controlled by the president. Voters hold the president accountable for policy successes and failures; thus, the president needs the authority to set policy. In a democracy, the policymaker should be accountable to the people through their elected representatives. If this is true for defense policy, why not for monetary policy? Finally, monetary and fiscal policy can only be coordinated effectively if run by one agency.

Alan Greenspan, Paul Volcker's successor, first appointed in 1987 and reappointed through 1997, maintained independence from the executive branch. This independence was maintained despite congressional pressures to fold the Fed into the executive branch and despite the burden of managing monetary policy during the most severe contraction since the Great Depression. Today, with fiscal policy tied up with huge structural deficits, the Fed is the principal agent for short-term stabilization policy. Greenspan assured Congress that he would resist executive branch pressure and protect the Fed's independence. Still, Congress tries from time to time to undermine the Fed's independence by stipulating tighter congressional control and by demanding closer accounting of Fed actions.

is called the **discount rate.** This is the only interest rate that the Fed actually sets directly. Thus, to discourage bank borrowing of reserves, it raises the discount rate; it lowers the rate to encourage borrowing, which drives reserves up. Bank borrowing from the Fed is, in fact, relatively unimportant, so a discount rate change is not critical. As a rule the Fed changes the discount rate only to signal the market that it has already changed its other policy tools or to realign its discount rate with other market rates after the latter have changed. By far the most important tool of monetary control is open-market operations.

Having said this, another interest rate that the Fed watches quite closely and that is very sensitive to Fed open-market operations is the federal funds rate. The *federal funds rate* is the rate banks charge each other in the market where they lend each other reserves on an overnight basis. They do this to be certain that they have just adequate reserves at the end of the day in order to satisfy the Fed's legal reserve requirement.

MONEY AND THE CIRCULAR FLOW MODEL

Discussion of the Fed, the monetary base, the banking system, and the money supply can be summarized by a money-supply schedule. If the Fed's control of the money supply were absolute, then the quantity of money would be shown as constant. The money supply would be independent of other variables, such as interest rates or income. The supply of money would be set by policymakers and not influenced by the internal workings of the private market economy.

However, this view, although not too far off, is a little too simplistic. Private markets do affect the money supply. Given the monetary base set by the Fed, banks want to make more loans when interest rates are high than when they are low. More loans will increase the multiple expansion of money. Thus, the quantity of money supplied will rise when rates of interest are high and fall when rates are low though these effects may be modest. Figure 15–2 illustrates this by an upward-sloping money-supply schedule.

The Workings of the Money Market

The money-supply schedule can now be combined with the demand-for-money schedule from Chapter 14. Recall that interest rates reflect the cost of holding money so that the quantity of money demanded varies inversely with interest rates. Putting supply and demand together enables us to analyze the effects on the money market of actions by the Fed, the government, or the private sector. As in all supply-and-demand analysis, it is assumed that the market is in equilibrium. In Figure 15–3, quantity supplied equals quantity demanded at point *A*.

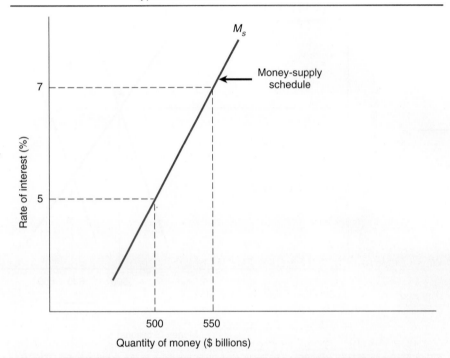

FIGURE 15–2   The Money Supply and the Interest Rate: A Hypothetical Case

The Fed controls the monetary base through open-market operations, legal minimum-reserve requirements, and the discount rate. The monetary base is clearly linked to M1 and M2. The quantity of money supplied then depends on the multiple-expansion process. The extent of bank loans tends to rise with interest rates so that the quantity of money supplied falls when interest rates rise. Because the decline in the quantity of money is small in response to an increase in interest rates, the money-supply schedule is an *inelastic* function of the market interest rate. In the figure, the money-supply schedule, M_s, slopes upward—high interest rates, say, 7 percent, bring money expansion through more loans and the quantity of money supplied rises, say, to $550 billion.

What happens when the Fed buys U.S. government securities on the open market? How will this affect the money market? When the Fed buys securities, it creates FRNs or bank reserves. This, in turn, begins a multiple expansion of the money supply. In Figure 15–3 a shift to the right (M'_s) in the money-supply schedule takes place. A surplus of money now will exist at an initial interest rate of 7 percent. In our example the surplus is $150 billion.

To profit from loans made possible by the infusion of new reserves and a lower federal funds rate, banks will offer lower interest rates to customers. Borrowers, at the margin, were happy with the old rate of 7 percent, but banks now want them to borrow more, and this will require lower interest rates. As interest rates fall, the two

FIGURE 15–3   A Fed Open-Market Purchase of U.S. Securities

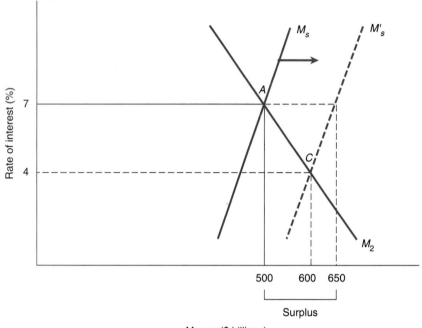

A Fed purchase of U.S. securities results in a multiple increase in the money supply. The money supply schedule shifts rightward from M_s to M'_s. At the original interest rate, 7 percent, the surplus of money puts downward pressure on interest rates. As rates fall, the two blades of the scissors respond: The quantity of money demanded rises from $500 billion, and the quantity of money supplied falls from $650 billion. The new equilibrium is at point *C*, with interest rate 4 percent and quantity of money $600 billion. The money-supply increase has lowered equilibrium interest rates.

blades of the scissors respond: The quantity of money demanded rises from $500 billion, and the quantity of money supplied declines from $650 billion. Both responses reduce the surplus. The new equilibrium point is point *C*. At *C* interest rates fall to 4 percent from 7 percent, and the money supply increases from $500 billion to $600 billion.

The effect of the Fed's open-market purchase of securities is to increase the money supply, resulting in lowering the interest rate. This shows how Federal Reserve open-market operations can alter interest rates. Interest rates, as we saw in Chapter 14, are an important channel through which the Fed influences the pace of economic activity.

What happens when there is a change in behavior in the private sector that decreases the demand for money? Suppose many firms anticipate a slowdown in sales. They will reduce their inventory stocks. Firms usually borrow money in order

FIGURE 15-4   An Expected Decline in Sales Reduces Money Demand

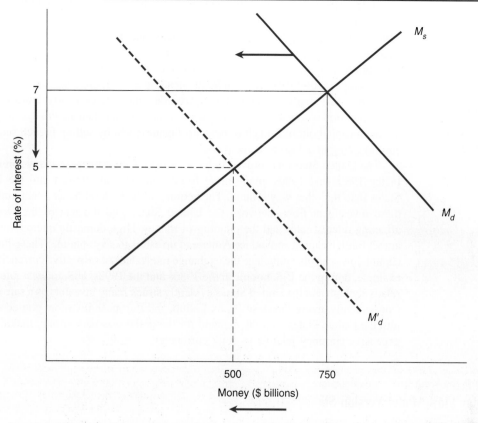

Firms reduce their demand for money as they draw down their inventory stocks of goods in anticipation of a drop in sales. A decline in money demand (to M'_d) lowers equilibrium interest rates from 7 percent to 5 percent, and lowers the equilibrium quantity of money from $750 to $500 billion.

to finance inventory stocks. Because firms are reducing inventories, they will demand fewer loans. This means a lower demand for money. Figure 15–4 illustrates a decline in money demand by a shift to the left from $750 billion to $500 billion in the schedule. This, in turn, produces a surplus of money at the 7 percent original interest rate. The surplus of money, caused by lower demand, drives interest rates down to 5 percent and reduces the equilibrium quantity of money supplied to $500 billion. Thus, the private sector can affect the position of the money-demand schedule and, therefore, equilibrium in the money market.

Consider another example of a change originating in private markets that influences the money market. Suppose consumer and business spending suddenly increase. How will a boom in private spending affect the money market? In order to increase expenditures, households and firms need more money for transactions. This means that money demand will increase at every interest rate: The money-demand schedule shifts to the right. Draw the figure and show yourself that both the equilibrium quantity of money and the equilibrium rate of interest will increase. The increase in demand for money raises interest rates and the equilibrium money supply. Thus, increased spending by the private sector, assuming the Fed takes no counteraction, will increase market interest rates and even slightly increase the money supply. This example shows that private market spending alters money market equilibrium.

Notice that many investors today consider alternatives nearly worldwide. A Saudi investor who can make a higher return in Japan than in France may shift financial capital out of French francs into Japanese yen by selling French securities and investing in a Japanese enterprise.

The United States has proved to be an attractive investment to many foreigners. In the 1980s and 1990s, many more foreign investments flowed into the United States than the other way around. The actions of the Federal Reserve can influence these investment flows between the United States and the rest of the world by affecting interest rates and the quantity of money. High domestic interest rates can attract foreign capital and induce American investors to stay at home. These financial capital flows can also influence the exchange rate values of respective currencies. For example, during the U.S. booms in the 1980s and the 1990s, U.S. interest rates were relatively high and the United States evidently struck many investors as a safe haven. Consequently, many Japanese, Arab, Latino, and European investors poured money into the United States, and the demand for the dollar was very strong, making it an expensive currency relative to other currencies.

Circular Flow Model Version Six

If the money market is integrated into the circular flow model, the interactions between the money market and markets for goods and services can be understood. The key variable connecting these two markets is the interest rate. What effect does an increase in the money supply have on the circular flow of income? We saw that the purchases of securities by the Fed caused an increase in the money supply that, in turn, lowered interest rates. How do lower interest rates affect the circular flow of income?

The Money Market Affects the Circular Flow
When the interest rates fall, borrowing becomes less expensive. Firms now find that marginal investment projects—such as machinery, equipment, factories, or accumulations of new inventories of goods and materials—that were previously too expensive are now profitable. Firms now borrow funds for marginal investment projects.

---

[1]Instructor note: This material is difficult. It brings the money market together with the circular flow model (which is essentially the goods market) to form a two-market economy. (This is basically a rudimentary IS-LM model.) It may be too complex, given time constraints, for some classes.

Thus, when interest rates fall, the rate of investment pouring into the circular flow accelerates.

When interest rates fall, households also find that purchases of goods such as refrigerators, houses, and cars are cheaper to finance. But when consumers borrow more at lower interest rates, they save less, because the yield on savings is lower. Thus, with lower interest rates, savings withdrawals from the circular flow decline, and consumption expenditures from income rise. When the stimulus to investment is combined with the stimulus to consumption, the pace of spending rises as interest rates fall. Circular flow model version six shows the effects on investment and saving when interest rates change (Figure 15–5).

But this does not tell the whole story. How will declining interest rates affect the circular flow of income? As interest rates fall, the rates of both investment and consumer spending rise. Consumer spending rises both because borrowing to spend is cheaper and because the return to savings (via loanable funds) falls. An increase in investment spending injected into the economy accelerates the circular flow and increases consumption spending from current income even more. This consequently decreases savings and therefore curbs withdrawals from the circular flow. The circular flow begins to swell, continuing until the economy comes to rest at a new, higher level of spending.

Even though savings rates per dollar of income are lower, the total level of realized savings rises. This higher level of realized savings is due to increased income, which resulted, in turn, from the new, higher level of investment spending at equilibrium. All these changes are a result of lower interest rates, which were lowered by monetary expansion. International financial flows will decline as lower domestic interest rates make the United States a less attractive investment. The expansion will also increase imports and disrupt the trade balance.

A reduction in the money supply raises interest rates and slows the circular flow of spending. Higher rates mean that money costs more to potential business and personal spenders. Durable-good purchases drop off, and private business investment falls; the circular flow of spending slows. Thus, the money supply affects the circular flow of income. The major channel is the Fed's influence on interest rates. When there is an increase in the money supply, the circular flow of income is stimulated; when there is a decrease in the money supply, the circular flow of income is depressed.

Expenditures Affect the Money Market

Conversely, changes in expenditures that originate in the circular flow affect the money market. In other words, it is a two-way street between the money market and the circular flow of income. Changes in the money supply influence the circular flow of income via interest rates. Changes in expenditure behavior alter money market equilibrium.

Suppose firms increase their inventory in anticipation of expanded sales. Inventory policies may change for many reasons: good political news, improved winter weather conditions, new technology, reduced trade barriers. Increased spending on

FIGURE 15–5   The Circular Flow Model Version Six: without Government but with Banking

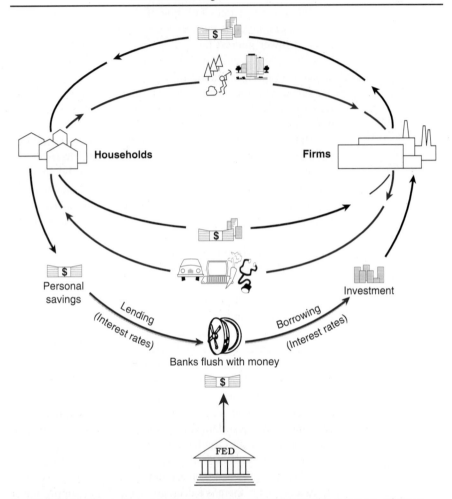

Investment injections by firms into the circular flow rise with lower interest rates, whereas savings withdrawals by households fall. These effects are illustrated by the interest rate arrow from savings by households to banks and by the interest rate arrow from banks to investment by firms. Because the Fed can affect interest rates through its open-market operations, it can influence the circular flow of income.

inventories increases investment injections into the circular flow. This added investment injection generates an economic expansion, an increase in national expenditures. As this increase in spending occurs, firms and households begin to demand more money to finance the increased spending.

Money demand rises because households and firms use more money to sustain higher spending rates. If you owned an auto dealership and expected a boom in car

FIGURE 15–6 Dual Direction of Cause and Effect—Money to Expenditures and Back

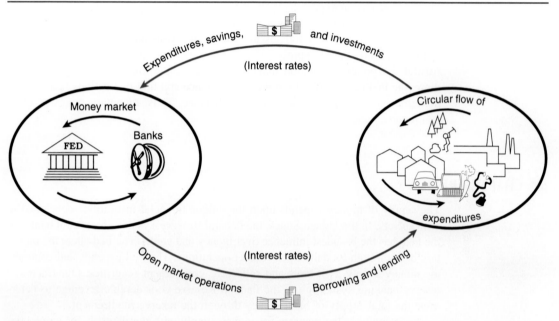

Actions in the money market affect the expenditure patterns of the economy; expenditure patterns of the economy affect the money market. This dual direction of cause and effect can make monetary policy difficult to implement.

sales, you would expand your stock of auto models. Larger inventory holdings have financial implications for your business. To finance the increased stock of cars, you would probably have to borrow more money from your local bank. Thus, the demand for money would rise. The same holds for families. To buy more houses and consumer durable goods, they borrow money. This leads to an increase in money demand.

As money demand rises, interest rates increase. Thus, an expansion in the circular flow of expenditures affects the money market. The expansion produces an increase in money demand, causing money to become relatively scarce, raising the rate of interest. Higher domestic interest rates and increased spending will raise international investment flows and U.S. imports. Thus, the trade balance and exchange rate will be influenced by the domestic economy as well.

In summary, changes in the money market, through influence on interest rates, affect the circular flow of expenditures. Changes in the circular flow affect the money market. Figure 15–6 shows this very important and complex dual direction of cause and effect. It plays an important role in the conduct of monetary policy and its effect on the economy.

The Fed attempts to stabilize the pace of economic activity by responding with corrective measures when tendencies toward recession or inflationary expansion are spotted. However, the Fed can misread the signals in spending patterns by the private sector. If the Fed expects a given level of money demand, but more is forthcoming, this can cause an unexpected pinch of money and drive up interest rates beyond the Fed's wishes. Conversely, if money demand is lower than the Fed expects, this can lead to lower interest rates and possibly too much expansion. The economy the Fed is trying to stabilize does not present a stationary target. For this reason, the Fed is often frustrated in policy application, and its critics blame it for missing the target. Furthermore, the Fed may worry about the trade balance and find that actions favorable to domestic balance may worsen the trade balance. Thus, monetary policy is often controversial and difficult.

CHAPTER REVIEW

The supply of money depends upon the unique financial institutions developed in each society. In the United States, the Federal Reserve System (the central bank), or the Fed, has the broadest influence over money and credit. The Fed alters the monetary base through its daily open-market operations. The Fed expands and contracts the money supply as it buys and sells U.S. government securities. Our fractional reserve banking system gives the Federal Reserve considerable leverage to determine the total supply of bank money through the reserve requirement.

By combining the diagram for money supply with the diagram for money demand, the Fed's effect on the money supply and on interest rates can be seen. The private sector can have an effect on the demand for money. Expansions in the private economy increase interest rates, whereas contractions lower interest rates.

The application of monetary policy, like fiscal policy, is quite controversial. Dual direction of cause and effect links the money market to the circular flow of income. This dual direction of cause and effect helps to explain some of the difficulties faced by the Fed in trying to stabilize the economy.

🎵 MULTIPLE-CHOICE SELF-TEST 🎵 🎵 🎵 🎵 🎵 🎵 🎵 🎵 🎵 🎵 🎵 🎵 🎵 🎵

1. The Federal Reserve System has the power to do all but which of the following?
   a. Require that banks hold a certain fraction of their deposits as reserves.
   b. Print the legal tender for the United States.
   c. Allow banks to borrow reserves from it and set the interest rate banks must pay for these loans.
   d. Create U.S. government securities to sell.

2. A Fed purchase of government securities leads to:
   a. An increase in bank reserves and an increase in the money supply.
   b. An increase in bank reserves and a decrease in the money supply.
   c. A decrease in bank reserves and a decrease in the money supply.
   d. A decrease in bank reserves and an increase in the money supply.

3. If the Fed raised reserve requirements for banks:
   a. This would cause a decrease in the money supply.
   b. This would cause an increase in the money supply.
   c. This would increase the size of the money multiplier.
   d. This would improve the safety of banks, but have no effect on the money multiplier or the money supply.

4. If banks face a reserve requirement of 10 percent, then when the Fed reduces bank reserves by $20 million, the money supply can be estimated to decline by about:
   a. $2 million.
   b. $20 million.
   c. $200 million.
   d. None of the above—no prediction is possible.

5. A reduction in interest rates results in:
   a. A larger quantity of money supplied.
   b. An increase in withdrawals from the circular flow.
   c. A higher quantity of money demanded.
   d. A decrease in injections into the circular flow.

6. Higher domestic interest rates tend to:
   a. Attract fewer foreign investors.
   b. Weaken the domestic currency relative to foreign exchange.
   c. Strengthen the currency and attract foreign capital.
   d. Stimulate imports and discourage exports.

🖎 STUDY QUESTIONS

1. If the reserve requirement is 10 percent and if banks keep another 5 percent as reserves on their own, how much will the money supply increase if the Fed buys $2,000 in U.S. securities?

2. How is the money multiplier affected by an increase in the reserve requirement from 20 percent to 25 percent?

3. What are the pros and cons in the debate over Fed independence?

4. What happens to a bank if all its depositors, thinking it will fail, rush to the bank to withdraw their funds?

5. How does the Fed control the money supply? Discuss its three tools and their effectiveness.

6. Show how an investment boom in the circular flow can affect the money market, and show how a Fed open-market operation can affect the circular flow.

7. Give a concrete example of how a shock in the circular flow model can change the money market and surprise the Fed.

8. Suppose the Fed disagrees with the president about the pace of economic activity. The Fed tries to slow the economy down by selling U.S. securities on the open market. At the same time, the government increases deficit spending in an attempt to stimulate the economy. Assess the consequences of these simultaneous, independent policy measures.

🎯 PROBLEM

Concerned about inflation rates above 10 percent, in 1981 the Fed engaged in extensive sales of federal securities.

1. If the Fed had a reserve requirement of 5 percent of deposits, then by how much would the Federal Open Market Committee's sale of $25 million of government securities shrink the money supply?

2. Show the effect of the Fed sale of securities on a graph of the money market. How is the new equilibrium different from the old?

3. How did this change in the money market affect the circular flow? Explain. Draw a diagram of the circular flow, labeling the various flows for the changes that would have resulted (e.g., increases, decreases).

CHAPTER 16

Why Do Economists Seem to Disagree So Much?

꿔 CHAPTER PREVIEW

When two economists speak before the media, they may sit together, but often they seem to speak apart. Economists, like other people, disagree about the role of government, and their difference of opinion is natural. Liberals tend to favor a larger domestic role for government and more activist trade policies; conservatives usually favor a smaller role and a more laissez-faire attitude. Economists' views on defense spending are also diverse and often opposed. Republicans want to maintain defense spending to stave off potential threats. Democrats see opportunities for a resource shift toward social spending.

Differences in political opinion do not mean that economists disagree about objective policy analysis. On the contrary, you will recall that economists distinguish between normative questions and positive questions; positive economics, as covered in this book, involve positive questions. To refresh your memory, *normative questions* are those that involve value judgments. Normative questions use verbs such as *ought to* or *should*, as in "Should the income tax be more progressive?" or "Ought able-bodied adults receiving welfare work?" One can only answer such normative questions after making personal value judgments. *Personal value judgments* involve philosophy, religion, and your own personal belief system. You and your neighbor can disagree forever about what is and is not "fair."

Positive economic analysis focuses, instead, on *positive questions,* which use verbs such as *is* or *are,* as in "Will a more progressive income tax system result in more tax evasion?" or "Do welfare payments to able-bodied adults discourage work effort?" These positive questions are answerable without regard to value judgments. They are scientific questions in the sense that they are *testable,* which means that, in principle, one could devise a test to prove whether these questions are right or wrong. One could design an experiment in which one measures the extent of tax evasion under different degrees of progressivity to see if the assertion that more progressivity leads to more evasion is correct. In contrast, there is no test to prove whether the tax system should or should not be progressive, because this involves a matter of opinion. As a matter of pure logic, normative questions cannot be resolved by positive analysis. Positive economic analysis can only answer positive questions.

The purpose of this chapter is to show that the vast majority of disputes among economists reflect differences about normative questions involving value judgments and not about positive economic analysis of value-free questions. There is tremendous consensus among economists about which positive questions should be asked, such as the importance of opportunity costs of policies, the essential nature of trade-offs, the laws of supply and demand, the role of capital formation in economic growth, the consequences of sustained increases in the money supply, the importance of incentive effects, and so forth.

As we shall argue in this chapter, when they take off their "economist hats," economists are just like other people who disagree about how the world should be. Normative questions concerning "what the fair income distribution should be," and "how much unemployment should be tolerated," and "how much society should tax the rich" require value judgments. Positive economic analysis, as you are taught in this book, is not about value judgments, but about thinking through the consequences of various policies, considering costs and benefits, and identifying winners and losers, not about choosing among alternatives.

One way to think about this is that once you are a well-trained economist, you are able to serve as a "hired gun." You can "shoot," that is, do sound economic analysis of proposals, for anyone—regardless of their normative judgments. Put another way, if you were listening to a tape recording of a meeting in the White House about economic policy, you could more quickly identify the voices of the economists in the room by the very nature of their analysis than you could identify which party is in office.

The economists invariably will be the ones making comments such as, "Well, on the one hand, this could happen, and on the other hand, that will happen." or, "Well that is an interesting proposal, but consider the opportunity costs involved." or, "It is true your measure will provide benefits, but are these benefits worth the costs?" or, "Let's see what the research says will be the consequences of that proposal for our constituents." Economists are interested in outcomes, unintended consequences, costs and benefits, trade-offs, and so forth. In government, the economists who advise elected officials trust the elected officials to reflect the normative views of those who elected them. The economists' job is to help the elected official achieve the goals he wants, at least cost.

Although positive economics is a scientific endeavor, we do not mean to imply here that economists have resolved all scientific questions in the field. This is not so. In fact, some very important positive scientific questions remain very much open to dispute. In this chapter, we will be discussing some of these unresolved scientific questions. Economists are very good at identifying important scientific questions, but are less effective in always providing satisfactory answers to them. An area in which there is considerable disagreement involves the short-term consequences of fiscal and monetary policies. This chapter deals with different analytical viewpoints on fiscal and monetary policy.

The political spectrum of economists reflects that of society, running from conservative libertarians, such as Walter Williams at George Mason University, to Marxists, such as Howard Sherman at the University of California, Riverside. Naturally, economists, like everyone else, argue about the value of government social programs and the appropriate level of regulation. Why did Michael Boskin, adviser to President George Bush, want to fight inflation with slow expansion, while Laura D'Andrea Tyson, liberal adviser to President Bill Clinton, advocates rapid growth?

When Republican presidential candidate Robert Dole, during the 1996 campaign, proposed cutting federal income tax rates by 15 percent, over 100 economists, including Nobel Prize winners Robert Solow and Franco Modigliani, signed a document repudiating the proposal as unaffordable and irresponsible. Soon, a host of other economists, headed by Nobel laureate Gary Becker and Stanford's John Taylor, supported the Dole proposal, Becker going so far as to describe it as "simple application of Economics 101." As it turns out, those against the Dole proposal were mainly Democrats and those for it, Republicans. Economists hold political views just as do the rest of us; their political endorsements and positions reflect these political views as well as their economic understanding.

How can such gross differences of opinion be explained? And if such deep differences persist, then how can you be expected to understand economics? Is there anything to learn except differences of opinion? First and most important, most public disputes among economists do not involve *positive* scientific questions of how the economy works. Most disputes are over the same sort of opinion disagreements we all hold, those that reflect nonscientific *normative* values such as:

- Should we tax the rich and give to the poor?
- Do we want a larger strategic defense arsenal?
- Is unemployment a more serious problem than is inflation?

Just as other people's views run the political spectrum from right to left, so do the opinions of economists.

1. Why, in public, do economists always seem to disagree? How much science is there to economics, the queen of the social sciences?
2. Both Keynesians and supply siders advocate tax cuts. Are their reasons the same?

CONCEPTS REINTRODUCED

NEW CONCEPTS

Laffer Curve
Trickle-Down Economics
Percolate-Up Economics
Dynamic Scoring
Keynesian Economics
Multipliers
Automatic Stabilizers
Income Velocity of Money
Monetarism
Equation of Exchange
Quantity Theory of Money
New Classical Macroeconomics (NCM)
Rational Expectations
Supply-Side Economics
Real Business Cycles
Aggregate Production Function
Technological Shocks

🎓 CHAPTER OBJECTIVES

After studying this chapter, you should be able to:

1. Tell what happens, according to Keynesians, to national income when government spending increases. What if the spending is financed by taxes? If it is financed by borrowing?

2. Tell what happens, according to the monetarists, to national income when government spending increases. If it is financed by borrowing? By taxes? By increasing the money supply?

3. Contrast the concepts of the *multiplier* as used by Keynesians and the *income velocity of money* as used by monetarists.

4. Tell how proponents of new classical macroeconomics (NCMs) use the concept of *rational expectations theory* to predict people's response to monetary policy, and contrast this to *monetarist theory.*

5. List some of the policies a *supply-side* economist would recommend to increase real national income.

ECONOMISTS AND THEIR POLITICAL VIEWS

Economists hold differing *political views* (normative) on national economic policy. Some economists favor tighter money. Some want looser money. Some want a balanced-budget amendment to the Constitution. Some want flexible and discretionary fiscal policy. Rarely do economists stand shoulder to shoulder in support of a given policy. Some favor activist trade policies—such as managed trade and industrial policy—whereas others prefer free trade and hands-off government. What is the nature of these pervasive disagreements over national economic policy?

Economists disagree about the conduct of Federal Reserve policy. Some favor an independent Fed, some do not. Some prefer a monetary aggregate target; some an interest rate target. Why is it that Milton Friedman often favors slower money growth to combat inflation, whereas James Tobin often advocates increased money growth to stimulate the economy?

In America today, conservatives tend to believe in a stronger defense to protect democracy against foreign dangers. Conservatives favor fewer federal social programs. On the other hand, liberals believe that international tensions are raised by massive U.S. defense spending. Liberals support government help for the poor, children, and the homeless. They believe that wealth and income should be redistributed to offset perceived inequities of competitive markets. Conservatives believe that many of the social welfare programs increase the recipients' dependence on government giveaways. Some conservatives want free trade in North America, whereas liberals want managed trade and protection of unskilled Americans whose wages are low or whose jobs are threatened. Some conservatives believe that foreign trade, especially purchases by Americans of goods produced abroad, threatens America's way of life.

Economists are not endowed with superior opinions—even about political economy. A Nobel Prize in economics makes an *opinion* on defense spending no more credible than an *opinion* on defense spending from a Nobel laureate in medicine.

In order of importance, *different policy prescriptions* from economists reflect:

- Different opinions and philosophies about political and social issues (value judgments).
- Different assessments of the magnitude of various effects.
- Different analysis of the workings of the economy.

Differences in value judgments among economists are similar to differences in value judgments by everybody else. Differences about the magnitudes of effects reflect the difficulty of measuring certain effects. The theoretical impact or direction of a policy action may be agreed about. For example, ordinarily an increase in price will lead to a decrease in demand. Economists agree about this theoretical effect. But they may then disagree about the magnitude of the effect. Will a 2 percent tax on cigarette smoking that raises cigarette prices reduce demand so much that smoking declines a lot? Or will smokers, resistant to modest price increases, cut back only very little, so that the tax does little to actually reduce smoking? This disagreement about magnitudes explains some of the public disagreements among economists, though not as many as do the disagreements that are pure differences in normative opinions.

Economists do have some disputes about scientific questions in the discipline, just as do geologists, physicists, and chemists in their disciplines. An area under considerable dispute today among economists is the short-run consequences of fiscal and monetary policies. Thus, some disputes in macroeconomics reflect these types of differences—scientific disputes about positive questions. This is where the student needs to accept the reality that economics is a living discipline. Economists do not have all the answers to the important positive questions. There is still much research to be done.

In terms of *macroeconomic theory,* U.S. economists generally fall into four groups—Keynesians, monetarists, new classical macroeconomists (NCMs), and supply siders.

The Role of the Media

Often when economists are heard in the public arena, their opinions appear to override their analysis. This fact in part reflects the nature of media, especially of television, coverage. A "balanced" news story must cover two views—one for and one against. Also, when the media want the views of economists on a hot political issue, a tax proposal, or a food stamp bill, they interview "influential" economists who are often associated with political heavyweights. The economists then speak *for* the politician, the party, or the industry. In fact, the given economist expresses an opinion that may actually conflict with dispassionate economic analysis. In this role, the economist works for, say, a politician—whether the president of the United States, a senator, a congressperson, or a candidate—and is speaking as both a politician and a scientifically trained economist. Oil industry economists speak for the oil industry; bank economists speak for banks; labor union economists speak for unions; and so on. These economists wear two hats— the scientific hat *and* the policy hat.

The media tend to overemphasize opinion and disagreement, because this makes the "story" more exciting. Often, television news reporters will solicit the views of a left-wing flamethrower and a right-wing flamethrower, rather than the views of the 95 percent of economists in the middle who may have reached a solid scientific consensus on the issue. Flamethrowers provide better "sound bites" to go with dramatic pictures. This is not to say that economists are without fault in creating the image of persistent disputants—exaggerating differences to draw attention. The very nature of the discipline has long lent it a pugilistic and adversarial flavor.

Scientific Disputes

Although public disputes among economists usually represent differences of *opinion,* important disagreements in analysis do persist. The most important source of *analytical* disagreement among economists involves the magnitudes of various effects in the national economy. Consider a proposal to lower the marginal tax rate on income (the tax on additional dollars earned) from 50 percent to 20 percent. Simple mathematics tells us that if the marginal tax rate is only 20 percent rather than 50 percent, on an additional $100 you earn, you are going to take home $80 after taxes rather than $50. Economic analysis tells us that such an increase in after-tax earnings may change your behavior. Would it encourage you to work harder and earn more income? Or would you become so rich that you would decide to enjoy more leisure time? Naturally, some individuals will work harder to earn $80 than to earn $50. Why then would economists disagree over a proposal to lower tax rates from 50 percent to 20 percent?

First, taxation involves a question of equity. Is it fair to charge 20 percent tax rates on income earned by everyone, regardless of their income level? You may think so; you may think not. It's your opinion. Second, a tax rate cut proposal involves other changes in the budget. Will the lost funds be collected elsewhere? Will spending be less? Will deficits increase? But also, this tax rate cut proposal raises an interesting scientific argument among economists. They ask further questions: Will the average person work harder as a result of the lower marginal tax rate? How much more production will result from additional work effort? Most economists agree that a lower marginal tax rate on income will typically raise work effort and production. But they disagree about the magnitude of the response to the change in taxes. In economic jargon: What is the responsiveness (elasticity) of work effort from an increase in after-tax income?

This example is of significant historical importance. In 1980 Arthur Laffer and others advised President Ronald Reagan to cut the top marginal tax rate on income from 70 percent to 50 percent and to cut all other tax rates by 10 percent. Laffer argued that work effort would increase a great deal and generate enough new tax revenue at the lower rate to offset the revenue lost from the rate cut. Laffer illustrated his idea on the back of a cocktail napkin in a Washington, D.C., lounge. We reproduce the **Laffer curve** in Figure 16–1.

After the Republican congressional landslide of 1994, many freshmen congress-persons could be heard echoing Laffer's ideas in their proposals for tax cuts. They claimed that congressional staff who estimate revenues had failed to allow for Laffer-type incentive effects by using static budgeting rather than *dynamic budgeting* methods. They argued that some tax cuts could "pay for themselves" as a result of changes in individual behavior.

Economists agree that a cut in marginal tax rates may create added work incentive. At the same time, most disagree with Laffer that the work-effort responses (elasticities) are strong enough to produce sufficient revenues to more than offset losses from the rate cuts.

Some political analysts call this Laffer idea **trickle-down economics.** That is, lower tax rates on the incomes of the rich will cause investment and expansion, which will in turn generate benefits that will "trickle down" to the poor. The 1980s saw the relative position of the poorest 20 percent of Americans deteriorate, whereas the top 20 percent became better off. Bill Clinton attacked the trickle-down policies of the Reagan and Bush administrations and promised to ratchet top marginal tax rates back up. Alan Blinder and Laura D'Andrea Tyson, Clinton's advisers, favor **"percolate-up" economics,** advocating higher taxes on the rich and more spending by government on infrastructure, on poverty programs, and on education and retraining. The result was to raise top marginal rates from 32 percent to 39.6 percent.

Republicans reintroduced the debate over marginal tax rate cuts by proposing 15 percent across-the-board cuts in federal income taxes, arguing that this would put more money in the hands of taxpayers and would partly pay for itself by the Laffer effect—raising work effort and income and thus actual tax revenues collected at the lower rates. The means of accounting for the increased revenues resulting from this Laffer effect, called **dynamic scoring,** is controversial.

Normally, when the Congressional Budget Office or the Office of Management and Budget tries to forecast the consequences of a tax cut, it looks at the instantaneous consequences, implicitly assuming limited changes in behavior of individuals being taxed. For example, it might estimate the effects of a tax rate cut by multiplying the rate times the base of the tax and call the result the *anticipated loss in revenue*. Economic theory, though, tells us that if we lower taxes on a particular activity, people will change their behavior by engaging in more of that activity. This dynamic response may take some time; however, if we want to know the eventual consequences of a tax rate cut, we may need to take into account this dynamic in evaluating, or scoring, the tax. Thus, *dynamic scoring* refers to more detailed, long-range, and, therefore, problematic, analysis of a proposal.

FIGURE 16–1   The Laffer Curve

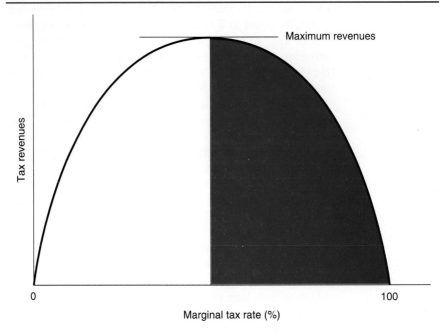

At a zero marginal tax rate the government collects zero revenue. At a 100 percent tax rate, it also collects zero. In between revenues are not zero, so they must rise to a peak and fall. Laffer argued that U.S. tax rates were so high that the economy was beyond the maximum point. If so, then a tax rate cut could increase revenues. The top rate fell under Reagan from 70 percent to 32 percent. President Clinton increased the top rate to about 40 percent.

Economists do disagree over some analytical points, because some scientific issues remain unresolved, as well as over quantitative values. In economics, as with any scientific inquiry, and especially in dealings with human interaction, not all is now known. Thus, disputes on analysis are inevitable. The four major theories of analysis that are applied to the national economy—Keynesian, monetarist, new classical macroeconomics (NCM), and supply side—are well-known in the public arena. Prominent economists support each view.

These four approaches can lead to different views on economic policy. Although each approach is based on scientific analysis, it is important to know that political liberals typically favor the Keynesian activist view, and political conservatives normally favor one of the other views. With the use of the circular flow model, the four views can be interpreted. Thus, even strongly held views that generate much conflict can be explained with the help of the same model. The circular flow model (Figure 16–2) shows the injections of investment, government

FIGURE 16–2   The Completed Circular Flow Model

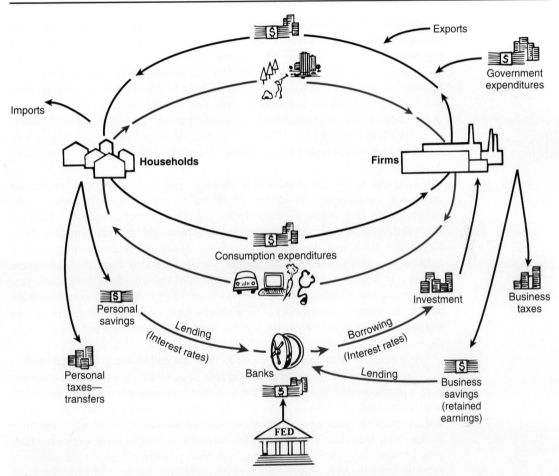

The completed circular flow model illustrates the goods and services and the dollar flows between businesses and households. It also shows the role of the foreign sector, fiscal policy, private spending, and monetary policy. Different views are held about the relative importance of these various factors.

expenditures and exports, withdrawals of savings, taxes and imports, and the influence of money via interest rates.

THE KEYNESIANS

Keynesians focus on shocks to the expenditure decisions of firms, households, and government. Keynesians analyze short-run expansions and contractions that result from changes in these expenditure patterns. But the Keynesian view goes beyond that.

Keynesian Theory and the Circular Flow

Keynesians think that the fiscal effects of the government budget are quite important. To a Keynesian, such as James Tobin, Henry Aaron, or Alan Blinder, an increase in government deficit spending can have a major effect on expanding the circular flow of income. How? Suppose the government increases spending and borrowing to finance this increase. To a Keynesian, this decision to increase government spending and borrowing stimulates economic activity. This action leads to a multiple increase in the circular flow of expenditures, culminating in an increase in national income that exceeds the original fiscal stimulus. If the government decided to finance new spending by new taxes, then Keynesians would expect only a small effect on overall spending.

Using the Keynesian circular flow model (Figure 16–3), you can see that the increase in government expenditures stimulates the pace of spending, whereas the increase in net taxes slows the pace of spending. These effects tend to be offsetting. But a deficit-financed increase in government expenditures is a net stimulant. Thus, Keynesians think that fluctuations in national expenditures can be magnified or reduced by government financial actions. Keynesians also think that investment spending is volatile and influenced by very complex uncertainties, inexplicable random events, and changing business expectations of profitability. Keynesians think that the economy is sensitive to outside shocks from investments and exports, and that these shocks occur frequently, causing the flow to fluctuate from one period to the next.

As a result of their analytical view, Keynesians emphasize government budget decisions as important determinants of the pace of economic activity. If the economy is in a recession, Keynesians advocate increasing government spending or cutting taxes to stimulate the economy. Liberal politicians, who favor expansive government budgets, prefer Keynesian economists such as Alan Blinder, Robert Solow, and Alice Rivlin. And, importantly, during slumps Keynesians tend to favor expansive budgets, because they think these budgets will have positive effects on the economy. Liberals favor the view that the government is helping the economy by increasing spending and cutting its taxes. These economists also worry a good deal about distributive justice: What fraction of income goes to the poorest citizens? They favor policies that help marginal workers and people thrown out of jobs by foreign competition. Thus, government spending programs and retraining and education policies fit right into the Keynesian stimulus idea. That the policy implications of Keynesian analysis appeal to liberals is readily apparent.

The Keynesian view was developed in response to the Great Depression of the 1930s by English economist John Maynard Keynes. Keynes believed that the Depression was the result of inadequate planned spending by the private sector. He advocated increases in deficit spending to compensate for sluggish private spending. Keynes thought that the Depression occurred because firms cut their investment spending, reducing injections. When individuals, fearing a personal budget crisis in the face of the crunch, increased savings, the lower consumption expenditures caused national income to fall even more.

FIGURE 16–3 The Circular Flow Model: Keynesian Version

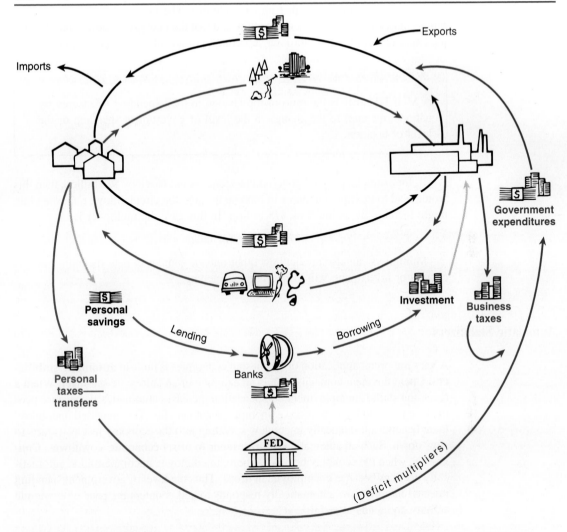

Keynesians focus on the shocks to the flow of total expenditures that cause the short-term fluctuations in the equilibrium level of spending. To them, changes in fiscal policy have important consequences for the circular flow. Whereas money matters, its effects are imprecise and unreliable. We illustrate these ideas with the color-highlighted arrows connecting government spending and tax activity to the money flow.

Keynes's solution to the Depression, which can be seen from the circular flow model, is straightforward: Increase government spending and cut taxes. Since the 1930s, as a result of the importance of **Keynesian economics,** government fiscal actions as conscious responses to slumps in private economic activity have become increasingly important. The original idea of Keynesian stimulation depended on the concept of the **multiplier** effect on expenditures. The idea is that deficit spending pumps more income into the circular flow and that the new expenditures create multiple expansions in the flow through subsequent rounds of consumption spending.

A MULTIPLIER is the ratio of the change in total spending (measured by national income) to the change in the level of government spending or the level of taxation.

If, for example, planned government spending increased by $25 billion, then this would lead to multiple increases in income through the circular flow; final spending might increase by as much as $75 billion. In this case the multiplier is

$$\$75 \text{ billion} \div \$25 \text{ billion} = 3$$

Multipliers can also predict how other outside sources of new spending, such as exports or investment, will affect national income.

Automatic Stabilizers

A very important application of Keynesian economics is built-in **automatic stabilizers.** Unemployment compensation is an example of an automatic stabilizer. When a recession starts, unemployment compensation increases automatically, because people lose jobs and begin to receive unemployment benefits. The increased unemployment benefits automatically inject new spending into the economy just as it starts to slow down. Such an automatic stabilizer tends to offset economic slowdowns. Conversely, when the economy begins to boom, unemployment compensation automatically declines because unemployment drops. Thus the level of government spending injected into the flow automatically responds to and counters the pace of economic activity and tends to stabilize it.

AUTOMATIC STABILIZERS are rules built into the government's budget that cause spending to increase (and tax revenues to decrease) when the economy goes into slumps and that cause expenditures to decrease (and taxes to increase) when the economy goes into booms. These budgetary changes occur quickly, because they do not require new legislation.

Automatic stabilizers have proliferated since the Depression. They include Social Security benefits, food stamps, farm subsidies, and AFDC. They have become so massive that, whenever the economy enters into a recession, the government budget automatically runs a huge deficit; when the economy expands, federal deficits automatically decline. Ironically, government deficits grew to the largest levels in postwar history during the terms of *Republican* presidents Gerald Ford, Ronald Reagan, and George Bush. The deficits grew because these leaders fought inflation with recession, by imposing—with the help of the Fed—tight policies. In recessions, automatic stabilizers kick in to raise government spending and to reduce government revenues. The result is large deficits. Reduced tax revenues and increased transfers were great enough to cause after-tax disposable income to rise, even though national earnings were falling. This was the case in the recession of 1974–1975 and in the recessions of 1980, 1981–1982, and 1990–1991.

This is not to imply that large deficits are simply a result of automatic stabilizers. As discussed in Chapter 13, discretionary fiscal measures, such as planned increases in the level of defense spending and the decision to index Social Security benefits, have contributed to deficits as well.

The advent of automatic stabilizers has had other unexpected consequences. One is that Keynesian economics itself has declined in influence, partly because automatic stabilizers were so successful. Why is this so? Keynes's basic policy contribution showed that government deficits could stimulate an economy in recession. However, when the economy is actively stimulated, automatic stabilizers work against the stimulus. Suppose, in a move to stimulate the economy, taxes are cut by 10 percent. Just as economic activity expands, people lose eligibility for entitlement programs. Thus, automatic-stabilizer expenditures fall and automatic tax revenues rise. Attempts to stimulate the economy are cushioned and offset by built-in automatic stabilizers. The converse is true if the economy slows down. Forces to create recessions have to be extremely powerful in order to slow spending enough to counter the offsetting stimulus from built-in automatic stabilizers.

With large automatic stabilizers, the size of the discretionary spending multiplier effect is very small. Even though most economists accept the theoretical idea of Keynesian multipliers, they disagree about the variability, magnitude, and predictability of the multipliers. Statistical estimates of government spending multipliers today are around 2, meaning that a $1-billion increase in government deficit spending will produce a $2 billion change in GDP.

Critique of the Keynesian Theory

Many economists think that Keynesian multipliers are small because of the need to finance a deficit by increased borrowing. What are the consequences of increased government borrowing? To some extent, this increased borrowing competes for funds with private investors. Using supply-and-demand reasoning you can see that an increased deficit raises total demand for loans and money. This raises interest rates, and at the margin, firms will reduce their private investment spending. Thus, increased federal borrowing *crowds out* private investment spending. Here we encounter another disagreement over magnitude: How large is the crowding-out effect? To Keynesians, crowding out is small, but to others it is large. Another drain on Keynesian multipliers is the tendency for an expansion to lead to more imports rather than to more domestic spending. This cushions the domestic stimulus.

A practical political difficulty with implementation of Keynesian fiscal policy is getting a complex organization like Congress to act decisively and in a timely fashion.

Keynesians do not ignore the role of money in the economy. They recognize that the Fed, through monetary policy, can have strong influence on what happens. However, to Keynesians, these effects are inexact and less predictable than the multiplier effects of the budget. Within this view, the private economy cushions itself from monetary effects, and at times, such as in a recession, this cushion is so effective that the Fed becomes helpless. Keynesians argue that monetary policy in these instances is like "pushing on a string."

THE MONETARISTS

Some of the more virulent arguments in macroeconomics have been between Keynesians and monetarists. *Monetarists,* such as Allan Meltzer, Milton Friedman, and Jerry Jordan, focus on the effect of money on the circular flow model. In order to understand how money passes through the circular flow, recall the analogy of water flowing through a pipe into a bathtub and then flowing out through the drain. In the economy, money corresponds to water. Money pours into the circular flow via the banking system, around the circular flow system, and out through Fed withdrawals. Money flows through the economy just as water flows through the pipes to the bathtub and out through the drain.

It is the relationship between the quantity of money flowing into the economy and the level of income generated by the flow that is important to monetarists. How is the quantity of money related to the level of income generated? Well, back to the water flowing through the tub. Suppose you asked: How much water passed through the bathtub over a period of time? You could freeze the water in the tub and count the gallons at a moment in time. But that procedure would give you the wrong answer. It would not show how much water had passed through the tub over a period of time— say, an hour. In addition to knowing the quantity of water flowing through the pipes, you need to know how fast the water is flowing. Similarly, to know how much income is generated in the economy, you must know both the *quantity* of money flowing through and the *rate of flow* of the money. The rate of flow of money through the economy is called the **income velocity of money.** If one thousand $1 bills are circulating in the economy and each $1 bill is spent an average of five times as it passes through the circular flow—exchanging hands from firms to households and back to firms again—then total expenditures are 5 times $1,000, or $5,000. In terms of yearly expenditures, a given quantity of money can generate a larger level of income, because money is spent several times throughout the year in generating income. In the course of one year, a dollar may be spent 7, 8, or 10 times. Monetarists focus on the quantity of money in the economy and the velocity of the money moving through the economy.

𝜋 𝜋

INCOME VELOCITY OF MONEY is the ratio of national income to the quantity of money in circulation. *Velocity* measures the average number of times money changes hands in generating national income per year.

Quantity Theory of Money

The formula that captures the essence of **monetarism** is the equation of exchange. First, the income velocity of money is defined as the ratio of income to the quantity of money:

$$\text{Velocity of money} \equiv \text{national income} \div \text{quantity of money}$$
$$\text{or} \tag{16-1}$$
$$V \equiv Y \div M$$

[We use three dashed lines to stress that this is a *definition* of the velocity of money; thus Equation (16–1) is an example of an "identity" rather than an "equality."]

To monetarists, the velocity of money over the long run is relatively stable. This means that most sustained fluctuations in economic activity originate with fluctuations in the quantity of money. To arrive at the **equation of exchange,** we rearrange Equation (16–1) and for simplicity we set V as a constant. The central monetarist proposition for the quantity theory of money is

$$MV_0 \equiv Y \tag{16-2}$$

Equation (16–2), the equation of exchange, says that the quantity of money M times the constant value of velocity V_0 equals money GDP, or national income Y.

The **quantity theory of money** rests on the monetarist view that the velocity of money is, if not constant, at least predictable. If velocity is constant, then changes in the level of expenditures can occur only if the quantity of money changes. This can be seen from Equation (16–2): Y can increase only if M increases.

Back to the water flowing through the tub: If the speed of the water pouring into and out of the tub stays the same, then over time the amount of water flowing through can vary only if the quantity of water pumped through increases or decreases. Thus, monetarists think that fluctuations in the quantity of money are the principal sources of fluctuations in the pace of economic activity.

Monetarists think that fiscal policy is unimportant in expanding or contracting the circular flow. They think crowding out is considerable. Suppose the government increases its spending by borrowing from the public through issuance of new U.S. securities. In this case, the government expenditure increase will be a stimulus.

Suppose government increases spending by $15 million. To finance this increase, the government borrows $15 million. To monetarists, this increase in borrowing $15 million will crowd out close to $15 million of private investment spending. In terms of the circular flow model, monetarists argue that this means that government expenditures increase by $15 million, and that investment spending decreases by nearly as much—with little "net" expansion of the economy occurring (Figure 16–4). Notice that this crowding-out argument between monetarists and Keynesians is an argument about the magnitude of a response: How much will investment fall when government borrowing rises?

What if the Fed changes monetary policy when the deficit increases? Suppose that when the government borrows the $15 million, the Fed "pumps" $15 million of new money into the economy with open-market operations. When the Fed pumps $15 million into the economy by buying U.S. securities, the Fed "monetizes the deficit." The government borrows the $15 million from the Fed; the Fed adds $15 million to the money supply. This increase in the quantity of money prevents government expenditures from crowding out investment. The net effect on the economy of a deficit financed by newly printed money is expansionary. Thus, monetarists look not at the government budget per se (whether it is in deficit or not), but at whether the Fed is increasing or decreasing the money supply. To monetarists, this latter effect is the most important.

Monetarism appeals to conservatives rather than to liberals because conservatives prefer a small domestic government budget. Thus conservatives find monetarism appealing, because it tells them that government deficits cannot be used, on their own, to stimulate the economy. In fact, deficits can be destructive if the Fed is compelled to buy the government debt obligations and thus inflate the money supply. This is a view conservatives hold anyway. Monetarism simply confirms their personal preference.

Output and Prices

Another important distinction between monetarists and Keynesians deals with their view of the effect money has on production and output. Monetarists think that fluctuations in the level of spending primarily cause fluctuations in the prices of inputs and products, not in the quantities of inputs hired and the goods and services sold. Keynesians think that fluctuations in economic activity principally cause fluctuations in the quantities of goods and services sold and in the input services employed, as well as in the prices of inputs and products. We can use the equation of exchange and the circular flow model to see this dispute more clearly. In the equation of exchange [Equation (16–2)], national income is the dollar value of income generated in the production of GDP. Therefore, national income is equal to the sum of all final goods and services produced, valued by their market prices. And thus, national income can be thought of as equal to the sum of prices times quantities. We can express this fact in equation form:

FIGURE 16–4   The Circular Flow Model: Monetarist Version

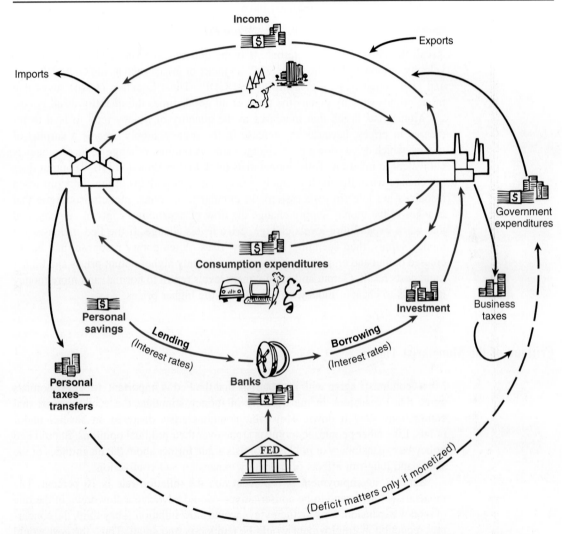

The monetarist emphasis is on the effect of Fed monetary policy on total spending. This is shown with the color-highlighted arrows connecting the Fed and banking to the flow of spending. Deficits are only important if they are monetized by Fed purchases of government debt. Except in the short run, increases in money lead to inflation and not to changes in output.

National income = prices × quantities of goods and services

or   (16–3)

$$Y = PQ$$

Intuitively, national income has two parts: prices and quantities. Thus, combining Equations (16–2) and (16–3), we have

$$MV_0 = PQ \qquad (16\text{–}4)$$

Recall the definition of the terms: M is the quantity of money, V_0 is the constant velocity of money, P is the price level (an index of prices such as the GDP deflator), and Q is output (e.g., a measure of real GDP). Thus, Equation (16–4) states that money times velocity equals the price of all goods times the quantity of all goods.

Monetarists argue that increases in the quantity of money tend to lead to increases in prices, because an increase in the money supply creates a surplus of money, which drives down its exchange value. A falling exchange value of money is equivalent to inflation. Thus, monetarists think that in Equation (16–4) output does not change when the money supply changes, except perhaps in the short run when resources are idle (in a recession). In circular flow terms, monetarists argue that changes in the money supply change the flow of expenditures, given velocity, and that when expenditure levels change, price levels change. If the Fed increases the money supply, then spending in the flow rises. A temporary response may be increased output and employment, but eventually only higher output prices and higher input costs result. Output and employment levels return to normal, and more money just leads to cheaper money, as reflected in the higher prices.

Critique of the Monetarist Theory

Most economists agree with monetarists that the Fed is important. Most economists agree that expansions in the quantity of money stimulate the economy and that contractions slow it down. However, nonmonetarists disagree on several major points. Like other people, economists argue over their political opinions: Should Fed policy be expansionary or not? Economists argue further about the magnitudes of the short- and long-run effects of monetary expansion and contraction.

Suppose unemployment is 8 percent and the inflation rate is 10 percent. The monetarists—who tend to be conservative—would advocate a slowdown in the rate of money expansion. This, in their view, would slow inflation. They think the concurrent reduction in employment would be temporary and small. Thus, the cost would be short-term and the benefits of reduced inflation would be long-term.

Keynesians—who tend to be liberals—disagree with this view for two reasons:

1. They disagree with the *opinion* that we should pay for reduced inflation with higher unemployment and slower economic growth.
2. They disagree about the *magnitude* of the effect on unemployment and lower living standards of the money contraction. Keynesians think that these real effects on unemployment and living standards last for a long time and are severe.

Both monetarists and Keynesians agree in principle that there are fiscal effects and that there are monetary effects. However, they disagree about the relative importance of fiscal and monetary policy, about the real short-term effects, and about political choices. Again, the main dispute is over the magnitude of the effects of monetary contraction.

NEW CLASSICAL MACROECONOMICS AND SUPPLY-SIDE ECONOMICS

In recent years NCM economists and supply-side economists have challenged the premises of both the Keynesians and the monetarists. Although the two are not yet one coherent model, NCM[1] and supply-side economics begin with similar premises: anti-Keynesianism, micro-based analysis, strict monetarism, a new concept—"rational expectations"—and belief in the importance of technology shocks. The NCM approach can also be described with the circular flow model. It can be seen to be an offshoot of the evolution of Keynesian and monetarist economics. NCM purports to explain stagflation, that is, simultaneous inflation and sluggish economic activity.

The NCM approach begins with three important empirical assertions about Keynesian and monetarist economics:

1. Multipliers are small, thus deficits are rejected as important stabilization tools.
2. The quantity of money influences prices and wages rather than standards of living and employment of inputs, even in the short run.
3. Output fluctuations result primarily from technology shocks to the supply side, that is, to productive capacity.

NCMs take the view that fiscal multipliers and real effects of monetary policy are small, perhaps even negligible, so that cyclical fluctuations must result from supply-side shocks. These convictions are based partly on a new theoretical model of macro behavior.

Rational Expectations

The main theoretical pillars of **new classical macroeconomics (NCM)** are the *theory of rational expectations* and the *model of production.* In the late 1970s an explanation was needed for the increasingly virulent inflation persisting in America despite high unemployment. Simultaneous high inflation and high unemployment contradict both traditional Keynesian and monetarist precepts.

---

[1]NCM received its name because many of the theoretical ideas are similar to views held by economists before John Maynard Keynes wrote *The General Theory* in 1935, in which he introduced the Keynesian model. The earlier, pre-Keynesian economists, often called *classical economists,* modeled macroeconomies much like microeconomic models and utilized the quantity theory of money. The new breed of economists, who have rejected many of the ideas of Keynes and, instead, use assumptions similar to those of their earlier forefathers, are called *new classical macroeconomists.*

Traditional Keynesian and monetarist analysis tells us that a stimulus, either fiscal or monetary, prods economic activity, and a depressant slows things down. During expansions, prices rise. In contractions, prices fall or rise less rapidly. Thus, prices rise when unemployment is low and rise very slowly or fall when unemployment is high. During the 1970s, however, prices and unemployment rose together. This outcome is counterintuitive to both the traditional Keynesian and monetarist views.

The NCM analysis begins with a circular flow model in which economic fluctuations occur as a result of numerous shocks to the system. Shocks come from surprise changes in the federal budget, surprises in foreign trade, surprises in the weather, surprises in scientific inventions, changes in educational policy, and so on. The most important shocks are to technology, however. All these shocks cause market participants (buyers and sellers) to modify their behavior in their own self-interest. The NCM assumes that markets, driven from equilibrium by surprises, return to an equilibrium quickly and efficiently.

Like monetarists, NCM economists think that monetary policy shocks are important. Monetarists think Fed actions produce recessions and expansions that alter real economic activity in the short run, because people are fooled by the Fed's actions. The NCM economists disagree. They think that, "on average," market participants

INFLUENTIAL ECONOMISTS

PRESENT-DAY ECONOMISTS

"Practical men, who believe themselves to be quite exempt from any intellectual influences, are usually the slaves of some defunct economist." J. M. Keynes, *The General Theory,* 1935.

Keynes was rarely wrong, but many present-day economists (not yet defunct) have great influence on events. Here are a few you may have read about.

James Buchanan—"The Buck" received the 1989 Nobel Prize for his development of the *theory of public choice,* in which economic models of individual choice are used to examine the motivations of government bureaucrats and politicians.

Paul Samuelson—The first American Nobel Prize winner taught basic national income analysis to President John F. Kennedy in the White House, thus laying the foundation for the famous Keynesian tax cut of 1964.

Milton Friedman—The father of modern monetarism set the stage for Fed use of monetary targets in the fight against inflation. His economic approach favors fiscal and monetary policy rules over discretion by the Fed and the executive branch.

James Tobin—A leading Keynesian theoretician. Tobin is a practitioner of the need for policy discretion in an imperfect world.

Laura D'Andrea Tyson—The first woman to chair the Council of Economic Advisers, she advocates industrial policy, choosing strategic industries for special subsidies, and managed trade. Tyson wrote *Who's Bashing Whom,* a critical appraisal of Japanese trade policies.

accurately forecast Fed actions and quickly adjust their behavior to prevent any real changes in economic activity (Figure 16–5).

Suppose the Fed plans to reduce unemployment by raising the growth of money through open-market purchases of government securities. Borrowers and lenders can anticipate such a monetary expansion; they recognize that eventually new money growth leads to an increase only in prices. They begin to anticipate that result by adjusting their prices instantly, thus avoiding even a transitional period of lower unemployment. The Fed cannot affect output and employment, even in the short run. The market participants instantly react to offset Fed actions. The only time the Fed can cause real effects is when it acts capriciously and thus surprises the market participants.

To the extent that the Fed follows a predictable course—expands the money supply when the economy slows down and slows down money-supply growth when the economy picks up—market participants can predict and offset Fed actions. This may seem farfetched. Can we really expect enough shoppers, farmers, and investors to be Fed watchers who fully anticipate normal Fed actions and then to speedily adjust their behavior to prevent real effects? According to NCM, market participants can anticipate the Fed, because they have **rational expectations.** Thomas Sargent, a principal advocate of rational expectations, explains the view with an analogy to his favorite football team, the Minnesota Vikings. If their archrivals, the Chicago Bears,

---

Charles Schultze—Director of the Office of Management and the Budget under President Lyndon B. Johnson and chair of the Council of Economic Advisers under President Jimmy Carter, Schultze is the most knowledgeable liberal on budgetary policy. He initiated the anti-inflation policy of 1979.

Gary Becker—Nobel Prize winner in 1995 and adviser to Republicans, Becker expanded the boundaries of economics to encompass study of decision-making units, such as the family, traditionally left to sociology. A supply sider, he focuses on efficiency effects of government policies. He is also a strong advocate of the position that a larger role for government has led to slower economic growth.

Alice Rivlin—As first chair of the Congressional Budget Office, this Keynesian's professionalism made her agency the most prestigious official fiscal-analysis group in Washington. She was appointed second in command in President Bill Clinton's Office of Management and Budget.

Michael Boskin—As chairman of President Bush's Economic Council, Boskin led the fight to use economic incentives, rather than command-and-control methods, to stem pollution, advised Eastern Europeans as they tried to adopt private markets, grappled with the federal budget deficit problem, advocated the cut in capital gains taxes, and resisted pressures to protect U.S. industry from Japanese trade.

Barbara Bergman—A liberal labor economist, her studies of women in the labor force, revealing wage and job discrimination, heavily influence Congress. Bergman's caustic sense of humor serves as an effective policy tool.

Herbert Stein—As chair of the Council of Economic Advisers under President Richard M. Nixon, he supported conservative positions on tight money and balanced budgets. His caustic tongue served him well in attacks on supply siders for optimistic forecasts in 1980.

FIGURE 16–5   The Circular Flow Model: NCM Version

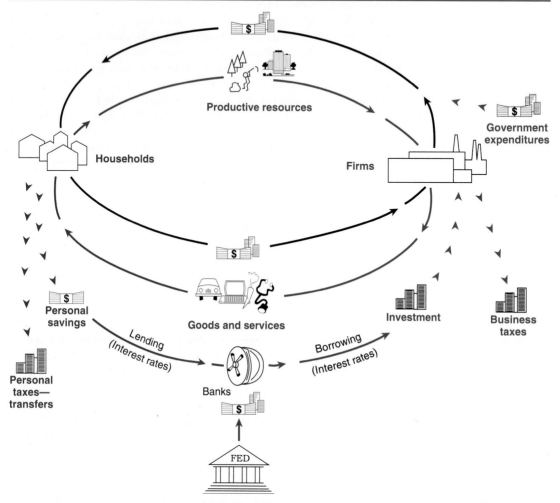

NCMs reject the view that monetary expansion has sustained effects on the real flow of goods and services and input of productive resources (indicated by the color-highlighted arrows). Fluctuations result from random shocks; especially technological shocks, to investment, savings, government spending, taxes, and transfers (shown by the color-highlighted arrows). Monetary policy and fiscal policy are unimportant, unless they surprise private markets.

always ran the same play on first down, wouldn't the Vikings figure that out and always prepare to offset that play? Of course they would. Similarly, market participants plan for systematic reactions by the Fed to fluctuations in the circular flow and begin to defend themselves against such policies. Thus, rational expectations and instant market reactions imply that the Fed has no real short-term effect on output and employment unless it truly surprises markets.

According to the concept of RATIONAL EXPECTATIONS, market participants intuitively anticipate systematic policy actions and their consequences for the economy. Thus, on average, private market forecasts are accurate, and planned monetary policy is ineffectual.

Robert Lucas, founder of the rational expectations school of thought, explains that accurate models must assume rational expectations, because market participants anticipate policy and its consequences for the economy. Were market participants to misforecast policy effects frequently, then they would be driven from the market by failures based on their false predictions.

Supply-Side Economics

The principal policy implication of NCM is that anticipated fiscal and monetary policy actions cannot systematically drive the economy away from the course set by private market participants. If the fiscal deficits have no effect on spending levels and if monetary policy only affects price levels, then what causes fluctuations in national output? What causes fluctuations in unemployment? This brings us to **supply-side economics.** Supply-side economists, following the early policy analysis of Arthur Laffer, believe that an important determinant of the level of national output and real spending is the effect that fiscal policy has on the incentives of producers and consumers rather than on the circular flow of spending. Supply siders view government tax, transfer, and spending policies as possible deterrents to work, savings, and capital formation. They argue that reversal of these policies would encourage work effort, savings, and investment activity. Real economic activity—production, employment, and output—would pick up; real economic growth without inflation would be the outcome of less government.

The key concept in supply-side economics is the **real business cycle**—the idea that business cycles are caused by real, as opposed to Keynesian or monetarist, financial forces. Supply siders say that we should forget budget deficits and open-market operations, and should focus instead on forces that determine the production of goods and services. The real-business-cycle theorists focus on a model developed in the 1950s by Robert Solow: the **aggregate production function.** The idea comes from microeconomics: Workers use capital to produce output. Rules, laws, regulations, and knowledge combine to determine the technological mix of inputs in generating output. **Technological shocks,** both positive and negative, occur all the time, causing shifts in output and employment that exactly resemble business-cycle fluctuations. An example of a positive shock is the invention of high-definition television. All of a sudden, a low-cost, new, and attractive product becomes available; consumers snap it up and production rises. An example of a negative shock is the Americans with Disabilities Act. Costs of producing a building rise because the new law mandates expensive additions such as ramps and easily accessible restrooms. Some proposed marginal projects can't justify such expenses, and output growth slows down. New pollution-compliance costs are another example of a negative supply-side shock. It is important to realize that although measures like the Clean Air Act and the Americans with Disabilities Act may be socially worth the cost, such measures, in part, do shock production and may cause cyclical down ticks.

We can analyze the supply-side position in terms of the circular flow model. NCM argues that multipliers are small and that the quantity of money affects only dollar values, not the quantities of goods and services flowing in the opposite direction. This counterclockwise dollar flow could rise and fall without having a major impact on the clockwise flow of physical goods and services. When dollars increase, prices and wages rise, but real incomes and real expenditures stay the same. In order to stimulate the physical flow of goods and services in the opposite direction from the dollar flow, government restrictions, regulations, and taxes may be altered. Less government would influence work effort and provide savings incentives and the desire to accumulate capital. A government might invest in research and development (R&D) or in technological research in fiber optics or some other cutting-edge science. Supply siders propose the following kinds of programs:

- Reduce high marginal income tax rates on the wealthy, so that people will have a greater incentive to work and to use their financial capital more productively.
- Reduce tax burdens on income that is saved in order to encourage people to save more. Specifically, reduce taxes on capital gains, on inheritance, on wealth, on interest-earning obligations, and so forth.
- Deregulate the economy so that businesses are not constrained by unnecessary environmental and safety regulations, red tape, and so on.
- Reduce taxes on businesses, especially on investment, so that firms will be encouraged to accumulate new machinery, equipment, and factories.
- Encourage R&D spending, perhaps with subsidies and tax breaks.

The theoretical tools used to bolster these proposals are micro-type tools, such as supply-and-demand analysis, applied to individual markets and activities. For example, study of capital formation focuses on incentives such as the after-tax real cost of funds to potential capital users.

Thus, NCM and supply-side economists take the view that the real part of the circular flow model, the part operating clockwise, is uninfluenced by monetary policy (Figure 16–6). Keynesian multiplier effects to stimulate the economy are

☑️ FIGURE 16–6   The Circular Flow Model: Supply-Side Version

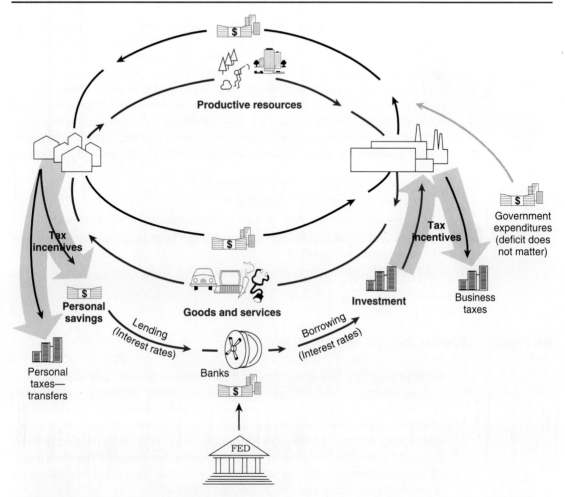

To supply siders, conventional monetary and fiscal policies operate on demand and are less important than policy effects on incentives to save and spend (indicated by the color-highlighted arrows). These incentive effects operate directly on the goods and services and the input of productive resources flow rather than indirectly on the dollar spending flow.

very small. The micro-based incentive system and its effect on production are more important. Clearly, this particular economic model appeals to businesses big and small. Nothing is nicer than being told that what you want to happen—such as lower taxes on people, on businesses, and on accumulated wealth—is also good for the country. Some business executives have found NCM–supply-side economics quite attractive.

Critique of NCM and Supply-Side Theory

As in the case of the Keynesian and the monetarist models, most disagreement among economists is about the magnitude of effects and the policy options rather than about the supply-side theory. The narrower micro focus is warranted if the spending-level effects of fiscal multipliers and monetary policy are small.

Lower taxes on earned income may raise the incentive to work. Lower taxes on savings will raise the incentive to save. Deregulation of industry will raise unfettered business activity. Reduced taxes on capital formation will encourage more capital accumulation. Subsidies to research and development will raise spending on R&D. Crucial questions arise in each case, however, over the magnitudes of responses:

- How big will the work incentive response be?
- How much more saving will people do?
- Will new production increase enough to warrant the reduction in regulations?
- Will the investment incentives result in relatively large increases in investment or in rather small increases?
- How considerable are technological shocks?

DIFFERENT APPROACHES TO NATIONAL POLICY

We have seen how to use the circular flow model to describe four approaches to national economic activity: Keynesian, monetarist, NCM, and supply-side. In each case, economists disagree partly about theory and partly about magnitudes of effects. Liberals, conservatives, and extreme conservatives disagree even more about policy actions based on these theories. The liberal and conservative views on specific issues are greatly simplified here in order to highlight some principal differences on political views and personal opinions rather than on economic theory. The five main areas of political disagreement in macroeconomic policy are:

1. **Inflation versus unemployment.** Liberals tend to emphasize the social costs of unemployment over the damage from inflation. Compared to inflation, unemployment affects fewer people more harshly. Few of us escape the effects of inflation, especially if it is unanticipated. Liberals tend to lean toward expansionary policies, whereas conservatives view inflation as more damaging to business and growth, and thus more troublesome than unemployment. Most conservatives argue that the unemployment costs of slowing the economy are short term and are worth the price of reducing inflation.

2. **Big government versus little government.** Conservatives favor limited government spending, so that people can enhance their own freedom through the marketplace. Liberals advocate an active role for government in helping disadvantaged and underprivileged people.

3. **Equity versus efficiency.** Liberals emphasize equity over efficiency. They are concerned more with an equitable distribution of income than with economic growth. Conservatives are more concerned with rapid growth than with equal distribution. Conservatives argue that rapid growth pulls up everyone's income together—all boats rise with the tide. Both are concerned with equal opportunity.

4. **Active versus passive policy.** Keynesians, who dominated policy in the Kennedy years, 1961–1964, and in the Carter years, 1977–1980, employed active adjustments in both monetary and fiscal policies to offset undesirable fluctuations in the economy. They used tax cuts, defense-spending increases, and frequent changes in money growth. In the 1980s monetarists and NCMs, such as Murray Weidenbaum and Jerry Jordan under President Reagan and Michael Boskin and John Taylor under President Bush, advocated very cautious hold-the-course policies and argued that activist policies destabilize the economy by forcing frequent adjustments to policy shocks by private markets. Clinton activists, including Laura D'Andrea Tyson and Robert Reich, advocate industrial policy, worker retraining, and investment in infrastructure.

5. **The role of defense in foreign policy.** Conservatives support large-scale strategic defense spending to protect democracy against unexpected threats from around the world. Liberals think that expensive strategic defense systems do not reduce world tensions and are too costly. They prefer the money to be spent on domestic infrastructure.

In order to emphasize the distinction between (normative) political and philosophical opinions on the one hand and objective (positive) analysis on the other, we have used the terms *conservative* and *liberal* as if various political views fell into neatly labeled categories. People's views and opinions are far more complex. Indeed, a person can hold a conservative view on some issues and a liberal view on others. Major battles can occur between individuals within a very narrow band of the political spectrum. Political and philosophical views are far more complex than we have indicated here.

𝒥𝒦 CHAPTER REVIEW

Economists are most frequently heard in the media when they are wearing their *political hats* and speaking for political parties. Thus, they appear to disagree about economic theory when in fact, they are, just as everyone else, expressing normative judgments about politics and philosophy.

Economists do disagree, however, over the *magnitudes* of some effects. As one example, Arthur Laffer wanted President Reagan to cut marginal income tax rates by 30 percent. He thought this would generate immediate and huge increases in economic activity. Most economists thought he exaggerated the speed and magnitude of the effect. Alan Blinder advised President Clinton to raise top tax rates.

Economists disagree over the size of the multipliers. Keynesians like Robert Eisner think deficits are important because they have multiplier effects on national spending levels; monetarists like Jerry Jordan think deficits are counterproductive because they crowd out private investment; supply siders like Edward Prescott think deficits are unimportant, but they also think taxes affect incentives.

Although all economists agree on the importance of positive economic analysis, they still disagree on some important theoretical issues: (1) the extent to which stimulations and contractions in the circular flow lead to changes in real living standards and (2) the quantity of real inputs hired as opposed to merely changes in the cost of living and the prices at which things are valued. Monetarists and supply siders think that expansions and contractions in the circular flow cause changes in inflation. Keynesians think that quantity effects of fiscal policy on demands are important and large. Real-business-cycle theorists think technological shocks to production primarily cause cyclical fluctuations. These arguments are over the theory of how things work, as well as over the magnitudes of effects.

🎵 MULTIPLE-CHOICE SELF-TEST 🎵 🎵 🎵 🎵 🎵 🎵 🎵 🎵 🎵 🎵 🎵 🎵 🎵 🎵 🎵

1. Keynesians advocate that the federal government raise and lower its budget deficit in response to changes in the circular flow because they believe:

   a. Multipliers are large, and the economy does not correct its output and employment levels quickly.

   b. Multipliers are large, and the economy corrects its output and employment levels quickly.

   c. Multipliers are small, and the economy does not correct its output and employment levels quickly.

   d. Multipliers are small, and the economy corrects its output and employment levels quickly.

2. If an increase in government spending appears to cause a large increase in national income, a monetarist would say:

   a. This is consistent with the claim that money multipliers are large.

   b. This was coincidental; probably investment had increased for some other reason.

   c. This probably happened because the Fed added to the money supply in order to help the government finance its bigger deficit.

   d. The crowding-out effect was small because the economy was not at full employment.

3. Suppose the money supply is $100 billion, investment spending is $50 billion, the government budget deficit is $110 billion, and the income velocity of money is 5. The level of national income must be:

   a. $1,050 billion.

   b. $500 billion.

   c. $260 billion.

   d. $200 billion.

4. The rational-expectations concept explains people's reaction to an expected increase in the money supply as follows:

   a. Because they know this Fed policy will cause inflation, they raise prices immediately rather than expanding output.

   b. Because they expected this policy change, they will already have increased output and employment.

   c. Because they expected this policy change, they will reduce output in response.

   d. Because they expected this policy change, they will not allow it to affect either their prices or their output decisions.

5. According to a supply sider, the effect of a tax cut on the level of output would be:

   a. A sizable increase, because the tax cut increases total spending.

    b.   Small or negligible, because the increased deficit will crowd out private investment.

    c.   A sizable increase, because firms and households will earn higher returns from increased work and investment.

    d.   Small or negligible, because fiscal and monetary policies may affect prices, but not output.

6.   If asked to analyze a sudden cyclical upturn, real-business-cycle theorists would look for:

    a.   A recent increase in pollution regulations.

    b.   A monetary policy stimulus.

    c.   An anticipated increase in the budget deficit.

    d.   A technological innovation.

✎ STUDY QUESTIONS

1.   On which aspects of national economic activity do Keynesians and monetarists agree?

2.   Evaluate the Laffer proposal to cut top personal income tax rates from 70 percent to 50 percent.

3.   Use the circular flow model and the quantity theory of money to analyze the effects of an increase in the money supply.

4.   Compare and contrast the views of Keynesians and NCM economists on the issue of the consequences of federal budget deficits.

5.   What are some normative and some positive arguments about which monetarists and supply siders disagree on the role of federal spending and tax policy?

🌿 PROBLEM

Suppose that national income is $200 billion and the Fed raises the money supply from $20 billion to $22 billion.

1. Use the quantity equation to explain what monetarists believe will happen as a result.

2. What would Keynesians say?

   Suppose you are chair of the President's Economic Council and that the economy is in a recession. What policies would you recommend for the Federal budget? For monetary policy? Justify your recommendations on the basis of the theory of the macroeconomy that you think is best.

CHAPTER 17

Inflation and Unemployment

𝒥𝒥 CHAPTER PREVIEW

Unemployment and inflation are stubborn concerns that frequently confront U.S. policymakers. The unemployment rate in 1975 was 8.5 percent; the inflation rate was 9.1 percent. Again, in 1980 the unemployment rate was 7.1 percent; the inflation rate was 13.5 percent. President Jimmy Carter added the inflation rate to the unemployment rate to form the "misery index," showing the seriousness of this combination, which is called *stagflation*. In 1986 inflation had fallen to 1.1 percent, but unemployment was stuck at 7.0 percent. In the aftermath of the 1990–1991 recession, unemployment rose to 7.4 percent while inflation fell to 2.9 percent. By 1996 unemployment and inflation were relatively low: Unemployment was 5.4 percent and inflation 3.3 percent.

Stagflation can be particularly troublesome, because the standard remedies suggested by traditional economic analysis for countering inflation and unemployment are exactly the opposite. Whatever short-term measure we suggest for curtailing inflation is the wrong medicine for the unemployment problem. Inflation calls for contractionary monetary and fiscal policies. Unemployment calls for expansionary policies. Obviously, we cannot stimulate and contract the economy at the same time. In the early 1980s attempts were made to alter the mix of policies—contract monetary policy to slow inflation and cut tax rates to stimulate employment. These measures were only partly successful.

1. Are inflation and unemployment beyond our control?
2. Is unemployment a legitimate national concern, or does it affect only a few?

𝕁𝕃 CONCEPTS REINTRODUCED

𝕁𝕃 NEW CONCEPTS

Friedman's Law
Demand-Pull Inflation
Cost-Push Inflation
Frictional Unemployment
Structural Unemployment
Cyclical Unemployment
Natural Rate of Unemployment (Un)
Efficiency-Wage Theory
Okun's Law
Stop-Go Policies
Cost-of-Living Adjustments (COLAs)

🏛 CHAPTER OBJECTIVES

After studying this chapter, you should be able to:

1. Define *demand-pull* and *cost-push* inflation by stating the nature of each.
2. List three types of unemployment, and give examples of each.
3. Define the natural rate of unemployment.
4. Give examples of monetary and fiscal policies that show a stop-go trend.

THE CAUSES OF INFLATION

That inflation is a problem can be of little doubt. According to John Maynard Keynes, in 1931, "Lenin is said to have declared that the best way to destroy the capitalist system was to debauch the currency." This refers to the political cost of inflation in a private market economy, and no doubt the notorious Marxist Vladimir I. Lenin recalled the German hyperinflation of the 1920s. As we noted in Chapter 11, uneven inflation distorts the price system, raises effective tax rates when the tax system is progressive, and confuses long-term planning. Inflation also has a political cost: It weakens public confidence in the health of the economy.

Inflation is the cheapening, or depreciation, of money. The role of the money supply is central to understanding inflation. When you go to the store to buy jeans, you think of yourself as demanding jeans. However, to economists you are also supplying money. When you enter into a transaction, the store supplies jeans and demands money, and you supply money and demand jeans. During inflation the store will supply fewer and fewer jeans in exchange for a given quantity of money. Thus, the price of jeans rises. When the general level of all prices rises, then money "depreciates" and we have inflation. Thus, the exchange price of money is the inverse of the price level P: $1/P$, where P is the level of prices. When P rises, the exchange price of money falls. When the consumer price index (CPI) rose from 1.954 to 2.174, the purchasing power of $1, measured in 1972 dollars, fell from $0.51 to $0.46.

Envision a standard supply-and-demand model and ask, What might cause the price of money to fall? or What might cause the price level to rise? There are two possible answers:

1. The price of money falls if the money supply rises too rapidly.
2. The price of money falls if demand for money falls relative to supply.

Figure 17–1 illustrates the market for money. The exchange price of money is $1/P$. In Panel A an increase in the supply of money raises the price level from 1.954 to 2.174. This is equivalent to reducing the equilibrium exchange price of money from $0.51 to $0.46. In Panel B a demand for money decrease is shown to lead to an increase in the price level from $1/1.954$ to $1/2.174$ and, therefore, to cheaper money.

FIGURE 17–1   Inflation and Money

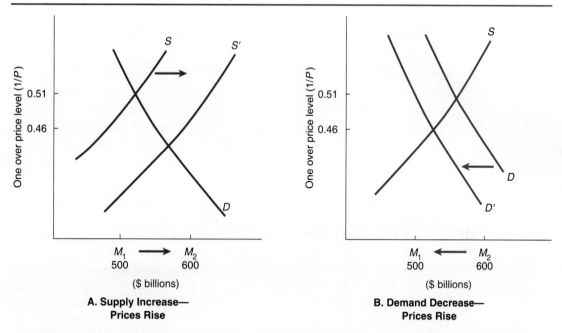

An increase in prices of all goods is equivalent to a decrease in the exchange price of money and, you will recall, reflects the value of money in terms of goods and services. Thus, money demand and supply depend on $1/P$ where the price level P can be measured by the CPI or the GDP deflator. An increase in money supply reduces its exchange price, which is equivalent to raising the price level of goods. The price level can also rise if money demand falls relative to supply.

The theory of supply and demand tells us that an increase in supply or a decrease in demand will lead to a one-time change in the price of the good. Because inflation is a sustained rise in prices, we must go one step farther to explain the cause of inflation. For inflation, the growth of the money supply must persistently exceed the growth of money demand. Thus, logically, inflation comes from either a slowdown in the growth rate of money demand or an increase in the growth rate of money supply.

Friedman's Law

Milton Friedman devoted much of his professional career to analyzing the causes of inflation. He believes the main cause of inflation is rapid growth of the money supply induced by the monetary authority—in the United States, the Fed. The central themes of Friedman's analysis of the United States economy are:

- The Fed controls the money supply.

- The rate of inflation depends on the growth rate of the money supply with a long and variable lag.

Friedman's Law is an essential ingredient to understanding inflation.

According to FRIEDMAN'S LAW, inflation follows excessive monetary growth with a long (about two-year) and variable lag. In more scientific terms, the rate of price-level change follows the rate of monetary growth, but after a long and variable lag. Insufficient monetary growth would lead to deflation.

However, despite its importance to the relationship between money growth and inflation, one must be cautious in applying Friedman's Law.

The Fed is not an isolated agent such as the proverbial hermit on a mountaintop. Like all central banks, the Fed is a political organization. The Fed is heavily influenced by Congress and the executive branch. In a democracy, public institutions respond to the will of the people. Thus, the Fed is not long able to ignore the pressures of the political system. The Fed may respond by inflationary policies to political pressures, which are in turn caused by other economic forces.

In addition, while inflation slows money growth, the lag is not precise. Fluctuations in the money supply occur that do not lead to inflation. Also, fluctuations in inflation occur that are not directly attributable to the money supply. At times, inflation occurs within six months of monetary expansion; at other times, not until three years later. Thus, considerable variability characterizes the inflation–money growth relationship.

TOOL KIT

FRIEDMAN'S LAW

The inflation rate is a result of too much money growth by the Fed. It takes approximately two years for inflation to result from excessive money growth. This lag is, however, quite variable. Inflation is sustained only by persistent money growth. Because people can adapt to persistent inflation, most serious problems are caused by erratic Fed policies that make inflation hard to predict. The illustration (Figure 17–A) depicts Friedman's Law.

Figures on money growth during recent years are available at the library. What do you predict the future inflation rate will be?

Third, money growth affects the economy in the short term in other ways, apart from any ultimate inflation effect. Recall, from Chapter 15, that a burst of money growth can drive interest rates down suddenly and, in the process, stimulate business investment spending.

Inflation as Seen from the Goods Market

Economists disagree about and debate the underlying relationship between the growth rate of the money supply and economic growth. This debate has a long history. J. K. Galbraith, in *Money: Whence It Came and Where It Went* (first published in 1975), recalled a debate of the early 19th century:

> In the debate [of 1811], indistinct but wholly recognizable is a difference of opinion which continues to this day. Where does economic change originate? Does it begin with those who are responsible for money—in this case with those who made loans and thus cause the supply of notes and deposits to increase? . . . Or does change begin with production? . . . In short, does money influence the economy or does money respond to the economy? The question is still asked.

As you saw in Chapter 15, the money market and the circular flow of income are linked by a dual direction of cause and effect (see Figure 15–5). Go back to Figure 15–2, which shows that economic expansion can lead to money-demand growth and thus to an increase in the equilibrium quantity of money. In principle, the economy influences money, and money influences the economy. Therefore, although economic expansion and monetary expansion are coincident, do we necessarily know whether the cause originated in the money market or in the goods market?

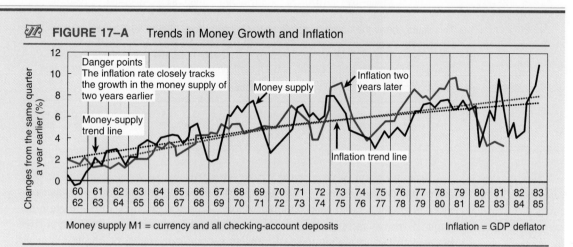

FIGURE 17–A Trends in Money Growth and Inflation

Money supply M1 = currency and all checking-account deposits

Inflation = GDP deflator

Source: Adapted from Milton Friedman "The Needle Got Stuck," *Newsweek* (July 25, 1983), p. 66.

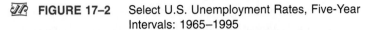

FIGURE 17–2   Select U.S. Unemployment Rates, Five-Year
Intervals: 1965–1995

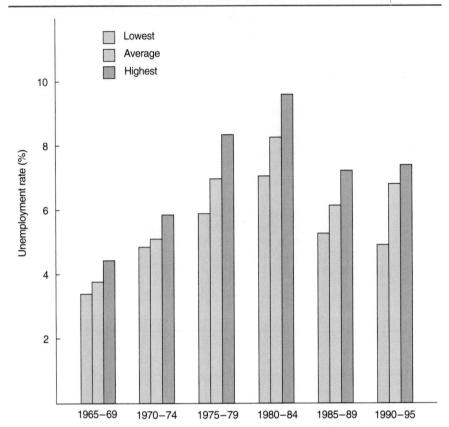

This figure shows the upward trend in unemployment from 1965 to 1985, when it began to fall, whether measured by lowest, average, or highest rate. Three facts stand out: (1) Unemployment rarely falls below 5 percent, (2) the rate fluctuates within those five-year intervals by as much as 3 percent, and (3) the average annual unemployment rate drifted upward from 1965 to 1985—then leveled out.

Source: *The Economic Report of the President* (Washington, D.C.: U.S. Government Printing Office, 1996); and Joint Economic Committee, *Economic Indicators* (Washington, D.C.: U.S. Government Printing Office, February 1997).

From the point of view of the market for goods and services, nearly all product prices rise during inflation. This suggests that national demand for goods and services is growing faster than national supply. We can now study inflation from the point of view of supply and demand for goods and services. The price level rises because costs, in growing too fast, prevent supply from rising, or because demand growth is outstripping supply. Thus, supply-and-demand analysis suggests two types of inflation: **demand-pull inflation** and **cost-push inflation.**

DEMAND-PULL INFLATION occurs when the national demand for goods and services outstrips the productive potential of the economy or national supply, causing prices to rise.

COST-PUSH INFLATION takes place when cost increases slow the growth rate of national supply, causing shortages and price increases.

Identifying the demand-pull and cost-push causes of inflation from the perspective of the market for goods and services does not contradict Friedman's Law. Instead, some root causes for pressures on the Fed to expand the money supply are suggested. This perspective helps explain some of the "blips" in inflation that are not directly explainable by money growth.

Consider 1973–1974 and 1979–1980, when OPEC countries suddenly increased the price of oil. These were significant depressive shocks to the supply potential of the American economy. These shocks led to both a contraction in economic activity and an increase in the level of prices.

How does the Fed respond to a depressive supply shock? There are two possibilities:

1. Slow money growth to stop inflation.
2. Increase money growth to offset the contraction in output of goods and services.

The second action will raise prices beyond the level caused by the initial supply shock itself, because the Fed expands national demand. Thus, a sudden increase in costs (resulting, in this example, from an oil shortage) leads to a shortage of goods and services and an increase in production costs and product prices. If the Fed responds to the contraction in output by printing more money, then it reinforces the increase in prices, exacerbating inflation.

Although it is evident that money plays a significant role in the inflationary process, the basic causes of inflation are more complicated. The root causes of inflation can originate on the supply side or on the demand side of the market for goods. Money has short-run effects on interest rates and on expenditures. This means that contracting the money supply to slow inflation may be extremely painful and politically unacceptable. To deal with this complex policy issue more carefully, we must first analyze the causes of unemployment.

THE ANATOMY OF UNEMPLOYMENT

The bar chart in Figure 17–2 illustrates the unemployment rate for selected intervals from 1965 to 1995. Any analysis of the causes of unemployment must deal with the three facts evident in this figure:

1. Even when the economy is bristling with activity, the unemployment rate is far from zero: around 4.5 percent in the 1960s, 7.5 percent in the 1970s, 6.0 percent in the 1980s, and 5.5 percent in the early to mid-1990s.
2. Unemployment varies over the business cycle from a low of about 5 percent to a high of about 10 percent.
3. The average annual unemployment rate increased from the 1960s until the middle of the 1980s when it began to level off.

Despite numerous policy attempts to lower unemployment, the stubborn problem of high unemployment persists.

The American political system has long accepted the social goal of full employment. President Harry Truman signed into law the Employment Act of 1946 in which Congress and the president agreed to high employment as an official goal of national policy. In 1974 President Gerald Ford, with the concurrence of Congress, signed the **Humphrey-Hawkins Act** in which the full-employment objective was reaffirmed as a national policy goal. Unemployment reached 7.5 percent in 1992, and, even though the NBER had declared the recession over, the Clinton–Gore campaign ran on the platform of getting the economy back to full strength. Their campaign headquarter's wall was adorned with a sign warning the campaign staffers that the polls favored them because of their aggressive economic recovery stance. The sign said, "It's the economy, stupid." President Bill Clinton's 1992 economic plan included a $31-billion stimulus package designed to create new jobs, but once he was in office, the reality of the budget deficit's relentless growth compelled the administration to raise taxes and limit spending. Nonetheless, the economy enjoyed a long expansion through the middle of the decade.

The Causes of Unemployment

One way to think about unemployment is to analyze the unique nature of labor. Consider how a producer responds when products don't sell. Suppose you sell tennis equipment. What do you do during the winter when people stop buying your goods? You hold onto your inventory of tennis balls and rackets until sales pick up again in the spring. In fact, many products can be held in inventory stocks until markets pick up. When steel sales slow down, mills idle their machinery until things pick up again in a few months. The capital is little harmed for being idle. However, the same is not true for labor. If you were a steelworker and the mill slowed down, you might be laid off. That day, week, or month of work you lose can never be reclaimed. Workers can't be kept in a freezer and put to use when needed. Thus, idle labor, or unemployment, is something that is lost forever and never recaptured.

Furthermore, the laid-off worker needs money to survive, live in a home, and feed a family. Thus, unemployment presents a unique kind of social and economic problem. Unlike material and machinery inputs to the production process, labor services cannot be held in inventoried stocks for use when demand picks up again.

Generally the unemployment rate is not composed of a single pool of persons out of work for a long period of time. Instead, in recessions layoffs become more frequent and the intervals between work periods become longer. When new workers enter the labor force, they are counted as unemployed during their job search. When the unemployment rate is high, new workers spend more search time than when unemployment is low. If you and other potential workers spend a bit longer looking for a job, when the statisticians from the labor department measure the unemployment rate, the average rate will be higher. Fluctuations in the unemployment rate reflect longer *durations* of unemployment for more workers, rather than a sudden increase in permanent unemployment for one small pool of people.

Still, unemployment is more pervasive for certain groups—particularly for young people and for African Americans and Latinos. It is also a bigger problem in some industries and for some types of jobs. Furthermore, during recessions over 15 percent of the unemployed are out of work for quite a long period of time—over six months. Nevertheless, analysis of job-loss duration suggests one key aspect of U.S. unemployment: Increased unemployment means an increase in the average time period between jobs and a longer search interval.

Statistical evidence suggests the need for different types of policy responses to different types of unemployment, and this has led economists to define three distinct types of unemployment: frictional, structural, and cyclical. Some unemployment is the **frictional unemployment** characteristic of the labor market. People need time to enter the labor force and to move from one job to another. New workers need time to find their first jobs, and other people need time to change jobs. This kind of unemployment is only slightly related to the business cycle or to gradual changes in the structure of the economy. Creation of more efficient employment and job-search agencies for new workers could possibly reduce the frictional unemployment rate. The Humphrey-Hawkins Act, which accepted 4 percent as a full-employment target, implicitly acknowledged inevitable frictions.

FRICTIONAL UNEMPLOYMENT occurs because people need time to enter the labor force or to move from one job to another. At any time, a certain fraction of new entrants into the labor force and workers who leave old jobs will be unemployed while they search for new jobs.

However, unemployment in the United States is much too large, even during cyclical upswings in the national economy, to be caused by frictions. A second type of unemployment that can be much more long-lasting and socially disturbing than frictional unemployment is **structural unemployment.**

STRUCTURAL UNEMPLOYMENT is caused by a mismatch between labor skills and jobs. The structurally unemployed are those whose skills are not suitable for the types of jobs available. The level of structural unemployment is largely unrelated to cyclical fluctuations in the level of national economic activity.

Unemployment fluctuates over short intervals by millions of workers. During the recession of 1980–1982, over 11 million Americans were counted as officially unemployed. They constituted as much as 11.5 percent of the labor force at the trough of the recession. By 1986 the rate of unemployment fell to 7.0 percent, and by 1989 it fell to 5.2 percent, as the economy enjoyed a robust expansion. Then the 1990–1991 slowdown saw unemployment rise again, reaching 7.5 percent in 1992. By 1996 unemployment had fallen to 5.4 percent. Such high and variable unemployment is attributed to cyclical fluctuations in the pace of economic activity. This brings us to the third type of unemployment—**cyclical unemployment.**

CYCLICAL UNEMPLOYMENT is associated with downturns in the pace of national economic activity. When demand for output is slack, firms in many industries lay off workers for a temporary period. In some industries, workers are let go, and in some cases, firms themselves fail and jobs disappear.

The Natural Unemployment Rate

One approach to analyzing the causes of unemployment and the policies for dealing with it is to identify the dividing line between structural and cyclical unemployment. To do this, economists use the concept of the **natural rate of unemployment (Un),** a term coined in 1968 by Milton Friedman.

The NATURAL RATE OF UNEMPLOYMENT (Un) is the lowest rate of unemployment that can be maintained by stabilization policies without accelerating the inflation rate.

The concept behind Un is not new, and it has been given many different names. It has also been assigned different values. Arthur Okun, chairman of the Council of

Economic Advisers to President Lyndon B. Johnson in the mid-1960s, used the term *normal unemployment*. He felt that the economy could expand, via fiscal and monetary stimulus, until unemployment reached 4.5 percent. Then, inflation would accelerate if attempts were made to pressure the economy to expand any more. The target rate for full employment in the 1974 Humphrey-Hawkins Act is 4 percent, implying a Un of 4 percent. The fact that unemployment drifted upward from the 1950s to the mid-1980s, however, suggests to many economists that Un itself changes. In 1974 MIT's Robert Hall argued that Un was 5.5 to 6 percent. Friedman believes that scholars are unable to state the exact value of Un.

Structural Unemployment

Unfortunately, unemployment rates over the last 25 years, even at business-cycle peaks, have been higher than 4 percent to 5 percent. This implies that changes in the structure of U.S. labor markets or the nature of the nation's workers have exacerbated the structural unemployment problem. Structural unemployment often reflects the obsolescence of certain job-specific skills.

For example, suppose you hold a very specific, technical job in the textile industry. As a result of foreign competition, your firm starts losing demand, and you are laid off. Much of your skill and training is job-specific: You were trained at certain tasks. Suppose there are job openings in the computer-hardware industry, but they are for workers with skills in electronics. You have the wrong skills for these jobs, so that even though there is demand for labor, you do not fit the job description. Under these conditions you will be unemployed for structural reasons. Economists today think that between 3 and 3.5 percent of American workers are structurally unemployed.

Two important changes in the composition of the American labor force throughout the 1970s contributed to the growth of structural unemployment: (1) the baby-boom generation and (2) adult women entering the labor force. Children born after World War II, the "baby boomers," entered the labor force in the early 1970s. Younger workers, especially teenagers, traditionally spend more time unemployed than older workers. According to the Council of Economic Advisers, by the late 1970s workers aged 16 to 24 accounted for 40 to 50 percent of total unemployment.

A second major change in the composition of the American labor force through the 1970s and 1980s was the massive increase in the number of working adult women. The percentage of eligible adult women who, according to official statistics, joined the labor force rose from 43 percent in 1970 to 54 percent in 1985. This increase partly reflected the thrust of the women's movement and partly the decline in growth of living standards of American families. Unemployment rates for females have traditionally exceeded those of males, partly because many of the jobs held by women have higher turnover rates. Some attribute this job placement of female workers to discrimination; others to different adult lifetime work patterns. An increase in the proportion of young people and women in the workforce increases the average unemployment rate.

Certain laws and customs also contribute to high structural unemployment. Two of the more important are minimum-wage laws and unemployment insurance. It is important to distinguish *analyzing* unemployment as a by-product of these laws, customs, and market actions from *judging* such activities.

Minimum-wage laws are designed to assure workers enough income to avoid poverty. Higher minimum wages lower employment. If the minimum wage forces a producer to pay a worker more than the worker adds to the value of production, then some workers will not be employed. Especially controversial are minimum-wage laws that apply to teenagers. The skill level among many teenagers entering the labor market is relatively low; high school dropouts, for example, are inexperienced, and they have had inadequate education and little job training. Faced with the prospect of hiring unskilled teenagers at a relatively high minimum wage, many employers would simply prefer to avoid hiring them altogether. Furthermore, many teenagers will seek employment, lured by the relatively high minimum wage. They may drop out of school to find a job. Because they are not very productive, they fail in their search, and teenage unemployment rises. In 1982 white teenage unemployment was 20 percent, compared to white adult unemployment of 8 percent. Nonwhite unemployment rates were 16 percent for adults and 44 percent for teenagers. Just prior to the 1996 presidential campaign, Congress voted and President Clinton signed a new minimum-wage law increasing the U.S. minimum wage from $4.25 to $5.15 an hour over a two-year period.

Unemployment compensation also increases the unemployment rate. Unemployment compensation is a collective insurance policy against the risk of losing income when unemployed. However, a by-product of unemployment insurance is that people are less distressed about losing a job and can take longer in searching for a new job. Thus, a side effect of unemployment compensation is an increase in the time spent unemployed.

Many economists have become increasingly concerned about the loss of high-paying manufacturing jobs in the United States. The proportion of the labor force in manufacturing fell steadily throughout the late 1970s and the 1980s. Manufacturing output itself has not fallen, but employment in manufacturing has. In an innovative and widely cited series of books, Robert Reich, who later became Secretary of Labor, argued that Americans were losing well-paid "muscle jobs" in manufacturing because of effective competition from Japan and Germany and because of increased reliance on new technologies such as robotics. Although demand for highly skilled analytical and conceptual work by American workers continues, low-skilled physical labor in the United States has lost its comparative advantage to low-wage workers in Asia, Latin America, and elsewhere. One consequence has been an increase in the disparity of income distribution, with some Americans becoming poorer because of low earnings and increased unemployment whereas others, especially college graduates and professionals, enjoy higher earnings.

The solutions to this problem are not obvious. President Clinton's team leaned toward increased training, skill development, tax incentives for new investment, and government-spending increases on public-sector capital infrastructure. Laura D'Andrea Tyson in *Who's Bashing Whom?* lays some of the blame on the Japanese for exporting manufacturing goods to the United States while protecting their own firms and workers from United States import. She advocates strategic quotas and tariffs to force the Japanese to open their home markets to foreign competition. These various proposals are heavily debated.

Cyclical Unemployment

When monetary and fiscal policies are utilized to slow the economy, the rate of unemployment increases: More people are added to the rolls of the unemployed and more people spend a longer time between jobs. Research indicates that 90 percent of cyclical unemployment results from job losses and layoffs. Keynes argued that this cyclical unemployment is largely involuntary. But Martin Feldstein argues that some cyclical unemployment results from either (1) *explicit contracts* between unions and corporations or (2) *implicit contracts,* (i.e., unwritten rules agreed to by custom) between employee and employer. These contracts are voluntary. He cites industries, such as auto and construction, in which workers implicitly accept the risk of layoffs when demand for product is low. They will accept this risk if they are assured of being rehired in good times and if wages paid during the good times provide adequate compensation for the layoff losses. Feldstein argues that because these contracts are satisfactory to both parties, we should not attempt to eliminate such unemployment by stimulating the economy. In his view these contracts convert the problem of temporary involuntary unemployment into a rational labor-inventory policy.

If unemployment is involuntary, then why are unemployed workers unable to force down wages so that firms find it economical to hire them? University of California, Berkeley, economists George Akerlof and Janet Yellen argued that firms may hold wages higher than necessary during cyclical downturns in order to maintain worker morale and to attract and hold the best workers. They call this idea **efficiency-wage theory** because it may be efficient to pay high wages even during a cyclical slump when wages could be allowed to fall. Efficiency wages induce workers to be loyal and work harder than purely competitive wages do; the latter would fall in recession and clear the labor market. The efficiency-wage theory explains how involuntary unemployment can persist during cyclical downturns.

Economists have not yet come to a consensus about the relative importance of voluntary and involuntary unemployment. Some argue that only unemployment above 7 percent is involuntary; others argue that unemployment above 5 percent is involuntary. Regardless of the cause of unemployment, its costs include significant lost output and slower growth. In the late 1960s Arthur Okun established an empirical relationship between the level of unemployment and the level of real GDP in the U.S. economy. We call this relationship **Okun's Law.**

OKUN'S LAW states that for every 1 percent of unemployment above Un (the natural unemployment rate) real GDP will be 3 percent lower than its potential.

In 1992 unemployment was 7.5 percent. If we use 5.0 percent as Un, the difference is 2.5 percent. Thus, $2.5 \times 3 = 7.5$ percent loss of real GDP. In 1992 GDP was $6,244 billion. Thus, according to Okun's Law, the loss in real GDP from cyclical unemployment was $468 billion. In 1992, $468 billion extra could have balanced the federal budget, with $187 billion left over!

ARE INFLATION AND CYCLICAL UNEMPLOYMENT RELATED?

Figure 17–3 illustrates yearly pairs of unemployment and inflation from 1960 to 1996. Through this 36-year period the combination of inflation and unemployment appears to display a pattern: The pairs seem to follow a cycling path of clockwise loops. Five such loops appear in the figure. The loops appear to be rising and, until the last loop, drifting to the right. Does this pattern suggest a systematic relationship between these two major indicators of economic performance? Although economists disagree about many aspects of macro policy and analysis, a rough consensus has emerged that Un drifted upward from 4.5 percent to 6.5 or 7 percent, then started to drift back down toward 5.0 or 5.5 percent. As we discussed above, this upward then downward drift probably reflects changed structural factors[1] especially the post–World War II baby-boom generation working its way through the labor market. If this is correct, then this means that somehow the economy is driven in cyclical *clockwise loops about Un.* One explanation involves changes in monetary and fiscal policies—changes that are called **stop-go policies.**

Go Policy

To illustrate a hypothetical loop, first assume that unemployment is at the natural rate Un, which we will assume to be 4.7 percent, and that inflation is at 6 percent. This state of affairs is represented in Figure 17–4 as point *A.* Suppose Un had drifted upward to this 4.7 percent level, so that the stabilization authorities (the Fed and the administration) misinterpret this rising natural rate as a cyclical slowdown. To reduce the unemployment rate below Un, the authorities institute expansionary policies. These expansionary policies—increased money growth and larger federal deficits— stimulate the circular flow. The unemployment rate falls to 3 percent as production expands. At the same time, this stimulus to the circular flow creates new demand for goods in excess of capacity, and thus inflation begins to creep up to 8 percent (point *B*). Because the inflation response to expansion operates with a long lag, the rise in inflation is modest at first. This first phase of the cycle is shown as the movement from *A* to *B* in Figure 17–4. This move consists of a sharp move to the left and a gradual drift upward.

---

[1]This section is more difficult analytically than other material in this chapter. It may be inappropriate for some classes. The analysis is based on work by Yale's James Tobin and is designed to explain the pattern of inflation-unemployment pairs. The pattern is one of clockwise loops that Tobin attributes to "myopic" stop-go monetary policies.

FIGURE 17–3   Inflation and Unemployment, 1960–1996

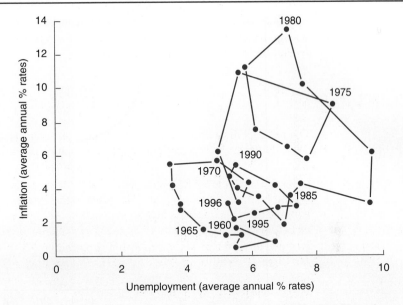

This figure shows actual inflation and unemployment pairs from 1960–1996. The pairs seem to be looping: Unemployment declines as inflation accelerates (1976–1979); inflation rises more slowly as unemployment picks up (1979–1980); inflation falls and unemployment rises (1981–1982). Inflation and unemployment fall together from 1984 to 1986. This cycle then starts over again.

Source: *The Economic Report of the President* (Washington, D.C.: U.S. Government Printing Office, February 1997).

How have expansionary policies caused production and employment to rise? We gave two basic reasons in earlier chapters. In Chapter 16 we showed that increasing the money supply encourages loans by driving down interest rates. Lower rates make marginal loans feasible for some firms and some households. Investment increases as a result, and multiple increases in spending take place. In Chapter 13 we showed that increased deficit spending raises demand for products sold to the government and raises after-tax personal incomes, which fosters increases in consumer spending as well. Now increased spending leads to depletions of inventory stocks, and firms start to place new orders and expand production of input goods. These responses require increased demand for labor, and employment starts to rise. From the point of view of covering costs, firms are selling more and raising prices as well. Consequently, profits are up, and firms can afford to expand by hiring more employees.

But, how long can continued expansionary policies hold unemployment down below Un? By raising expenditures and prices, expansionary policies cause firms to expand output and employment. Remember Friedman's Law: Expansionary monetary policy eventually leads to more inflation. Inflation begins to erode the gains from expansion in two ways:

FIGURE 17–4 The Looping Begins with a Go Phase

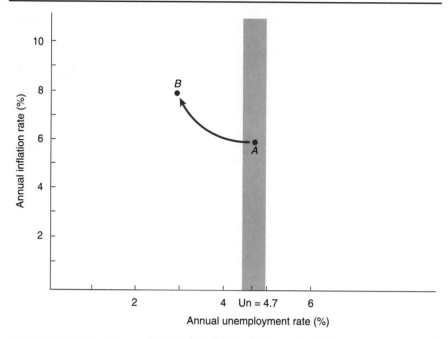

Expansionary policies increase the circular flow of expenditures, driving unemployment down from Un at 4.7 percent to 3 percent and inflation up from 6 percent to 8 percent.

1. Increased prices depreciate the purchasing power of money. The initial increase in the real money supply begins to diminish and then vanish as the purchasing power of money falls. This means interest rates rise again, loans decline, and the expansion sputters.

2. Workers realize an inflation is occurring and react by demanding higher wages. Their argument is that they have to keep up with the cost of living. As wages rise, the temporary benefit from higher product prices erodes and firms reduce employment, moving the economy back toward Un. This is illustrated by the movement from B to C in Figure 17–5. This move consists of a sharp upward move and a gradual drift to the right.

We have now seen that output and employment seem to increase quickly when policy expands and that inflation responds more slowly. Once inflation takes hold, the gains from expansion dissolve, both because the value of the money supply falls and because wages catch up to price increases. This explains why the economy moves from A to B to C. At C, unemployment is back to Un, a level resulting from largely structural causes. But inflation has risen to 10 percent, up from 6 percent. The main problem facing the country at B and more so at C is now perceived to be inflation, not unemployment.

FIGURE 17–5   Inflation Erodes Gains from Expansion

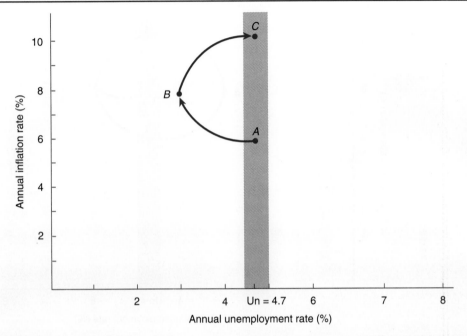

The unemployment gains, from Un to 3 percent as a result of expansionary policies, erode—driving unemployment back up to 4.5 percent. Inflation takes hold, with a long and variable lag, rising up to 10 percent. This moves the economy from *B* to *C*.

Stop Policy

Suppose the stabilization authorities now decide to counterattack inflation. Then monetary and fiscal contraction are imposed at point *C* to slow inflation. These *stop policies* slow down the economy. Again, output and employment seem to respond quickly to contractionary policies, with slower inflation occurring later. First, the economy moves from *C* to *D* in Figure 17–6. Unemployment rises to 6 percent, output declines, and the economy enters a recession. Inflation falls from 10 percent at *C* to 8 percent at *D*. Eventually, inflation will fall from *D* (8 percent), but this may require a sustained period of recession and high cyclical unemployment. If the political system loses patience with abnormally high unemployment as the economy moves from *C* to *D*, then renewed expansion may occur before the economy drops back to *A*. This would ignite a new round of accelerating inflation. Then, the economy would move into a new, higher loop toward *E*. If not, the economy might be allowed to settle at point *A*.

As indicated by the historical record in Figure 17–3, the economy rarely goes back to the initial point (point *A* in Figure 17–6). Instead, it seems that after a bout of inflation, markets adjust to an inflation environment. Market participants seem to

FIGURE 17–6   As Inflation Declines, Unemployment Rises

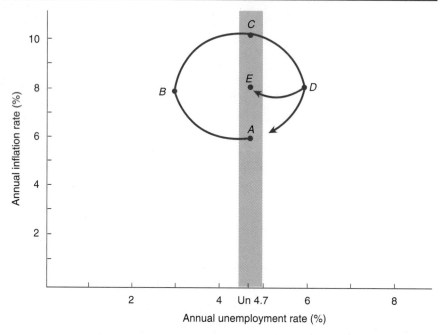

Alarmed by 10 percent inflation at point *C,* the authorities begin stop policies that slow the economy. Thus, inflation falls from 10 percent to 8 percent initially, but unemployment rises quickly from 4.5 percent to 6 percent. The economy moves to *D.* Eventually the economy returns to Un at 4.5 percent after people adapt to inflation at 8 percent. But rather than returning to *A,* the economy moves to *E,* above the start of the first loop, because society has become accustomed to higher inflation.

adapt themselves to higher inflation. They then build this higher inflation into their personal decisions and their lifestyles. Strong unions and Social Security recipients manage to protect their incomes with formal **cost-of-living adjustments (COLAs).**

Congress in 1995 created a special commission, including Michael Boskin (chair), to show how the CPI might be modified to remove an evident upward bias of about 1.5 percent to 2.0 percent. Reducing the CPI bias would reduce the growth rate of COLAs tied to the CPI. This would, in turn, reduce the growth of entitlements and balance the federal budget over time. The committee cautiously reported a 1.1 percent upward bias.

COLAs (cost-of-living adjustments) are automatic adjustments in incomes paid to individual recipients and are tied to the inflation rate, usually measured by the CPI. COLAs are built into many wage contracts and government income-maintenance programs such as Social Security.

Producers become more flexible in their pricing policies, automatically raising prices as labor costs go up. Lenders build an "inflation premium" into their interest rates. Thus, when the economy enters into a new expansionary ("go") phase of the cycle, it begins above *A* (at a point like *E*). If a new round of go policy were to begin, then it would lead to unemployment below Un, with inflation accelerating and ultimately rising even above point *C*.

The empirical evidence, which was shown in Figure 17–3, is consistent with this stop-go story. The U.S. economy was at the top of the loops in 1956–1957, 1970–1971, 1974–1975, 1980–1981, and 1989–1990. The first peak, 1956–1957, was followed by the recession of 1957–1958. The last four peaks were all followed by contractionary policies to slow inflation: Nixon's price controls in 1972, Ford's WIN (Whip Inflation Now) program in 1975, Reaganomics in 1981–1982, and the Greenspan tightening of 1989–1992, then a leveling off from 1992–1996.

The stop-go story we have told is one way in which unemployment and inflation may be intimately interrelated. It clearly places the burden of stabilization on the political system, blaming politicans for the instability by lowering unemployment below Un with expansionary (go) policies, then reacting too heavily against inflation with contractionary (stop) policies, and finally causing inflation by expanding too strongly (go) again to their own slump. However, stop-go policies may prevent short-term political conflict.

🏛 CHAPTER REVIEW

Inflation has many root causes. Some originate outside the economy and produce supply shocks, such as the two OPEC price increases of the 1970s. Some originate inside the economy, such as large federal deficit spending at times when the economy is already growing rapidly, as during the Vietnam War period. Regardless of the shocks, however, inflation follows sustained growth of the money supply. This fact is summarized by Friedman's Law.

There are three principal types of unemployment: frictional, structural, and cyclical. Economists argue about the relative importance of cyclical unemployment and about the ability of policies to deal with it successfully. Most economists believe that structural unemployment has become increasingly prevalent over the last 30 years. Recent concerns have focused on the lack of high-wage jobs for physical labor, possibly as a result of trade and technological change. Un (the natural unemployment rate) increased from around 4.5 percent in the early 1960s to around 7.0 percent in the mid-1980s and may now be around 5.0 percent.

Inflation and unemployment are intimately connected. Stop-go policies have contributed to the accelerating inflation and high unemployment suffered in the late 1960s, the 1970s, and the 1980s, and to the clockwise loops about Un.

🎵 MULTIPLE-CHOICE SELF-TEST 🎵🎵🎵🎵🎵🎵🎵🎵🎵🎵🎵🎵🎵🎵🎵

1. *Demand-pull inflation* is defined as inflation resulting from:
   a. An increase in the demand for money.
   b. An increase in the demand for loans.
   c. Increases in total spending that cannot be matched by increases in output.
   d. Imbalances in the growth of money demand and money supply.

2. Cost-push inflation occurs when:
   a. The economy's capacity to produce output is reduced or grows more slowly, resulting in cost increases.
   b. The Fed increases the money supply too rapidly.
   c. The Fed increases the money supply too slowly.
   d. The supply of loans expands too rapidly.

3. Structural employment is:
   a. The lowest rate of unemployment that can be maintained without accelerating the rate of inflation.
   b. Caused by a mismatch between the skills of unemployed workers and the skills required in jobs for which there are openings.
   c. The unemployment that exists as workers search out the right job.
   d. The rising and falling unemployment that occurs because the structure of the economy causes it to have bouts of prosperity and recession.

4. The unemployment that is due to people's taking some time while unemployed to search out the right job for themselves is called:
   a. Cyclical.
   b. Structural.
   c. Natural.
   d. Frictional.

5. The stop-go policy story shows government:
   a. Perpetually trying to fight the current, biggest business-cycle problem.
   b. Trying to create business cycles.
   c. Trying to reduce unemployment but seldom showing much concern about inflation.
   d. As the primary force offsetting what would otherwise be large swings in the business cycle.

𝕴𝕴 STUDY QUESTIONS

1. How are unemployment compensation and minimum-wage laws related to Un?

2. Does the Fed cause inflation, or does it react to political pressure as part of the inflation process?

3. Explain how stop-go policy leads to stagflation.

4. "Inflation is always and everywhere caused by monetary policy." Discuss.

5. Discuss potential solutions for structural unemployment and the loss of high-wage jobs in manufacturing.

𝕴𝕴 PROBLEM

Identify the kind of unemployment involved in each of the following situations (structural, cyclical, or frictional, and voluntary or involuntary).

1. Employment in shoe manufacturing is falling fast; employment in the finance industry is rising rapidly, but the shoe workers are remaining unemployed.

2. Janet Chung is going back to work outside the home after 15 years of homemaking. Unsure what jobs she is best suited for, she explores numerous alternatives. Her job search ends highly successfully after three months.

3. It's the 1960s. Large numbers of women like Mrs. Chung are entering the labor force, and the average duration of unemployment lengthens.

4. Mort Sykes has just endured seven months of unemployment, waiting for times to get better so that he'll be rehired as a machine tool operator. Because his wage at this work is at least 25 percent higher than wages for alternative jobs that are available, he would rather wait it out than take another kind of job.

5. Leroy Johnson lost his job in Cincinnati and moved to Houston, where he had heard jobs were easier to find. Unfortunately, this took place in 1986 and Houston also had no jobs for Leroy. After nine months of looking, he was living on the streets.

CHAPTER 18

Rising Living Standards or Stagnation?

♫♫ CHAPTER PREVIEW

In the early 1960s President John F. Kennedy's economic adviser Robert Solow declared that our knowledge of macroeconomics was largely complete: We had only to dot the i's and cross the t's. For the previous 15 years the trend in economic growth had been substantial and upward, punctuated by only brief pauses.

This growth continued to the early 1970s, then the next 20 years told a different story. The growth rate of the economy continued upward, but the trend in that growth rate flattened out. Although no sudden, remarkable collapse occurred, a gradual, sporadic slowdown in the rate of growth became evident by the late 1970s. By 1979, output per worker, which had risen at 4 percent a year in the 1950s, was actually falling; inflation was in double digits (13 percent); and unemployment was 5.5 percent. Economists began to wonder: Do we know anything about economic growth? Where did we go wrong? What does the future hold?

The early 1980s started with a severe recession that was deeper than any we had experienced since the Great Depression. Unemployment rose to 11 percent, and growth of real GDP was actually negative for over a year and a half. A tremendous expansion, which began in 1983, set the record for uninterrupted growth and continued until the recession of 1990–1991, but income distribution deteriorated so that poorer Americans, disproportionately more blacks and Chicanos, seemed to be left behind. At the same time, the United States was absorbing large numbers of new immigrants from Latin America and from Asia. From 1991 to 1996 we enjoyed a sustained expansion, but the real growth rate seemed to have slowed by about one-third from 3.5 percent to 2.5 percent. Have we learned from these experiences? Can we apply the lessons to the future?

1. Will scarcities in crucial resources, such as oil or land, bring economic growth to a halt?
2. Does growth in one region require exploitation of workers in another?
3. Can growth rates return to the high post–World War II levels?

CONCEPTS REINTRODUCED

NEW CONCEPTS

Minimum Subsistence
Malthusian Trap
Production Function
Neoclassical Growth Models
Total Factor Productivity (TFP)
Technological Change
Incentives to Save
Incentives to Invest
Paradox of Thrift
Infrastructure Investment
Command and Control
Managed Trade

🎞 CHAPTER OBJECTIVES

After studying this chapter, you should be able to:

1. Define *labor productivity* and *total factor productivity.*
2. Explain how total output can grow even without growth in productivity.
3. Define Malthus's view of *population growth* and his view of the *growth of resources.*
4. Contrast neoclassical growth models with the Malthusian model.
5. List some of the factors that lead to output growth in the neoclassical model.
6. Explain the slowdown in productivity growth in the United States after 1973.

THE MIRACLE

The growth rate of real GDP in the United States from 1950 to 1973 averaged about 4 percent per year. Although 4 percent may seem to be a small fraction, at this rate real GDP doubles approximately every 18 years. Growth of population can explain part of the 4 percent growth rate, because more workers naturally contribute to growth potential. Growth in the labor force after World War II accounts for about one-fourth of real economic growth.

This means that growth of output per worker increased at a rate of about 3 percent per year. As we saw in Chapter 11, output per worker is called *labor productivity.* To people living and working in the United States throughout the 1950s and 1960s, this growth in labor productivity, in effect, meant that in each year they earned a 3 percent bonus over and above what they had earned in the previous year. This bonus meant they could buy more goods and services, better medical care, improved housing, new automobiles, better entertainment, and so forth. Thus, a 3 percent labor-productivity growth rate implied a quarter century of rising living standards at a rate of 3 percent a year.

Rising living standards also mean that society is able to become more generous with economic assistance. Rapid growth permits expansion of social services without the stresses that would result from higher tax burdens on fixed incomes. In the United States from 1950 to 1980, more support was directed to retired citizens. In fact, the Social Security benefits paid during the 1960s and the 1970s exceeded the contributions of the retired. Also, many new poverty, educational, social, health, and welfare programs were introduced and expanded.

From 1973 to 1981, the growth in productivity fell from the 3 percent range of the earlier quarter century to less than 0.5 percent. Despite a long recovery from the severe recessions in 1980 and 1982, productivity growth in the United States remained low throughout the 1980s and early 1990s. This did not mean that output per worker fell in the 1970s, 1980s, and 1990s, nor that people became worse off. It did mean that the extra benefits, the bonuses generated by productivity growth that had characterized the previous quarter century, slowed greatly. In the aftermath of this slowdown in productivity growth, U.S. institutions underwent significant social changes.

The breaking point between the rapid-growth period and the slow-growth period occurred around 1973. Some analysts think that this date is important in that it marks the first major foreign oil price shock of the 1970s. In 1973, OPEC, an oil-producing cartel led by Saudi Arabia, quadrupled oil prices in one instant. Again in 1979–1980, OPEC quickly "jacked up" prices. In the aftermath of both price shocks, Western economies suffered major recessions. In the view of some economists, the 1974–1975 recession was made worse by contractionary policies imposed in 1974 by the Fed and by the Ford administration, and the 1980–1982 recession was also exacerbated by tight monetary policies.

However, careful analysis of labor and capital growth and of technological change reveals that the basic causes of the productivity slowdown probably occurred before 1973. To many analysts, the causes of the slowdown dated from the middle and late 1960s. Institutional characteristics of the growing industrial economies after World War II, the waging and financing of the Vietnam War from 1965 to 1971, and the need to integrate the baby-boom generation into the economy were three major factors.

Whatever the causes, the productivity growth slowdown became reality by the 1970s and 1980s, as can be seen from Table 18–1. Growth figures for major industrialized economies from the 1960s to 1986 are shown in Table 18–1. Note that for each country, growth after 1973 was slower than growth over the earlier period. From the end of World War II to 1973 was a rapid-growth period for the countries represented in the table. Any explanation for the slowdown in labor productivity growth must apply to all countries.

The sudden deterioration in the economic well-being of industrialized countries and the ensuing social stresses and changes in economic behavior highlight the importance of economic growth as a major issue in national policy. We now turn to a discussion of U.S. social and political responses to the growth slowdown.

First, American families altered their lifestyles. Because living standards were no longer rising as rapidly and because families had children growing in age and

TABLE 18–1 International Comparisons of Labor Productivity Growth, 1960–1986

Country	1960*–1973	1973–1979	1979–1986
United States	2.2	0.3	0.6
West Germany	4.9	3.4	2.0
Japan	8.6	3.2	2.8
France	5.9	3.5	2.5
United Kingdom	3.3	1.3	1.9

*Period 1 starting dates differ: Germany—1961, Japan—1967, and France—1965.
Source: Hulten, Charles R. (ed.), "Introductions," *Productivity Growth in Japan and the United States,* National Bureau of Economic Research, Studies in Income and Wealth, vol. 53, 1990, Table 2, p. 7.

need, many felt compelled to increase the family work effort. Women, including those with young children, entered the labor force in large numbers. Frank Levy, in *Dollars and Dreams,* carefully analyzed the consequences of sluggish income growth for various groups. By 1980 three-quarters of women with two or more young children were working full-time. Young people, originally tagged *yuppies* (young, upwardly mobile professionals), married later in life, had fewer children, and lived in small condominium apartments rather than in large houses like those of their parents. Those yuppies whose childless lifestyle became evident were later labeled *dinks* (double income–no kids). As a result of increased work effort, the actual growth rate of the economy continued at the 4 percent pace throughout the 1970s and 1980s. In other words, actual GDP continued to grow in constant dollars, but this growth was achieved by greater work effort. The greater work effort offset the decline in output that would otherwise have accompanied the labor productivity slowdown.

Political and social institutions also felt pressures from the decline in productivity growth. Because families had to work harder to maintain living standards, increased spending for social programs became politically unpopular. In addition, because the economy was growing at a slower rate, the level of unemployment began to creep up. This rising unemployment induced expansionary policies. In turn, these expansionary policies in the 1970s contributed to spiraling inflation. This was discussed in Chapter 17. Inflation lowers the purchasing power of the dollar and has costs of its own. Inflation also raises effective tax rates, because people move into higher tax brackets. Bracket creep, under progressive taxation, causes average tax rates to rise faster.

For business, inflation can be even more damaging. Tax deductions, which businesses receive from writing off purchases of capital, decline when the inflation rate rises, because the deductions are based on the original cost of the capital. In the 1970s the rate of physical capital formation—such as machinery, equipment, factories, plants, warehouses, office buildings, and farms—grew more slowly than warranted by growth in the labor force. By the late 1980s people began to fear that the American dream was coming to an end. Would young people enjoy the high and growing living standards of their parents, or would they have to work harder just to keep up?

Thus, many of the stresses associated with poverty, inflation, high unemployment, greater work effort, and slower capital formation can be traced to the productivity growth slowdown.

WHY DID PRODUCTIVITY GROWTH SLOW?

There is only partial agreement on the specific causes of the productivity slowdown. Some analysts attribute the slowdown to increased tax burdens imposed on American businesses and households during the 1970s. As a primary cause, however, this does not stand up to analysis. Effective tax rates, after correcting for legislative changes and tax avoidance, actually showed a slight decline in the 1970s. Also, there were massive business tax cuts in 1981, which apparently failed to produce the promised explosion of productivity.

A popular explanation for the slowdown was the energy price shocks, which began in 1973. Again, this argument has not stood up to analysis. Energy is a very small fraction of the cost of doing business in major manufacturing industries—less than 2 percent. It is difficult to attribute a major two-decade-long slowdown in productivity to an increase in the price of something that is such a small fraction of costs. Furthermore, these industries were already showing significant slowdowns prior to the OPEC action of 1973.

In addition to the tax and energy explanations, many analysts attribute the slowdown to increased burdens placed on industry by government regulation, especially pollution control. However, this explanation may not hold up completely either. As we have seen, the slowdown occurred in many other industrialized countries, including countries with much lower effective tax rates than those of the United States, less government regulation, and less burdensome pollution controls. Let us now discuss some important conceptual ideas related to growth before we return to the key causes of the industrial slowdown.

FROM MALTHUS TO SOLOW AND BACK AGAIN

Early 18th-century European philosophers of world events, now called *classical* economists, analyzed the long-run prospects for society's well-being. Some felt prospects were poor. These pessimistic views earned economics the title "dismal science." The Industrial Revolution, which began in the middle of the 18th century, ran counter to the expectations of these pessimists. The success of modern industrialized societies caused the pessimistic views of the followers of Thomas Malthus to be supplanted by the neoclassical approach of modern economists, such as Paul Samuelson, Robert Solow, and Dale Jorgenson—who are called *neoclassical* economists.

The Malthusian Trap

At the turn of the 19th century, an imposing and severe English cleric, Parson Thomas Malthus, turned to analysis of poverty and growth. This man introduced an explosive idea, one that to this day dominates popular thinking, about the long-run prospects of life on earth. Parson Malthus articulated the thought that resources develop more slowly than does population. In Malthus's view, people reproduce geometrically—2 people produce 4; 4 times 4 produces 16; 16 times 16 produces 256; 256 times 256 produces 65,536; and so forth.

Exploding population growth is in sharp contrast to the ability of the earth to reproduce resources. To Malthus, the limited resource was agricultural land. He argued that whereas population grew at a geometric rate, compounding the number of people from one period to the next, arable land could grow only at an arithmetic rate: 2, 4, 6, 8. . . . Land grew, because new land could be claimed from the forests and marshes. But the growth rate of arable land was bound to be slower than the population growth rate. Consequently, as population grew faster than food, living standards eventually had to decline. Malthus argued that the decline would stop only after living standards fell so low that the birthrate would be adequate only to offset the death rate—population would stop growing. This meant that people would fall into **minimum subsistence** living.

Malthus was a pessimist, for he argued that only starvation, warfare, or perhaps moral restraint could prevent the geometric growth of population. Only at the bare subsistence level will people stop reproducing faster than their food supply. Any time living standards start to rise, population will grow faster than the food supply, bringing the living standard back to minimum subsistence. Consequently, in Malthus's view, the world finds itself always forced back to a position of stagnation at minimum subsistence into the **Malthusian trap.** Fortunately, modern societies avoided the disastrous Malthusian scenario. For much of the world, Malthus was wrong.

The MALTHUSIAN TRAP refers to the minimum subsistence level to which humans were predicted to descend as a result of geometric population growth and arithmetic resources growth.

The logic of the Malthusian theory is irrefutable: If the population grows at a faster rate than that of the resources people need to survive, then people's standard of living will ultimately fall to minimum subsistence. Fortunately for most people, this did not happen to the societies Malthus was studying. He thought that living standards in England and in Europe in general would steadily decline. Just the opposite has been the case! Living standards in Western industrialized nations have improved dramatically from the days of Malthus. This has been true despite the *logic* of his argument. Malthus's argument was missing two crucial elements—technological change and the laws of supply and demand—making it largely irrelevant to the Western experience.

First, through new technologies, even a limited growth in land results in rapid growth in production of food and other goods. The land may be tilled, fertilized, and drained to be used more productively. Today's American farm problem is overproduction and surplus labor, which is the polar opposite of the problem envisioned by Malthus. Second, Malthus failed to recognize that people do not reproduce geometrically and that land does not grow only according to arithmetic law. Rather, people are thinking, rational beings who develop their resources and obey the laws of economics. As particular resources become scarce, the market prices of these resources rise. These price increases in turn choke off the growth of demand for the products and generate pressures for the development of substitutes. This encourages the conservation of the scarce products. Malthus, in ignoring these two important features of economics, produced a model that predicted exactly the opposite of reality.

Whereas Malthus predicted substandard living conditions and permanent stagnation, European countries, the United States, Japan, and other nations have enjoyed abundance, unprecedented growth, and prosperity.

Still, Malthus's nightmare has been realized today in many less developed countries where starvation and minimum subsistence are reality. In many places in the southern hemisphere we see that unchecked population growth, destructive political and economic systems, and inadequate agricultural development still lead to deprivation and starvation.

However, even the terrible conditions in countries such as Ethiopia probably reflect economic policies and political decisions more than they do Malthusian law. It is also clear that ruthless political policies designed to cripple a revolt can include starving a populace into submission.

Some economists argue that government-imposed price ceilings on food products bankrupt farmers and drive them from the land. The result is underproduction of food and, eventually, starvation. When water and fertile land become scarce as a result of drought conditions, governments may be tempted to reduce food prices to help poor consumers. But such policies are counterproductive, because they discourage farmers, who are confronted with the reality of increasingly scarce and costly inputs—water and fertile land. Faced with increased costs and lower farm prices, the farmers are driven out of business.

Solow and Jorgenson

The work of Robert Solow typifies modern (neoclassical) analysis of growth economics. Rather than starting from a perspective of predetermined production constraints as Malthus did, the neoclassical economist starts with the notion that decision makers apply economic principles to determine production levels.

Solow's analysis of growth begins with the idea, first discussed in Chapter 16, of a **production function.** The neoclassical production function focuses on the relationship between output and the inputs needed to generate output. In other words, various combinations of all the available inputs capable of being used in the production process determine output. Output is measured in the broadest possible terms, say, total GDP. At any moment in time, some given level of technology constrains the amount of output that will be generated by the available inputs. The idea is that inputs produce output according to exact physical rules, expressible in mathematical terms. Most important, these rules are flexible enough to allow variations in the *proportions* of inputs used in production.

The PRODUCTION FUNCTION expresses the physical relationship between the quantities of various inputs and the quantity of real output, as determined by the state of technology and by human application of that technology. It exhibits variable proportions of inputs in the production process.

The simplest **neoclassical growth models,** which are models using production functions, focus on the two inputs, called *capital and labor.* Labor, of course, is the quantity and quality of various human inputs used; capital is the machinery and equipment, industrial plant, structures, and inventory used. Given the technological relationship between these physical inputs and the output expressed by the production function, the neoclassical economist assumes that in a competitive market economy the quantities of capital and labor used will depend on their relative costs. Thus, the decisions made by producers will focus on choosing the least costly combination of capital and labor inputs needed to produce the maximum amount of output. In other words, output of the economy depends on the state of *technology,* on the *costs* of different kinds of inputs, and on *cost-minimizing* behavior by producers.

One of the important points of this neoclassical approach to growth economics is that as a particular input—say, energy or land—becomes relatively scarce, its cost rises relative to that of other inputs. As this input becomes more costly, rational producers conserve it in order to produce with the least costly combination of inputs. Thus, the scarce input will be automatically rationed and preserved. The neoclassical approach corrects the major flaws of Malthusian models, namely, rigid physical relationships, which led to false inferences. The neoclassical framework also allows analysis of technological change. Studies of growth and output per input unit of labor and capital have shown that the growth rate in output cannot be explained simply by the growth in physical inputs.

Utilizing the Solow-type neoclassical framework, Dale Jorgenson, Zvi Griliches, and others analyzed the growth rates of the United States, Canada, Germany, Japan, and the United Kingdom from the end of World War II to 1960 and from 1960 to 1973.

In order to isolate measurable components of input growth, in addition to labor, we require a new concept, which is more complete than *labor productivity.* This new concept is called **total factor productivity (TFP).** TFP is the ratio of output on the numerator to a weighted average of inputs on the denominator. In productivity studies, economists usually weight each input by its "cost share" in production. For instance, if labor represented 75 percent of the cost of all inputs, capital 20 percent of total costs, and energy 5 percent, the denominator would be

$$(0.75 \times \text{labor}) + (0.2 \times \text{capital}) + (0.05 \times \text{energy})$$

If labor grew at 5 percent, capital at 10 percent, and energy at 30 percent, the denominator would be

$$(0.75 \times 0.05) + (0.2 \times 0.1) + (0.05 \times 0.3)$$

Inputs, weighted by cost shares, would have grown at 7.25 percent. To compute the percentage growth rate in TFP, we take the *difference* between output growth and weighted input growth.[1] Thus, if output had grown at 9.5 percent, we would conclude that TFP had grown at 2.25 percent (9.5 percent − 7.25 percent).

---

[1]Mathematically inclined students will know that to calculate the percentage rate of change of a ratio of rates of change, one computes the difference between the two rates of change.

TOTAL FACTOR PRODUCTIVITY (TFP) growth is the difference between the percentage rate of growth of output and the percentage rate of growth of all appropriately weighted inputs. The input weights reflect the relative importance in production of each input; usually, the weights are cost shares.

Using TFP and other methods, Jorgenson and Griliches found that growth of inputs could usually explain about 70 percent of the growth in output. They found that in the first period, 1950–1960, U.S. output grew at a 3.7 percent rate and in the second period, 1960–1973, it grew at a 4.3 percent rate. Inputs grew at 2.3 percent in the first period and 3 percent in the second. A substantial proportion of output growth could be explained by the growth in physical inputs. On the other hand, on average during the first period 1.4 percent and during the second period 1.3 percent of output growth were not explained merely by new physical inputs.

What made output growth approximately 30 percent faster than physical input growth? Several factors are cited—economies of scale, increased specialization, improved management techniques. Most economists attribute such TFP growth to **technological change.** In the view of modern economists, economic growth exceeds the growth in both labor and capital because of improved technology. It is this change in technology that allows for improved types of capital and labor and for a better mix of the two. The Jorgenson studies indicate similar results for the other countries.

TECHNOLOGICAL CHANGE is a change in the production process that causes an increase in output to exceed the increase in the quantity of inputs in the production function.

Table 18–2 presents detailed growth rates for the United States from 1950 to 1992. Growth originally at over 3.5 percent fell to less than 1.5 percent (column 1). Column 2 shows labor productivity growth, and column 3 shows total factor productivity growth. Compare the TFP growth rates before and after 1973. You can see a significant slowdown from the 1 percent to 1.5 percent range down to the 0 percent to 0.5 percent range. Evidently, the fall in the rate of technological change and the fall in the growth rate of the quantity of capital input caused the U.S. economy to stall after the early 1970s. Meanwhile, parts of the rest of the world are catching up.

The most important growth episodes in the 1960s and 1970s took place in Asia. Japan grew at a 9.8 percent rate in the 1960s and at 6 percent in the 1970s. Meanwhile, by adopting modern capitalist market models, convertible currencies, and export-oriented policies, the *Four Tigers*—Hong Kong, Taiwan, Singapore, and South Korea—grew at a 9.3 percent rate, and the neighboring Association of South East Asian Nations (ASEAN) countries—Thailand, Cambodia, the Philippines,

Indonesia, and Malaysia—grew at over 8 percent. Francis Fukuyama, in *The End of History and the Last Man,* compares growth in Taiwan to that in the People's Republic of China. Both started at about the same base in 1949. By 1989 Taiwan's percapita GDP was $7,500. That of the People's Democratic Republic (PDR) reached $350, much of that due to market-oriented reform attempts in agriculture. A similar comparison is made by Fukuyama for North Korea and South Korea. At parity in 1960, South Korea turned to competitive pricing in international markets. By 1989, South Korean GDP was about four times that of North Korea.

The 1989 collapse of communist regimes throughout Eastern Europe and the former Soviet Union brought forth even more evidence for the success of market-oriented economies. East Germany was decades behind West Germany. Hungary, which had been nearly identical to Austria at the turn of the century, had a living standard less than one-third as high, even after adoption of comparatively liberal market-oriented policies during the 1970s and the 1980s.

Vigorous moves toward private markets, flexible market-determined prices, competitive management practices, stable budgets, convertible currencies, and stable monetary policies in many Latin American countries, as well as in some Eastern European countries, ushered in the 1990s. The strongest turns to Western-style capitalism were made by Mexico and the Czech Republic. Mexico still has serious political problems, but the Czech Republic may be the next "tiger" of the future.

Productivity Growth

Although the slowdown in growth of productivity among advanced industrialized countries in the 1970s and the 1980s has been a major puzzle, one of the ironies of the slowdown is that it has renewed interest in the West in the Malthusian models, just as the East and Latin America were turning toward neoclassical growth. Despite the more

TABLE 18–2   Output and Productivity Growth Rates for the United States, 1950–1992

		Productivity	
Years	**Output**	**Labor**	**Total Factor**
1950–1954	3.64	2.25	1.28
1954–1963	3.28	2.40	1.50
1963–1972	3.82	2.13	1.09
1972–1978	3.31	1.26	0.62
1978–1987	2.44	0.79	0.12
1987–1992	1.31	0.75	0.37

Source: Gordon, Robert J., "The Jobless Recovery: Does It Signal a New Era of Productivity-Led Growth?" *Brookings Papers on Economic Activity* 1, William C. Brainard and George L. Perry (eds.), Table 4, p. 288, 1993.

sophisticated neoclassical analysis, noneconomists have focused on the potential limits to growth from the use of fixed resources, such as oil. Even though the Malthusian doctrine has been discredited by both economic history and analysis, it still lingers. It seems to have a certain appeal to the pessimistic side of human nature. In response to the oil price shocks of 1973–1974 and 1979–1980, Malthusians emphasized the declining sources of petrochemical products in projecting a slowdown in economic growth. They argued that hydrocarbons, in particular coal and energy-producing products, being limited in supply, will eventually grind modern industrialized economies to a halt. Some noneconomists, scientists as a general rule, have even gone so far as to predict that industrial growth will end around the year 2000.

What two factors do these noneconomists ignore? First, they ignore technology. When energy products become scarce, new technologies develop that conserve these scarce resources. Second, scarcity itself causes an increase in the price of these inputs, and this generates market pressure to conserve them as well.

Are we running out of oil? The obvious answer is Yes! As Joe Kalt at the JFK School of Government says, "We started running out of oil the day the first black shiny stone was thrown into a fire and some Stone Age man noticed that it burned rapidly and gave off heat." From that point on, we began to use coal and other energy-producing materials to warm us and eventually to run our factories. Paradoxically, however, the fact that we *are* running out of a resource does not mean we *will* run out. Supply, demand, and technology have historically worked to our benefit to avert exhaustion of scarce products. This may seem quite abstract and unlikely. After all, how can we expect to replace something as vital and necessary as oil *and* continue to perform as modern industrialized societies?

An interesting illustration of this is the case of Germany during World War II. Germany found itself cut off from natural rubber supplies. Rubber had to be replaced so that vehicles could still be driven on wheels. In order to satisfy the need for natural rubber the Germans invented and manufactured synthetic rubber. This is but one example of how inventiveness in technology can produce alternatives and substitutes when a product becomes increasingly scarce and its price rises significantly. Economists do not accept the naive view that there are fixed limits to growth. Instead, economists concentrate on the relationship between the growth rates of various inputs and on their implications for output. Evidence from the experience of the postwar period indicates that technological change plays a major role in determining economic growth.

DEMAND-SIDE AND SUPPLY-SIDE POLICIES

We will now analyze growth with the circular flow model, shown in Figure 18–1. The money market is connected to the flow via the savings-withdrawal process and the investment-injection process with a colored line that passes through the banks. Recall that monetarists believe that the primary source of fluctuations in the circular flow of expenditures comes from financial activity originating in the money market. The light-colored line, indicating the flow of physical goods and services and of

𝒥𝑅 FIGURE 18–1   Circular Flow Model with Money Market Linkage

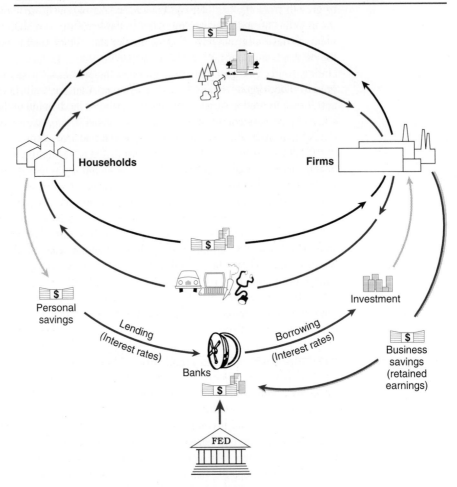

The circular flow model here shows the connection between the money market and the circular flow model with the private sector only.

input services, moves in the opposite direction from the dollar flow. Recall that supply siders concentrate on how producers respond to incentives. Thus, the circular flow model accommodates Keynesian, monetarist, and supply-sider views. This model helps to analyze growth policy actions by government and by the Fed.

The Demand Side

Consider traditional demand-side policies designed to increase the rate of expenditures. Increases in the rate of federal deficit spending, which do not completely crowd out private investment, expand the flow of spending by increasing effective demand. Alternatively, increases in the money supply by the Fed reduce interest rates, which stimulate spending by making borrowing cheaper. The amount of stimulus depends on quantitative responses in the economy, and the magnitudes are arguable. This stimulus also raises effective demand. Thus, both expansionary monetary and fiscal policy increase effective demand.

Increases in effective demand lead to increases in expenditures, which in turn lead to increases in production, unless the economy is at full capacity. Despite the result of potential growth, demand-side policies have come under severe criticisms from conservative economists. Traditional Keynesian analysis focuses on effective demand. Martin Feldstein, economic adviser to President Ronald Reagan in the early 1980s, faulted Keynesian economics for ignoring the supply side. Feldstein argued that increasing expenditures with federal deficit spending encouraged consumer demand but did not foster stable growth. His argument was that demand-side expansion ignores the need for capital goods. We have seen the need for capital goods to achieve growth propounded in neoclassical models.

Feldstein argued that Keynesians ignored capital formation and that deficit spending favored consumption over investment, because deficits increase interest rates, thereby crowding out investment expenditures. In Feldsteins's view, if an expanding economy does not foster capital formation, its productive potential is lowered. He and others believed that the slowdown in productivity during the 1970s was caused by slower capital formation in earlier years. This slowdown in capital formation was attributable to deficit spending designed to favor the consumer.

Feldstein also argued that the capital produced in the late 1960s and the 1970s unduly favored residential construction. Although housing is included in the capital stock and requires borrowing, it contributes little to productive potential. Thus, demand-side policies that favor consumer spending and housing skew the mix of GDP away from capital formation.

Keynesians, under Presidents John F. Kennedy, Lyndon B. Johnson, Jimmy Carter, and Bill Clinton, did favor demand expansion. But, in their defense, the policies under those administrations included tax incentives for capital formation. It is therefore unlikely that Keynesian policies caused the slowdown in capital formation. On the other hand, public demands for social spending—Social Security, AFDC, medical care, and other programs—did favor consumption over investment. In addition, the slowdown in capital formation probably reflected increased defense spending throughout the late 1960s to fight the Vietnam War. Total capital formation did not slow in the 1970s. At the same time, growth of the labor force was so rapid that it outstripped growth in nonresidential capital formation.

The Supply Side

Supply siders focus on the importance of productive capacity to meet effective demand. This again brings us to the neoclassical production function: capital, resources, labor inputs, and technological change. Under what circumstances will aggregate demand expansion lead to new production? Supply siders advocate a favorable climate for capital formation and for improvement in the quality of the labor force. Because capital formation requires the availability of finance, supply siders focus on savings and **incentives to save.** They are also concerned about the transmission of savings to capital. Thus, they also focus on capital spending by firms and **incentives to invest.**

The primary policy initiative of the Reagan administration's first term was a tax reform package called the *Economic Recovery Tax Act (ERTA)* that was passed in 1981. ERTA, designed to foster savings and investment, reduced tax rates on personal income and taxes on personal savings for retirement. Business taxes for firms investing in new capital were also reduced. ERTA was set up to stimulate long-term growth. Tax measures were written into law to stimulate savings rather than to encourage consumption by individuals. Incentives were provided for firms to increase investment spending. The real after-tax interest earned by savers was raised by providing special financial accounts known as *individual retirement accounts (IRAs).* At the same time, tax credits and other breaks for firms undertaking new investment expenditures lowered the real after-tax cost of capital goods.

In principle, these measures should have led to increased capital formation. Unfortunately, investment activity actually collapsed during the Reagan administration of the early 1980s. Two important factors contributed to this collapse:

1. *The drastic increase in the real cost of borrowing money.* Even though they had some tax incentives, firms found the real cost of obtaining funds far too great to undertake more investment expenditures. Between 1979 and 1982 real interest rates increased from less than 1 percent to around 10 percent.

2. *A severe contraction in the economy, which occurred between 1980 and 1982.* Effective demand declined so dramatically that firms feared they could not sell their products.

TOOL KIT

THE RATE OF RETURN ON SAVINGS

What rate of return will you earn on your savings? Inflation, taxes, fluctuations in stock and bond markets, the length of time you hold the asset, and the rules that govern its payment are among the many factors that influence the answer. For this reason, a robust market exists in specialists who advise people on their investments. Be warned, however! Your circumstances are unique. There are no simple answers or rules for everyone.

In a world without inflation, taxes, and uncertainty, you would know the yield on various assets and could choose savings to fit your goals. Suppose a stock paid a dividend yielding 7 percent annually. If you preferred 7 percent to current consumption, you would buy the asset. Simple enough. In the real world, though, you have to contend with inflation, taxes, and uncertainty.

The decline in effective demand, coupled with the increase in the real cost of borrowing, swamped any potential supply-side effects, and investment fell. This does not mean that supply-side effects are unimportant. Just as effective demand is important, the mix of GDP is important for balanced growth.

As discussed in Chapter 13, by the middle of the 1980s, the imbalances and inequities of the federal income tax system had become evident. The Tax Reform Act of 1986 was designed to raise tax revenues from business, to lower tax payments from persons, to lower *marginal* tax rates for everyone, and to level the playing field so that private sector decisions would not be tax-determined. The result was a nearly flat-rate tax system that, in the long run, might foster a more balanced type of capital formation.

President Bill Clinton in 1993, however, proposed a complete repudiation of the 1986 act: raising top marginal tax rates from 29 percent to 39.6 percent, reintroducing many "loopholes," such as enterprise zones and selective investment tax credits, and limiting certain capital gains breaks. The new Republican majority after 1994 began again to push for a flatter tax system as did Republican presidential candidate Robert Dole.

Potential for Policy Conflict

We have reviewed the damage done by the productivity slowdown of the 1970s, the early failure of the Reagan policies to produce effective growth, the subsequent 1986 change in the tax law, and the reversals by the Clinton administration in 1993–1994. Policy proposals that favor growth often produce potential conflicts and unexpected errors. A particular policy may seem attractive in terms of one objective, such as

Suppose you expect annual inflation to be 4 percent. You can expect a real yield on the 7 percent asset of 3 percent. Now suppose you are in the 33 percent marginal tax bracket, implying that you will pay 33 percent of your interest yield in taxes. Unless indexed to inflation, the tax rate will apply to the nominal interest rate, 7 percent. The real after-tax yield is now less than 1 percent, only 0.69 percent. In equation form

$$(1 - 0.33) \times (0.07) - 0.04 = 0.0069$$

Suppose the capital gains tax rate were reduced to 15 percent, as was advocated by President George Bush. If you held a stock that paid no dividends but appreciated at 7 percent a year instead, then the appreciated value on your stock would be taxed at the lower capital gains rate of 15 percent, and only once you sold the stock to realize the gain. Suppose you sold stock to realize income of 7 percent a year; the real after-tax yield would be nearly 2 percent, 1.95 percent:

$$(1 - 0.15) \times (0.07) - 0.04 = 0.0195$$

If you held onto the stock longer, you could defer the capital gains tax payment, that is, delay payment until some time in the future. Deferring taxes reduces their impact, because you can always be earning income on the money until the tax bill comes due.

growth or price stability, but can lead to damaging effects in terms of another objective. The debates of the 1990s over tax policy are similar to the earlier debates.

Taxes: Growth versus Equity

A policy conflict arises when taxes on individuals and businesses are cut in order to stimulate growth. The Reagan administration cut the high marginal tax rates for everyone, but did so disproportionately for wealthy individuals and businesses both in 1981 and in 1986. Dole proposed another set of cuts in 1996 after Clinton had raised top rates. The justification for reducing high marginal tax rates is simple. High marginal tax rates may discourage wealthy people from saving, because the after-tax yield on savings will be too low. Lower marginal tax rates can encourage saving and lead to more funds available for capital formation. Similarly, lower corporate tax burdens, at the margin, foster construction of new buildings and equipment. Thus, it is attractive to try to reduce the tax rates on the wealthy and on businesses.

On the other hand, any change in the tax laws alters the equity of the tax system. Although reduction of tax burdens on wealthy individuals may favor growth, it raises questions about the fairness of the tax system. Some balance is needed between the two conflicting policy objectives of growth and equity.

Disinflation and Real Interest Rates

A second policy conflict arises when the Fed tries to restrain inflation. Inflation damages long-run planning; therefore, less inflation favors growth. Because contractionary monetary policy reduces inflation, it provides a favorable climate for growth. Unfortunately, monetary contraction that slows inflation also has perverse consequences in the short run for capital formation, because tight money drives up interest rates.

The disinflation generated by tight money from 1979 to 1982 raised the real cost of money. The high real interest rates discouraged capital formation. Again, slow monetary growth combined with stringent regulatory controls imposed by the Fed on banks to drive inflation rates down from 6.1 percent in 1990 to 3.1 percent in 1991. High real interest rates and a sharp recession were part of the result. Thus a significant policy conflict arises. This conflict explains in part why anti-inflation policies are politically so difficult to sustain.

The Paradox of Thrift

A third policy conflict concerns thrift. The Reagan administration, in its first year, introduced legislation favoring saving. The logic was that saving provides the needed financial base for production of new capital. Unfortunately, this logic does not take into account the **paradox of thrift.** The paradox of thrift illustrates that the policies that appear favorable to growth can have perverse effects.

The paradox of thrift works as follows: To provide funds for capital formation, policies that encourage saving are instituted. From circular flow analysis, we realize that increased savings result in increased withdrawals from the circular flow. Unless these withdrawals are successfully channeled into new investment spending, effective demand falls. Thus, it is possible that a favorable savings policy will lead to a slow-down in the rate of spending. Rather than stimulating capital formation, an increased savings rate may slow spending so much that capital formation will decline.

Capital formation depends not only on the availability of funds but also on the prospects for profit. If firms find their profits declining as the economy goes into a contraction, they will pull back and cut their investment expenditures. Thus, a policy to encourage thrift may lead to a slowdown in the economy, a decline in capital, and even a decline in realized savings.

A similar conflict confronted President Clinton. **Infrastructure investment** by the federal government would create jobs, spur growth, and, according to Alicia Munnell (an economics researcher for the Boston Federal Reserve System), even foster private domestic investment. Unfortunately, increased federal spending, even for infrastructure, would exacerbate the budget deficit and possibly cause interest rates to rise in bond markets, which could discourage investment. Should the govern-ment save more by cutting the deficit and thus stimulate investment, or should it save less by increasing infrastructure investment?

Environment versus Growth

Economic growth, as it is usually defined, is not an end in and of itself. In fact, to some the perverse side effects of industrial expansion, such as environmental pollu-tion, are bad enough to outweigh the benefits of growth. The **slow-growth move-ment,** especially virulent in the western United States in the late 1980s and the early 1990s, reflects concern for balancing environmental protection against unfettered expansion. From an economist's perspective, the choice between clean air on the one hand, for example, and faster cars on the other is a legitimate social choice for the use of scarce resources. The appropriate mechanisms for achieving a desirable mix are subject to analysis. Typically the choice is between legal-administrative (**command-and-control**) approaches and indirect incentive programs.

It is necessary, in either case, to realize that environmental programs are costly and must compete with other needs for scarce resources. These competing needs can best be met by a healthy and expanding economy, not by a sluggish, contracting one in which workers cannot find jobs. For example, conversion away from a transporta-tion system dependent on the internal combustion engine could be very expensive and could so significantly reduce standards of living that it would be resisted by the population. Environmental measures undertaken without regard to other social costs would be disastrous.

Another important conflict between environmental concerns and economic well-being is the xenophobia in some regions against migration by other Americans, on the ground that newcomers lower the quality of life of residents. In Seattle, Washing-ton, for instance, migrants from California are treated like pariahs who have no right to move to the Emerald City, Seattle. Some residents seem to think that selection of who is entitled to live in an area is decided by incumbents. Neighborhood member-ship is perceived to be part of one's personal property right. Californians themselves expressed a similar xenophobia in 1994 when they voted in favor of Proposition 189. By a margin of two to one, they voted to outlaw certain social support benefits, including health care and education, to illegal immigrants in the state. Such attitudes are extremely hazardous to economic growth and rising living standards.

For example, research reveals that the substantial improvement in the well-being of African Americans from the end of World War II to the 1990s has reflected their ability to migrate to regions of the country where their labor earns a higher return. Thus, selfish attitudes that restrict Americans' mobility will stifle increases in living standards. A danger of the slow-growth movement is that it will advocate counterproductive measures in terms of enhancing the environment as well as measures that are destructive to those who wish to work their way up the ladder of economic well-being.

Trade and Recessions

The relationship between growth and international trade has yet to be analyzed. When an economy is in a contraction, unemployment is increasing and industries decline. Tremendous political pressures arise to protect firms and jobs from foreign competition. The recessions in the early 1980s and the early 1990s are good examples of this phenomenon. The decline in the auto and steel industries fostered considerable political pressures to erect trade barriers, especially against Japanese auto and steel producers in the 1980s. Quotas, "voluntary" in nature, were accepted by the Japanese. These quotas, instigated by the U.S. government in order to placate demands of the auto industry and its workers, led to limits in auto supplies and increases in domestic and foreign car prices. In the mid-1990s, the United States again tried to pressure the Japanese to open their markets to U.S. automobile products. This included pressure for voluntary quotas and threats of punitive 100 percent tariffs on luxury automobiles, such as the Lexus, sold in the United States. In the short view, such protectionist measures seem to favor domestic industry, allowing it to thrive in the face of recession.

In the 1990s President Bush and President Clinton made numerous concessions to domestic producers of textiles, automobiles, and farm products to protect them, at least for a while, against competition with Mexico. The *North American Free Trade Agreement (NAFTA)* was in fact a monument to **managed trade**—a carefully crafted 2,000-page document. NAFTA carefully reduced protective barriers for U.S. firms, and even erected some new ones, over a 10- to 15-year period. President Clinton introduced new side agreements to protect both jobs and the environment. With these constraints imposed, NAFTA passed and marked the beginning of freer trade that led in 1995 to passage of the General Agreement on Trade and Tariffs (GATT) by all major trading nations worldwide. GATT will mean lower tariffs and better methods of adjudicating disputes.

Free trade provides flexibility of resources—labor, capital, and finance—and therefore provides an advantageous long-run environment for growth. Further, with huge domestic borrowing by both public and private sectors, the United States was strained for funds in the 1980s and the 1990s and needed foreign capital in order to continue expansion. In contrast, when trade is constrained, fewer choices are available for producers seeking to minimize costs. Likewise, fewer choices are available for consumers trying to spend their income in the most effective way possible. Thus, private academic economists heavily favored NAFTA and GATT. In the extreme, when trade is prohibited altogether, we live on an island of our own and produce only our own goods. This is neither feasible nor desirable.

CHAPTER REVIEW

Malthusians warn us of the dangers of unchecked population growth applied to limited resources driving down living standards. But industrial nations are better analyzed with neoclassical models in which inputs determine outputs in variable proportions. Neoclassical models focus on aggregate production functions that postulate the possibility of technological changes, allowing output growth to outpace input growth. This encourages analysis of technological change and adaptability.

For growth, the mix of GDP can be as important as its level, because capital formation is a necessary ingredient for growth. We have seen, however, that policies that foster growth can conflict with equity and can be ineffective, as illustrated by the paradox of thrift. Finally we saw that less restricted trade, embodied in NAFTA and GATT, expands opportunities for growth.

𝒯𝓇 MULTIPLE-CHOICE SELF-TEST 𝒯𝓇 𝒯𝓇 𝒯𝓇 𝒯𝓇 𝒯𝓇 𝒯𝓇 𝒯𝓇 𝒯𝓇 𝒯𝓇 𝒯𝓇 𝒯𝓇 𝒯𝓇 𝒯𝓇 𝒯𝓇 𝒯𝓇 𝒯𝓇

1. *Labor productivity* is defined as:
   a. The quantity of labor in the economy divided by the quantity of capital.
   b. Real output of the economy divided by the quantity of labor.
   c. The quantity of capital in the economy divided by the quantity of labor.
   d. The quantity of labor in the economy divided by real output.

2. Key parts of Thomas Malthus's model of economic growth include all but which of the following?
   a. Population grows at a more rapid rate than land inputs.
   b. Population growth is most likely to be slowed only by extreme poverty.
   c. Technological advances are the only hope for increases in living standards.
   d. The likely long-run outcome for the world is a very large population living at a minimum subsistence level.

3. A basic reason the Malthusian model didn't correctly predict the future for Western economies is that:
   a. The world's stocks of natural resources have increased more rapidly than Malthus's model predicted.
   b. Malthus didn't realize that technological advances would allow the production of more output from given quantities of inputs.
   c. Population in these economies stopped growing.
   d. Land was far more abundant than Malthus realized.

4. A basic feature of modern growth models is that:
   a. Capital and land are usually the main inputs considered.
   b. They assume that population growth will slow as income rises.
   c. They use production functions that show that capital, not land, is the crucial input for increasing output.
   d. They show that the same amount of output can be produced with different combinations of inputs, depending on input prices.

5. Growth in output per worker (labor productivity) of Western nations has been due to *all but* which of the following?
   a. Growth in the quantity of capital.
   b. Technological change: improved machines.
   c. Growth in the quantity of labor.
   d. Advances in the ability to use natural resources of various types.

6. *Four Tigers* refers to:
   a. The Asian nations that grew rapidly in the 1960s and the 1970s.
   b. The leaders of Eastern Europe who overthrew the communists.
   c. The signers of NAFTA.
   d. The innovators who introduced TFP.

☡ STUDY QUESTIONS

1. How would Malthus and Solow approach the growth problems of Third World countries?

2. Congress considers a plan to reduce the tax rate on personal incomes over $250,000 a year from 50 percent to 20 percent. Analyze this proposal in terms of growth and equity.

3. How would individuals react to an increase in the after-tax return on savings? Is it possible for the economy as a whole to react in a different way?

4. Is growth always better served by more capital formation? Discuss the need for balanced input growth.

5. What economic measures would you recommend to a newly freed eastern European nation such as Poland, the Czech Republic, Slovakia, or Hungary?

☡ PROBLEM

Some of the differences between Malthus's model and modern growth models can be seen by exploring how a very simple kind of production function works. Here is a production function that is a highly simplified version of the ones that economists like Jorgenson and Griliches have used to explain U.S. economic growth:

$$Q = A \times K \times L$$

where

Q = Quantity of output.
A = Rate at which inputs can be turned into output. (Thus, it measures the state of technology, and it gets larger as technology improves.)
K = Quantity of capital in the economy.
L = Number of workers in the economy.

1. Suppose the current state of technology is such that $A = 20$ and there are 25 machines and 100 workers in the economy. What will be the total output produced by the economy? What will be the labor productivity in this economy?

2. Could the economy produce this same output if it had only 25 workers? What other things could change in the production function to make this possible? Can you figure out a change in K that would make it possible? A change in A?

3. If the economy had only 25 workers but 100 machines, what would be the output per worker? If A increased from 20 to 25, reflecting a technological advance in firms' ability to use machines and labor, what would the output per worker become?

CHAPTER 19

Issues in Stabilization Policy

工 CHAPTER PREVIEW

You're a developer. Should you take out a million-dollar loan now to finance a new housing project or should you wait until interest rates fall? The decision depends on your forecast. Will government borrowing decline? Will the Fed accelerate money growth? Will personal incomes be up and banks be flush with money when you're ready to sell your new houses? Or will a recession hit, forcing you to unload your new houses and to declare bankruptcy? You need to understand macroeconomics and stabilization policy to have even a chance at intelligent decision making.

Macroeconomics culminates in stabilization policy. Executives, politicians, and commentators regularly try to anticipate the direction and impact of federal budget policy and of Fed monetary policy—a difficult and frustrating task. A comic recently said, "Economists accurately

forecast nine out of every seven recessions.''
Nevertheless, today's decisions depend on forecasts of tomorrow. Buying a house, building a
factory, ordering materials, investing in stocks—
all require forecasts, and such forecasts depend
crucially on policy and its consequences.

1. Will the federal government balance its
   budget? How would this affect the bond and
   stock markets?
2. What policies, in addition to monetary and
   fiscal policy, can government use to improve
   the nation's economic performance?
3. Are the Federal Reserve System and the
   executive branch of government capable of
   managing the economy? Or, would we be
   better off if we were to require them to obey
   fixed policy rules?

CONCEPTS REINTRODUCED

Bracket Creep 239
Crowding Out 294
Deficit Spending 414
Expected Real Rate of Interest 308
Fiscal Policy 289
Fisher Effect 309
Friedman's Law 379–380
Open-Market Operations 326
Efficiency-Wage Theory 389
Stop-Go Policies 390

NEW CONCEPTS

Targets
Instruments
Mundell-Tobin Effect
Ricardian Equivalence
Incomes Policies
Workfare
Indexation
Industrial Policies

𝓜 CHAPTER OBJECTIVES

After studying this chapter, you should be able to:

1. List two targets of monetary and fiscal policy.
2. List some of the instruments that can be used to attempt to reach policy targets. Are these instruments of fiscal policy or of monetary policy?
3. Describe some of the conditions that limit the effectiveness of fiscal and monetary policy instruments in the "real world."
4. State the target of an *incomes policy,* and list some of the instruments that such a policy might use.

THE MIX OF MONETARY AND FISCAL POLICY

In principle, a nation's leaders can coordinate monetary and fiscal policies to achieve several stabilization objectives. For instance, they may wish to increase the pace of economic growth, keep the inflation rate in check, and hit a particular target rate of unemployment; they could choose a careful mix of money supply growth and federal budget policy to achieve these multiple objectives. In actual practice, it is very difficult to implement policy coordination.

Fiscal policy, once thought to be an excellent device for stabilizing the business cycle, is now seen to be burdened with conflicting social goals and controversy. Many now think that fiscal policy is an awkward device for stabilization purposes. Rather than setting a budget to achieve macroeconomic stability, the public sector sets spending levels that are complex political compromises between various groups in Congress and in the White House that may have conflicting spending priorities. Tax rules often become vehicles for political and social agendas—capital gains tax cuts to help investors, tax cuts for the middle class, tax credits for the poor. In the last 15 years, the major problem confronting budget policy has been persistent and large structural budget deficits leading to a federal debt in 1997 that is six times larger than it was in 1979: $5,457.0 billion.

Thus, with countercyclical fiscal policy tied up with budget problems, the burden of economic stabilization policy often falls on monetary policy, which in the United States is undertaken by the Fed. If, as in some countries, the central bank is under the control of the government, monetary policy can turn out to be counterproductive as a stabilization device, but in the United States the monetary policy authority is largely independent of the executive branch.

In the past, economists have often criticized the Fed for its stop-go policies (see Chapter 17), which can exacerbate cyclical swings rather than ameliorate them. Large, chronic federal government borrowing, coupled with relatively tight monetary policy, leads to high interest rates. High interest rates can have two effects. One is to attract foreign financial capital and thus trade deficits. The other is low rates of capital formation. The latter implies slow growth. The former implies increased national rates of borrowing from the rest of the world and, therefore, increased foreign claims on future U.S. production. Commentators often view the U.S. policy mix with alarm.

Instruments and Targets

A rule can be designed to attain some stabilization goal. To illustrate this principle with a noneconomic example, consider Juan, a student who wants to go home for Christmas. He needs a policy to achieve his goal of getting home. We can analytically break his problem down into two targets: to go home and to get there by Christmas. Thus, he has a directional target (get home) and a timing target (arrive by Christmas). Juan has a car with two instruments: the steering wheel and the accelerator. How does Juan, the policymaker, implement his two instruments to hit his two targets?

The answer is to match the appropriate instrument to the appropriate target. Juan's solution is obvious: The steering wheel guides the car home. The gas pedal sets the necessary speed to arrive home by Christmas.

This simple analogy illustrates the need to coordinate fiscal and monetary policy to achieve national goals. Suppose, for example, we have two national economic policy goals:

1. To achieve a nonrecessionary and noninflationary national income level.
2. To achieve a desired mix of investment and consumption in GDP.

Assume that the mix of GDP between investment and consumption is determined by the rate of interest. This assumption simplifies our problem by restricting us to two **targets:** national income and interest rates. For simplicity, assume that monetary policy consists of open-market operations and that fiscal policy consists of choosing a given level of deficit spending. To achieve these two targets, the authorities have two **instruments:** open-market operations and deficit spending. How should these two instruments be used to achieve the target national income and the target interest rate?

Because we have two instruments and two targets, we match instruments to targets. We let money growth determine the level of national income, so that we match open-market operations to national income. In this model, deficits lead to crowding out through interest rate increases. Thus, the deficit (or surplus) instrument is matched to the target interest rate. The instruments are then set to values that will hit the targets to achieve the desired levels of income, and the mix between investment and consumption. The Fed buys securities until the money supply hits the desired level of national income, and the government sets its deficit so that the investment-consumption mix of GDP is on target.

This economic example illustrates how to match policy instruments to targets and thus achieve national goals. In practice, as noted above, implementation and coordination of fiscal and monetary policies are far more difficult.

- The social goals of economic policy are complex, conflicting, and subtle. It is not sufficient to achieve a target level of national income. We may also wish to achieve specific results in employment, residential construction, defense spending, the trade balance, and smokestack industrial policy.
- Politics obviously dominate federal budget decisions. The actual budget reflects compromises between various constituencies—heavy industry, unions, women's groups, the new right. Thus, the budget is not a simple instrument that is used to hit a well-defined target. A flare-up in the Persian Gulf, for instance, may dictate a costly naval presence, exacerbating deficit spending.
- Fiscal policy is difficult to implement in a timely fashion. It takes a long time to change the budget, and often even longer to actually spend more money or cut the budget. Consequently, fiscal policy may be too clumsy an instrument for use in stabilizing national income. Implementing fiscal policy can take so long that it exacerbates cycles rather than ameliorating them.
- Consensus on the macroeconomic model is limited. How would a Keynesian match instruments to targets in our example above? How would a supply sider match these instruments?
- The Fed, unlike Congress, can exert policy with the narrow focus of a stabilization goal. Still, monetary policy is not without critics who think that the Fed's use of stop-go policies actually destabilizes the economy. Are such stop-go policies necessary? Some think that the Fed should focus on international monetary considerations such as stabilizing exchange rates. Often Fed policy is shrouded in mystery, and the realized consequences of an action take a long and unpredictable time to occur.

The Poor Mix

As noted above, fiscal and monetary policy are not as well coordinated in fact as the instruments-and-targets illustration suggests they could be. Instead, the trend in fiscal policy has been toward increases in mandated benefits programs, especially in Social Security, health, medical care, and income-support programs. Despite cuts in defense spending, the largest single item in the budget, and tax increases in 1984, 1985, 1990, and 1992, deficit growth from 1980 to 1992 outstripped GDP growth and after a brief pause is expected to explode again early in the next century. These persistent increases in the deficit-GDP ratio have caused the accumulated debt to grow from $0.89 trillion to $5.5 trillion in 17 years. Interest payments on this debt now comprise the fourth largest item in the federal budget, $240 billion in 1997.

How did we get ourselves into this budget morass of chronic deficit spending? Fiscal policy has become the arena in which our society works out its social conflicts. Since the mid-1970s, the budget has been the arena of class warfare in the United States. Less bloody than an actual war, budget war has nonetheless left us with a difficult legacy. How did we get here, and what have we tried to do to avoid or cushion the pain? Six of the more important events and issues should be understood:

1. *Reaganomics 1982–1986.* President Reagan passed one of the most dramatic economic policies of modern times in America. He froze tax hikes by lowering tax rates on both personal and corporate income. Personal income tax rates fell from a top marginal rate of 70 percent to 30 percent. Corporate rates were reduced from 48 percent to 32 percent. Even after four tax hikes, federal revenue remained between 19 and 20 percent of GDP in the middle of the 1990s. Reagan was less successful in obtaining reductions in domestic spending, though growth in some programs was slowed down.

2. *The Reagan defense buildup.* From 1982 through 1987 U.S. defense spending was a greater percentage of GDP than at any post–World War II time except during the height of the Vietnam War. Defense absorbed 7 percent of GDP during the middle 1980s. To some this was the final blow that crushed the former Soviet Union, for its leaders tried to match the U.S. buildup, but its economy could not take the pressure and buckled. Still, it contributed to unprecedented debt accumulation.

3. *Bipartisan increases in social spending.* Administrations of both parties during the '60s, '70s, and '80s expanded social spending, especially for the middle class. The largest program by far is Social Security, which cost $370 billion in 1997. The fastest growing items, though, are medical care and health entitlements. Even though these programs, along with food stamps, AFDC, and other income support programs, are touted as support for the poor, most of the money ends up helping the middle class. Since this is where the votes are, political economy tells us that we should not be surprised by this resultant distribution of benefits.

4. *Payroll taxes ratcheted upward.* The only tax Congress has had an easy time increasing seems to be the payroll tax that supports the Social Security programs. Laws passed in the early 1980s allowed these taxes to increase automatically each year into the 1990s. Payroll taxes accounted for 11 percent of total federal revenues in 1950, 30 percent in 1970, and 35 percent by 1997.

5. *Gramm-Rudman-Hollings law.* In a dramatic attempt to control its own deficit spending, Congress tried to force fiscal discipline on itself in the late 1980s by passing legislation that would automatically cut spending across the board if Congress failed to make discretionary cuts on its own. The eventual goal of the Gramm-Rudman-Hollings legislation was to balance the budget by 1991. In 1990 the law was dropped in a Republican-Democratic deal. President Bush and the Democrat-controlled Congress agreed to exchange a tax increase for future caps on domestic spending programs. The deficit in 1991 was $269 billion, not zero.

6. *Balanced budget amendment to the Constitution.* The midterm elections of 1994 saw a startling switch of control in the U.S. Congress. For the first time in 40 years, both houses of Congress were nominally controlled by the Republican party. In an attempt to impose outside discipline on spending and the deficit, the Chairman of the House, Newt Gingrich, and his crew of Republican freshmen proposed a balanced-budget amendment to the Constitution. The amendment failed to garner the two-thirds majority vote needed to pass in the Senate because

of unified Democratic opposition, but it remains on the agenda for national discussion.

Our analysis in Chapter 13 suggested that deficits can crowd out private investment spending by raising interest rates or by attracting loans from abroad, which causes a trade deficit. But, as we now know, fiscal policy is tied up with debates over management and the size of structural deficits.

Without fiscal policy for stabilization, more pressure falls on monetary policy. The Federal Reserve Board imposed anti-inflation policies throughout the 1980s and 1990s that dictated relatively tight money. Tight money, combined with large deficits, produces high interest rates. Because high interest rates discourage domestic capital formation and encourage financial capital flows from abroad, the mix of policies was poor. This mix, tight money and loose deficits, still bodes ill for the future and raises doubts about the wisdom of our policy coordination.

DEBATES OVER STABILIZATION POLICY

Should the Fed, the president, and Congress have discretion in setting policy, or should they be bound by rules? Some people advocate a constitutional amendment to balance the budget and limit the growth of government. Others want the Fed to follow fixed rules set by Congress. Some want Congress itself bound by fixed tax and spending limits. Should the Fed focus on long-run effects or short-run effects of its policies? What is the relative importance of stabilization effects and incentive effects of fiscal policy? Does a tax cut affect the economy principally through a circular flow spending boom or through incentives that influence specific consumers and producers?

Rules versus Authority

A long-standing debate involves the degree of discretion allowed monetary and fiscal authorities: the Fed, the executive branch, and Congress. Compared to 30 years ago, the weight of opinion among economists has shifted from favoring discretion in policy toward establishing rules that restrain policymakers. In recent years, three rules have been proposed:

1. *A monetary policy rule:* Require the Fed to increase the money supply at a steady annual growth rate within narrowly designated limits (e.g., 4 to 5 percent).
2. *A balanced-budget amendment to the Constitution:* By constitutional amendment, set the size of the federal budget as a percentage of GDP and limit the growth of the total budget to the same rate of growth of GDP.
3. *Fix the goal of the Federal Reserve:* Set zero inflation as the only goal of Federal Reserve policy.

These three political economy proposals—which remove discretion from the policy-making apparatus—are controversial. Those who favor removal of policy discretion argue that politicians all too often favor deficits, larger government, and inflationary monetary expansion. Only fixed rules can prevent abuse of policy. Policy is too complex, sluggish, and unpredictable, so that discretionary measures may foster instability and are thus impractical and counterproductive. Those who oppose rules fear reductions in programs and fear that authorities will hide behind simple rules. Although discretion may be difficult, authorities must aim for the best course possible. They can only do this if allowed to react to events as they occur. Furthermore, they argue that, in a democracy, policy should reflect the desires of the people rather than arcane rules set in stone at a time when the future could not be perceived.

However, rules and discretion need not be diametrically opposed. In a world in which policymakers have discretion, performance can be evaluated only if the authority's goals are enunciated by a decision rule. Shouldn't an authority state the rule that governs its plans? Also, if rules are set, shouldn't those rules, under certain circumstances, permit deviations from a fixed path? A rule need not be inflexible. For example, a balanced-budget rule could require an average long-term balance, rather than a yearly balance. Similarly, a rule governing monetary policy could allow for some discretion by the Fed.

Monetary Policy: Long Term versus Short Term

The complexity of stabilization policies is becoming increasingly evident. Monetary policy, that is, decisions by the Fed to increase or decrease the money supply, has complex consequences for interest rates. In the short term, increased money keeps interest rates down. However, monetary expansion has very different long-term consequences. After a long and variable lag, excessive increases in the money supply produce inflation, and thus an increase in interest rates. This is paradoxical. Monetary expansion drives interest rates down in the short run. By inducing expected inflation, though, monetary expansion drives interest rates up in the long run. What then is the effect of monetary policy on interest rates? If the Fed cuts the money supply, will rates rise because money is scarce, or will rates fall because expected inflation has declined?

A crucial aspect of this question is the effect of money on the expected real rate of interest. (The expected real rate of interest, you will recall from Chapter 14, is the key cost variable that affects investment decisions.) The market interest rate reflects both the expected real rate of interest and the expected inflation rate. The *Fisher Effect* said that an increase in expected inflation causes a proportional increase in the market interest rate, so that the expected real rate of interest remains unchanged.

Robert Mundell and James Tobin independently came up with a counterargument to the Fisher Effect, the **Mundell-Tobin Effect.** Although a sustained inflation eventually leads to a commensurate increase in interest rates, according to their theory, over a shorter term interest rates will not rise enough to compensate lenders for inflation.

A sustained increase in the money supply produces a sustained inflation. A sustained inflation generates expected inflation, and this raises interest rates. But an increase in expected inflation also reduces the demand for money. (Because people expect money to depreciate in the future, they choose to hold less money now.) This lower money demand pulls interest rates down to partly offset the increasing effect of inflation. Thus, market interest rates rise at a slower rate than the increase in expected inflation. If expected inflation is subtracted from interest rates, the difference is the expected real rate of interest. It will have to decline; this is the Mundell-Tobin Effect. It implies that monetary policy has real stabilization effects on growth and investment through the real expected interest rate.

The MUNDELL-TOBIN EFFECT says that expected inflation increases market interest rates less than proportionately to an increase in the money supply. This is because high expected inflation lowers money demand. Thus, an increase in money growth drives down the expected real rate of interest.

A numerical example can show how this works. Inflation is 0 percent, and interest rates are 3 percent. Suppose inflation is expected to rise from 0 percent to 10 percent. According to the Mundell-Tobin Effect, interest rates will rise by less than 10 percent—say, from 3 percent to 11 percent—an increase of 8 percent. By definition, the expected real rate of interest is the difference between the market interest rate and the expected inflation rate. The 11 percent interest rate minus the 10 percent expected inflation gives an expected real rate of interest of 1 percent. From the point of view of the expected return on investment and yield on savings, the real return fell from 3 percent to 1 percent. Sustained inflation does lead to higher market interest rates, but these rates are not high enough to stop the real cost of borrowing from falling. The Mundell-Tobin Effect also works in reverse when disinflation occurs. From 1979 to 1983, when Fed tight-money policy reduced inflation, real interest rates rose. Disinflation brought on high real interest rates, reflecting the Mundell-Tobin Effect in reverse.

Monetarists believe the Fed should focus on long-term inflation and disregard short-term interest rate fluctuations. Keynesians favor policies that focus on short-term interest rates. The Fed may have to choose: It cannot achieve short-term targets if it focuses only on long-term inflation effects. Conversely, if it focuses on short-term interest rate effects, it may ignore long-term consequences for inflation.

Ricardian Equivalence and Fiscal Policy

Suppose the president asks you, as chair of his Council of Economic Advisers, to advise him on the economic effects of a tax cut for the middle class. Although he naturally, as a politician, likes tax cuts, he is concerned about the chronic, high budget deficits. What key points would you make in your analysis of the issue?

First, your answer would depend on which type of economist you are—Keynesian or new classical macroeconomist. Your analysis of how the economy works will determine your answer to the president. A Keynesian would make the following point: By increasing after-tax disposable income, a middle-class tax cut will increase consumer spending and thus stimulate the economy. However, a new classical macroeconomist would tell the president that the effects depend on how consumers perceive the cut. If they think it is permanent, then they will increase spending and stimulate the economy. However, if they think the cut is only temporary, then they will not change their spending habits, knowing that they would have to revert to normal spending patterns very soon. President Bush tried to boost spending with a temporary cut in the form of suspending tax withholding in the winter months.

Harvard economist Robert Barro has suggested a third view: If people believe that a tax cut now will simply lead to a later increase in taxes, they may not spend more in response to the tax cut. Suppose consumers believe that the real cost of the government is the total resources that it uses up when it spends, rather than simply the explicit taxes it imposes. Then a tax cut, not accompanied by a spending cut, does not reduce the real cost of government. It merely shifts the cost of expenditures to the future. A tax cut without any reduction in spending means an increase in the deficit. Thus, the government borrows more to pay for spending what had been financed with taxes. How will consumers respond to this cost shifting to the future?

In Barro's view, consumers, who are rational and forward looking, will not just spend more when a tax cut increases their disposable incomes; they will also anticipate a future tax increase large enough to pay for today's lower taxes. This future cost must include taxes to pay for the interest on the newly borrowed money. If consumers correctly perceive this long-run effect, then they will not increase spending at all in response to the tax cut! Of course, one might argue that if the government defers its spending far enough into the future, then today's taxpayer will ignore it, thinking it will fall on a future generation. But, wait. The future generation is this generation's offspring. Thus, current consumers may hold down their spending to provide adequate funds for their children to pay taxes. This argument is called **Ricardian Equivalence** after David Ricardo, who first identified the idea 300 years ago. Today's consumer will not spend more in response to a tax cut, because they "know" that they or their offspring will have to pay the taxes eventually. They decide to put aside the savings now rather than spending the tax cut.

Nonstabilization Policy Measures

The applications of monetary and fiscal policy have many limitations—they are sluggish, clumsy, and controversial. Some economists suggest other techniques for dealing with unemployment and inflation. One important category of policies, which is popular in Europe, is **incomes policies.** Wage and price controls are usually implemented during war in order to stifle inflation. During World War II the government established a wage-and-price control board to monitor large companies, big unions, and strategic industries. During peacetime, the only major U.S. attempt at controls was imposed during the Nixon administration in 1971. Presidents John F. Kennedy, Gerald Ford, and Jimmy Carter tried modest "jawboning" and guidelines, but these more relaxed measures were ineffective.

> INCOMES POLICIES, designed to restrict wage and price increases, range from "jawboning" by the president to laws that limit wage and price increases.

Most U.S. economists are skeptical of incomes policies. Incomes policies distort relative prices and private markets. Under President Richard M. Nixon's imposition of wage and price controls, shortages did develop, and critics take this as evidence against incomes policies. Some examples of circumvention of the Nixon controls were:

- The lumber industry regularly exported lumber from the United States to Canada, then reimported it for sale in the United States at higher, more profitable, uncontrolled prices.
- Although poultry feed was not subject to price controls, chickens were. As feed became more expensive, it ultimately became unprofitable and uneconomical to feed chickens. As a result, millions of baby chicks were slaughtered instead of being raised for market. Shortages of chicken soon became pervasive.
- Because it became more profitable to sell fertilizer and chemical pesticides abroad at uncontrolled prices than to sell them at home to American farmers at controlled prices, domestic agricultural production suffered for want of these important inputs.

Nevertheless, supporters of wage and price measures believe controls can be effective complements to stabilization policy. Such measures play an important role in Europe. Germany, Austria, France, and others often negotiate wages and prices in meetings between unions, business, and government.

Direct Job Creation

Attempts to lower unemployment without accelerating inflation have often failed. The natural rate of unemployment (Un) rose steadily from 1965 to 1987 and seems to have leveled off and fallen since. Can policy attack unemployment and poverty directly without stimulating the overall economy? This depends on the cause of a high national rate. Does the increase in Un reflect increasing structural unemployment emanating, for example, from the effects of unemployment compensation and minimum-wage laws as they impact on teenagers? If so, reversing these measures could lower Un. Economist Janet Yellen, from the University of California, Berkeley, and now a key presidential advisor, argued that firms intentionally hold wages too high to employ all potential workers. Firms do this to encourage employees to be productive. Yellen calls these high wages **efficiency wages.** Efficiency wages may contribute to cyclical unemployment. Thus, according to some economists, existing social programs such as aid to the unemployed should be kept.

They recommend that the government intervene in labor markets as an employer of last resort. Such *direct-job-creation* programs were used during the Great Depression on a modest scale. Some critics argue that direct job creation in the 1930s shifted labor from private jobs to meaningless, make-work public jobs. Others, however, are less pessimistic about direct job creation and believe that government can provide skills and training to the hard-core unemployed and, in the process, complete useful projects. The Scandinavian countries provide interesting examples of retraining and relocating of workers through government programs. Sweden, for instance, spends less on unemployment compensation than on retraining and placement. The result is unemployment rates close to 1 percent rather than the 5 percent rates in America and 10 percent rates in parts of Europe. Note that once unemployed Swedes are offered new jobs, they are dropped from the welfare roles even if they reject the jobs.

In the 1970s a major direct-job-creation attempt was written into law in the Comprehensive Employment and Training Act (CETA). This act funded local governments for employing difficult-to-hire workers. In some cases, local agencies used CETA money to employ people they would have employed anyway at their own expense, rather than using CETA monies to expand their workforces. This dampened CETA's ability to increase overall employment, and the program was discontinued by the Reagan administration.

During the 1980s many states, led by California, began to replace welfare programs, where feasible, with **workfare** programs in which benefits were tied to participation in training and work programs. The Clinton welfare reform team proposed that the federal government provide jobs to working-age welfare recipients as a last resort. Nevertheless, President Clinton signed the Republican congressional welfare reform, which excluded job guarantees.

Inflation Damage Control

Proposals that minimize the damage done by inflation without actually reducing it are suggested from time to time. Some of these proposals protect the private sector, and others alter government revenues. COLAs insulate private individuals from the ravages of inflation, and **indexation** of taxes lowers government revenues as it protects taxpayers from bracket creep. Tax indexing consists of modifying the tax laws to adjust tax brackets, leaving effective tax burdens on constant dollar income the same. In Israel and Brazil, indexation, though widely used, has not been successful in slowing inflation, unless accompanied by contractionary stabilization measures. Nevertheless, indexation may succeed in redistributing the discomfort.

> INDEXATION consists of modifying contracts and tax brackets so that
> their dollar terms adjust to the inflation rate as measured in an index, such
> as the CPI.

COLAs prevent erosion of incomes from inflation. The COLA on Social Security benefits, tied to raises in the CPI, insulates recipients from loss of purchasing power as a result of inflation. Similarly, unions like to insert COLA clauses into their wage contracts. Although COLAs help some people, their prevalence promotes inflation, because additional wage, income, and price increases automatically follow. Recall the discussion in Chapter 17 about attempts to remove the upward bias in the CPI that was resulting in excessive COLA increases in many benefit programs. A new congressional commission, the Boskin Commission, in December 1996, argued that the CPI overstates inflation by 1.5 percent, so that a 3.5 percent CPI is really only a 2 percent rate of inflation if correctly measured.

Industrial Policy

Faced with apparently well-orchestrated government and business alliances from Japan, a united Europe, and the new industrial countries of Asia, many in the United States are searching for a new formula for becoming more competitive on international markets. Dramatic purchases by foreigners of land in Hawaii, hotels in Los Angeles, and even the Rockefeller Center in New York have attracted attention to the idea that the United States needs to adopt a closer planning relationship between business and government to stem the tide of foreign competition and to secure a preeminent position in the world.

What is **industrial policy,** and would it work here? Though the idea of an industrial policy is complex, to some it means an alliance between business and government in which government endorses and supports national business interests in competition with the rest of the world.

> INDUSTRIAL POLICIES are government-controlled and government-
> designed measures for advancing and promoting certain business interests
> in order to enhance U.S. competitiveness abroad. These policies include
> selecting particular product lines, such as superconductors, that will receive
> subsidies, tariff production, tax breaks, and so on.

To be operational, a centrally planned and coordinated industrial policy requires that the government pick winners and losers among various sectors and firms and then help the winners by subsidies, tax breaks, tariffs, and so on. Advocates of industrial policy point to Japan's success at projecting its automobile industry abroad and to France's joint business and government efforts to develop its airline industry—especially the airbus. Meanwhile, American firms seem to flounder about, operating on their own, often hampered by U.S. government taxes, red tape, controls, and constraints.

Some of these arguments reflect little more than businesses looking for special breaks, favoring comparisons to foreign programs only when it is to their advantage. Some reflect a distorted view of the degree of harmony elsewhere and a tendency to see the "greener pasture on the other side of the fence." Some reflect socialist attitudes that government can allocate resources better than the private market mechanism can when dealing with extremely large and long-term programs.

Cries for improved competitiveness have been driven partly by chronic U.S. trade deficits, especially with Japan. Americans buy far more goods and services produced by the rest of the world than foreigners buy from U.S. producers. These trade deficits, stubborn and large during the 1980s, suggest to many that the United States is either incompetent or treated unfairly by other countries—countries that want to trade here but will not allow U.S. firms to trade there.

However, it seems likely that the trade deficits primarily reflect domestic spending and borrowing practices. Domestic demands for borrowed funds to finance large, chronic federal budget deficits, coupled with low U.S. savings rates and corporate borrowing, attract foreign loans. Foreign money is drawn to the United States by domestic U.S. borrowing. This flow of loan money into the United States, as shown in other chapters, requires a net flow of foreign goods into the country in order to balance accounts. One result is that foreign lenders have American cash with which to make investments in the United States. Thus, U.S. budget deficits cause the U.S. trade deficit and the apparent inability of American firms to compete abroad.

In fact, the U.S. government does work with business in many sectors. The Commerce, Agriculture, Transportation, Energy, and Interior Departments all do specific work to help, advocate, and coordinate various needs of the economy. The Council of Economic Advisers, the Office of Management and the Budget, and the Treasury Department all coordinate fiscal and other government policies for the benefit of the private sector.

To improve coordination of government policies, President Bill Clinton formed the new National Economic Council, headed by a financier. A business consultant who is a strong advocate of industrial policy advises the president on domestic policy. Thus, a turn toward a more active, government-led industrial policy to compete with Japan and Germany may well be under way. Subsidies for high-technology producers in Silicon Valley and for major airline production companies, such as Boeing in Seattle, are in the offing.

Many critics of industrial policy warn of inefficiencies that can result from close, even cozy, ties between government and business. Recall complaints of $400 hammers purchased by the Military Industrial Complex. Nonetheless, we may rightly ask: How much central planning is appropriate and how much is necessary? Obviously, when we observe the collapse of centrally planned regimes in Eastern Europe, in the former Soviet Union, and in Asia, we must realize that centralization can be debilitating to incentives, morale, and initiative. But given apparent successes in Japan and Germany, the appropriate balance will always be a hotly debated issue.

Federal Reserve Policy and Rational Consumers

Suppose you are the top economic adviser to the Board of Governors of the Federal Reserve Bank and the chair asks you to recommend policies for dealing with the potential recession that might occur soon. What would you advise?

After seeing how money affects interest rates and the pace of economic activity, you might well advise the chair to "lean against the wind" and increase money growth to stimulate spending and offset the recession.

There is, however, a very different modern view. It has to do with how the private sector perceives Fed policy. Recall Friedman's law: Money growth leads to inflation, with a long and variable lag. If individuals are rational and forward looking, as were Mr. Barro's agents in the tax-cut example, then they will be evaluating possible Fed actions: (1) They realize that money growth leads eventually to inflation and (2) having observed the Fed in the past, they will anticipate its antirecession conduct. Putting these two perceptions together, private citizens will anticipate both what the Fed will do and how its actions will eventually affect inflation.

Individuals build this new inflation information into their decisions and adjust their own plans accordingly. In the language of Chapter 17, the private economy will naturally gravitate to the "natural rate of unemployment" without letting Fed money policy actions get in the way. This is a very strong version of policy anticipation and suggests that Fed actions have little sustained effect on output and employment. In other words, there is a natural tendency for the real economy to achieve a path of output and employment over time. These will depend on shocks that hit the economy, causing slumps, but the Fed is not capable of altering them with monetary policy.

Policy Credibility and Time Consistency

This raises the notion of credibility. We argue above that rational and forward-looking economic agents, consumers, workers, and producers can anticipate and offset Fed policy when the Fed follows a discernible pattern in its monetary policy. One is tempted then to argue that the Fed could, if it wanted to have real effects, simply fool the public by behaving unexpectedly. In fact, policymakers are often tempted to do something like this.

Suppose the Fed establishes a long-range policy of stable monetary growth of 10 percent per year without deviations from this rate. Further suppose the Fed makes its policy credible, so that individual economic agents expect this policy and behave in their own best interests, as if the Fed were always going to adhere to its 10 percent rule.

Now, suppose a recession occurs. The president goes to the chair of the Board of Governors and requests a more rapid than normal growth of money, reasoning that this will drive down interest rates and stimulate the economy. One might argue that this unexpected stimulus will pump up the economy and get it going, because people expect only 10 percent growth.

Alas, there is a fly in the ointment. If the Fed does this when the first recession occurs, then the announced policy will lose its credibility! The Fed will have been able to fool the public once, but after that people will know that the Fed will increase money growth beyond the 10 percent rate when recessions hit, and the announced policy will no longer be credible.

CHAPTER REVIEW

Theoretically, conventional monetary and fiscal policy can be coordinated to achieve several goals—which means matching instruments to targets. The practical application of policy has been less successful, hampered by politics, controversy, and possibly ignorance. Some people advocate fixed rules of policy behavior that balance the budget by constitutional amendment or expand the money supply at a fixed rate. The complexity of policy effects is illustrated by the Mundell-Tobin Effect with which we analyzed monetary expansion and interest rates.

Policymakers apply nonstabilization measures from time to time, such as wage and price controls, direct job creation, and tax indexing. In recent years, economists have noticed the ability of firms and consumers to anticipate actions of policymakers, like the central bank and the Treasury. The private sector may be able to offset expected policy actions by anticipating them. This complicates the job of policymakers who may want to try to trick the public by announcing tougher policies than they actually are willing to implement. Because policy always involves an amalgam of scientific economic analysis and philosophical and political opinion, we will always have to settle for an uneasy ambiguity in policy analysis.

𝕿 MULTIPLE-CHOICE SELF-TEST 𝕿 𝕿 𝕿 𝕿 𝕿 𝕿 𝕿 𝕿 𝕿 𝕿 𝕿 𝕿 𝕿 𝕿 𝕿

1. The targets of macroeconomics policy might include which of the following?
   a. Tax credits for investment.
   b. Contractionary monetary policy.
   c. A 3 percent rate of inflation.
   d. Increasing the federal deficit by $50 billion.

2. If some NCM economists wanted to achieve the two targets of reduced inflation and an increase in investment, their preferred combination of instruments would be:
   a. A reduction in the growth rate of the money supply and an increase in the federal deficit.
   b. A reduction in the growth rate of the money supply and a decrease in the federal deficit.
   c. An increase in the growth rate of the money supply and an increase in the federal deficit.
   d. An increase in the growth rate of the money supply and a decrease in the federal deficit.

3. Using fiscal policy to achieve a goal of decreasing current inflationary pressures on output will be difficult or impossible if:
   a. Legislators feel they cannot decrease major spending programs because such programs are needed and feel they cannot raise taxes because of supply-side concerns.
   b. The time before the reduction in government spending will actually occur is estimated to be two years.
   c. The crowding-out effect has been so considerable that any decrease in government deficits will be immediately replaced by increased investment.
   d. Any of the above is the case.

4. *Income policies* are defined as:
   a. Rules requiring that wages and benefits be increased in proportion to the rate of inflation.
   b. Nonstabilization policies.
   c. Policies that set limits on rates of wage and price increases in an attempt to reduce the rate of increase.
   d. Policies that attempt to change the equilibrium level of national income.

5. Direct-job-creation programs:
   a. Are an attempt to lower the natural unemployment rate.
   b. Include CETA, started by the Reagan administration.
   c. Are seen by critics as an attempt to avoid the use of expansionary fiscal and monetary policy.
   d. Can reduce cyclical, but not structural, unemployment.

𝕴𝕴 STUDY QUESTIONS

1. "Monetary expansion increases interest rates." Discuss. Be sure to consider expected inflation and expected real interest rates.

2. How would a Keynesian coordinate fiscal and monetary policy to hit target income and interest rate levels?

3. How would a monetarist coordinate stabilization policies?

4. How successful are forecasts of inflation, GDP, and interest rates? Discuss several difficulties economists have in forecasting these magnitudes.

5. Analyze indexation, direct job creation, and wage and price controls as policies for improving social well-being.

𝕴𝕴 PROBLEM

Suppose that the nation of Chad has a personal income tax indexed to inflation as measured by Chad's CPI. The CPI has risen in the last year from 100 to 120. Chad's income tax table last year was as follows:

Taxable Income		
Above	**But Less than or Equal to**	**Tax Rate**
—	10,000 francs	0%
10,000 francs	20,000 francs	10%
20,000 francs	40,000 francs	20%
40,000 francs	—	30%

1. Change the tax table as required by the indexing law.

2. Calculate the income tax liability of a family whose income was 50,000 francs last year and 60,000 francs this year.

3. How much did this family's real income rise? How much did its real tax liability increase?

4. Suppose the CPI had been 200 at the start of the year and had risen to 240 by the end. Would this have changed the calculations? If so, in what direction?

CHAPTER 20

The Exchange Rate and the Balance of Payments

CHAPTER PREVIEW

By 1979 one U.S. dollar, worth 358 Japanese yen in 1970, had slid so far that it could buy only 210 yen. Six years later, in 1985, the dollar had strengthened to 238 yen. The long slide in the dollar's relative currency value throughout the 1970s reflected the relatively rapid U.S. inflation vis-à-vis the yen. A similar slide took place in the dollar's relative value vis-à-vis the deutsche mark (DM), another important international currency. One U.S. dollar, which had bought 3.65 DM in 1970, was worth only 1.82 DM in 1980. As with the yen, the dollar bounced back in the early eighties and reached 2.94 DM per dollar by 1985. The strength of the dollar relative to the two most important alternative international currencies, the yen and the deutsche mark, during the 1980s was attributed by news analysts and economists to high U.S. interest rates brought on by large budget deficits and to an evident worldwide belief that America was a safe haven for financial investments.

Then, in the late 1980s, the dollar slide of the 1970s returned; by 1996 $1 would buy 112 yen or 1.54 DM. This reversal reflected fears that continuous federal budget deficits might eventually force a new round of U.S. inflation through monetization of the debt and the recognition that U.S. economic policy might require a recession soon. Figure 20–1 (see page 441), from *Newsweek* magazine, March 20, 1995, illustrates the dollar slide from 1985 to 1995 vis-à-vis the yen. Are the cited events really the causes of the movements, or are they merely coincidental? You will have a better sense of the answer after finishing this chapter.

Wide fluctuations in currency values can generate fortunes and take them away overnight. Banks can fail, exporters can go under, investors can go broke. These problems are all part of the fast-paced world of international finance.

The United States imported $799 billion worth of foreign goods in 1996 and exported $612 billion worth of its own goods. Will this trade gap in merchandise persist? Is this a bargain for the United States, or is it a cause for concern? U.S. farmers complain that the high dollar makes it hard for their products to compete in overseas markets. The United Auto Workers Union argues that the strong dollar gives Japanese automobile makers a cost advantage of several thousand dollars per car in the U.S. market.

1. What factors determine the value of one currency against another?
2. What roles do government policies play in international finance?

CONCEPTS REINTRODUCED

Crowding Out 294
Demand Curve 52
Fiscal Policy 289
Interest Rates 307
Supply Curve 74
Exchange Rate 313
Nonconvertible Currency 314

NEW CONCEPTS

Foreign Exchange Markets
Central Bank Intervention
Floating Exchange Rates
Fixed Exchange Rates
Balance of Payments
Current Account
Capital Account
Merchandise Trade Balance
Bretton Woods International Monetary System
Managed Floating

ℐℛ CHAPTER OBJECTIVES

After studying this chapter, you should be able to:

1. Calculate the price in dollars given an exchange rate for dollars, some foreign currency, and a price in a foreign currency; calculate the price in foreign currency given a price in dollars.

2. Contrast fixed and floating exchange rates by stating who or what controls the exchange rate in each case.

3. List the components of the U.S. balance of payments, including the components of the current and capital accounts.

4. Explain how interest rates, national incomes, and price levels affect the supply of and demand for foreign currencies.

THE FOREIGN EXCHANGE MARKET

Currencies of various countries are bought and sold each business day in the **foreign exchange markets** of New York, London, Paris, Frankfurt, Tokyo, and other financial centers. Although these markets are not located at any specific sites within a city, they are networks of relationships among central banks, commercial banks, and other currency traders. Foreign currency transactions take many different forms. Tourists purchase hundreds of dollars' worth of foreign currencies during their travels abroad. Importers buy millions of dollars' worth of foreign currencies to pay for their purchases of foreign goods. Exporters cash in their foreign currency revenues for the currencies of their own countries. Large commercial banks trade millions of dollars' worth of currencies with each other in a single day. These interbank transactions are usually negotiated over the telephone, and the funds are electronically transferred by computers.

ℐℛ ℐℛ

FOREIGN EXCHANGE MARKETS are markets in which the currencies of different nations are bought and sold.

Transfers from one currency to another are made at the exchange rate between the two currencies on that date. Table 20–1 shows the exchange rate between the U.S. dollar and a variety of important foreign currencies on October 17, 1996. Each of these exchange rates is written as the number of dollars per unit of the foreign currency—the dollar price of the foreign currency. Exchange rates may also be quoted as the foreign currency price of dollars: one dollar cost 111.8 Japanese yen or 5.207 French francs on this date.

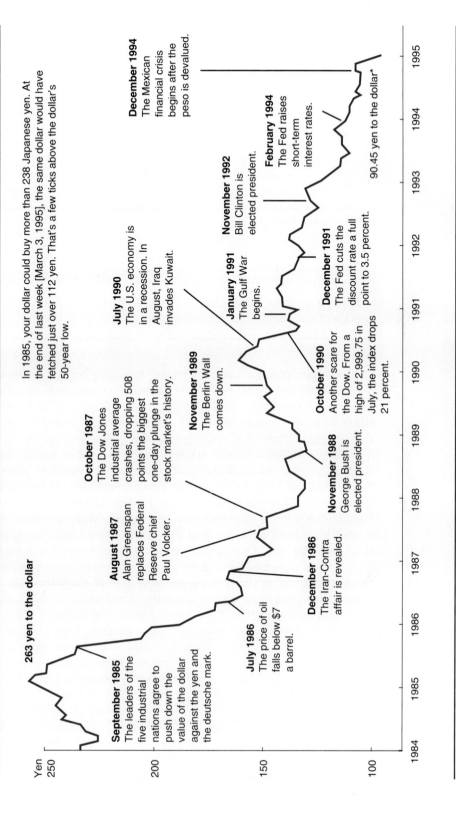

FIGURE 20–1 The Dollar's Long Slide, 1984–1995

Yen

263 yen to the dollar

In 1985, your dollar could buy more than 238 Japanese yen. At the end of last week [March 3, 1995], the same dollar would have fetched just over 112 yen. That's a few ticks above the dollar's 50-year low.

September 1985
The leaders of the five industrial nations agree to push down the value of the dollar against the yen and the deutsche mark.

July 1986
The price of oil falls below $7 a barrel.

December 1986
The Iran-Contra affair is revealed.

August 1987
Alan Greenspan replaces Federal Reserve chief Paul Volcker.

October 1987
The Dow Jones industrial average crashes, dropping 508 points the biggest one-day plunge in the stock market's history.

November 1988
George Bush is elected president.

November 1989
The Berlin Wall comes down.

July 1990
The U.S. economy is in a recession. In August, Iraq invades Kuwait.

October 1990
Another scare for the Dow. From a high of 2,999.75 in July, the index drops 21 percent.

January 1991
The Gulf War begins.

December 1991
The Fed cuts the discount rate a full point to 3.5 percent.

November 1992
Bill Clinton is elected president.

February 1994
The Fed raises short-term interest rates.

December 1994
The Mexican financial crisis begins after the peso is devalued.

90.45 yen to the dollar*

*As of March 10, 1995.

Sources: Federal Reserve, Bloomberg *Newsweek* (March 20, 1995) pp. 24–25.

♪♪ TABLE 20–1   U.S. Dollar Exchange Rates, New York, October 17, 1996

Foreign Currency	U.S. $ Price	Currency per $
German DM	0.649	1.54 DM
Japanese yen	0.0089	111.8 yen
British pound	1.5845	0.6311£
French franc	0.1920	5.207 Fr.
Canadian dollar	0.7383	1.3544 C$
Mexican peso	0.1285	7.7820 p.

Source: *The Wall Street Journal* (October 17, 1996).

♪♪ ♪♪

Recall from page 313 in Chapter 14 that an EXCHANGE RATE is the price of one currency in terms of another.

Banks earn profits in currency trading by selling foreign currencies at prices slightly higher than the prices they pay for them. In large interbank transactions, the difference between these two rates is typically less than 1 percent. It is usually much higher for smaller transactions. Banks and other currency traders can also earn *speculative* profits if the price of a currency they are holding goes up. They incur losses if it goes down. Millions of dollars are won and lost by currency traders who gamble on the prospect of a change in the value of a currency relative to other currencies. During 1982 and 1983 the value of the Hong Kong dollar fell by about 60 percent relative to the U.S. dollar. Some American bankers who sold their holdings of Hong Kong dollars prior to these exchange rate changes avoided millions of dollars of losses. This episode was also a good illustration of how a wide variety of events can affect exchange rates. The main reason for the drop in the value of the Hong Kong dollar was the widespread uncertainty about the future roles of Great Britain and the People's Republic of China in the administration of the colony. On the basis of treaties established in the 19th century, Britain had administrative control over the colony that expired in 1997. The Chinese took over at that time. This new arrangement is viewed with apprehension by some in the Hong Kong business community.

At times some currencies cannot be traded at all. For example, the Hungarian forint and Soviet ruble were not convertible into Western currencies at all in 1989. As noted in Chapter 14, a nonconvertible currency becomes a terrific barrier to trade, because potential traders are forced to barter rather than use money as a means of exchange. In 1990 McDonald's announced the opening of a hamburger restaurant in Moscow. Trade with the Commonwealth of Independent States was so difficult and complex that this one business deal took over 15 years to plan, and despite a $50-million investment, McDonald's did not anticipate any return at all. The demand for the product was undeniable, however, as Muscovites during the dead of winter waited three to four hours in line, dressed in their finest furs, to fork over a week's pay for a Big Mac, fries, and a shake!

ECONOMIC ANALYSIS OF THE FOREIGN EXCHANGE MARKET

In thinking about foreign exchange markets in economic terms, it is useful to consider the sources of demand for and supply of foreign currencies. We demand foreign currencies so that we can buy items of value in foreign countries. An American firm importing French bicycles needs French francs and buys them with U.S. dollars. Foreigners sell their own currencies when buying items in the United States. A British investor wanting to purchase shares of General Motors stock needs U.S. dollars and pays for them with British pounds.

Building upon these simple ideas, we can apply demand-and-supply analysis to foreign exchange markets. For simplicity, we consider only two countries, the United States and Great Britain. The exchange rate is the U.S. dollar price of British pounds—the number of dollars it takes to buy a pound. We call this exchange rate *e*. The *lower* the exchange rate, the *higher* the value of the dollar in terms of the pound. If the value of the dollar goes up against the pound, we say that the dollar has *appreciated* relative to the pound. If the value goes down, we say that the dollar has *depreciated*.

Changes in the exchange rate *e* affect the quantities of foreign currencies demanded and supplied. In particular, as the dollar price of pounds goes up, the quantity of pounds demanded by Americans goes down. If the cost of pounds goes up, then the prices of British goods—which are specified in terms of pounds—will go up in dollar terms. This makes these items more expensive to American buyers. If Americans demand fewer of these items, the quantity of pounds they demand will also go down. Similarly, as the value of the pound goes up relative to the dollar, American goods become less expensive to the British. If they demand more of these items, and hence require more dollars, the quantity of pounds they supply will also go up. These ideas are summarized in Figure 20–2.

Because the exchange rate is such an important price, it is a potential target for manipulation by the government. Specifically, a central bank can influence exchange rates by buying and selling its own currency in exchange for foreign currencies. This practice is called **central bank intervention** in the foreign exchange market, and every central bank in the world has engaged in it at one time or another.[1] In other words, to drive its currency up in value, the central bank must add to the demand for it; to drive it down, the central bank must add to the supply of it. Central banks can pick from a wide variety of potential intervention strategies, but two important polar cases can be identified. Each can be understood using the supply-demand diagram.

---

[1] Some of the most important central banks in international financial relations are the U.S. Federal Reserve, the Bank of England, the Deutsche Bundesbank of Germany, and the Bank of Japan.

FIGURE 20–2   Demand and Supply of British Pounds

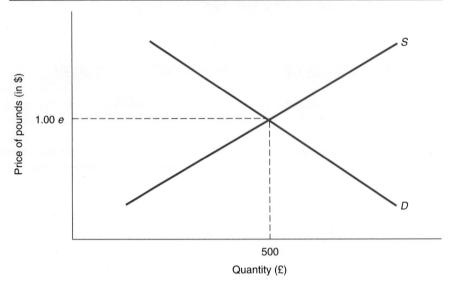

The exchange rate is the dollar price of pounds. The supply of pounds is shown by *S;* the demand for pounds by *D.* The equilibrium exchange rate of $1 is at the intersection of these demand-and-supply curves.

CENTRAL BANK INTERVENTION in the foreign exchange market is intended to influence exchange rates. To drive its currency up in value, a central bank buys it with foreign currencies; to drive it down, a central bank sells it in return for foreign currencies.

Under FLOATING EXCHANGE RATES the central bank allows market supply and demand to determine exchange rates.

A country maintains **floating exchange rates** if its central bank does not try to influence the exchange rate, no matter how much the demand and supply of foreign currencies fluctuate. The quantities of foreign currency demanded and supplied must be in equilibrium. If the supply or the demand curve shifts, the exchange rate will have to float up or down to restore equilibrium. Suppose that there is a sudden decrease in British demand for U.S. stocks and bonds, and that as a result the supply of pounds falls (shifts in) from S_0 to S_1, as shown in Figure 20–3. This causes the dollar to depreciate from exchange rate $1 to $1.25. (*Depreciation* of the dollar—and thus *appreciation* of the pound—entails an *increase* in the dollar price of pounds.)

FIGURE 20–3   Depreciation of the Dollar

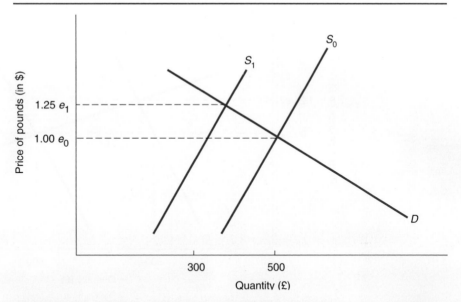

The supply of pounds shifts from S_0 to S_1. Under floating exchange rates, this causes the dollar to depreciate (and the pound to appreciate) from the exchange rate $e = \$1$ to the exchange rate $e = \$1.25$.

A country maintains **fixed exchange rates** if its central bank holds the exchange rate e at some specified level, no matter how much the demand and supply of foreign currencies fluctuate. For instance, e could be set so that $1.00 is equivalent to £1.00. This seems to imply that the foreign exchange market could be out of equilibrium much of the time—if the demand and the supply curves do not intersect at the specified exchange rate. However, if a central bank is committed to holding its currency at the specified exchange rate, it must stand ready to buy or sell at that rate as much foreign currency as the market requires. Thus, the central bank will make up the difference between market demand and market supply of foreign currencies, so that the *total* quantities demanded and supplied are equal. The central banks of some countries on occasion announce a fixed exchange rate, but do not intervene in the foreign exchange market to support it. The emergence of *black markets* for foreign currencies in those countries is the inevitable result.

Under FIXED EXCHANGE RATES the central bank holds the value of the currency constant against some foreign currency or currencies.

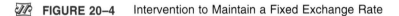

FIGURE 20–4   Intervention to Maintain a Fixed Exchange Rate

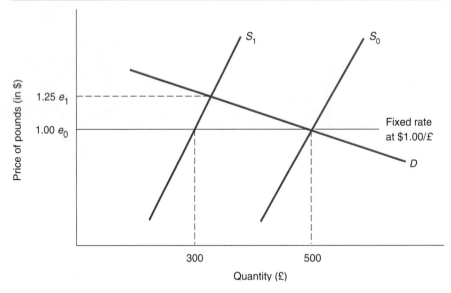

The supply of pounds shifts from S_0 to S_1. To support the dollar at the fixed exchange rate of $1, the Fed must sell the amount of 200£.

The foreign currencies that a central bank keeps on hand for intervention are called its *foreign currency reserves.* If the central bank holds the value of its currency higher than is necessary for equilibrium, the currency is *overvalued.* If its value is held lower than is necessary for equilibrium, it is *undervalued.* These ideas are illustrated in Figure 20–4. Suppose that the initial equilibrium exchange rate is $e = \$1$, but that there is the same decline in the supply of pounds as in Figure 20–3. If the exchange rate is allowed to move to its new equilibrium level, it will go from $1 to $1.25. However, the Fed can hold the value of the dollar at the now overvalued level of $1 per pound by buying dollars at $1£. By adding to the supply of pounds, and adding to the demand for dollars, the Fed supports the value of the dollar relative to the pound. However, there is one drawback: The Fed, like any central bank, may have only a limited amount of foreign currency in reserve, and it can actually run out if it is forced to support the dollar too long![2]

In summary, any event that causes the net demand or supply of foreign currencies to change has an effect under both fixed and floating exchange rates. That event causes our currency to *depreciate* under floating exchange rates. It forces our central bank to sell foreign currency reserves (to prevent depreciation of our currency) under fixed exchange rates. Similarly, that event causes our currency to *appreciate* under

---

[2]A central bank may sometimes borrow foreign currencies from other central banks in order to have enough reserves on hand to support the value of its currency.

floating exchange rates and forces our central bank to buy foreign currency reserves (to prevent appreciation of our currency) under fixed exchange rates.

THE BALANCE OF PAYMENTS

We now need to look more closely at the kinds of transactions that require foreign currencies. Every year Americans conduct an almost endless variety of economic transactions with foreigners:

- American citrus growers sell oranges and grapefruits in Canada.
- German investors buy Treasury bills from the U.S. government.
- American tourists buy dinners at restaurants in Mexico City.
- Japanese automobile companies build plants in the United States.
- McDonald's opens a restaurant in Moscow.

A statistical record of all these transactions is maintained by the government. The record is called the **balance of payments**. Each of the transactions listed above is included in our balance of payments. To understand how balance-of-payments accounts work, first notice that there are two sides to every transaction: Someone always gives up one item of value in exchange for some other item of value. Suppose that American automobile dealers import $1 million worth of cars made by Honda in Japan. Honda provides a shipment of automobiles worth $1 million, but in return is given $1 million by the dealers. Any entry in our balance of payments that involves the sending of some item of value to another country is entered as a *credit,* with a plus (+) sign. Paying the $1 million to Honda generates a $1-million credit in our accounts. Any entry that involves the receiving of some item of value from another country is entered as a *debit,* with a minus (−) sign. Receiving the $1 million worth of cars generates a $1-million debit in our accounts.

The BALANCE OF PAYMENTS is a record of all the transactions between a country and the rest of the world during a given year.

Every transaction covered in the balance of payments involves a credit and a debit of exactly the same amount. Moreover, the balance-of-payments accounts always record both sides of every transaction. Thus the accounts necessarily sum to zero! But we always seem to hear about a problem with the U.S. balance of payments. Why the big fuss if the accounts always add up to zero?

The answer is that important *categories* within the accounts *can* be out of balance. The two basic categories in the balance of payments are the **current account** and the **capital account.**

The CURRENT ACCOUNT includes all transactions that either contribute to national income or involve the spending of national income.

The CAPITAL ACCOUNT covers international trade in real and financial *assets.* These include corporate stocks and bonds, government securities, bank deposits, currencies, real estate, and productive capital.

If either of these accounts has a negative total *(a net debit),* we say that it is in *deficit.* If it has a positive total *(a net credit),* we say it is in *surplus.* In principle, these two accounts must sum to zero: The current account surplus must equal the capital account deficit. However, to account for errors and omissions in the data, a third category called *statistical discrepancy* is included. It is calculated as the negative of the sum of the current and capital accounts. This guarantees that all three will sum to zero. Table 20–2 shows the details of these categories of the U.S. balance-of-payments accounts for 1995.

The Current Account

Table 20–2 identifies four major categories in the current account and shows that the United States had a current account deficit of 148.2 billion in 1995. This deficit reflected an even larger deficit in the most important category within the current account, the **merchandise trade balance.** Included in this category are all traded goods— manufactured items, agricultural commodities, chemicals—and all other

TABLE 20–2   U.S. Balance of Payments, 1995 (in $1 billions)

1. Current account:			−148.2
Merchandise trade balance		−173.5	
Merchandise exports	575.9		
Merchandise imports	−749.4		
Net military transactions		3.6	
Net income from services and investments		56.8	
Net private and official transfers	−35.1		
2. Capital account:			116.6
U.S. holdings of foreign assets, increase (−)		−307.9	
Foreign holdings of U.S. assets, increase (+)		424.5	
3. Statistical discrepancy			−31.6
Sum of items 1, 2, and 3			00.0

Source: *Economic Indicators* (October 1996).

physically tangible products. Table 20–2 includes the two sides of this balance— *merchandise exports* and *merchandise imports.*

The merchandise trade balance is *the* trade balance discussed by the press. It is important because it reflects in a very broad sense our ability to produce goods that are competitive in world markets. The large and growing U.S. merchandise trade deficits in recent years—$122.1 billion in 1985, $145 billion in 1986, $109 billion in 1990, and $173.5 billion in 1995—are thus serious cause for concern.

Net military transactions are similar to merchandise trade, but are kept separate because military sales and purchases have less to do with economic conditions and more to do with U.S. foreign policy decisions.

Net income from services and investments reflects American interest, dividend, and profit income from investments abroad, less foreign income from investments in the United States. It includes the foreign profits of U.S. multinational corporations, less the U.S. profits of multinational corporations based abroad. It also reflects the incomes from services performed abroad by Americans, less service incomes earned by foreigners in the United States. These incomes include wages, fees, and royalties, as well as payments for insurance, freight, banking, travel, communications, and other services.

Net private and official transfers are the net payments of pensions, grants, and gifts between the residents or governments of the United States and other countries. The fact that net transfers were negative in 1994 means that transfers from the United States to foreigners exceeded transfers from foreigners to the United States.

The Capital Account

Table 20–2 divides the capital account into two categories— changes in foreign assets held by U.S. citizens and changes in U.S. assets held by foreigners. Increases in *U.S. holdings of foreign assets* generate debits (minuses) in the account, because Americans are buying items of value from abroad. Similarly, increases in *foreign holdings of U.S. assets* generate credits (pluses) in the account. Table 20–2 shows a U.S. capital account surplus of $116.6 billion in 1995. Americans acquired $307.9 billion worth of assets abroad, whereas foreigners acquired $424.5 billion worth of assets in the United States.

Many capital account items are linked to current account items. Recall the U.S. automobile dealers who import $1 million worth of cars made by Honda. Suppose they pay for the shipment with checks drawn on their bank accounts. This creates a $1-million debit in the U.S. current account: The dealers have acquired $1 million worth of cars from abroad. It also creates a $1-million credit in the U.S. capital account: Honda has acquired $1 million from the United States. Honda can deposit the checks in its own U.S. bank account.

Now suppose that Honda buys $1 million worth of U.S. Treasury bills using these dollars. In this case, there is no additional effect on the U.S. capital account. Honda holds more U.S. Treasury bills, but its U.S. dollar bank deposits have gone down by an identical amount.

Foreign investments by multinational corporations in plants and equipment are included in the capital account. International loan transactions and central bank intervention in foreign exchange markets are included as well. However, profits on foreign investments and interest on foreign loans are part of national income, and thus appear in the current account.

Statistical Discrepancy

Table 20–2 shows that *statistical discrepancy,* the sum of the capital and current accounts, was −$31.6 billion in 1995. This means that financial flows between countries of $31.6 billion are not captured in the official statistics. What caused these enormous unexplained financial flows? This is more expenditure than the GDPs of many countries! How could there possibly be so much inaccurate or omitted data?

Some potential answers were supplied by *The Wall Street Journal.* It reported that the statistical discrepancy probably reflected a variety of factors, including "political unrest, crime, sloppy paper work, and deception among bankers."[3] People from unstable countries may secretly try to get their funds out of their countries and into the United States. None of their secret transactions is included in the accounts. Imports brought in by smugglers, whether drugs or other illegal products, are also usually omitted from the accounts.

The Link between the Current and the Capital Accounts

The balance of payments always sums to zero, but the current account and the capital account each can be in surplus or deficit. Moreover, surpluses or deficits in these accounts can have very important implications for an economy. To understand this, we start with the capital account.

Investors who buy assets of another country—who invest their funds in that country—acquire *claims* on the future income of that country. Their claims on its future income become a part of their wealth. A Japanese firm that holds U.S. Treasury bills has a claim on the U.S. government. In the future, the government will have to borrow more funds, or collect more taxes, to pay the interest and repay the principal on this borrowing from the Japanese firm. Thus, in the national balance-of-payments account, our capital account deficit shows the claims we have acquired on foreigners this year, less the claims foreigners have acquired on us. In a very general way, it simply shows the net amount we have loaned to foreigners this year.

Because the current and capital accounts sum to zero, the current account surplus must equal the capital account deficit. (This would be the case in the published accounts if there were not errors and omissions in the data.) In other words, if we in

---

[3]Richard F. Janssen, " 'Discrepancy' in the Balance of Payments Grows and Grows, but Remains a Puzzle," *The Wall Street Journal* (July 29, 1980).

the United States earn more from our exports of goods and services than we spend on imports of goods and services (a current account surplus), we must be lending the difference to foreigners (a capital account deficit). This is the only way they could actually pay for all their imports from us. On the other hand, if we run a current account deficit, we must be running a capital account surplus. Because our exports are insufficient to pay for all our imports, we must be borrowing from foreigners to make up the difference.

The United States has been doing just that—borrowing from foreigners at unprecedented rates to finance its current account deficits—over the past 16 years. We can find out how much borrowing simply by adding up the current account deficits. If we start in 1989, we have $103.8 billion in 1989, $92.7 billion in 1990, $7.4 billion in 1991, $61.5 billion in 1992, $99.9 billion in 1993, $148.4 billion in 1994, and $148.2 billion in 1995. This is the same way that countries such as Mexico, Brazil, and Poland got into their foreign debt problems—by running current account deficits for many consecutive years.

The United States is enjoying lots of foreign goods and services right now, in exchange for which foreigners are acquiring claims on our future income. Is this a serious problem for our economy? Not *necessarily.* A current account deficit can be beneficial if it enables a country to purchase and install productive capital that will generate income in the future. However, if the deficits are simply being used to permit levels of spending that cannot be sustained over the long run, then the country may be in trouble. Deficits caused mostly by increases in consumption and military spending—neither of which adds to our productive capacity—can be dangerous to our economy in the long run.

DETERMINANTS OF DEMAND AND SUPPLY OF FOREIGN CURRENCIES

People demand foreign currencies in order to buy goods, services, or assets abroad. Foreigners supply their currencies in order to purchase our goods, services, and assets. Thus, there is a link between the balance of payments and the foreign exchange market. Any item that enters the accounts as a credit generates a *supply* of foreign currency; any item that enters the accounts as a debit generates a *demand* for foreign currency. In addition, total credits equal total debits in the accounts, and total quantities of foreign currency demanded and supplied must be equal. But what factors determine the demand and supply of foreign currencies?

Interest Rates

Interest rates influence the demand for and supply of foreign currencies through their effects on capital account transactions. Suppose that interest rates rise in our country, but not in other countries. This means there is now a higher rate of return on bonds and other assets in our country. Financial investors worldwide will want to move their funds into assets in our country. This increases the demand for our currency and decreases the demand for other currencies. Our currency appreciates as a result.

Macroeconomic policies in the United States from 1979 to 1982 provide a classic example of the importance of interest rates. Contractionary monetary policy was used to bring down inflation, but resulted in a deep recession. Combined with expansionary fiscal policy, this drove interest rates to historic highs. Because interest rates were persistently higher in the United States than abroad, investors shifted their funds into the United States to enjoy the higher rates of return. The resulting increase in the demand for dollars put strong upward pressure on the value of the dollar relative to other currencies, such as the German DM and the British pound, and forced up foreign interest rates as well. The higher foreign interest rates worsened the recession around the world. The episode seemed to confirm an old adage: "When the United States sneezes, Europe catches pneumonia."

In the 1990s, Japan began to suffer its own monetary difficulties and was seen also to be very sensitive to economic actions in the United States. Such a large part of Japanese exports are to the United States that any slowdown in the United States can cause serious financial repercussions in Japan. Coupled with hard protectionist trade bargaining by U.S. negotiators, the Japanese, like the Europeans, began to recognize the power U.S. economic forces could have on their own economic well-being.

National Incomes

The national incomes of countries around the world can affect the supply of and demand for foreign currencies through the current account. If national income rises in the United States because of expansionary monetary or fiscal policies, our consumption of all goods and services—domestic and foreign—will increase. This in turn increases our demand for the foreign currencies we need to pay for imports. Likewise, if national incomes rise abroad, foreign demand for our goods and services will increase. This increases the supply of foreign currencies.

Because levels of national income are so closely related to demands for goods and services, changes in national incomes will have important effects on merchandise trade balances and current account balances. In 1992 and 1993, the United States recovered from recession much more quickly than did other countries. As a result, U.S. demand for imports grew faster than foreign demand for U.S. exports, and the U.S. trade balance and current account were pushed further into deficit. At the same time, the increased U.S. demand for foreign products was helping other countries to recover from the recession.

Price Levels

Price-level changes in various countries also influence the demand for and supply of foreign currencies through the current account. If inflation is much higher in one country than in others, then over time the goods and services produced by that country will become less and less competitive. Consumers around the world will tend to shift away from its products and to search for cheaper substitutes. Eventually, its currency will be forced to depreciate. Under floating exchange rates, market forces accomplish this directly. Under fixed exchange rates, a conscious policy decision to change the exchange rate is needed. In either case, the exchange rate is the great equalizer. If persistent wage and price inflation in a country makes its products more and more expensive, depreciation of its currency can bring its costs back into line with those in other countries.

On the other hand, suppose that inflation rates are not very different, but that our currency appreciates for some other reason. The result is that our products become less competitive. In the early 1980s this was a problem for the United States. The appreciation of the dollar caused by high U.S. interest rates made U.S. products less competitive at home and abroad. The merchandise trade deficit and the current account deficit worsened. Unemployment in the United States was temporarily higher than it would have been otherwise. At the same time, appreciation of the dollar made U.S. consumers better off, because it made foreign goods and services less expensive. Japanese televisions, French wines, Brazilian coffee, and German automobiles were all cheaper than they would have been otherwise.

This episode also provides some further insights into the effects of federal budget deficits on the economy. Recall from Chapter 13 that one of the potential effects of federal deficits is the crowding out of private capital formation. In the early 1980s this did not seem to be a serious problem in the United States, despite the high interest rates. Our enormous capital account surpluses covered the borrowing needs of both the federal government and private corporations. However, by creating a large demand for dollars, these inflows of foreign funds drove up the value of the dollar. U.S. farmers, automobile manufacturers, and even powerful corporations such as Caterpillar were seriously hurt by the high dollar. Their products were priced out of markets at home and abroad! The long slide of the dollar in the late 1980s and early 1990s actually helped U.S. exporters. Thus, federal budget deficits can cause serious dislocations within the economy, even if private domestic investment is not directly affected.

INTERNATIONAL MONETARY SYSTEMS

There have been several different international monetary arrangements over the past century. None has been marked by either purely fixed exchange rates or purely floating exchange rates. Rather, our international monetary systems have been compromises of various sorts between the two extremes.

The Bretton Woods System

From 1946 to 1973, all countries outside the Communist bloc participated in the **Bretton Woods international monetary system.** The arrangement was established at a conference at Bretton Woods, New Hampshire, in June 1944. Based on past experience, its founders had definite ideas about the kind of system they wanted to build. Under the *international gold standard* from 1880 to 1913, the values of all major currencies had been fixed in terms of gold. This provided financial stability, but was too inflexible over the long run. One problem was that expansion of money supplies around the world depended upon new discoveries of gold rather than on intentional stabilization policies. On the other hand, exchange rates floated during the 1920s and the 1930s. This was a time of financial chaos, particularly in Europe. Many observers blamed the floating rates for the financial crises of the era.

The system created at Bretton Woods was intended to provide the stability and discipline of a gold standard, but also some of the flexibility of floating exchange rates. The dollar was at the center of the system; it was the *key currency:*

- The value of the dollar was fixed in terms of gold. Every other country held its currency at a fixed exchange rate against the dollar. These exchange rates could be adjusted if necessary.

It is in this sense that Bretton Woods was called an *adjustable-peg* system. If a country lost (or gained) too much foreign currency in an effort to hold its exchange rate fixed, it would be permitted to change the value of its currency against the dollar and, thus, against all other currencies.

- To maintain confidence in the value of the dollar, the U.S. Treasury stood ready to exchange gold for dollars on request.

TOOL KIT

BUYING IN FOREIGN CURRENCIES

Your big trip abroad is coming up, and you want to get the most for your money. When and where should you exchange your U.S. dollars for the currencies of the countries you will be traveling in?

One simple rule is that it is best to keep most of your funds in dollars until you actually need foreign currency. First, because you always pay to convert from one currency to another, you do not want to convert much more than you will actually use. Second, banks abroad tend to offer better exchange rates than do banks in the United States. Moreover, the larger banks in major financial centers tend to offer the best exchange rates because they have to compete with each other. A tiny hotel

high in the Italian Alps will probably not give a very good exchange rate. Of course, you will need to hold some foreign currency to cover your minor daily expenses. Airports are convenient places to buy small amounts of local currency, though their exchange rates are not always the best.

Corporate travel managers suggest that your best bet is actually to use a credit card for your big expenses abroad. Credit cards are safer than cash, and the major ones are accepted far from the beaten path. More important, the price is hard to beat. None of the major cards charge more than 1 percent above the wholesale exchange rate on their currency conversions. In contrast, banks

If investors knew they could get gold for their dollars at any time, they would not be reluctant to hold dollars.

- The dollar became the most important *medium of exchange* in international transactions.

  It was held by central banks as their main reserve currency and was used in almost all private transactions.

- The **International Monetary Fund (IMF)** was established as an overseer for the exchange rate system and international monetary relations.

  Countries trying to support the values of their currencies could borrow reserves from the IMF. If they wanted to adjust their exchange rates against the dollar, they had to get permission from the IMF first.

  The system looked good on paper, but it had several flaws in practice. One was that countries were usually reluctant to make the necessary adjustments to their exchange rates. Governments that were losing foreign currency reserves viewed depreciation of their currencies as a serious political liability, an admission of defeat in economic policy. (There is a strong statistical relationship between depreciation and changes of government—both peaceful and violent—in developing countries.) Depreciation also added to the pressure for inflation—because it raised the prices of imported goods and services. On the other hand, countries that were acquiring

---

typically charge 3 percent or more above wholesale rates, and traveler's checks usually cost an additional 1 percent. The only drawback to using a credit card is that the exchange rate on a purchase is not determined until the bill is processed, which can take several days or more. If foreign exchange markets are volatile during that period, the exchange rate could turn against you, and you might end up paying more than you had anticipated.

Whether you use credit cards or cash, you have some discretion in deciding when to purchase your foreign currency, or even when to travel. If you try to time your transactions to take advantage of exchange rate changes, you are in effect speculating in the foreign exchange market. If you think the dollar will go up in value in the near future, it would be better to hold your dollars as long as you can; if you think the dollar will be going down, buy the foreign currency now.

So, is the dollar going up or down? Well, there is good news and bad news. The good news is that you can get a rough indication of how a major currency is expected to perform against the dollar by looking at its *forward* exchange rate—the price that currency traders set now for delivery of that currency in one month, two months, or longer. If the forward price of a currency is lower than its current price, it is a good bet that it will fall in value in the future.

The bad news is that it is very difficult to do much better than the forward rate. Exchange rate advisory services on Wall Street try to forecast whether future exchange rates will be higher or lower than the current forward rates. Over a one-month horizon, the very best of these firms get the right answer only about 50 percent of the time. The good news for the rest of us is that, by flipping a coin to make our forecasts, we can do about as well as the best financial analysts in the country.

foreign currency reserves were even less inclined to make exchange rate adjust-ments. They did not face the grim discipline of running out of foreign currency reserves. Appreciation also made their products less competitive, which would hurt employment and profits in important industries.

The problems of the Bretton Woods system that actually led to its downfall were related to the U.S. dollar. Because the dollar was at the center of the exchange rate system, the United States was informally obligated not to change its value against gold or other currencies. However, inflation was higher in the United States than in many other industrial countries in the late 1960s and early 1970s. This made U.S. goods and services less and less competitive. The current account of the U.S. balance of payments deteriorated. Private investors lost confidence in the dollar, and the U.S. Treasury lost huge amounts of gold as foreigners traded in their dollars. In 1971 President Richard M. Nixon decided to renounce formally our obligation to provide gold on demand. To support the value of the dollar, foreign central banks had to buy massive amounts of dollars. After two more turbulent years, in 1973 the major economies all switched to a form of floating exchange rates.

Managed Floating

Many observers argue that the shift to floating exchange rates was inevitable. The adjustable-peg system was just not flexible enough to handle the stresses in the world economy in the early 1970s, such as the oil price shocks and U.S. inflation. On the other hand, although floating exchange rates would adjust automatically to these problems, they had the disadvantage of being potentially volatile, creating uncer-tainty in international trade and thus acting as a hindrance to it. For these reasons, most countries were not willing to let their currencies float freely at all times. The arrangement that emerged can thus be best viewed as **managed floating.** All central banks have intervened in foreign exchange markets to stabilize exchange rates from time to time. The larger countries have typically not tried to hold their exchange rates at rigidly set levels. An important exception was the group of countries forming the European Monetary System (EMS). From the early 1970s to the mid-1980s, these countries tried to float as a bloc against the U.S. dollar. By 1992 Western European countries had hoped to adopt a fully integrated economic system with a unified currency arrangement and the removal of almost all internal barriers to trade. Prob-lems arose, however, because some Eastern European nations now wanted to be in on the action and because Germany had financial problems trying to integrate the East into the West.

Many smaller countries continue to peg their currencies to the dollar, the deutsche mark, or the yen. Exchange rate policies have also varied within certain countries over time. In the United States, the Carter administration intervened in foreign exchange markets quite often. The Reagan and Bush administrations were, on the other hand, more committed to letting market forces determine exchange rates in all but the most volatile circumstances. President Bill Clinton's team intervened in exchange rate markets with moral suasion as well as transactions policy. Mexico tried to manipulate the peso and had to devalue it in 1995, causing financial shocks throughout emerging countries.

One major benefit of the switch to floating rates in the early 1970s was that it allowed U.S. goods and services to become more competitive. Although the dollar was officially lowered in value against other currencies in 1971 and 1973, it continued to depreciate over the next decade. In fact, the rate of depreciation more than compensated for higher inflation in the United States. This was reflected for a time in improved U.S. current accounts. However, largely because of the shift in our monetary-fiscal policy mix from late 1979 on, the dollar appreciated markedly, wiping out those competitive gains. U.S. farmers and manufacturers were hard-hit. In 1986–1987, the dollar reversed course and began to fall relative to many foreign currencies. The dollar continued its slide through the mid-1990s. Wide fluctuations in exchange rates accompany significant shifts in trade and investment flows. The final outcome depends on the course of the federal budget deficits and monetary policies, as well as on foreign economic policies and performances.

CHAPTER REVIEW

A country can maintain fixed exchange rates, floating exchange rates, or some kind of compromise arrangement. If it wants to hold its exchange rate fixed, its central bank must be prepared to buy or sell foreign currencies to support that exchange rate unless it accepts a nonconvertible currency. If it wants to let the exchange rate float, it lets day-to-day market supply-and-demand conditions determine the value of its currency.

The balance of payments is a record of all transactions between a country and the rest of the world in a given year. The current account includes all transactions related to the earning or spending of national income. The capital account covers international trade in assets. By definition, the balance of payments sums to zero. This implies that the current account deficit must equal the capital account surplus. If our imports of goods and services exceed our exports, we must borrow from other countries to finance that deficit.

The foreign exchange market is influenced by factors that affect the demand-and-supply of goods, services, and assets. Of particular importance are interest rates, which if high enough can draw funds into a country and thus drive up the value of its currency. Two other factors—national income levels and national price levels—are linked to foreign exchange markets through their effects on demands and supplies of goods and services.

In the period since World War II, there have been two major international monetary arrangements: the Bretton Woods system from 1946 to 1973 and managed floating from 1973 to the present. Under Bretton Woods, exchange rates were fixed but could be adjusted if central banks were losing or gaining too much foreign currency. The major economies switched to managed floating exchange rates in 1973 because of new stresses in the world economy and because of some of the inherent difficulties in the Bretton Woods system.

✿ MULTIPLE-CHOICE SELF-TEST ✿✿✿✿✿✿✿✿✿✿✿✿✿✿✿✿

1. Exchange rates determined by the laws of supply and demand are called:
   a. Managed exchange rates.
   b. Floating exchange rates.
   c. Legal exchange rates.
   d. Fixed exchange rates.

2. Which one of the following would appear in the current account of the U.S. balance of payments?
   a. A Japanese investor buys some U.S. Treasury bills.
   b. *The New York Times* buys newsprint from a Canadian paper company.
   c. Brazil pays back part of its debt to some U.S. banks.
   d. The Federal Reserve sells dollars to a European central bank.

3. If interest rates in the United States and Great Britain are initially at 5 percent, but U.S. interest rates rise to 10 percent, we should expect that:
   a. There would be no significant change in exchange rates.
   b. The British pound and the dollar would both fall in value against gold.
   c. The dollar would depreciate against the British pound.
   d. The dollar would appreciate against the British pound.

4. In the late 1960s and early 1970s, inflation in the United States as compared to other industrial countries:
   a. Was higher, which caused the U.S. current account to deteriorate.
   b. Was lower, which caused the U.S. current account to improve.
   c. Was higher, but the dollar depreciated at an even faster rate.
   d. Was lower, but the dollar appreciated at an even faster rate.

5. A surplus in the capital account:
   a. Must be matched by the surplus in the current account, except for any statistical discrepancy.
   b. Is the usual state of the U.S. balance of payments.
   c. Suggests a trade imbalance of exports exceeding imports.
   d. Means, in effect, that Americans have been borrowing from foreigners in order to finance a high level of imports.

✿ STUDY QUESTIONS

1. Answer the following questions by considering the market for British pounds in the United States.
   a. There is a recession in Great Britain. Will the demand or the supply curve for pounds shift? In or out?

b. If there is no central bank intervention, will this cause the dollar to appreciate or to depreciate? Draw a supply-demand diagram of the foreign exchange market to show your result.

c. Suppose that the Fed wants to hold the exchange rate between the dollar and the pound fixed at its initial value, despite the British recession. Will the Fed have to buy or sell pounds? Explain.

2. Mexico had current account deficits of $3.2 billion in 1978, $5.5 billion in 1979, $8.2 billion in 1980, and $13.9 billion in 1981. Using this information, calculate how much the foreign indebtedness of the country increased over those four years. Explain your answer.

3. From 1990 to 1994, Mexican inflation averaged 12 percent per year. Over the same period, U.S. inflation averaged 3 percent per year. The Mexican government held the peso virtually fixed in value against the dollar during that period. Could this policy have contributed to the current account problems Mexico had? Explain.

💹 PROBLEM

Draw a demand-supply graph of the market for dollars (with the price of dollars expressed in Japanese yen) for each of the following events. Show the change in the equilibrium price and quantity of dollars traded because of each event.

1. Income grows fast in Japan, affecting Japanese demand for imported goods.

2. Interest rates in the United States fall, whereas they remain unchanged in Japan.

3. The United States experiences a sharp increase in inflation.

APPENDIX

Answers to Multiple-Choice Self-Tests and Problems

CHAPTER 1

Multiple-Choice Self-Test

1. *d.*
2. *a.*
3. *a.*
4. *b.*
5. *a.*

Problem

Jack's advice ignores the opportunity cost of the machinery. If Luis and Elena can sell the machinery, they may well be able to earn a better return by investing the proceeds in something else. Whether they own the machinery outright or borrowed to buy it, they should be equally concerned with whether or not their investment in the machinery will earn a good return. The opportunity cost of the funds they could get by selling the machinery is the same either way.

CHAPTER 2

Multiple-Choice Self-Test

1. *d.*
2. *b.*
3. *a.*
4. *c.*
5. *d.*

Problems

1. The new choice can involve both more food and more manufactured goods. If you have drawn your two production possibility curves correctly, you can see that there are many points on the new curve (after the increase in food production) that give Kenya both more manufactured goods and more food. The only point that stays the same is the point on the axis at which all productive resources are dedicated to manufactured goods.

2. There are many policy options: One is to let the market price rise enough to ration the more limited supply. Choosing a nonprice means of rationing discourages suppliers from finding new sources.

CHAPTER 3

Multiple-Choice Self-Test

1. *c.*
2. *b.*
3. *d.*
4. *c.*
5. *d.*

Problem

a. The elasticity of demand for bus trips is

$$(2,000/10,000)/(25/75) = 0.6$$

b. Since demand is inelastic (percent increase in price is less than percent decline in quantity), total revenue will increase.

c. Total revenue with $0.75 fare: $7,500.
Total revenue with $1 fare: $8,000.
The fare increases may not resolve the deficit problem as well as city officials may have hoped because the fare hike does reduce the number of trips. Therefore, revenue does not rise by 33 percent, the amount of the fare increase.

CHAPTER 4

Multiple-Choice Self-Test

1. *d.*
2. *b.*
3. *b.*

4. *c.*

5. *a.*

Problem

b.   Initial equilibrium is 600 houses at a price of $55,000.

c.   During recession, equilibrium is 500 houses at $50,000.

CHAPTER 5

Multiple-Choice Self-Test

1. *b.*

2. *b.*

3. *d.*

4. *c.*

5. *c.*

Problems

b.   Equilibrium price is $10,000; quantity is 8 tons.

c.   7 tons demanded; 10 tons produced; surplus, 3 tons.

d.   3 tons; $36,000.

e.   Net loss, $60,000.

f.   Taxpayers prefer option *d*; tobacco consumers prefer *e*.

CHAPTER 6

Multiple-Choice Self-Test

1. *c.*

2. *d.*

3. *b.*

4. *a.*

Problem

a.   Fixed cost stays at $500. The rest of the blanks should be:

Total cost	$800	$1,000	$1,200	$1,500	$1,900	$2,400
Marginal cost		200	200	300	400	500

At price $300, the firm should produce 4 units; at price $350, 4 units; at price $400, 5 units.

CHAPTER 7

Multiple-Choice Self-Test

1. *a.*
2. *c.*
3. *a.*
4. *c.*
5. *d.*

Problems

Total Revenue	Marginal Revenue	MR – MC
$ 90,000	$ 90,000	
160,000	70,000	$ 30,000
210,000	50,000	0
240,000	30,000	–20,000
250,000	10,000	–40,000
240,000	–10,000	–65,000
210,000	–30,000	–90,000

b.   Best output is 300 tons.

CHAPTER 8

Multiple-Choice Self-Test

1. *a.*
2. *c.*
3. *c.*
4. *d.*
5. *d.*

Problems

a.   Graph should show an increase in demand.
b.   Graph should show a decrease in supply.
c.   Graph should show a decrease in demand.
d.   Graph should show an increase in supply.

CHAPTER 9

Multiple-Choice Self-Test

1. *b.*
2. *b.*
3. *c.*
4. *a.*
5. *a.*

Problems

a.   Initially, 8 tons will be produced.
b.   Supply curve should shift up by $10,000.
c.   Additional cost will now be $7,500 per ton.
d.   Graph will give approximate answer. Exact answer is 7.25 tons at $63,750 per ton.

CHAPTER 10

Multiple-Choice Self-Test

1. *b.*
2. *c.*
3. *d.*
4. *b.*
5. *d.*

Problems

a.   The new production table should include the following figures: India, 0 tons corn, 110 tons rice; China, 75 tons corn, 195 tons rice; total, 75 tons corn, 305 tons rice.
b.   Each country's total consumption with trade is greater than it was able to produce and consume without trade. The production table is the same as the specialized production table for *a*, but consumption after trade would be India, 20 tons corn, 105 tons rice; China, 55 tons corn, 200 tons rice; total, 75 tons corn, 305 tons rice.

CHAPTER 11

Multiple-Choice Self-Test

1. *a.*
2. *d.*

3. *c.*
4. *b.*
5. *a.*
6. *b.*
7. *c.*
8. *d.*

Problem

If the CPI and your wages go up by 10 percent, you might gain a little. However, your answer may well depend on whether you buy the same bundle of goods as in the CPI, or whether your bundle has more or less of the goods that rose the most in price. If the wage increase pushed you into a higher tax bracket, then you are likelier to be a little worse off because of the inflation.

CHAPTER 12

Multiple-Choice Self-Test

1. *a.*
2. *a.*
3. *c.*
4. *d.*
5. *b.*
6. *c.*

Problem

Your diagram should look like Figure 12–5 in the text, with the following effects on each of the flows:

1. Withdrawal for personal savings declines.
2. A larger fraction of household income is spent on consumption.
3. Firms face higher demand, so they hire more productive resources and pay more income to households.
4. With higher income, households increase both personal savings and consumption expenditures.
5. This causes another round of increases in demand (3) and income (4). Increasing consumption leading to increasing production continues until equilibrium is reestablished.

CHAPTER 13

Multiple-Choice Self-Test

1. *b.*
2. *a.*
3. *c.*
4. *a.*
5. *c.*
6. *a.*
7. *d.*

Problem

a. The marginal tax rates are 15, 28, 33, and 28 percent.
b. Income, $20,000; total tax, $3,188.50; average tax rate, 15.94 percent.
    Income, $50,000; total tax, $11,843.50; average tax rate, 23.69 percent.
    Income, $100,000; total tax, $28,000; average tax rate, 28 percent.

CHAPTER 14

Multiple-Choice Self-Test

1. *c.*
2. *e.*
3. *c.*
4. *a.*
5. *d.*
6. *b.*
7. *b.*

Problem

1. You cannot tell exactly what the expected real rate of interest was unless you assume that investor's expectations of inflation agreed with the Council of Economic Advisers. You cannot tell the realized real rate of interest unless you know the realized rate of inflation. However if the CEA forecast is the expected rate, then the expected real return is 5.9% which is 10% minus 4.1%.
2. The 1996 expected real rate is $r - \pi^e = 5.4 - 3.3 = 2.1\%$. This is smaller than the 1990 rate, from problem 1, of 5.9%. Thus, the expected cost of capital had fallen and investment should rise.

CHAPTER 15

Multiple-Choice Self-Test

1. *d.*
2. *a.*
3. *a.*
4. *c.*
5. *c.*
6. *c.*

Problem

a. The sale of $25 million in securities reduces bank reserves by $25 million. That $25 million in reserves backed up $500 million in deposits ($25 nlillion/0.05), so the money supply is reduced by $500 million.

b. The graph should look like Figure 15–3 (A Fed Open-Market Purchase of U.S. Securities) except that the direction of shift of the money supply is reversed: the new equilibrium will be at a smaller money supply and higher interest rate.

c. Reducing reserves in the banking system raises interest rates and reduces the ability of firms to borrow funds for investment. The circular flow diagram should look like Figure 15–5 (The Circular Flow without Government but with Banking).

1. Flow of reserves from Fed to banks decreases.
2. Flow of borrowing by firms decreases.
3. Flow of investment decreases.
4. Flow of income (from firms to households) decreases.
5. Flows of consumption and savings decrease. Income, consumption, and savings continue to decrease until new equilibrium is reached.

CHAPTER 16

Multiple-Choice Self-Test

1. *a.*
2. *c.*
3. *b.*
4. *a.*
5. *c.*
6. *d.*

Problem

$MV = PQ$. The effect of an increase in the money supply will depend on the size of V, the velocity of circulation of money. If V does not change, then the new PQ should be $220 billion. ($PQ$ was $200 billion when M was $20 billion, so V was 10.) How the increase is divided between P and Q will depend on the state of the economy at the time when the change in money supply begins to have its effect. Because the time lag of the effect is unpredictable, somewhere between six months and two years, the effect on prices versus real output is unpredictable.

b.   Keynesians would say about the same thing, except that they would include the possibility that a money expansion would have little effect at all. They would suggest that the change would be mostly in output as long as there was unemployment in the economy and in prices only if the economy were already at full employment. The third possibility that Keynesians see is that neither P nor Q would change much, if the economy were in a contractionary period. Rather, V would fall. New reserves would not be turned into an expansion of the money supply, and investment would not increase because businesses don't invest as much in a period of declining income.

b.   An answer to this problem will differ for activist Keynesians and monetarists than for supply siders or new classical macroeconomists.

Activists tend to recommend counter-cyclical stabilization policies. Expansionary fiscal policy entails some combination of expenditure increases and tax cuts. Expansionary monetary policy calls for expansion also—raise the money supply via open market operations to reduce interest rates and thus raise investment expenditure and consumer demand for durable goods and housing.

Supply siders may focus on structural measures to improve incentives for labor market participation and skill development and for tax incentives to foster, as the margin, savings and investment.

CHAPTER 17

Multiple-Choice Self-Test

1.   *c.*
2.   *a.*
3.   *b.*
4.   *d.*
5.   *a.*

Problem

a.   Structural, involuntary.
b.   Frictional.

Structural.
d. Cyclical, voluntary.
e. Cyclical, involuntary.

CHAPTER 18

Multiple-Choice Self-Test

1. *b.*
2. *c.*
3. *b.*
4. *d.*
5. *c.*
6. *a.*

Problem

a. $Q = 20 \times 5 \times 10 = 1,000$; $Q/L = 1,000/100 = 10$.
b. If $L = 25$, then $Q = 1,000$ if $K = 100$ or if $A = 40$.
c. $Q/L = 1,000/25 = 40$; if $A = 25$, then $Q = 25 \times 10 \times 5 = 1,250$ and $Q/L = 50$.

CHAPTER 19

Multiple-Choice Self-Test

1. *c.*
2. *b.*
3. *d.*
4. *c.*
5. *a.*

Problem

a. The new tax table would include the following income brackets and tax rates: 0–12,000 francs, 0 percent; 12,000–24,000 francs, 10 percent; 24,000–48,000 francs, 20 percent; over 48,000 francs, 30 percent.
b. A family whose income last year was 50,000 francs would pay in tax:

$$10\% \ (20,000 - 10,000) + 20\% \ (40,000 - 20,000) + 30\% \ (50,000 - 40,000)$$
$$\text{Total tax} = 8,000 \text{ francs}$$

With income of 60,000 francs this year, the tax is:

$$10\% \ (24,000 - 12,000) + 20\% \ (48,000 - 24,000) + 30\% \ (60,000 - 48,000)$$
$$\text{Total tax} = 9,600 \text{ francs}$$

Neither income nor tax liability changed in real terms. Nominal income and tax liability increased 20 percent.

d. If the price indices had been 200 and 240, the tax table changes would have been the same: new tax bracket amounts would be 20 percent higher.

CHAPTER 20

Multiple-Choice Self-Test

1. *b.*
2. *b.*
3. *d.*
4. *a.*
5. *d.*

Problem

a. Demand curve shifts up and right; higher equilibrium price and quantity of dollars traded.

b. Demand curve shifts down and left; lower equilibrium price and quantity of dollars traded.

c. Demand curve shifts up and right *or* supply curve shifts up and left; lower quantity of dollars traded; equilibrium price may be higher or lower depending on which curve is shifted.

GLOSSARY

Acreage controls   Limits set by governments on the number of acres of farmland in production.

Active versus passive policy   The government can play an active role, controlling the direction of the economy, or a passive role, allowing the economy to follow its own path without intervening.

Aggregate production function   Robert Solow introduced the idea in the 1950s that one could represent the relationship between inputs in an entire economy (such as labor, capital, materials and energy) and outputs in the form of a simple functional relationship in which the quantity of output, measured by GDP or by total industrial output, is a function of the quantities of the various inputs, number of worker hours, quantity of machinery and structures, the volume of materials, etc.

Antitrust laws   Laws designed to promote open markets by limiting practices that reduce competition.

Automatic stabilizers   Measures built into a government's budget that cause its spending to increase and its tax revenues to decrease when the economy goes into slumps and that cause its expenditures to decrease and its taxes to increase when the economy goes into booms.

Balance of payments   A record of all the financial transactions between a country and the rest of the world during a given year.

Balanced budget   When total federal government outlays, which are expenditures on goods and services plus transfer payments plus interest on the debt, equals tax revenues from all sources, the budget is balanced.

Bank reserves   The total quantity of Federal Reserve notes held in bank vaults or checkable deposits by the Federal Reserve district banks.

Bracket creep   The process by which inflation drives personal incomes upward into higher tax brackets. In a progressive income tax system, this causes an increase in tax burdens. See also **Tax indexing.**

Bretton Woods international monetary system (1946–1973)   A system in which the value of the U.S. dollar was fixed in terms of gold, and every other country held its currency at a fixed exchange rate against the U.S. dollar. When trade deficits occurred, the central bank of the deficit country financed the deficit with its reserves of international currencies.

Business cycles   Periodic swings in the pace of national economic activity, characterized by alternating expansion and contraction phases.

Capital account   A category in a balance-of-payments account that covers international trade in real and financial assets (corporate stocks and bonds, government securities, bank deposits, currencies, real estate, and productive capital).

Capital gains   Implicit income received as a result of gains in the value of physical capital, such as buildings, land, and machinery, and in the value of, financial capital, such as stocks and bonds.

Capital gains tax   Tax applied to the income earned as capital gains. It is usually collected only when the gains are converted into cash form.

Capital-intensive production methods   Methods of production that use a high quantity of capital per worker.

Central bank intervention   Influence on exchange rates in the foreign exchange market when exchange rates are not fixed by law. For example, a central bank may buy its country's currency with foreign currencies to drive its currency up in value; to drive its currency down, the central bank would sell its currency in return for foreign currencies.

CETA   See **Comprehensive Employment and Training Act.**

Change in demand   A change in a nonprice determinant that causes a shift in the position of the demand curve.

Change in quantity demanded   Movement along the demand curve caused by a price change; no shift occurs in the curve itself.

Change in quantity supplied   Movement along the supply curve caused by a price change; no shift occurs in the position of the curve itself.

Change in supply   A shift in the position of the supply curve caused by a change in one of the cost determinants of supply.

Choice   The act of selecting among alternatives, a concept crucial to economics.

Circular flow model   A diagram showing the money and real exchanges in both the input and output markets as they flow between sectors of the economy.

COLAs   See **Cost-of-living adjustments.**

Common property   Property owned in common by a society.

Comparative advantage   The advantage in production of a good if a country's relative opportunity cost of producing that good is lower than in other countries.

Complements   Products related in such a way that a price change for one product leads to a shift in the opposite direction in the demand for another product. See **Substitutes.**

Comprehensive Employment and Training Act (CETA)   An act that provides federal funding for use by local governments in retraining and employing difficult-to-hire workers.

Consumer price index (CPI)   A measure of the average amount (prices) paid for a market basket of goods and services by a typical U.S. consumer in comparison to the average paid for the same basket in an earlier base year.

Consumption expenditures   The total dollar value of all goods and services purchased by the household sector for current use.

Contraction phase A part of a business cycle, in which GDP, employment, and production are on the decline.

Corn laws In 18th-century Britain, a set of barriers to the importation of foreign grains.

Cost-of-living adjustments (COLAs) Automatic adjustments in incomes that are tied to the inflation rate (usually measured by the CPI) and paid to individual recipients.

Cost-push inflation A condition in which a slowdown of the supply growth rate pushes costs upward. For example, plague reduces the labor force and thus productive potential—resulting in inflation.

CPI See **Consumer price index.**

Craft unions Exclusive combinations of workers in individual trades such as printing, shoemaking, and baking.

Credit The capacity to borrow money up to a specified limit under specified conditions.

Crowding in Increase of private investment through the income-raising effect of government spending financed by deficits.

Crowding out Decrease of private investment caused by the tendency for federal government, by deficit financing, to compete with firms or persons for borrowed funds. Firms and households, unable to borrow at a low rate of interest, curtail their investment and consumption spending.

Currency sterilization A central bank measure designed to insulate domestic money supply from foreign currency flows.

Current account A category in the balance of payments account that includes all transactions that either contribute to national income or involve the spending of national income.

Cyclical deficits Deficits in the federal budget caused when total outlays exceed tax revenues as a result of cyclical slowdowns in the economy (recessions). Cyclical deficits occur because when the private market economy slows down, tax revenues automatically fall and many transfer payments, such as income supports based on entitlement, automatically rise.

Cyclical unemployment Temporary layoff of workers due to downturns in the pace of economic activity.

Demand curve A graphic representation of the relationship between prices and the corresponding quantities demanded per time period.

Demand-pull inflation Price increases caused when the national demand for goods and services outstrip the productive potential of the economy or national supply.

Derived demand The demand for a resource is a reflection of the demand for the product or service it produces.

Discount rate The interest a private bank pays for a loan from the U.S. Federal Reserve System. See also **Federal Reserve System.**

Disequilibrium A condition in which the quantity demanded does not equal the quantity supplied at the going price. See also **Equilibrium.**

Disinflation   A slowdown in the rate of inflation.

Dividends   Profits of a firm that are distributed to the investors (stockholders).

Division of labor   Assignment of specific tasks to workers and productive resources; a reflection of economic specialization.

Dynamic scoring   Proposals to prediction supply side incentive responses to reductions in certain tax rates, such as a capital gains rate cut. If one thinks rate cuts generate increased economic activity then one should allow for the new revenues generated in evaluating (or scoring) a tax proposal.

Economic growth   A sustained increase in total output or output per person for an economy over a long period of time.

Economic problem   Three basic questions: What goods and services will be produced? How? For whom?

Economic Recovery Tax Act of 1981 (ERTA)   Legislation designed to foster savings and investment so as to encourage long-term growth through reductions of personal income tax rates, taxes on personal savings for retirement, and business taxes for firms investing in new capital.

Economic regulations   Laws to control entry into the market, prices, the extension of service by established firms, and issues of quality control.

Economic specialization   Concentration of activity in a few particular tasks or in producing only a few items.

Economics   The study of choice and decision making in a world with limited resources. See also **Normative economics; Positive economics.**

Efficiency wage theory   This idea, which was developed by George Akerlof and Janet Yellen, explains why even in the face of unemployment employers may keep wages high. They pay workers more than they need to in order to keep up morale of workers so that worker effort will be high and turnover low. This theory explains why unemployment can rise during a cyclical business slump without causing wages to fall. This theory is important because data implies that the unemployment rate rises during economic slowdowns and that wages do not fall cyclically.

Elasticity of supply   The percentage change in the quantity supplied divided by the percentage change in price.

Embargo   A deliberate cutoff of supply, typically intended as a political statement.

Employment Act of 1946   Legislation that set full employment and price stability as national policy goals and established the Council of Economic Advisers.

Entitlements   Government transfer payments made to individuals with certain designated characteristics and circumstances, such as age or need.

Equation of exchange   The quantity of money times the constant value of velocity equals GDP or national income: $MV = (GDP)$.

Equilibrium   A condition in which the quantity supplied equals the quantity demanded, so that the market clears at the existing price. In the circular flow, it is a state of matching flows in which the system has a tendency to neither rise nor fall. See also **Disequilibrium.**

ERTA   See **Economic Recovery Tax Act of 1981.**

Exchange rate   The price of one currency in terms of another.

Exchange value   The purchasing power of a unit of currency for goods and services in the marketplace.

Exclusion principle   Exclusion of others from use of a private good by its owner, unless they pay.

Expansion phase   A phase of a business cycle in which the economy is growing rapidly: output is increasing, employment is rising, industrial production is increasing, and prices are tending to rise.

Expected real interest rate   The rate that firms must plan to cover with their profits, the expected real cost of household credit, and the central determinant in decision making for savers and investors in the private sector.

Exports   All goods and services produced in a country and sold abroad.

Externalities   Costs or benefits that fall on third parties.

FDIC   See **Federal Deposit Insurance Corporation.**

Fed   See **Federal Reserve System.**

Federal debt   The current dollar sum of financial obligations equal to the accumulated past deficits minus surpluses of the U.S. government.

Federal Deposit Insurance Corporation (FDIC)   A federal regulatory agency that insures all deposit accounts in member banks up to $100,000.

Federal funds rate   The rate of interest banks charge on reserves borrowed on an over-night basis (in order to meet reserve requirements). This rate is very sensitive to the availability of reserves (and liquidity) in the banking system.

Federal Reserve bank accountability   The concept that the Board of Governors of the Federal Reserve system should be held accountable for the conduct of monetary policy. See also **Federal Reserve System.**

Federal Reserve Notes (FRN)   Paper money such as dollar bills that is issued by the Federal Reserve System. This is the money that is "legal tender for all debts, public and private." (The actual printing of these bills is undertaken by the Bureau of Engraving and Printing.)

Federal Reserve System (Fed)   The U.S. central bank consisting of 12 regional banks that are run by the Board of Governors, the members of which are appointed by the president for overlapping 14-year terms. The Fed is formally independent of the executive and congressional branches of government. Private bank members of the system own their assets.

Fiscal policy   Federal government expenditure, tax, and borrowing decisions that affect the level of national economic activity.

Fisher Effect   The theory that an increase in expected inflation causes a proportional increase in the market interest rate, so that the expected real rate of interest remains unchanged. See also **Mundell-Tobin Effect.**

Fixed costs   Costs that are predetermined and unavoidable.

Fixed exchange rates   Currency values of a given country that are held constant against a foreign currency or currencies by the central bank of the country.

Fixed inputs   Inputs that cannot be changed over a given time interval.

Floating exchange rates   Currency values of a given country that the central bank of the country allows to fluctuate in response to supply and demand.

Foreign currency reserves   Currencies of another country or countries that the central bank of a given nation keeps on hand for use in intervention.

Foreign exchange markets   Markets in which the currencies of different nations are bought and sold.

Four Tigers   Four Asian countries—Hong Kong, Singapore, Taiwan, and South Korea—which enjoyed very rapid economic growth (often rates in excess of 9 percent) from 1960 to 1990.

Fractional reserve banking   A practice common among banks, in which only a fraction of deposits are held on reserve. Most bank deposits are loaned out to parties willing to pay interest.

Free rider   One who receives something without paying.

Frictional unemployment   Unemployment due to workers leaving old jobs and seeking new ones.

Friedman's law   The theory that inflation follows excessive monetary growth with a long (about two year) and variable lag. The rate of price change follows the rate of monetary growth.

GDP   See **Gross domestic product.**

GDP deflator   A measure of the percentage increase in the average price of products in GDP over a certain base year (now 1972) published by the Commerce Department.

Goods and services markets   Exchanges in which products (manufactured goods and services) are sold.

Government budget rule   A concept that total government outlays (the sum of expenditures on goods and services, transfer payments, and interest on the debt) must equal total revenue (the sum of taxes and government loans).

Government expenditures on goods and services   Dollar payments, made by a government, in exchange for currently produced products or work received.

Government security   A loan contract in which a government promises to pay a lender a fixed rate of interest per year and to repay the original loan at a fixed future date.

Gramm-Rudman-Hollings Law (1985)   A U.S. law imposing across-the-board cuts in most federal spending categories unless Congress and the president agree to lower budget deficits. Designed to eliminate structural deficits by 1991, the original law was struck down by federal courts as unconstitutional. A new, corrected bill was passed in 1987 and was then repealed in 1990.

Gross domestic product (GDP)   The total market value, in terms of current dollars, of all final goods and services produced by U.S. citizens who are working in the United States or abroad in one year.

Humphrey-Hawkins Act (1974)   Congressional action to reaffirm the federal commitment to full employment. The national full-employment goal was defined as 4 percent.

Hyperinflations   Rapid out-of-control inflations, at double-digit (and higher) rates per month.

IMF   See **International Monetary Fund.**

Imports   Goods and services produced in and supplied to a country by foreigners. Many goods are complex composites produced in many places, and the exact percentage of foreign content that defines a good as an import is a legal question.

Income distribution   The distribution of income among people for a time period, such as one year.

Income velocity of money   The ratio of national income to the quantity of money in circulation. Velocity measures the average number of times money changes hands in generating national income per year (monetarist theory).

Income policies   Strategies to restrict wage and price increases, ranging from "jawboning" by the president to laws that set wage and price levels.

Indexation   Modifying contracts and tax brackets so that their dollar terms adjust to the inflation rate as measured in an index, such as the CPI.

Individual retirement account (IRA)   A special type of retirement account, designated by law, that encourages savings by allowing favorable tax treatment, such as a yearly deduction of $2,000 under 1985 tax law.

Industrial policy   Government-controlled and government-designed measures to advance and promote certain business interests so as to enhance U.S. competitiveness abroad. This policy includes selecting particular product lines (such as superconductors) to receive subsidies, tariff protection, tax breaks, etc.

Inferior good   A product or service for which demand decreases when income increases. See **Normal good.**

Inflation   Increase in the overall level of prices over an extended period of time.

In-kind benefits   Noncash forms of pay or assistance.

Interest payments on the federal debt   Dollar payments made by the U.S. Treasury Department to those who hold federal government debt instruments, called *U.S. Securities.* These securities are held by private banks and individuals, which include foreigners, businesses, federal government trust funds, and the Federal Reserve Bank.

International Monetary Fund (IMF)   The overseer for the exchange rate system and international monetary relations.

Investment expenditures   Dollar expenditures by firms or individuals on capital goods (factories, office buildings and other structures, machinery and equipment, inventories, and residential housing) used to produce other new goods and services.

Investment Tax Credit   A law that allowed corporations to reduce their tax payments by a percentage of the money they spent to purchasing new capital goods. Intended to stimulate investment spending, ITC, lowered effective tax rates for capital-intensive industries.

Involuntary unemployment   Unemployment in which potential workers, able and willing to work at the existing market wage rate, are unable to find jobs.

IRA   See **Individual retirement account.**

Keynesians   Followers of John Maynard Keynes who focus on short-run expansions and contractions that result from changes in expenditures by firms, households, and government. These economists emphasize the shocks to expenditure decisions caused by action initiated by decision makers outside the circular flow model.

Labor-intensive production methods   Use of a low quantity of capital per worker.

Labor market   Exchange of human skills and time for wages and benefits.

Labor productivity   The ratio of real output per unit of labor input. Growth is measured by a higher ratio of outputs to inputs.

Laffer curve   A graph that Professor Arthur Laffer drew on the back of a napkin in a lounge in Washington, DC, for the editorial writers of *The Wall Street Journal*, which depicted his argument that lower marginal tax rates on newly earned income would cause so much more work and investment by tax payers that tax revenues would rise rather than fall. The curve itself plots tax revenues as a function of marginal tax rates. As tax rates rise from zero to one hundred percent, tax revenues start at zero, rise, reach a peak, and then fall to zero—the main point being that very high tax rates discourage income generating activity.

Law of demand   An analytical tool that states: People purchase more of any particular good or service as its relative price falls and less as its relative price rises.

Law of diminishing marginal productivity   A maxim of economics that states: If all factors of production are held constant except one, equal additions of that one variable factor will eventually increase output in decreasing increments.

Law of supply   An analytical tool that states: At higher relative prices, the quantity supplied of a good will increase; at lower relative prices, smaller quantities will be supplied.

Legal tender   Paper dollars and coins mandated as acceptable means of payment by the government.

Libertarianism   The view that government should play a minimal role, rarely interfering in the personal lives of private citizens.

Loanable funds   Money that borrowers receive from lenders.

Long run   A period during which all inputs are variable. See also **Short run.**

M1   The total quantity of coins and paper currency classified as legal tender by government mandate that circulates in the hands of the public, plus all checking account balances the public maintains in financial institutions.

M2   All of M1 plus savings, small time deposit account balances (less than $100,000) in financial institutions, and small money market mutual funds owned by individuals.

Macroeconomics   The study of the sum total of economic activity, dealing with the issues of growth, inflation, and unemployment and with national economic policies relating to these issues. See also **Microeconomics.**

Malthusian trap   The minimum subsistence level to which humans were predicted to descend as a result of geometric population growth and arithmetic resource growth.

Managed floating   An international economic system in which central banks intervene in foreign exchange markets to stabilize their currency exchange rates. See also **Bretton Woods international monetary system.**

Managed trade   A trade policy in which governments agree to establish agencies to determine the rules and regulations establishing who may trade what with whom and under what conditions. NAFTA was a 600-page document setting out such conditions. See also **NAFTA.**

Marginal cost   The increase in total costs as one more unit is produced.

Marginal physical product of labor   The added output, measured in physical terms, that results from the addition of one new worker to the production process while all other inputs are held fixed.

Marginal revenue   The addition to total revenue as one additional unit is produced and sold.

Marginal revenue product of labor   The product of two variables: the marginal physical product of labor and the marginal revenue received from selling the added output.

Marginal tax rate   The tax rate charged on the taxpayer's last dollar earned; in a progressive tax system the marginal tax rate is always greater than the average tax rate.

Market economy   An extremely decentralized system in which many buyers and many sellers interact.

Markets   Networks in which buyers and sellers interact to exchange goods and services for money.

Market structure   A classification system that groups firms according to the competition they face in the marketplace.

Medium of exchange   The money or circulating good used in every transaction; in the United States, currency and checking (transaction) accounts held in various financial institutions.

Merchandise trade balance   A category in the current account of the balance of payments that includes all traded goods (manufactured items, agricultural commodities, chemicals, and all other physically tangible products).

Microeconomics   The study of the individual parts of the economy; the household and the firm; how prices are determined; and how prices determine the production, distribution, and use of goods and services. See also **Macroeconomics.**

Minimum wage   The lowest hourly wage, set by law, that can be paid.

Monetarists   Followers of Milton Friedman who focus on the effect of money and monetary policy on changing price and employment levels.

Monetary aggregates   The term economists use to refer to the total supply of money included in M1 and M2. See also **M1; M2; Near-monies.**

Monetary base   The total quantity of currency in circulation outside of banks plus the currency held by banks or deposited with the Fed.

Monetary units   The medium of exchange for all economic transactions.

Money   The accepted common medium of exchange for goods and services in the marketplace that functions as the unit of account, a means of deferred payment, and a store of value.

Money market mutual funds   Shares in institutional funds invested in financial instruments such as U.S. Treasury securities, certificates of deposit in financial institutions (CDs), and commercial paper (IOUs of big corporations).

Money multiplier   The ratio of a change in money balances to a change in reserve requirements in the bank system (10 percent reserve requirement).

Money supply   Legal currency and various transaction account balances held at financial institutions (M1) plus small savings and time deposit accounts of individuals (M2). See also **M1; M2.**

Monopolistic competition   A market in which large number of firms sell similar but differentiated products, with no significant barriers to entry.

Monopoly   A market in which there is only one supplier.

Multiple expansion   The increase in consumption expenditures generated by new investment expenditures.

Multiplier   The extent of economic stimulus (increase in national income) generated by a planned increase in deficit spending, through either an increase in government expenditures or a decrease in taxes or both (as in Keynesian theory). See also **Keynesians.**

Mundell-Tobin Effect   The theory that expected inflation increases market interest rates less than proportionately, because high expected inflation lowers money demand; an increase in expected inflation drives down the expected real rate of interest. See also **Fisher Effect.**

NAFTA   North American Free Trade Agreement was a carefully crafted agreement designed to foster trade by reducing various barriers between Mexico, Canada, and the United States. The agreement was originally established by the Salinas, Bush, and Mulroony governments but had not been approved by Congress by September 1993.

National Bureau of Economic Research (NBER)   A private research institute that collects, synthesizes, and analyzes thousands of series of historical data on the U.S. economy.

National income   The total value of all earnings of the inputs (wages, salaries, and fringe benefits of labor, rental income on all property, interest payments on loans, income of small individual proprietorships, and profit) that produce GDP.

Natural monopoly   A market condition in which one producer supplies all the market at lower costs than many producers could.

Natural rate of unemployment (Un)   The lowest rate of unemployment that can be maintained by stabilization policies without accelerating the inflation rate.

NBER   See **National Bureau of Economic Research.**

NCM   NCM refers to new classical macroeconomists who have revitalized the pre-Keynesian classical views of the workings of the economic system. See **Supply-side economics.**

Near-monies   Assets less easy than monetary aggregates to convert into a medium of exchange (large deposit accounts held by businesses, financial instruments created in the banking process, and financial instruments issued by government and other institutions). See also **M1; M2.**

New classical macroeconomics (NCM)   See **Supply-side economics** and **NCM.**

Nominal GDP   GDP measured in current prices. See also **GDP deflator; Gross domestic product; Real GDP.**

Nominal rate of interest   The cost inflicted by inflation's erosion of the value of stored dollars plus the forgone real interest rate; the opportunity cost of holding money.

Nonconvertible currency   A currency, such as the Polish zloty and the Soviet ruble in 1989, that cannot be traded outside its country of origin for other currencies. A nonconvertible currency is a barrier to trade because it forces potential traders to barter rather than to use the two currencies as a means of exchange.

Normal good   A product or service for which demand increases when income increases. See also **Inferior good.**

Normative economics   Analysis that contains value judgments, either implicitly or explicitly. See also **Economics; Positive economics.**

North American Free Trade Agreement   See **NAFTA.**

Okun's Law   A rule about the relationship between unemployment and GDP: For every 1 percent of unemployment above the natural rate, real GDP will be 3 percent lower than its potential.

Oligopoly   A market structure in which just a few firms control a high percentage of total sales.

Open-market operations   Purchases and sales of U.S. government securities by the Fed.

Opportunity cost   The highest valued sacrifice needed to get a good or service; the next most expensive forgone alternative.

Paradox of thrift   A seemingly contradictory aspect of a policy intended to encourage growth, in which increased saving increases withdrawals from the money flow. Unless the withdrawals are successfully channeled into new investment spending, capital formation will decline.

Peak   The highest point attained in a business cycle. A slowdown and leveling off of expansion occurs at the peak, and a downturn begins. See also **Trough.**

Personal savings   The difference between household income (after taxes) and consumption expenditures.

Positive economics   Objective analysis of the economy without implicit or explicit values or subjective feelings. Statements then can be verified with empirical evidence. See **Economics; Normative economics.**

Price   The amount of money (or other things) that must be given up to buy a good or service.

Price ceiling   An upper legal limit on price.

Price controls   Upper or lower limits on a price.

Price elasticity of demand   The percentage change in the quantity demanded divided by the percentage change in price measured along a demand curve or schedule.

Price floor   The lower limit imposed on a product's price by a price control law.

Price searcher   A business with some degree of monopoly power that can set price.

Price supports   Price floors on certain agricultural crops.

Price taker   A buyer or seller who takes the market price as given.

Private costs   Internal costs explicitly accounted for by a firm. See also **Social costs.**

Private good   A good exclusively owned that cannot be simultaneously used by others.

Privatization   The transfer of activities from the public sector to the private sector.

Production function   The physical relationship between the quantities of various inputs and the quantity of output, as determined by the state of technology.

Production possibilities curve   All combinations of the maximum amounts of goods that a society can produce with the available resources and technology.

Productive resources   The inputs of labor, land and natural resources, and capital used to generate new goods and services.

Profits   Total revenues minus total costs (including all implicit opportunity costs) for a given period of time.

Property rights   The conditions of ownership of an asset; the rights to own, use, and sell.

Protectionism   A foreign trade policy in which tariffs and quotas are imposed to restrict imports.

Public goods   Goods that cannot be withheld from people even if they don't pay for them; normally provided by government.

Pure competition   A situation in which many sellers sell the same product and no seller can set the price.

Quantity theory of money   The view that the velocity of money is nearly constant, or at least predictable, so that changes in the level of national expenditures result mainly from changes in the quantity of money. See also **Monetarists.**

Quota   A quantitative restriction on imports.

Rational expectations   The theory that market participants intuitively anticipate systematic policy actions and their consequences for the economy. Thus, on average, private market forecasts are thought to be accurate, and planned policy is considered ineffectual. See also **Supply-side economics.**

Real business cycles   The theory that cyclical fluctuations are caused by technological shocks, such as new inventions or environmental restrictions rather than by demand-side choices, such as fiscal and monetary policies.

Real GDP   The total market value of all final goods and services produced in one year, which is corrected for inflation to constant dollars in order to facilitate accurate comparison of GDP figures over time.

Real rate of interest   The dollar interest rate corrected for inflation; equal to the nominal rate minus the inflation rate.

Realized real interest rate   The nominal interest rate minus the realized inflation rate.

Rent controls   Fixed limits (usually upper) on rents that can be charged to tenants by owners according to a legal restriction; usually imposed by local governments.

Reserve currency   A currency of one country (for example, the U.S. dollar) that is used in transactions between two other countries.

Retailers   Sellers of items and services in relatively small quantities to consumers.

Retained earnings   Business profits that firms do not pay out to their stockholders; the earnings are usually reinvested by the firms.

Revenues   Price times quantity sold; total gross earnings of a firm before subtracting costs.

Right-to-work laws   Laws banning union membership as a requirement for continued employment.

Rising opportunity costs   The rise in per-unit costs as more is produced.

Rule of rational choice   For any decision, proceed if the additional benefits exceed the additional costs (including opportunity costs).

Savings and loan bailout   Measures established by Congress and the Bush administration to supply tax-generated funds for depositors in failed savings and loans.

Shortage   A market condition in which the quantity demanded exceeds the quantity supplied at a given price.

Short run   A period during which some inputs are fixed and cannot be varied. See also **Long run.**

Slow-growth movement   Opposition to economic growth by various groups of individuals and organizations, which in the late 1980s and the early 1990s favored slowing growth of cities and other communities. These groups believed that the side effects of growth, such as environmental pollution, outweigh the benefits of growth and expansion.

Social costs   A firm's private (internal) costs plus the external costs. See also **Private costs.**

Social optimum   An economic condition in which all costs are covered in the long run; price equals marginal cost.

Socialism   The view that government should own and control major industries, using the dollars earned to provide benefits to citizens.

Speculative profits   Income that foreign currency traders make if the price of a currency they are holding goes up.

Stagflation   An economic condition characterized by simultaneous inflation, slow growth, and high unemployment.

Structural deficits   Budget deficits built into the federal budget that will persist despite reasonable rates of economic expansion.

Structural unemployment   Unemployment of workers whose skills are no longer suitable for, or do not match, the types of jobs available.

Substitutes   Products related in such a way that a price change for one product leads to a shift in the same direction in the demand for another product. See **Complements.**

Supply curve   A graphic representation of the relationship between quantities supplied at each price for a given time period.

Supply-side economics   Focus on the effects on national output potential or supply through reduction of taxes and government regulation of business; expected to increase productivity and economic growth.

Surplus   A production condition in which the quantity supplied exceeds the quantity demanded at a given price.

Target prices   A special type of price support for agriculture.

Tariff   A tax on imports.

Tax-based incomes policies (TIPS)   A means of enforcing government-established wage and price guidelines by tying a company's tax liability to its pricing performance.

Tax indexing   Adjustment of tax brackets so that an increase in income due only to inflation does not increase real tax liability (offsets bracket creep). See also **Bracket creep.**

Tax Reform Act of 1986   An overhaul of the U.S. federal tax system that reduced personal income tax revenue and increased business tax revenue. Top marginal tax rates on personal income were cut from 50 percent to 28 percent, and the 15-bracket system was replaced with a 3-bracket system: 0 percent, 15 percent, and 28 percent. Corporate tax rates were reduced from 46 percent to 33 percent, but tax breaks such as investment tax credits were eliminated.

Technological change   An advance (usually scientific) that causes an increase in output to occur relative to the quantity of inputs in the production function.

Terms of trade   The relative prices of goods and services traded in international markets.

Theory of public choice   A theory developed by James Buchanan in which economic models of individual choice are used to analyze the motivations of government bureaucrats and politicians.

Time deposits   Savings held in a financial institution for a fixed time period (such as six months or a year).

TIPS   See **Tax-based incomes policies.**

Total factor productivity (TFP)   A measure of economic efficiency sometimes also called *multifactor productivity* is the ratio of total output to a weighted average of all inputs. As a rule, the weight of each input is its percentage share in total costs. This is a more general measure of economic efficiency than labor productivity, which is the ratio of output to total labor input.

Trade balance   The difference between exports and imports. If exports exceed imports, then the trade balance is in surplus. If imports exceed exports, the balance is in deficit. See **deficit.**

Trade-offs   The opportunity costs of selecting one thing rather than another.

Transfer payments   Outlays by a government for which no good or service is received in the current period.

Transaction accounts   The total funds that may be withdrawn on demand from financial institutions such as banks, savings and loans, and credit unions.

Transaction costs   The costs of making an exchange.

Transfer programs   Programs in which the government gives economic support to people without requiring recipients to supply any current goods or services in return.

Trough   A point in the business cycle corresponding to the end of a slowdown and the beginning of an expansion (the opposite of peak). See also **Peak.**

Twin deficits   A condition in which the federal budget deficit and the trade balance deficit tend to grow at the same time. Both started to become very large in the 1980s and the 1990s.

Unemployment   The difference between the number of people in the labor force and the number of people who are working. These figures are determined by the U.S. Department of Labor through a statistically detailed survey in which people are asked such questions as: Do you work currently? If not, what have you done to seek a job in the past few weeks? If you are on vacation or leave, do you still hold down a job? There are three kinds of unemployment: frictional, structural, and cyclical. See also **Cyclical unemployment; Frictional unemployment; Involuntary unemployment; Natural unemployment rate; Structural unemployment.**

Unemployment compensation   A federal program by which payments are made to workers who are laid off during economic slowdowns; both firms and employed workers pay into the system.

Usury laws   Upper limits set on interest rates that can be legally charged.

Variable costs   Costs of a production process that increase or decrease along with changes in level of production, as opposed to fixed costs. See also **Short run.**

Voluntary export restraint   A quota that is identical to an import quota, except that the affected foreign market agrees voluntarily to limit exports from its country to a market.

Workfare programs   State-run welfare programs in which welfare benefits are tied to participation in training and work programs when feasible for the recipients.

Working poor   Workers earning inadequate income as judged by government-established standards of poverty.

INDEX